JoJo's
BIZARRE ADVENTURE

04

PART 3
STARDUST CRUSADERS

荒　木　飛　呂　彦

HIROHIKO ARAKI

JoJo's Bizarre Adventure
PART 3 STARDUST CRUSADERS

CONTENTS

JoJo's

BIZARRE ADVENTURE

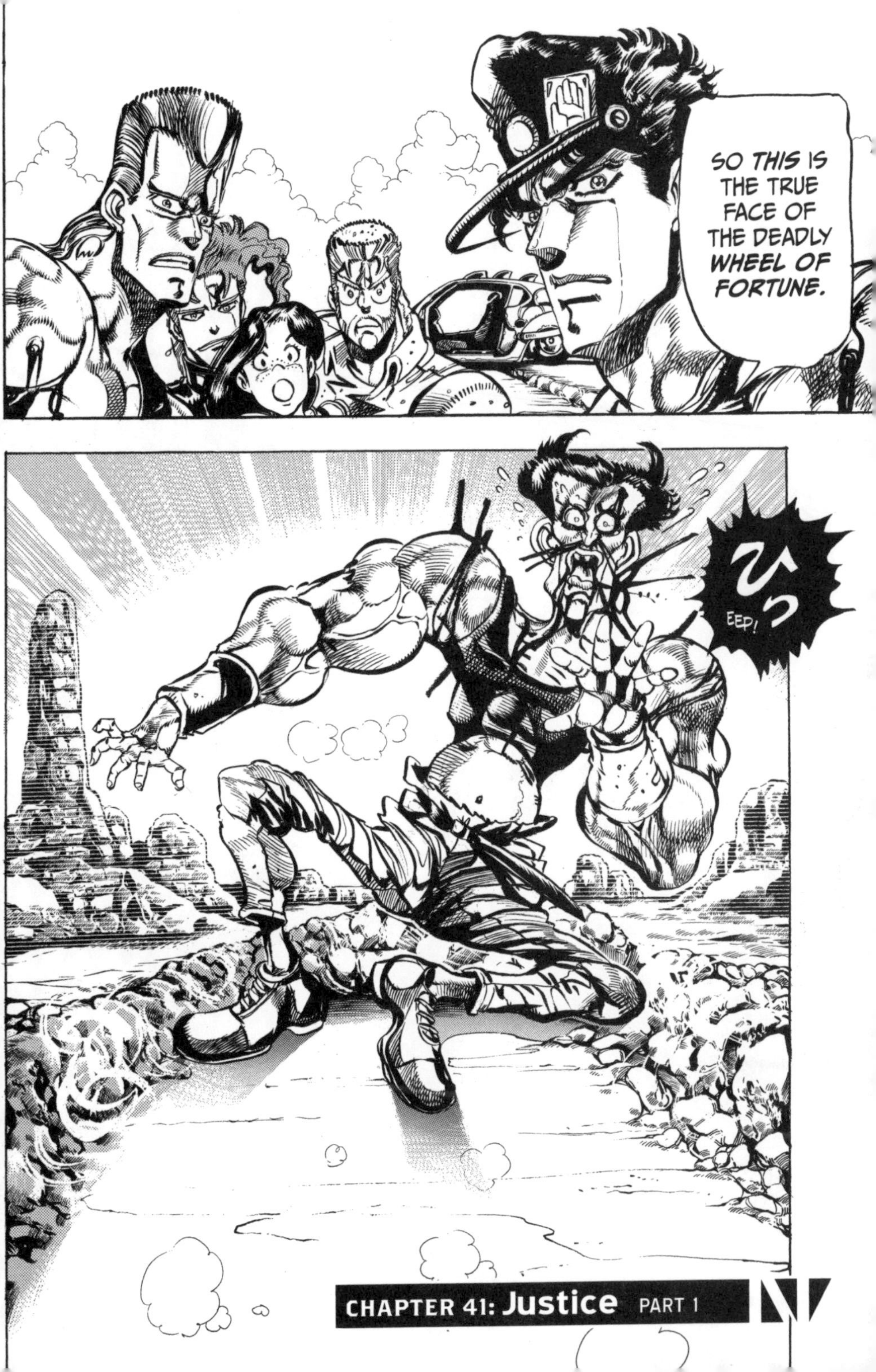
SO THIS IS THE TRUE FACE OF THE DEADLY WHEEL OF FORTUNE.
ひっ
EEP!
CHAPTER 41: Justice PART 1

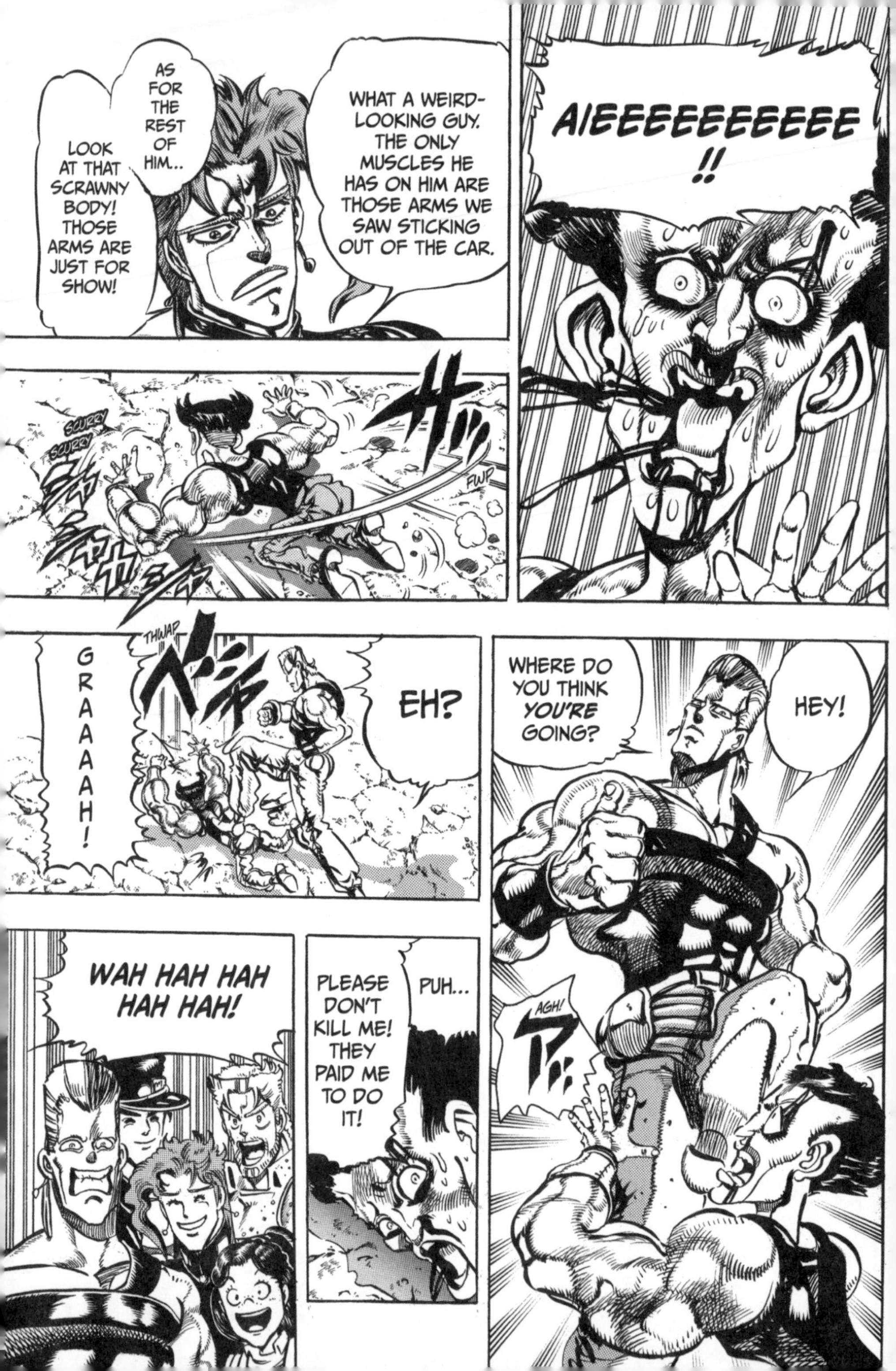
AIEEEEEEEEEEE!!
WHAT A WEIRD-LOOKING GUY. THE ONLY MUSCLES HE HAS ON HIM ARE THOSE ARMS WE SAW STICKING OUT OF THE CAR.
AS FOR THE REST OF HIM...
LOOK AT THAT SCRAWNY BODY! THOSE ARMS ARE JUST FOR SHOW!
FWP
SCURRY
SCURRY
HEY!
WHERE DO YOU THINK YOU'RE GOING?
AGH!
EH?
THWAP
GRAAAAAH!
PUH...
PLEASE DON'T KILL ME! THEY PAID ME TO DO IT!
WAH HAH HAH HAH HAH!

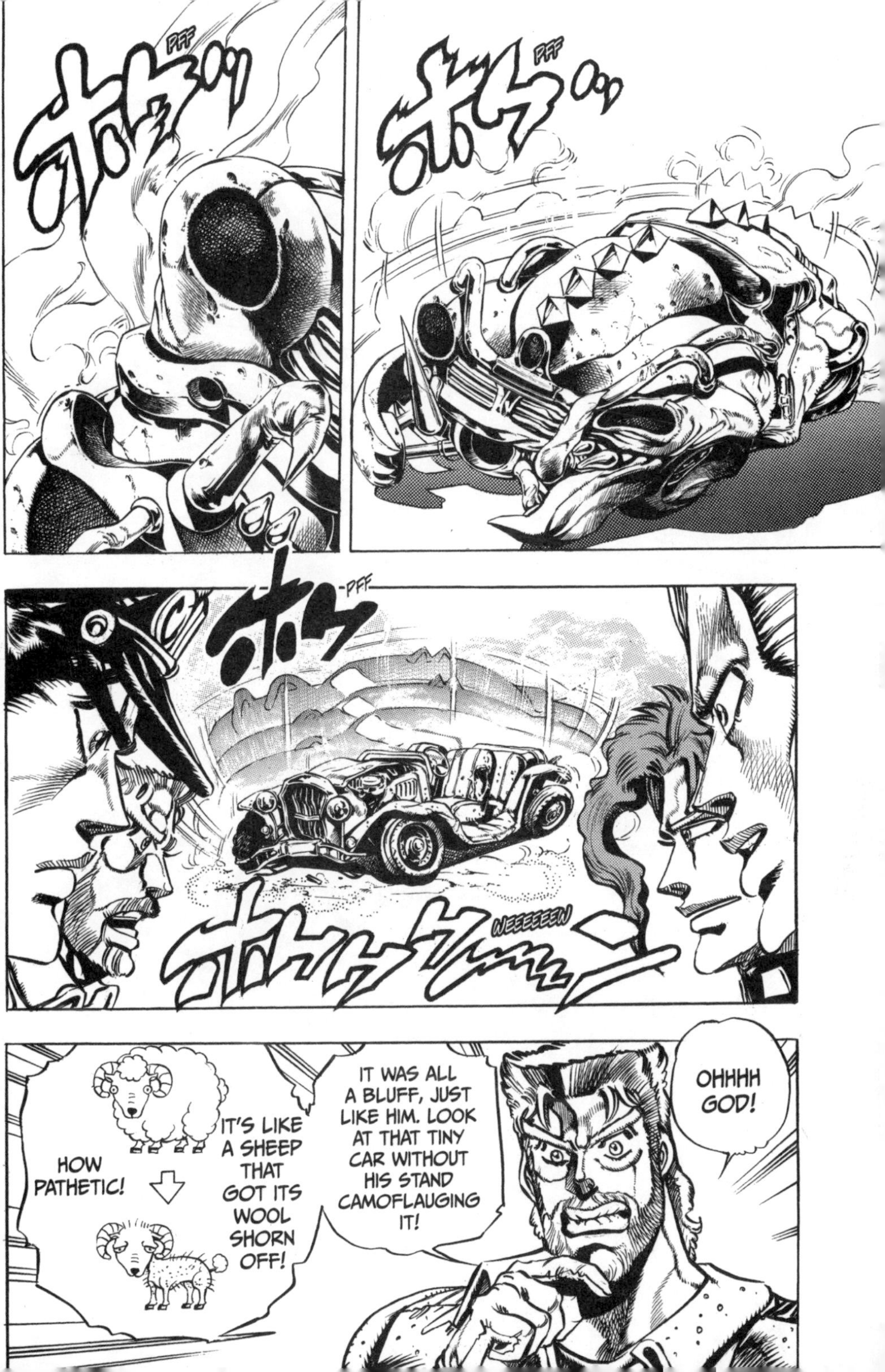
PFF
PFF
-PFF
WEEEEEEW
OHHHH GOD!
IT WAS ALL A BLUFF, JUST LIKE HIM. LOOK AT THAT TINY CAR WITHOUT HIS STAND CAMOFLAUGING IT!
IT'S LIKE A SHEEP THAT GOT ITS WOOL SHORN OFF!
HOW PATHETIC!

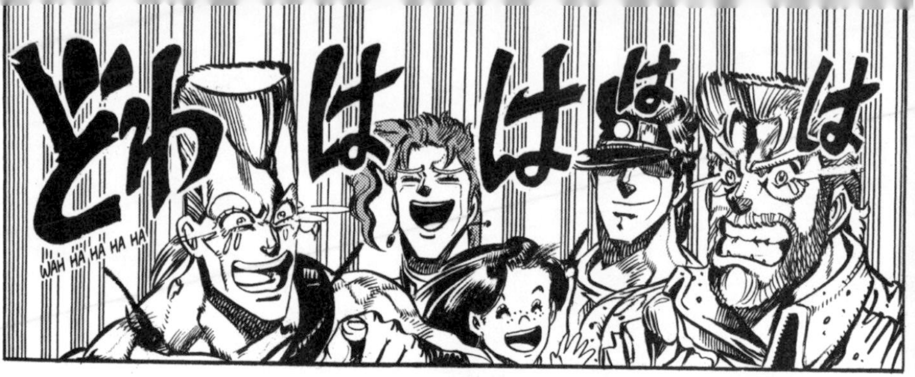
どわはははは
WAH HA HA HA HA

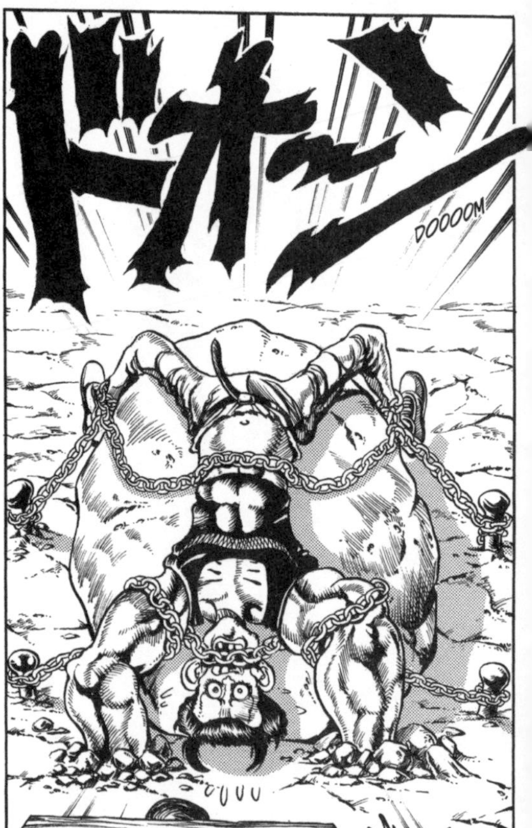
ドオン
DOOOOM
わたしは修行僧です。神聖なる苦行をじゃましてほどいたりしないでください。
UGGH NGG BLGGG!

*SIGN: I AM A MONK IN TRAINING. PLEASE DO NOT INTERFERE WITH THE SACRED RITE I AM UNDERGOING.

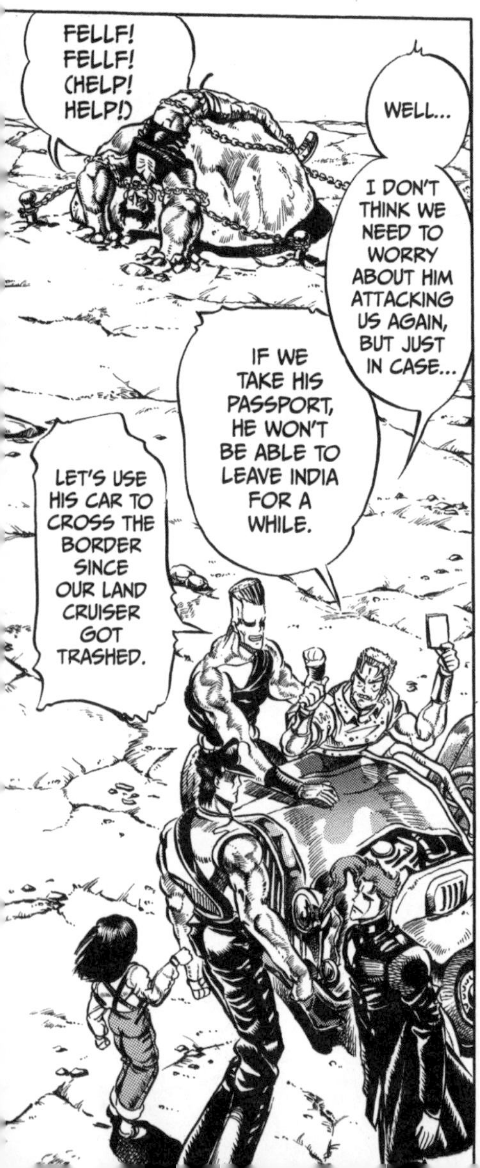
WELL...
I DON'T THINK WE NEED TO WORRY ABOUT HIM ATTACKING US AGAIN, BUT JUST IN CASE...
IF WE TAKE HIS PASSPORT, HE WON'T BE ABLE TO LEAVE INDIA FOR A WHILE.
FELLF! FELLF! (HELP! HELP!)
LET'S USE HIS CAR TO CROSS THE BORDER SINCE OUR LAND CRUISER GOT TRASHED.

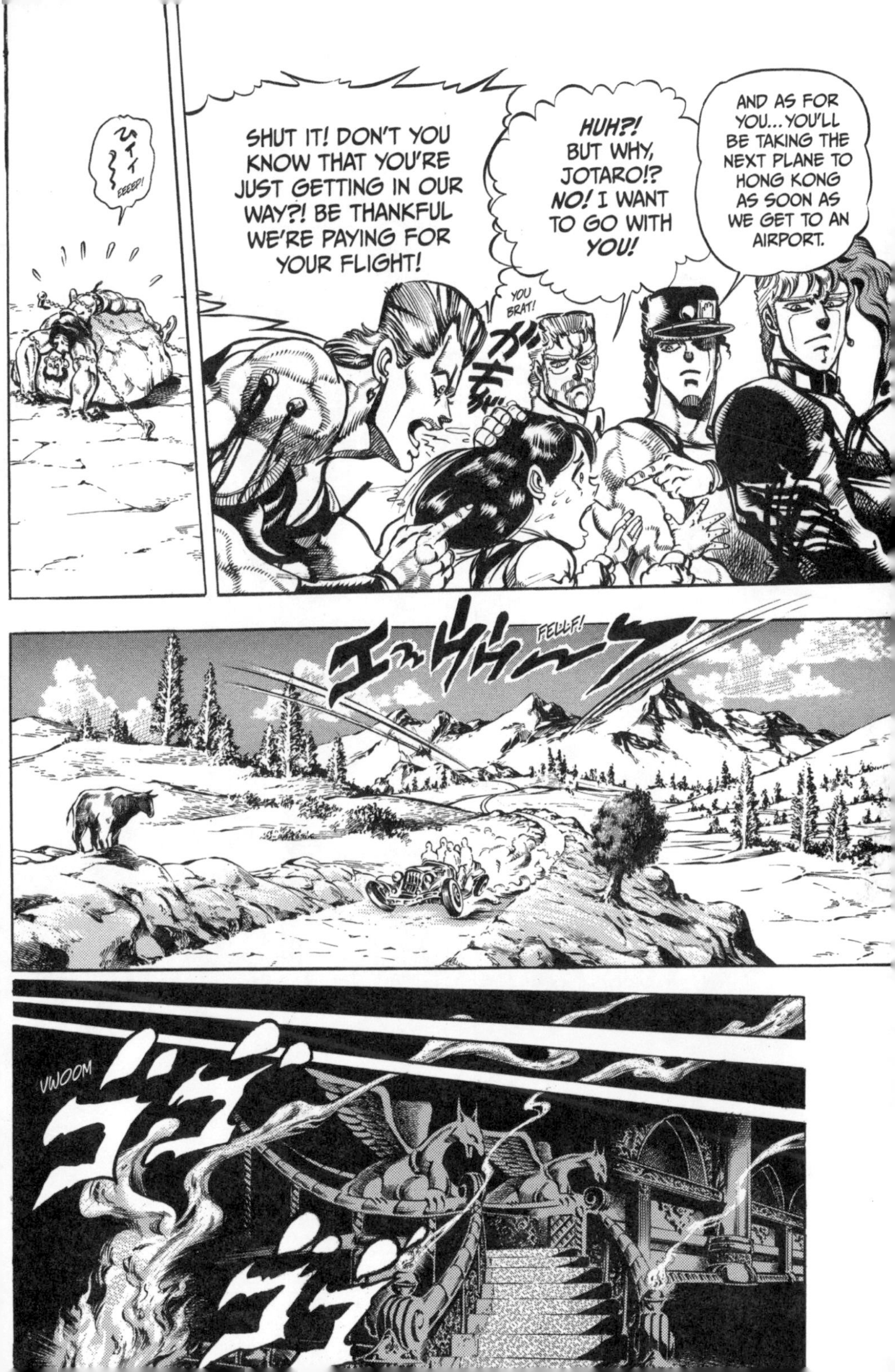
AND AS FOR YOU...YOU'LL BE TAKING THE NEXT PLANE TO HONG KONG AS SOON AS WE GET TO AN AIRPORT.
HUH?! BUT WHY, JOTARO!? NO! I WANT TO GO WITH YOU!
SHUT IT! DON'T YOU KNOW THAT YOU'RE JUST GETTING IN OUR WAY?! BE THANKFUL WE'RE PAYING FOR YOUR FLIGHT!
YOU BRAT!
EEEEP!
FEELF!
VWOOM

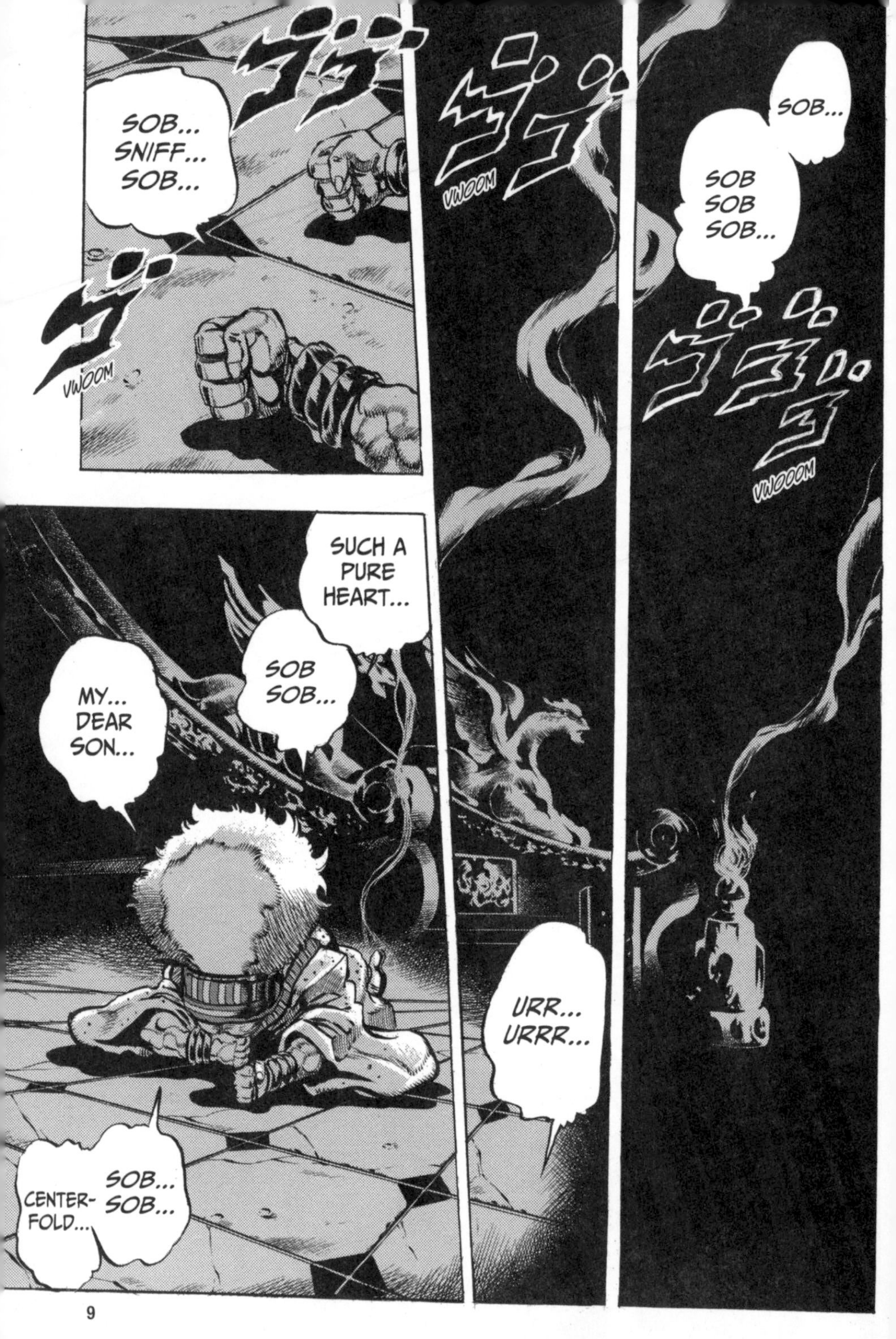
SOB...
SOB SOB SOB...
VWOOOM
VWOOM
URR... URRR...
SOB... SNIFF... SOB...
VWOOM
SUCH A PURE HEART...
SOB SOB...
MY... DEAR SON...
SOB... SOB...
CENTER-FOLD...

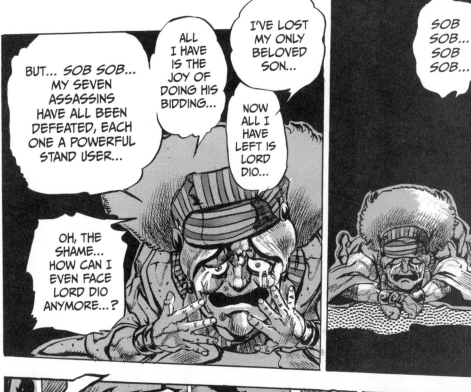

SOB SOB... SOB SOB...
I'VE LOST MY ONLY BELOVED SON...
NOW ALL I HAVE LEFT IS LORD DIO...
ALL I HAVE IS THE JOY OF DOING HIS BIDDING...
BUT... SOB SOB... MY SEVEN ASSASSINS HAVE ALL BEEN DEFEATED, EACH ONE A POWERFUL STAND USER...
OH, THE SHAME... HOW CAN I EVEN FACE LORD DIO ANYMORE...?
...
KUHHHH

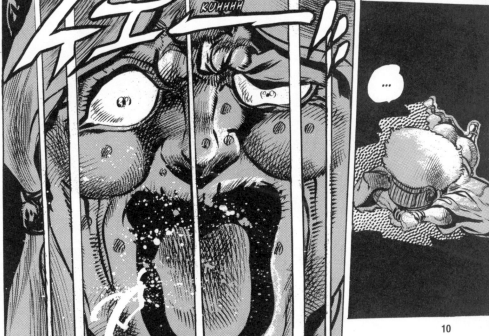

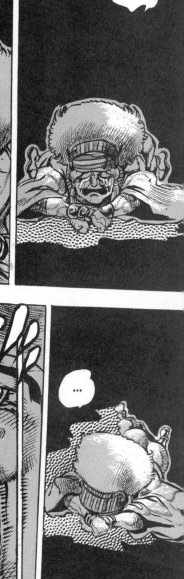

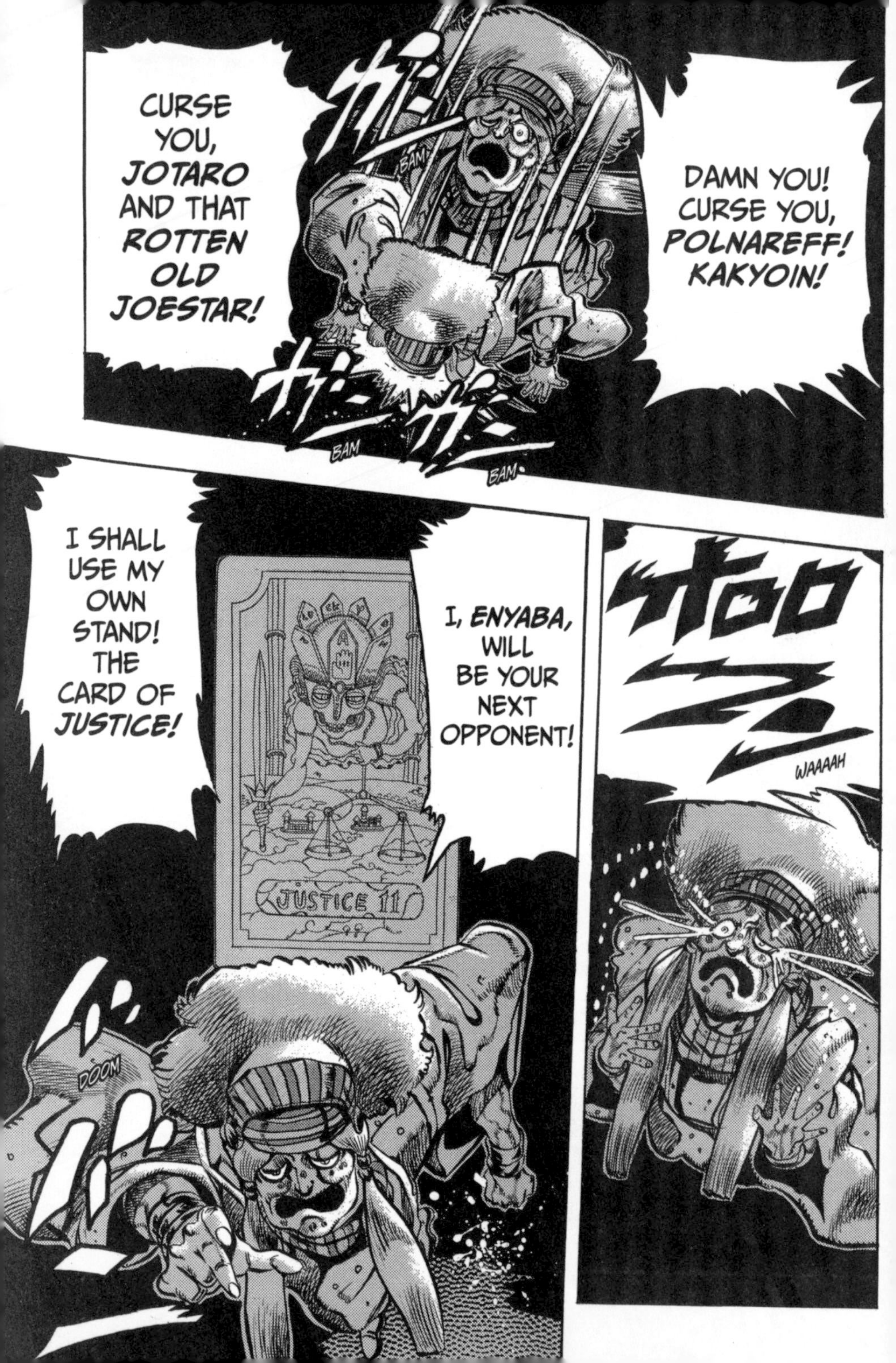
DAMN YOU! CURSE YOU, POLNAREFF! KAKYOIN!
BAM
CURSE YOU, JOTARO AND THAT ROTTEN OLD JOESTAR!
BAM
BAM
WAAAAH
I, ENYABA, WILL BE YOUR NEXT OPPONENT!
I SHALL USE MY OWN STAND! THE CARD OF JUSTICE!
JUSTICE 11
DOOM

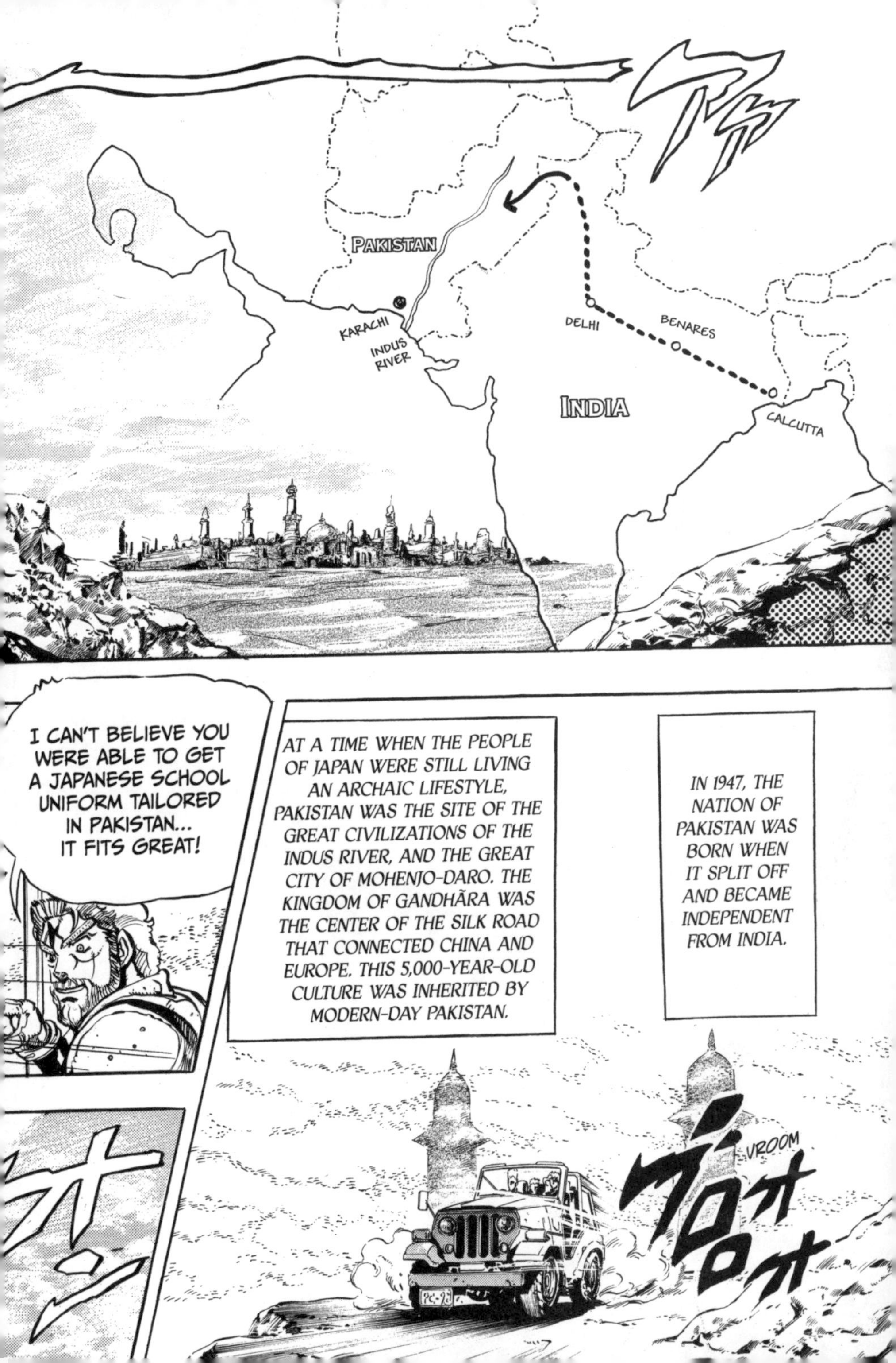
PAKISTAN
KARACHI
INDUS RIVER
DELHI
BENARES
INDIA
CALCUTTA
IN 1947, THE NATION OF PAKISTAN WAS BORN WHEN IT SPLIT OFF AND BECAME INDEPENDENT FROM INDIA.
AT A TIME WHEN THE PEOPLE OF JAPAN WERE STILL LIVING AN ARCHAIC LIFESTYLE, PAKISTAN WAS THE SITE OF THE GREAT CIVILIZATIONS OF THE INDUS RIVER, AND THE GREAT CITY OF MOHENJO-DARO. THE KINGDOM OF GANDHĀRA WAS THE CENTER OF THE SILK ROAD THAT CONNECTED CHINA AND EUROPE. THIS 5,000-YEAR-OLD CULTURE WAS INHERITED BY MODERN-DAY PAKISTAN.
VROOM
I CAN'T BELIEVE YOU WERE ABLE TO GET A JAPANESE SCHOOL UNIFORM TAILORED IN PAKISTAN... IT FITS GREAT!

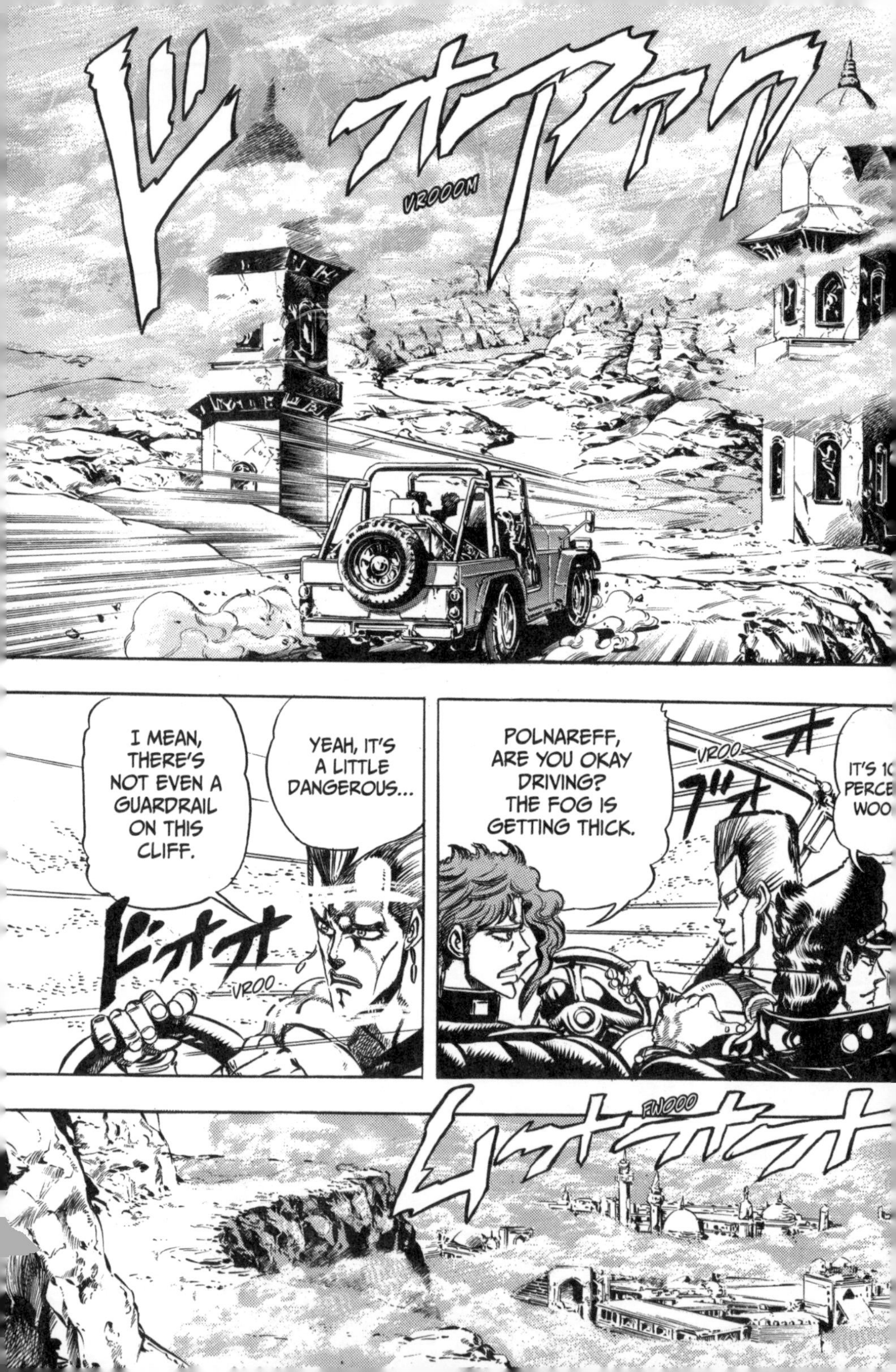
VROOOM
VROO
IT'S 10 PERCE WOO
POLNAREFF, ARE YOU OKAY DRIVING? THE FOG IS GETTING THICK.
YEAH, IT'S A LITTLE DANGEROUS...
I MEAN, THERE'S NOT EVEN A GUARDRAIL ON THIS CLIFF.
VROO
FWOOO

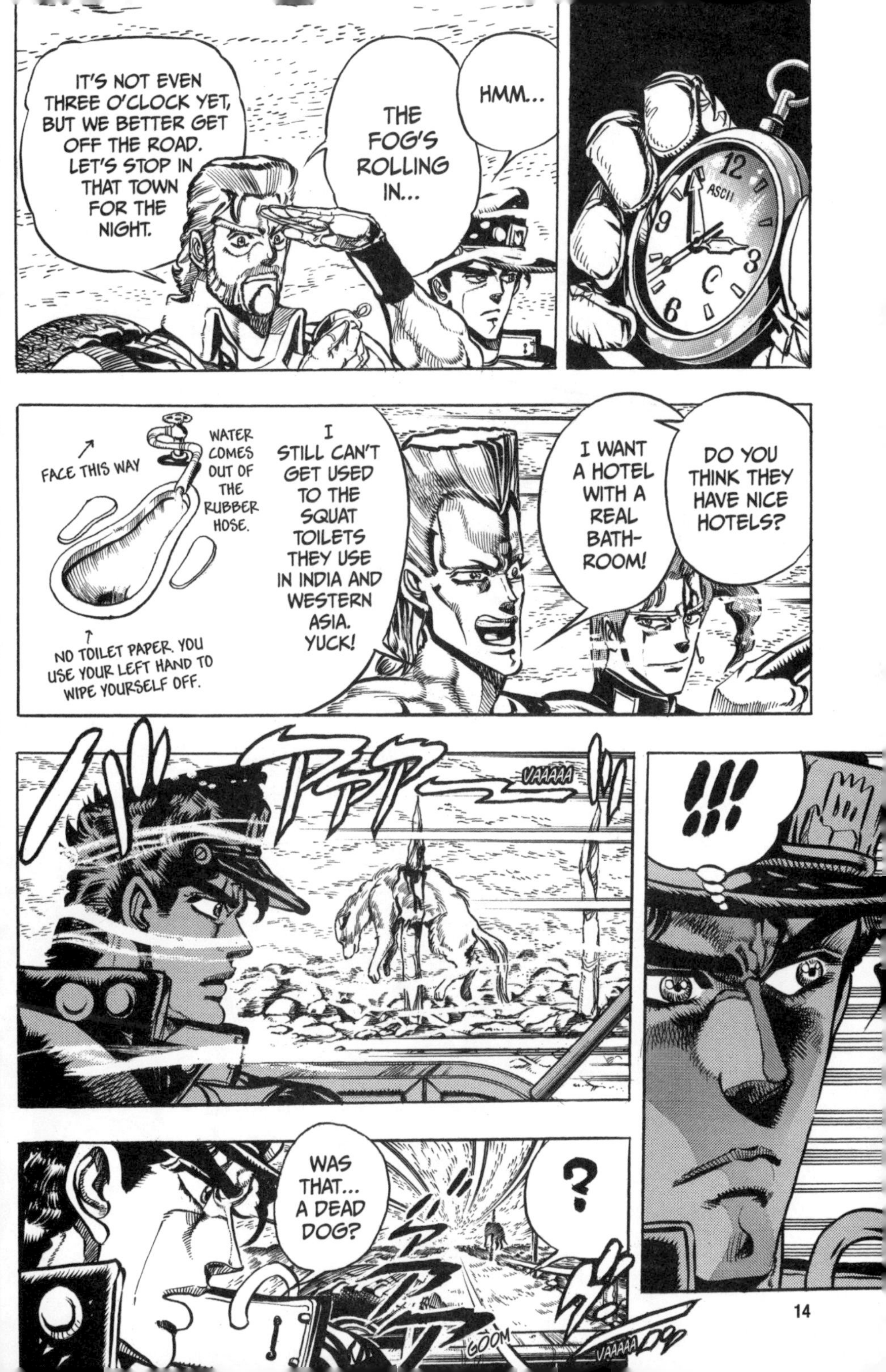
ASCII
HMM...
THE FOG'S ROLLING IN...
IT'S NOT EVEN THREE O'CLOCK YET, BUT WE BETTER GET OFF THE ROAD. LET'S STOP IN THAT TOWN FOR THE NIGHT.
DO YOU THINK THEY HAVE NICE HOTELS?
I WANT A HOTEL WITH A REAL BATH-ROOM!
I STILL CAN'T GET USED TO THE SQUAT TOILETS THEY USE IN INDIA AND WESTERN ASIA. YUCK!
WATER COMES OUT OF THE RUBBER HOSE.
FACE THIS WAY
NO TOILET PAPER. YOU USE YOUR LEFT HAND TO WIPE YOURSELF OFF.
!!!
VAAAAA
?
WAS THAT... A DEAD DOG?
GOOM
VAAAAA

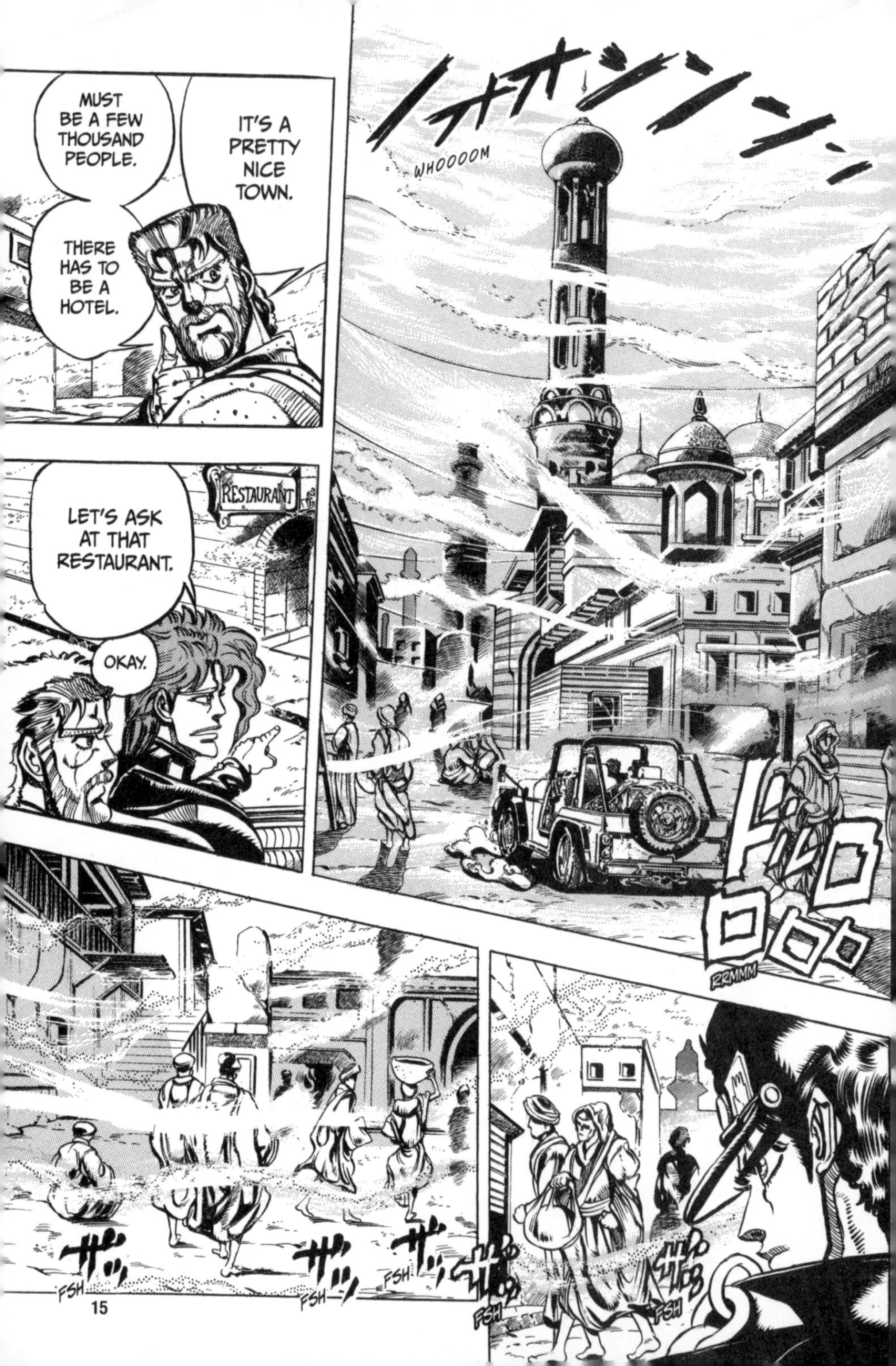
WHOOOOM
RRMMM
IT'S A PRETTY NICE TOWN.
MUST BE A FEW THOUSAND PEOPLE.
THERE HAS TO BE A HOTEL.
RESTAURANT
LET'S ASK AT THAT RESTAURANT.
OKAY.
FSH
FSH
FSH
FSH
FSH

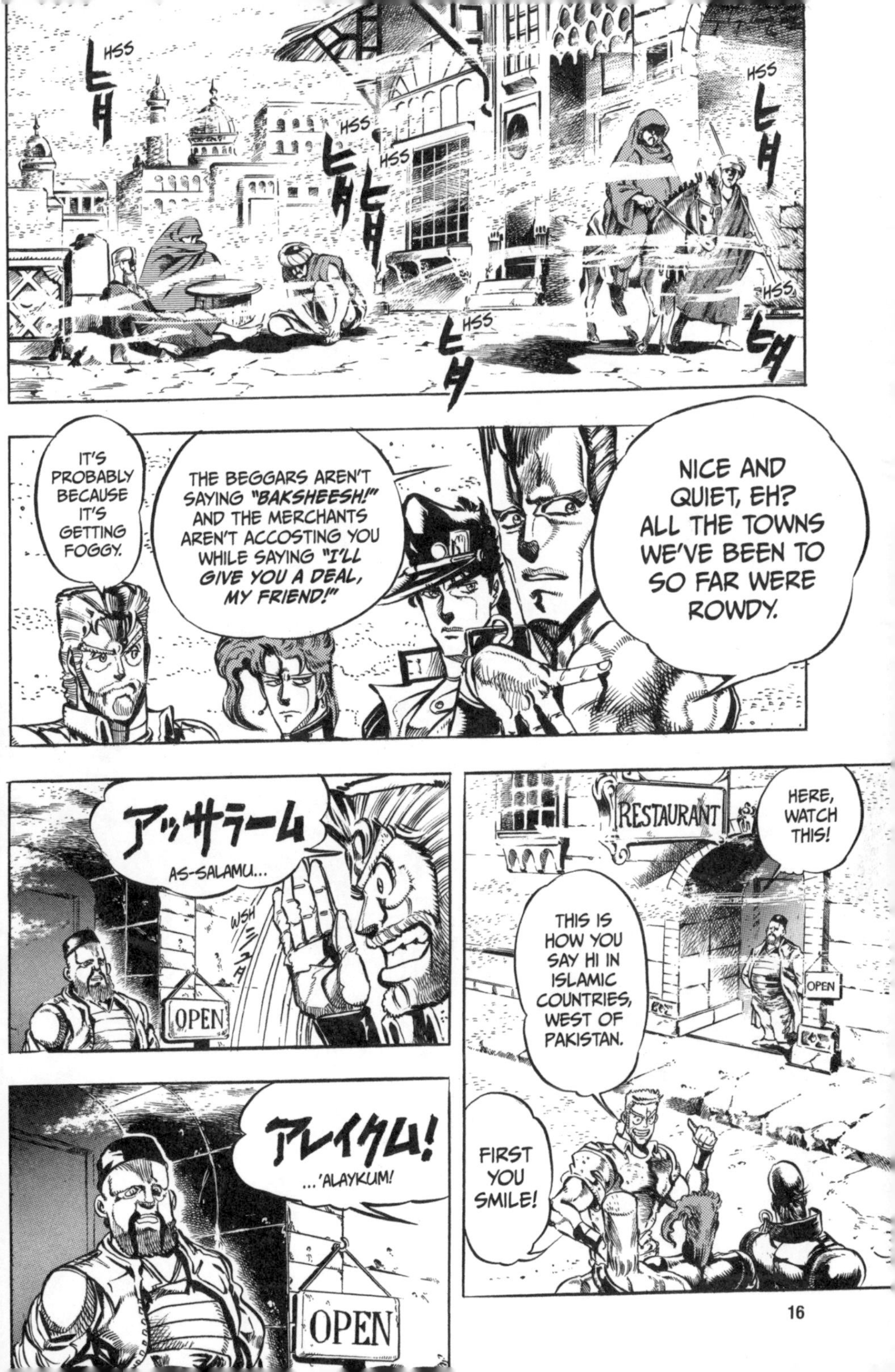
HSS
HSS
HSS
HSS
HSS
HSS
NICE AND QUIET, EH? ALL THE TOWNS WE'VE BEEN TO SO FAR WERE ROWDY.
THE BEGGARS AREN'T SAYING *"BAKSHEESH!"* AND THE MERCHANTS AREN'T ACCOSTING YOU WHILE SAYING *"I'LL GIVE YOU A DEAL, MY FRIEND!"*
IT'S PROBABLY BECAUSE IT'S GETTING FOGGY.
RESTAURANT
HERE, WATCH THIS!
THIS IS HOW YOU SAY HI IN ISLAMIC COUNTRIES, WEST OF PAKISTAN.
FIRST YOU SMILE!
OPEN
アッサラーム
AS-SALAMU...
WSH
OPEN
アレイクム!
...'ALAYKUM!
OPEN

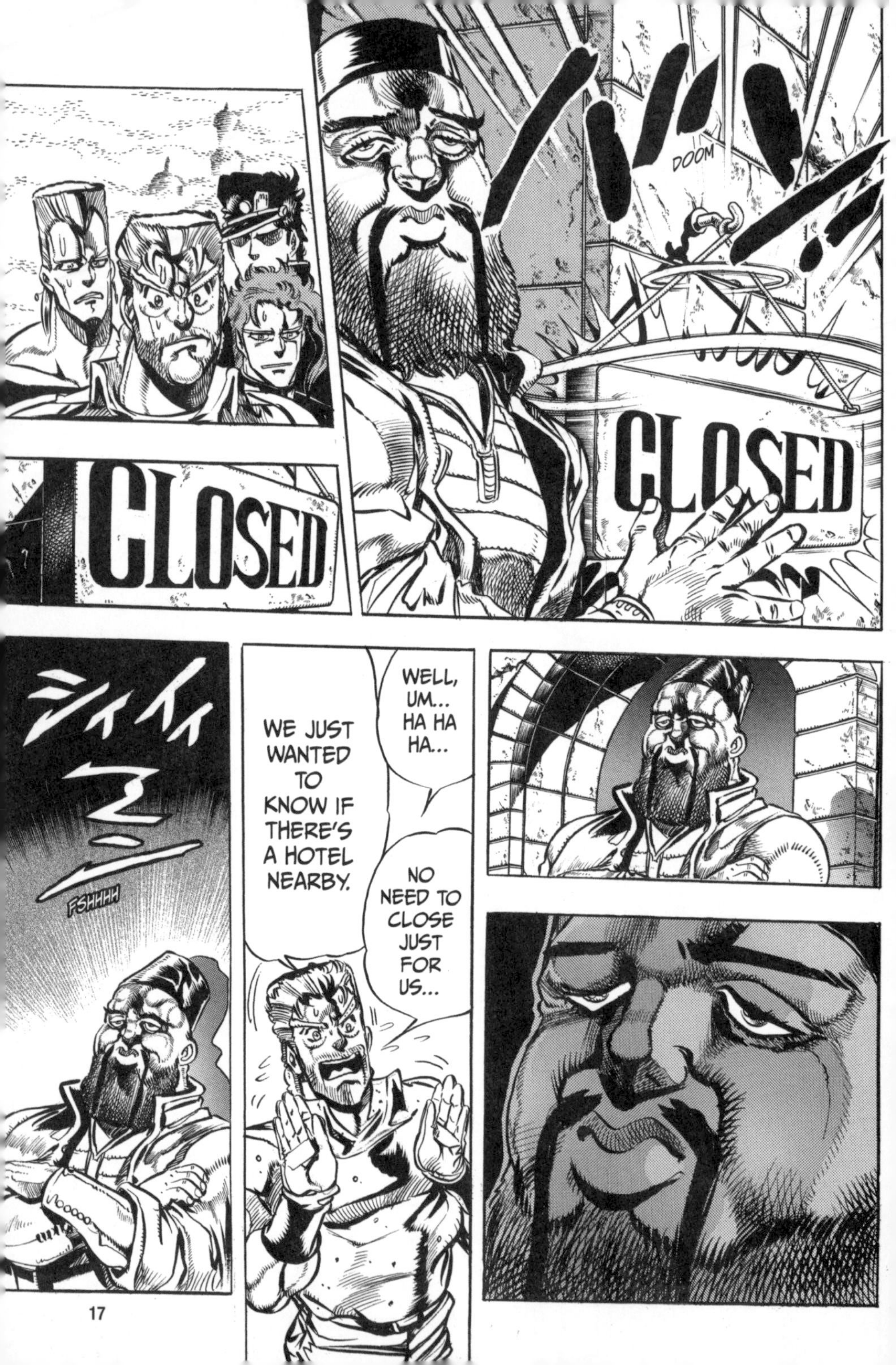
DOOM
CLOSED
CLOSED
WELL, UM... HA HA HA...
WE JUST WANTED TO KNOW IF THERE'S A HOTEL NEARBY.
NO NEED TO CLOSE JUST FOR US...
シィィーン
FSHHHH

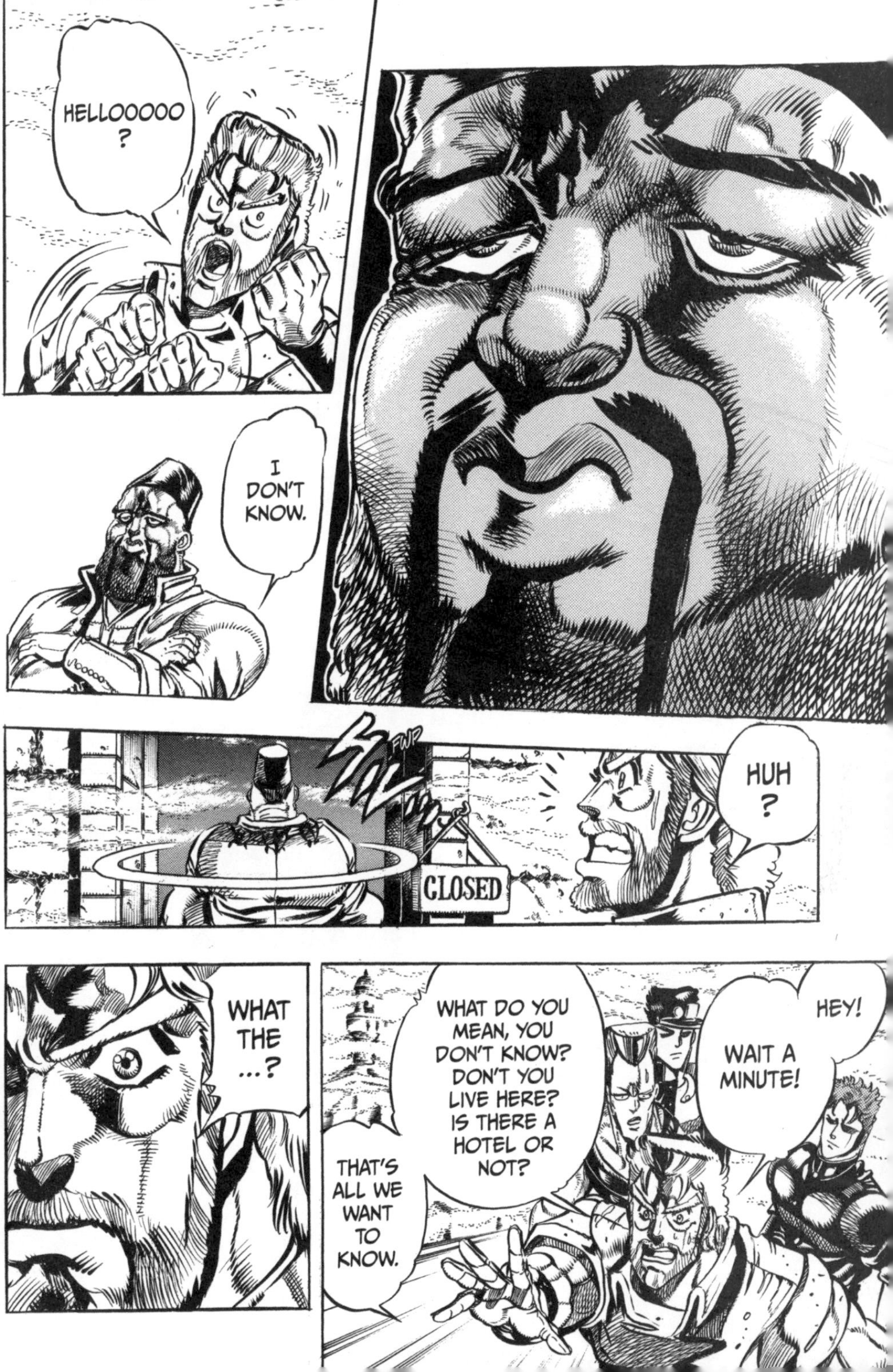
HELLOOOOO?
I DON'T KNOW.
HUH?
FWP
CLOSED
HEY!
WAIT A MINUTE!
WHAT DO YOU MEAN, YOU DON'T KNOW? DON'T YOU LIVE HERE? IS THERE A HOTEL OR NOT?
THAT'S ALL WE WANT TO KNOW.
WHAT THE ...?

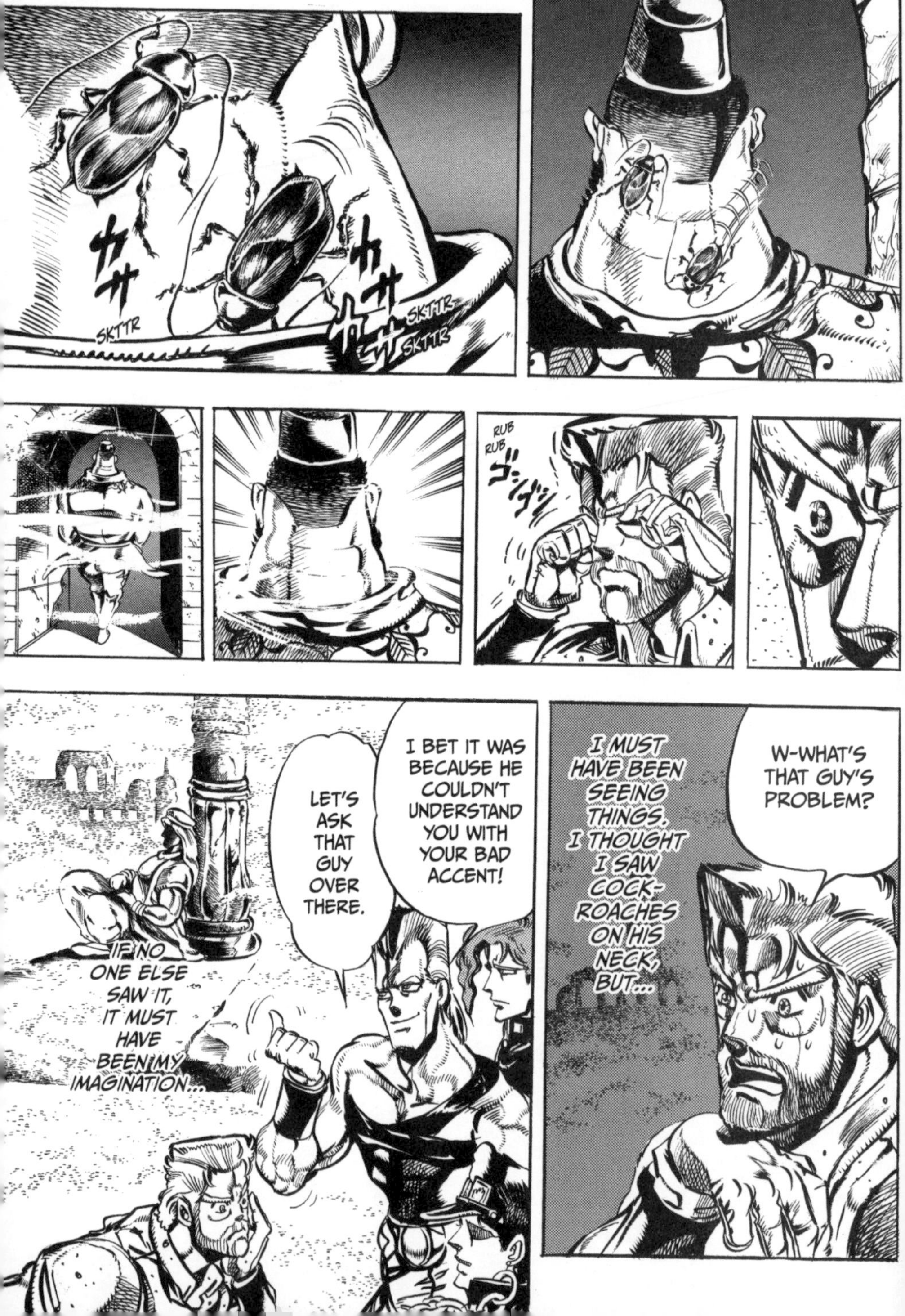
カサ
SKTTR
カサ
カサ
SKTTR
SKTTR
RUB RUB
ゴシゴシ
W-WHAT'S THAT GUY'S PROBLEM?
I MUST HAVE BEEN SEEING THINGS. I THOUGHT I SAW COCK-ROACHES ON HIS NECK, BUT...
I BET IT WAS BECAUSE HE COULDN'T UNDERSTAND YOU WITH YOUR BAD ACCENT!
LET'S ASK THAT GUY OVER THERE.
IF NO ONE ELSE SAW IT, IT MUST HAVE BEEN MY IMAGINATION...

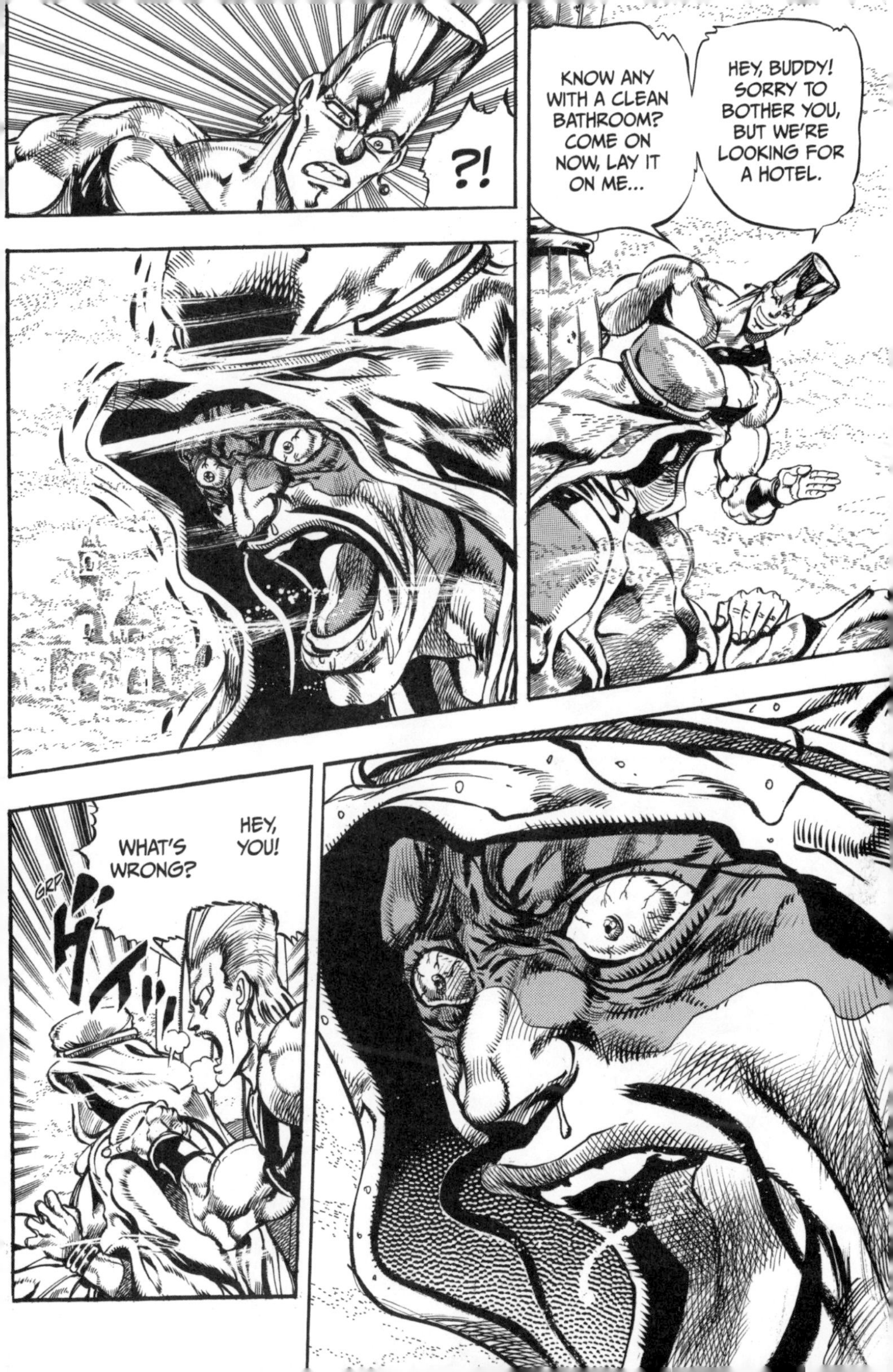
HEY, BUDDY! SORRY TO BOTHER YOU, BUT WE'RE LOOKING FOR A HOTEL.
KNOW ANY WITH A CLEAN BATHROOM? COME ON NOW, LAY IT ON ME...
?!
HEY, YOU!
WHAT'S WRONG?
GRP

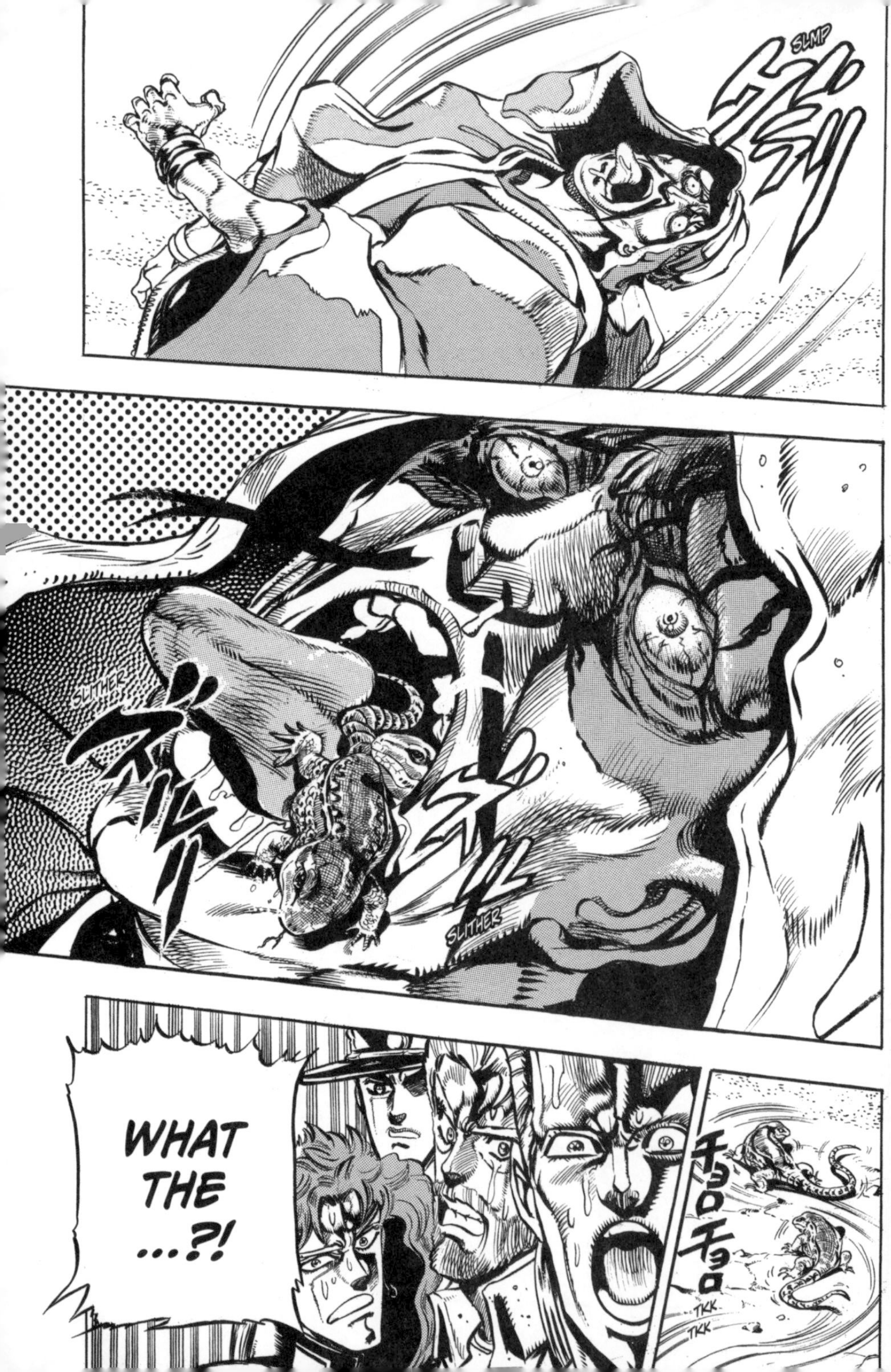
SLMP
SLITHER
SLITHER
チョロチョロ
TKK
TKK
WHAT THE ...?!

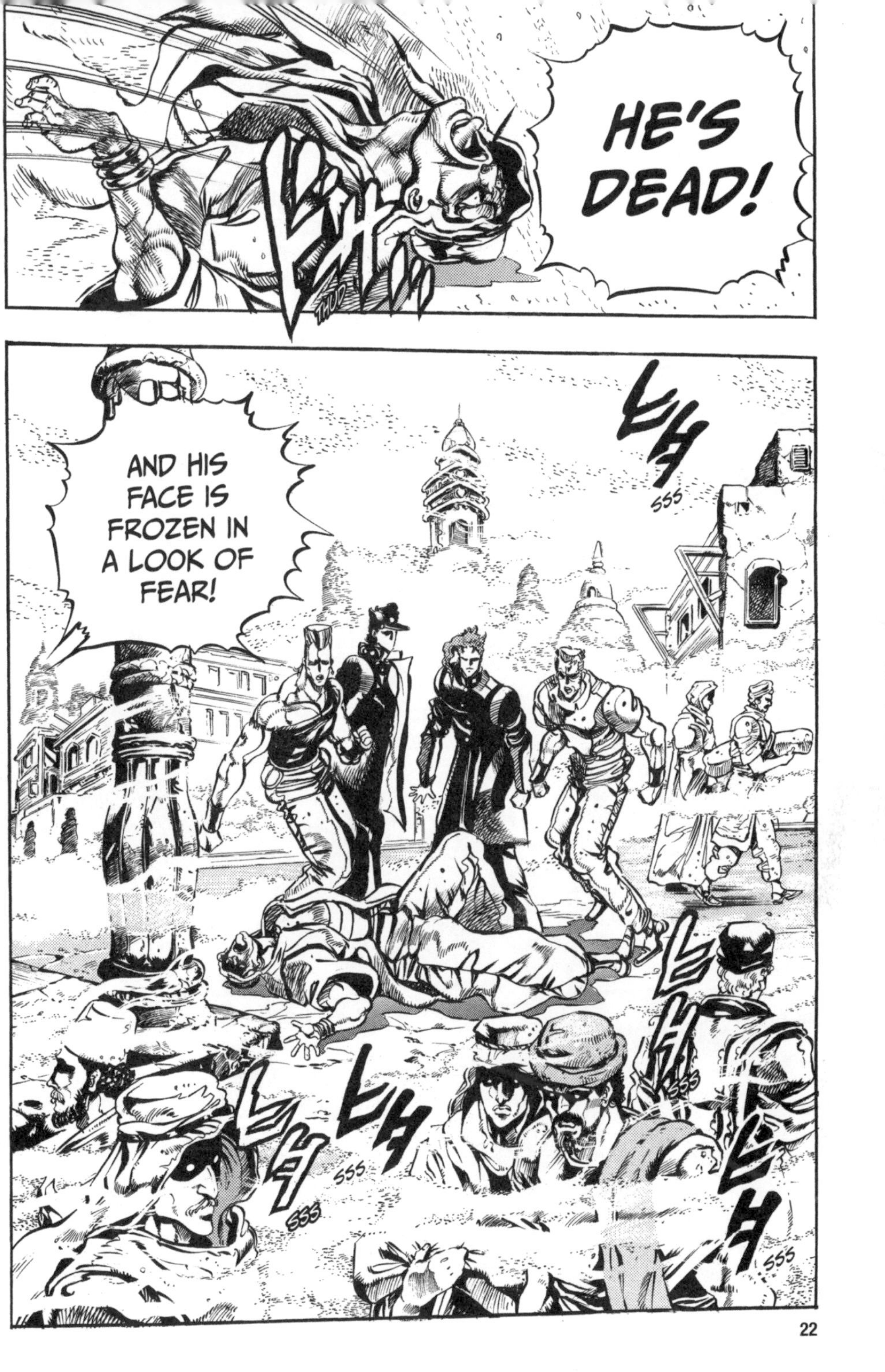
HE'S DEAD!
THUD
AND HIS FACE IS FROZEN IN A LOOK OF FEAR!
SSS
SSS
SSS
SSS
SSS

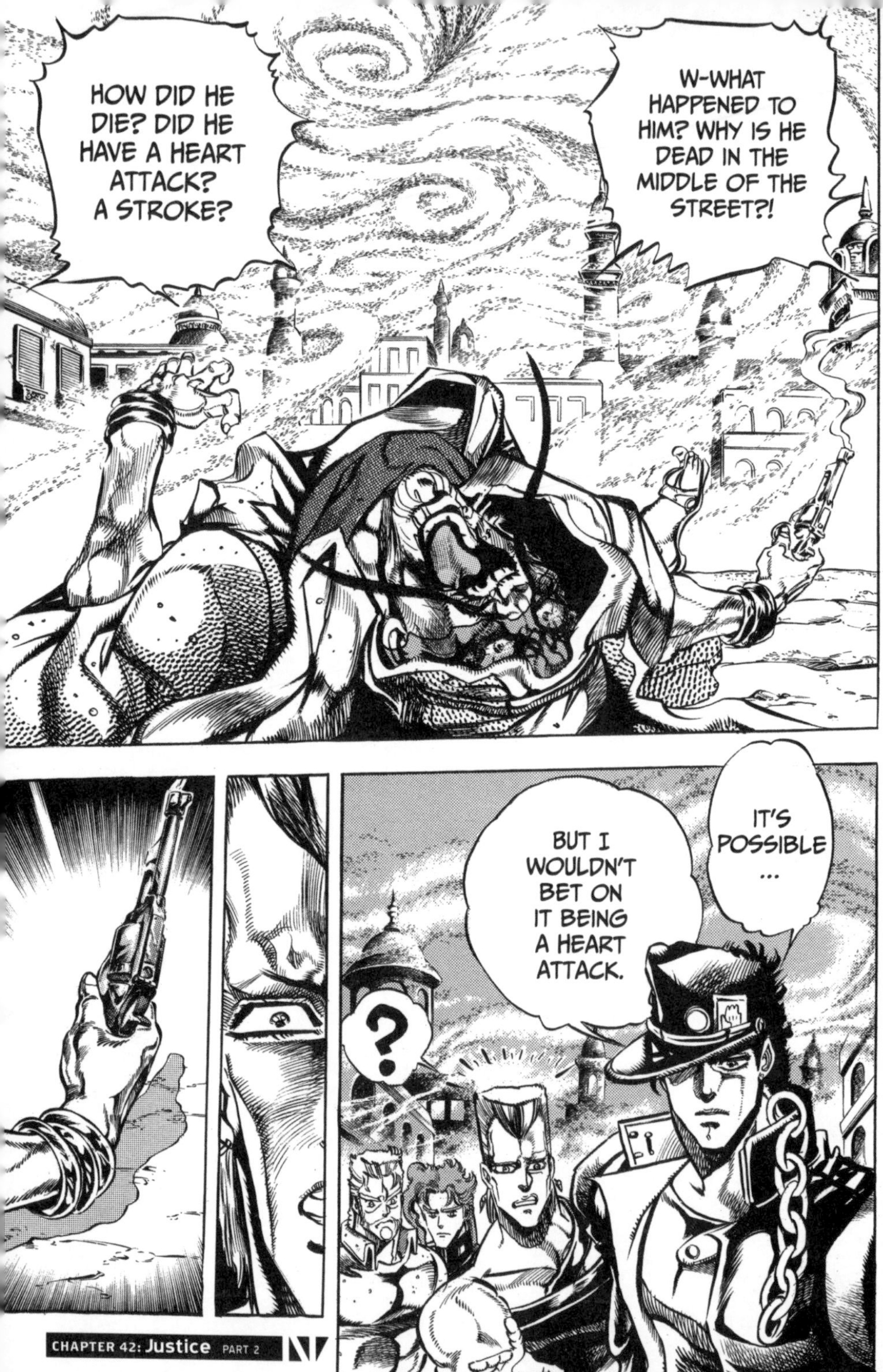
W-WHAT HAPPENED TO HIM? WHY IS HE DEAD IN THE MIDDLE OF THE STREET?!
HOW DID HE DIE? DID HE HAVE A HEART ATTACK? A STROKE?
IT'S POSSIBLE ...
BUT I WOULDN'T BET ON IT BEING A HEART ATTACK.
?

CHAPTER 42: Justice PART 2

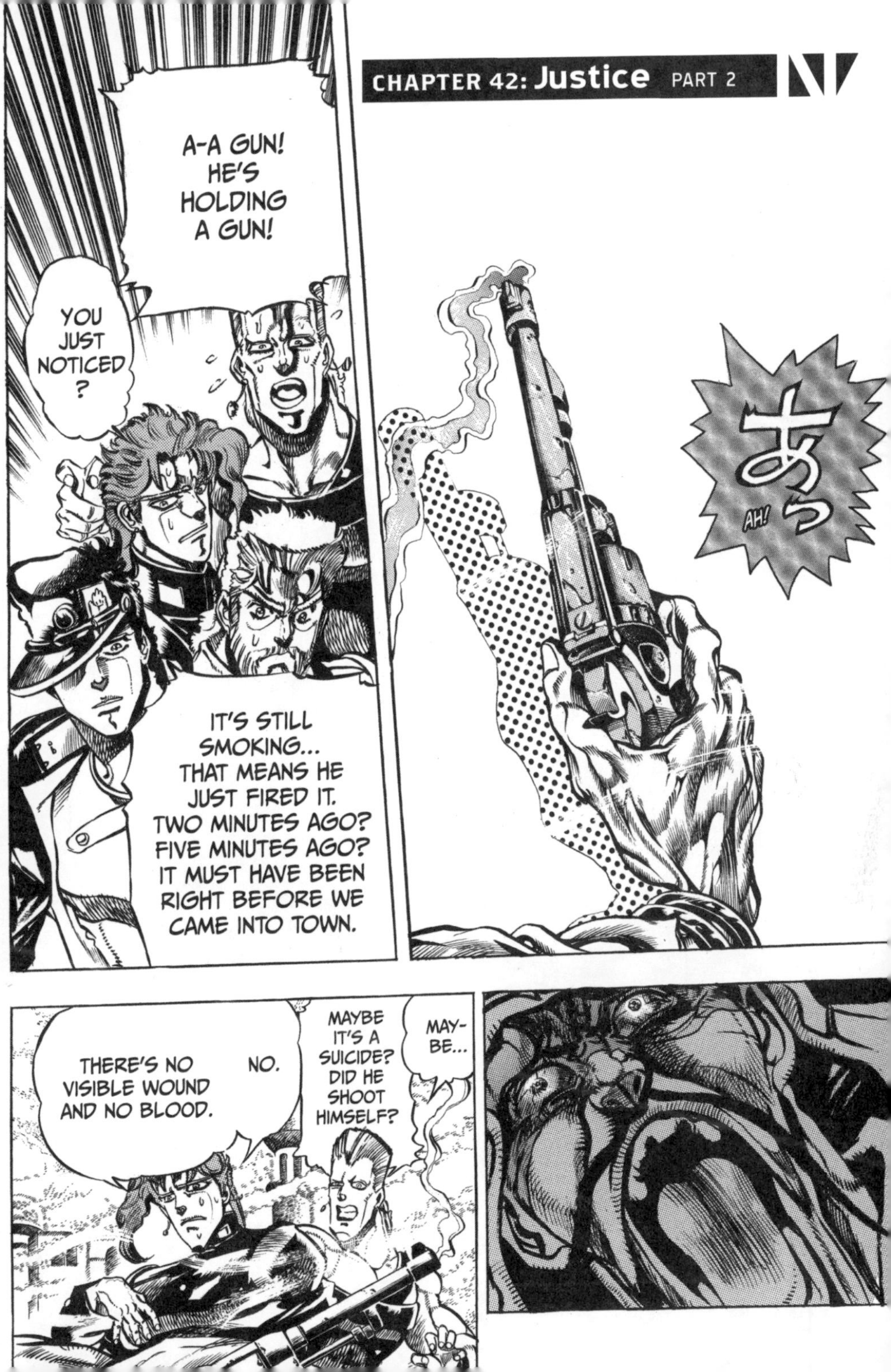

あち
AH!
A-A GUN! HE'S HOLDING A GUN!
YOU JUST NOTICED?
IT'S STILL SMOKING... THAT MEANS HE JUST FIRED IT. TWO MINUTES AGO? FIVE MINUTES AGO? IT MUST HAVE BEEN RIGHT BEFORE WE CAME INTO TOWN.
MAY-BE...
MAYBE IT'S A SUICIDE? DID HE SHOOT HIMSELF?
NO.
THERE'S NO VISIBLE WOUND AND NO BLOOD.

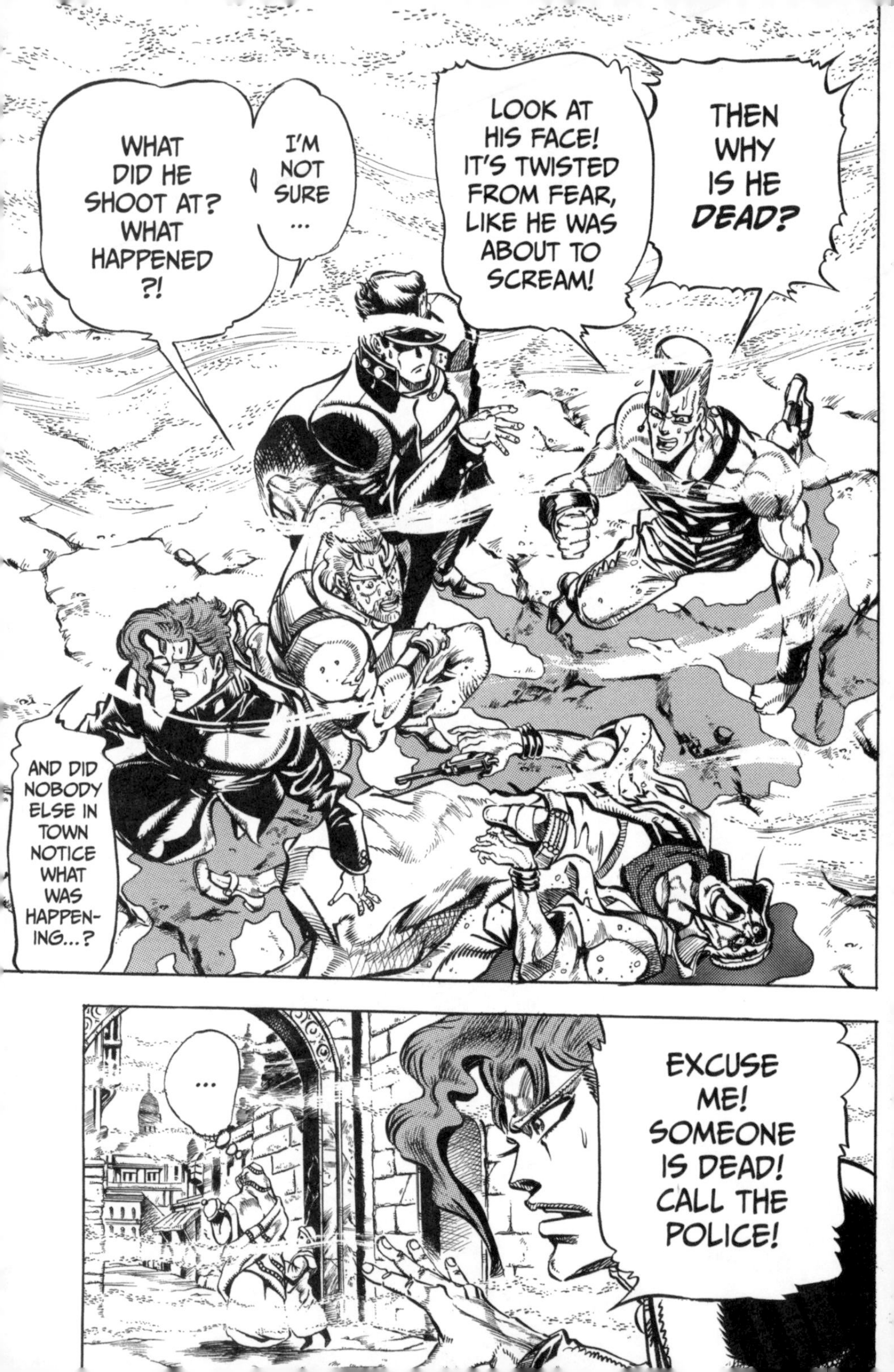
THEN WHY IS HE *DEAD?*
LOOK AT HIS FACE! IT'S TWISTED FROM FEAR, LIKE HE WAS ABOUT TO SCREAM!
I'M NOT SURE ...
WHAT DID HE SHOOT AT? WHAT HAPPENED ?!
AND DID NOBODY ELSE IN TOWN NOTICE WHAT WAS HAPPEN-ING...?
EXCUSE ME! SOMEONE IS DEAD! CALL THE POLICE!
...

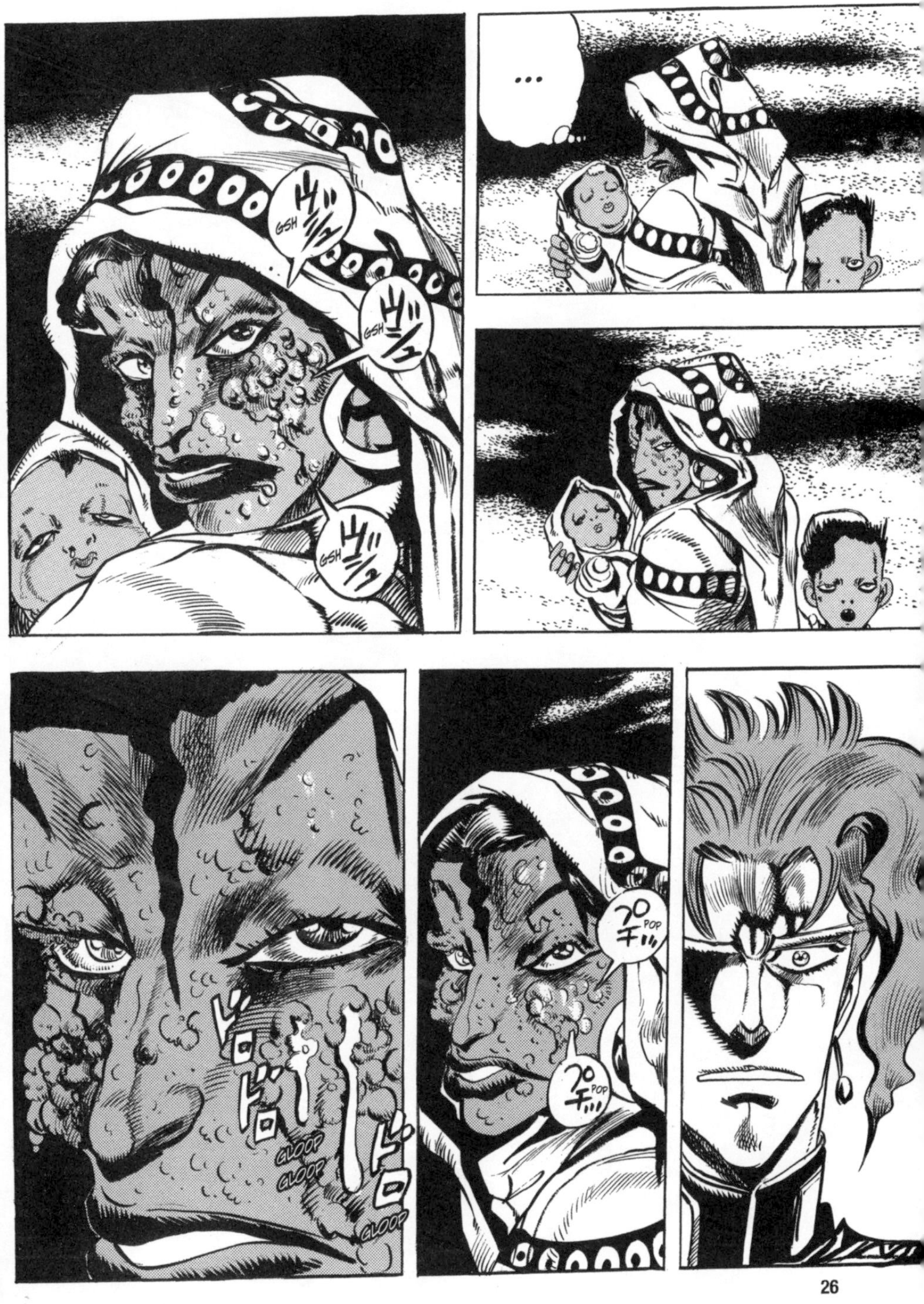
...
GSH
GSH
GSH
POP
POP
CLOOP
CLOOP
CLOOP

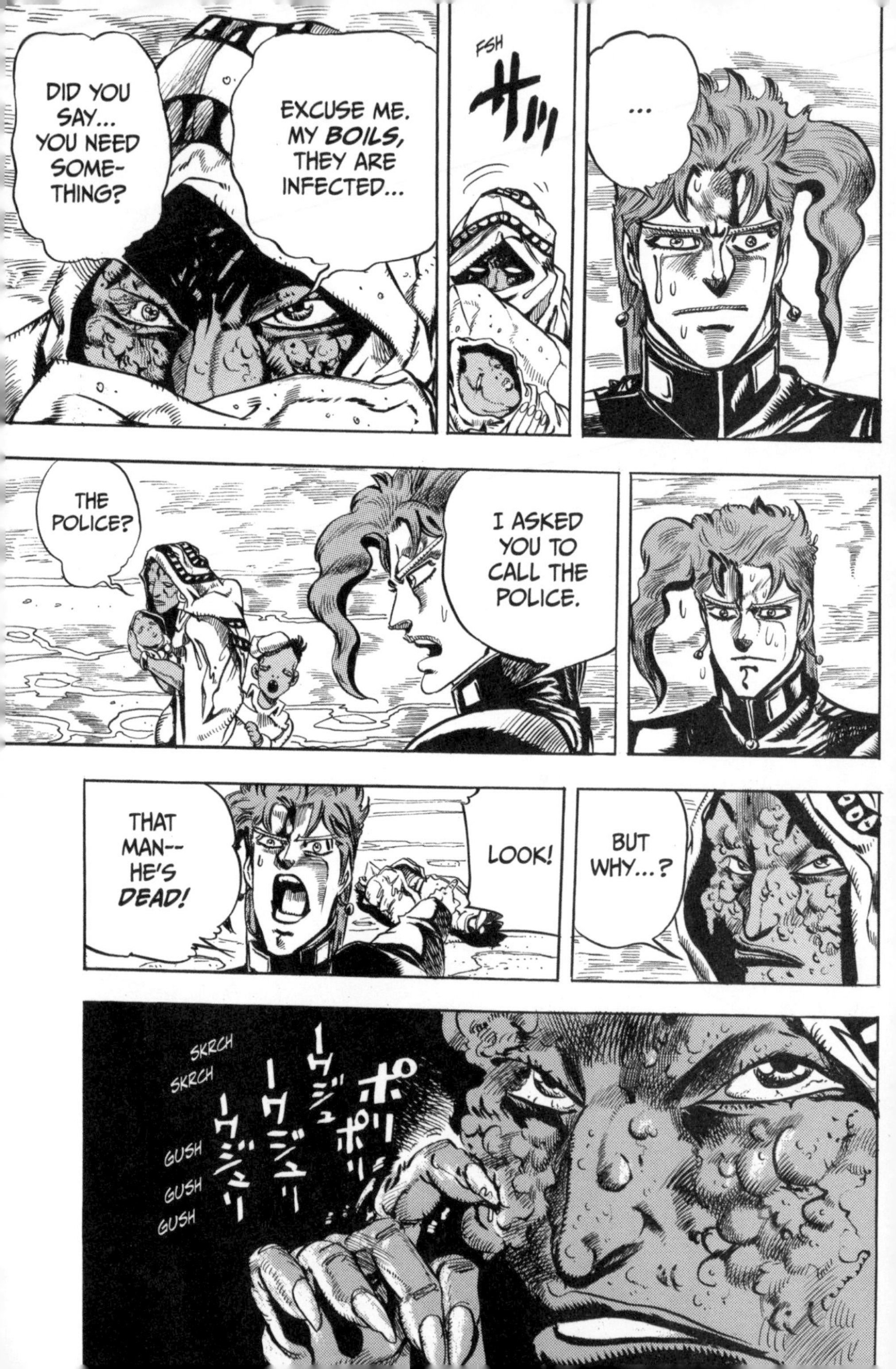
...
FSH
サッ
EXCUSE ME. MY *BOILS,* THEY ARE INFECTED...
DID YOU SAY... YOU NEED SOME-THING?
I ASKED YOU TO CALL THE POLICE.
THE POLICE?
BUT WHY...?
LOOK!
THAT MAN-- HE'S *DEAD!*
ポリ ポリ
SKRCH SKRCH
GUSH GUSH GUSH

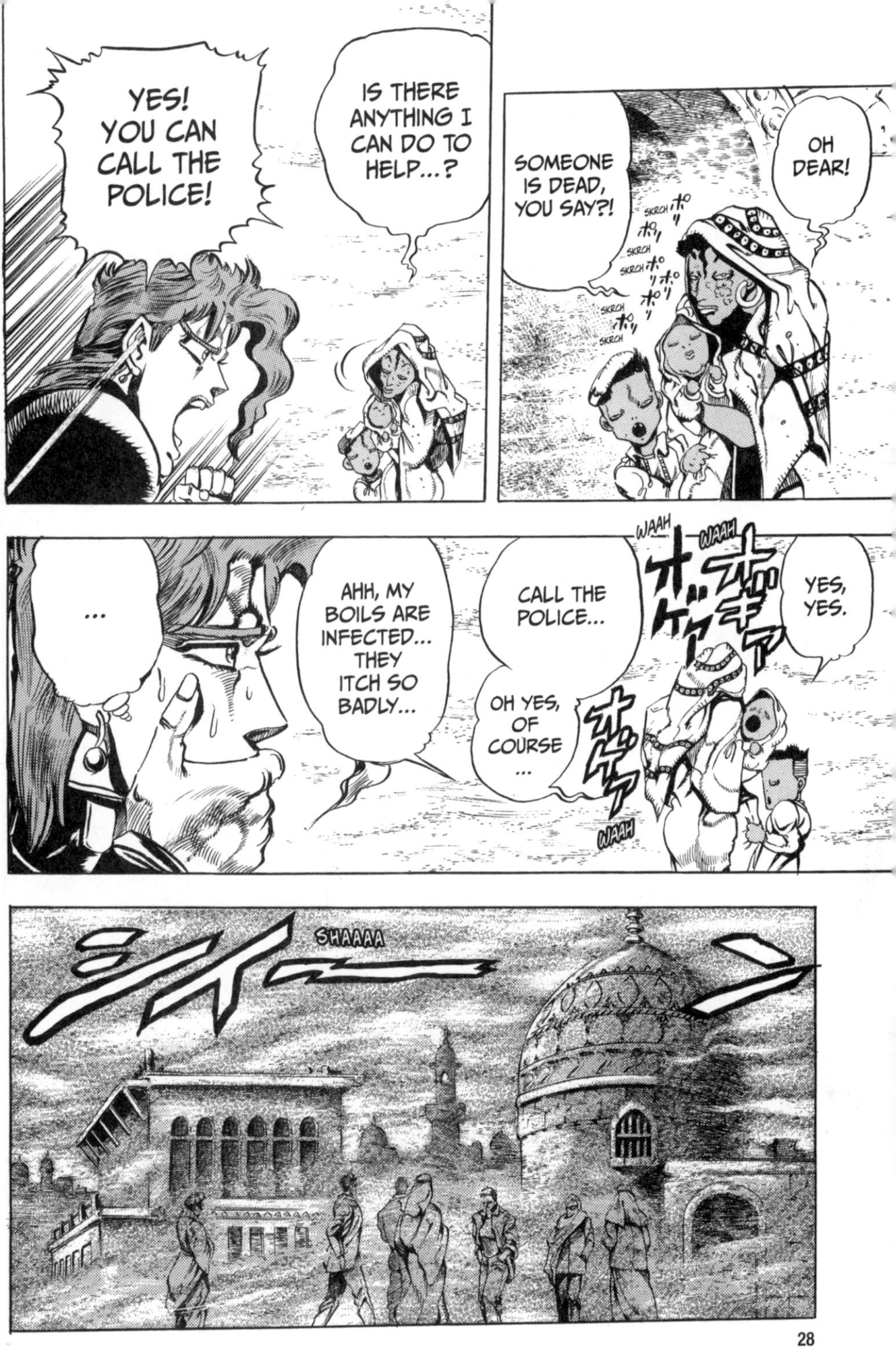

OH DEAR!
SOMEONE IS DEAD, YOU SAY?!
SKRCH
SKRCH
SKRCH
SKRCH
SKRCH
IS THERE ANYTHING I CAN DO TO HELP...?
YES! YOU CAN CALL THE POLICE!
YES, YES.
WAAH
WAAH
WAAH
CALL THE POLICE...
OH YES, OF COURSE ...
AHH, MY BOILS ARE INFECTED... THEY ITCH SO BADLY...
...
SHAAAA

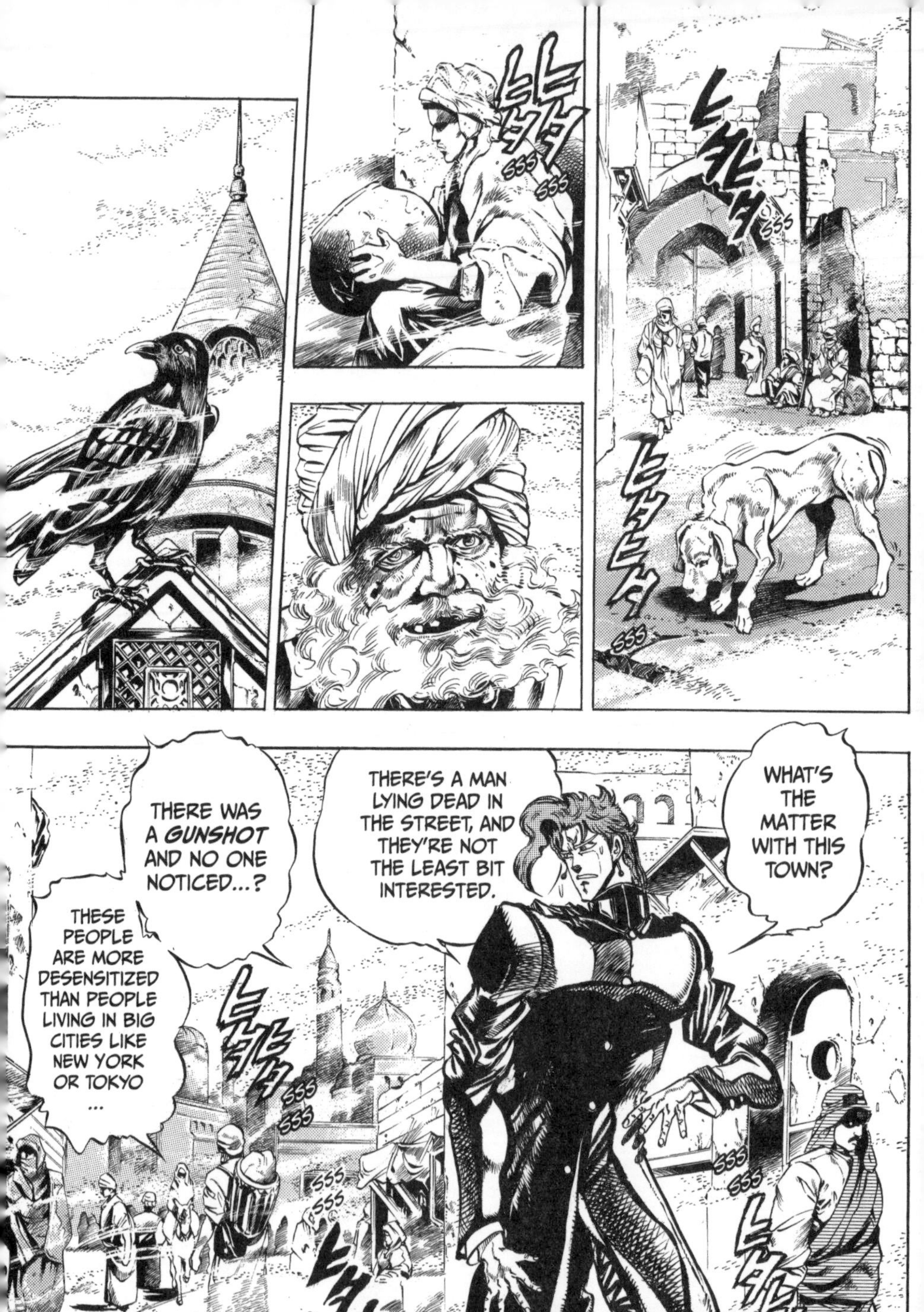
SSS
SSS
SSS SSS
SSS
WHAT'S THE MATTER WITH THIS TOWN?
THERE'S A MAN LYING DEAD IN THE STREET, AND THEY'RE NOT THE LEAST BIT INTERESTED.
THERE WAS A *GUNSHOT* AND NO ONE NOTICED...?
THESE PEOPLE ARE MORE DESENSITIZED THAN PEOPLE LIVING IN BIG CITIES LIKE NEW YORK OR TOKYO ...
SSS SSS
SSS SSS
SSS SSS

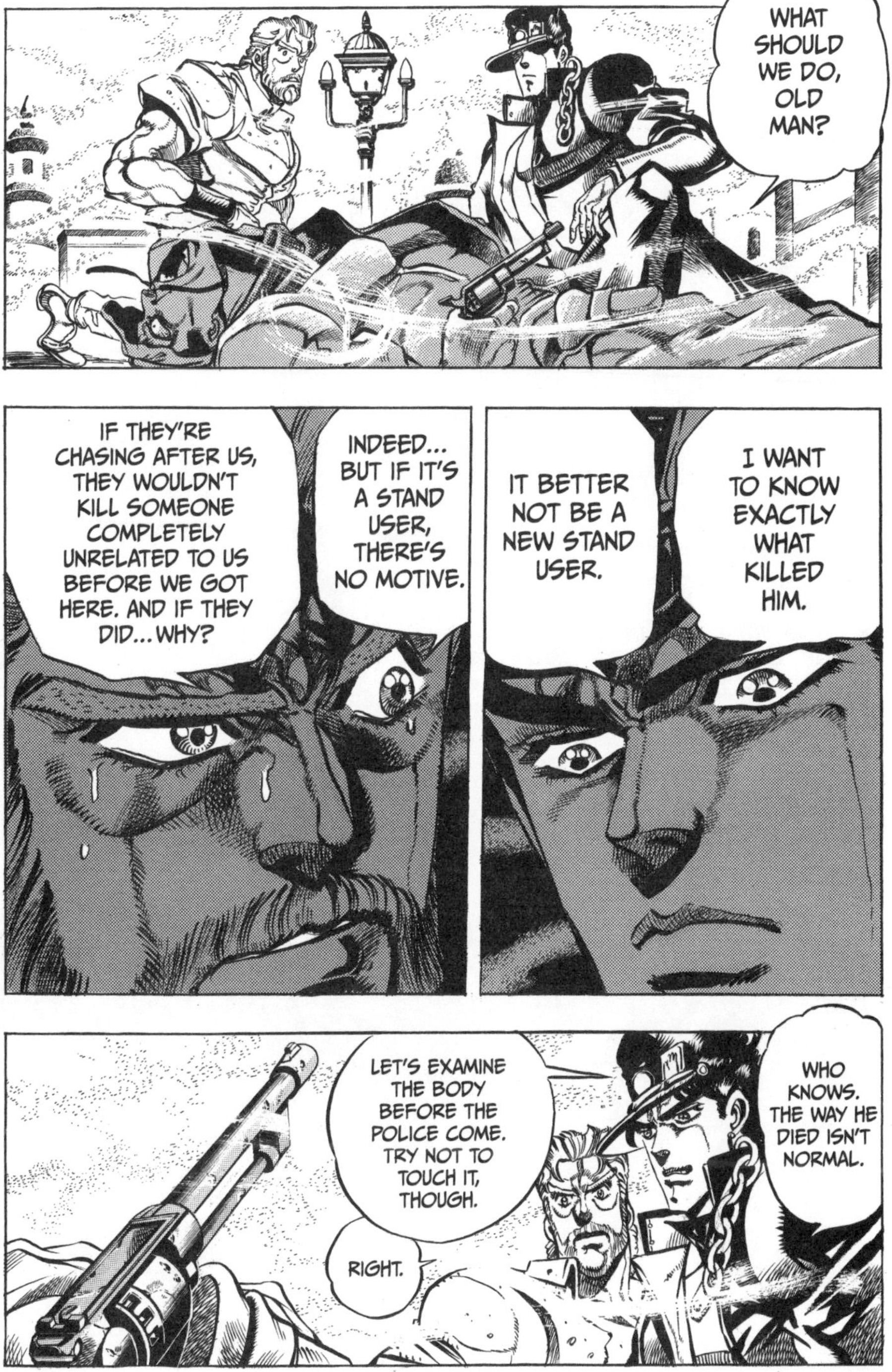
WHAT SHOULD WE DO, OLD MAN?
I WANT TO KNOW EXACTLY WHAT KILLED HIM.
IT BETTER NOT BE A NEW STAND USER.
INDEED... BUT IF IT'S A STAND USER, THERE'S NO MOTIVE.
IF THEY'RE CHASING AFTER US, THEY WOULDN'T KILL SOMEONE COMPLETELY UNRELATED TO US BEFORE WE GOT HERE. AND IF THEY DID...WHY?
WHO KNOWS. THE WAY HE DIED ISN'T NORMAL.
LET'S EXAMINE THE BODY BEFORE THE POLICE COME. TRY NOT TO TOUCH IT, THOUGH.
RIGHT.

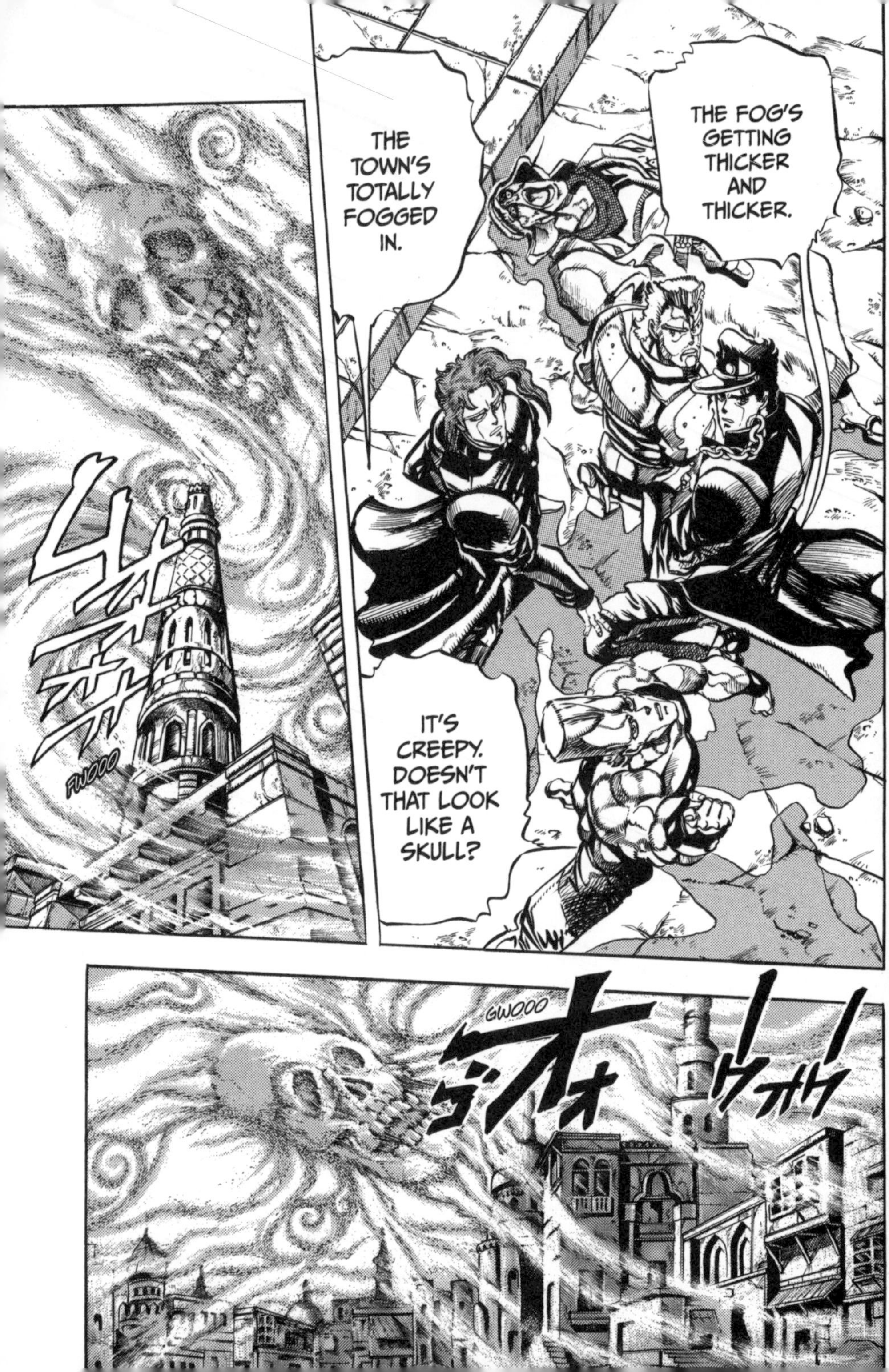
THE FOG'S GETTING THICKER AND THICKER.
THE TOWN'S TOTALLY FOGGED IN.
IT'S CREEPY. DOESN'T THAT LOOK LIKE A SKULL?
FWOOO
GWOOO

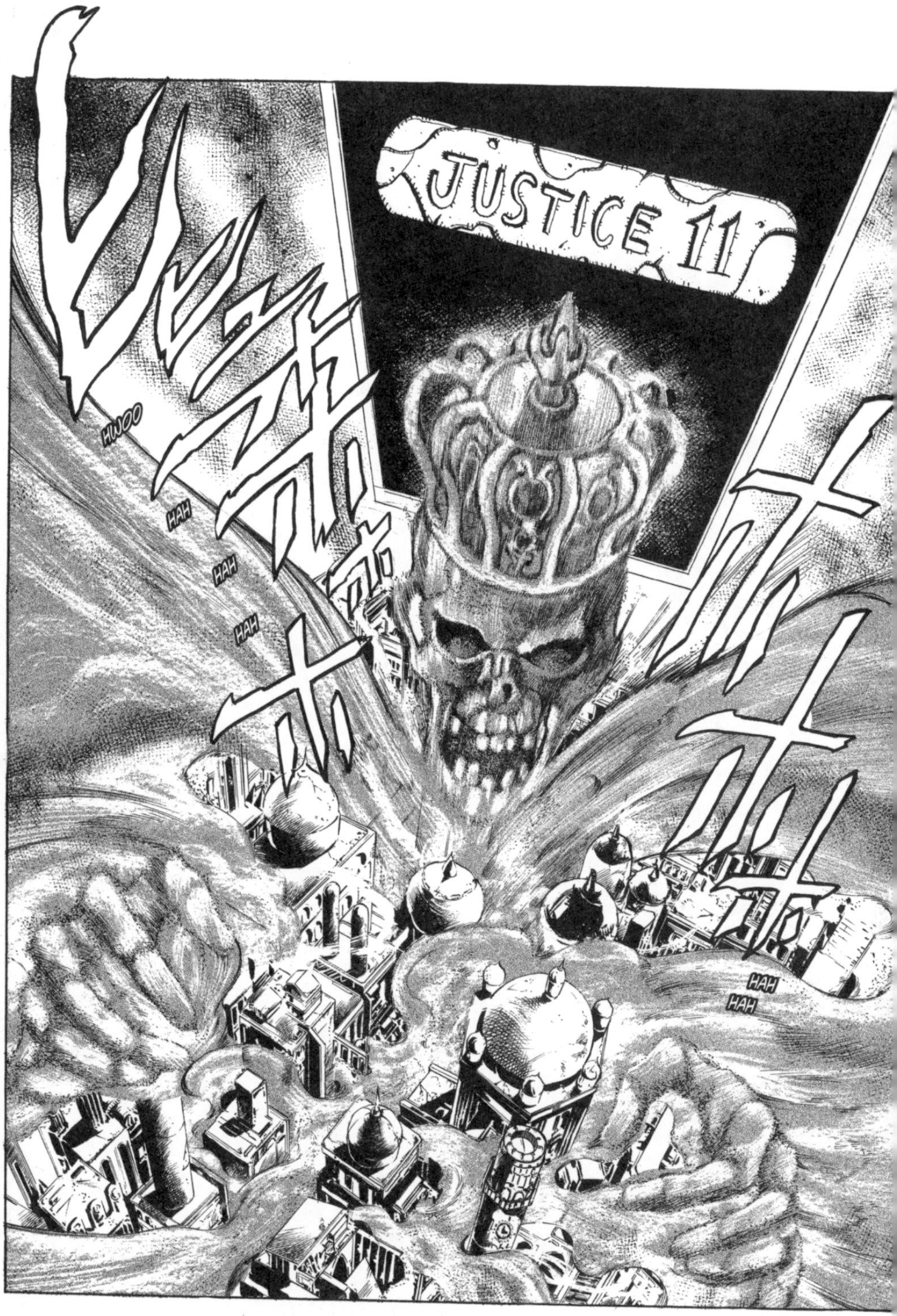
JUSTICE 11
HWOO
HAH
HAH
HAH
HAH
HAH

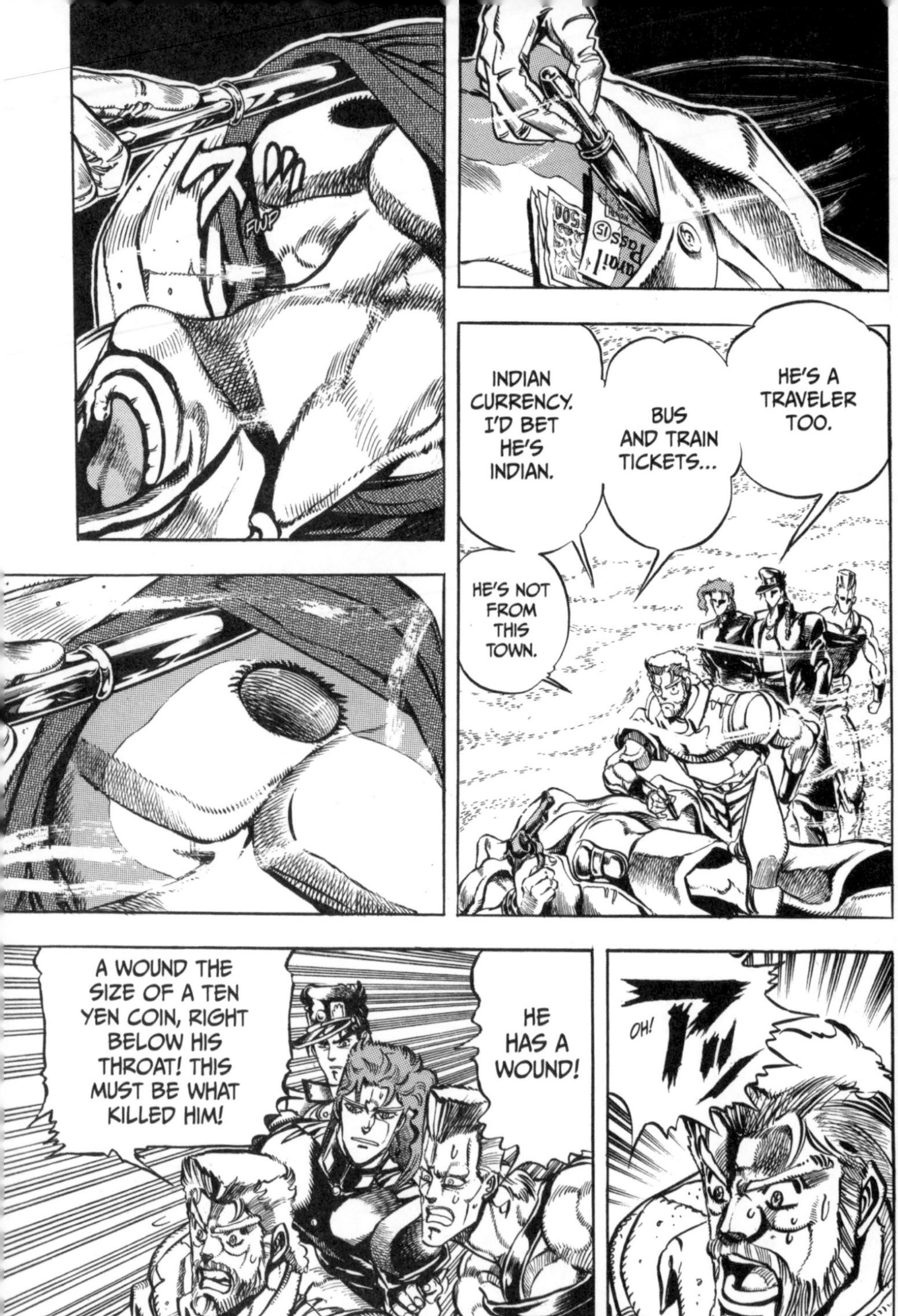
FWP
HE'S A TRAVELER TOO.
BUS AND TRAIN TICKETS...
INDIAN CURRENCY. I'D BET HE'S INDIAN.
HE'S NOT FROM THIS TOWN.
OH!
HE HAS A WOUND!
A WOUND THE SIZE OF A TEN YEN COIN, RIGHT BELOW HIS THROAT! THIS MUST BE WHAT KILLED HIM!

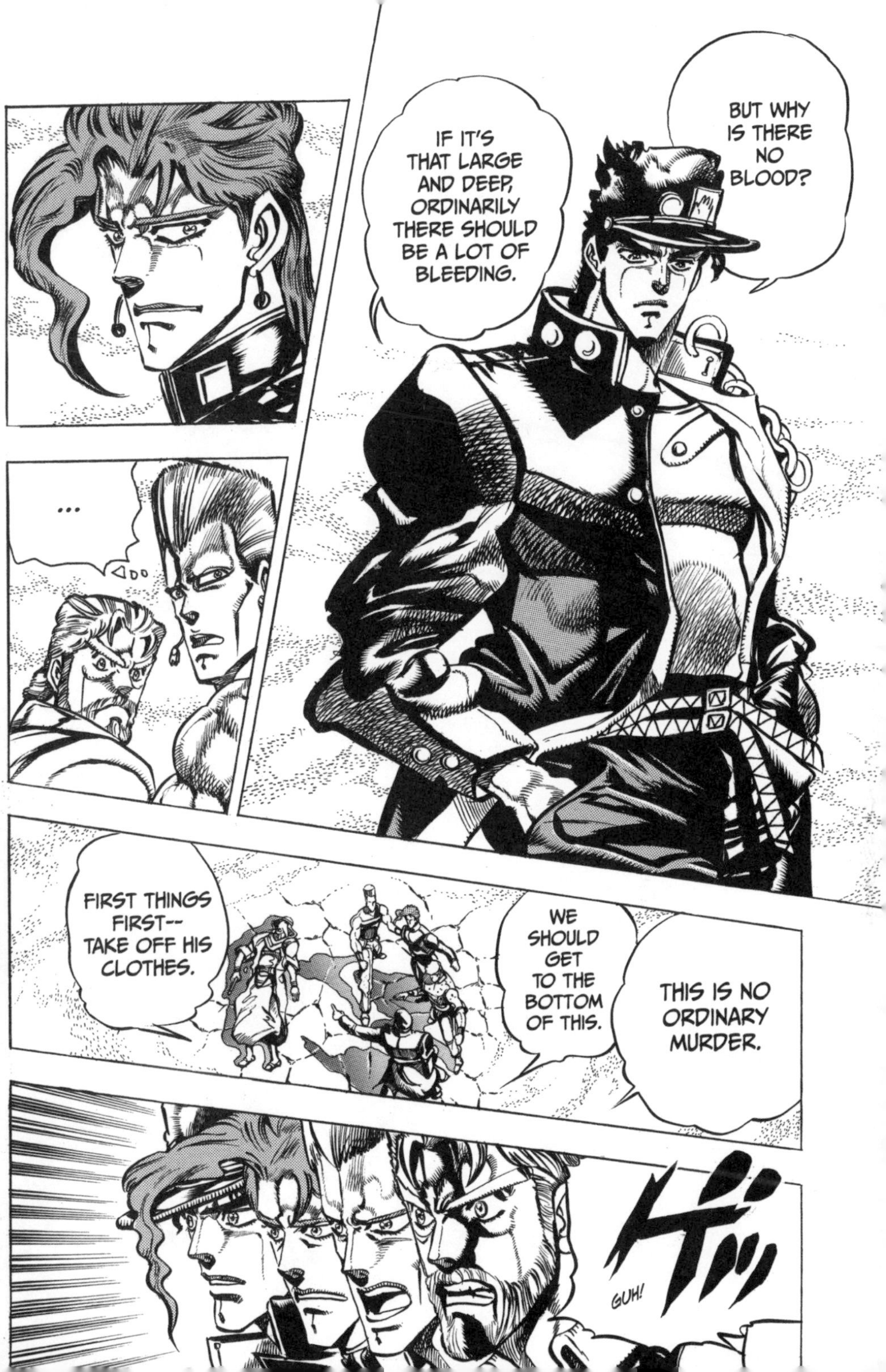
BUT WHY IS THERE NO BLOOD?
IF IT'S THAT LARGE AND DEEP, ORDINARILY THERE SHOULD BE A LOT OF BLEEDING.
...
THIS IS NO ORDINARY MURDER.
WE SHOULD GET TO THE BOTTOM OF THIS.
FIRST THINGS FIRST-- TAKE OFF HIS CLOTHES.
GUH!

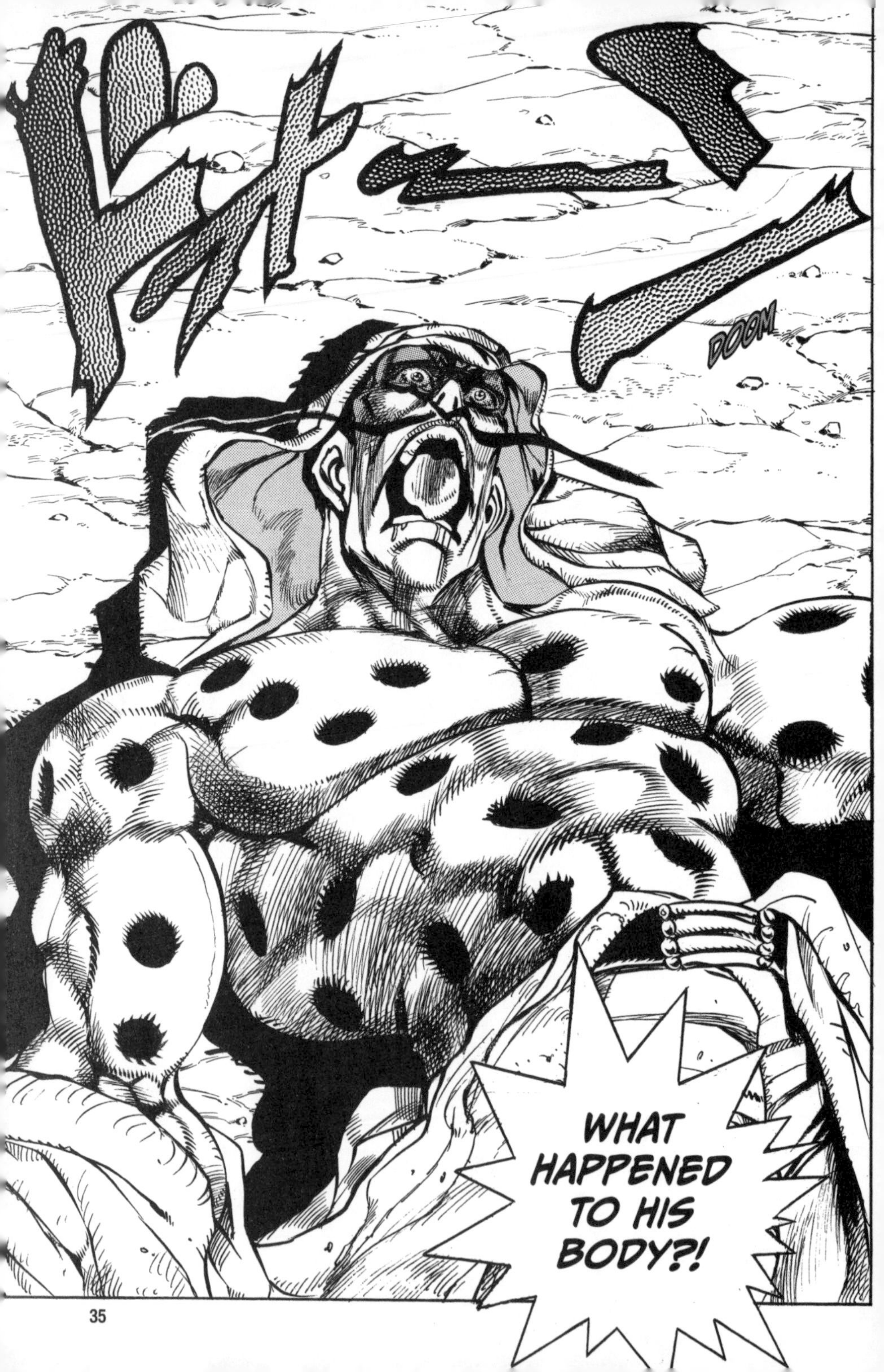
ドメメェーン
DOOM
WHAT HAPPENED TO HIS BODY?!

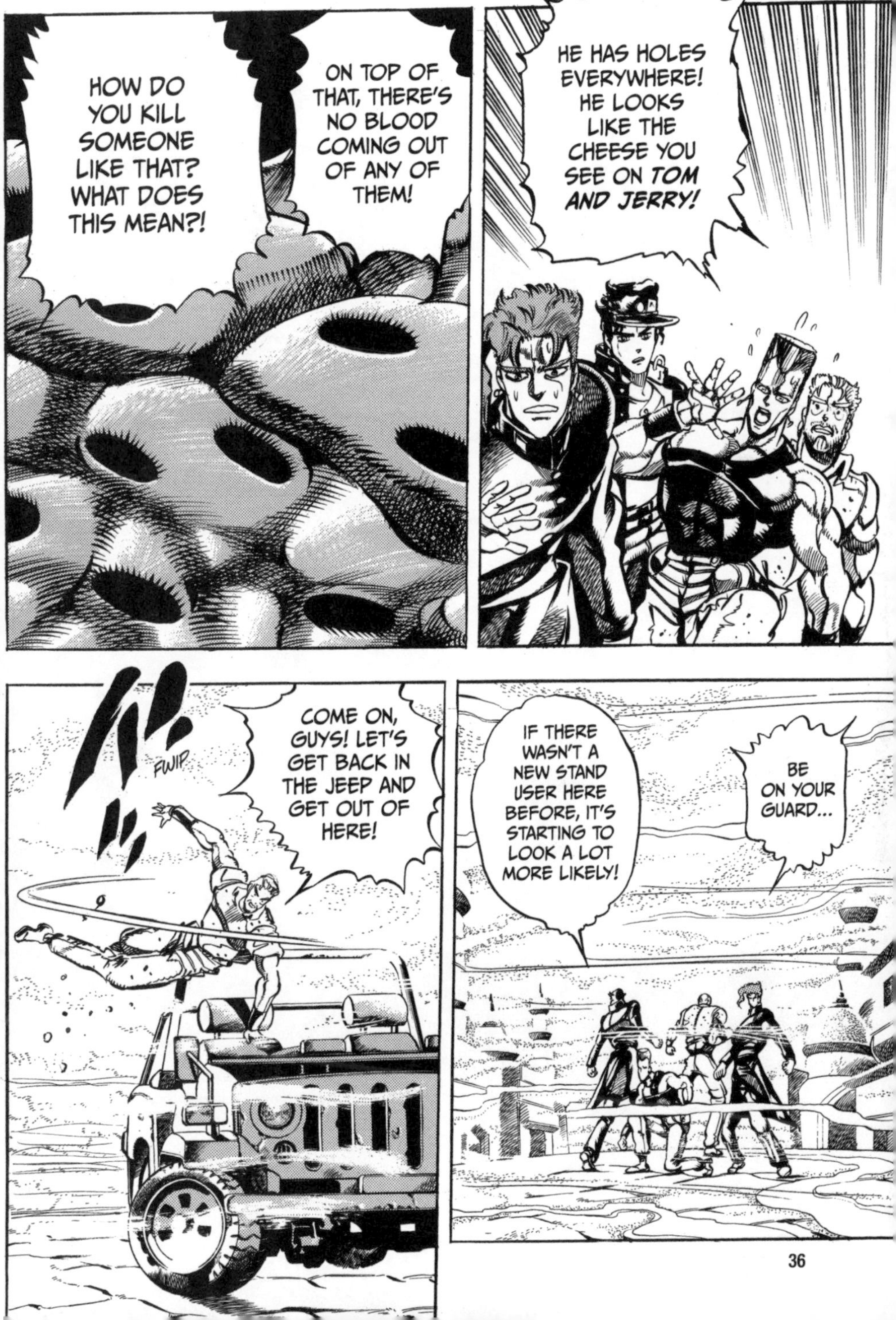
HE HAS HOLES EVERYWHERE! HE LOOKS LIKE THE CHEESE YOU SEE ON *TOM AND JERRY!*
ON TOP OF THAT, THERE'S NO BLOOD COMING OUT OF ANY OF THEM!
HOW DO YOU KILL SOMEONE LIKE THAT? WHAT DOES THIS MEAN?!
BE ON YOUR GUARD...
IF THERE WASN'T A NEW STAND USER HERE BEFORE, IT'S STARTING TO LOOK A LOT MORE LIKELY!
COME ON, GUYS! LET'S GET BACK IN THE JEEP AND GET OUT OF HERE!
FWIP

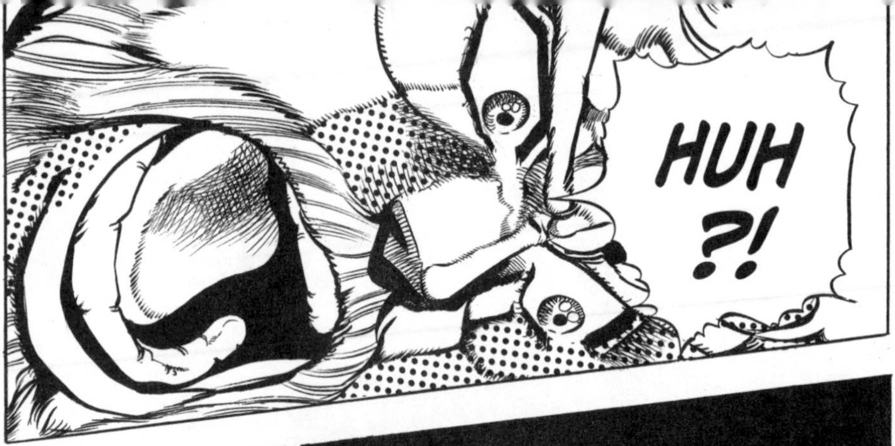
HUH ?!

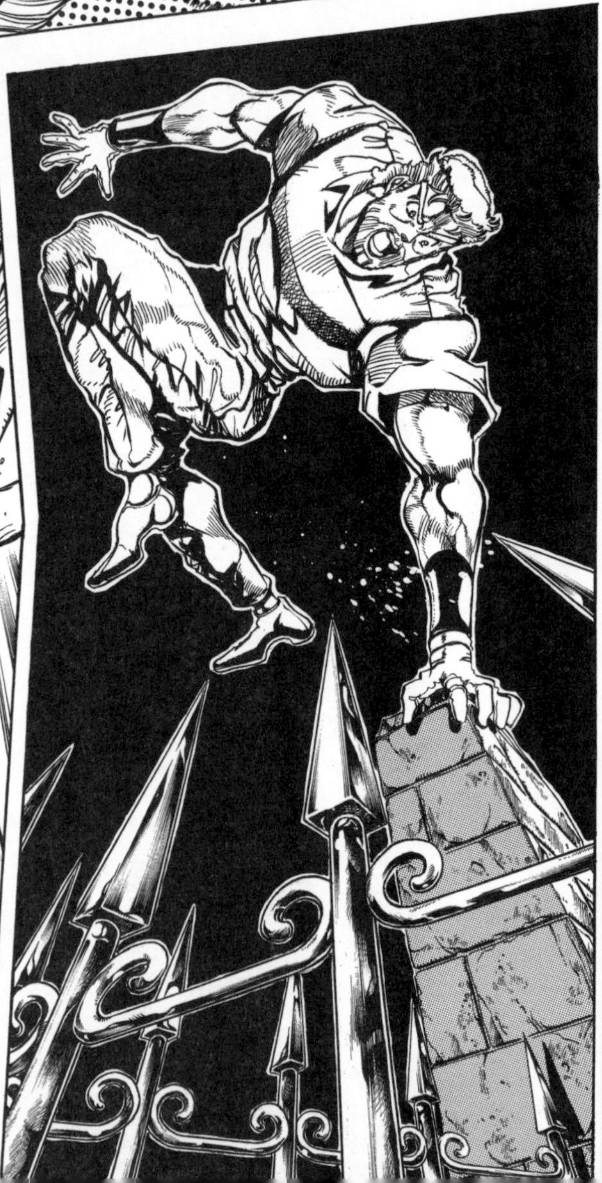

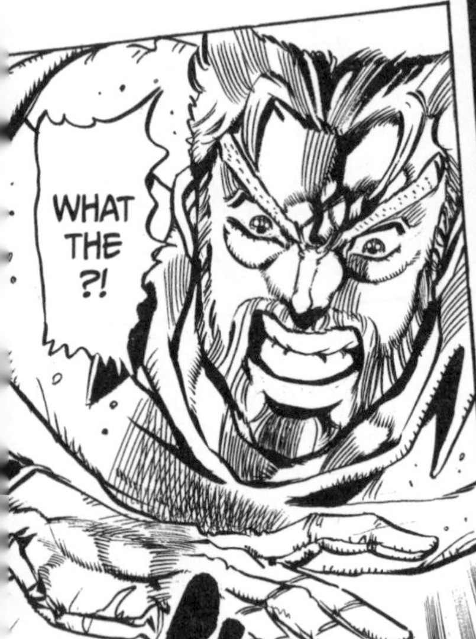
WHAT THE ?!
VWOO

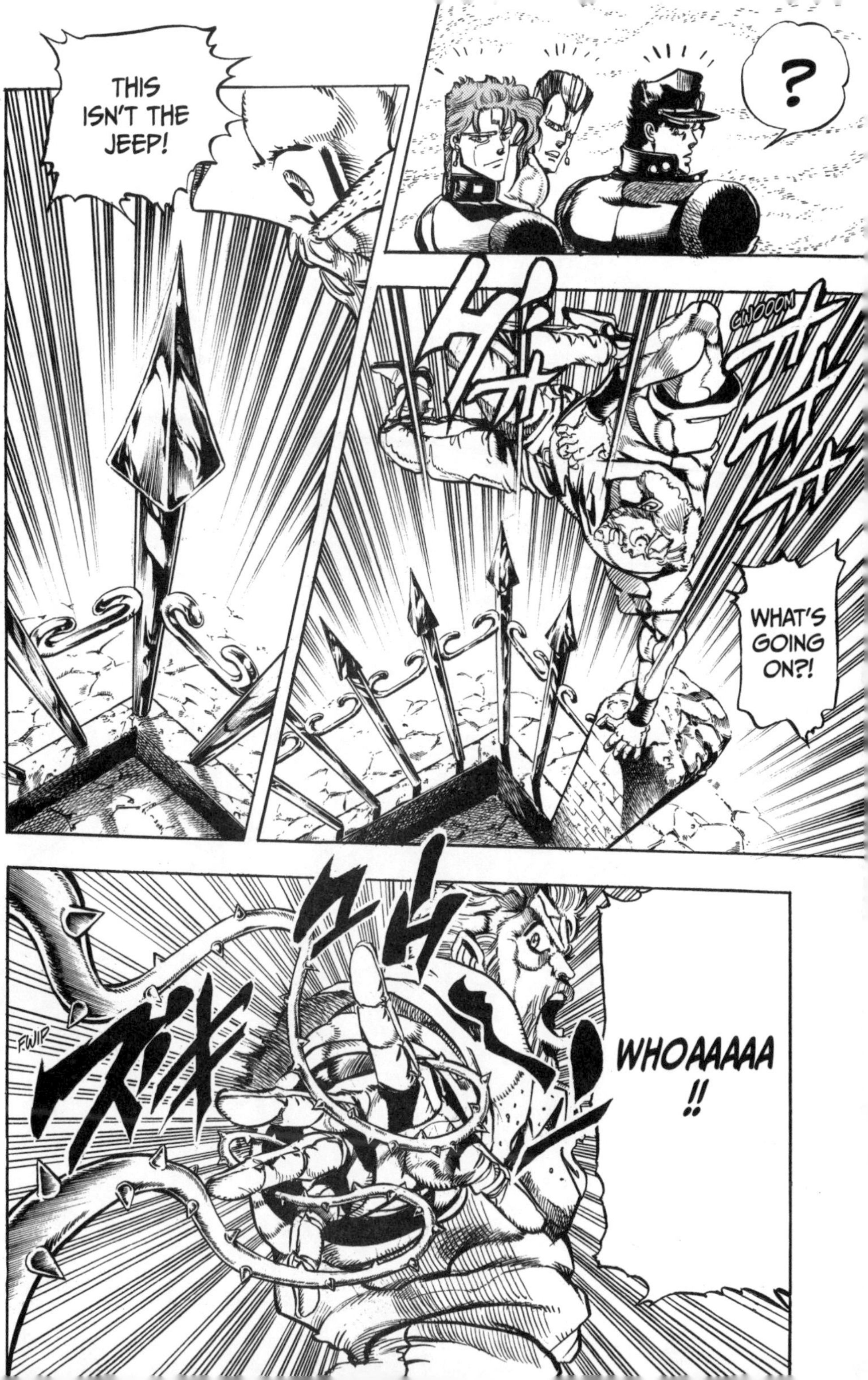
?
CWOOOM
WHAT'S GOING ON?!
THIS ISN'T THE JEEP!
FWIP
WHOAAAAA !!

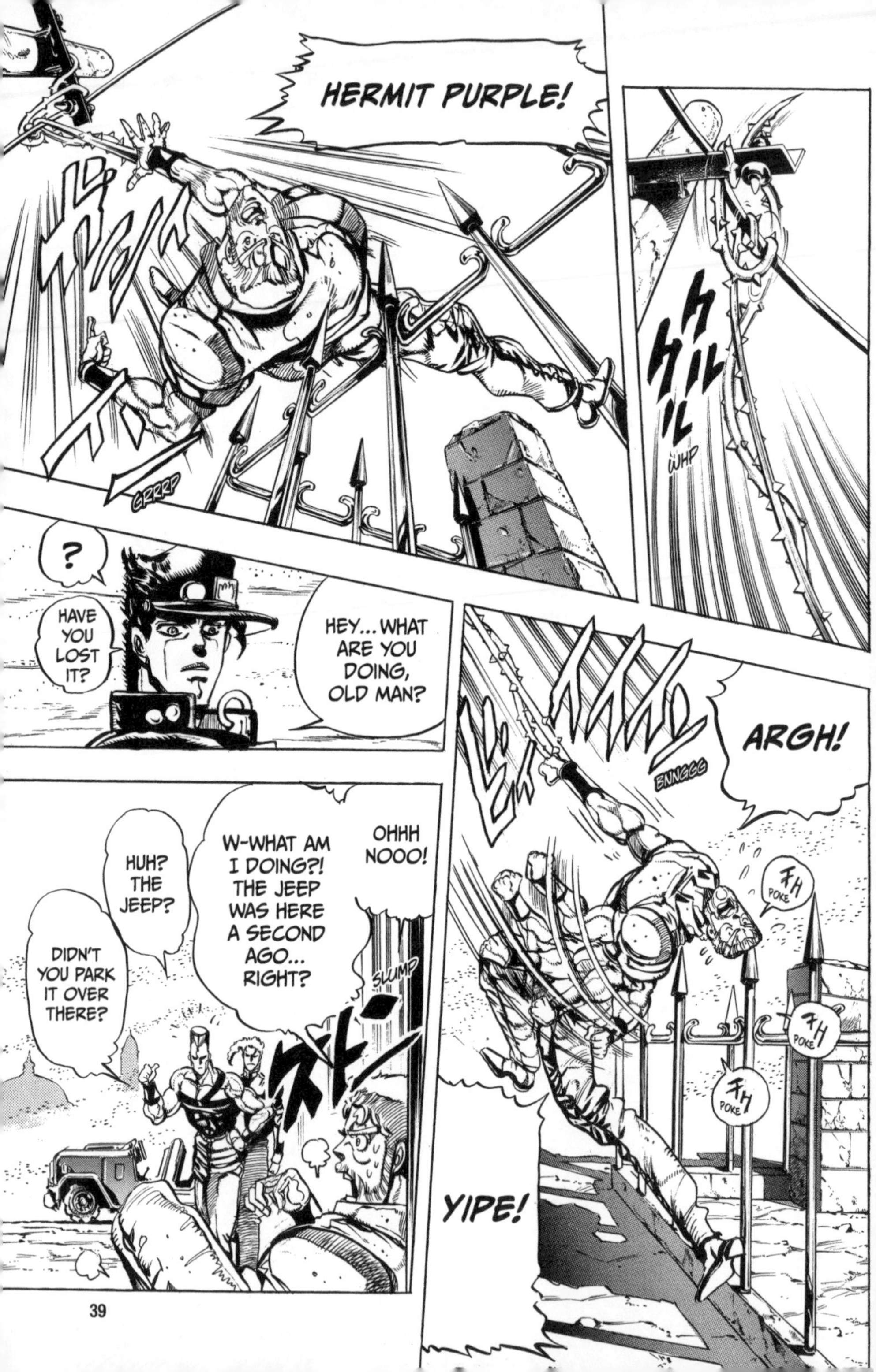
WHP
HERMIT PURPLE!
GRRRP
ARGH!
BNNGGG
POKE
POKE
POKE
YIPE!
HEY...WHAT ARE YOU DOING, OLD MAN?
?
HAVE YOU LOST IT?
OHHH NOOO!
W-WHAT AM I DOING?! THE JEEP WAS HERE A SECOND AGO... RIGHT?
HUH? THE JEEP?
DIDN'T YOU PARK IT OVER THERE?
SLUMP

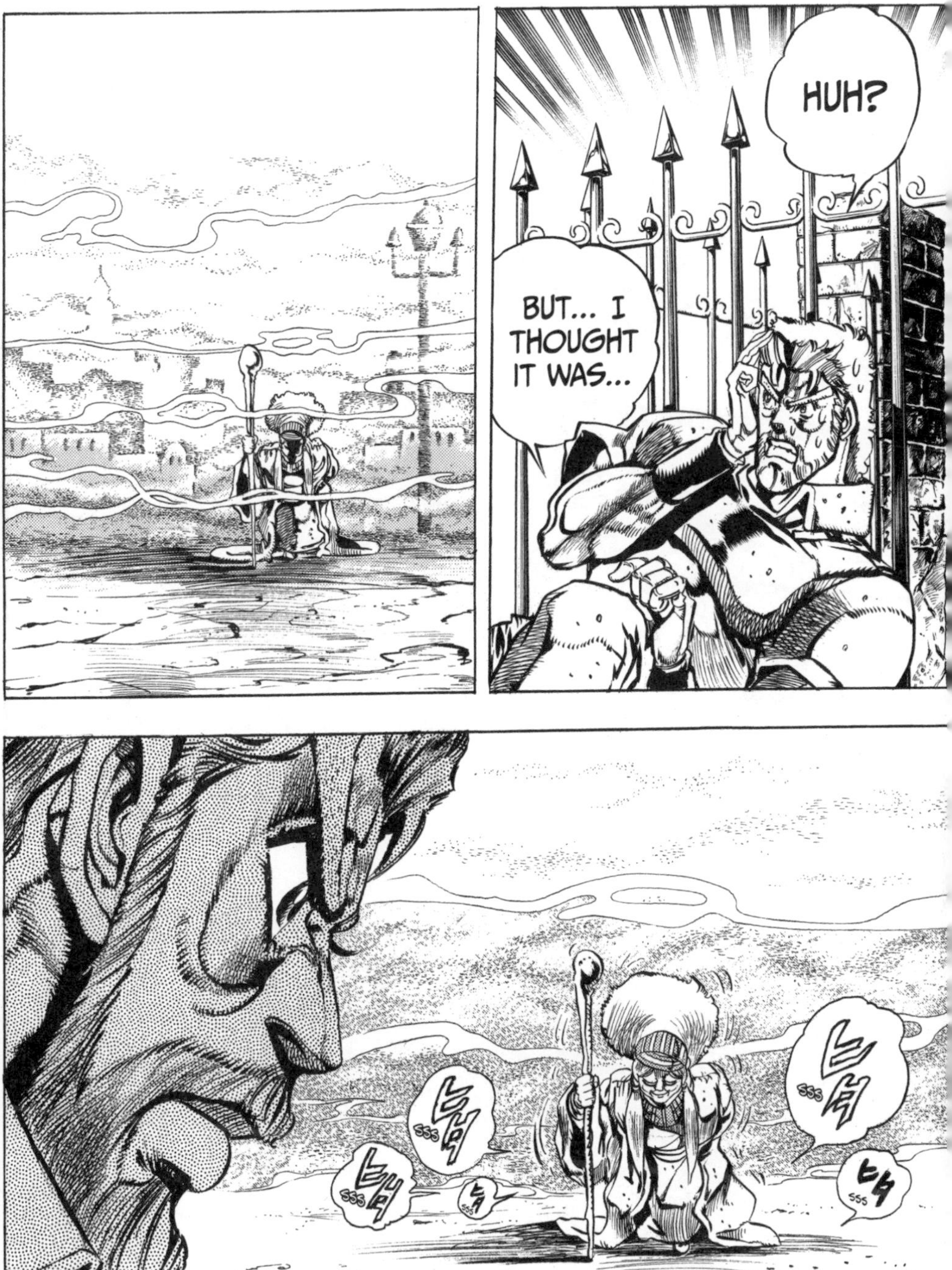
HUH?
BUT... I THOUGHT IT WAS...
sss
sss
sss
sss
sss

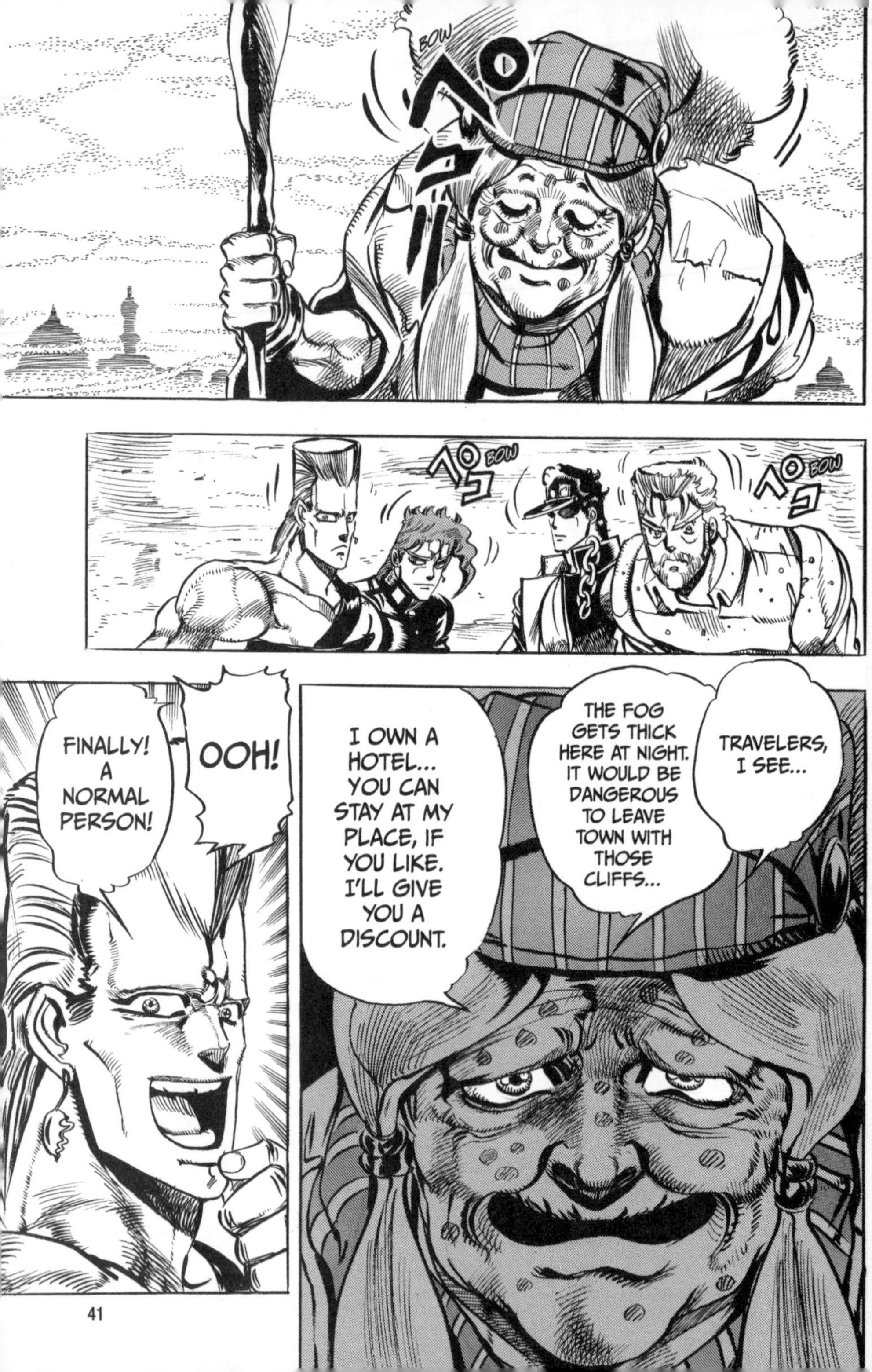
BOW
BOW
BOW
TRAVELERS, I SEE...
THE FOG GETS THICK HERE AT NIGHT. IT WOULD BE DANGEROUS TO LEAVE TOWN WITH THOSE CLIFFS...
I OWN A HOTEL... YOU CAN STAY AT MY PLACE, IF YOU LIKE. I'LL GIVE YOU A DISCOUNT.
OOH!
FINALLY! A NORMAL PERSON!

JUSTICE 11

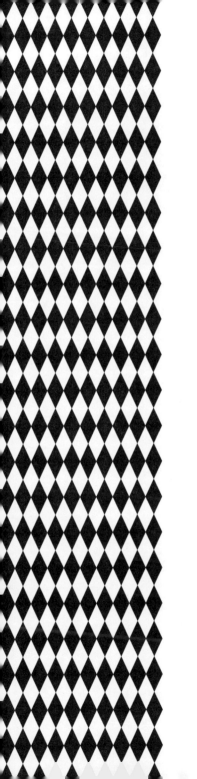

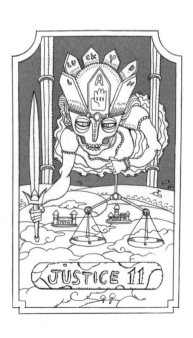

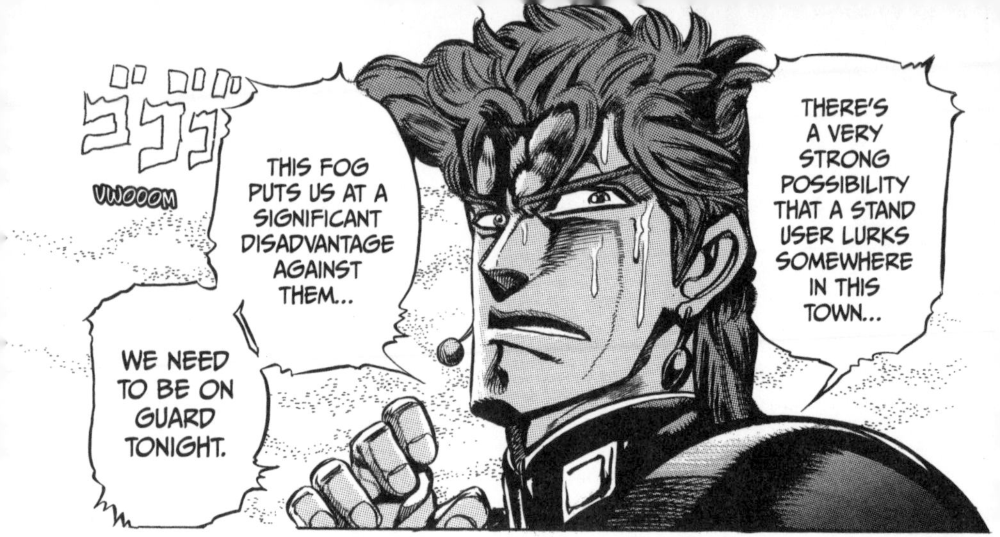
THERE'S A VERY STRONG POSSIBILITY THAT A STAND USER LURKS SOMEWHERE IN THIS TOWN...
THIS FOG PUTS US AT A SIGNIFICANT DISADVANTAGE AGAINST THEM...
VWOOOM
WE NEED TO BE ON GUARD TONIGHT.

CHAPTER 43: Justice PART 3

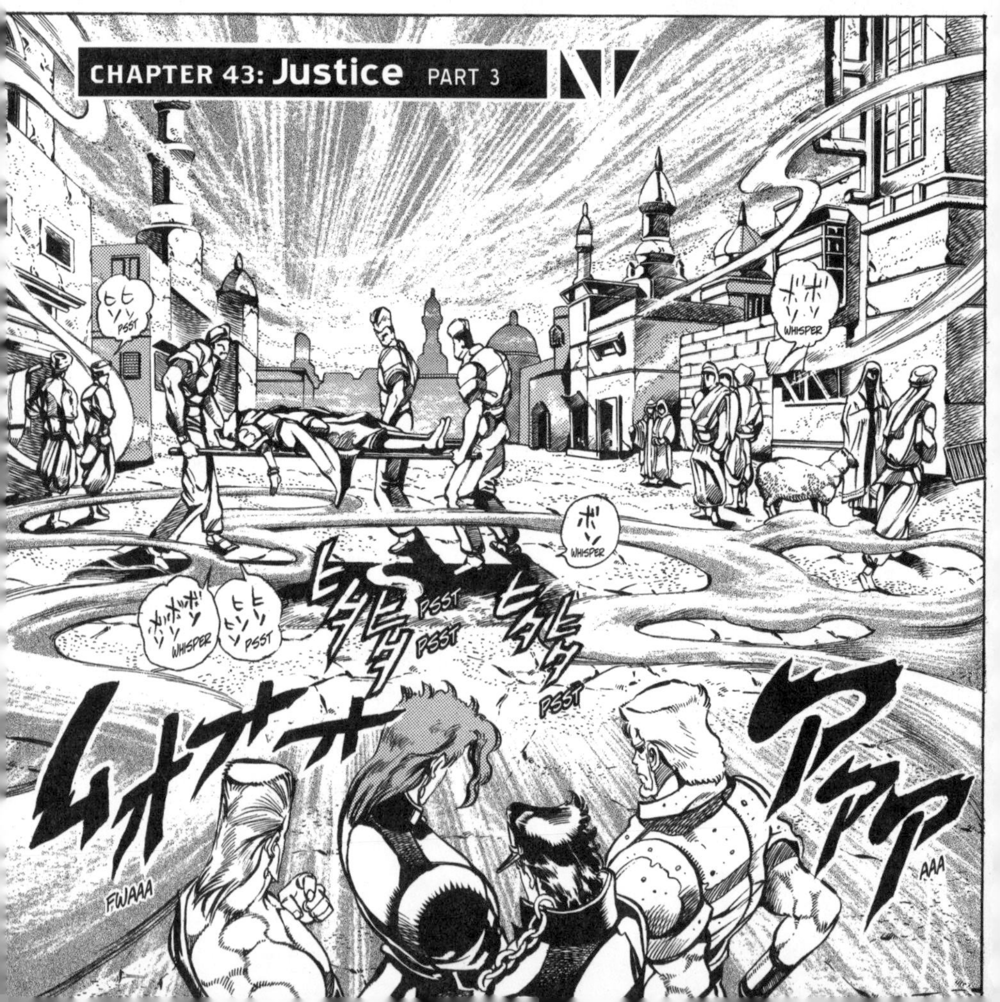
WHISPER
PSST
WHISPER
PSST
PSST
PSST
WHISPER
PSST
AAA
FWAAA

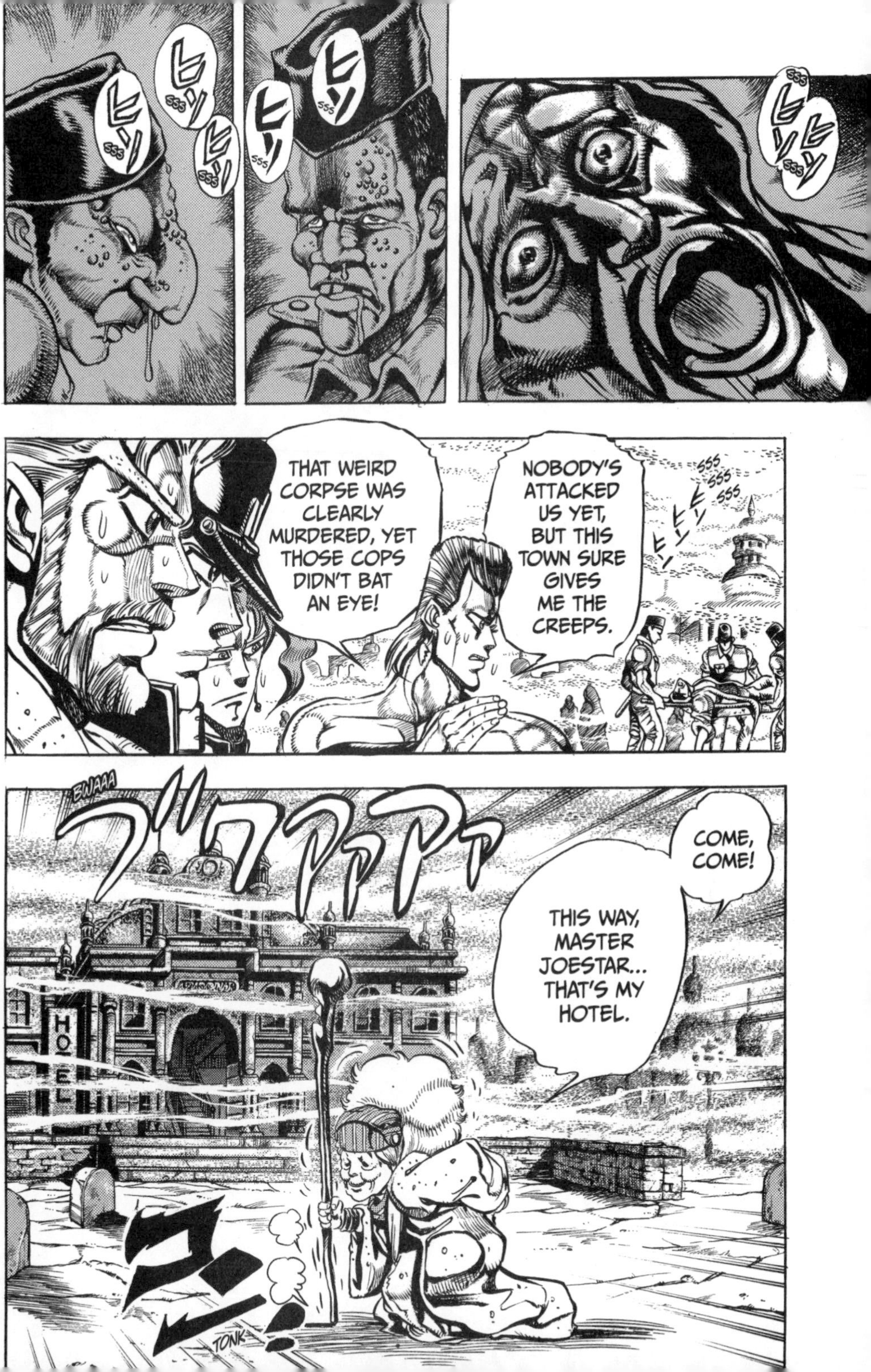ヒソ ヒソ
SSS SSS
ヒソ ヒソ
SSS SSS
ヒソ ヒソ
SSS SSS
ヒソ ヒソ ヒソ
SSS SSS SSS
NOBODY'S ATTACKED US YET, BUT THIS TOWN SURE GIVES ME THE CREEPS.
THAT WEIRD CORPSE WAS CLEARLY MURDERED, YET THOSE COPS DIDN'T BAT AN EYE!
COME, COME!
THIS WAY, MASTER JOESTAR... THAT'S MY HOTEL.
BWAAA
ブワァァァァ
HOTEL
TONK

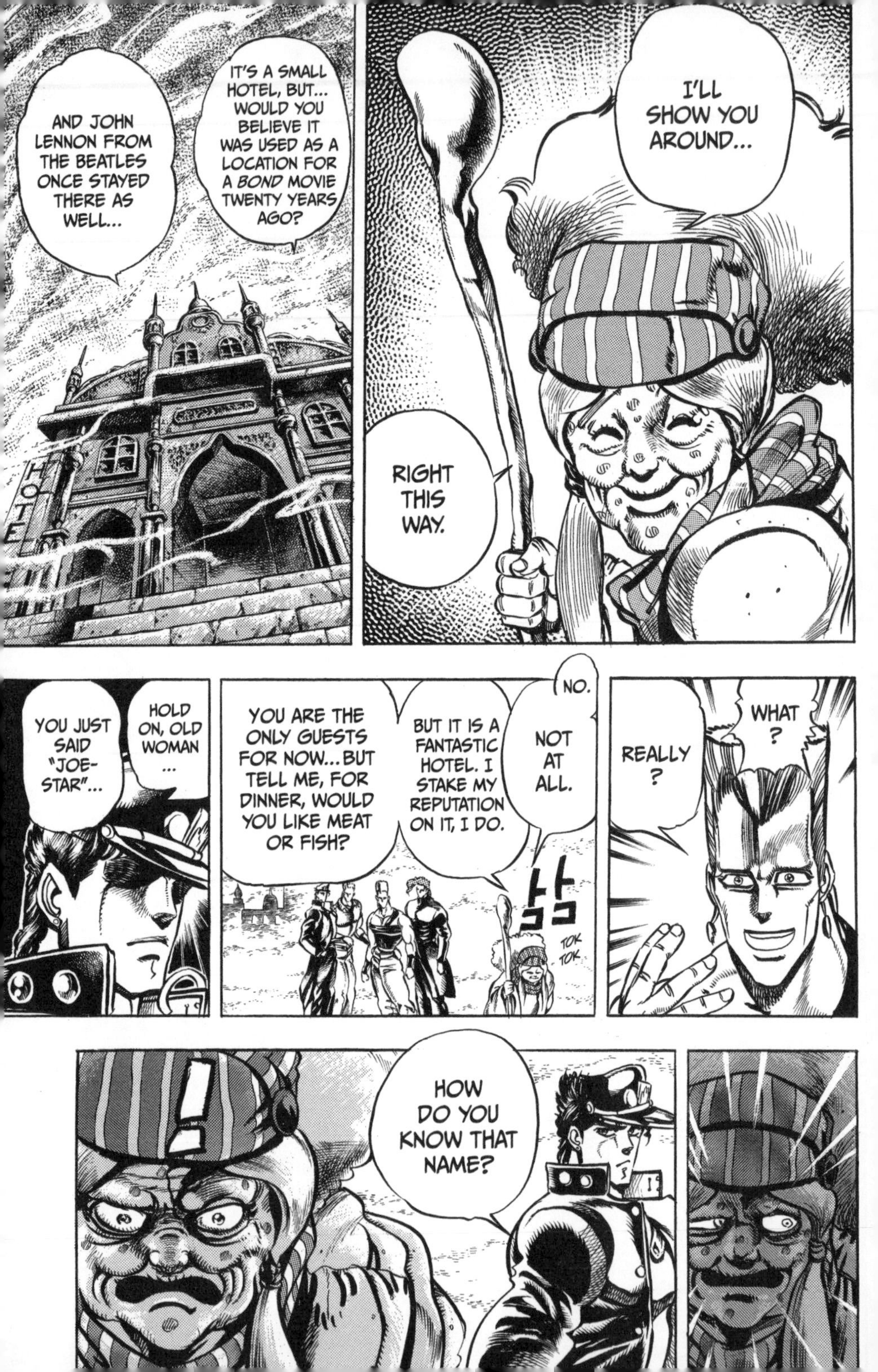
I'LL SHOW YOU AROUND...
RIGHT THIS WAY.
IT'S A SMALL HOTEL, BUT... WOULD YOU BELIEVE IT WAS USED AS A LOCATION FOR A *BOND* MOVIE TWENTY YEARS AGO?
AND JOHN LENNON FROM THE BEATLES ONCE STAYED THERE AS WELL...
HOTE
WHAT?
REALLY?
NO.
NOT AT ALL.
BUT IT IS A FANTASTIC HOTEL. I STAKE MY REPUTATION ON IT, I DO.
YOU ARE THE ONLY GUESTS FOR NOW... BUT TELL ME, FOR DINNER, WOULD YOU LIKE MEAT OR FISH?
TOK TOK
HOLD ON, OLD WOMAN...
YOU JUST SAID "JOE-STAR"...
HOW DO YOU KNOW THAT NAME?
!

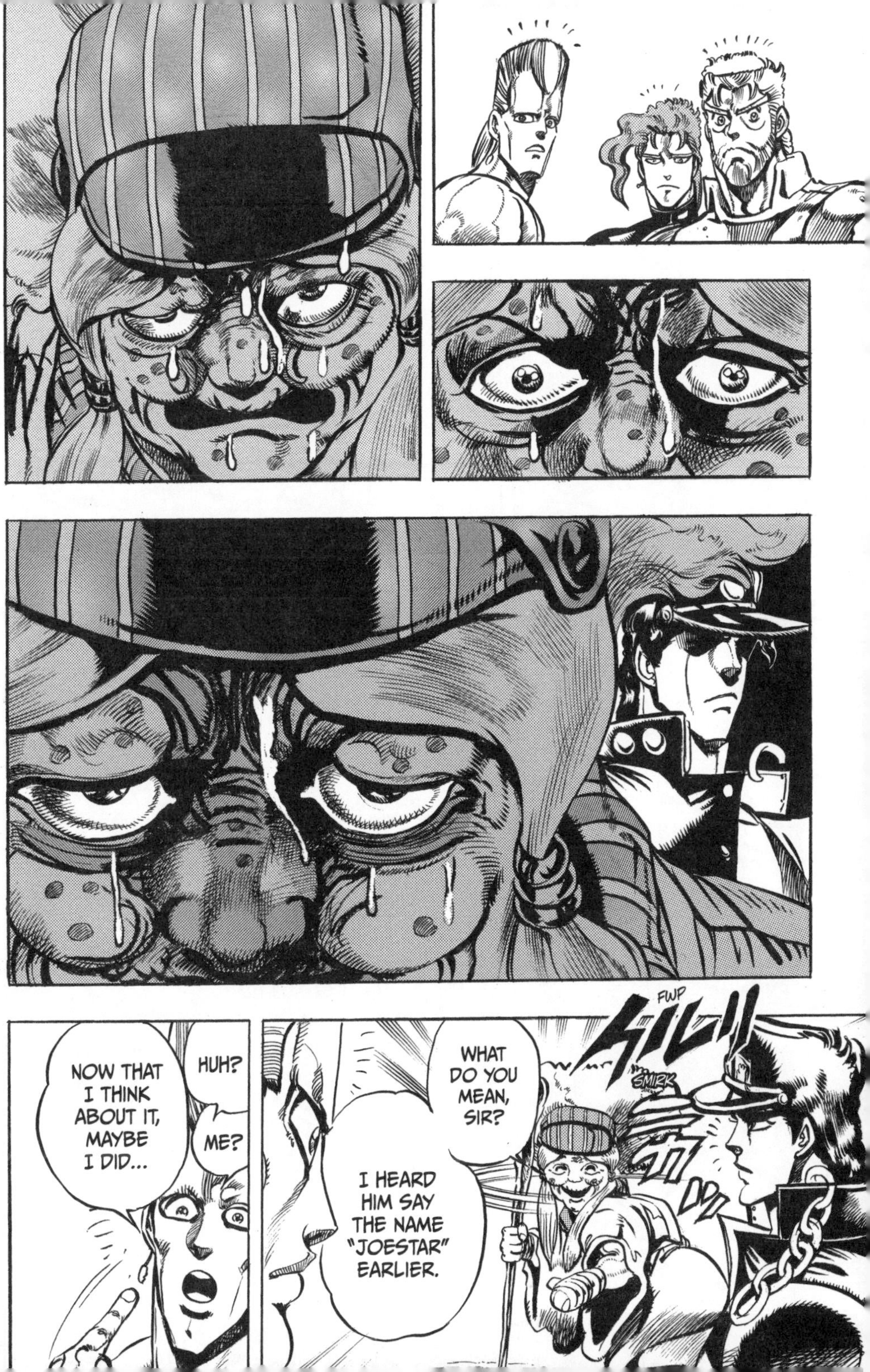
FWP
SMIRK
WHAT DO YOU MEAN, SIR?
I HEARD HIM SAY THE NAME "JOESTAR" EARLIER.
HUH?
ME?
NOW THAT I THINK ABOUT IT, MAYBE I DID...

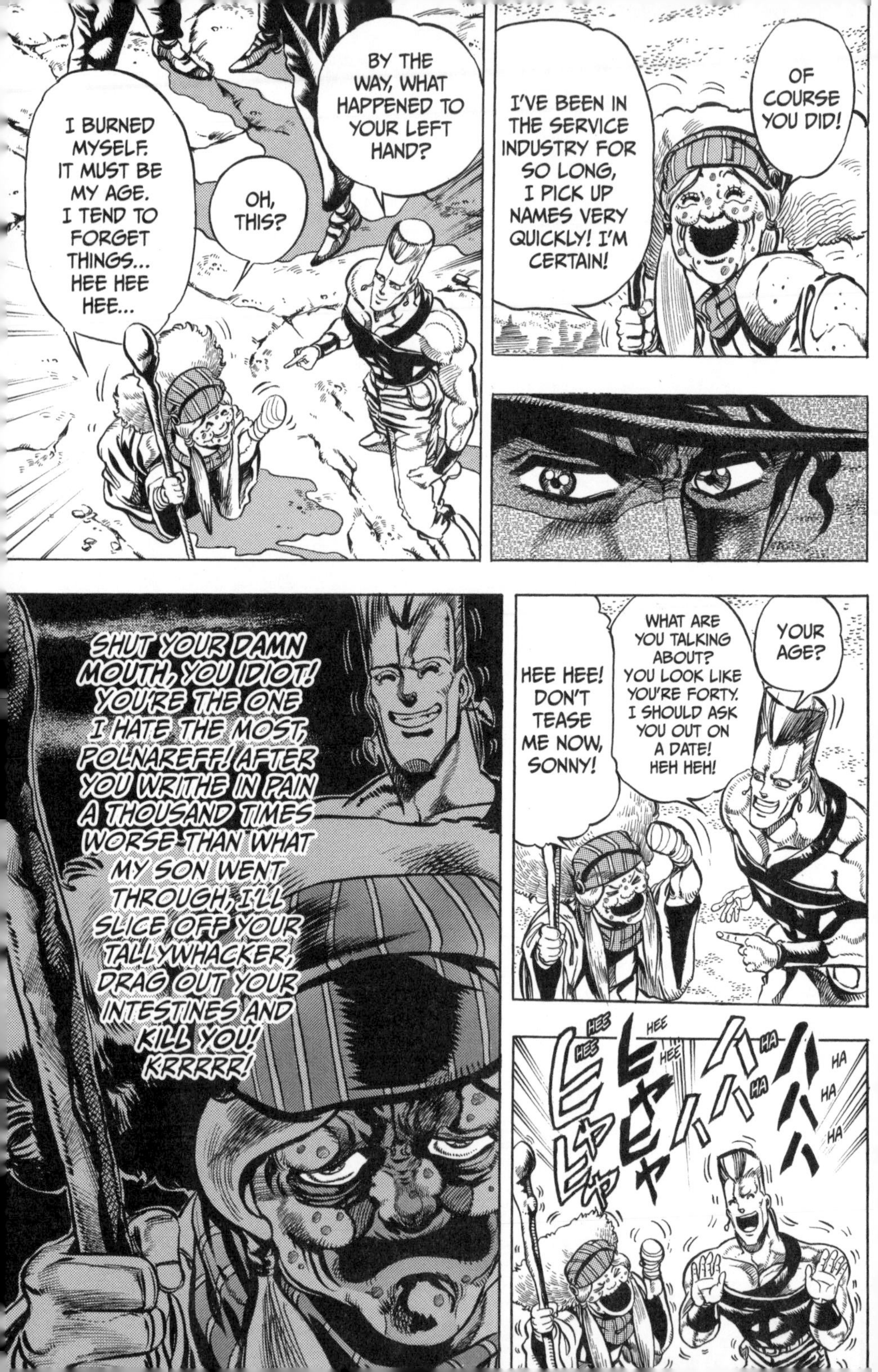
OF COURSE YOU DID!
I'VE BEEN IN THE SERVICE INDUSTRY FOR SO LONG, I PICK UP NAMES VERY QUICKLY! I'M CERTAIN!
BY THE WAY, WHAT HAPPENED TO YOUR LEFT HAND?
OH, THIS?
I BURNED MYSELF. IT MUST BE MY AGE. I TEND TO FORGET THINGS... HEE HEE HEE...
YOUR AGE?
WHAT ARE YOU TALKING ABOUT? YOU LOOK LIKE YOU'RE FORTY. I SHOULD ASK YOU OUT ON A DATE! HEH HEH!
HEE HEE! DON'T TEASE ME NOW, SONNY!
HA HA HA HA
HA HA
HEE HEE
HEE HEE
SHUT YOUR DAMN MOUTH, YOU IDIOT! YOU'RE THE ONE I HATE THE MOST, POLNAREFF! AFTER YOU WRITHE IN PAIN A THOUSAND TIMES WORSE THAN WHAT MY SON WENT THROUGH, I'LL SLICE OFF YOUR TALLYWHACKER, DRAG OUT YOUR INTESTINES AND KILL YOU! KRRRRR!

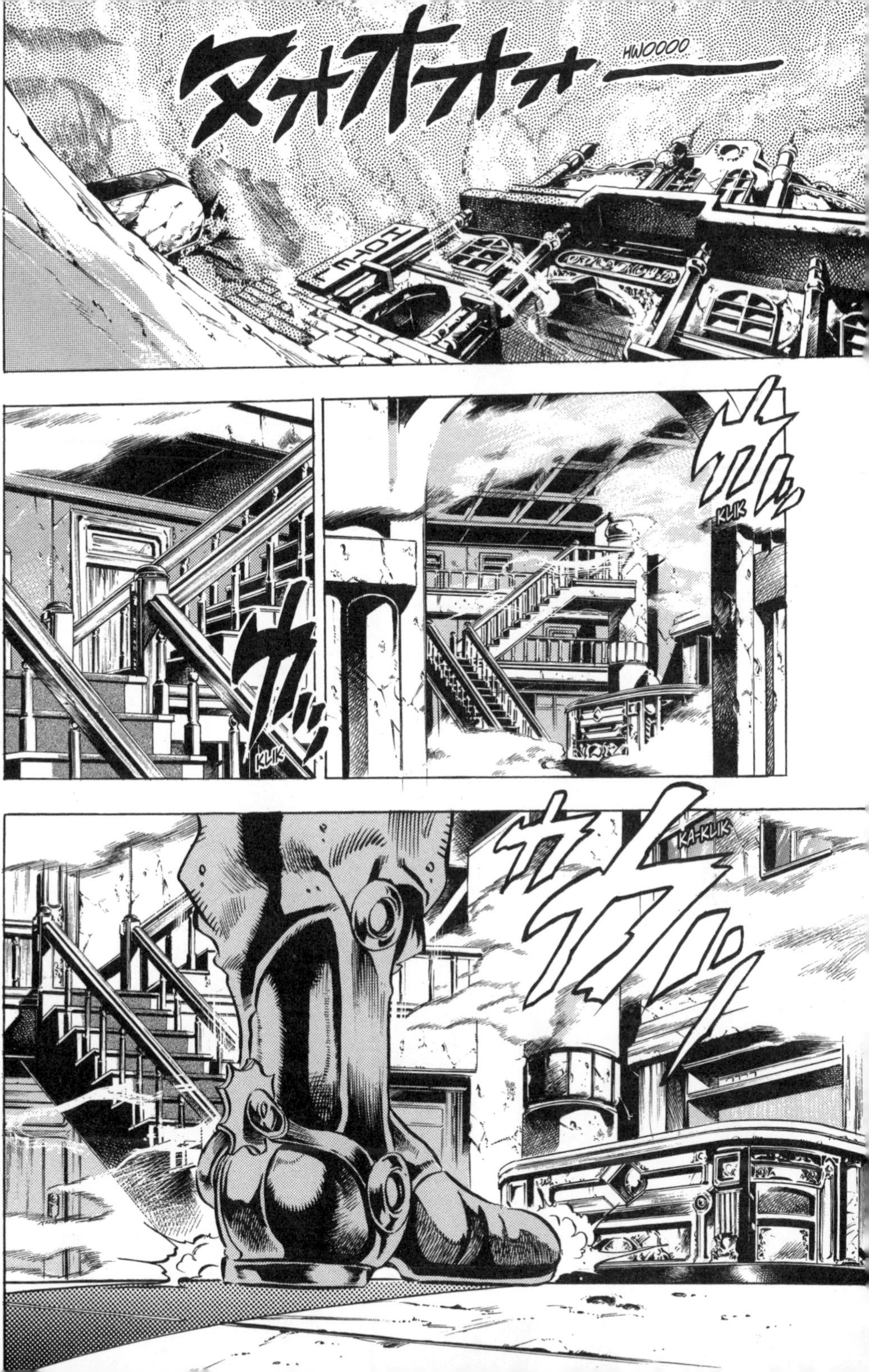
HWOOOO
KLIK
KLIK
KA-KLIK

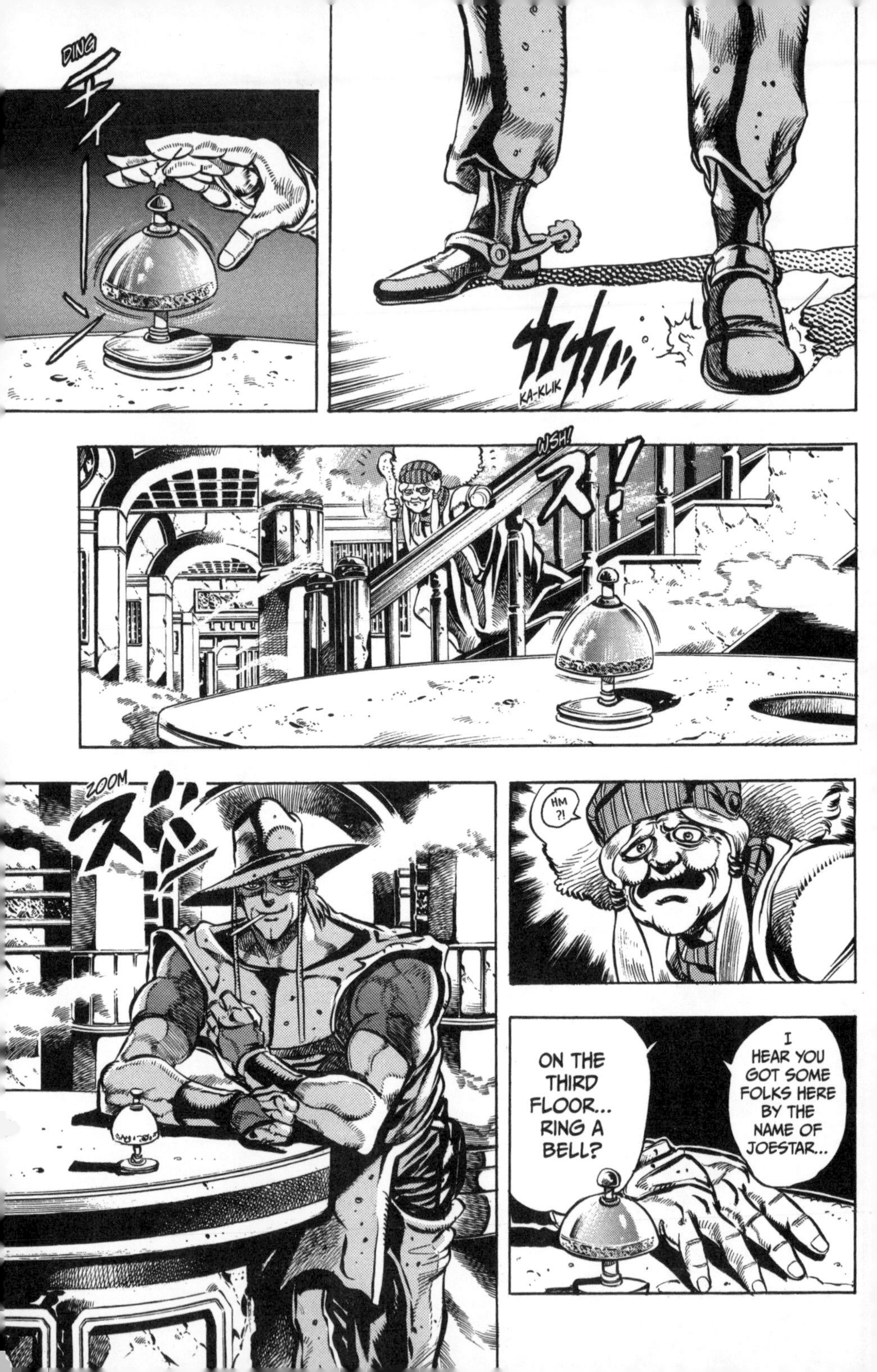
KA-KLIK
DING
WSH!
HM ?!
I HEAR YOU GOT SOME FOLKS HERE BY THE NAME OF JOESTAR...
ON THE THIRD FLOOR... RING A BELL?
ZOOM

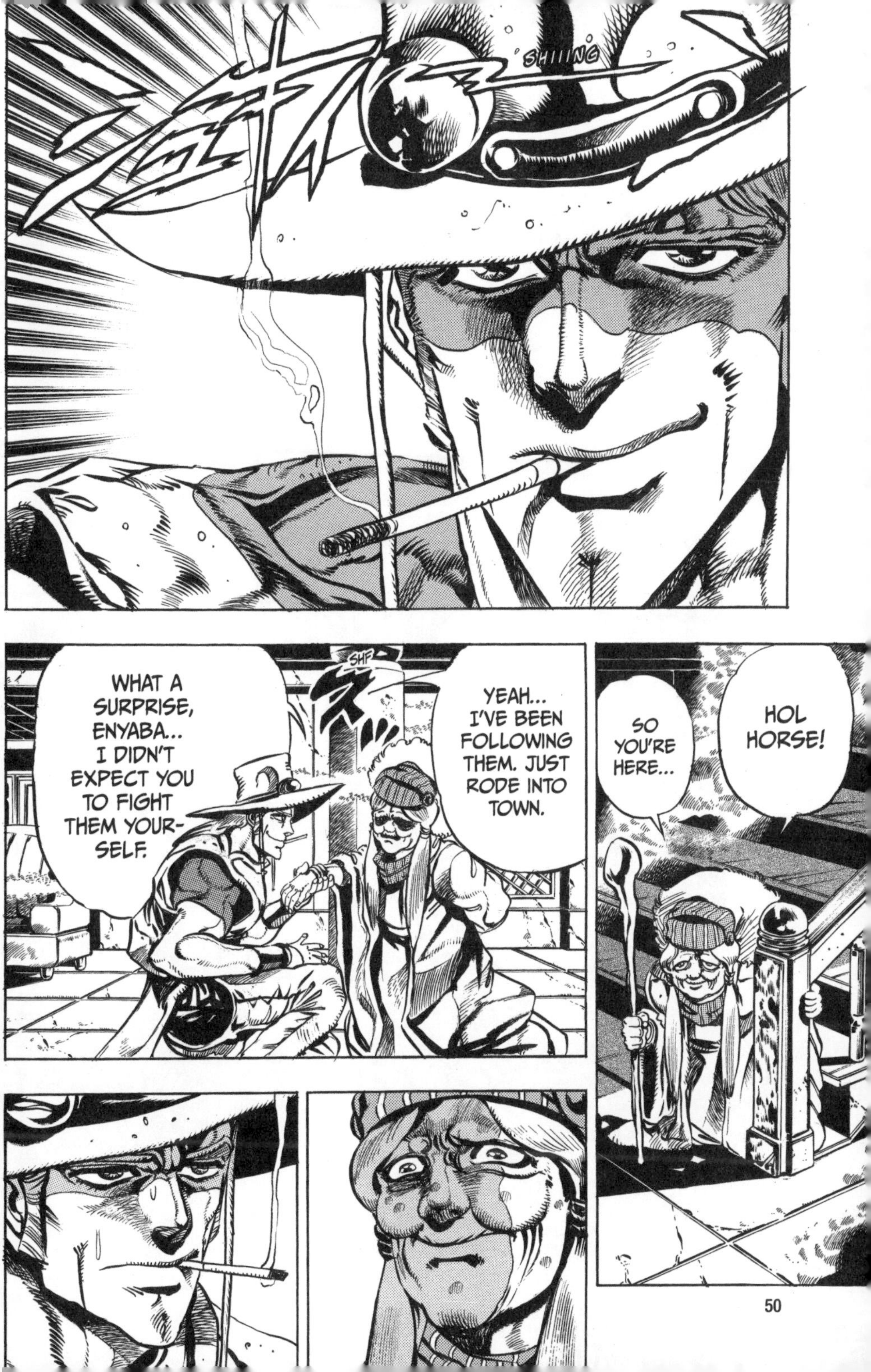
SHIIING
HOL HORSE!
SO YOU'RE HERE...
SHF
YEAH... I'VE BEEN FOLLOWING THEM. JUST RODE INTO TOWN.
WHAT A SURPRISE, ENYABA... I DIDN'T EXPECT YOU TO FIGHT THEM YOUR-SELF.

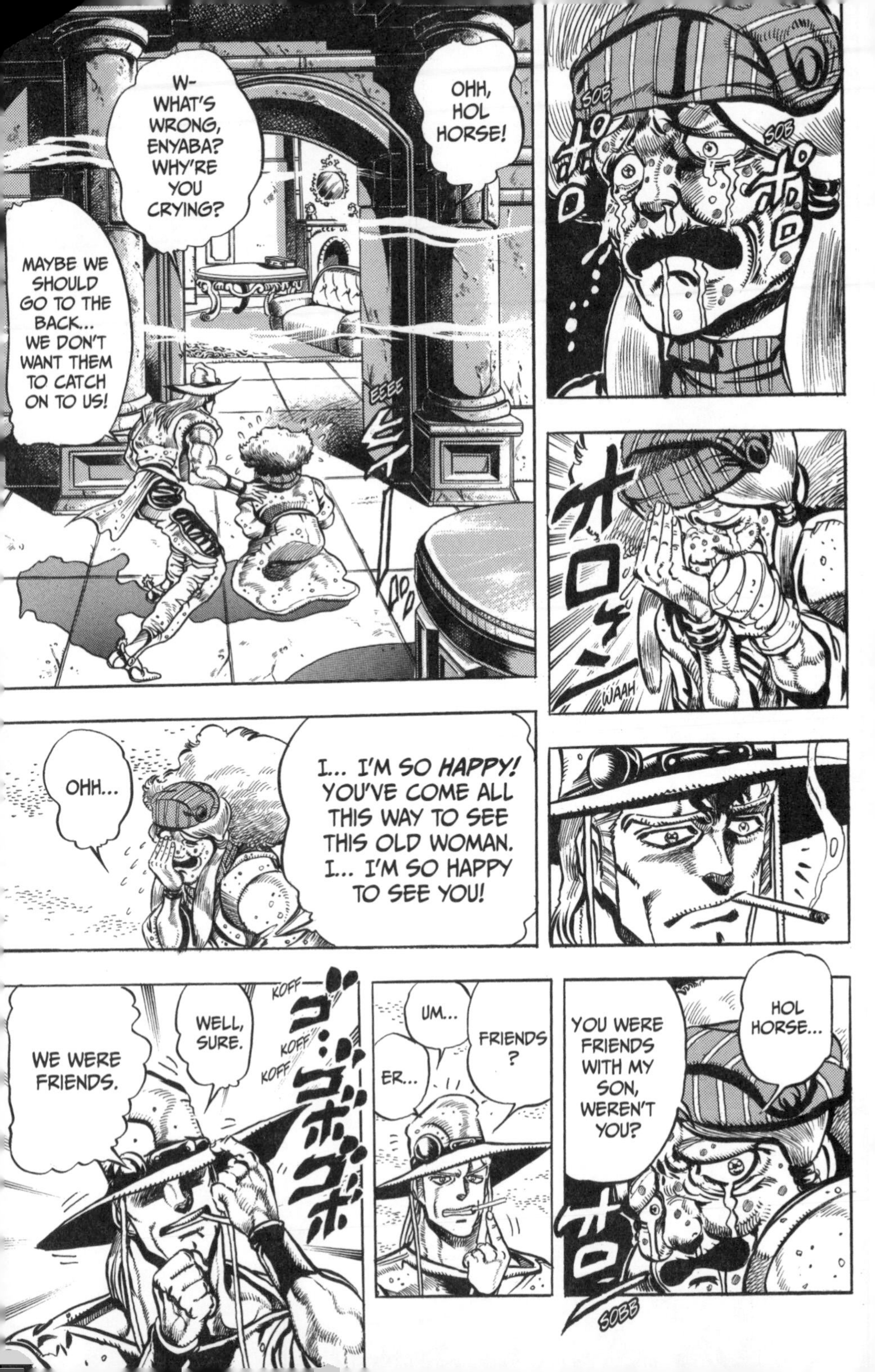
SOB
SOB
WAAH
OHH, HOL HORSE!
W-WHAT'S WRONG, ENYABA? WHY'RE YOU CRYING?
MAYBE WE SHOULD GO TO THE BACK... WE DON'T WANT THEM TO CATCH ON TO US!
EEEE
I... I'M SO *HAPPY!* YOU'VE COME ALL THIS WAY TO SEE THIS OLD WOMAN. I... I'M SO HAPPY TO SEE YOU!
OHH...
HOL HORSE...
YOU WERE FRIENDS WITH MY SON, WEREN'T YOU?
SOBB
FRIENDS?
UM...
ER...
KOFF
KOFF
KOFF
WELL, SURE.
WE WERE FRIENDS.

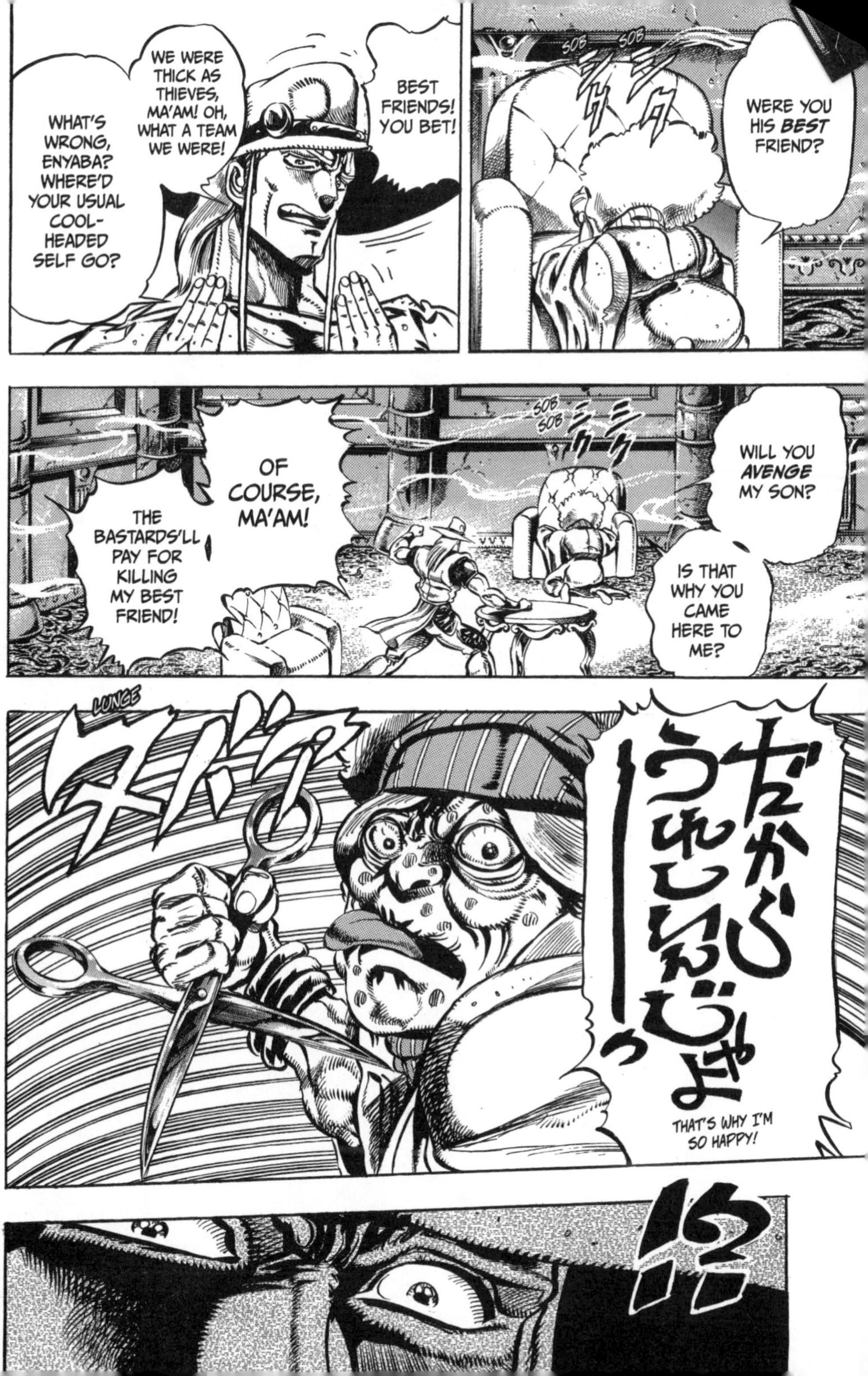
SOB SOB
WERE YOU HIS BEST FRIEND?
BEST FRIENDS! YOU BET!
WE WERE THICK AS THIEVES, MA'AM! OH, WHAT A TEAM WE WERE!
WHAT'S WRONG, ENYABA? WHERE'D YOUR USUAL COOL-HEADED SELF GO?
WILL YOU AVENGE MY SON?
IS THAT WHY YOU CAME HERE TO ME?
SOB SOB
OF COURSE, MA'AM!
THE BASTARDS'LL PAY FOR KILLING MY BEST FRIEND!
だからうれしいんじゃよーっ
THAT'S WHY I'M SO HAPPY!
LUNGE
!?

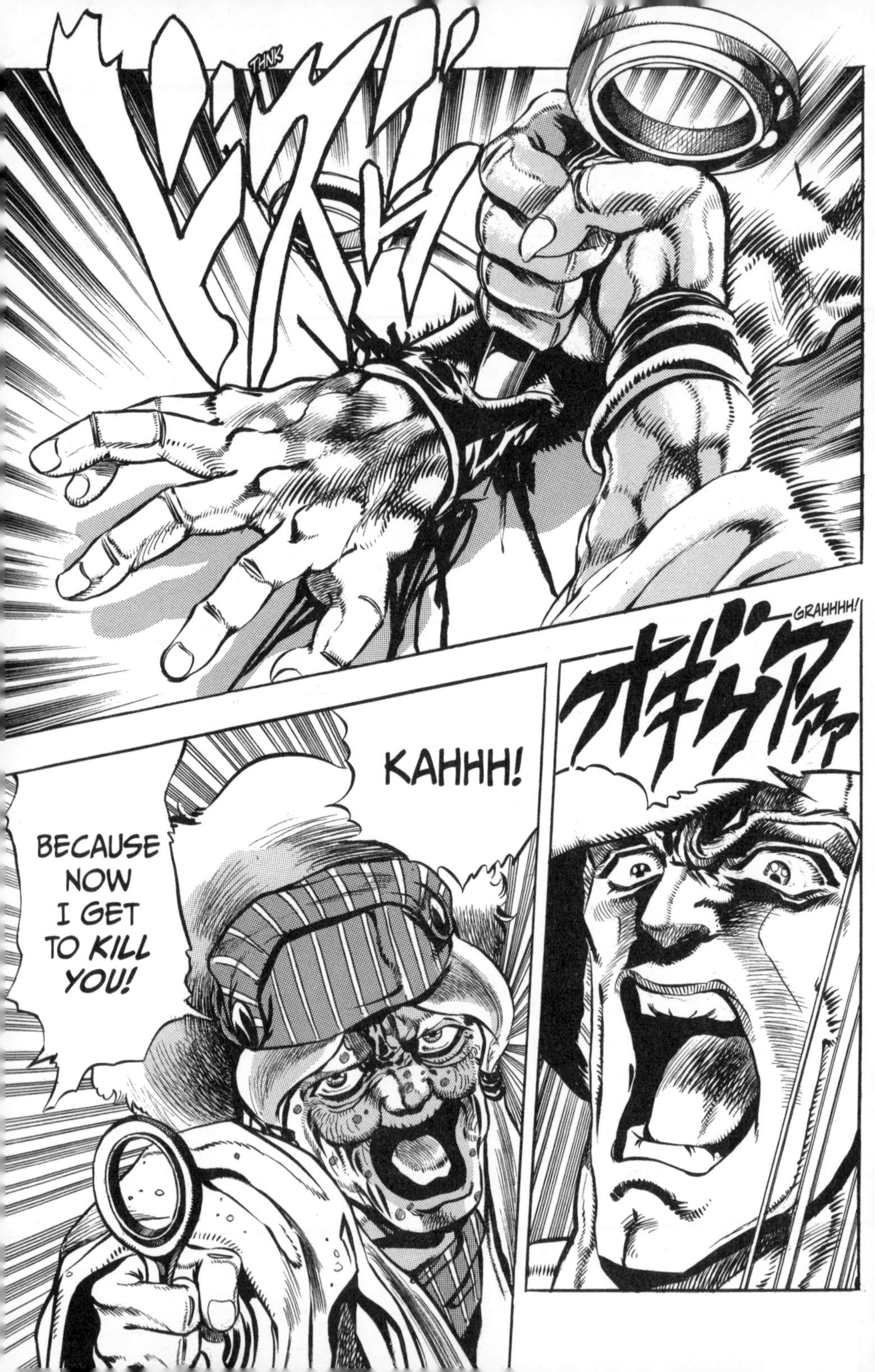
THNK
GRAHHHH!
KAHHH!
BECAUSE NOW I GET TO KILL YOU!

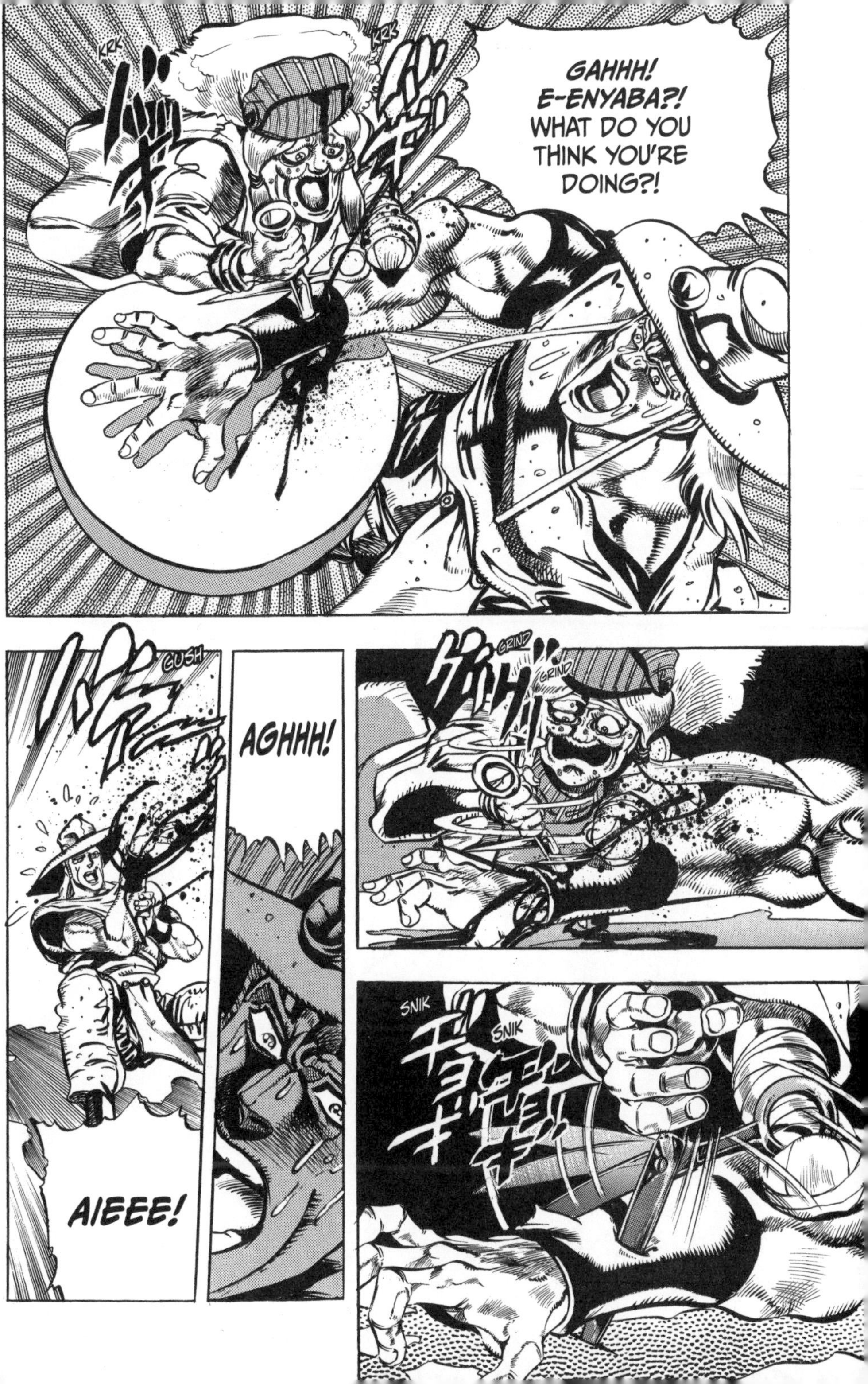
KRK
KRK
GAHHH! E-ENYABA?! WHAT DO YOU THINK YOU'RE DOING?!
GRIND
GRIND
SNIK
SNIK
AGHHH!
GUSH
AIEEE!

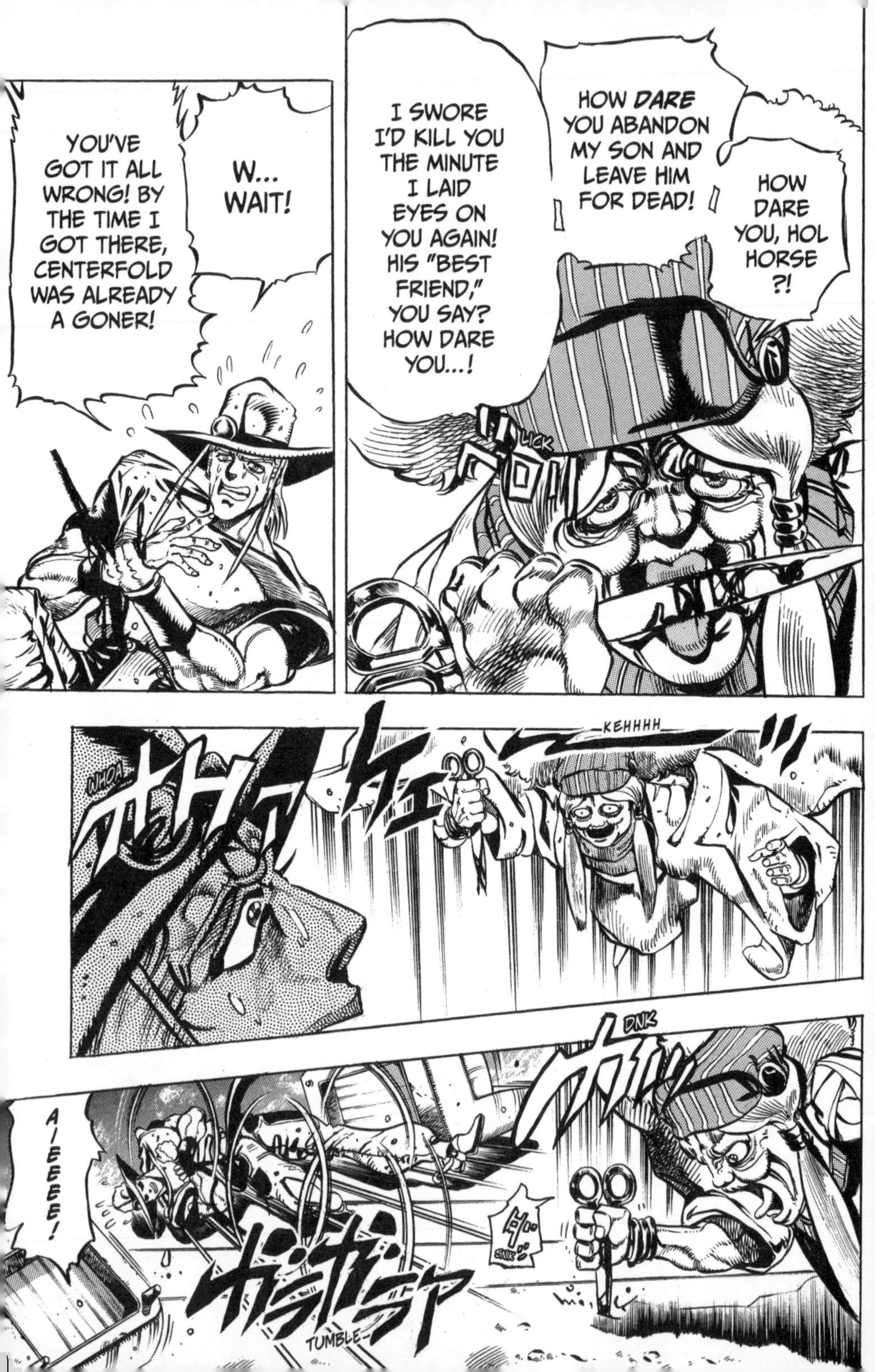
HOW DARE YOU, HOL HORSE?!
HOW DARE YOU ABANDON MY SON AND LEAVE HIM FOR DEAD!
I SWORE I'D KILL YOU THE MINUTE I LAID EYES ON YOU AGAIN! HIS "BEST FRIEND," YOU SAY? HOW DARE YOU...!
LICK
W... WAIT!
YOU'VE GOT IT ALL WRONG! BY THE TIME I GOT THERE, CENTERFOLD WAS ALREADY A GONER!
KEHHHH
WHOA
DNK
SNK
AIEEEEE!
TUMBLE

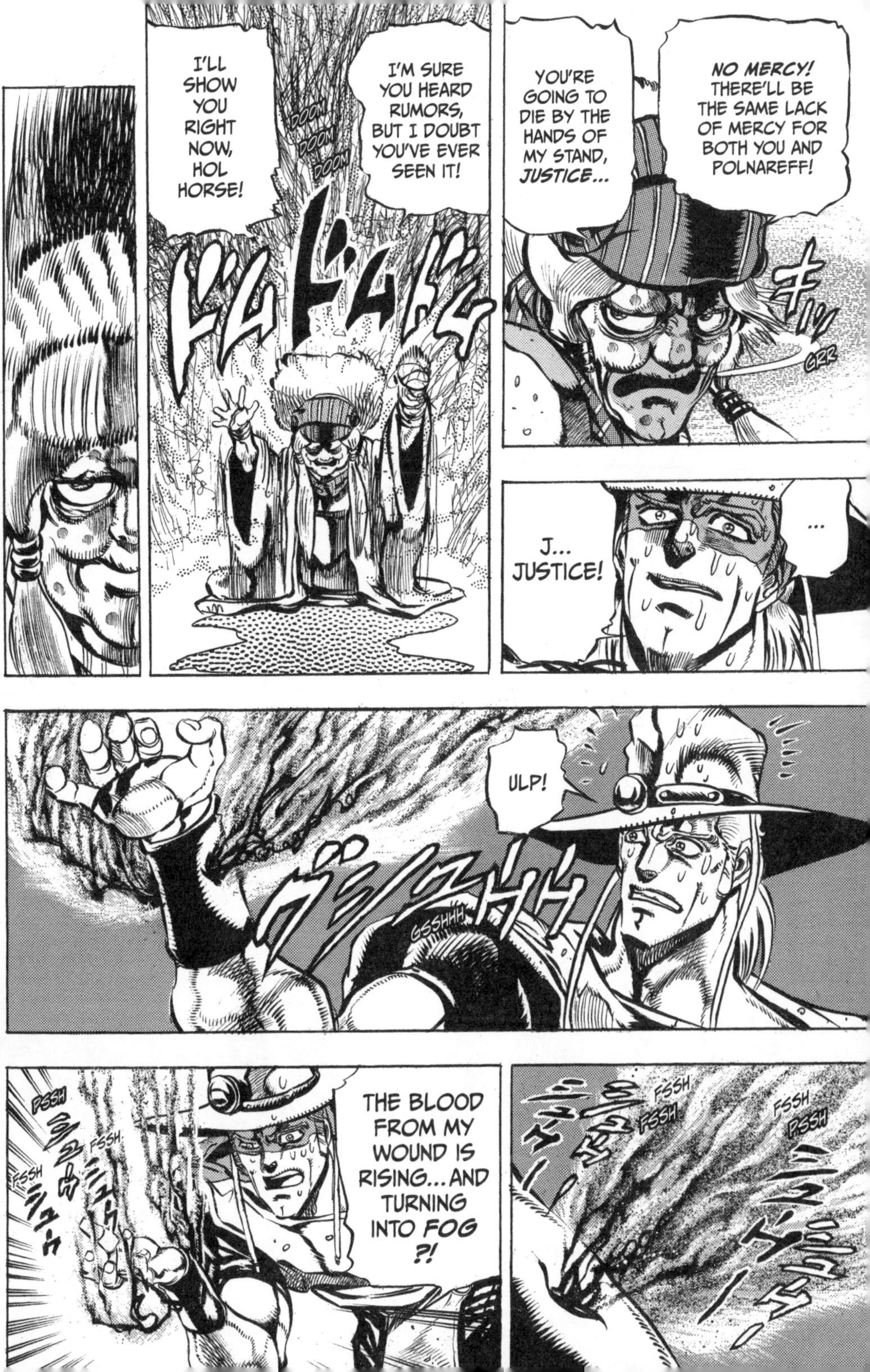
NO MERCY! THERE'LL BE THE SAME LACK OF MERCY FOR BOTH YOU AND POLNAREFF!
YOU'RE GOING TO DIE BY THE HANDS OF MY STAND, JUSTICE...
GRR
...
J... JUSTICE!
I'M SURE YOU HEARD RUMORS, BUT I DOUBT YOU'VE EVER SEEN IT!
DOOM DOOM DOOM
I'LL SHOW YOU RIGHT NOW, HOL HORSE!
ULP!
GSSHHH
FSSH FSSH
FSSH PSSH
THE BLOOD FROM MY WOUND IS RISING... AND TURNING INTO FOG ?!
PSSH
FSSH
FSSH

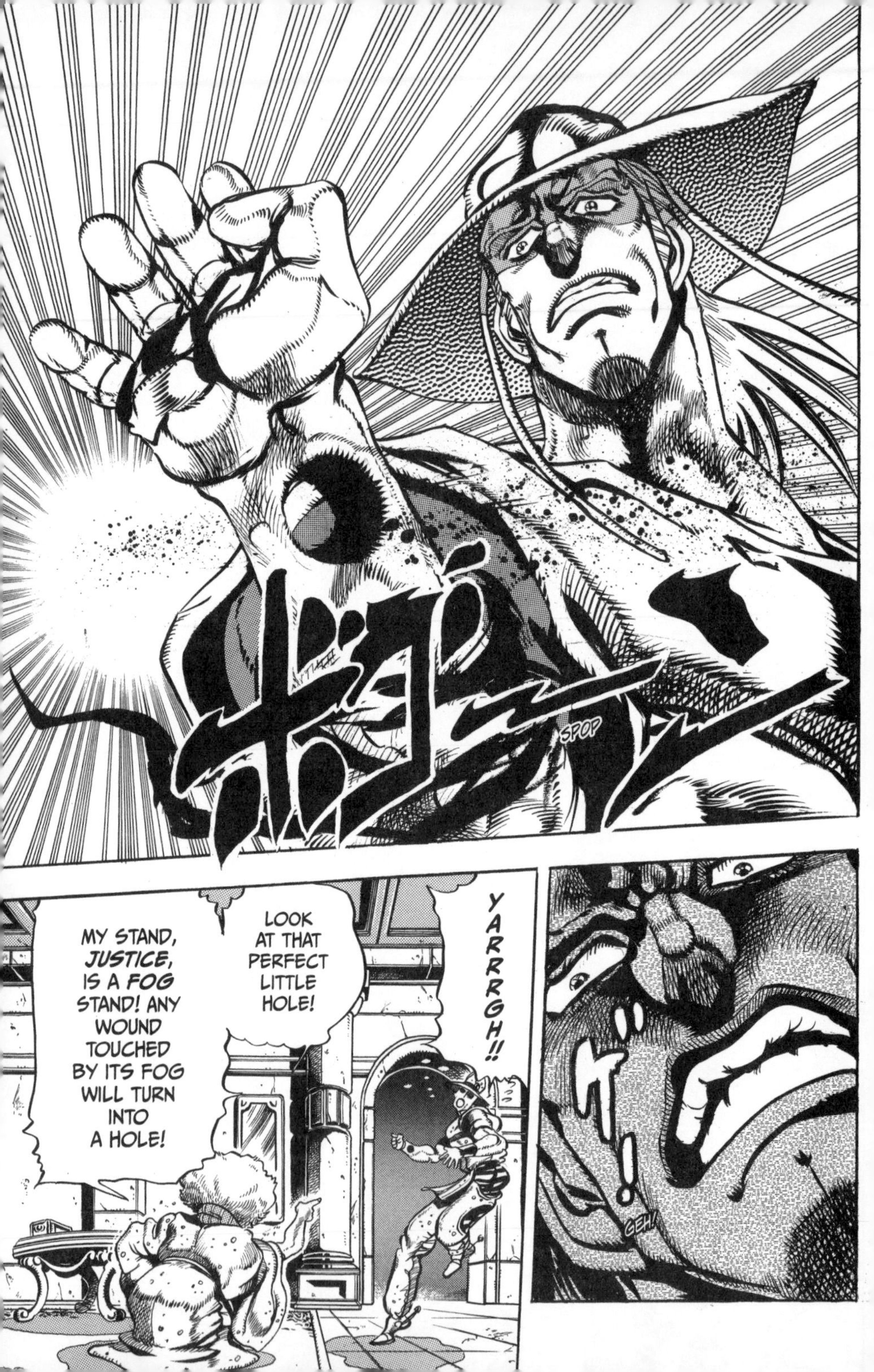
SPOP
GEH!
YARRRGH!!
LOOK AT THAT PERFECT LITTLE HOLE!
MY STAND, *JUSTICE*, IS A *FOG* STAND! ANY WOUND TOUCHED BY ITS FOG WILL TURN INTO A HOLE!

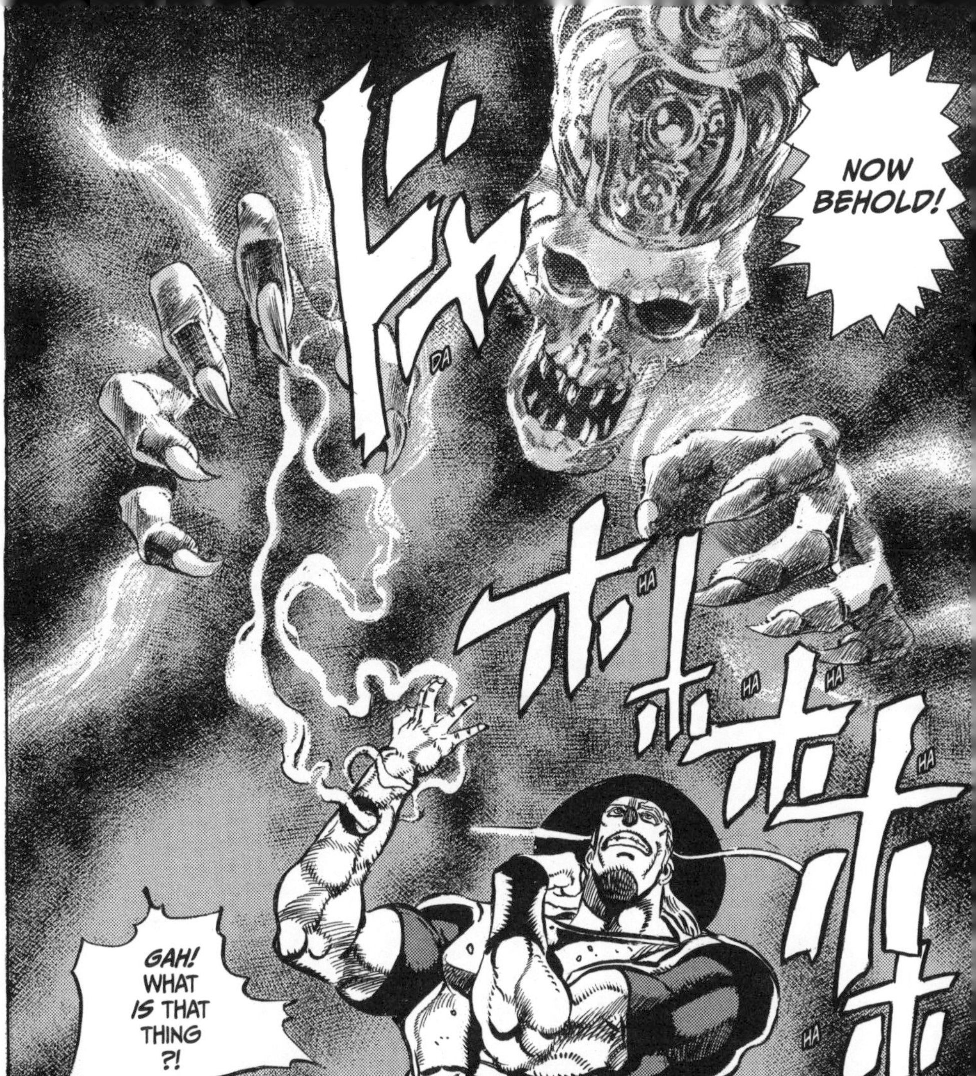
NOW BEHOLD!
DA
HA HA HA HA HA HA
GAH! WHAT *IS* THAT THING ?!
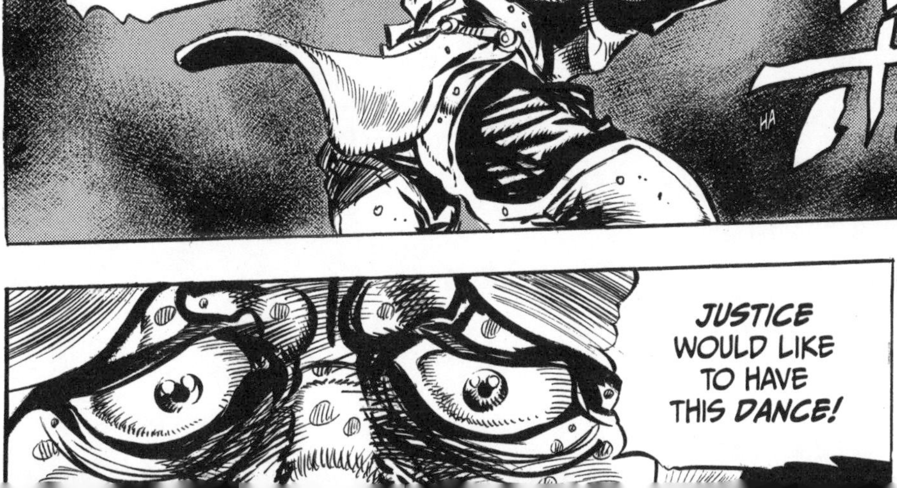
JUSTICE WOULD LIKE TO HAVE THIS *DANCE!*

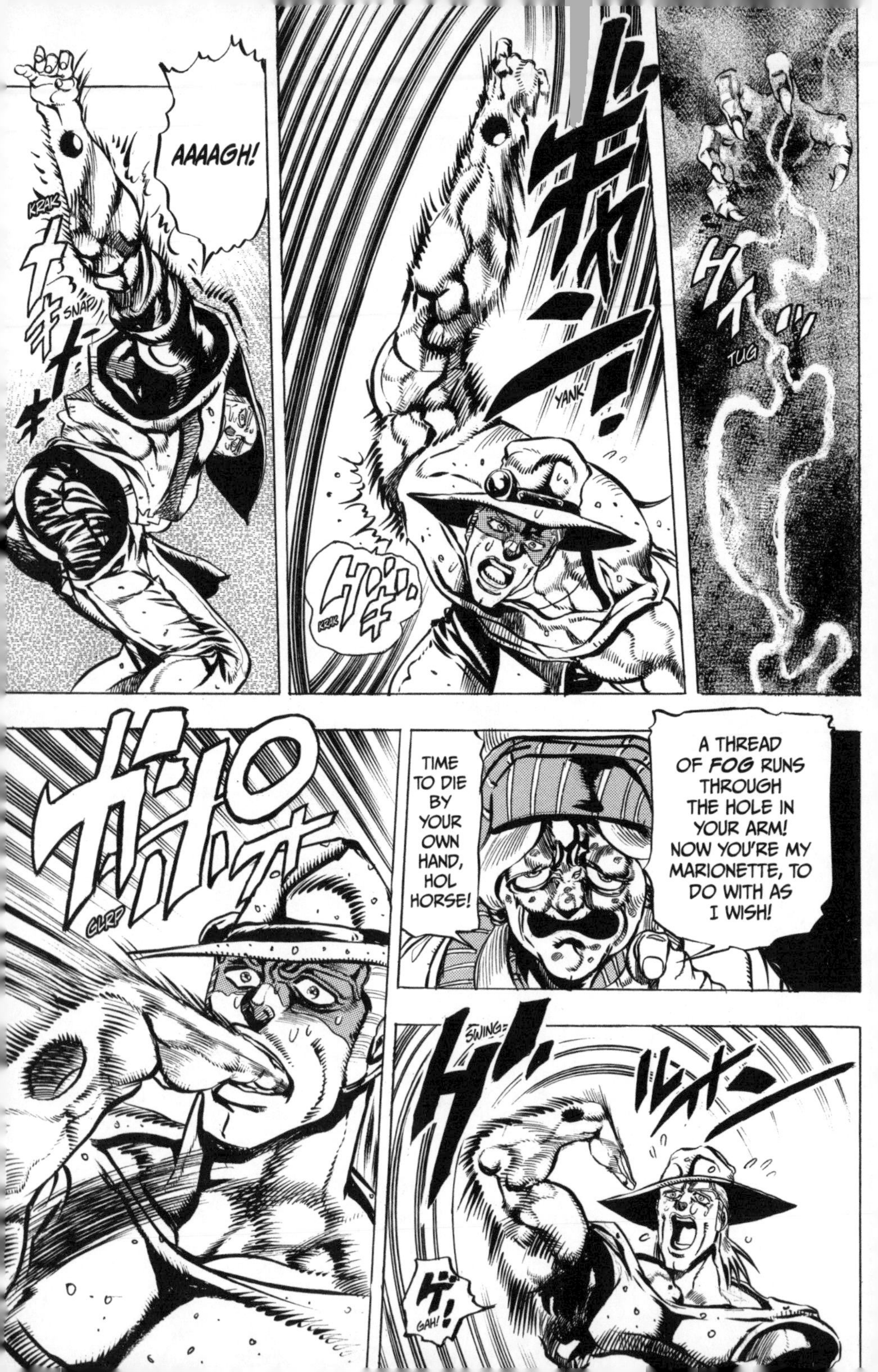

TUG
YANK
KRAK
AAAAGH!
KRAK
SNAP
A THREAD OF FOG RUNS THROUGH THE HOLE IN YOUR ARM! NOW YOU'RE MY MARIONETTE, TO DO WITH AS I WISH!
TIME TO DIE BY YOUR OWN HAND, HOL HORSE!
SWING
GAH!
CLRP

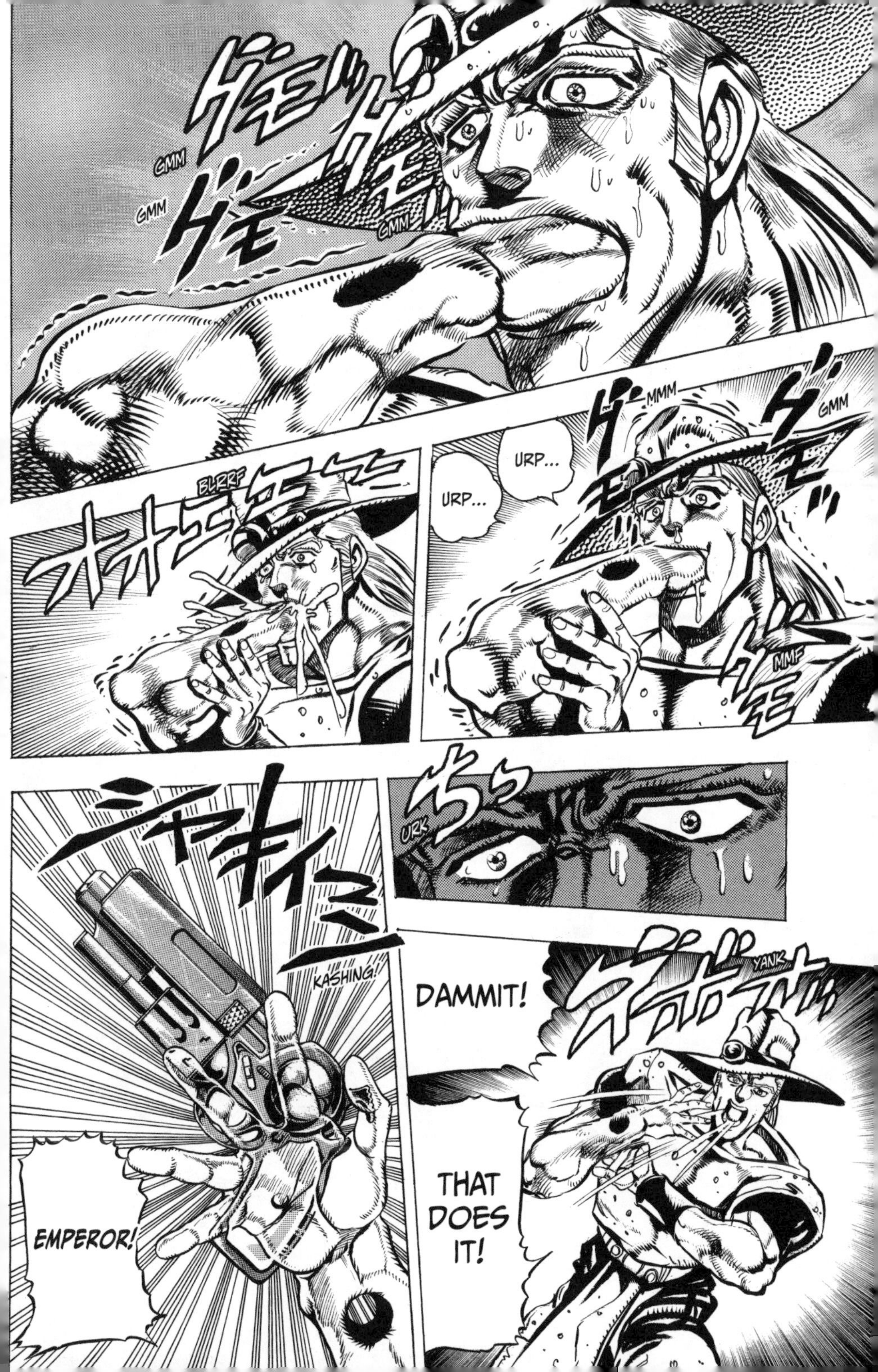
GMM
GMM
GMM
MMM
GMM
URP...
URP...
MMF
BLRRF
URK
YANK
DAMMIT!
THAT DOES IT!
KASHING!
EMPEROR!

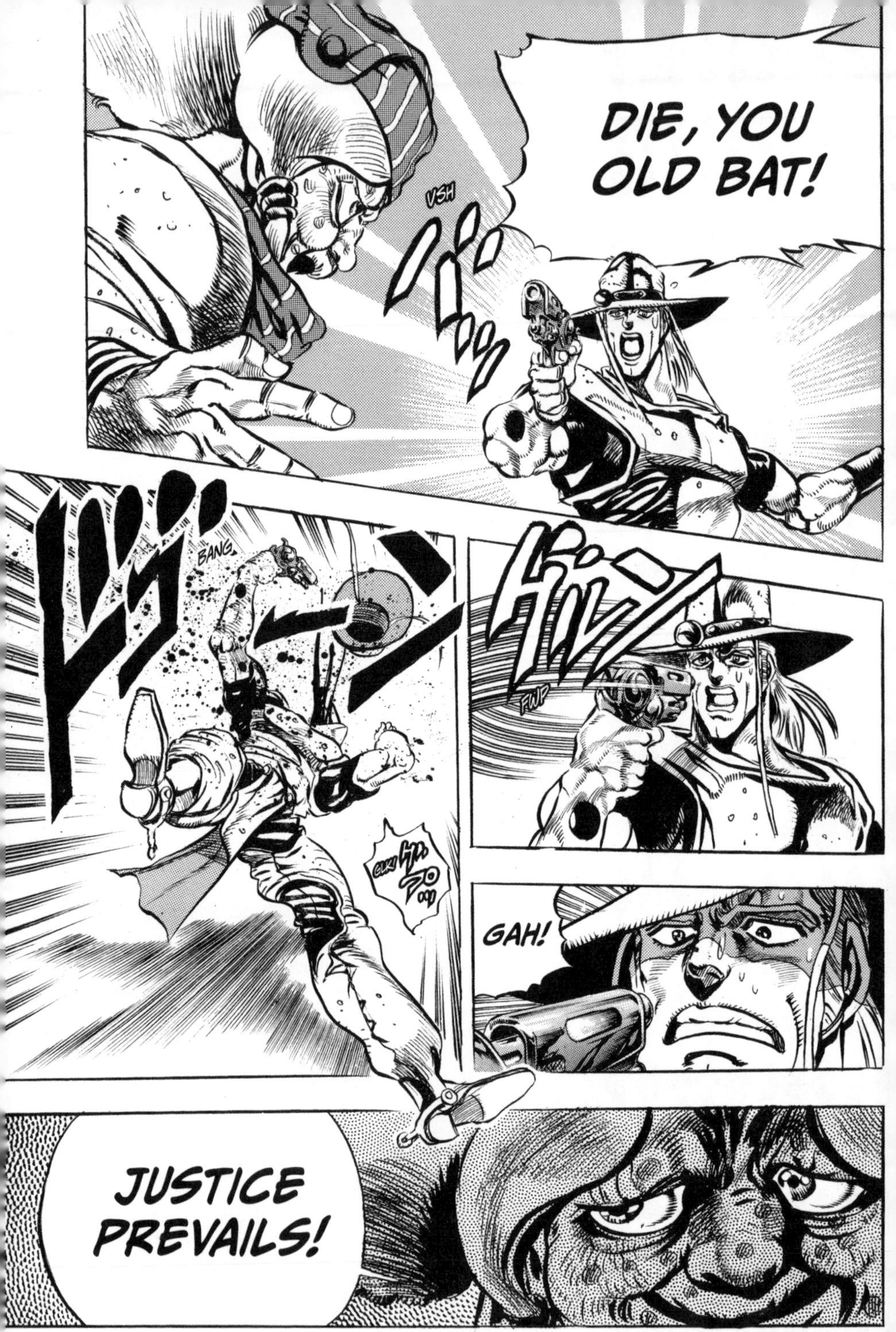
DIE, YOU OLD BAT!
VSH
FWP
GAH!
BANG
GLK!
JUSTICE PREVAILS!

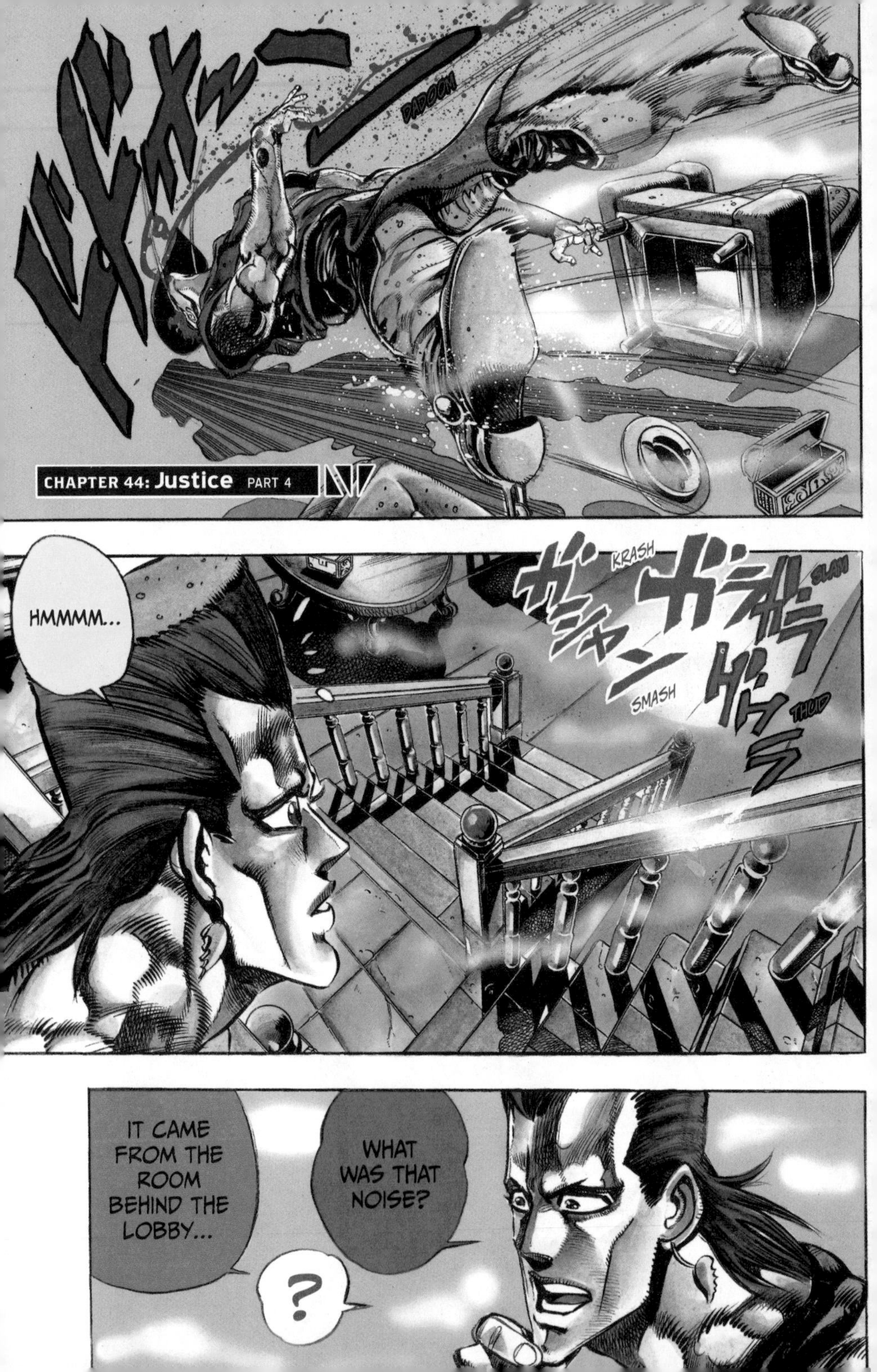
DADOOM
CHAPTER 44: Justice PART 4
HMMMM...
KRASH
SLAM
SMASH
THUD
WHAT WAS THAT NOISE?
IT CAME FROM THE ROOM BEHIND THE LOBBY...
?

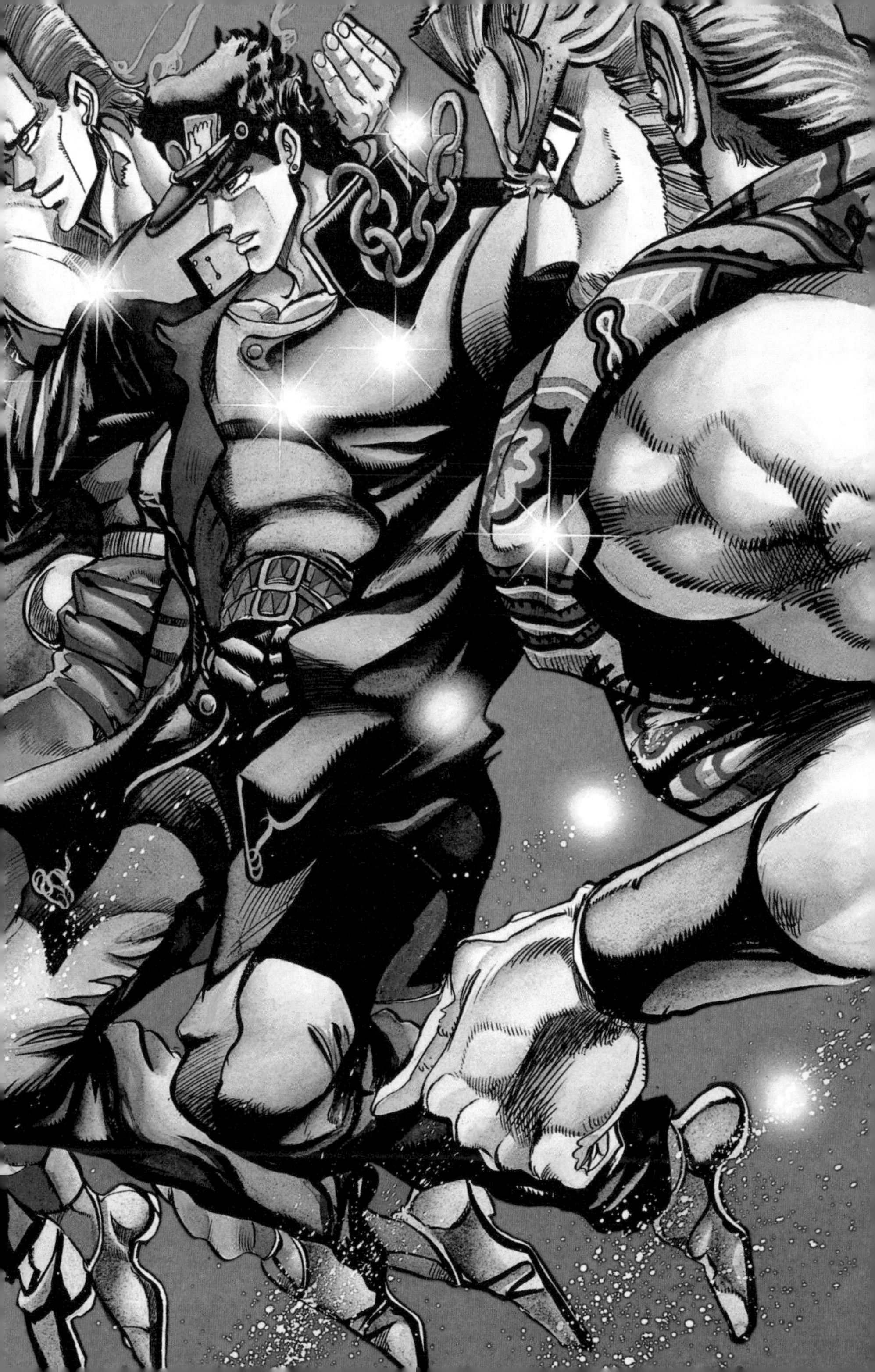

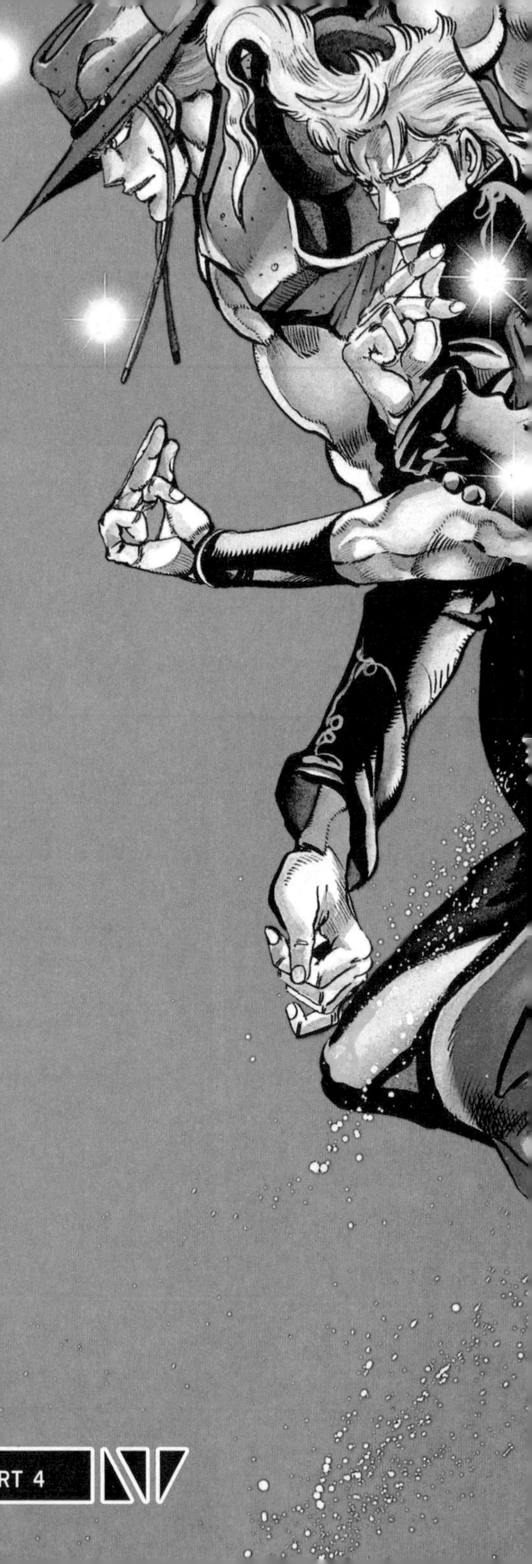

CHAPTER 44: Justice PART 4

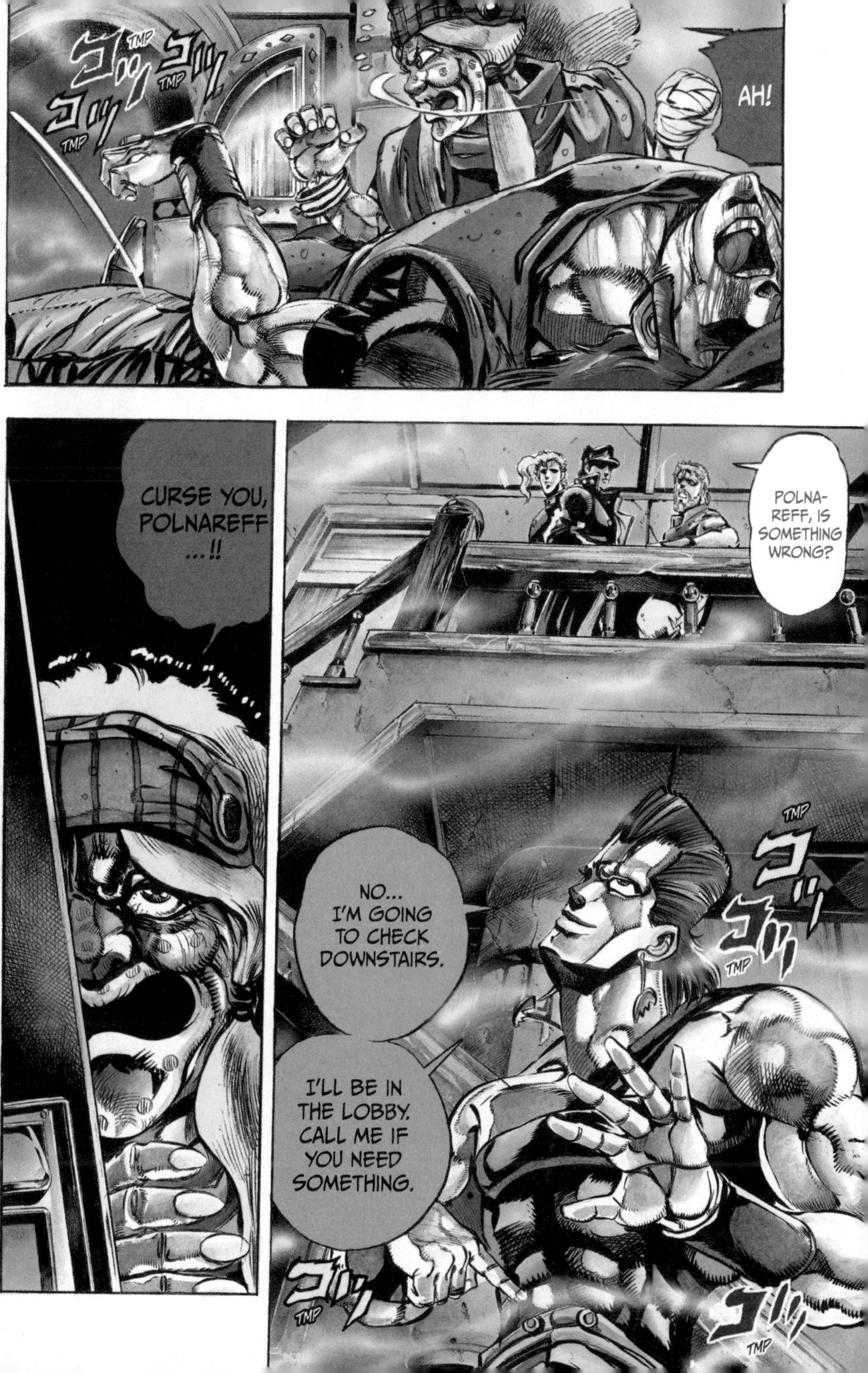
AH!
TMP
TMP
TMP
POLNAREFF, IS SOMETHING WRONG?
TMP
TMP
NO... I'M GOING TO CHECK DOWNSTAIRS.
I'LL BE IN THE LOBBY. CALL ME IF YOU NEED SOMETHING.
TMP
TMP
CURSE YOU, POLNAREFF ...!!

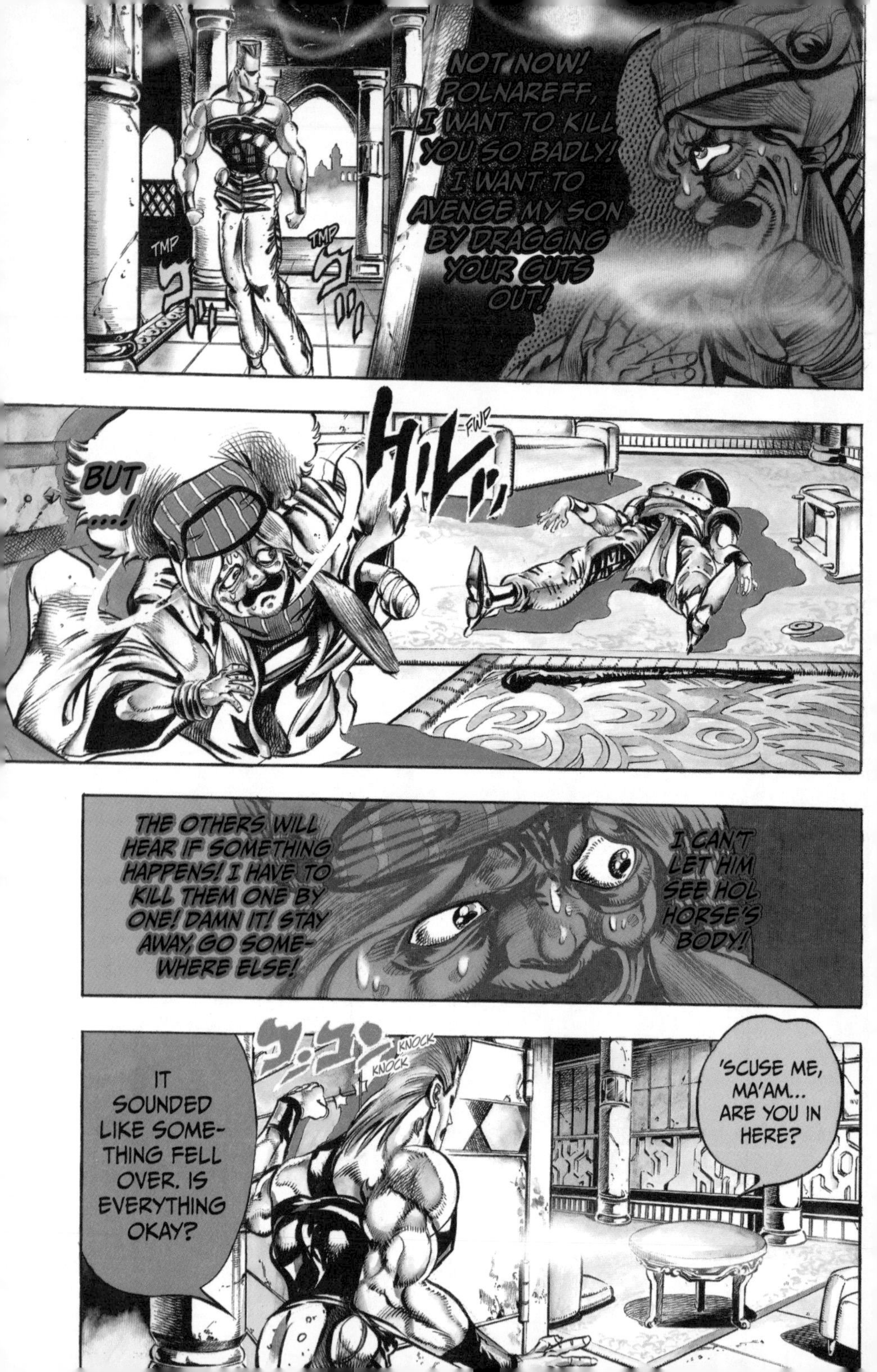
NOT NOW! POLNAREFF, I WANT TO KILL YOU SO BADLY! I WANT TO AVENGE MY SON BY DRAGGING YOUR GUTS OUT!
TMP
TMP
FWP
BUT ...!
I CAN'T LET HIM SEE HOL HORSE'S BODY!
THE OTHERS WILL HEAR IF SOMETHING HAPPENS! I HAVE TO KILL THEM ONE BY ONE! DAMN IT! STAY AWAY, GO SOME-WHERE ELSE!
'SCUSE ME, MA'AM... ARE YOU IN HERE?
KNOCK
KNOCK
IT SOUNDED LIKE SOME-THING FELL OVER. IS EVERYTHING OKAY?

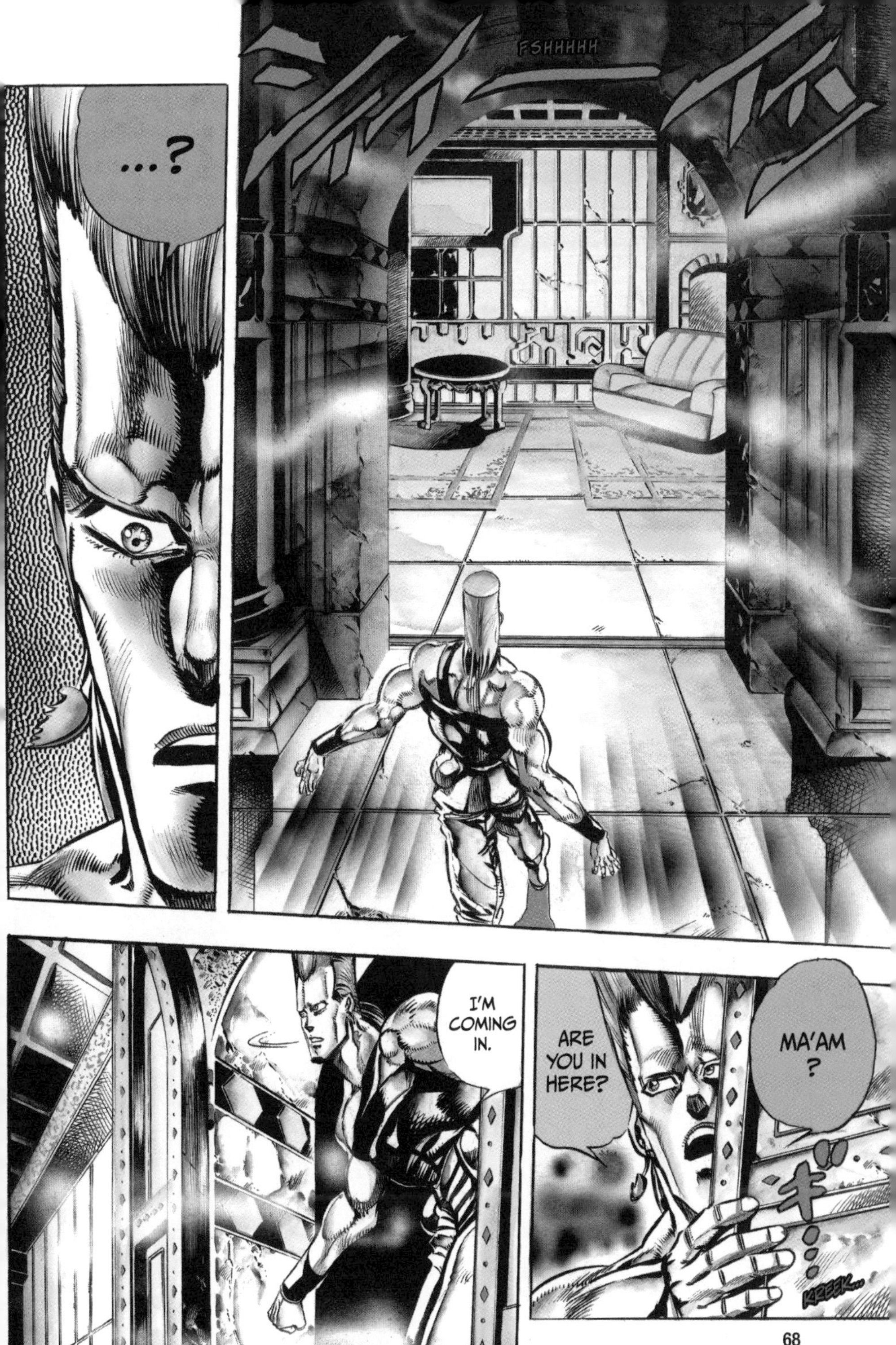
FSHHHHH
...?
MA'AM ?
ARE YOU IN HERE?
KREEK...
I'M COMING IN.

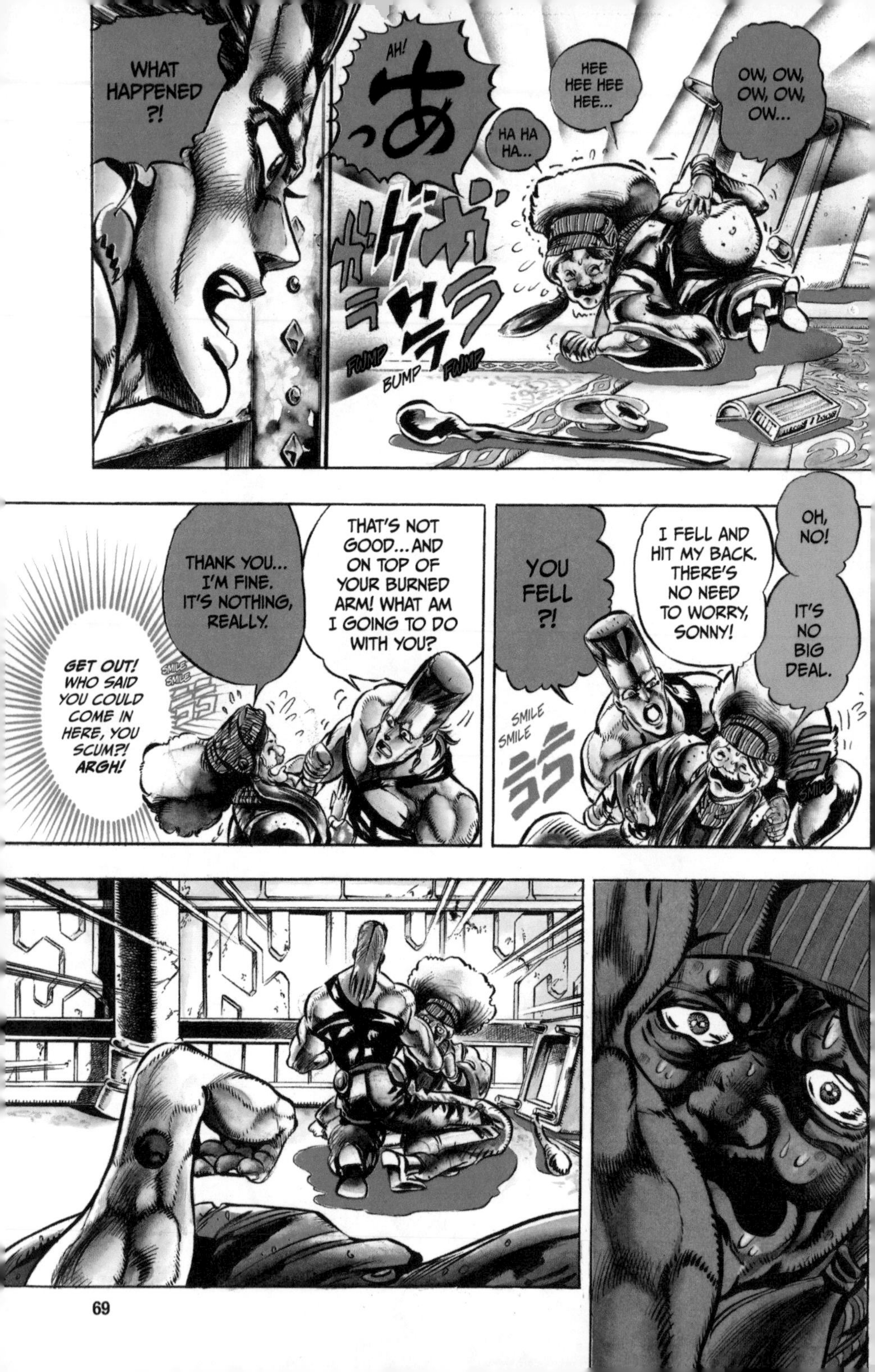
OW, OW, OW, OW, OW...
HEE HEE HEE HEE...
HA HA HA...
AH!
FWUMP
BUMP
FWUMP
WHAT HAPPENED ?!
OH, NO!
IT'S NO BIG DEAL.
I FELL AND HIT MY BACK. THERE'S NO NEED TO WORRY, SONNY!
YOU FELL ?!
SMILE SMILE
SMILE
THAT'S NOT GOOD...AND ON TOP OF YOUR BURNED ARM! WHAT AM I GOING TO DO WITH YOU?
THANK YOU... I'M FINE. IT'S NOTHING, REALLY.
GET OUT! WHO SAID YOU COULD COME IN HERE, YOU SCUM?! ARGH!
SMILE SMILE

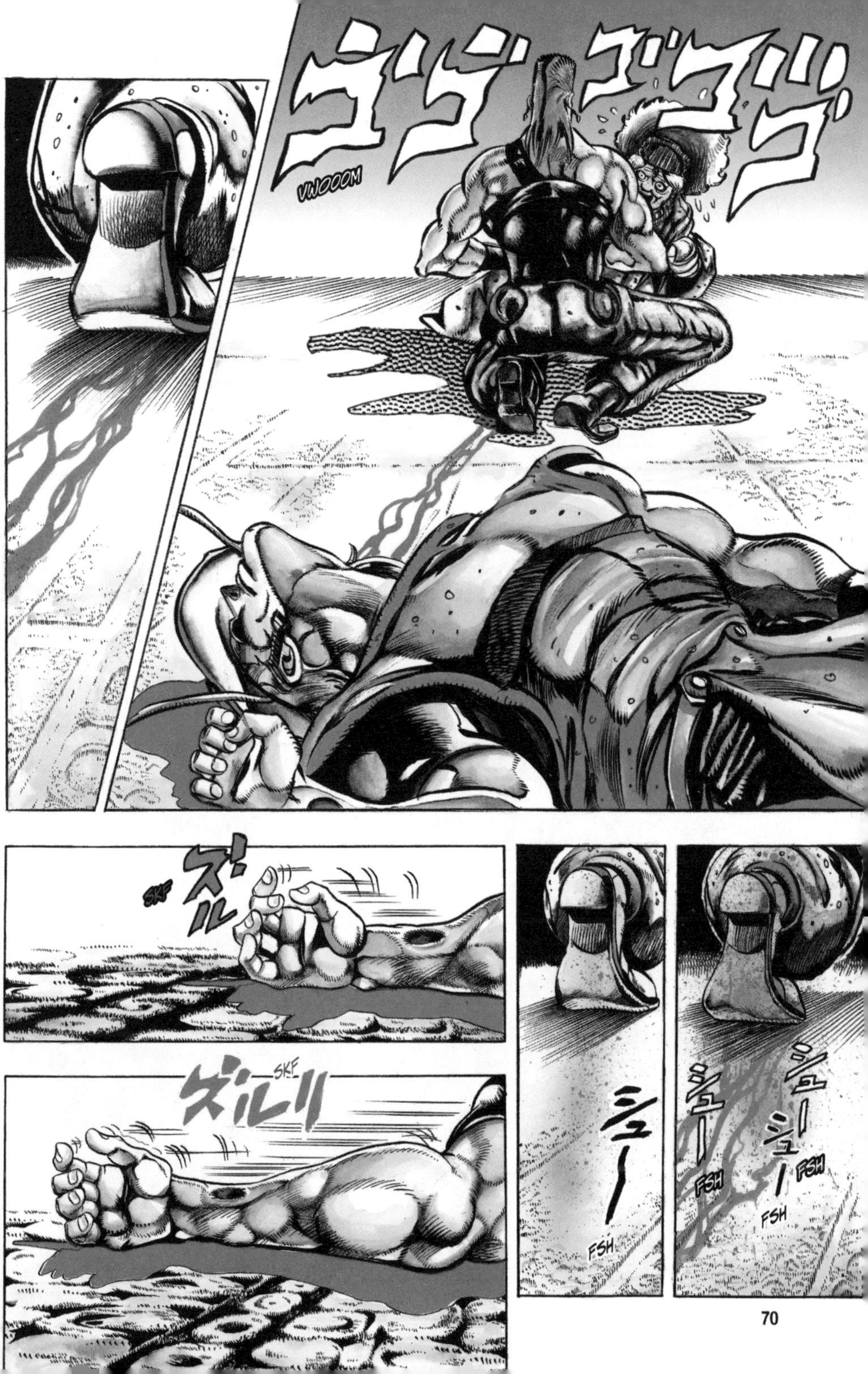
ゴゴゴゴ
VWOOOM
シューシュー
FSH
FSH
FSH
シュー
FSH
ズル
SKF
ズルリ
SKF

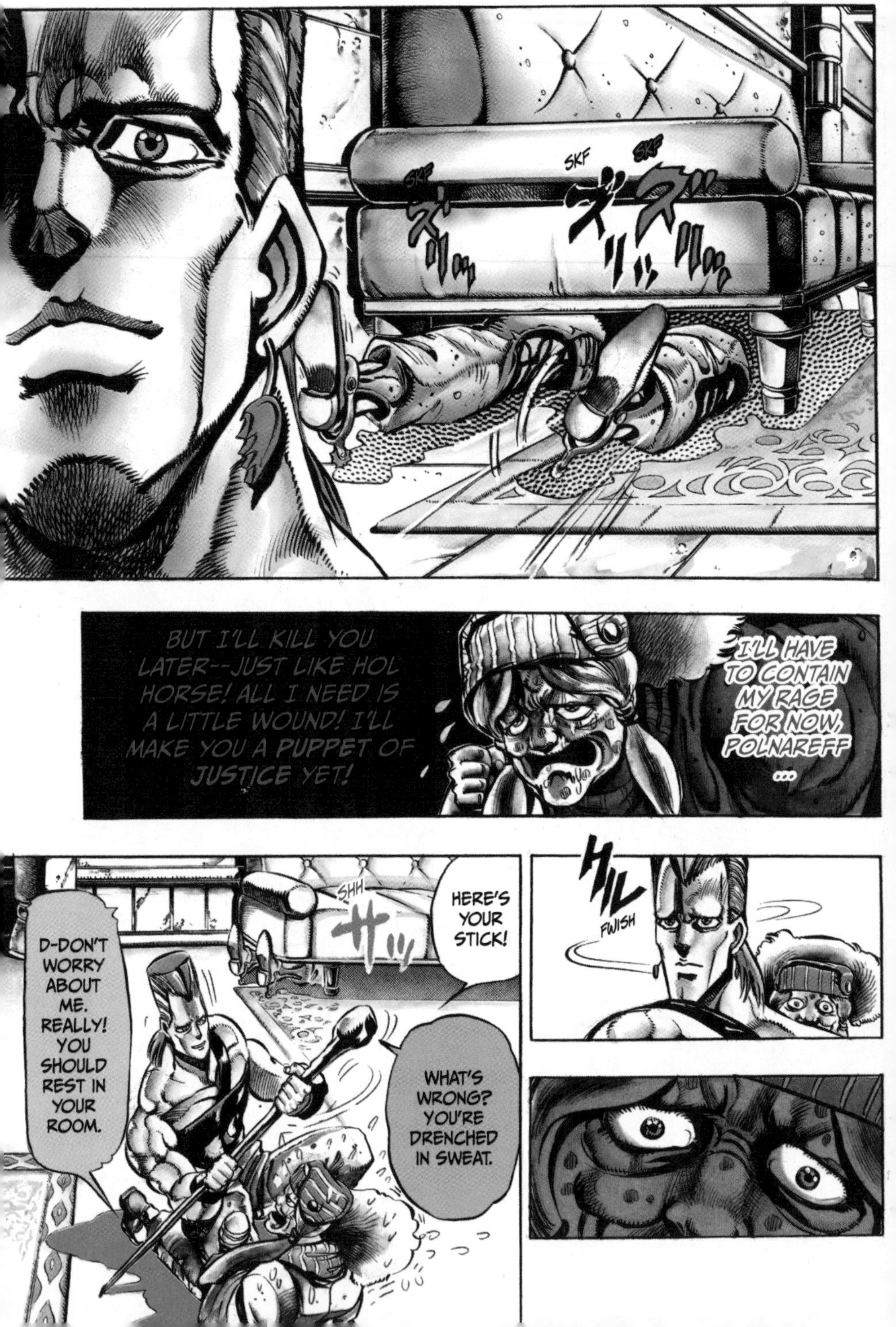
SKF
SKF
SKF
I'LL HAVE TO CONTAIN MY RAGE FOR NOW, POLNAREFF...
BUT I'LL KILL YOU LATER--JUST LIKE HOL HORSE! ALL I NEED IS A LITTLE WOUND! I'LL MAKE YOU A PUPPET OF JUSTICE YET!
FWISH
SHH
HERE'S YOUR STICK!
WHAT'S WRONG? YOU'RE DRENCHED IN SWEAT.
D-DON'T WORRY ABOUT ME. REALLY! YOU SHOULD REST IN YOUR ROOM.

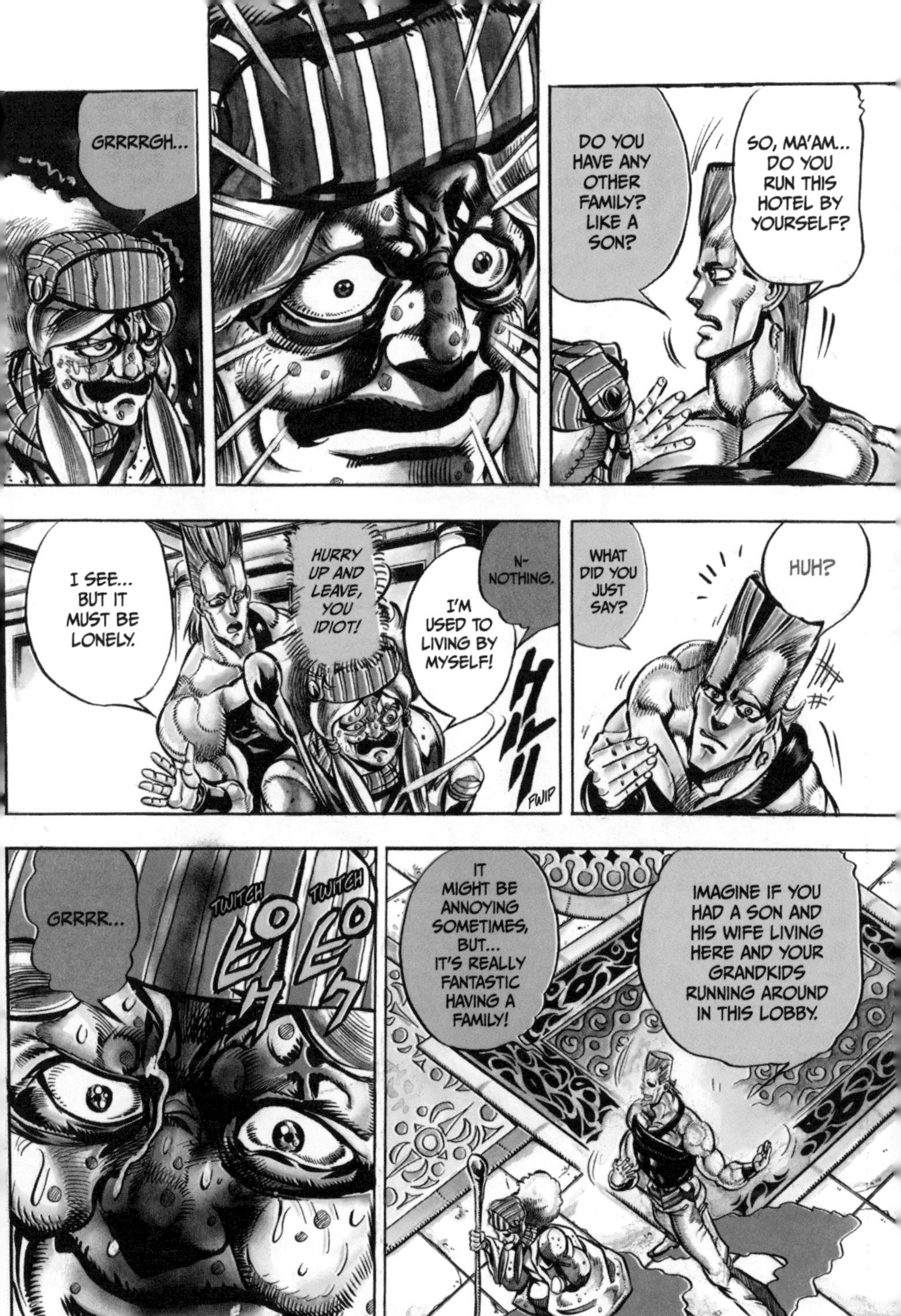
SO, MA'AM... DO YOU RUN THIS HOTEL BY YOURSELF?
DO YOU HAVE ANY OTHER FAMILY? LIKE A SON?
GRRRRGH...
HUH?
WHAT DID YOU JUST SAY?
N-NOTHING.
I'M USED TO LIVING BY MYSELF!
HURRY UP AND LEAVE, YOU IDIOT!
I SEE... BUT IT MUST BE LONELY.
FWIP
IMAGINE IF YOU HAD A SON AND HIS WIFE LIVING HERE AND YOUR GRANDKIDS RUNNING AROUND IN THIS LOBBY.
IT MIGHT BE ANNOYING SOMETIMES, BUT... IT'S REALLY FANTASTIC HAVING A FAMILY!
TWITCH
TWITCH
GRRRR...

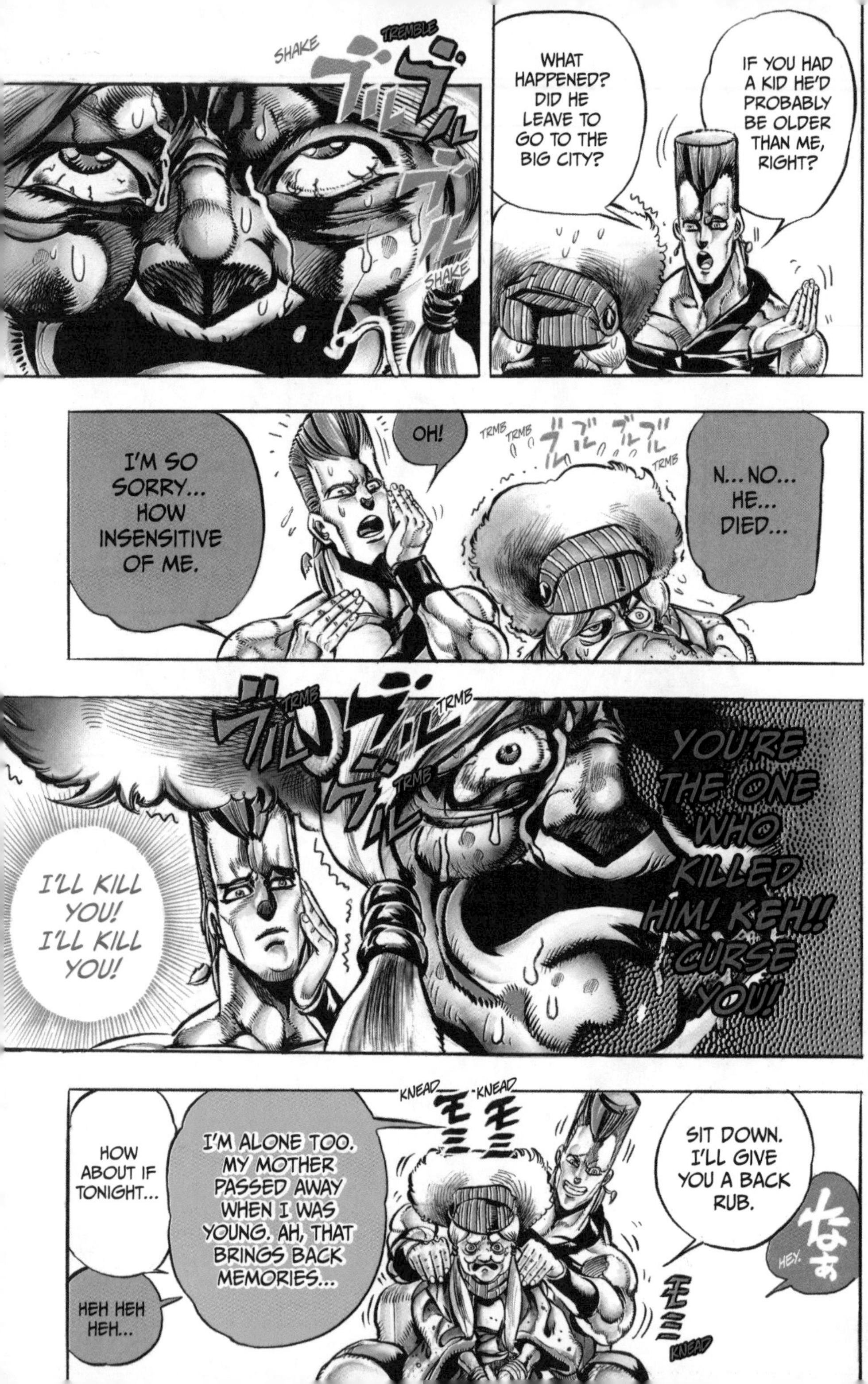
IF YOU HAD A KID HE'D PROBABLY BE OLDER THAN ME, RIGHT?
WHAT HAPPENED? DID HE LEAVE TO GO TO THE BIG CITY?
TREMBLE
SHAKE
SHAKE
TRMB
TRMB
TRMB
N... NO... HE... DIED...
OH!
I'M SO SORRY... HOW INSENSITIVE OF ME.
TRMB
TRMB
TRMB
YOU'RE THE ONE WHO KILLED HIM! KEH!! CURSE YOU!
I'LL KILL YOU! I'LL KILL YOU!
HEY.
SIT DOWN. I'LL GIVE YOU A BACK RUB.
KNEAD
KNEAD
I'M ALONE TOO. MY MOTHER PASSED AWAY WHEN I WAS YOUNG. AH, THAT BRINGS BACK MEMORIES...
HOW ABOUT IF TONIGHT...
HEH HEH HEH...
KNEAD

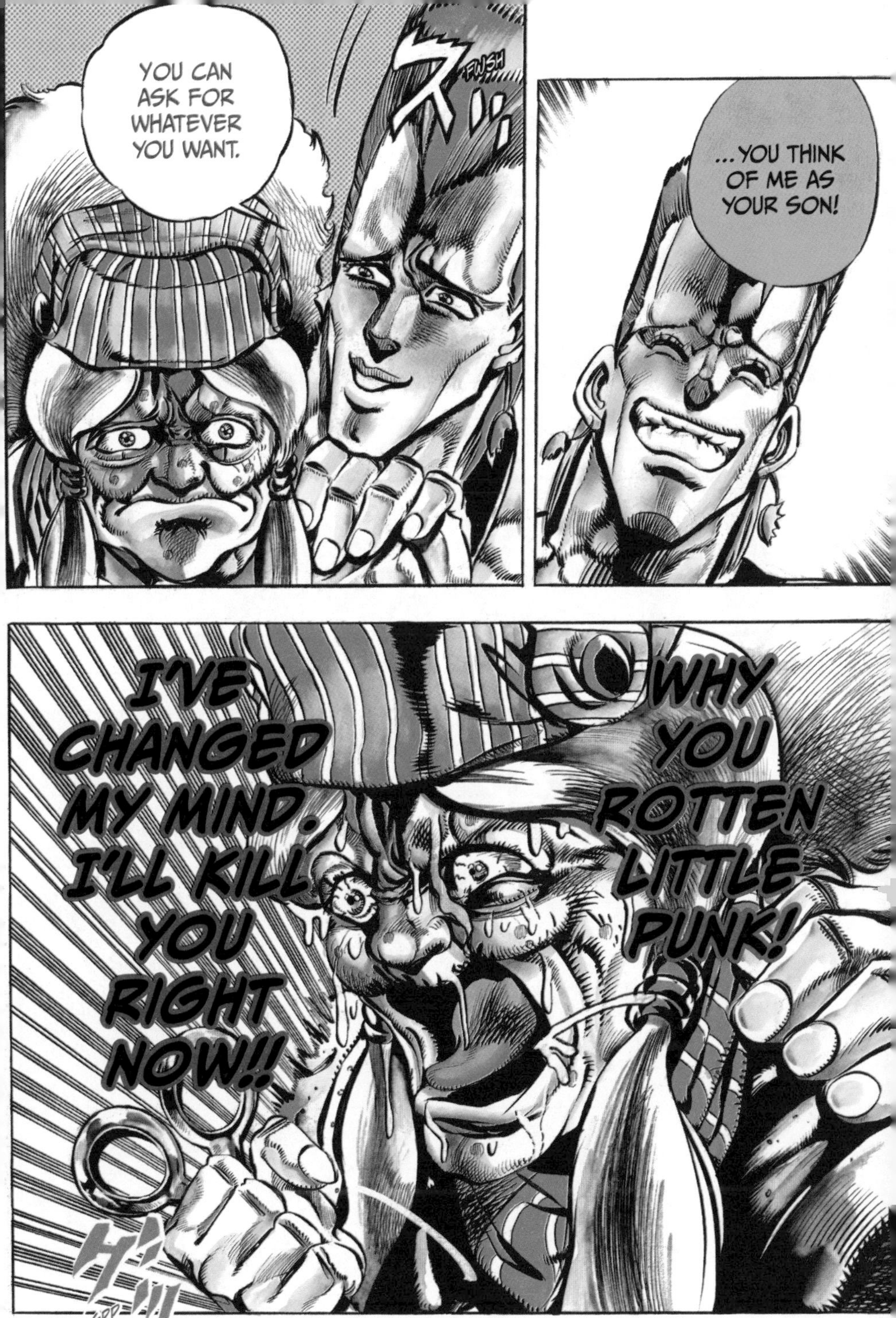
...YOU THINK OF ME AS YOUR SON!
FWSH
YOU CAN ASK FOR WHATEVER YOU WANT.
WHY YOU ROTTEN LITTLE PUNK!
I'VE CHANGED MY MIND. I'LL KILL YOU RIGHT NOW!!
GRP

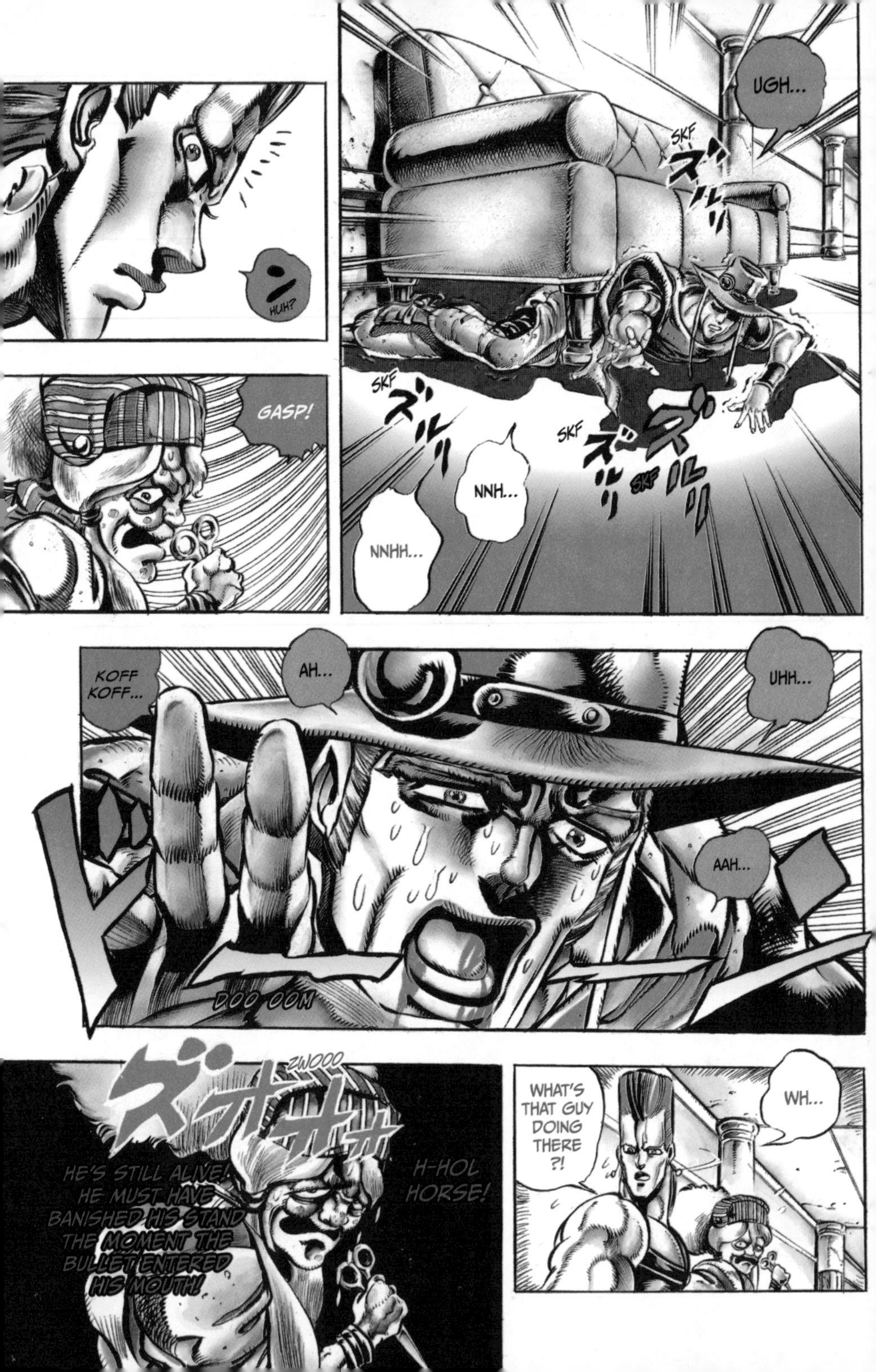
UGH...
SKF
SKF
SKF
SKF
NNH...
NNHH...
HUH?
GASP!
UHH...
AH...
KOFF KOFF...
AAH...
DOO OOM
WH...
WHAT'S THAT GUY DOING THERE?!
ZWOOO
H-HOL HORSE!
HE'S STILL ALIVE! HE MUST HAVE BANISHED HIS STAND THE MOMENT THE BULLET ENTERED HIS MOUTH!

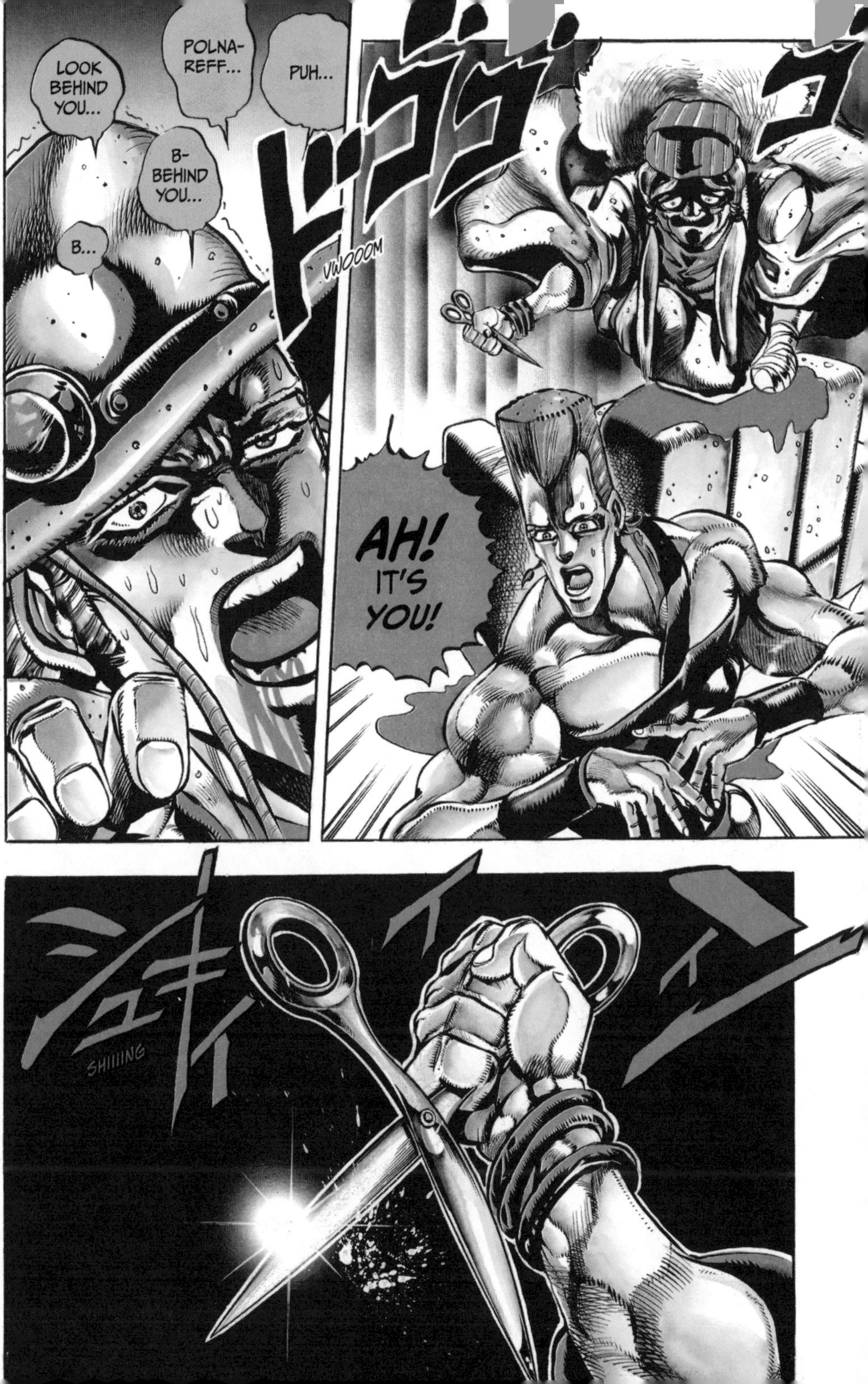
VWOOOM
AH! IT'S YOU!
PUH...
POLNA-REFF...
LOOK BEHIND YOU...
B-BEHIND YOU...
B...
SHIIIING

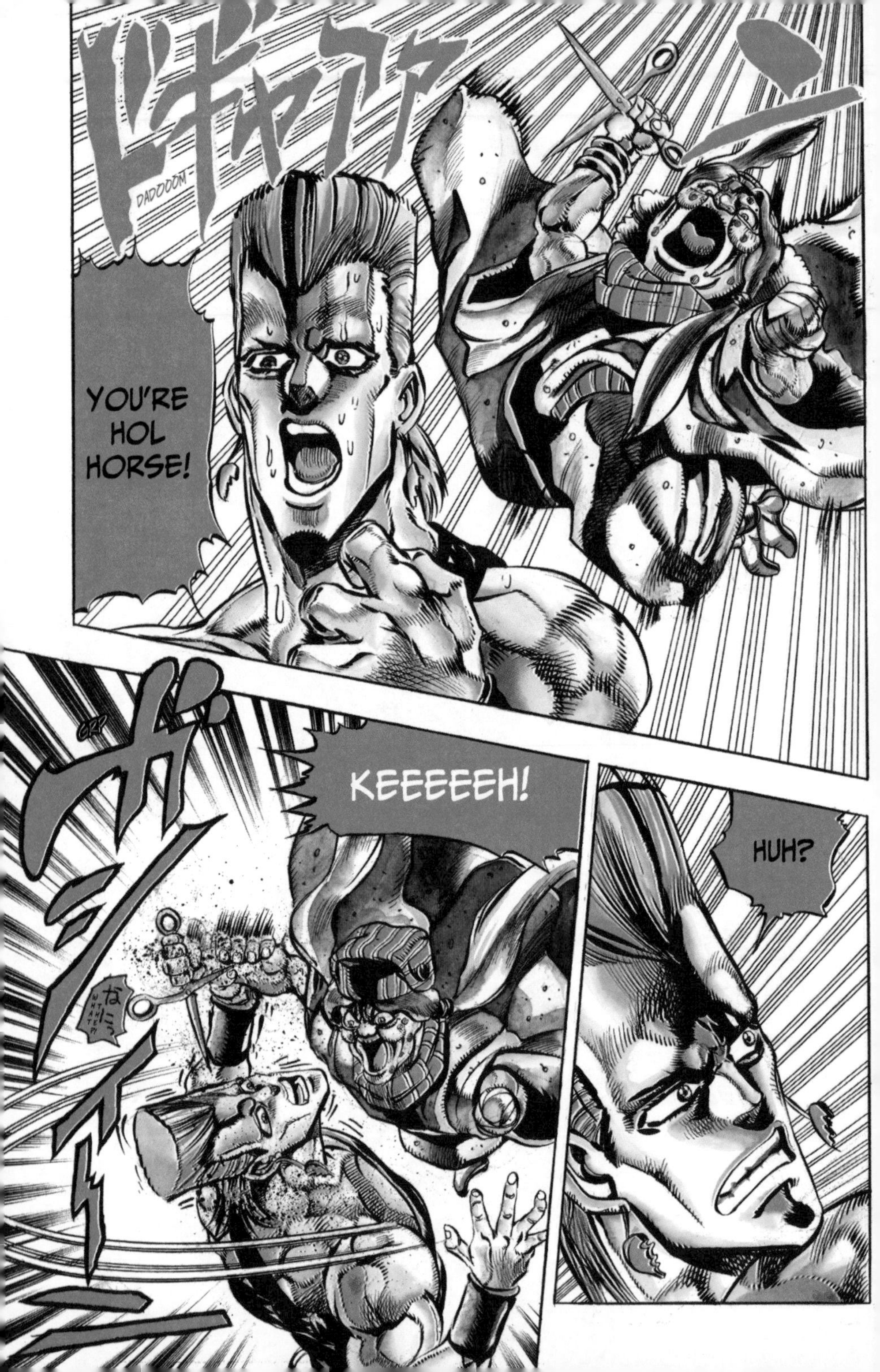

DADOOOM
YOU'RE HOL HORSE!
HUH?
KEEEEEH!
GRP
なにっ
WHAT THE?!

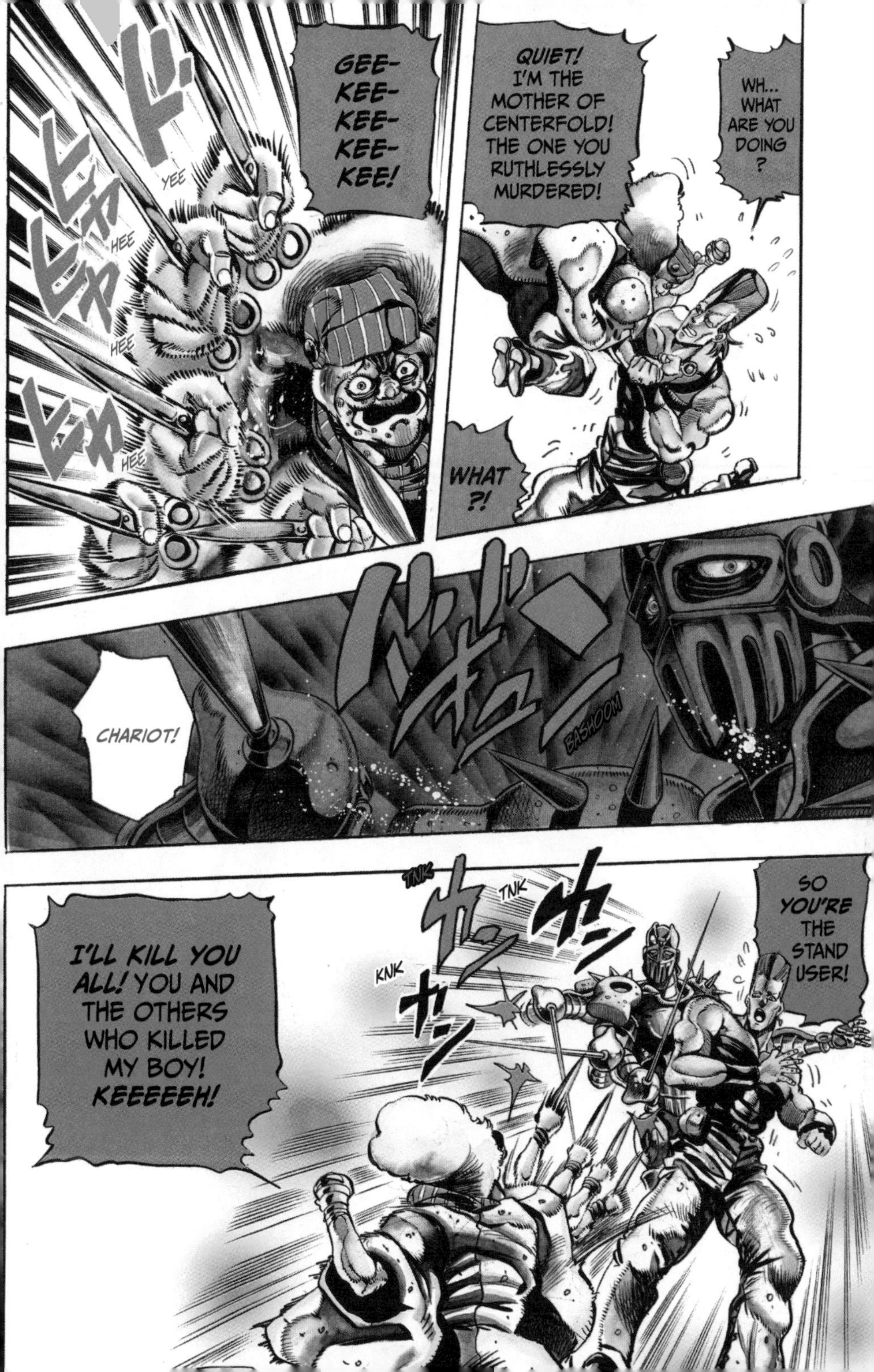
WH... WHAT ARE YOU DOING?
QUIET! I'M THE MOTHER OF CENTERFOLD! THE ONE YOU RUTHLESSLY MURDERED!
WHAT?!
GEE-KEE-KEE-KEE-KEE!
YEE
HEE
HEE
HEE
BASHOOM
CHARIOT!
SO YOU'RE THE STAND USER!
TNK
TNK
KNK
I'LL KILL YOU ALL! YOU AND THE OTHERS WHO KILLED MY BOY! KEEEEEH!

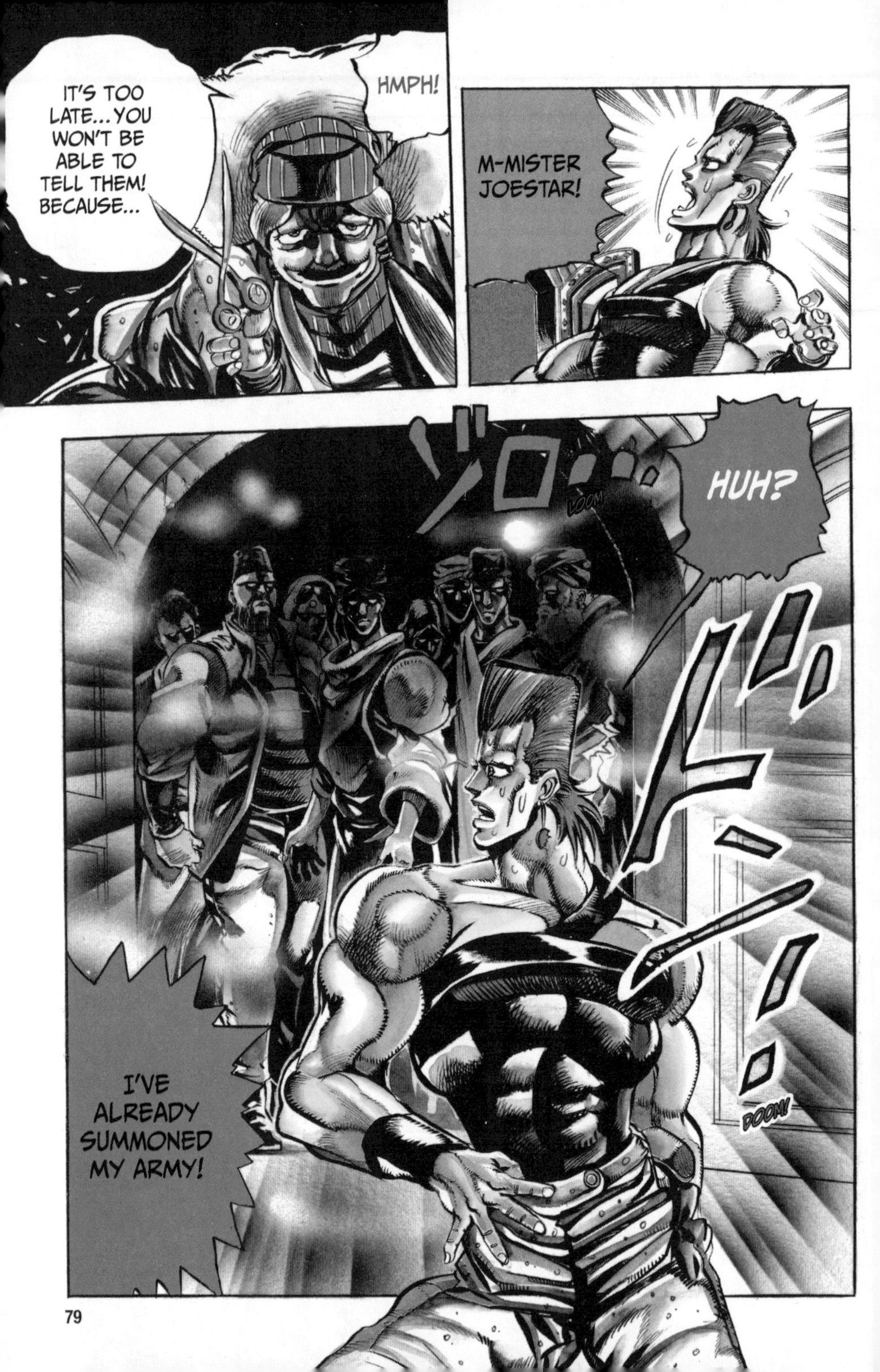
M-MISTER JOESTAR!
HMPH!
IT'S TOO LATE...YOU WON'T BE ABLE TO TELL THEM! BECAUSE...
LOOM
HUH?
DOOM!
I'VE ALREADY SUMMONED MY ARMY!

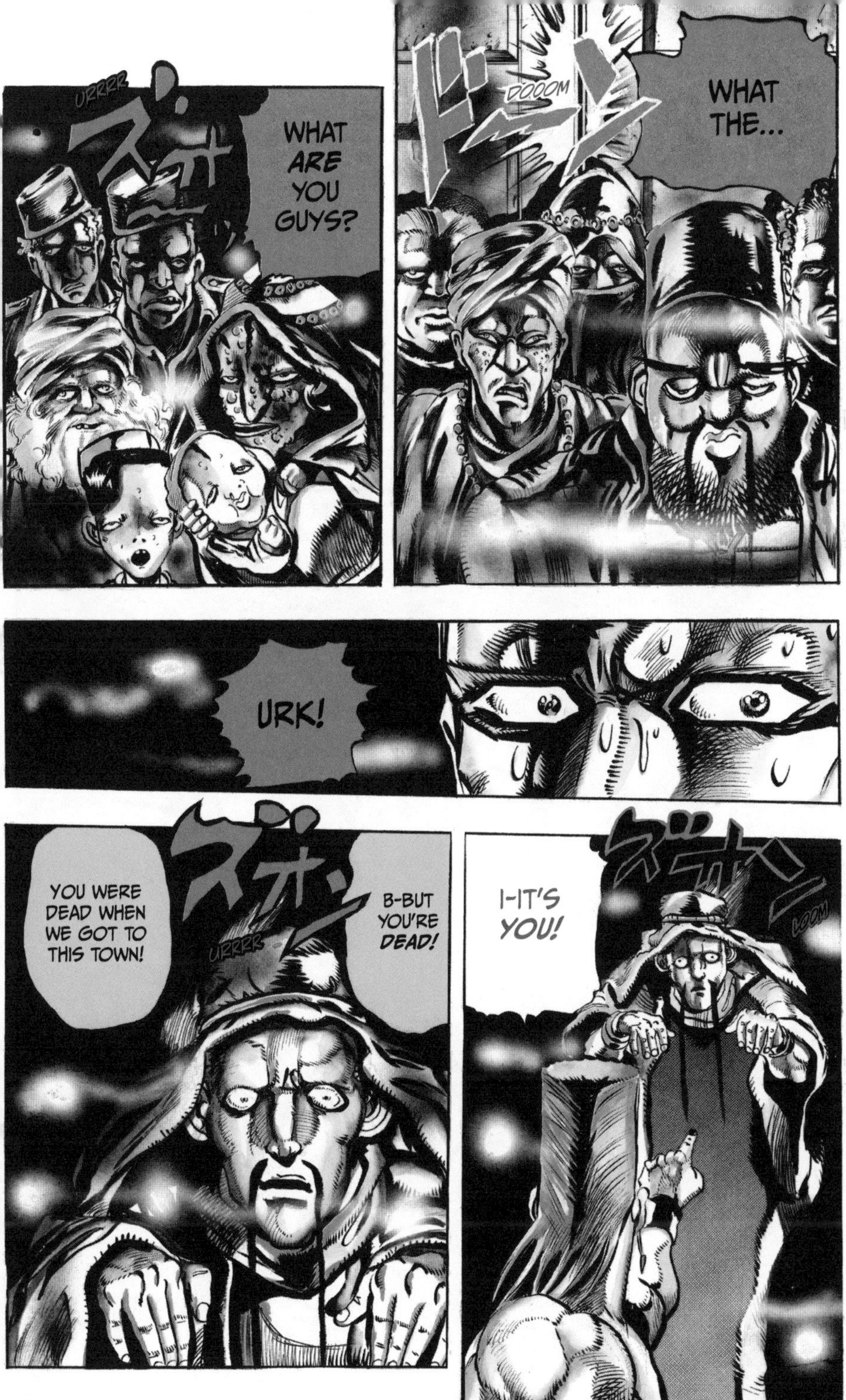
DOOOM
WHAT THE...
URRRR
WHAT ARE YOU GUYS?
URK!
LOOM
I-IT'S YOU!
B-BUT YOU'RE DEAD!
URRRR
YOU WERE DEAD WHEN WE GOT TO THIS TOWN!

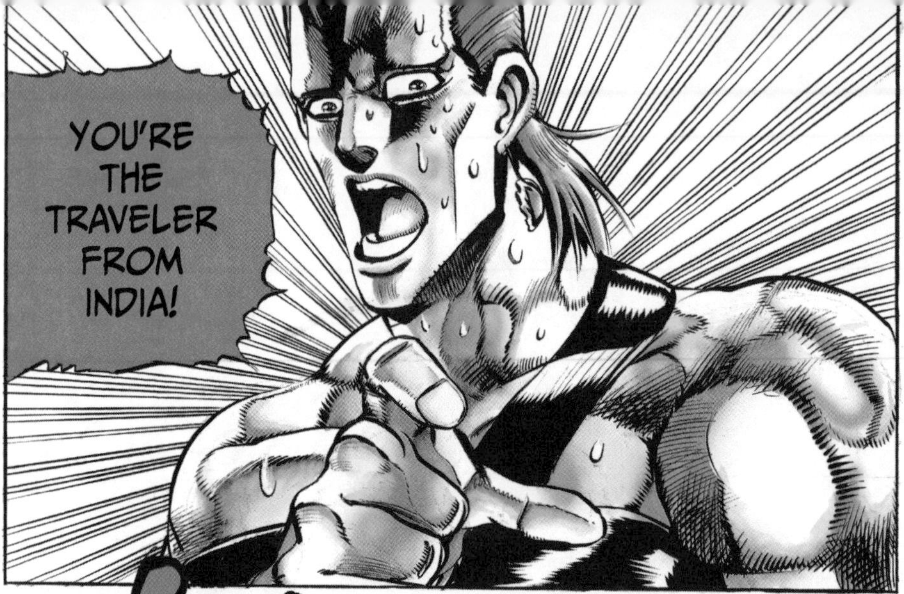
YOU'RE THE TRAVELER FROM INDIA!
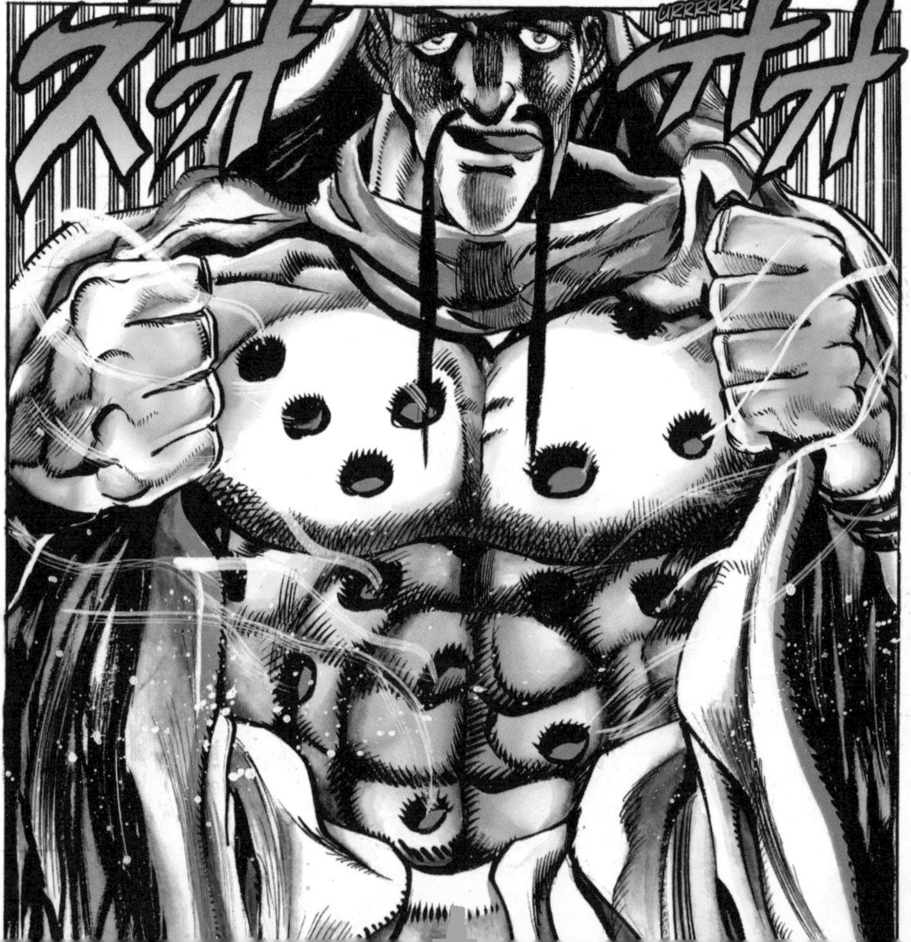
URRRRRR

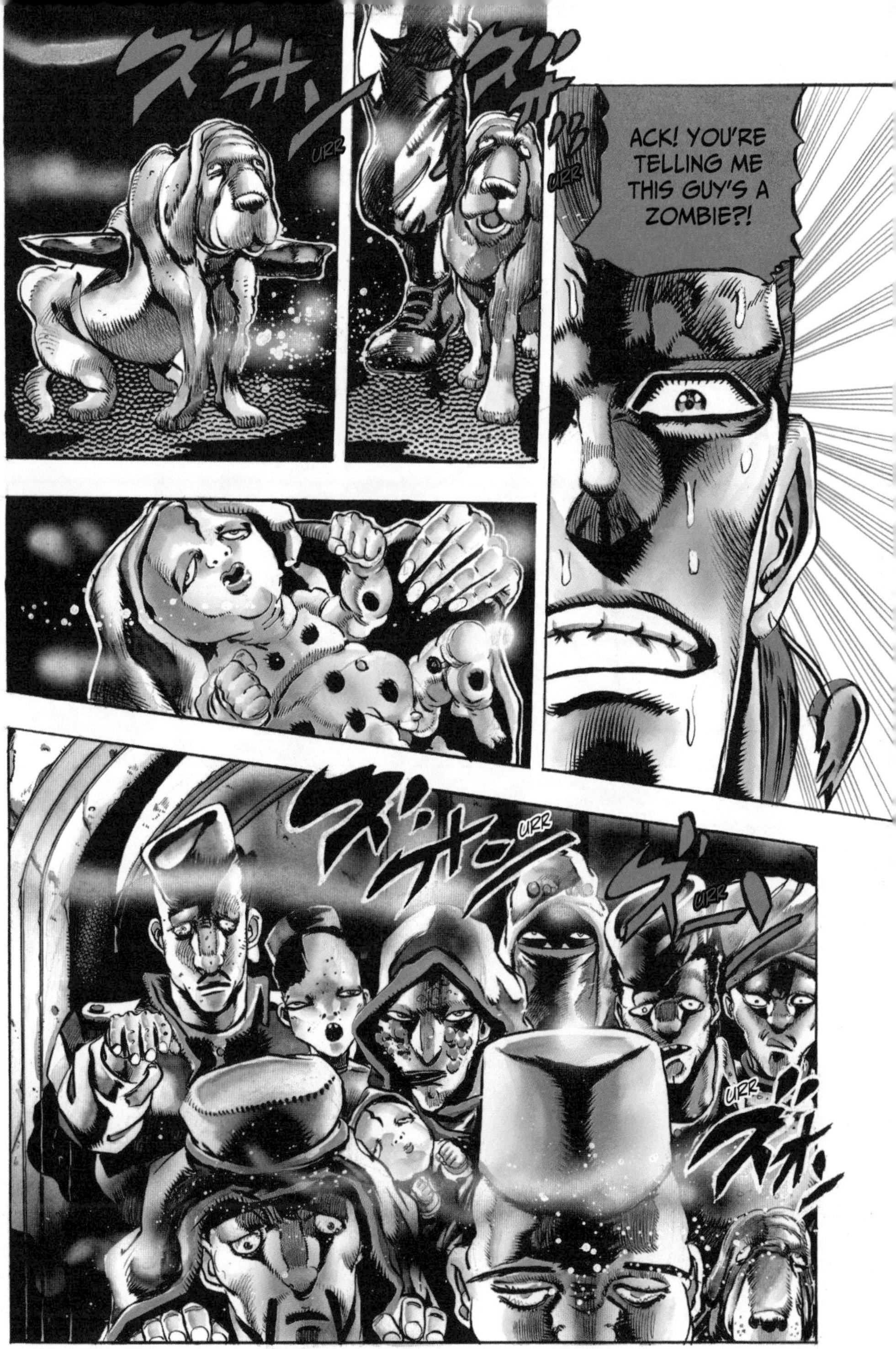
ACK! YOU'RE TELLING ME THIS GUY'S A ZOMBIE?!
URR
URR
URR
URR
URR

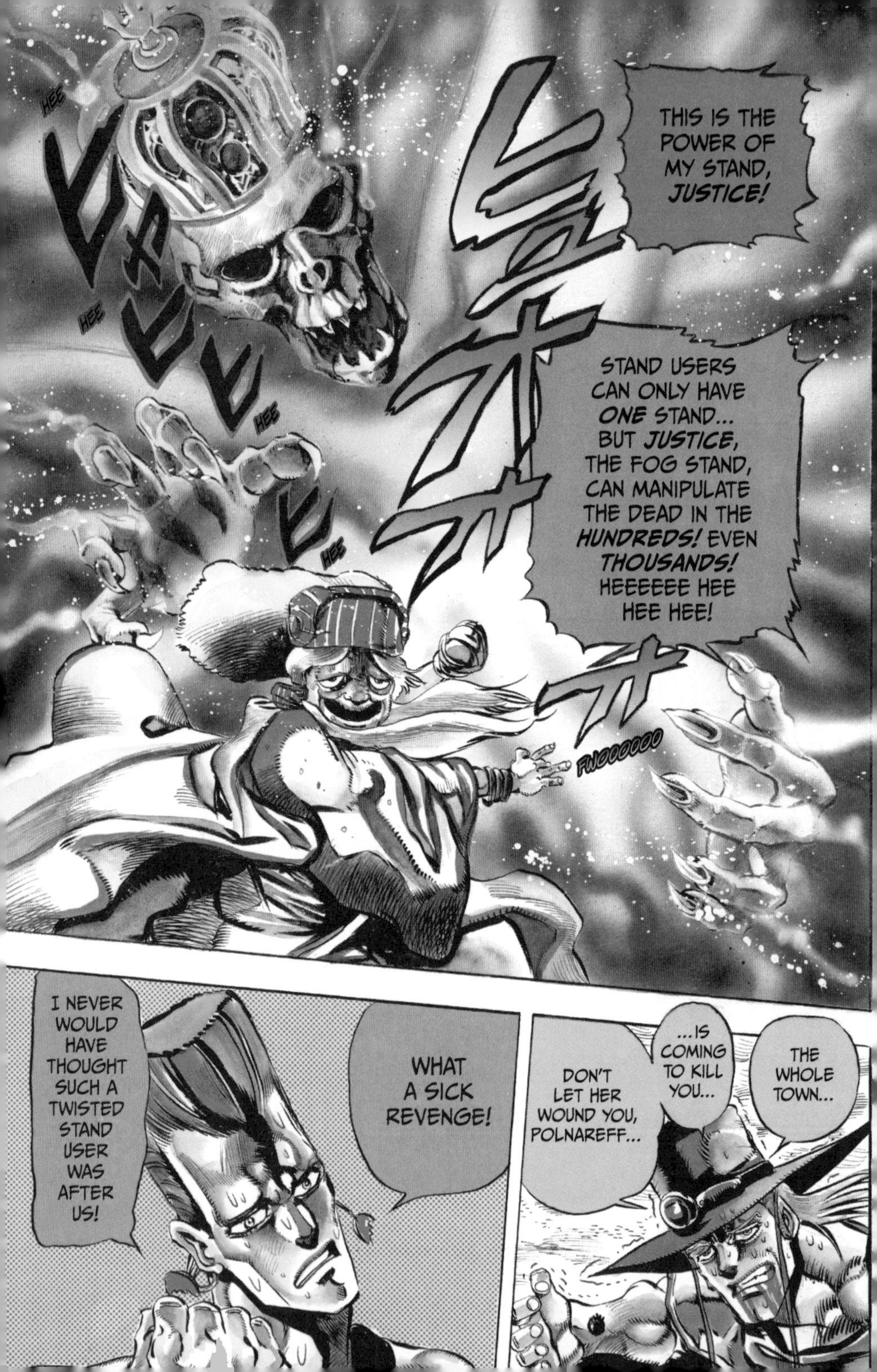
HEE
HEE
HEE
HEE
THIS IS THE POWER OF MY STAND, *JUSTICE!*
STAND USERS CAN ONLY HAVE *ONE* STAND... BUT *JUSTICE*, THE FOG STAND, CAN MANIPULATE THE DEAD IN THE *HUNDREDS!* EVEN *THOUSANDS!* HEEEEEE HEE HEE HEE!
FWOOOOOO
THE WHOLE TOWN...
...IS COMING TO KILL YOU...
DON'T LET HER WOUND YOU, POLNAREFF...
WHAT A SICK REVENGE!
I NEVER WOULD HAVE THOUGHT SUCH A TWISTED STAND USER WAS AFTER US!

CHAPTER 45: Justice PART 5

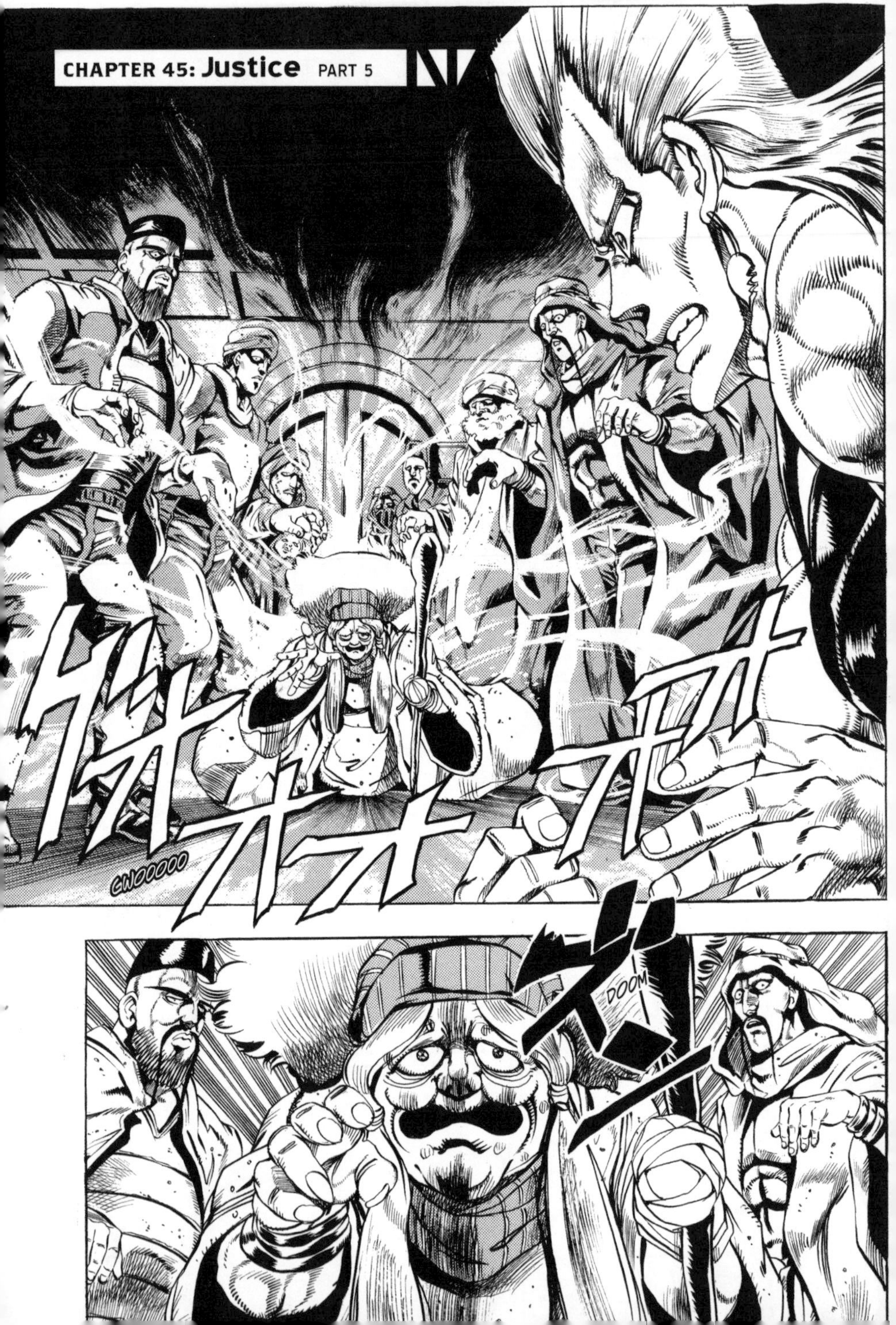
GWOOOOO
DOOM

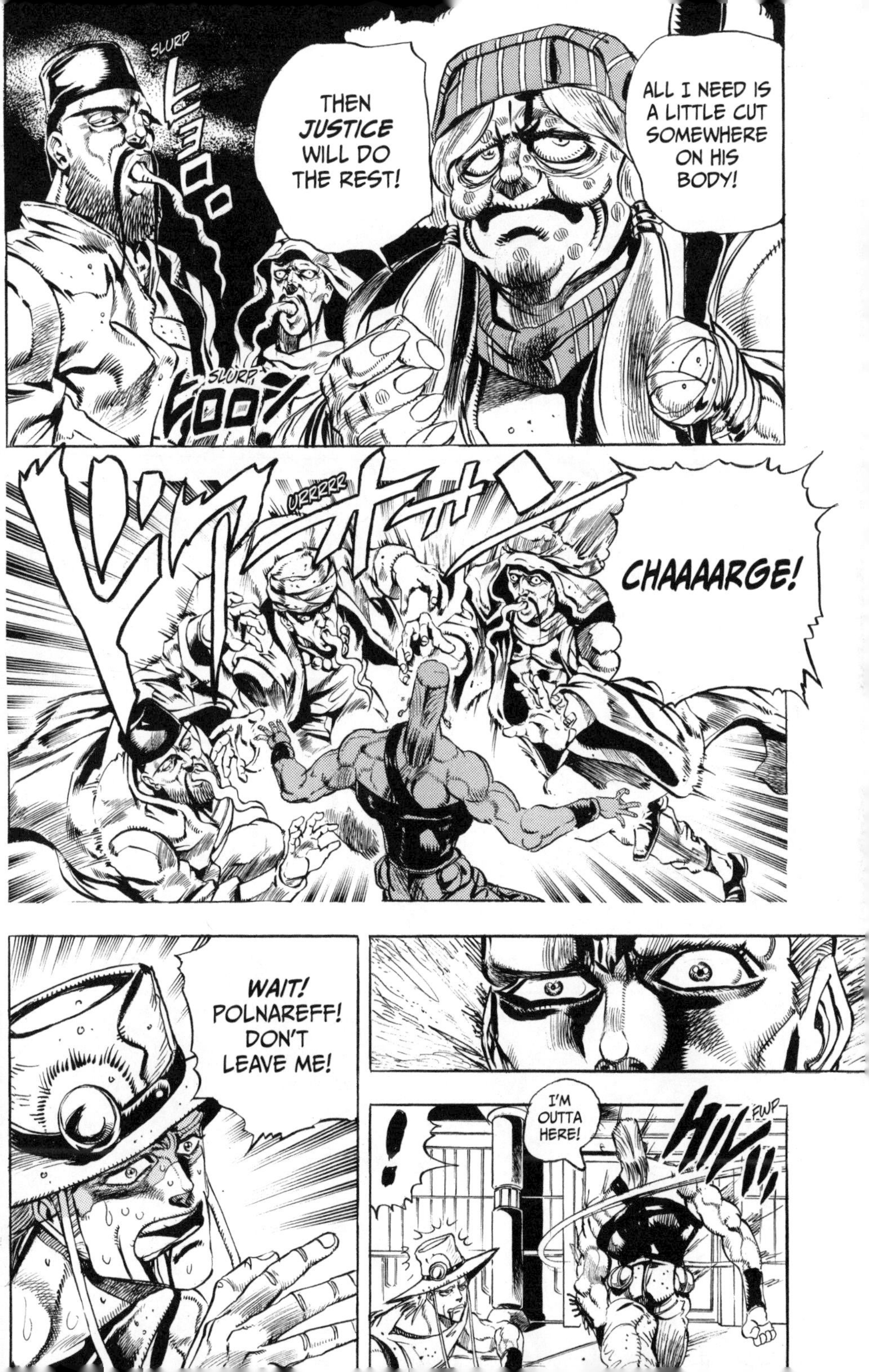
ALL I NEED IS A LITTLE CUT SOMEWHERE ON HIS BODY!
THEN JUSTICE WILL DO THE REST!
SLURP
SLURP
URRRRR
CHAAAARGE!
I'M OUTTA HERE!
FWIP
WAIT! POLNAREFF! DON'T LEAVE ME!

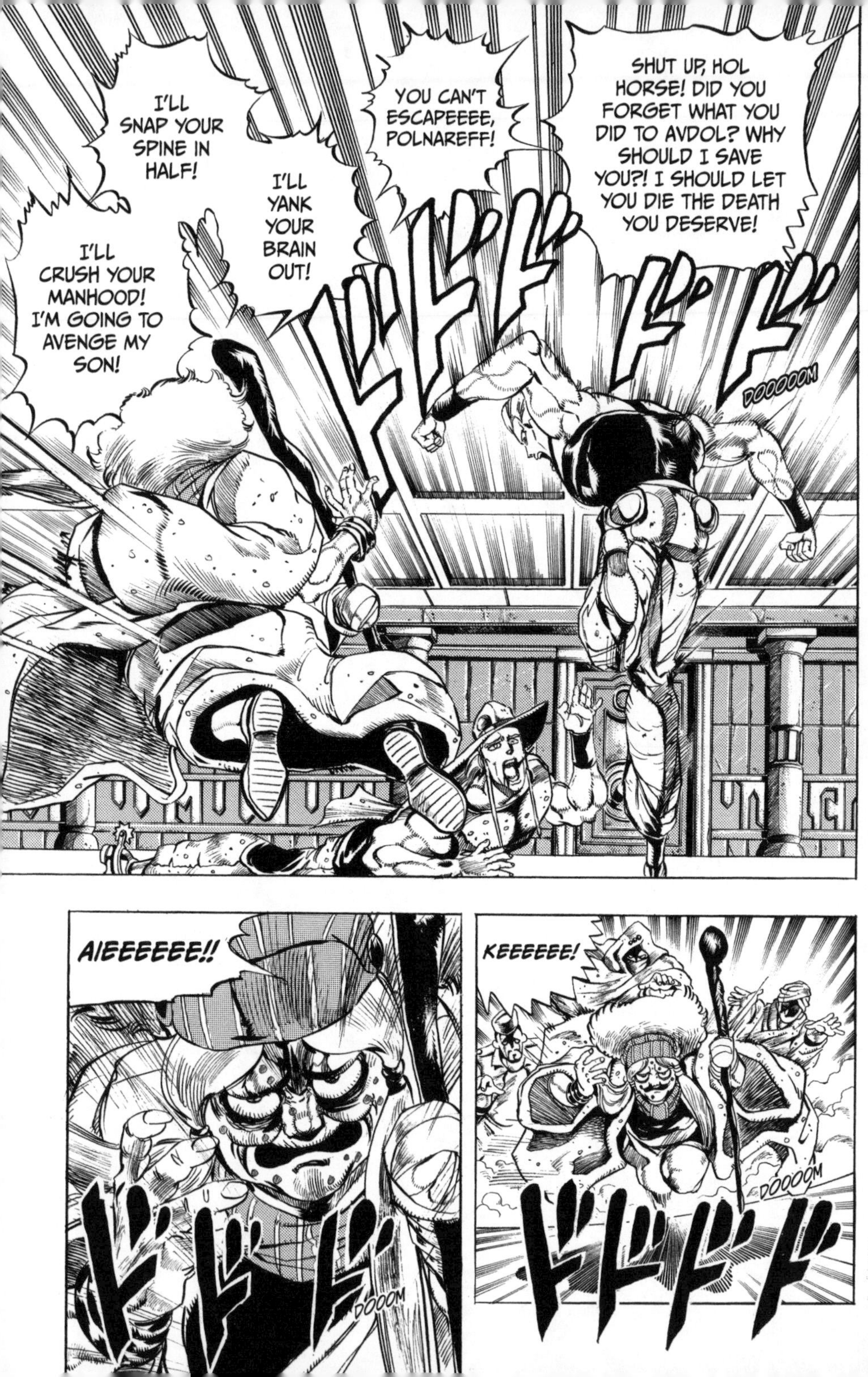
SHUT UP, HOL HORSE! DID YOU FORGET WHAT YOU DID TO AVDOL? WHY SHOULD I SAVE YOU?! I SHOULD LET YOU DIE THE DEATH YOU DESERVE!
ドドド
DOOOOOM
YOU CAN'T ESCAPEEEE, POLNAREFF!
ドドド
I'LL YANK YOUR BRAIN OUT!
I'LL SNAP YOUR SPINE IN HALF!
I'LL CRUSH YOUR MANHOOD! I'M GOING TO AVENGE MY SON!
KEEEEEE!
DOOOOM
ドドドドド
AIEEEEEE!!
ドドド
DOOOM

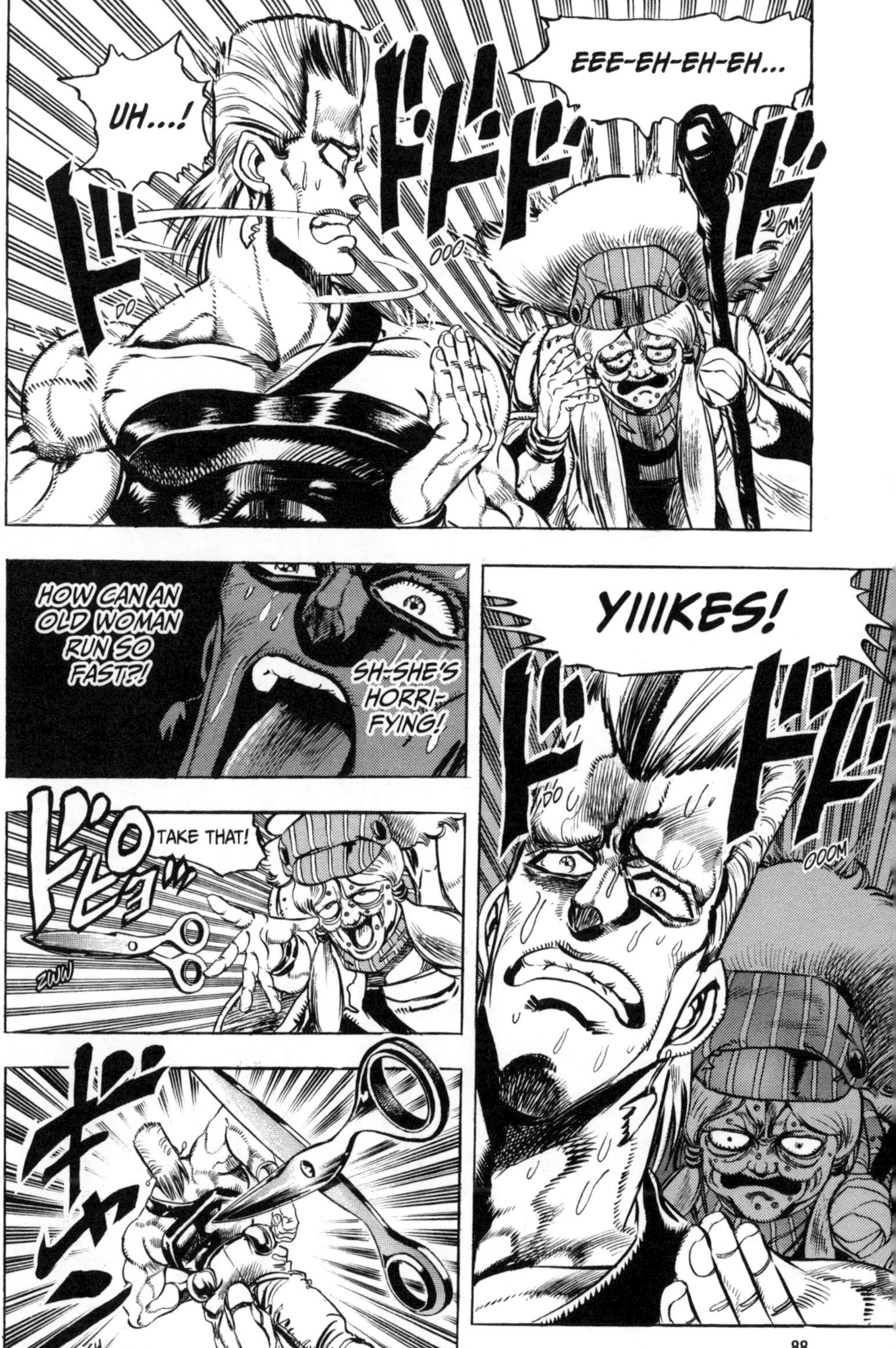
EEE-EH-EH-EH...
OM
OOO
UH...!
DO
YIIIKES!
DO
OOOM
SH-SHE'S HORRI-FYING!
HOW CAN AN OLD WOMAN RUN SO FAST?!
TAKE THAT!
ZWW
WOOSH

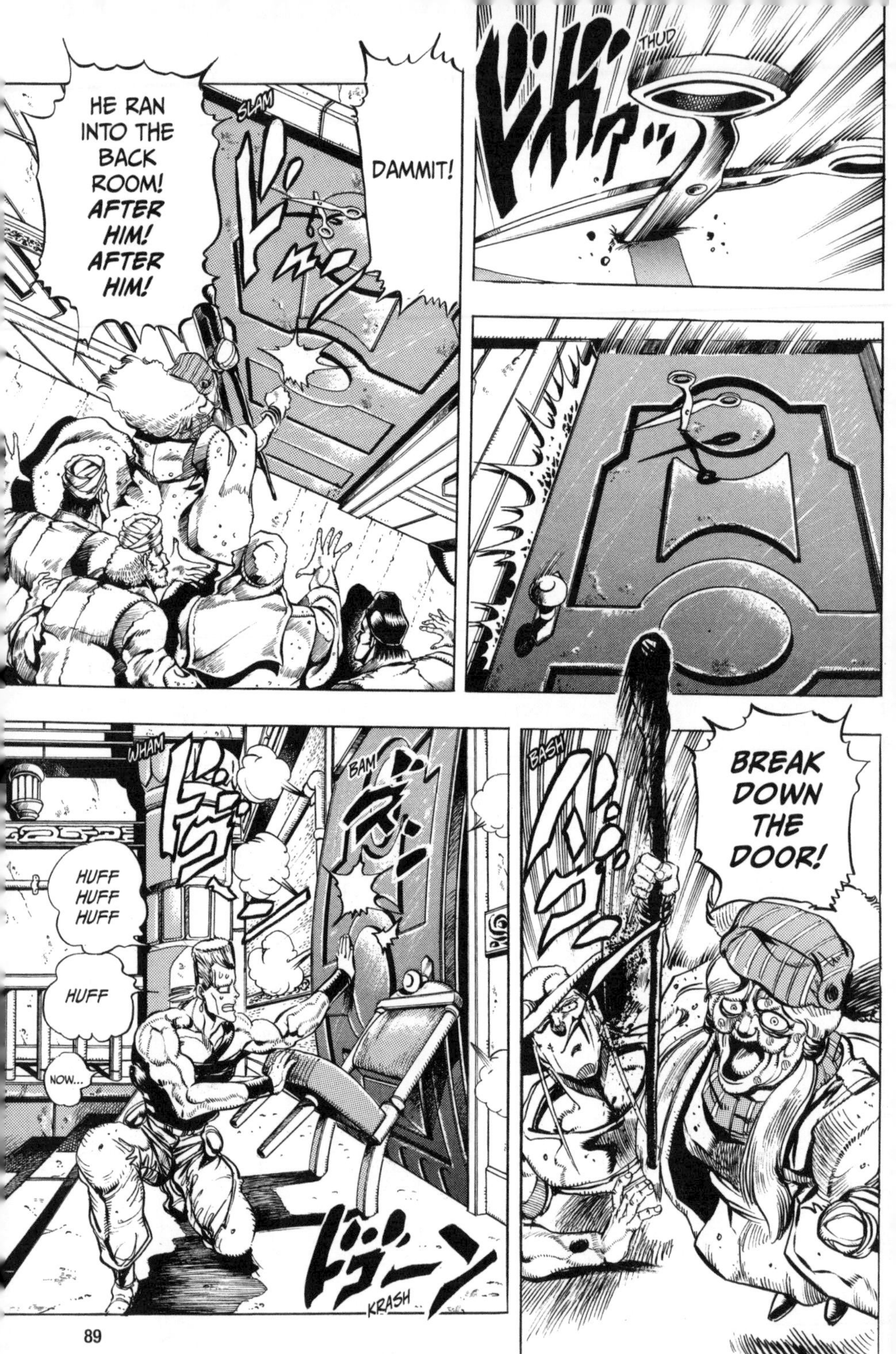
THUD
DAMMIT!
SLAM
HE RAN INTO THE BACK ROOM! AFTER HIM! AFTER HIM!
BREAK DOWN THE DOOR!
BASH
BAM
WHAM
HUFF HUFF HUFF
HUFF
NOW...
KRASH

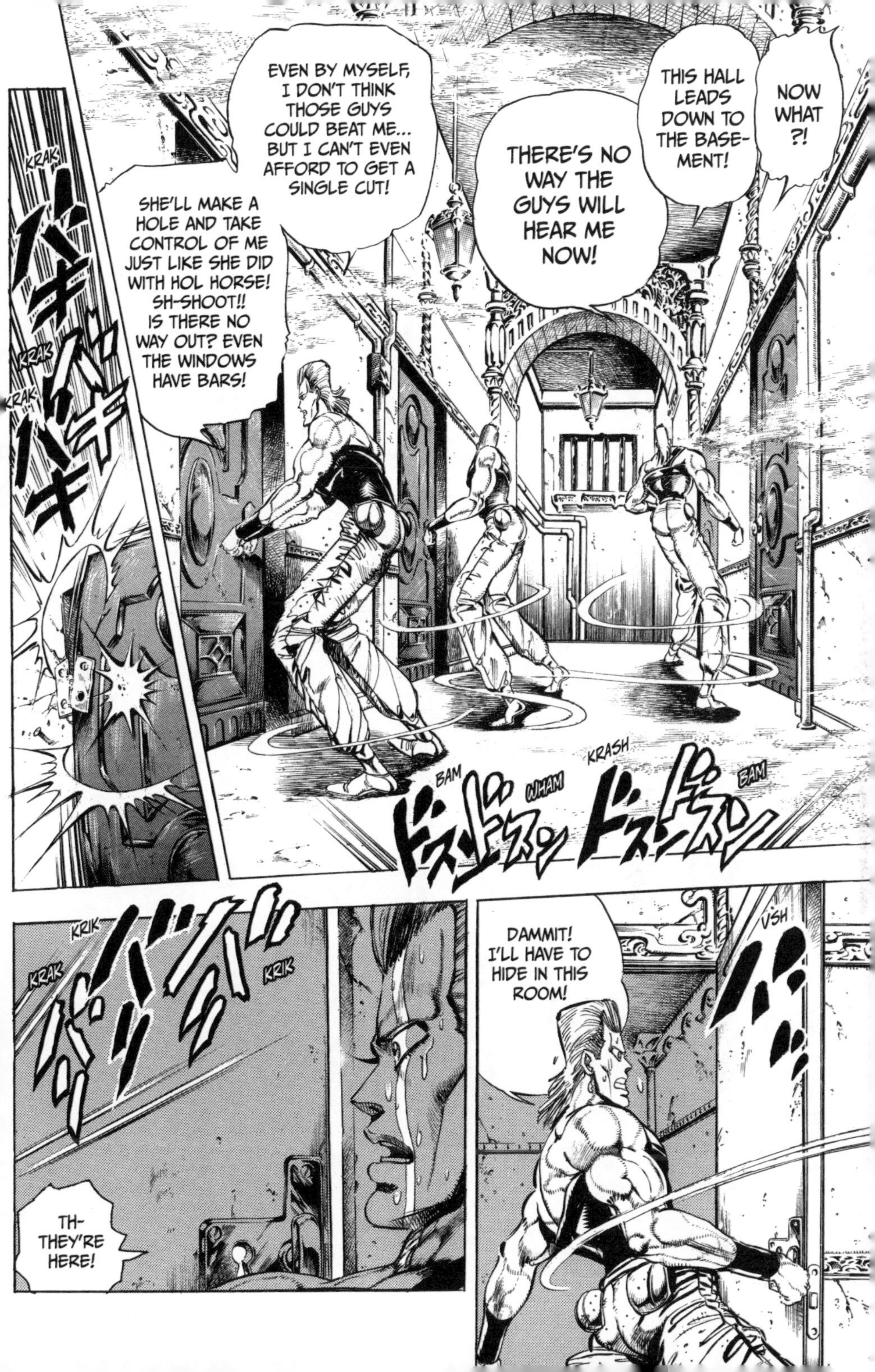
NOW WHAT ?!
THIS HALL LEADS DOWN TO THE BASE-MENT!
THERE'S NO WAY THE GUYS WILL HEAR ME NOW!
EVEN BY MYSELF, I DON'T THINK THOSE GUYS COULD BEAT ME... BUT I CAN'T EVEN AFFORD TO GET A SINGLE CUT!
SHE'LL MAKE A HOLE AND TAKE CONTROL OF ME JUST LIKE SHE DID WITH HOL HORSE! SH-SHOOT!! IS THERE NO WAY OUT? EVEN THE WINDOWS HAVE BARS!
BAM
KRASH
BAM
WHAM
KRAK
KRAK
KRAK
VSH
DAMMIT! I'LL HAVE TO HIDE IN THIS ROOM!
KRIK
KRAK
KRIK
TH- THEY'RE HERE!

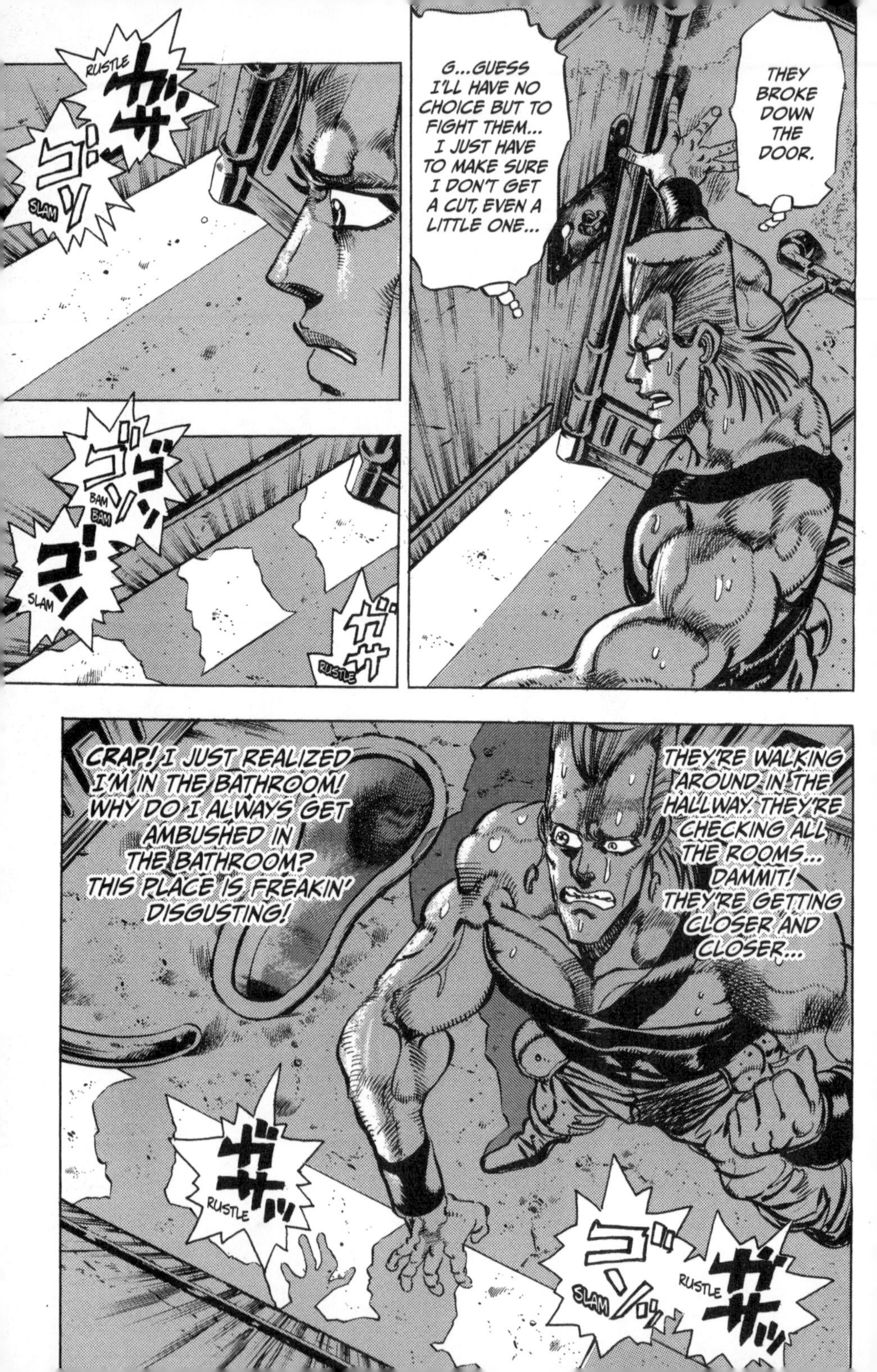

THEY BROKE DOWN THE DOOR.
G...GUESS I'LL HAVE NO CHOICE BUT TO FIGHT THEM... I JUST HAVE TO MAKE SURE I DON'T GET A CUT, EVEN A LITTLE ONE...
RUSTLE
SLAM
BAM BAM
SLAM
RUSTLE
THEY'RE WALKING AROUND IN THE HALLWAY. THEY'RE CHECKING ALL THE ROOMS... DAMMIT! THEY'RE GETTING CLOSER AND CLOSER...
CRAP! I JUST REALIZED I'M IN THE BATHROOM! WHY DO I ALWAYS GET AMBUSHED IN THE BATHROOM? THIS PLACE IS FREAKIN' DISGUSTING!
RUSTLE
SLAM
RUSTLE

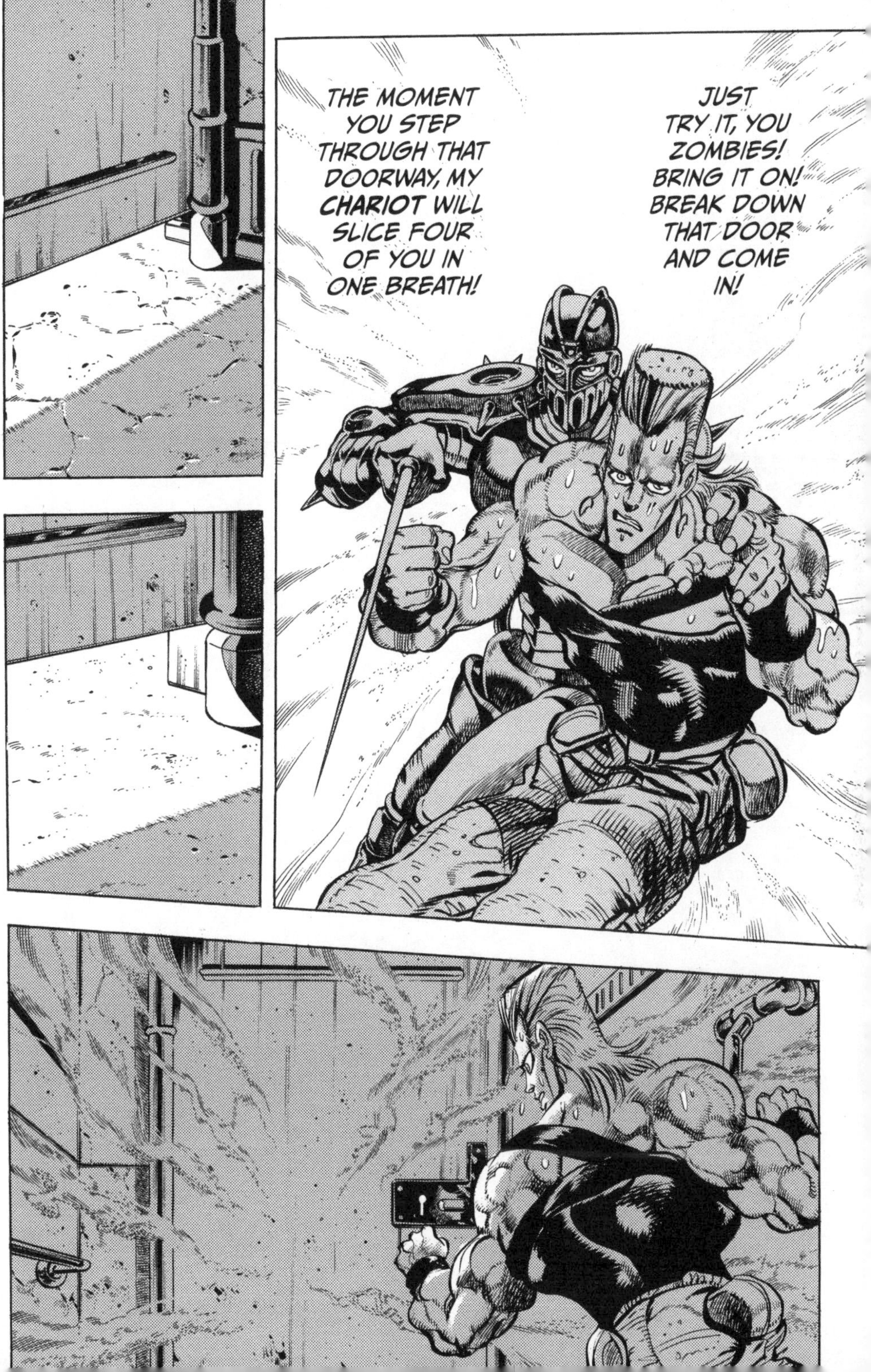
JUST TRY IT, YOU ZOMBIES! BRING IT ON! BREAK DOWN THAT DOOR AND COME IN!
THE MOMENT YOU STEP THROUGH THAT DOORWAY, MY CHARIOT WILL SLICE FOUR OF YOU IN ONE BREATH!

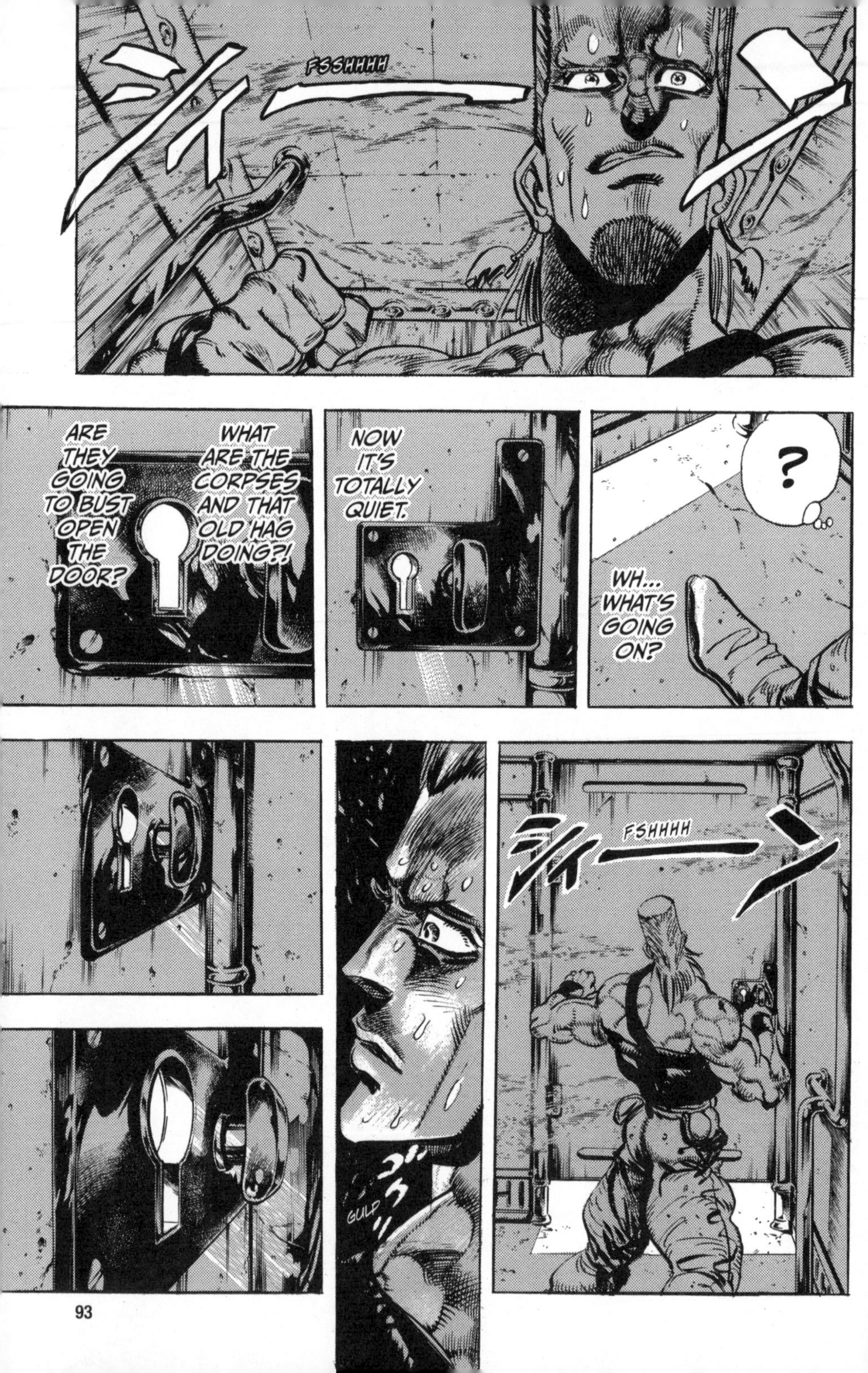
FSSHHHH
?
WH... WHAT'S GOING ON?
NOW IT'S TOTALLY QUIET.
WHAT ARE THE CORPSES AND THAT OLD HAG DOING?!
ARE THEY GOING TO BUST OPEN THE DOOR?
FSHHHH
GULP

WHAT'S TAKING SO LONG?! DO SOME-THING!

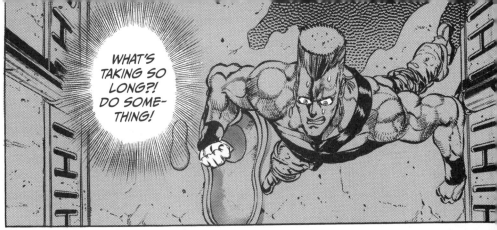

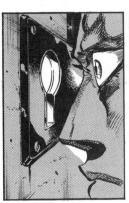

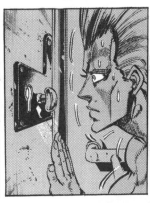

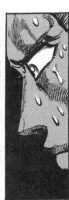

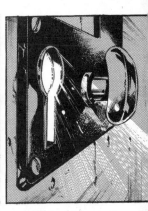

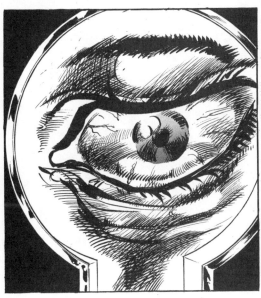

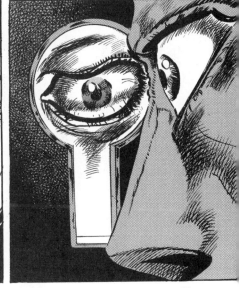

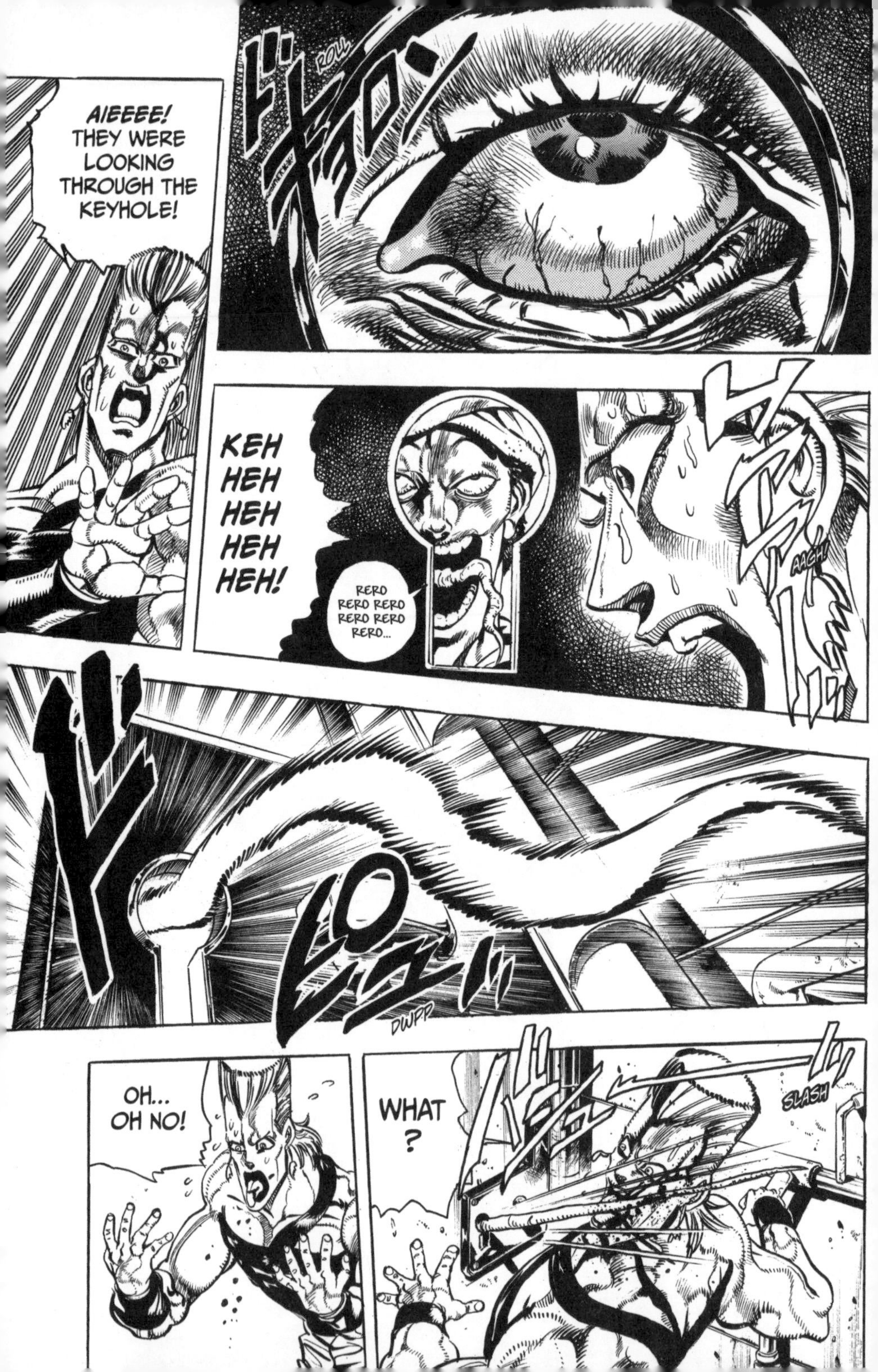
ROLL
AACH!
KEH HEH HEH HEH HEH!
RERO RERO RERO RERO RERO RERO...
AIEEEE! THEY WERE LOOKING THROUGH THE KEYHOLE!
DWPP
SLASH
WHAT?
OH... OH NO!

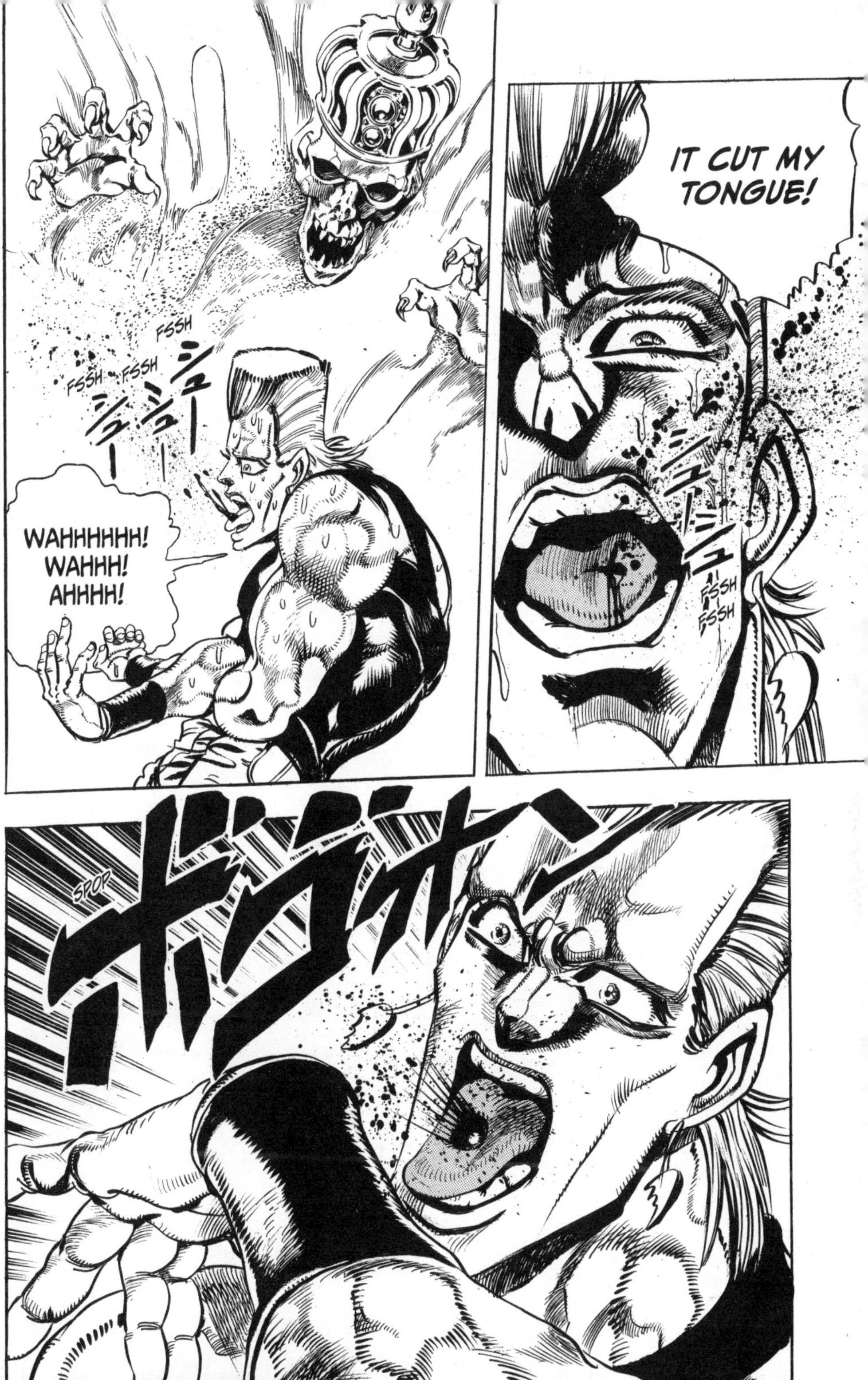
IT CUT MY TONGUE!
FSSH
FSSH
FSSH
FSSH
FSSH
WAHHHHHH! WAHHH! AHHHH!
SPOP

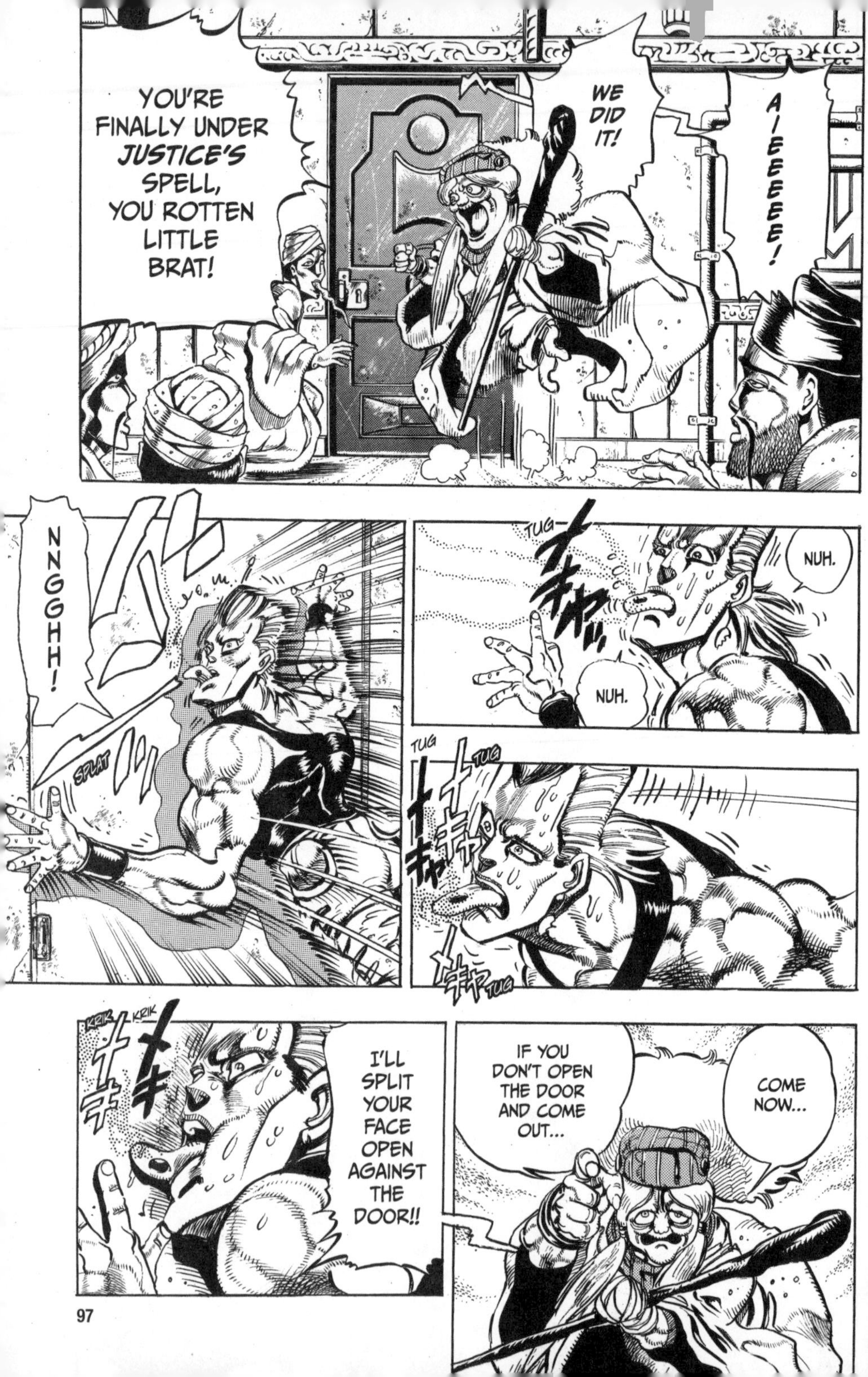
AIEEEEEE!
WE DID IT!
YOU'RE FINALLY UNDER JUSTICE'S SPELL, YOU ROTTEN LITTLE BRAT!
TUG
NUH.
NUH.
TUG
TUG
TUG
NNGGHH!
SPLAT
COME NOW...
IF YOU DON'T OPEN THE DOOR AND COME OUT...
I'LL SPLIT YOUR FACE OPEN AGAINST THE DOOR!!
KRIK KRIK

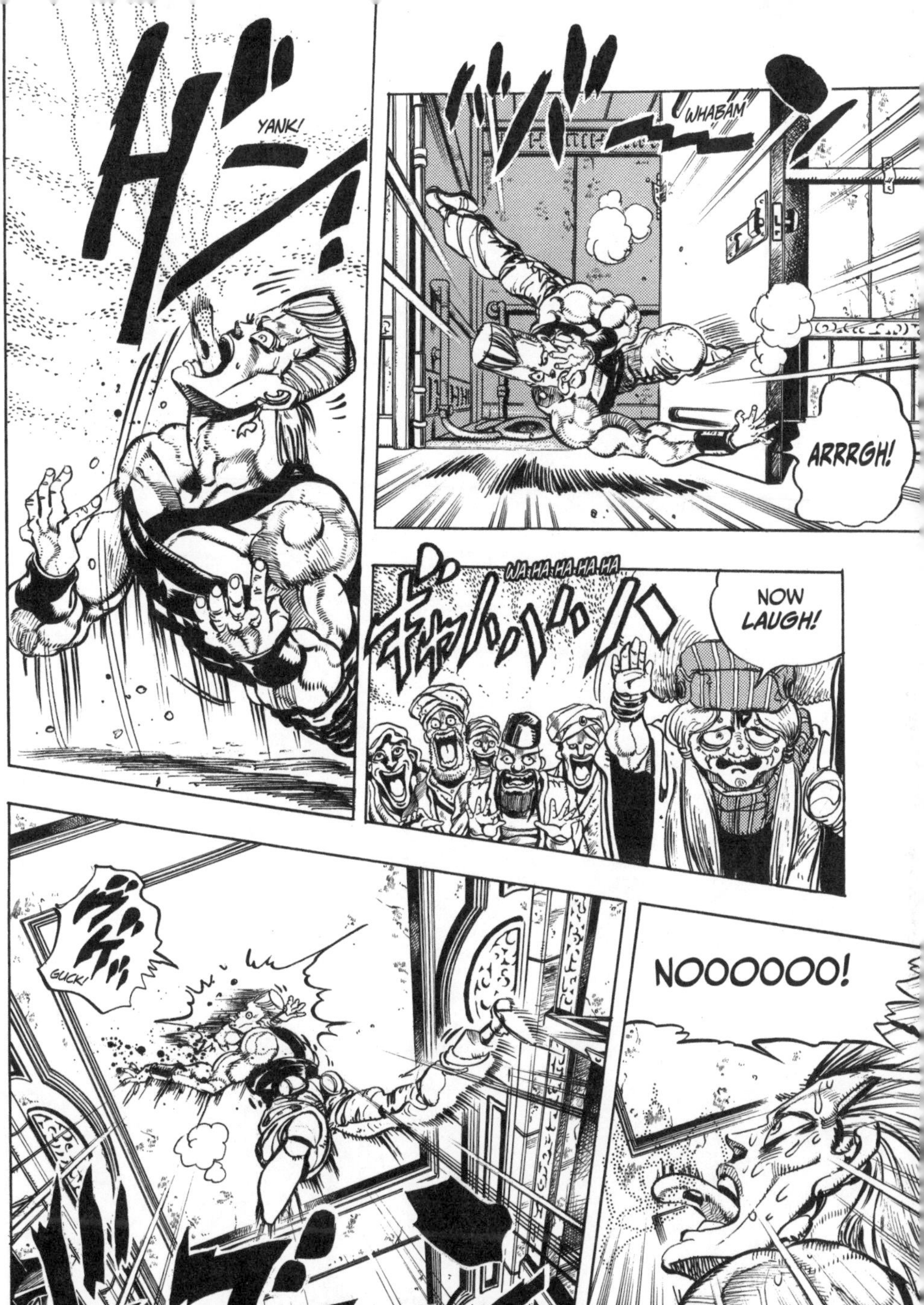
WHABAM
ARRRGH!
NOW LAUGH!
WA HA HA HA HA
YANK!
NOOOOOO!
GUCK!
KABAMMM

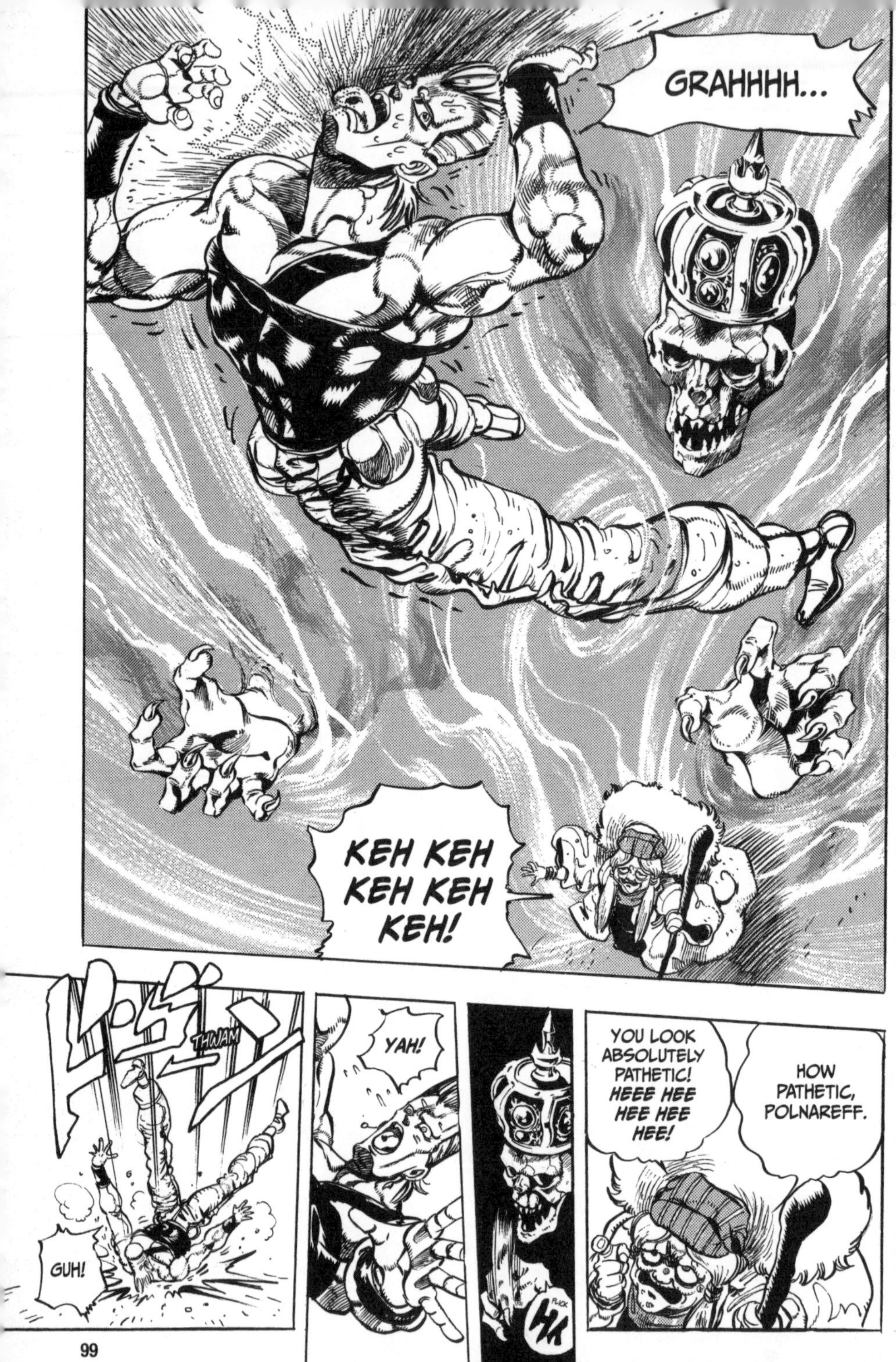
GRAHHHH...
KEH KEH KEH KEH KEH!
HOW PATHETIC, POLNAREFF.
YOU LOOK ABSOLUTELY PATHETIC! HEEE HEE HEE HEE HEE!
FLICK
YAH!
THWAM
GUH!

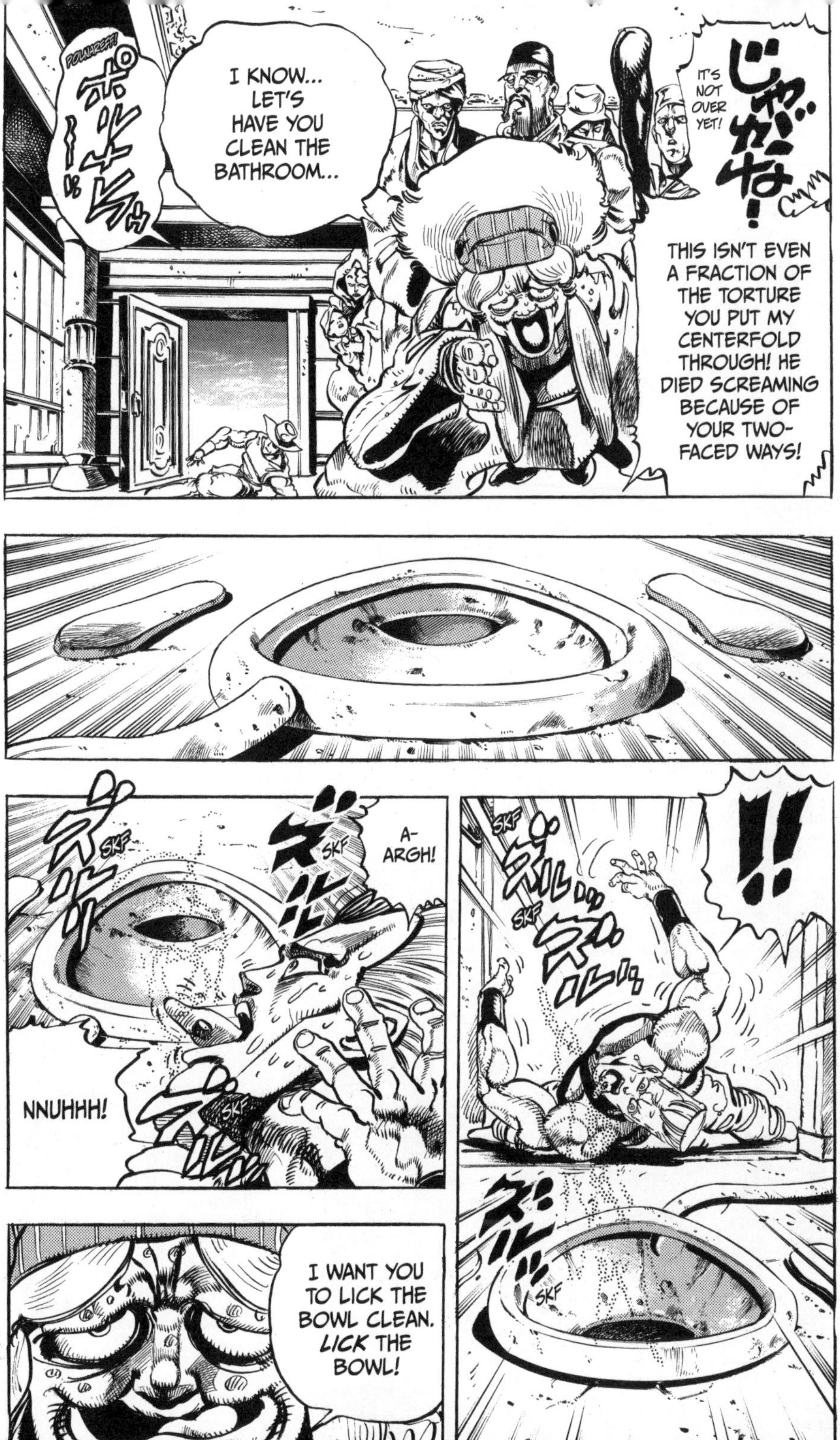
じゃがな!
IT'S NOT OVER YET!
THIS ISN'T EVEN A FRACTION OF THE TORTURE YOU PUT MY CENTERFOLD THROUGH! HE DIED SCREAMING BECAUSE OF YOUR TWO-FACED WAYS!
I KNOW... LET'S HAVE YOU CLEAN THE BATHROOM...
ポルナレフゥ
POLNAREFF!
!!
SKF
SKF
A-ARGH!
SKF
SKF
NNUHHH!
SKF
SKF
I WANT YOU TO LICK THE BOWL CLEAN. *LICK* THE BOWL!

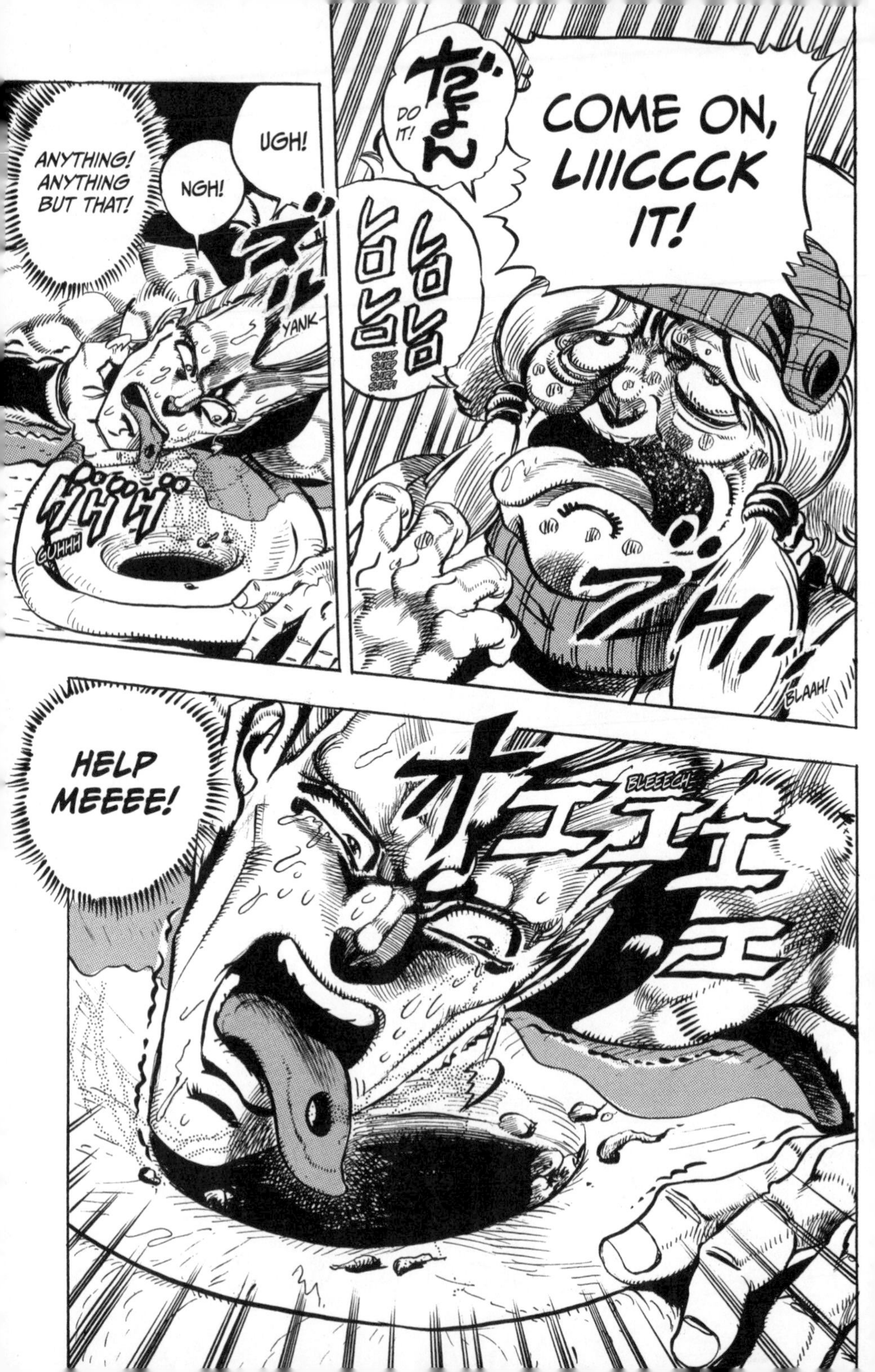
COME ON, LIIICCCK IT!
DO IT!
SLURP SLURP SLURP SLURP!
BLAAH!
UGH!
NGH!
ANYTHING! ANYTHING BUT THAT!
YANK
GUHHH
BLEEECH
HELP MEEEE!

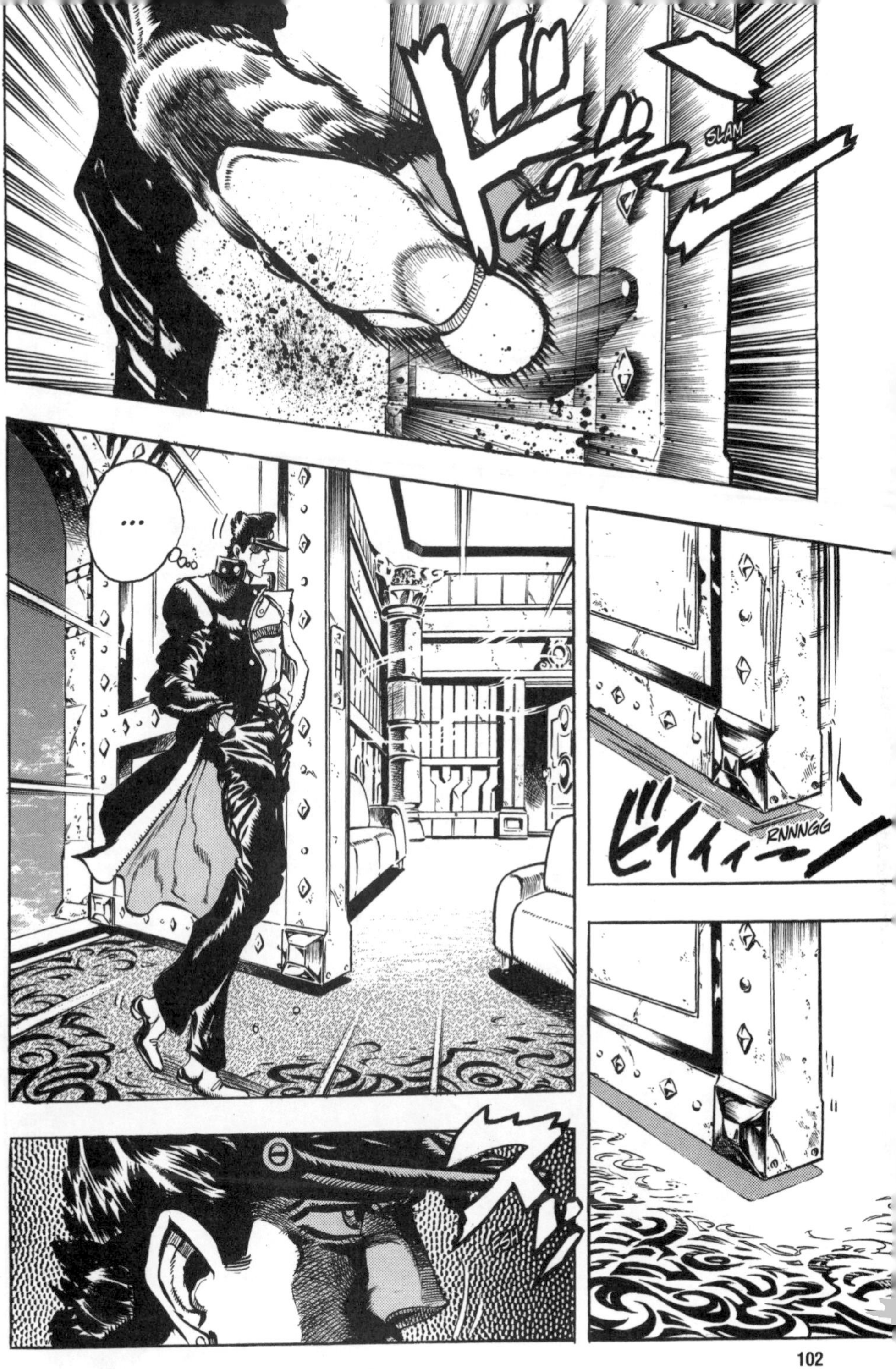
SLAM
ビイイイー
RNNNGG
...
FSH

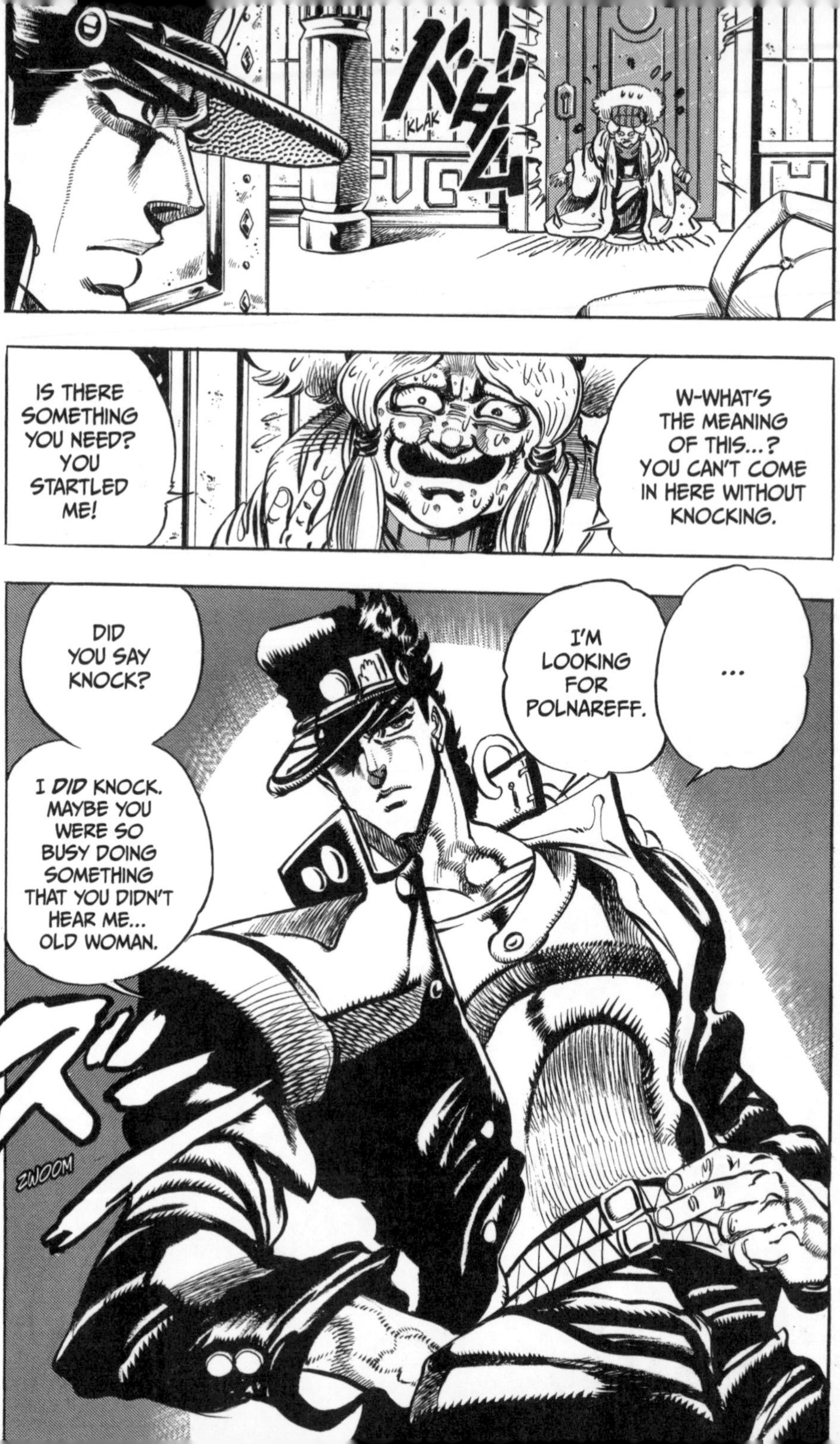
バダム
KLAK
W-WHAT'S THE MEANING OF THIS...? YOU CAN'T COME IN HERE WITHOUT KNOCKING.
IS THERE SOMETHING YOU NEED? YOU STARTLED ME!
...
I'M LOOKING FOR POLNAREFF.
DID YOU SAY KNOCK?
I *DID* KNOCK. MAYBE YOU WERE SO BUSY DOING SOMETHING THAT YOU DIDN'T HEAR ME... OLD WOMAN.
ズ
ZWOOM

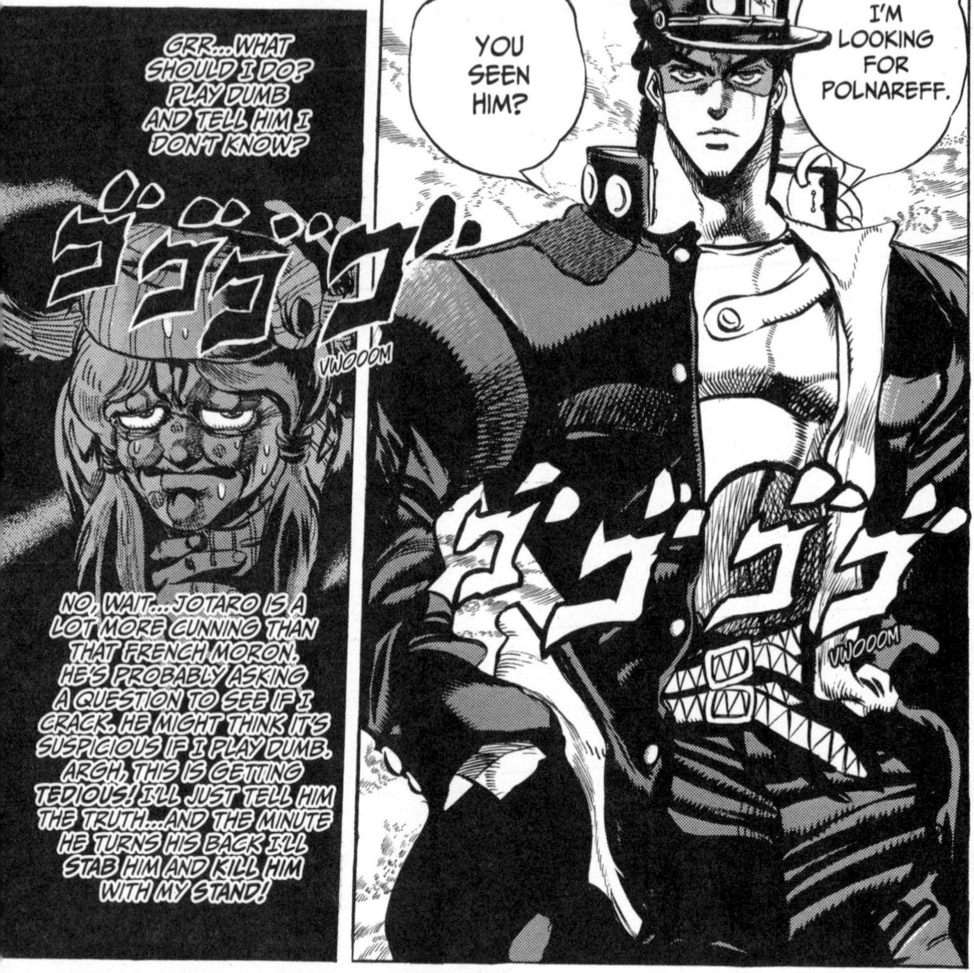
I'M LOOKING FOR POLNAREFF.
YOU SEEN HIM?
VWOOOM
GRR...WHAT SHOULD I DO? PLAY DUMB AND TELL HIM I DON'T KNOW?
VWOOOM
NO, WAIT...JOTARO IS A LOT MORE CUNNING THAN THAT FRENCH MORON. HE'S PROBABLY ASKING A QUESTION TO SEE IF I CRACK. HE MIGHT THINK IT'S SUSPICIOUS IF I PLAY DUMB. ARGH, THIS IS GETTING TEDIOUS! I'LL JUST TELL HIM THE TRUTH...AND THE MINUTE HE TURNS HIS BACK I'LL STAB HIM AND KILL HIM WITH MY STAND!

CHAPTER 46: Justice PART 6

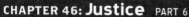

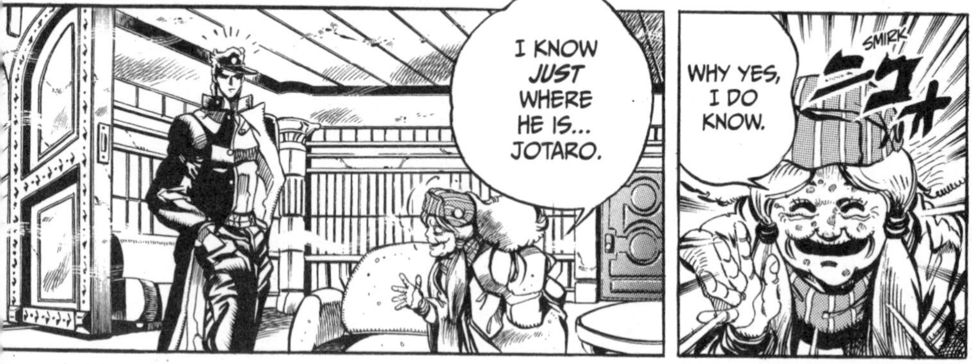
SMIRK
WHY YES, I DO KNOW.
I KNOW *JUST* WHERE HE IS... JOTARO.

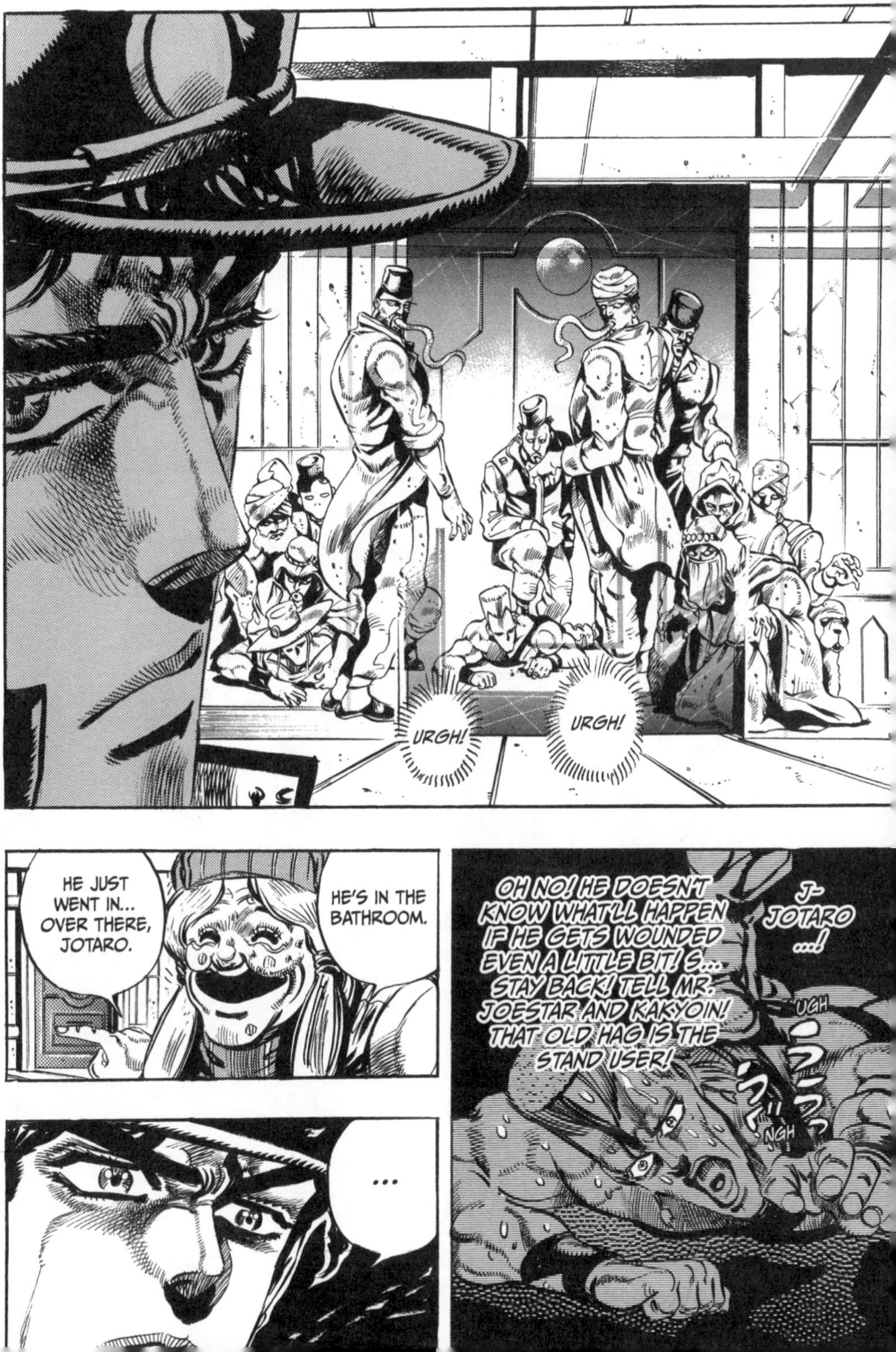
URGH!
URGH!
J-JOTARO...!
OH NO! HE DOESN'T KNOW WHAT'LL HAPPEN IF HE GETS WOUNDED EVEN A LITTLE BIT! S... STAY BACK! TELL MR. JOESTAR AND KAKYOIN! THAT OLD HAG IS THE STAND USER!
UGH
NGH
HE'S IN THE BATHROOM.
HE JUST WENT IN... OVER THERE, JOTARO.
...

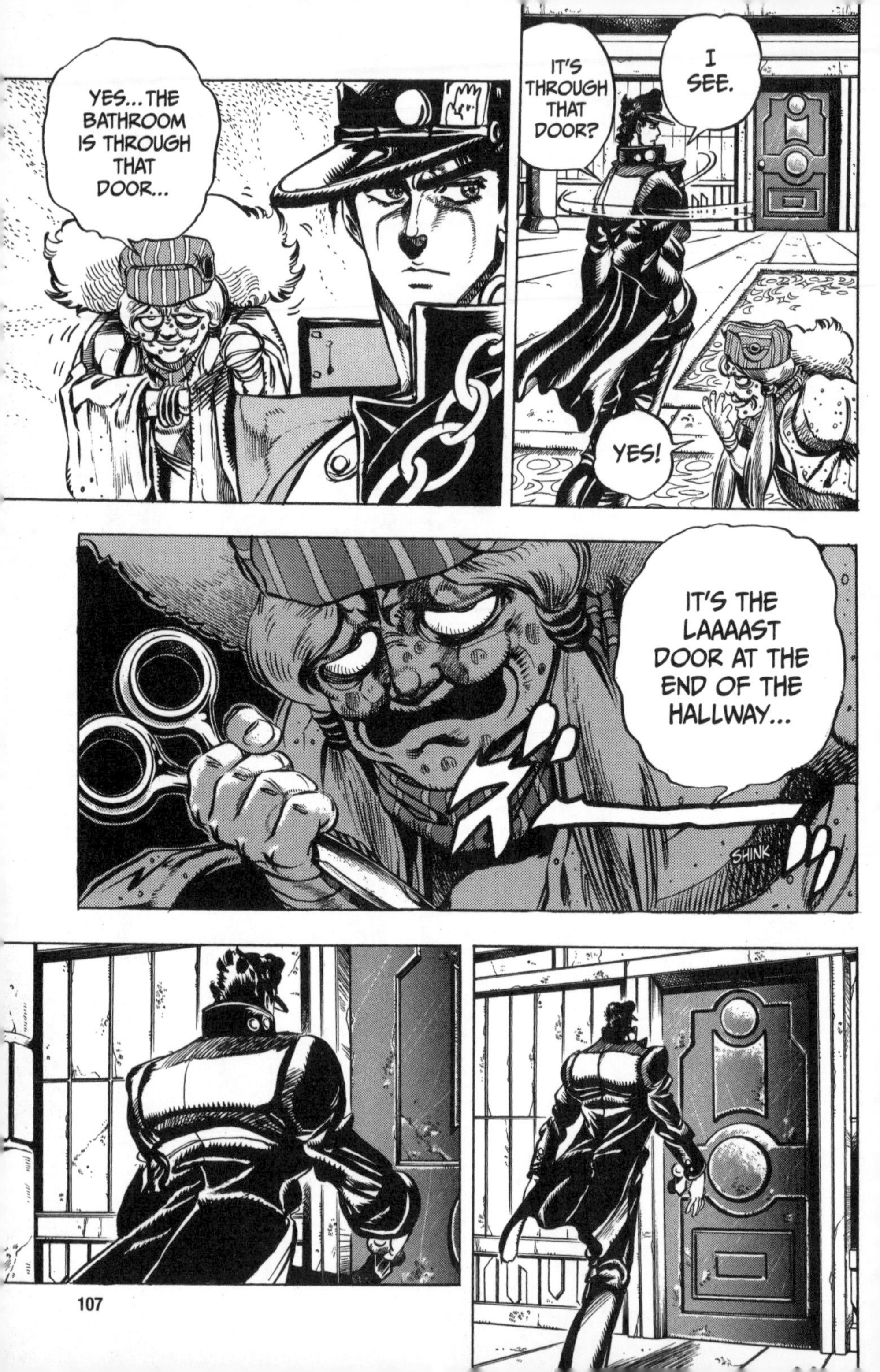
I SEE.
IT'S THROUGH THAT DOOR?
YES!
YES...THE BATHROOM IS THROUGH THAT DOOR...
IT'S THE LAAAAST DOOR AT THE END OF THE HALLWAY...
SHINK

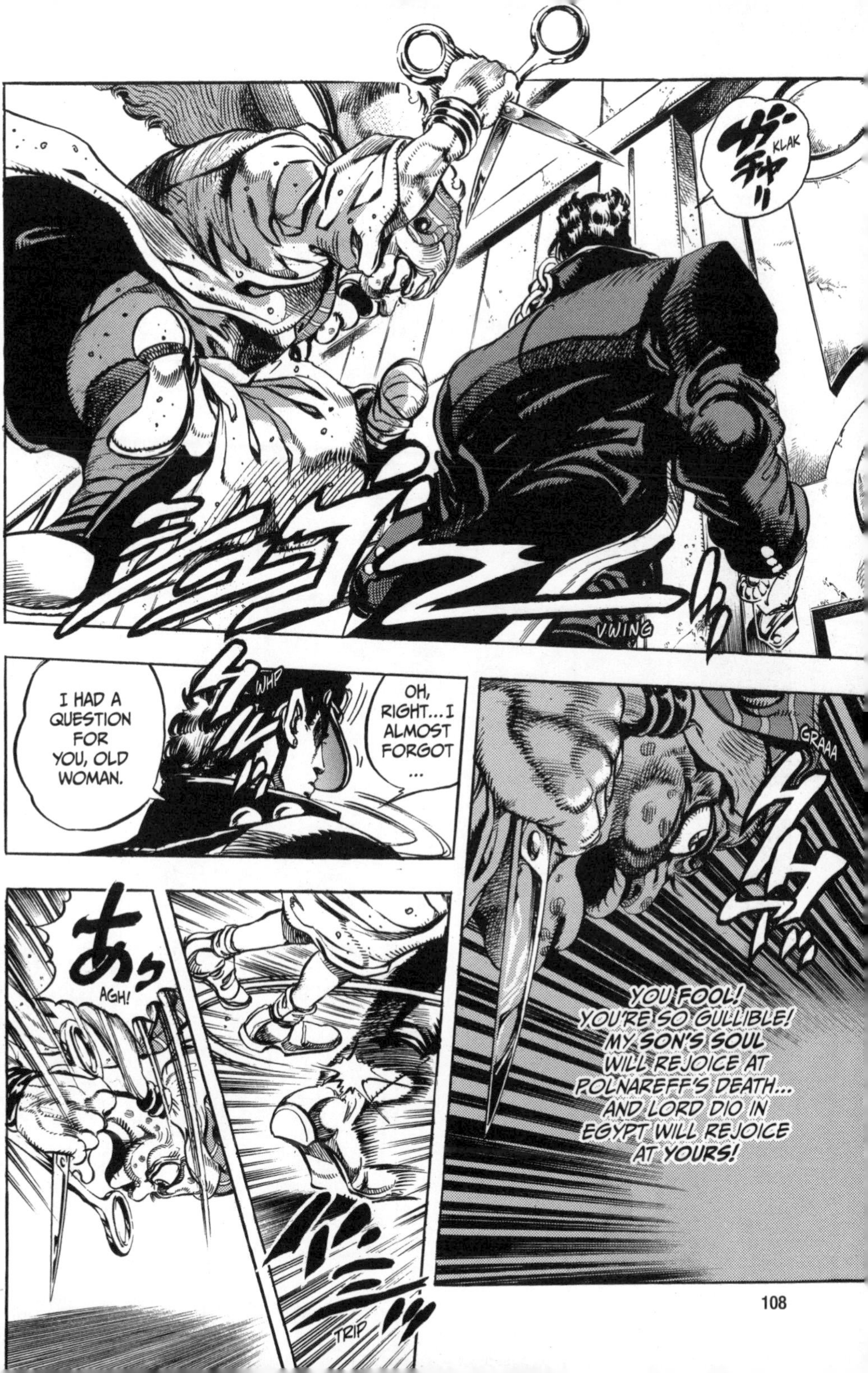
KLAK
VWING
GRAAA
YOU FOOL! YOU'RE SO GULLIBLE! MY SON'S SOUL WILL REJOICE AT POLNAREFF'S DEATH... AND LORD DIO IN EGYPT WILL REJOICE AT YOURS!
OH, RIGHT... I ALMOST FORGOT ...
I HAD A QUESTION FOR YOU, OLD WOMAN.
WHP
TRIP
AGH!

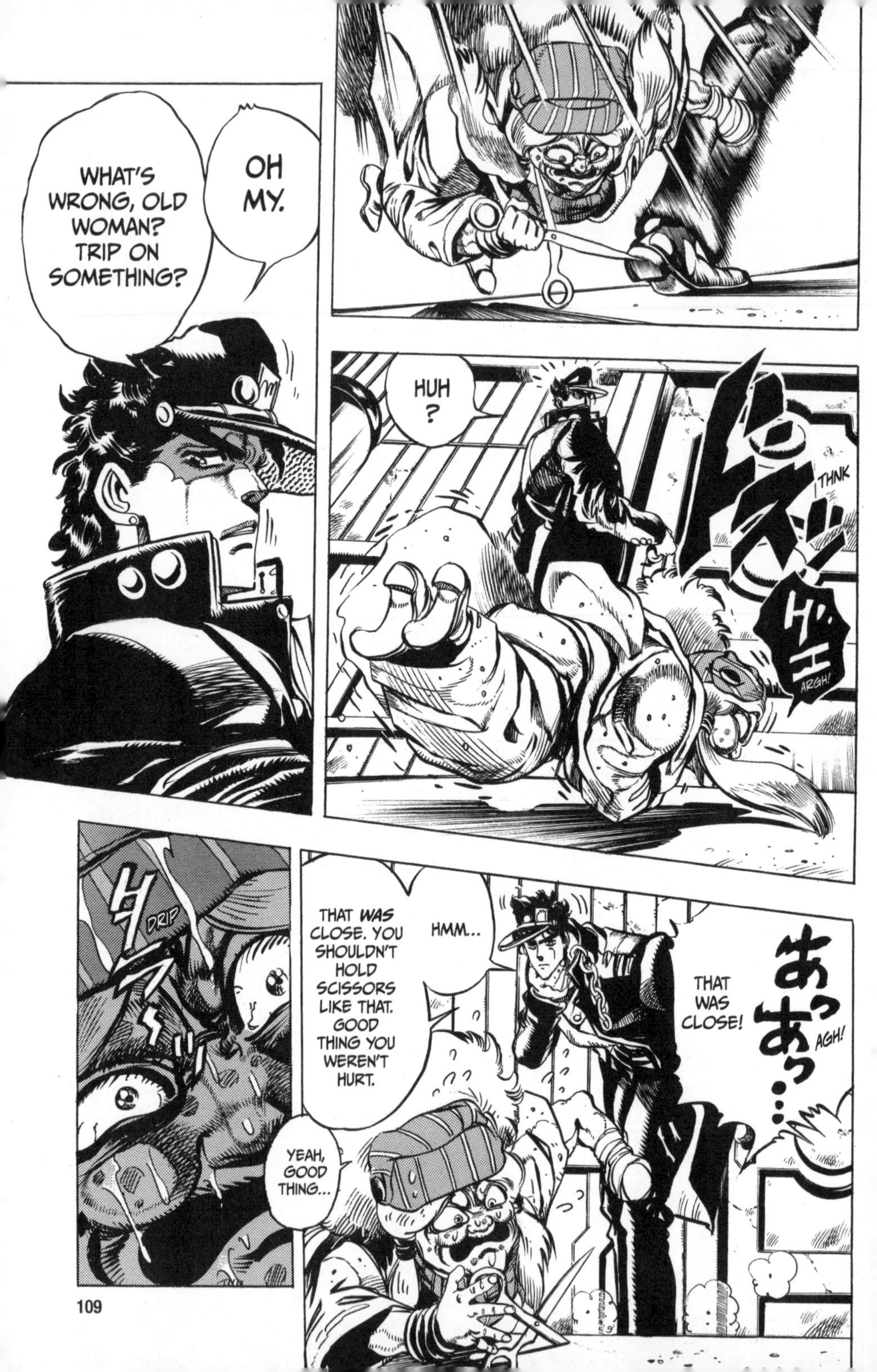
THNK
ARGH!
HUH?
OH MY.
WHAT'S WRONG, OLD WOMAN? TRIP ON SOMETHING?
AGH!
THAT WAS CLOSE!
HMM...
THAT ***WAS*** CLOSE. YOU SHOULDN'T HOLD SCISSORS LIKE THAT. GOOD THING YOU WEREN'T HURT.
YEAH, GOOD THING...
DRIP

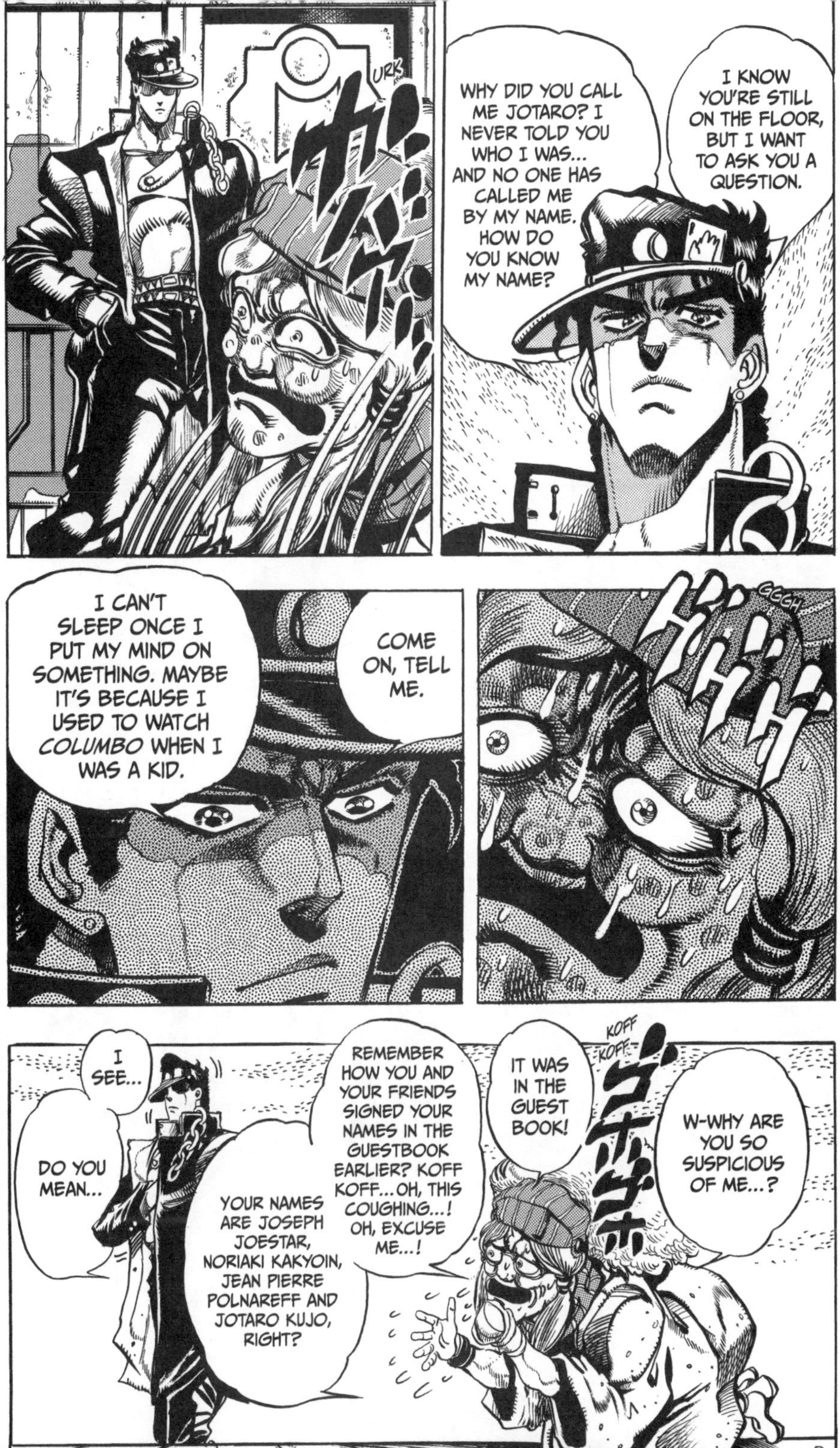
I KNOW YOU'RE STILL ON THE FLOOR, BUT I WANT TO ASK YOU A QUESTION.
WHY DID YOU CALL ME JOTARO? I NEVER TOLD YOU WHO I WAS... AND NO ONE HAS CALLED ME BY MY NAME. HOW DO YOU KNOW MY NAME?
URK
GGGH
COME ON, TELL ME.
I CAN'T SLEEP ONCE I PUT MY MIND ON SOMETHING. MAYBE IT'S BECAUSE I USED TO WATCH *COLUMBO* WHEN I WAS A KID.
W-WHY ARE YOU SO SUSPICIOUS OF ME...?
KOFF KOFF
IT WAS IN THE GUEST BOOK!
REMEMBER HOW YOU AND YOUR FRIENDS SIGNED YOUR NAMES IN THE GUESTBOOK EARLIER? KOFF KOFF...OH, THIS COUGHING...! OH, EXCUSE ME...!
YOUR NAMES ARE JOSEPH JOESTAR, NORIAKI KAKYOIN, JEAN PIERRE POLNAREFF AND JOTARO KUJO, RIGHT?
I SEE...
DO YOU MEAN...

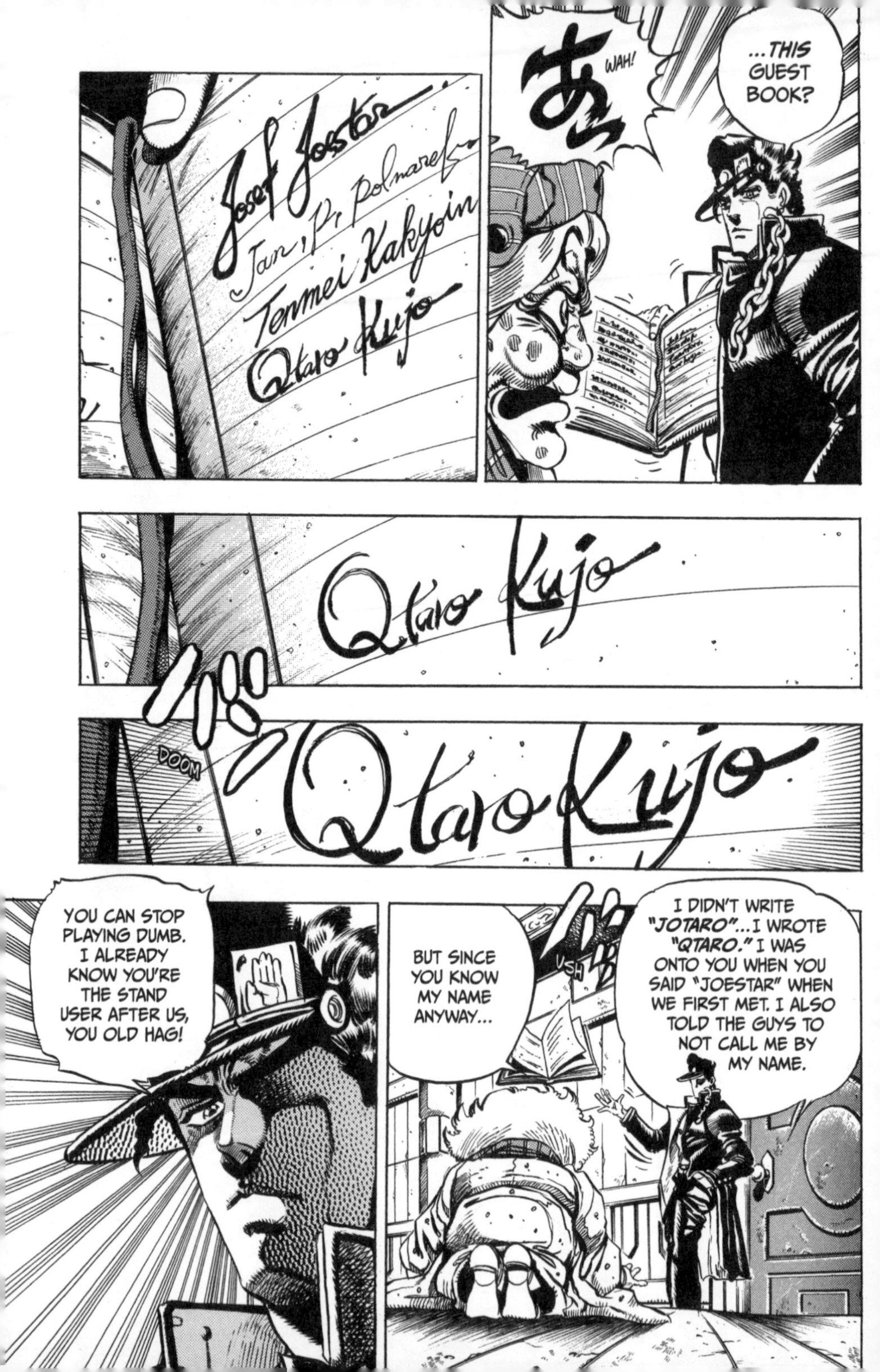
...THIS GUEST BOOK?
あ
WAH!
Josef Joestar
Jan, P, polnareff
Tenmei Kakyoin
Qtaro Kujo
Qtaro Kujo
DOOM
Qtaro Kujo
I DIDN'T WRITE "JOTARO"...I WROTE "QTARO." I WAS ONTO YOU WHEN YOU SAID "JOESTAR" WHEN WE FIRST MET. I ALSO TOLD THE GUYS TO NOT CALL ME BY MY NAME.
USH
BUT SINCE YOU KNOW MY NAME ANYWAY...
YOU CAN STOP PLAYING DUMB. I ALREADY KNOW YOU'RE THE STAND USER AFTER US, YOU OLD HAG!

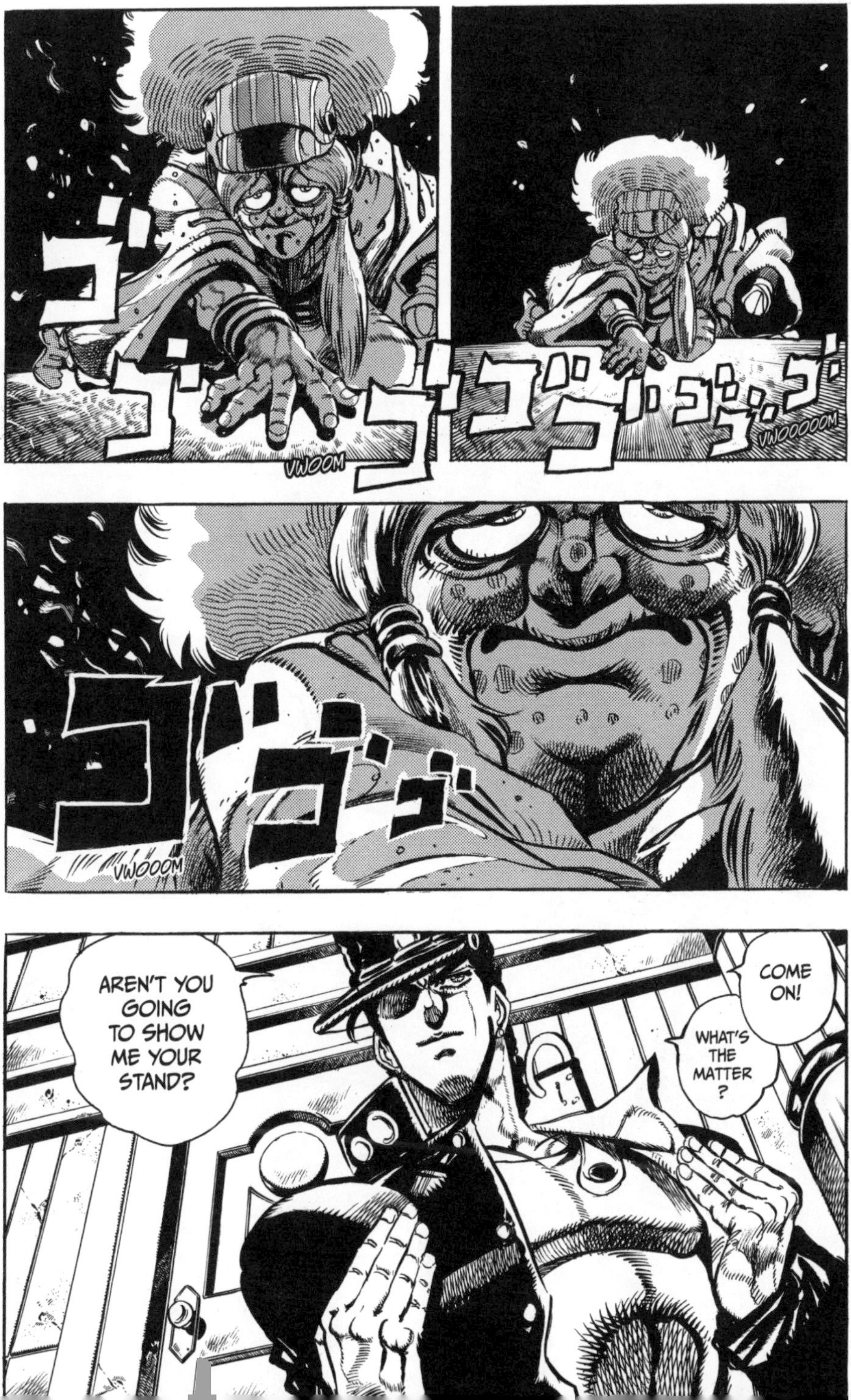
VWOOOOM
VWOOM
VWOOOM
COME ON!
WHAT'S THE MATTER?
AREN'T YOU GOING TO SHOW ME YOUR STAND?

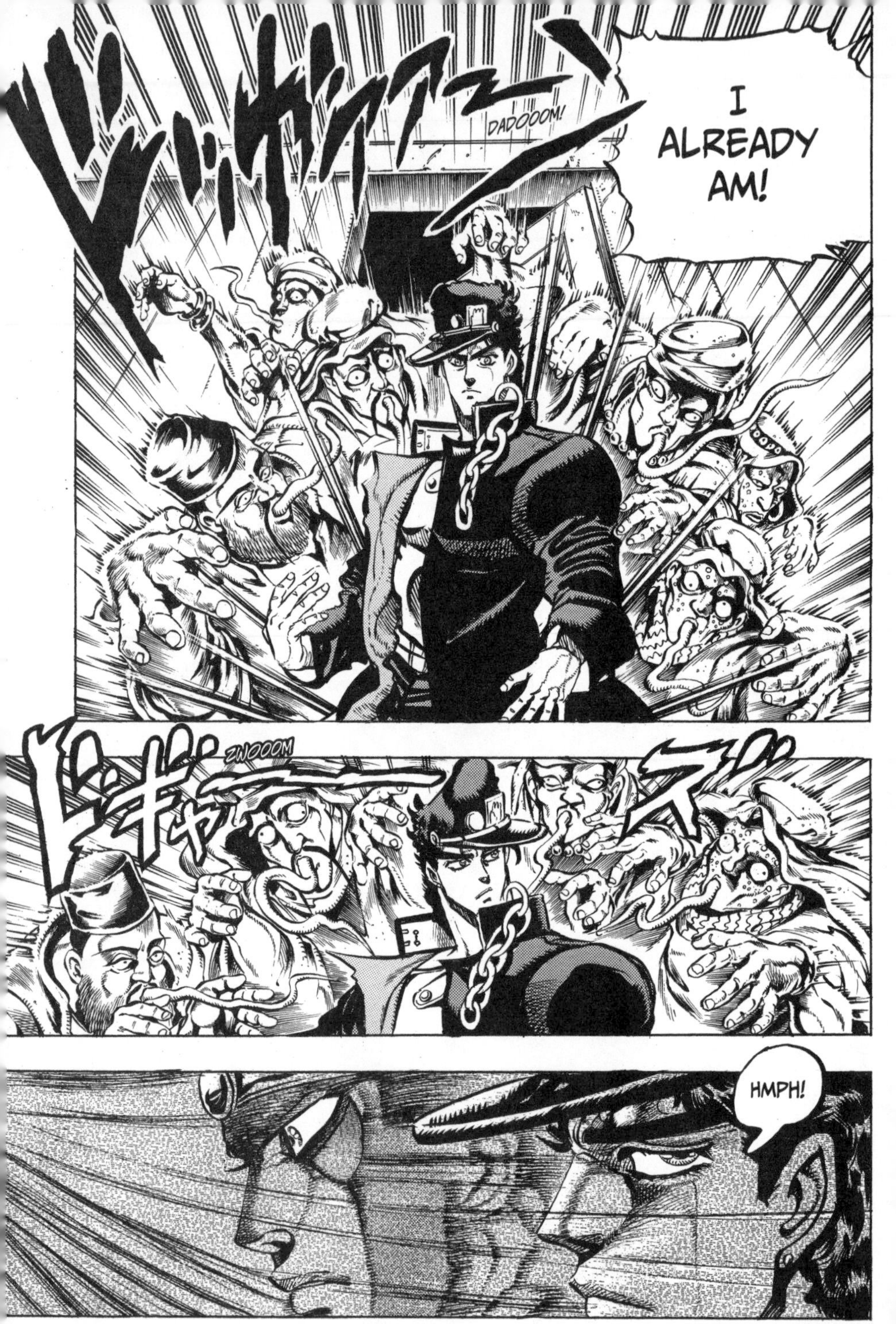
I ALREADY AM!
DADOOOM!
ZWOOOM
HMPH!

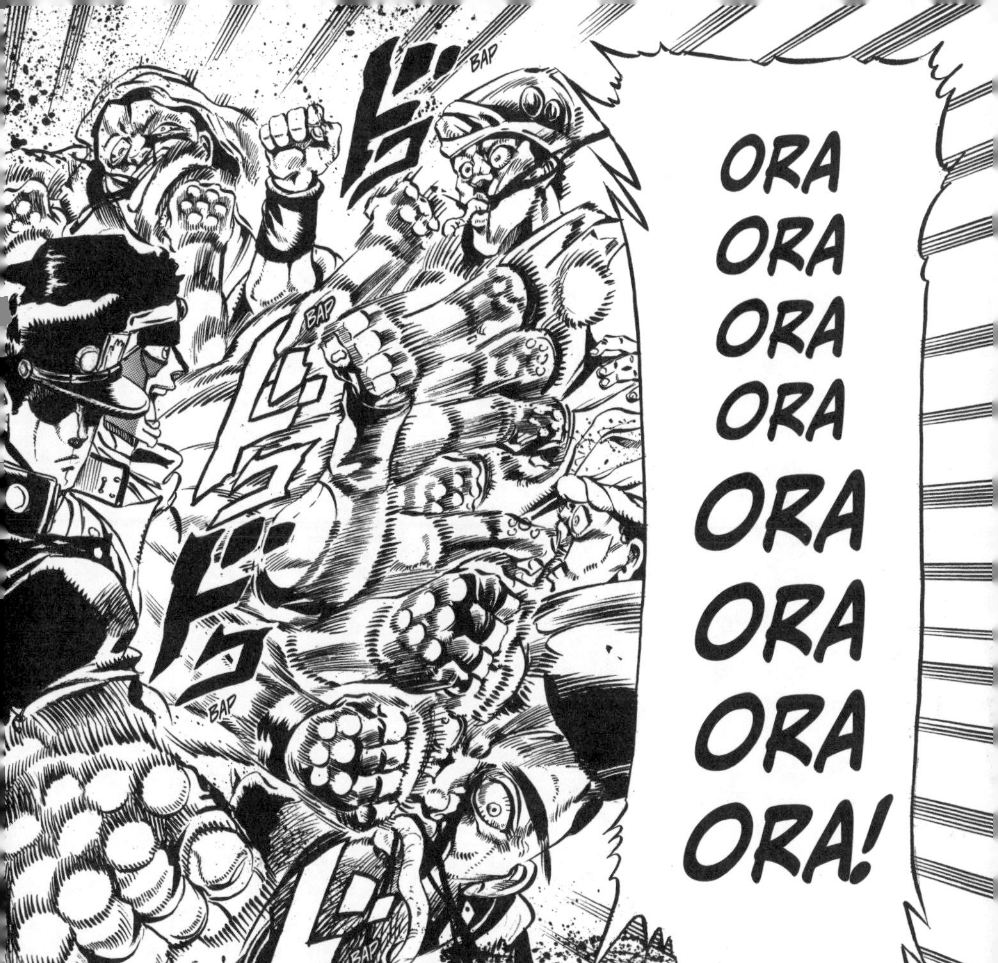
ORA ORA ORA ORA ORA ORA ORA ORA!
BAP
BAP
BAP
BAP
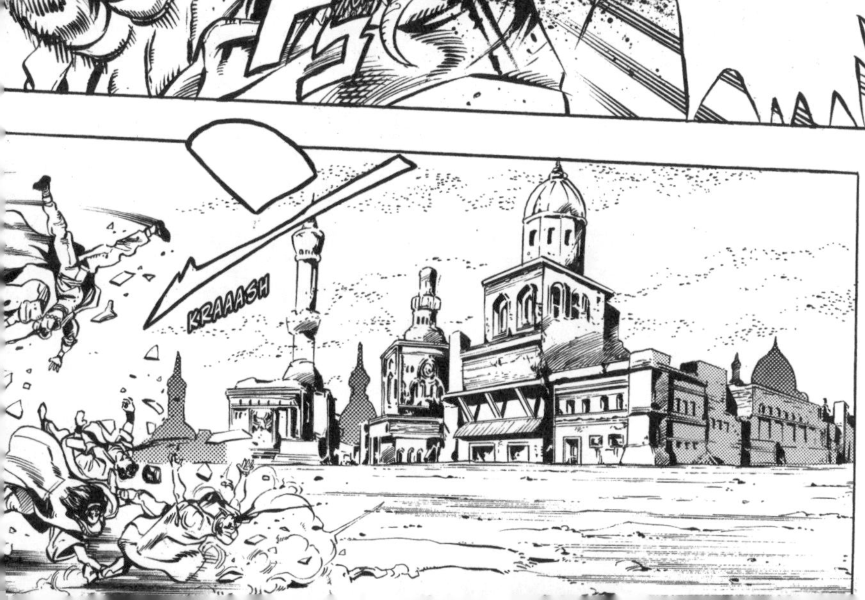
KRAAASH

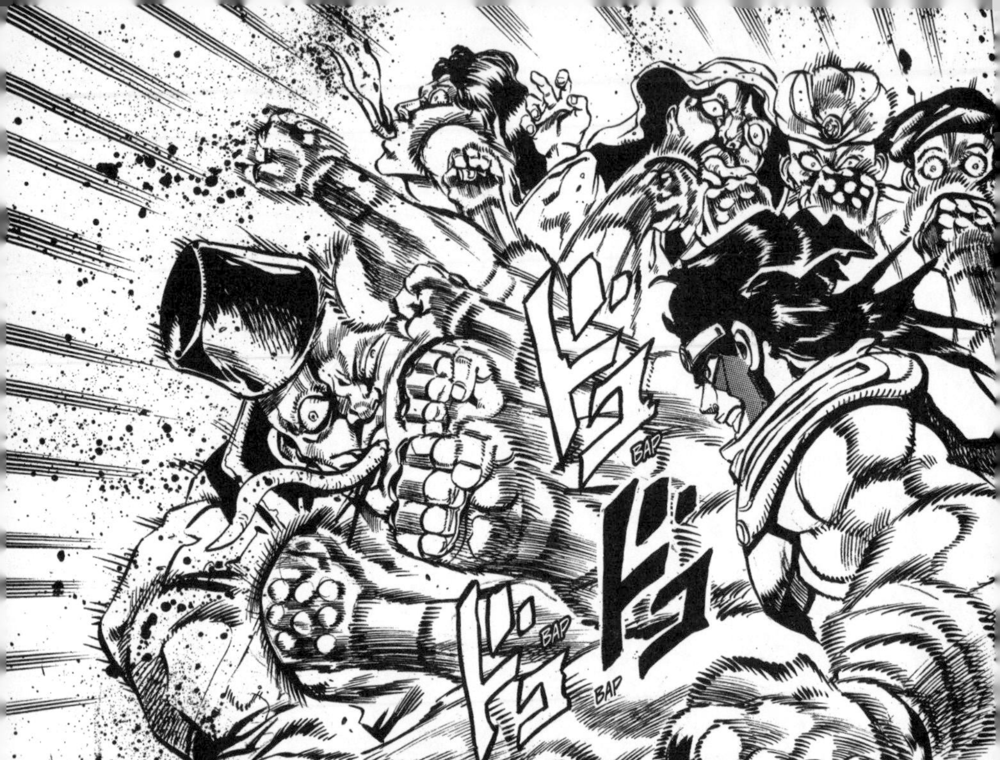
BAP
BAP
BAP
BAP
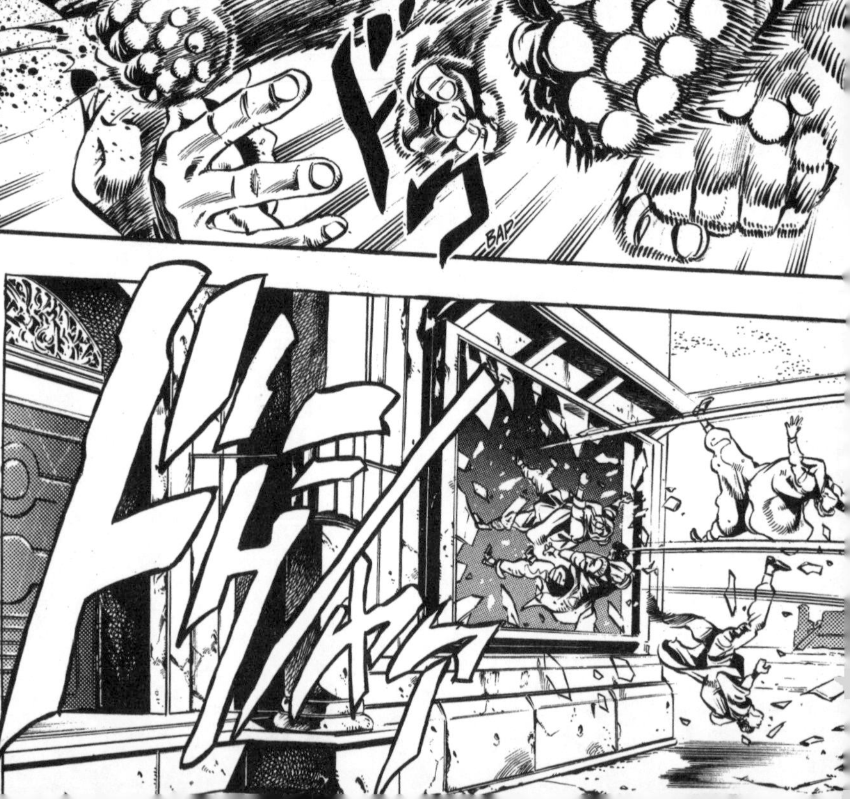

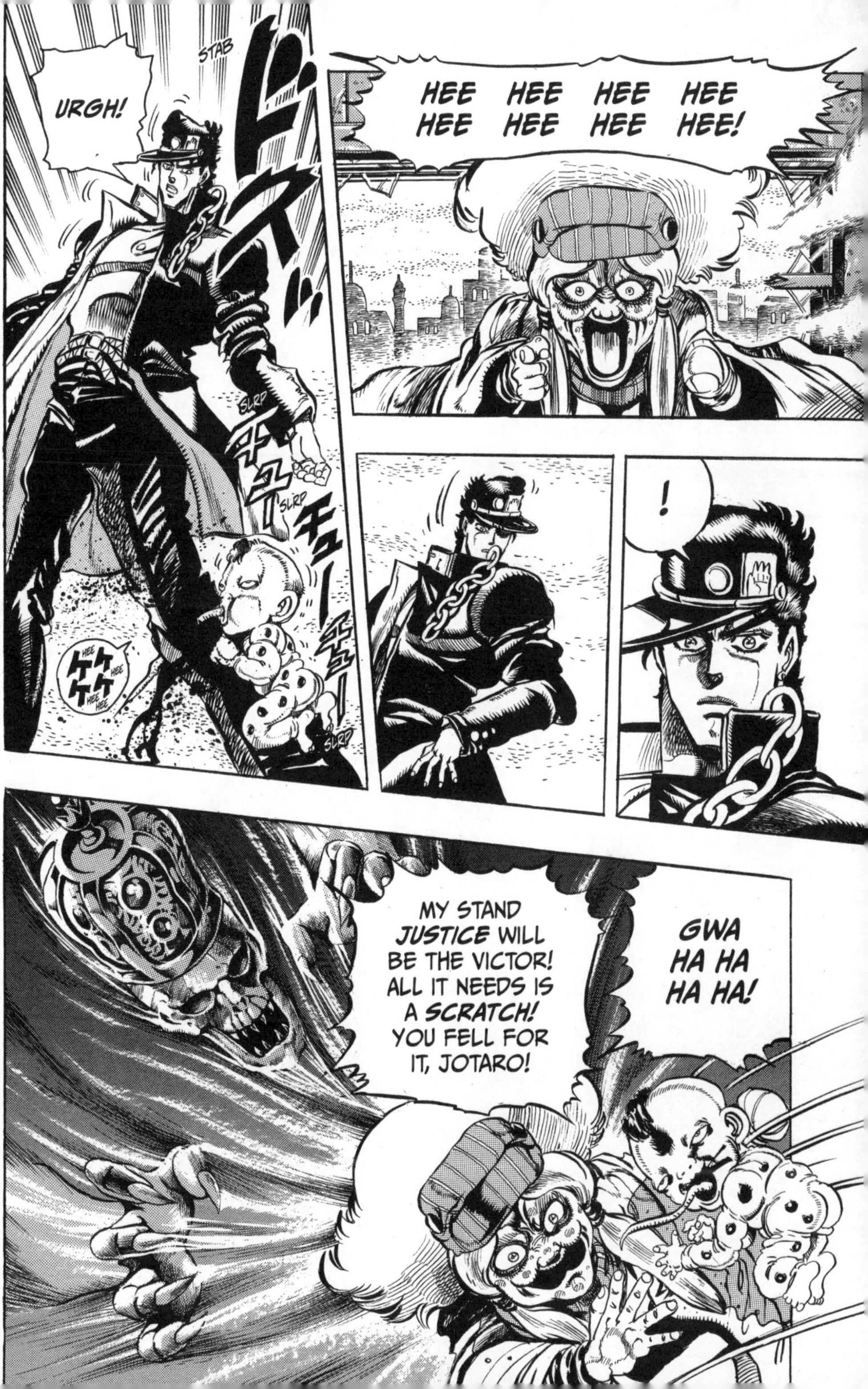
HEE HEE HEE HEE HEE HEE HEE HEE!
!
URGH!
STAB
SLRP
SLRP
SLRP
HEE HEE HEE HEE
GWA HA HA HA HA!
MY STAND JUSTICE WILL BE THE VICTOR! ALL IT NEEDS IS A SCRATCH! YOU FELL FOR IT, JOTARO!

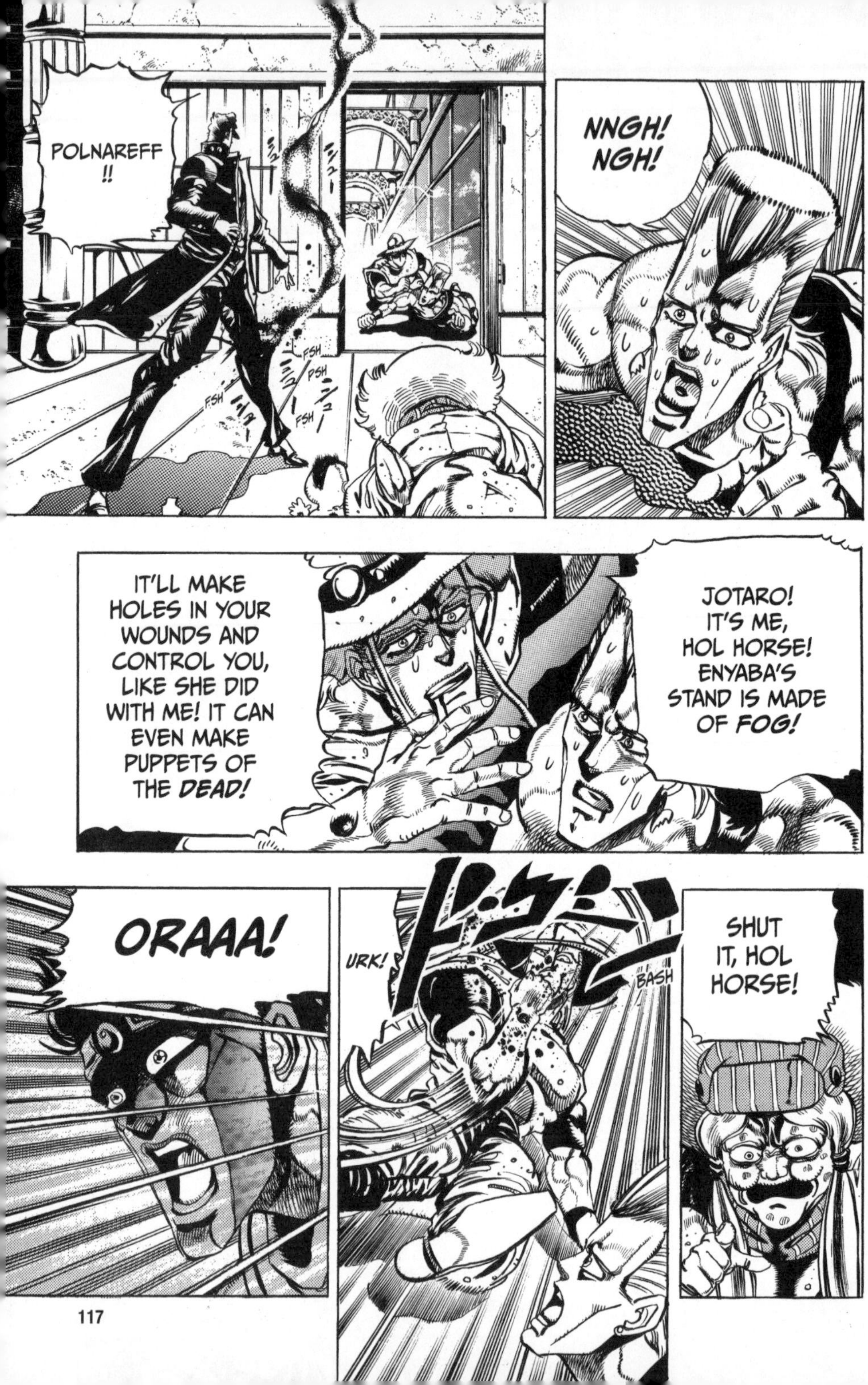
NNGH! NGH!
POLNAREFF !!
FSH
PSH
FSH
FSH
JOTARO! IT'S ME, HOL HORSE! ENYABA'S STAND IS MADE OF FOG!
IT'LL MAKE HOLES IN YOUR WOUNDS AND CONTROL YOU, LIKE SHE DID WITH ME! IT CAN EVEN MAKE PUPPETS OF THE DEAD!
SHUT IT, HOL HORSE!
BASH
URK!
ORAAA!

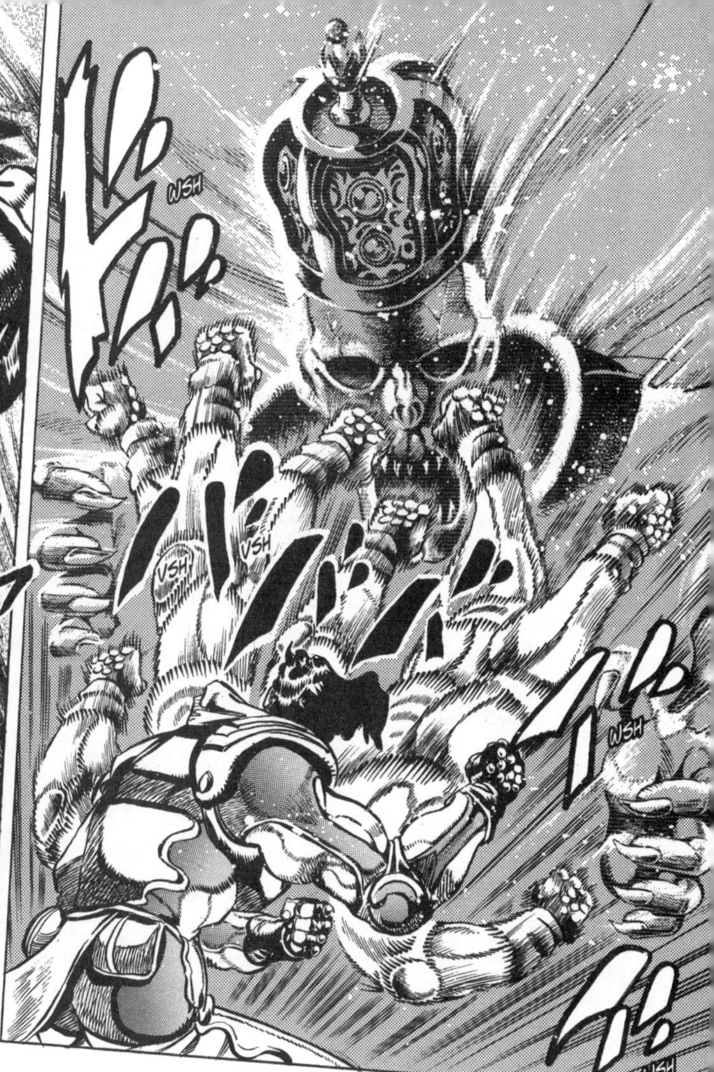
WSH
VSH
VSH
WSH
WSH

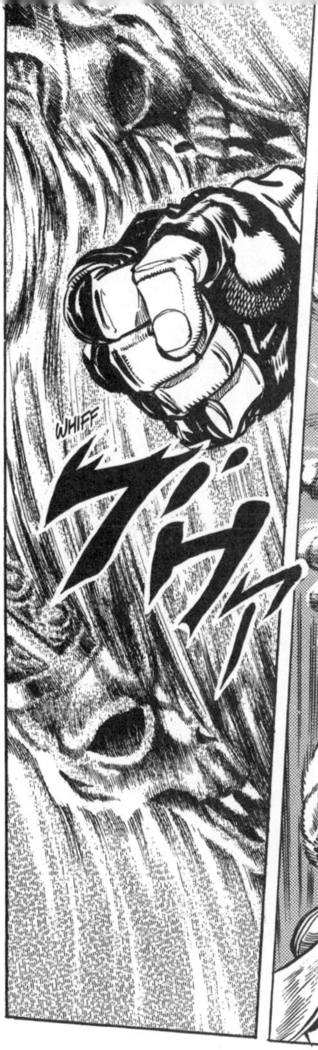
WHIFF

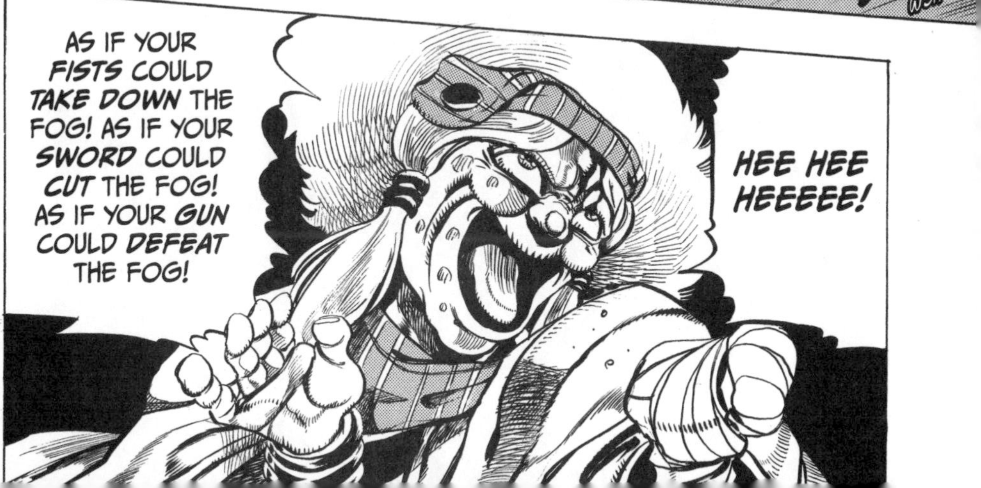
HEE HEE HEEEEEE!
AS IF YOUR FISTS COULD TAKE DOWN THE FOG! AS IF YOUR SWORD COULD CUT THE FOG! AS IF YOUR GUN COULD DEFEAT THE FOG!

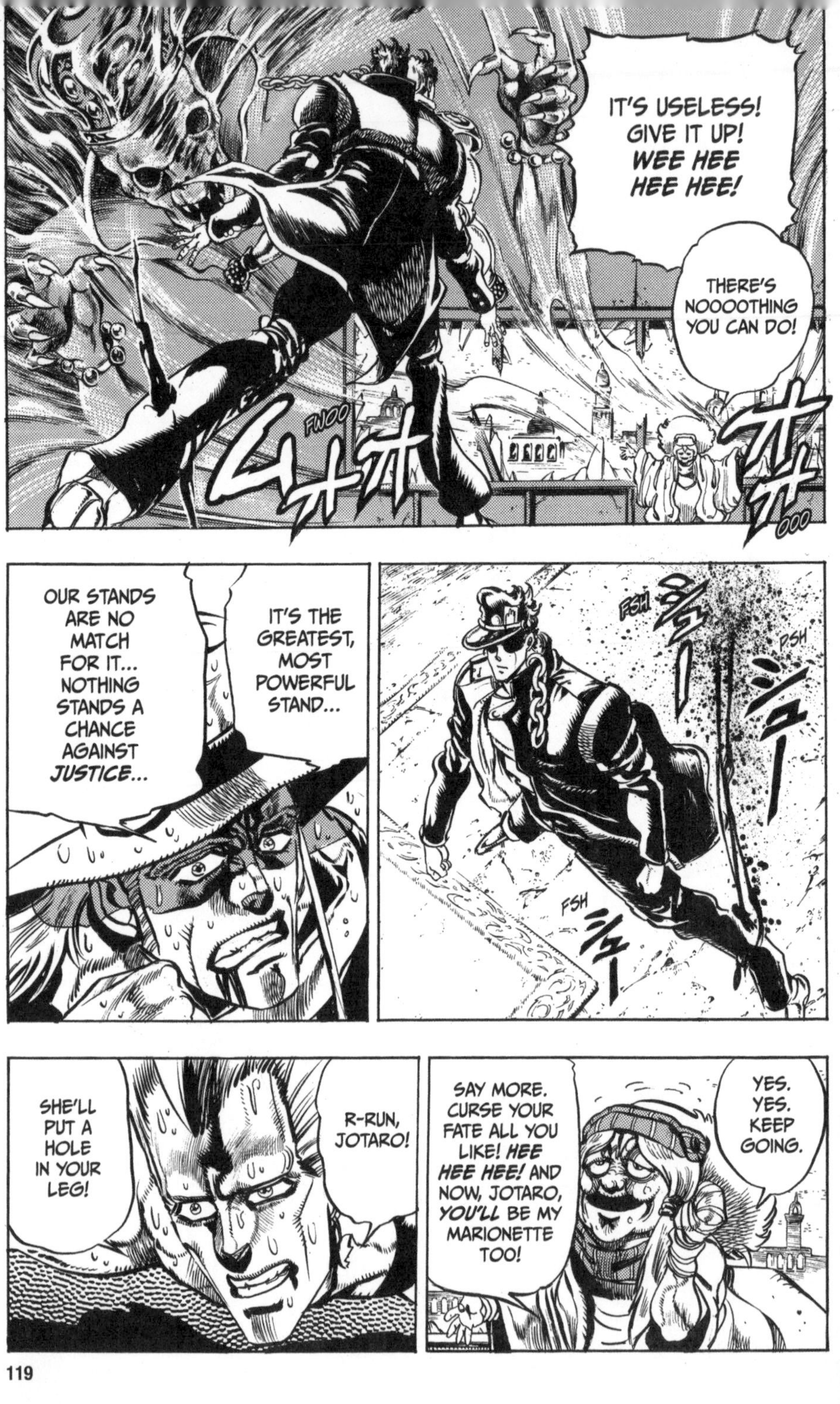
IT'S USELESS! GIVE IT UP! WEE HEE HEE HEE!
THERE'S NOOOOTHING YOU CAN DO!
OOO
FWOO
FSH
PSH
FSH
IT'S THE GREATEST, MOST POWERFUL STAND...
OUR STANDS ARE NO MATCH FOR IT... NOTHING STANDS A CHANCE AGAINST JUSTICE...
YES. YES. KEEP GOING.
SAY MORE. CURSE YOUR FATE ALL YOU LIKE! HEE HEE HEE! AND NOW, JOTARO, YOU'LL BE MY MARIONETTE TOO!
R-RUN, JOTARO!
SHE'LL PUT A HOLE IN YOUR LEG!

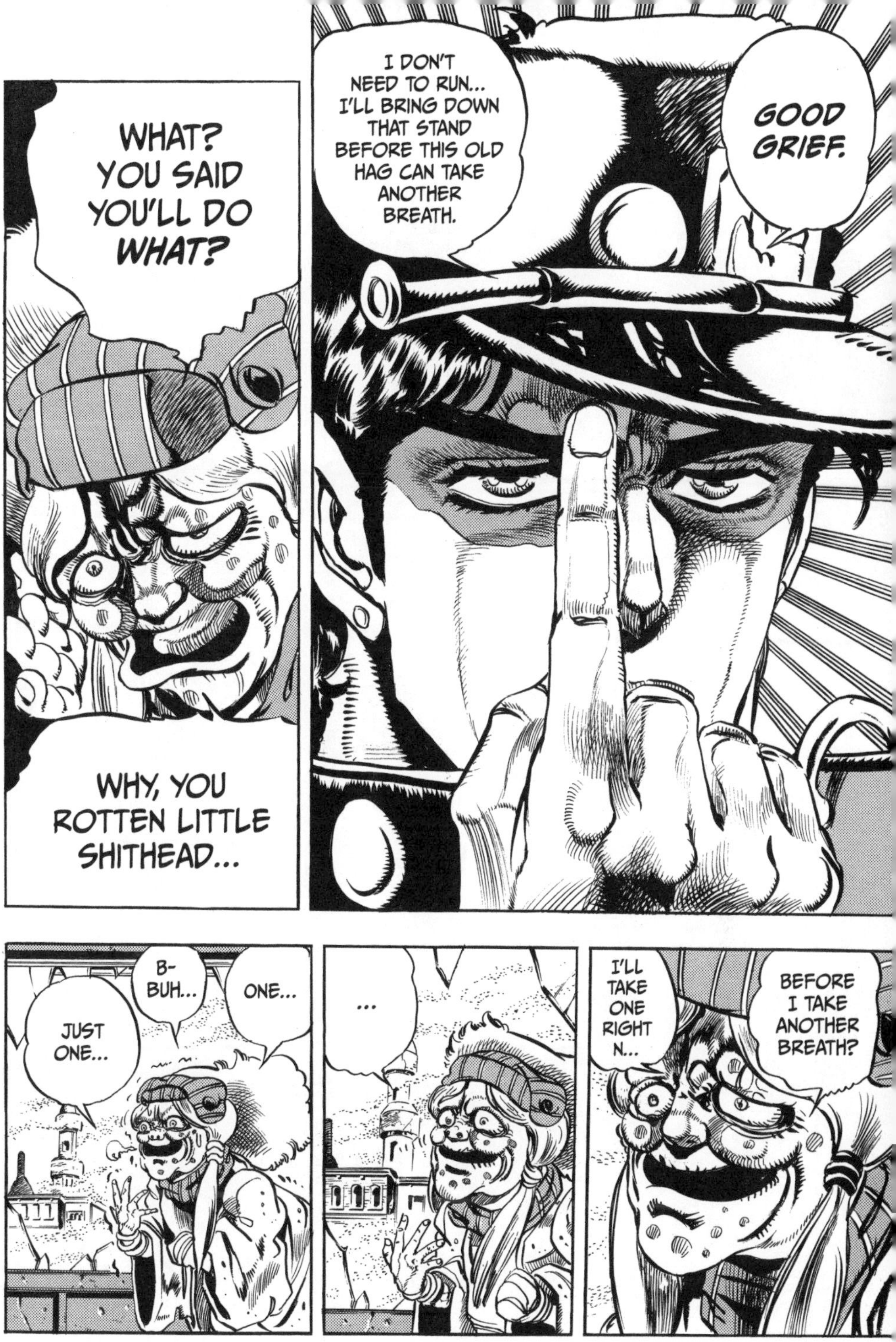
GOOD GRIEF.
I DON'T NEED TO RUN... I'LL BRING DOWN THAT STAND BEFORE THIS OLD HAG CAN TAKE ANOTHER BREATH.
WHAT? YOU SAID YOU'LL DO WHAT?
WHY, YOU ROTTEN LITTLE SHITHEAD...
BEFORE I TAKE ANOTHER BREATH?
I'LL TAKE ONE RIGHT N...
...
ONE...
B-BUH...
JUST ONE...

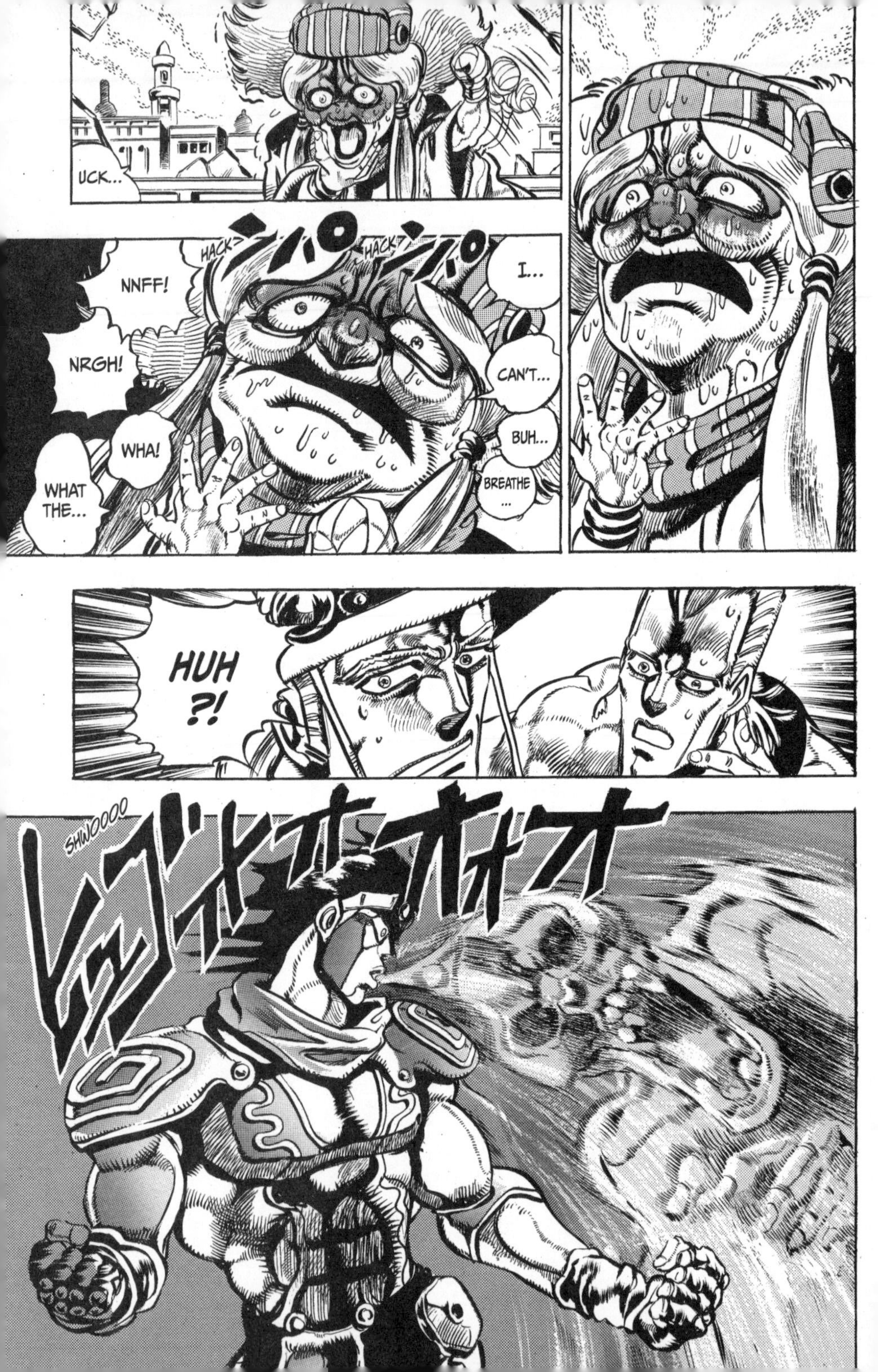
UCK...
HACK
HACK
I...
CAN'T...
BUH...
BREATHE...
NNFF!
NRGH!
WHA!
WHAT THE...
HUH ?!
SHWOOOO

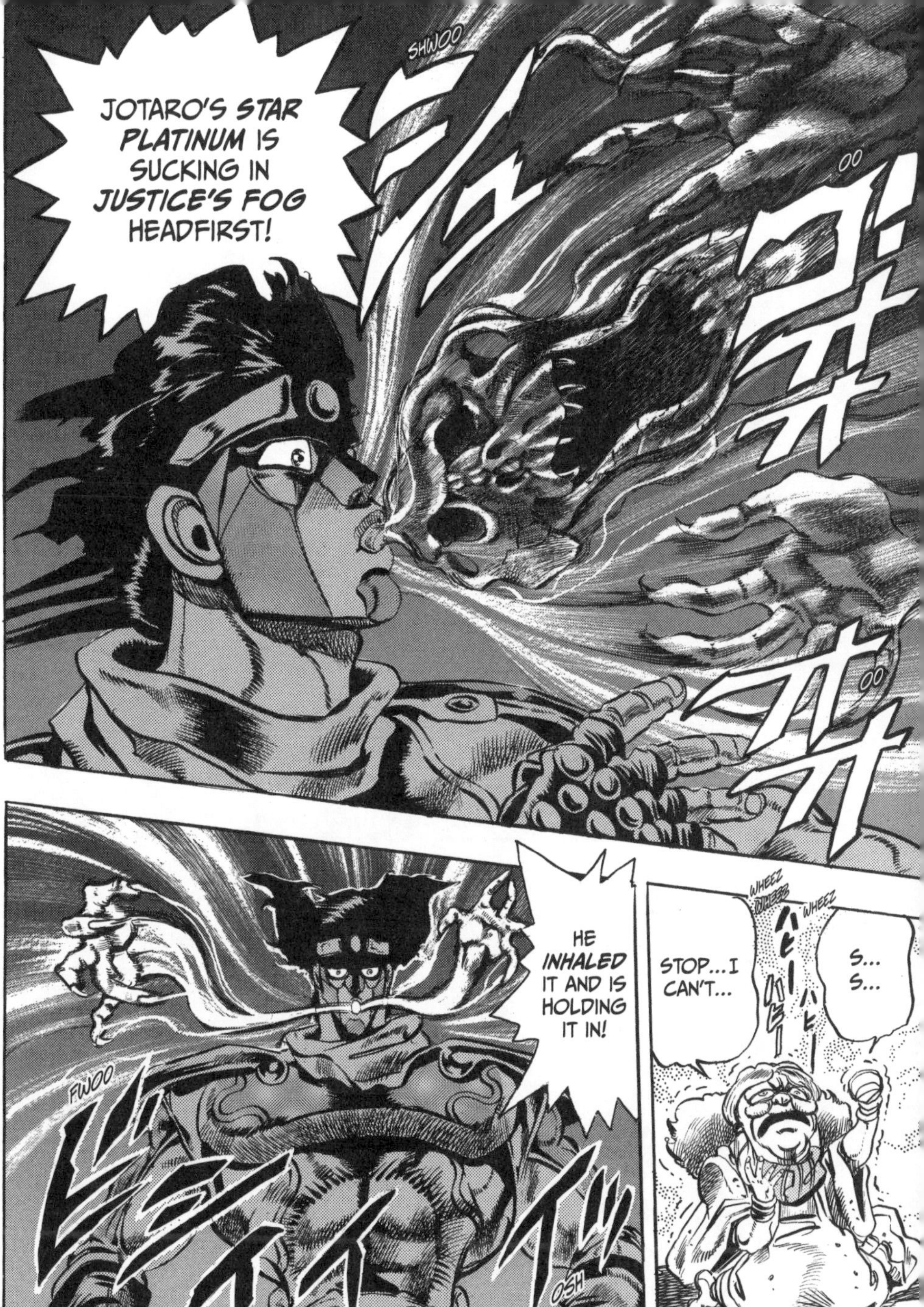
SHWOO
JOTARO'S STAR PLATINUM IS SUCKING IN JUSTICE'S FOG HEADFIRST!
OO
OO
WHEEZ
WHEEZ
WHEEZ
S... S...
STOP... I CAN'T...
HE INHALED IT AND IS HOLDING IT IN!
FWOO
OSH

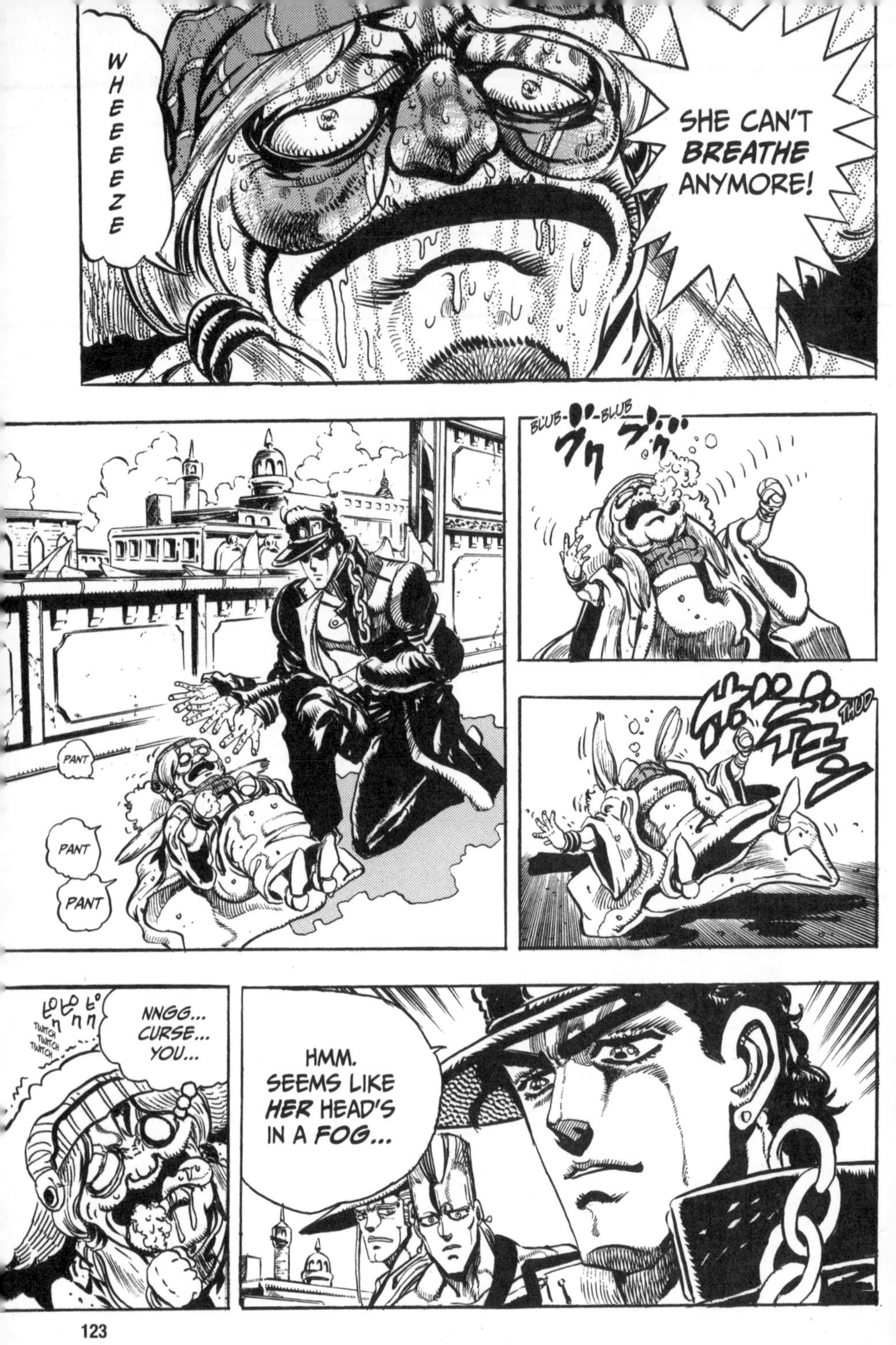

SHE CAN'T *BREATHE* ANYMORE!
WHEEEEEZE
BLUB-BLUB-BLUB
THUD
PANT
PANT
PANT
HMM. SEEMS LIKE *HER* HEAD'S IN A *FOG*...
NNGG... CURSE... YOU...
TWITCH TWITCH TWITCH

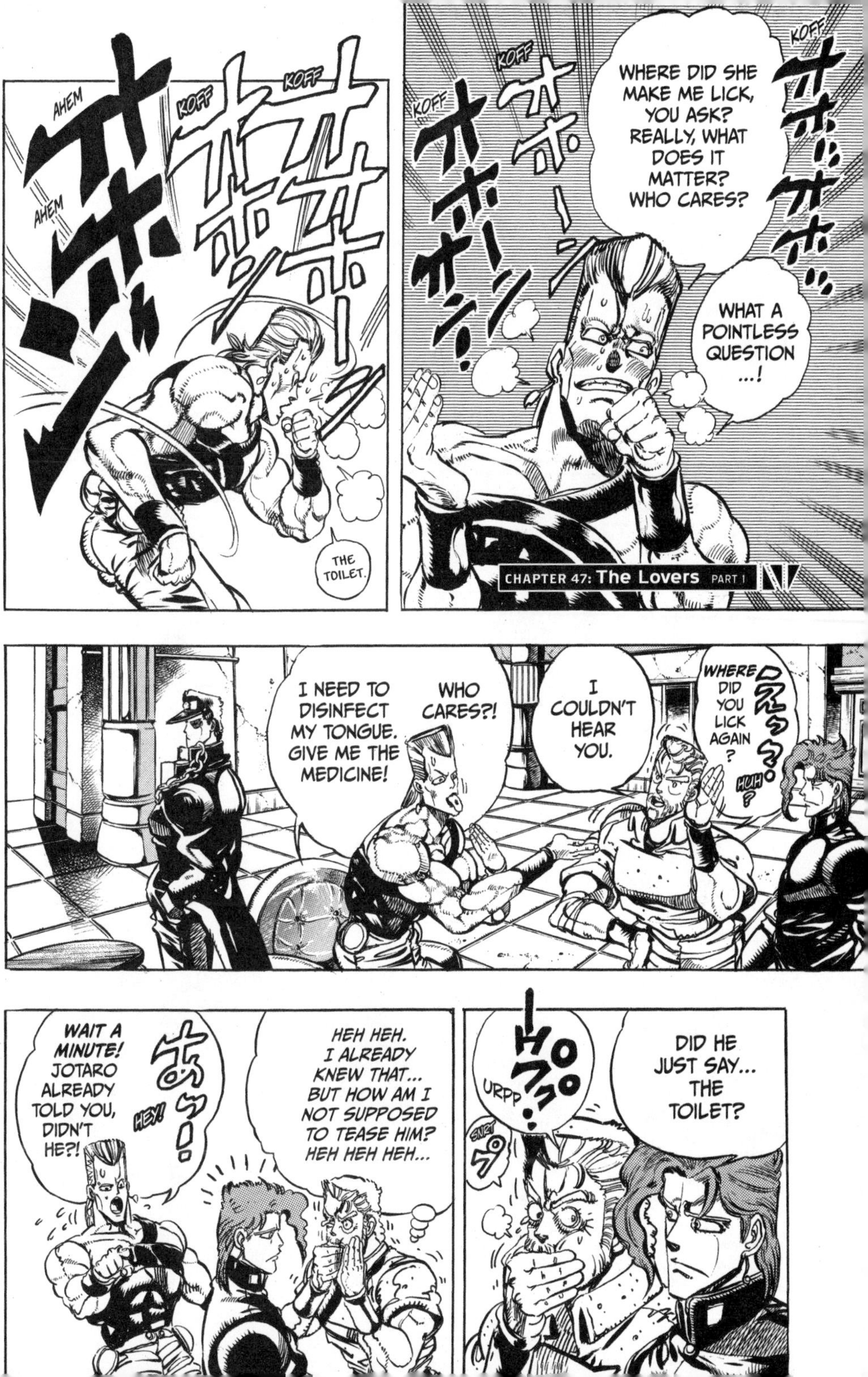
KOFF
KOFF
KOFF
WHERE DID SHE MAKE ME LICK, YOU ASK? REALLY, WHAT DOES IT MATTER? WHO CARES?
WHAT A POINTLESS QUESTION ...!
CHAPTER 47: The Lovers PART 1
KOFF
KOFF
AHEM
AHEM
THE TOILET.
WHERE DID YOU LICK AGAIN?
HUH?
I COULDN'T HEAR YOU.
WHO CARES?!
I NEED TO DISINFECT MY TONGUE. GIVE ME THE MEDICINE!
DID HE JUST SAY... THE TOILET?
URPP
SNRT
HEH HEH. I ALREADY KNEW THAT... BUT HOW AM I NOT SUPPOSED TO TEASE HIM? HEH HEH HEH...
HEY!
WAIT A MINUTE! JOTARO ALREADY TOLD YOU, DIDN'T HE?!

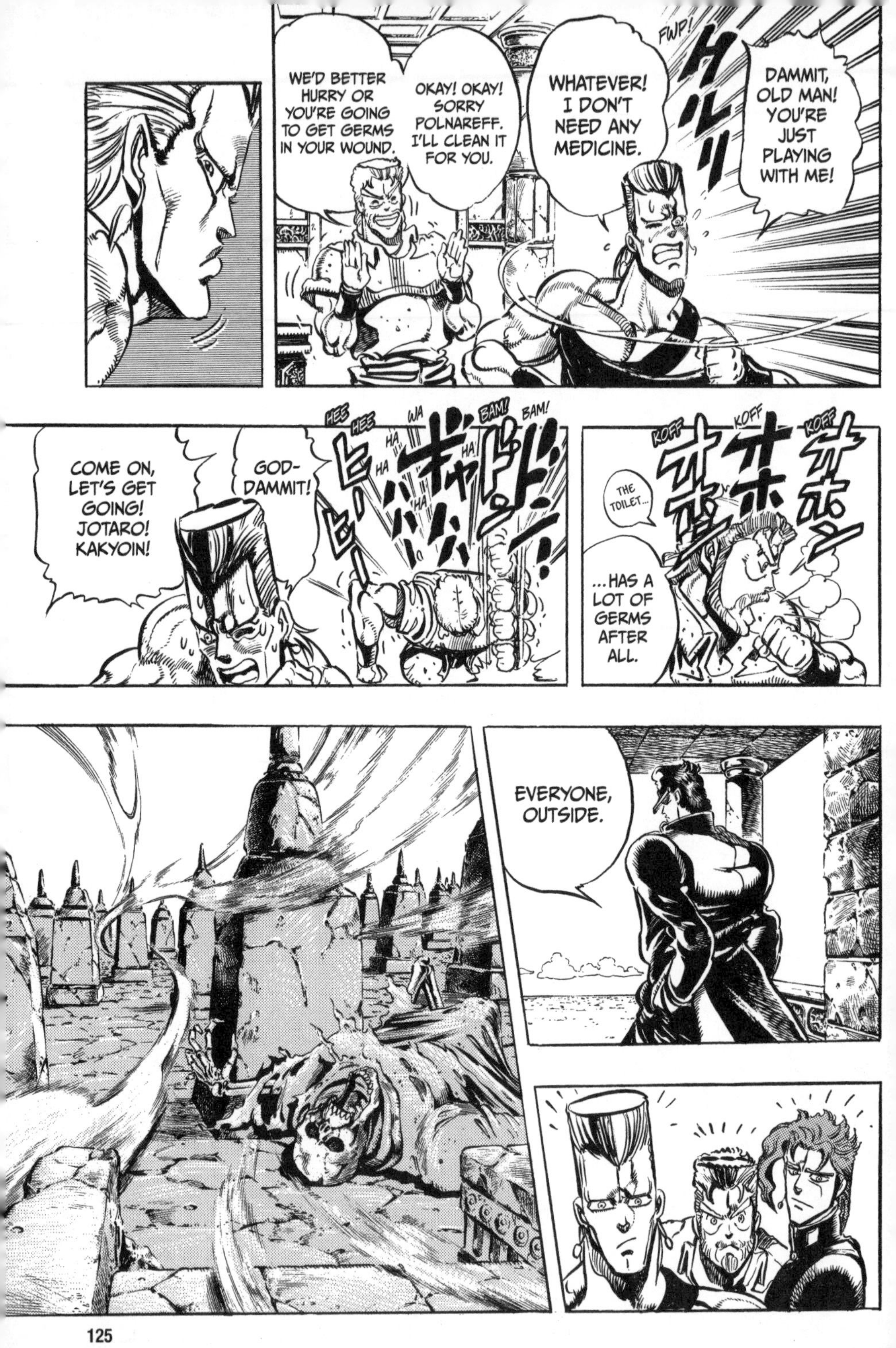
FWP!
DAMMIT, OLD MAN! YOU'RE JUST PLAYING WITH ME!
WHATEVER! I DON'T NEED ANY MEDICINE.
OKAY! OKAY! SORRY POLNAREFF. I'LL CLEAN IT FOR YOU.
WE'D BETTER HURRY OR YOU'RE GOING TO GET GERMS IN YOUR WOUND.
KOFF KOFF KOFF
THE TOILET...
...HAS A LOT OF GERMS AFTER ALL.
BAM! BAM!
WA HA HA HA HA
HEE HEE
GOD-DAMMIT!
COME ON, LET'S GET GOING! JOTARO! KAKYOIN!
EVERYONE, OUTSIDE.

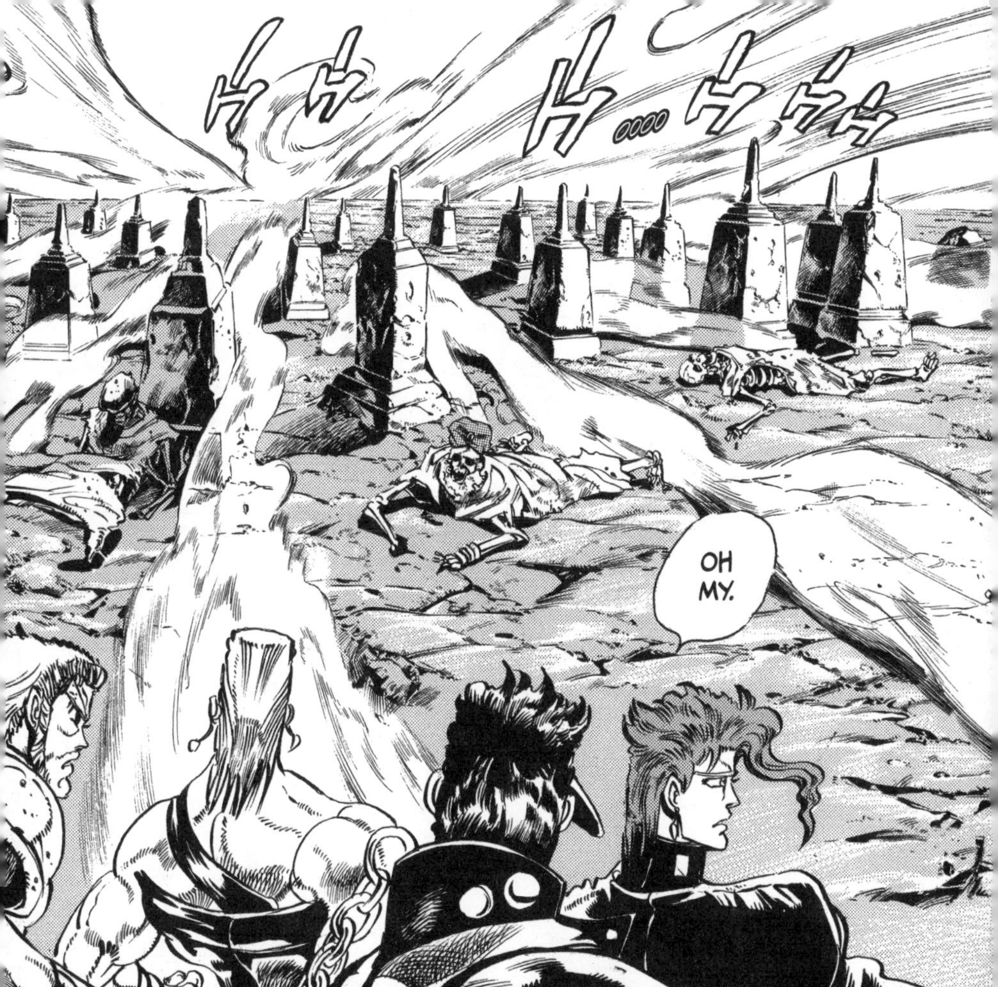
OH MY.

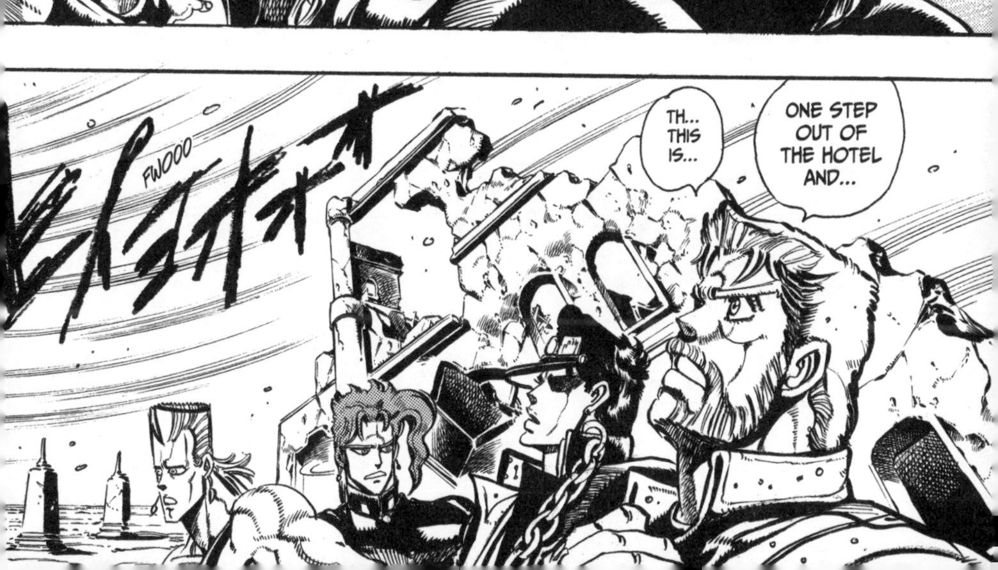
ONE STEP OUT OF THE HOTEL AND...
TH... THIS IS...
FWOOO

CHAPTER 47: The Lovers PART 1

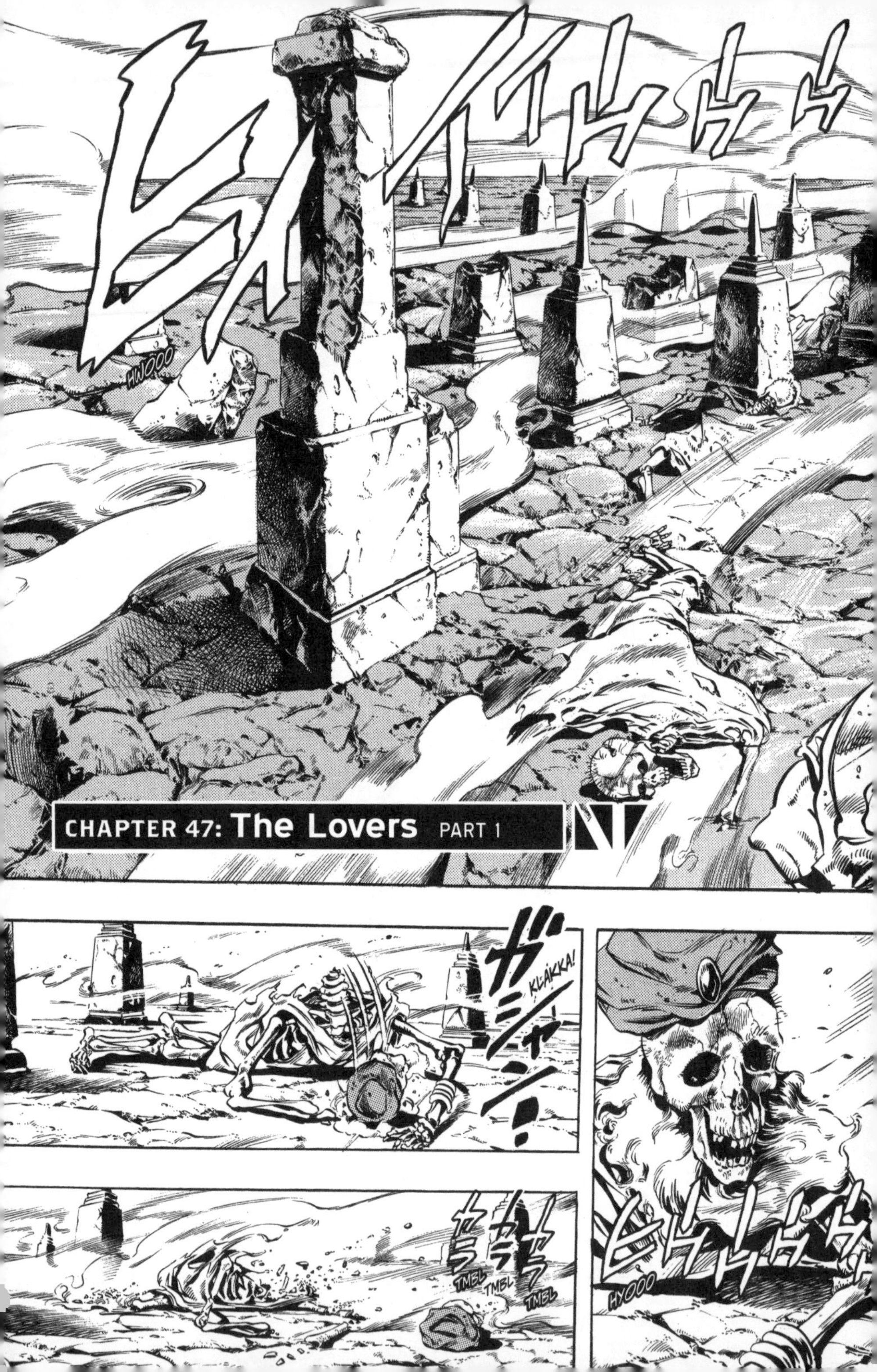
HWOOO
CHAPTER 47: The Lovers PART 1
HYOOO
KLAKKA!
TMBL
TMBL
TMBL

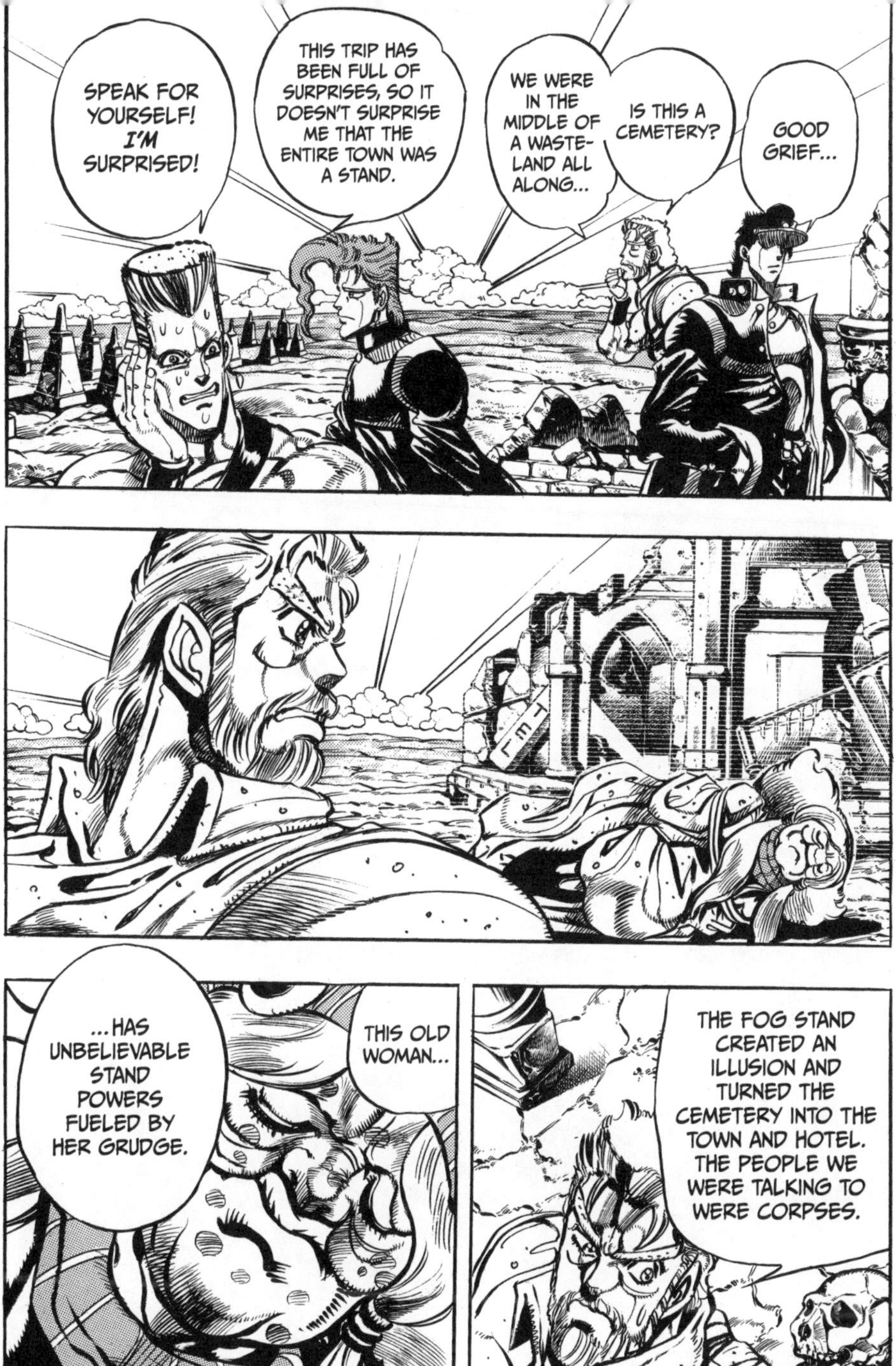
GOOD GRIEF...
IS THIS A CEMETERY?
WE WERE IN THE MIDDLE OF A WASTE-LAND ALL ALONG...
THIS TRIP HAS BEEN FULL OF SURPRISES, SO IT DOESN'T SURPRISE ME THAT THE ENTIRE TOWN WAS A STAND.
SPEAK FOR YOURSELF! *I'M* SURPRISED!
THE FOG STAND CREATED AN ILLUSION AND TURNED THE CEMETERY INTO THE TOWN AND HOTEL. THE PEOPLE WE WERE TALKING TO WERE CORPSES.
THIS OLD WOMAN...
...HAS UNBELIEVABLE STAND POWERS FUELED BY HER GRUDGE.

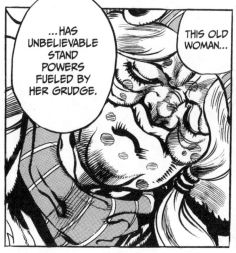

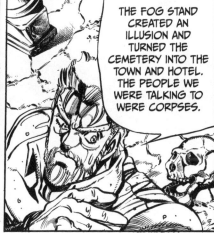

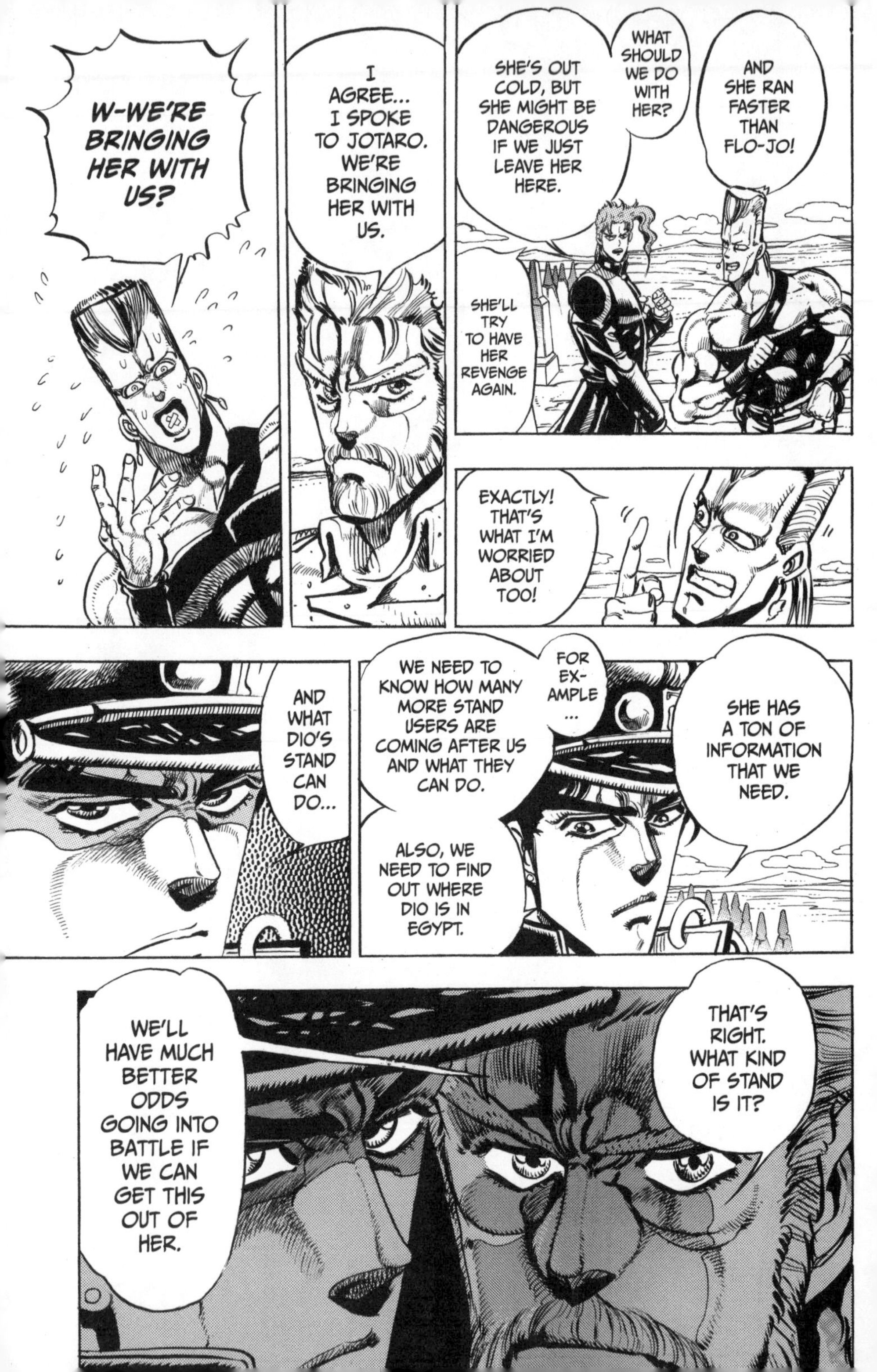
AND SHE RAN FASTER THAN FLO-JO!
WHAT SHOULD WE DO WITH HER?
SHE'S OUT COLD, BUT SHE MIGHT BE DANGEROUS IF WE JUST LEAVE HER HERE.
SHE'LL TRY TO HAVE HER REVENGE AGAIN.
EXACTLY! THAT'S WHAT I'M WORRIED ABOUT TOO!
I AGREE... I SPOKE TO JOTARO. WE'RE BRINGING HER WITH US.
W-WE'RE BRINGING HER WITH US?
SHE HAS A TON OF INFORMATION THAT WE NEED.
FOR EX-AMPLE ...
WE NEED TO KNOW HOW MANY MORE STAND USERS ARE COMING AFTER US AND WHAT THEY CAN DO.
ALSO, WE NEED TO FIND OUT WHERE DIO IS IN EGYPT.
AND WHAT DIO'S STAND CAN DO...
THAT'S RIGHT. WHAT KIND OF STAND IS IT?
WE'LL HAVE MUCH BETTER ODDS GOING INTO BATTLE IF WE CAN GET THIS OUT OF HER.

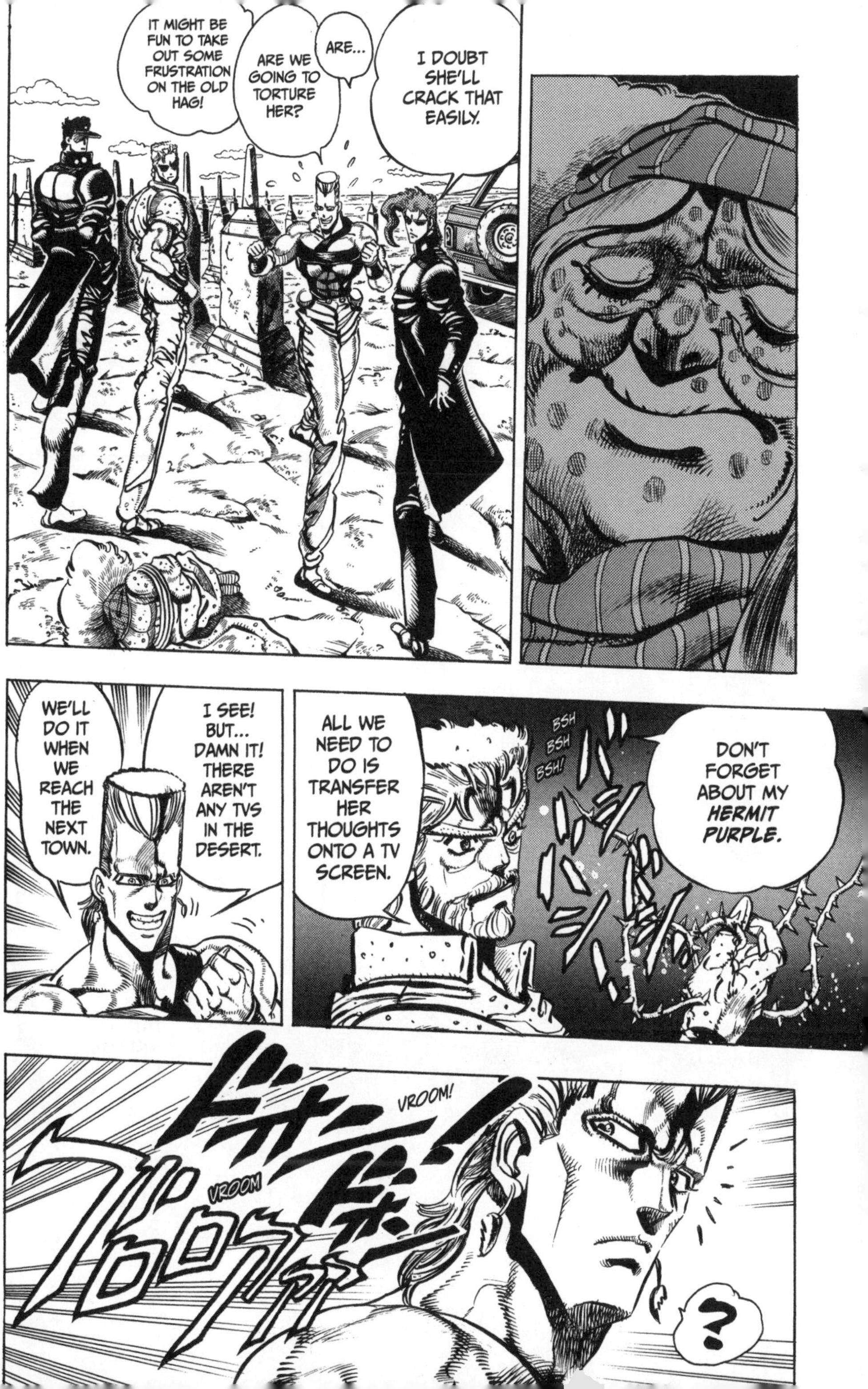
I DOUBT SHE'LL CRACK THAT EASILY.
ARE...
ARE WE GOING TO TORTURE HER?
IT MIGHT BE FUN TO TAKE OUT SOME FRUSTRATION ON THE OLD HAG!
BSH BSH BSH!
DON'T FORGET ABOUT MY *HERMIT PURPLE*.
ALL WE NEED TO DO IS TRANSFER HER THOUGHTS ONTO A TV SCREEN.
I SEE! BUT... DAMN IT! THERE AREN'T ANY TVS IN THE DESERT.
WE'LL DO IT WHEN WE REACH THE NEXT TOWN.
VROOM!
VROOM
?

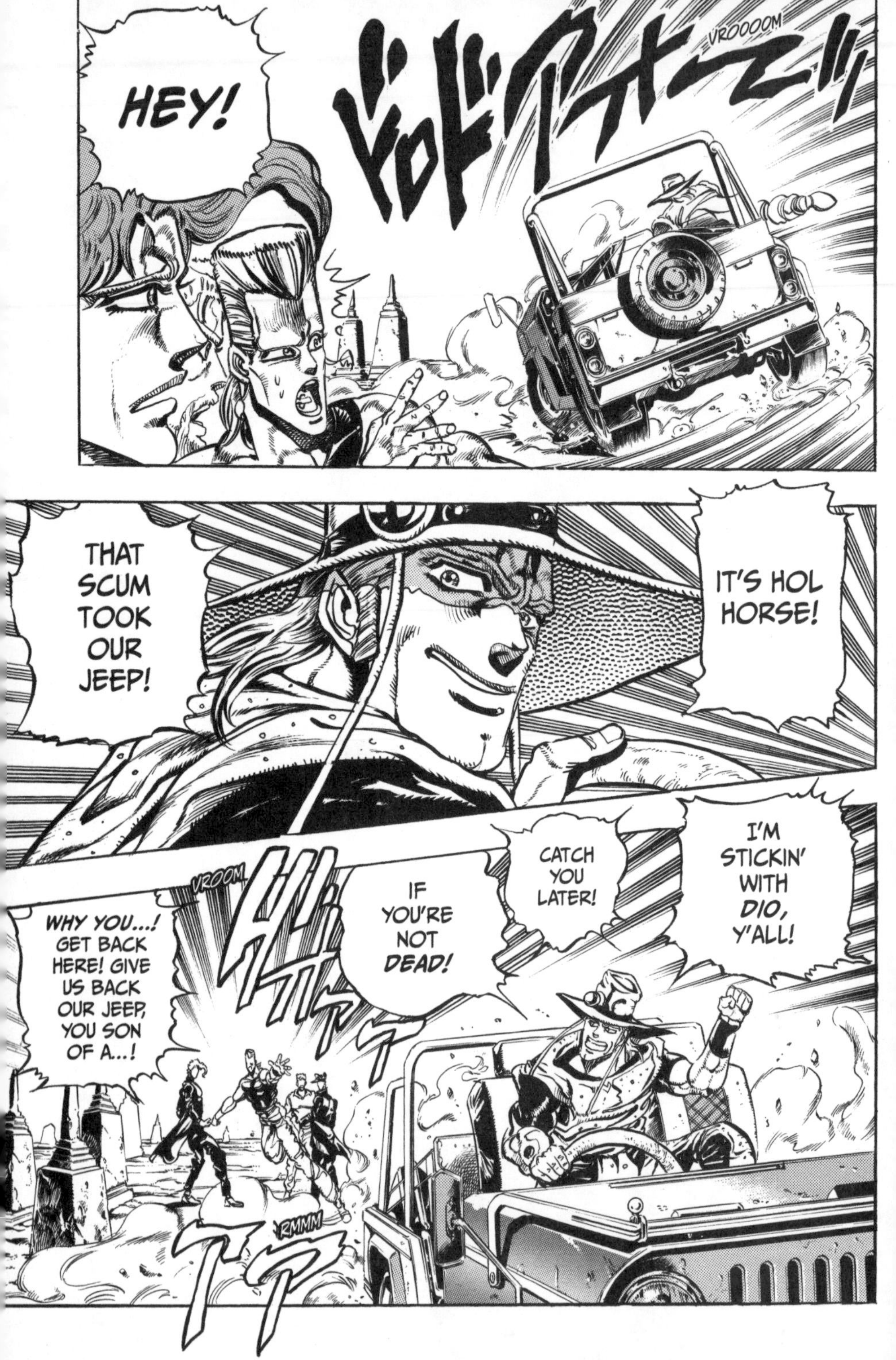
VROOOOM
HEY!
IT'S HOL HORSE!
THAT SCUM TOOK OUR JEEP!
I'M STICKIN' WITH *DIO*, Y'ALL!
CATCH YOU LATER!
IF YOU'RE NOT *DEAD!*
VROOM
WHY YOU...! GET BACK HERE! GIVE US BACK OUR JEEP, YOU SON OF A...!
RMMM

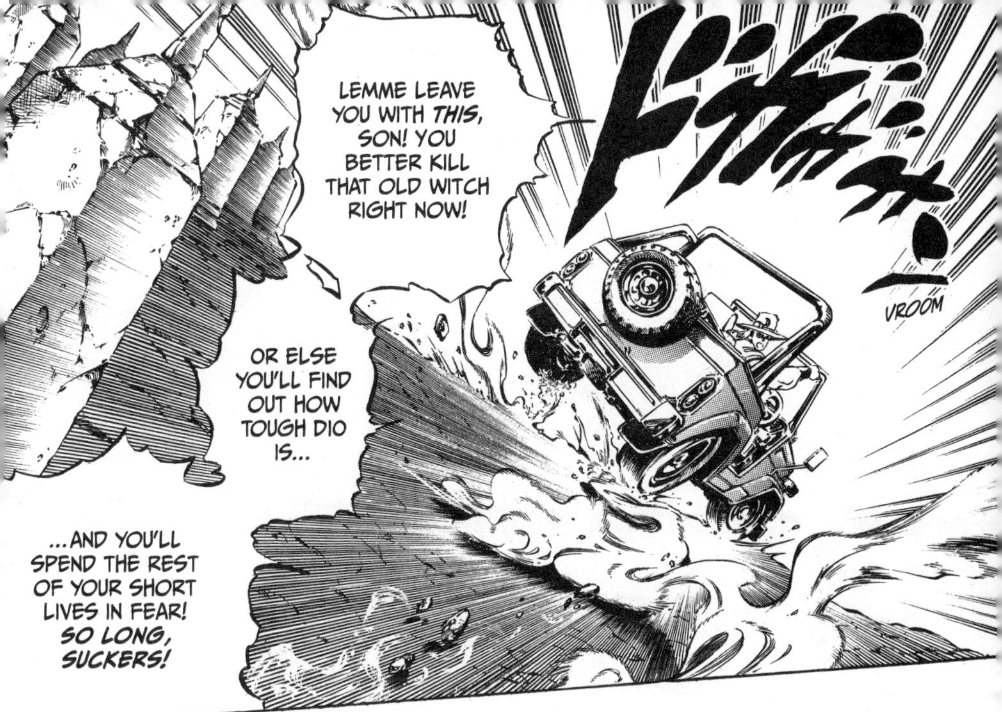
VROOM
LEMME LEAVE YOU WITH *THIS*, SON! YOU BETTER KILL THAT OLD WITCH RIGHT NOW!
OR ELSE YOU'LL FIND OUT HOW TOUGH DIO IS...
...AND YOU'LL SPEND THE REST OF YOUR SHORT LIVES IN FEAR! ***SO LONG, SUCKERS!***

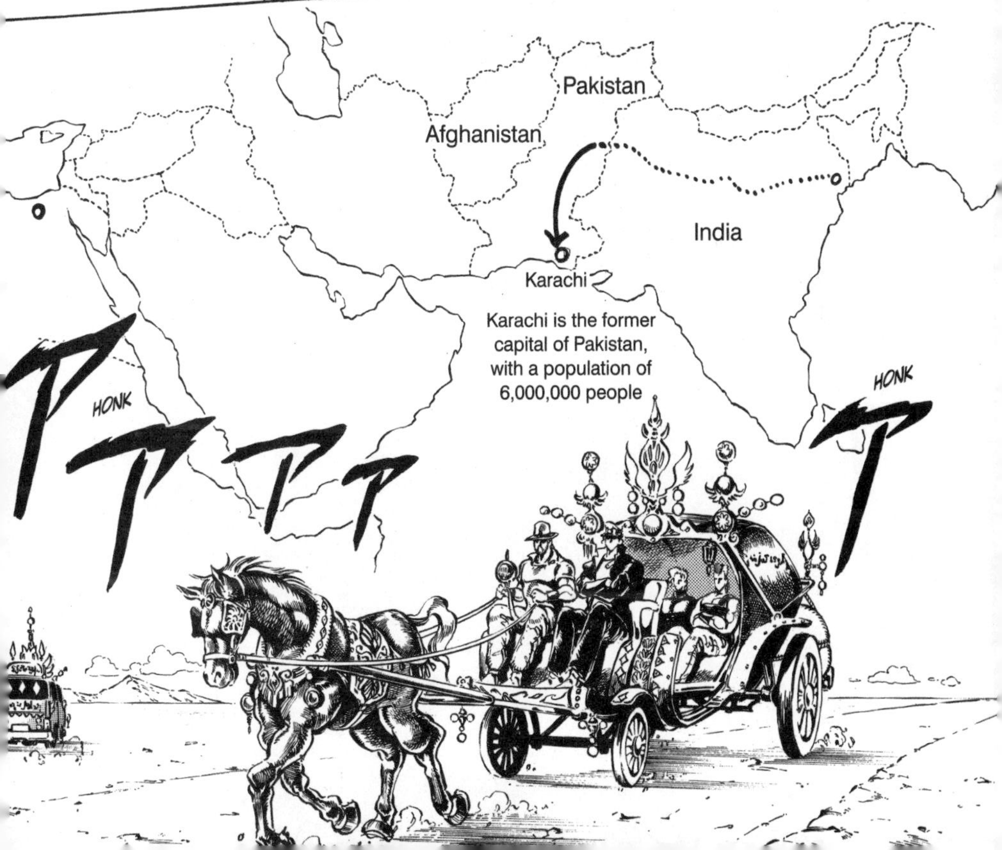
Pakistan
Afghanistan
India
Karachi
Karachi is the former capital of Pakistan, with a population of 6,000,000 people
HONK
HONK

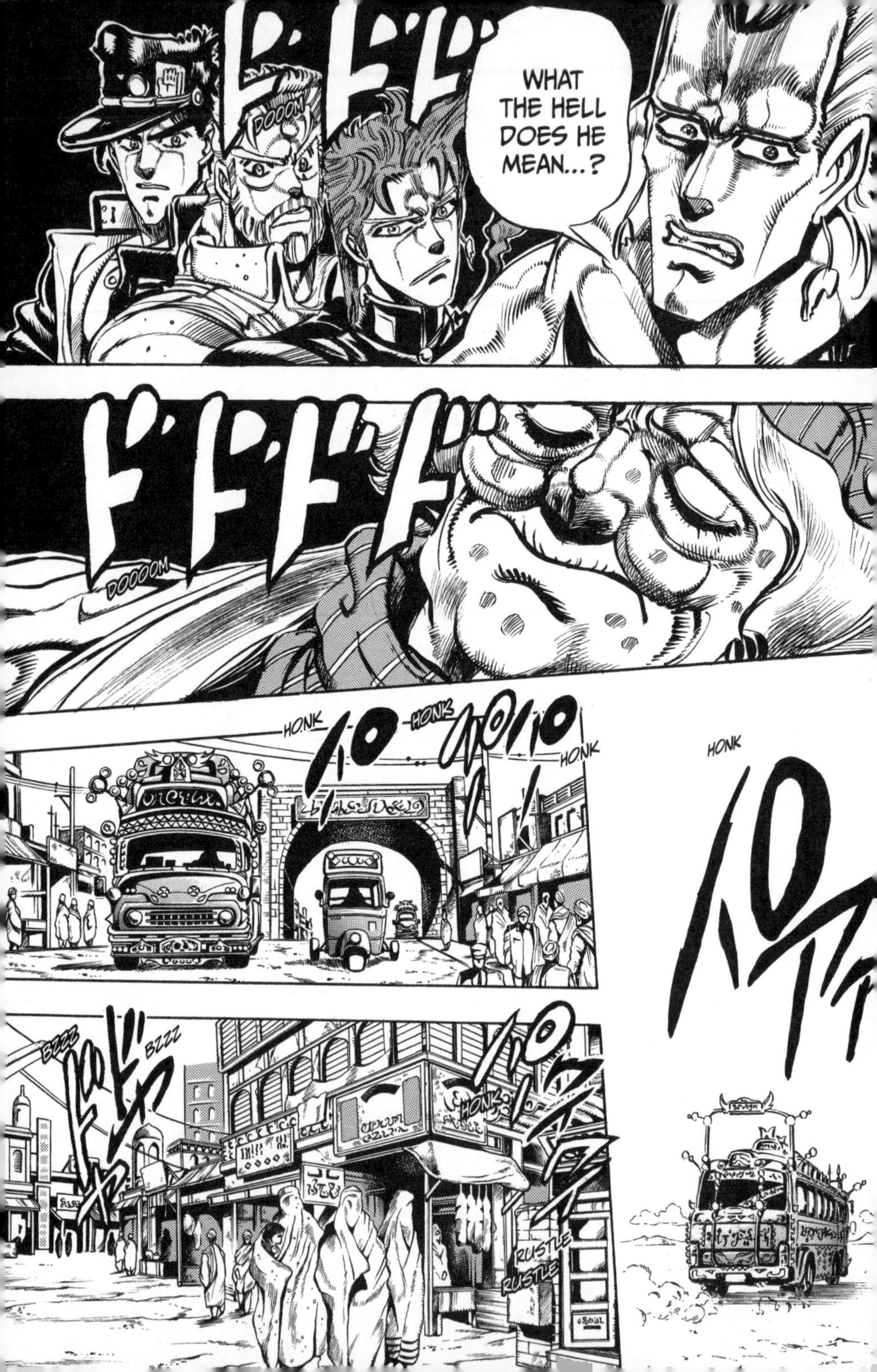
WHAT THE HELL DOES HE MEAN...?
DOOOM
DOOOOM
HONK
HONK
HONK
HONK
HONK
BZZZ
BZZZ
RUSTLE
RUSTLE

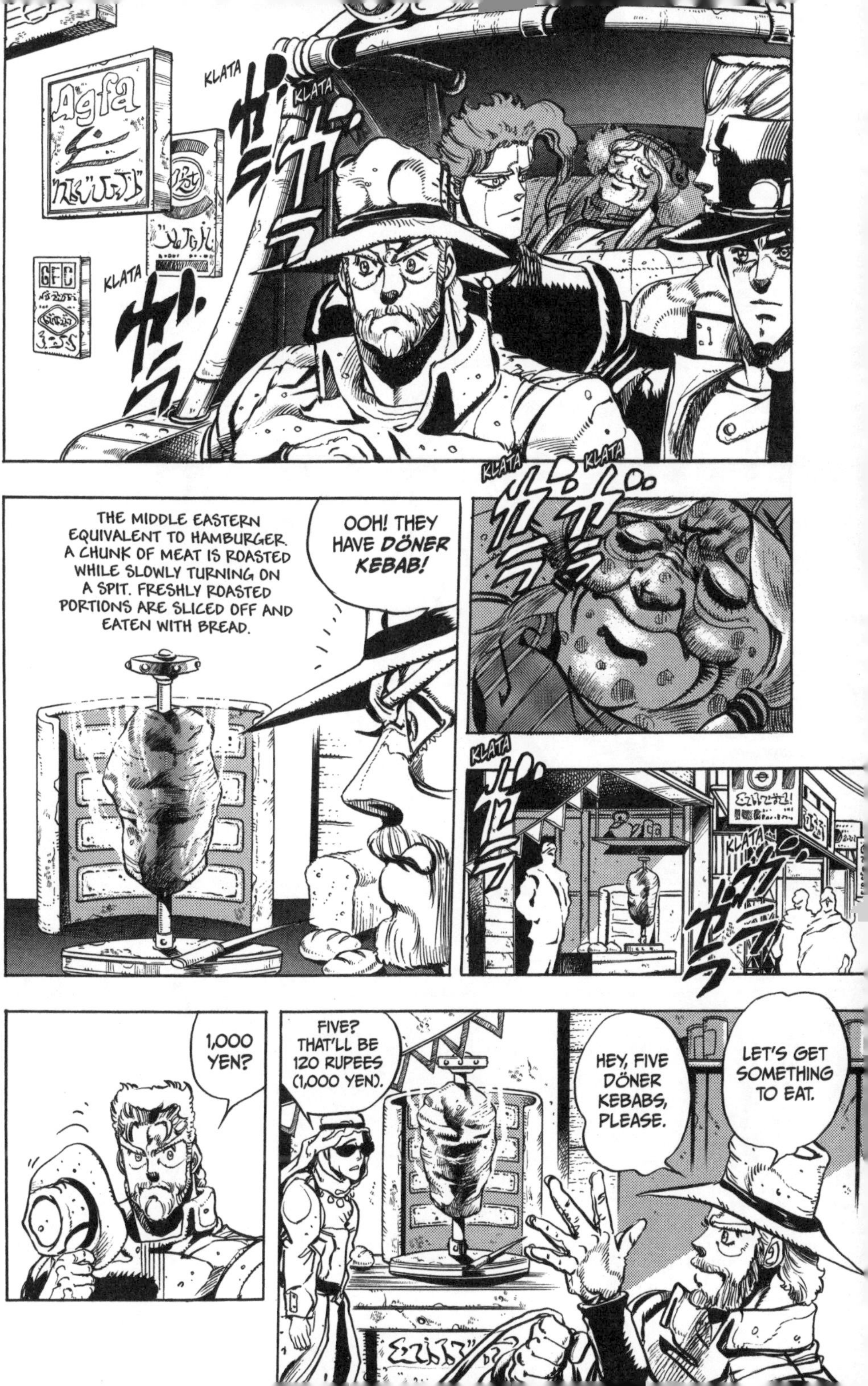
KLATA
KLATA
KLATA
Agfa
GFC
KLATA
KLATA
KLATA
KLATA
OOH! THEY HAVE DÖNER KEBAB!
THE MIDDLE EASTERN EQUIVALENT TO HAMBURGER. A CHUNK OF MEAT IS ROASTED WHILE SLOWLY TURNING ON A SPIT. FRESHLY ROASTED PORTIONS ARE SLICED OFF AND EATEN WITH BREAD.
LET'S GET SOMETHING TO EAT.
HEY, FIVE DÖNER KEBABS, PLEASE.
FIVE? THAT'LL BE 120 RUPEES (1,000 YEN).
1,000 YEN?

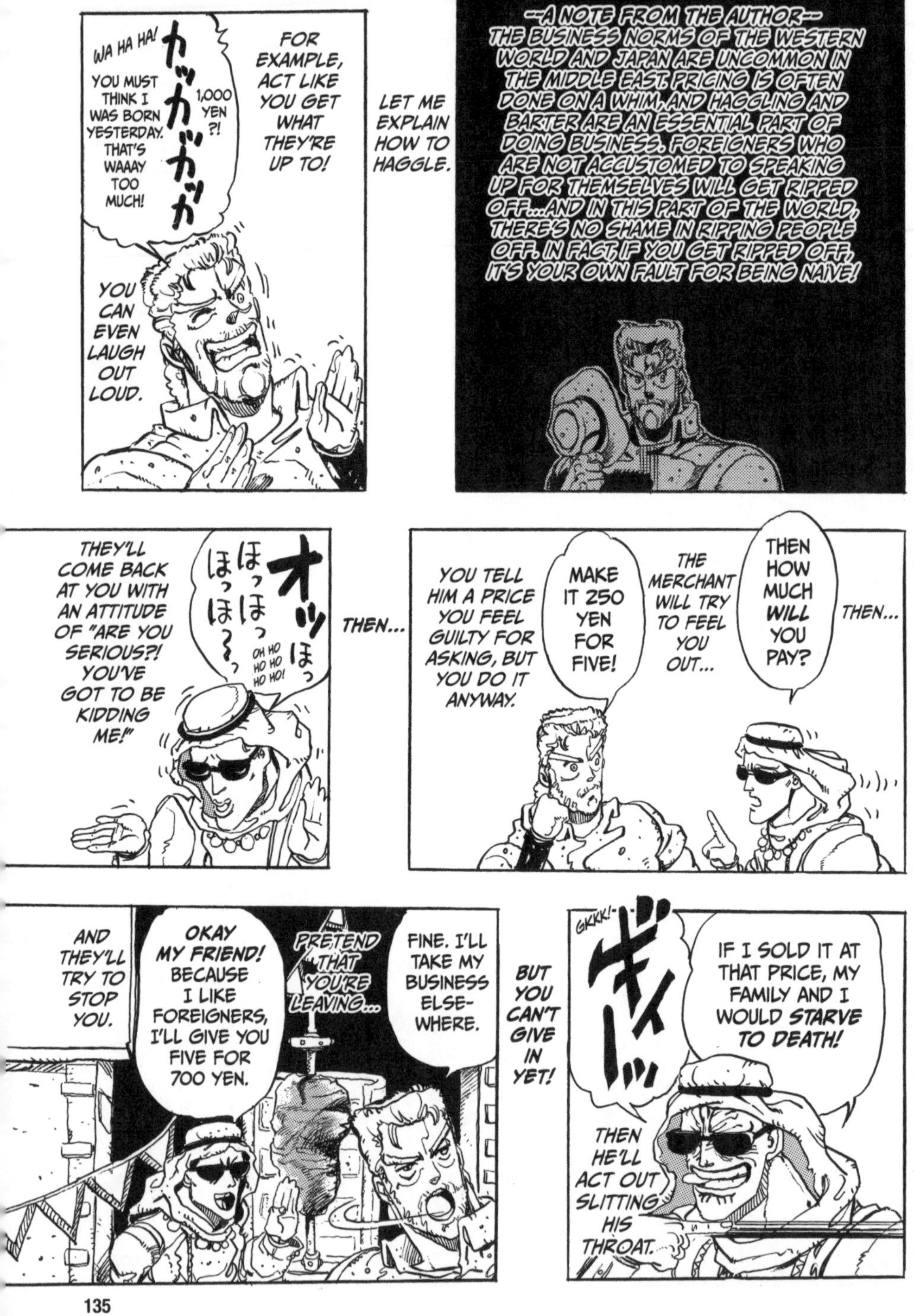
--A NOTE FROM THE AUTHOR-- THE BUSINESS NORMS OF THE WESTERN WORLD AND JAPAN ARE UNCOMMON IN THE MIDDLE EAST. PRICING IS OFTEN DONE ON A WHIM, AND HAGGLING AND BARTER ARE AN ESSENTIAL PART OF DOING BUSINESS. FOREIGNERS WHO ARE NOT ACCUSTOMED TO SPEAKING UP FOR THEMSELVES WILL GET RIPPED OFF...AND IN THIS PART OF THE WORLD, THERE'S NO SHAME IN RIPPING PEOPLE OFF. IN FACT, IF YOU GET RIPPED OFF, IT'S YOUR OWN FAULT FOR BEING NAÏVE!
LET ME EXPLAIN HOW TO HAGGLE.
FOR EXAMPLE, ACT LIKE YOU GET WHAT THEY'RE UP TO!
カッカッカッカ
WA HA HA!
YOU MUST THINK I WAS BORN YESTERDAY. THAT'S WAAAY TOO MUCH!
1,000 YEN?!
YOU CAN EVEN LAUGH OUT LOUD.
THEN...
THEN HOW MUCH WILL YOU PAY?
THE MERCHANT WILL TRY TO FEEL YOU OUT...
MAKE IT 250 YEN FOR FIVE!
YOU TELL HIM A PRICE YOU FEEL GUILTY FOR ASKING, BUT YOU DO IT ANYWAY.
THEN...
オッほっほっほっほ〜っ
OH HO HO HO HO HO!
THEY'LL COME BACK AT YOU WITH AN ATTITUDE OF "ARE YOU SERIOUS?! YOU'VE GOT TO BE KIDDING ME!"
IF I SOLD IT AT THAT PRICE, MY FAMILY AND I WOULD STARVE TO DEATH!
ギィッ
GKKK!
THEN HE'LL ACT OUT SLITTING HIS THROAT.
BUT YOU CAN'T GIVE IN YET!
FINE. I'LL TAKE MY BUSINESS ELSE-WHERE.
PRETEND THAT YOU'RE LEAVING...
OKAY MY FRIEND! BECAUSE I LIKE FOREIGNERS, I'LL GIVE YOU FIVE FOR 700 YEN.
AND THEY'LL TRY TO STOP YOU.

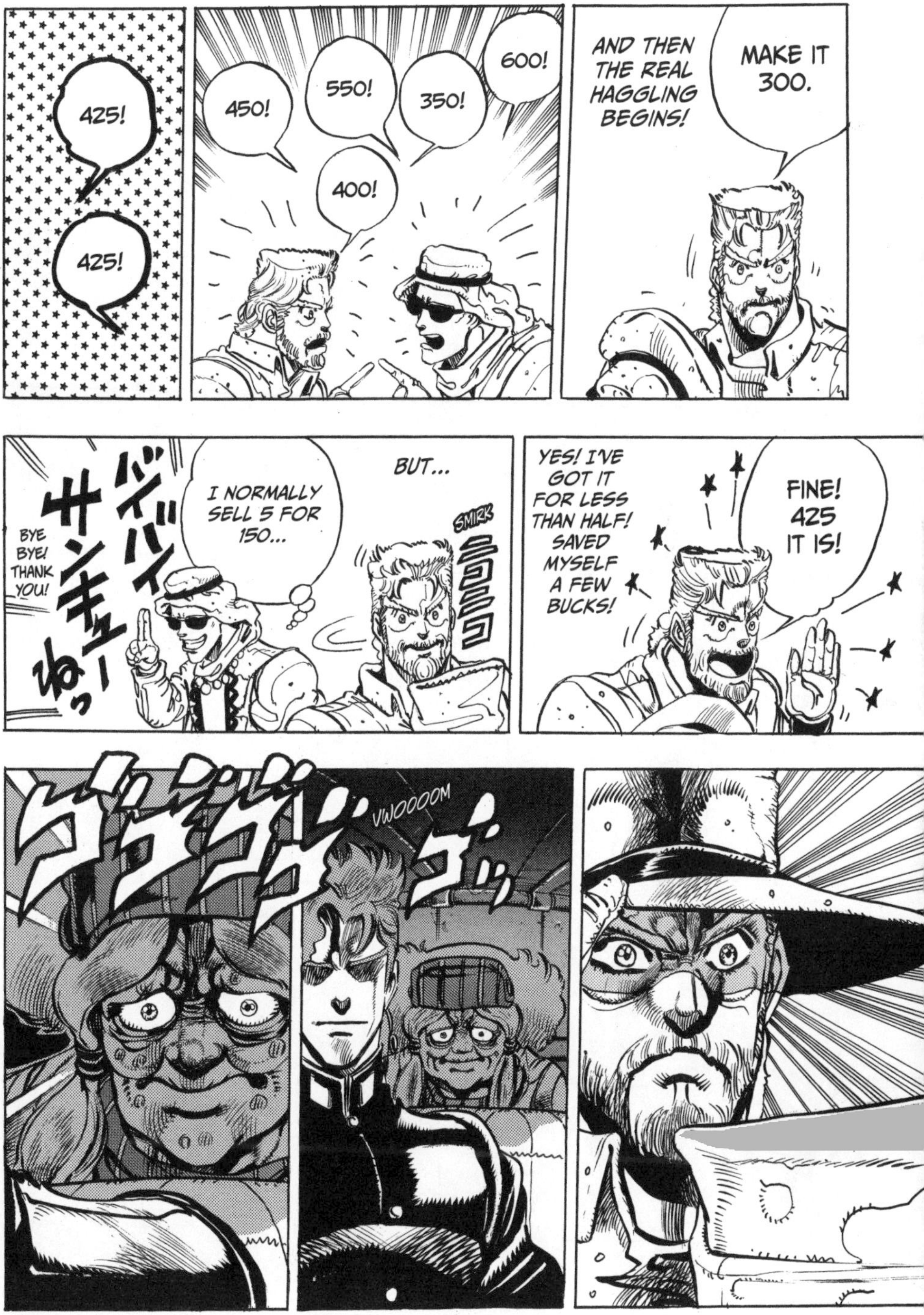
MAKE IT 300.
AND THEN THE REAL HAGGLING BEGINS!
600!
350!
550!
450!
400!
425!
425!
FINE! 425 IT IS!
YES! I'VE GOT IT FOR LESS THAN HALF! SAVED MYSELF A FEW BUCKS!
BUT...
SMIRK
I NORMALLY SELL 5 FOR 150...
バイバイサンキューねっ
BYE BYE! THANK YOU!
ゴゴゴゴゴッ
VWOOOOM

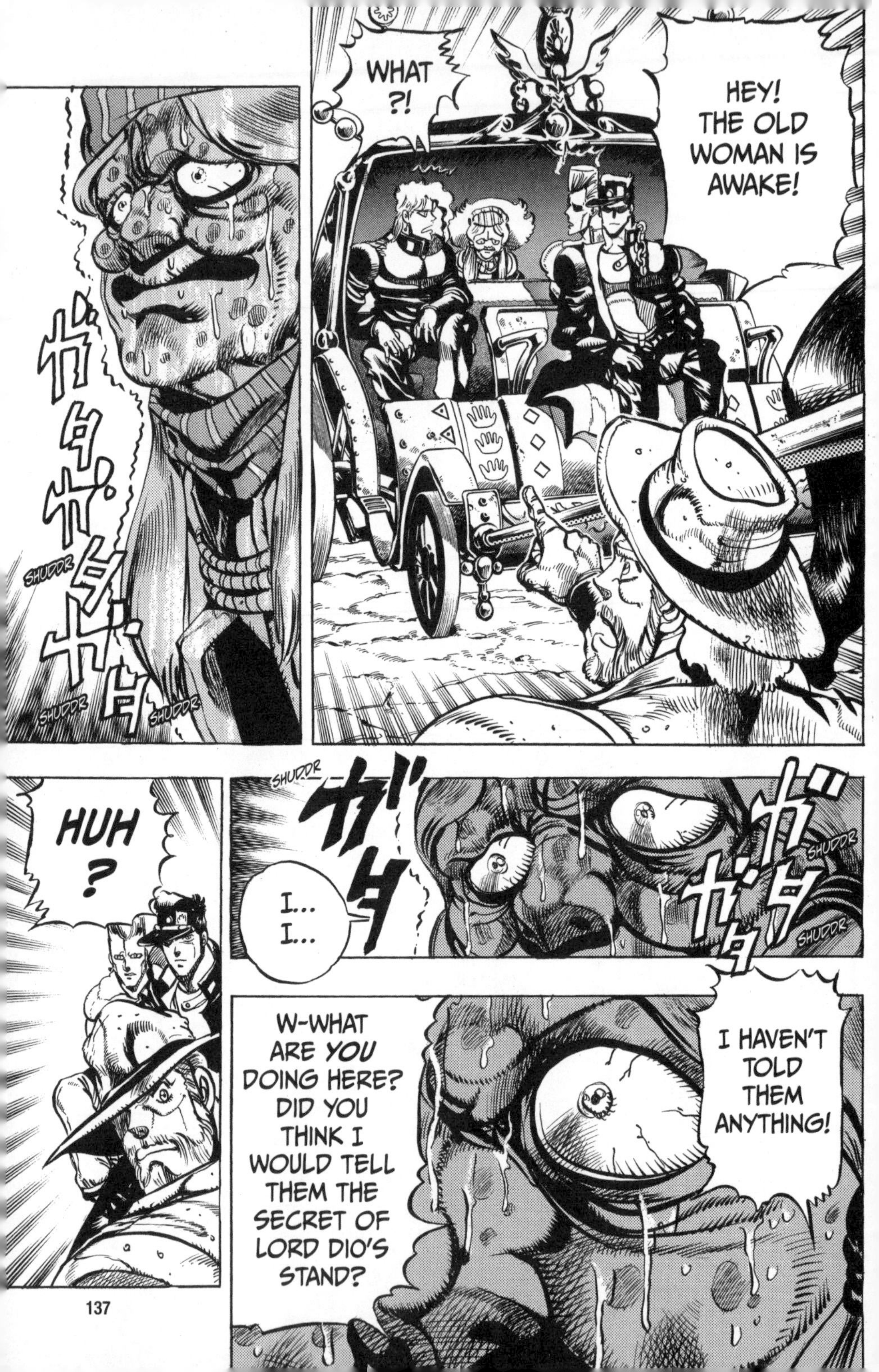
HEY! THE OLD WOMAN IS AWAKE!
WHAT ?!
SHUDDR
SHUDDR
SHUDDR
SHUDDR
SHUDDR
SHUDDR
I... I...
I HAVEN'T TOLD THEM ANYTHING!
W-WHAT ARE *YOU* DOING HERE? DID YOU THINK I WOULD TELL THEM THE SECRET OF LORD DIO'S STAND?
HUH ?

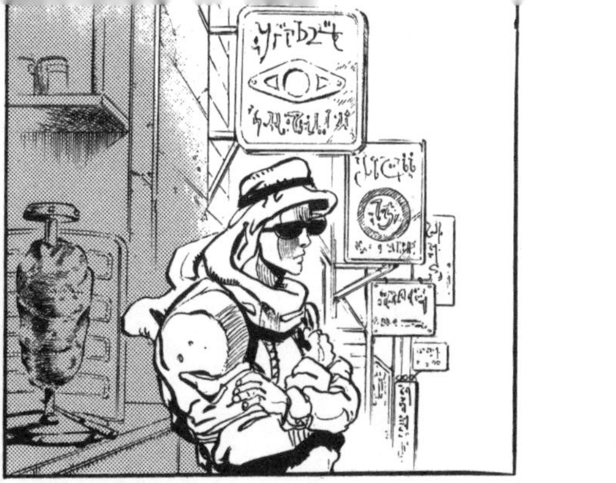

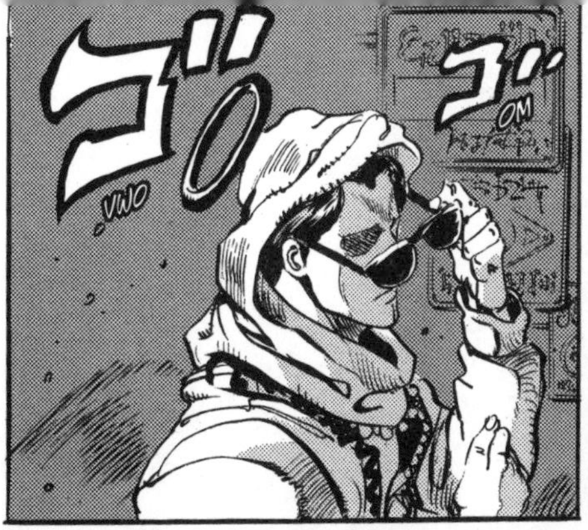
ゴ
VWO
ゴ
OM

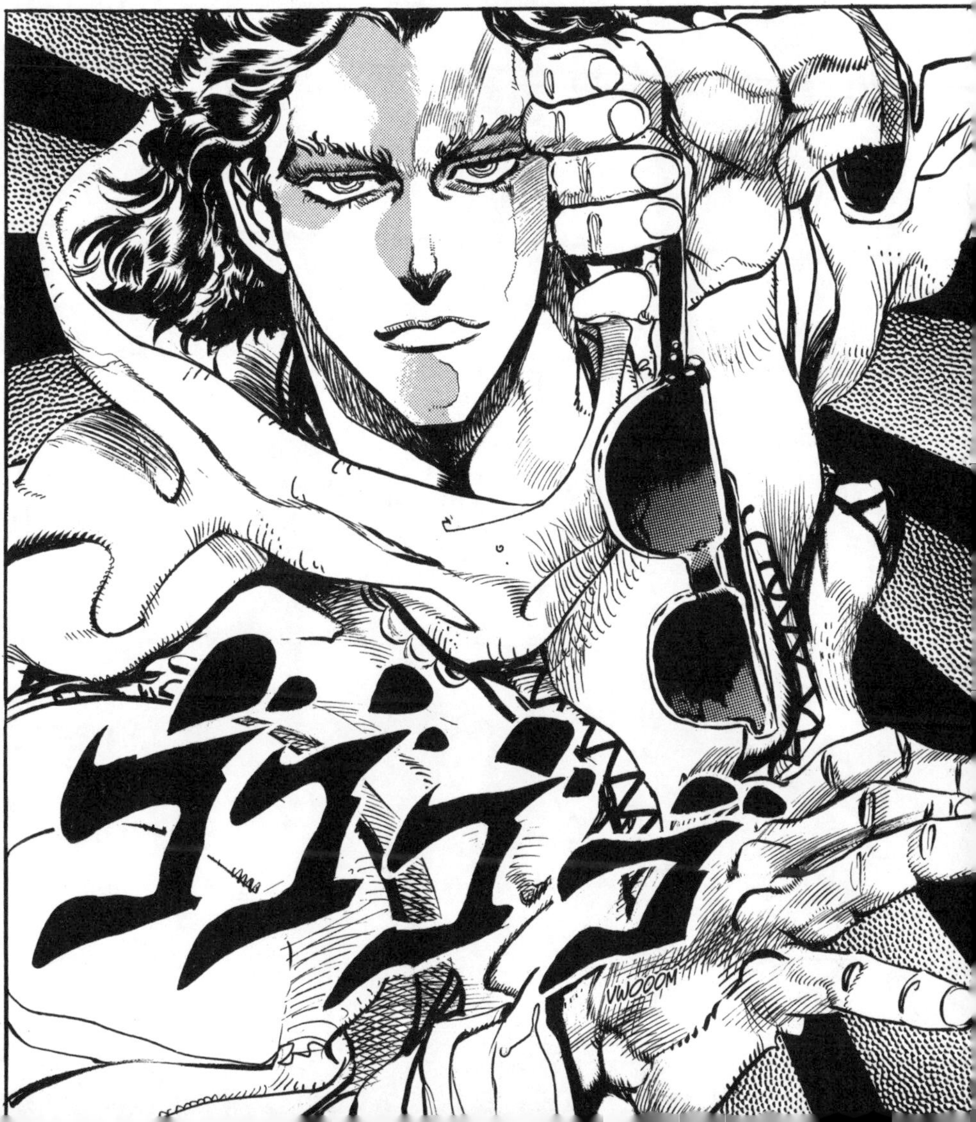
ゴゴゴゴ
VWOOOM

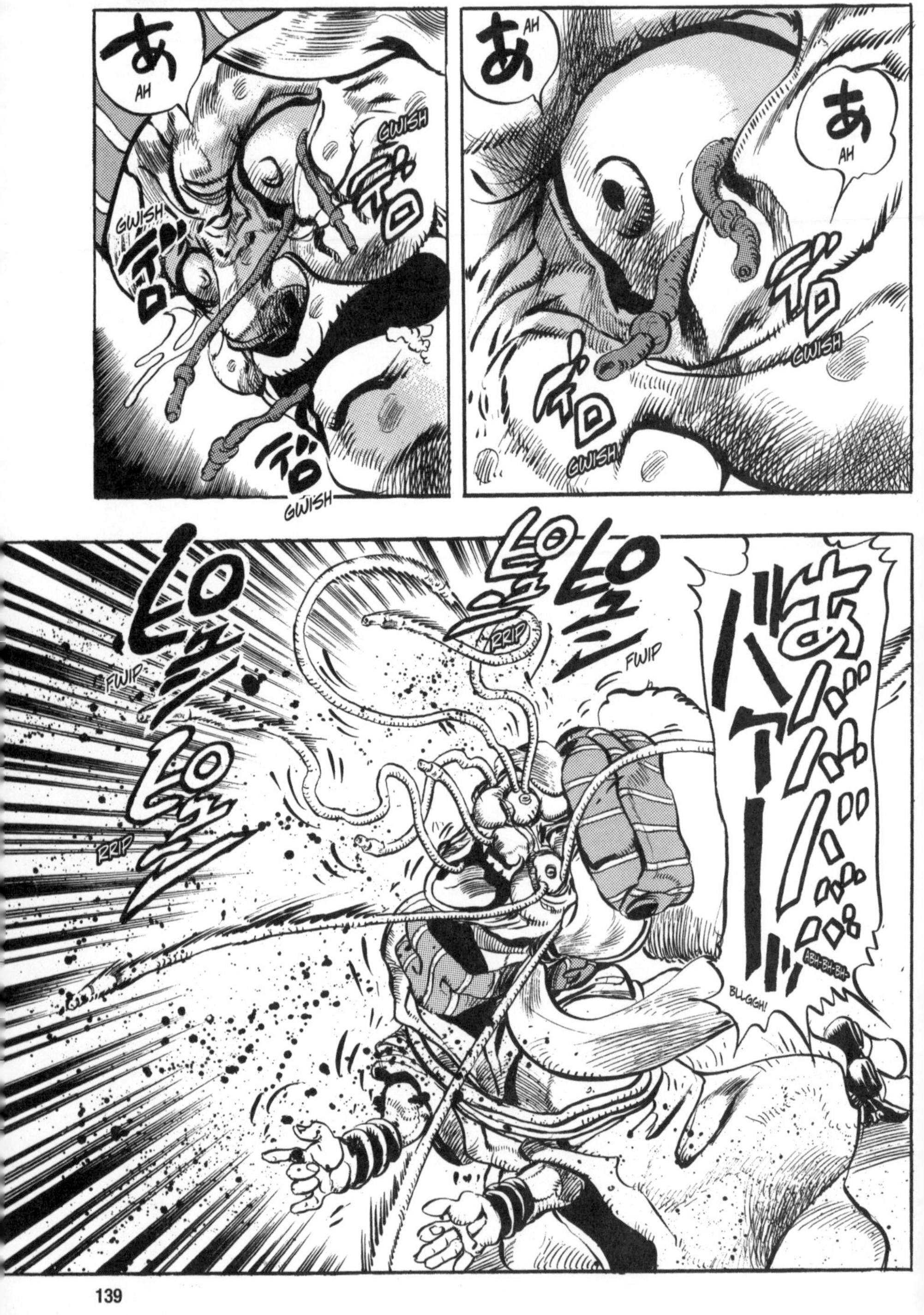

あ
AH
あ
AH
GWISH
GWISH
あ
AH
GWISH
GWISH
GWISH
ABH-BH-BH
BLUGGH!
FWIP
RRIP
FWIP
RRIP

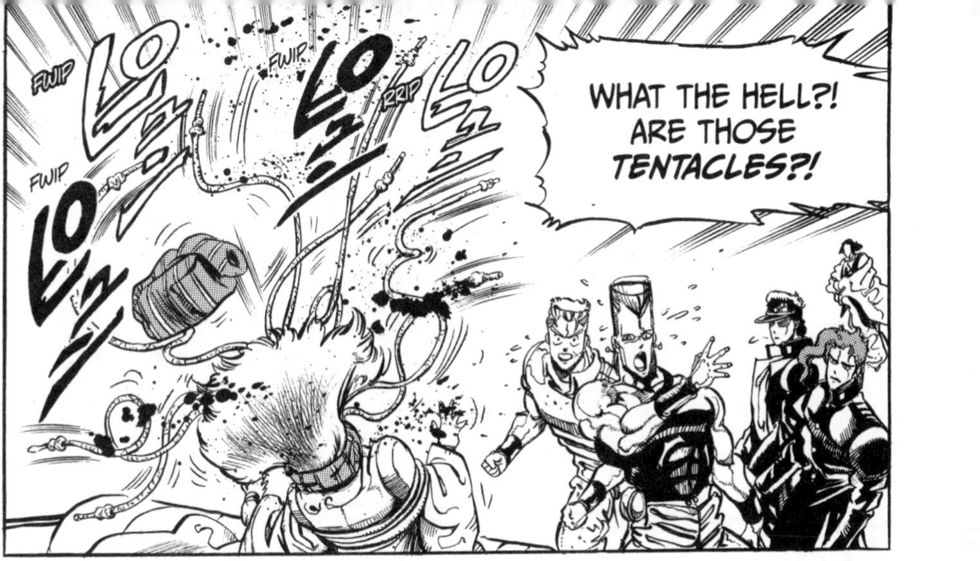
FWIP
FWIP
KRIP
FWIP
WHAT THE HELL?! ARE THOSE TENTACLES?!

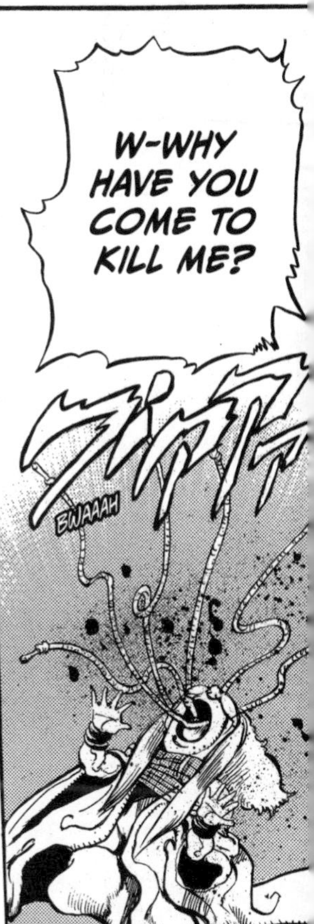
W-WHY HAVE YOU COME TO KILL ME?
BWAAAH

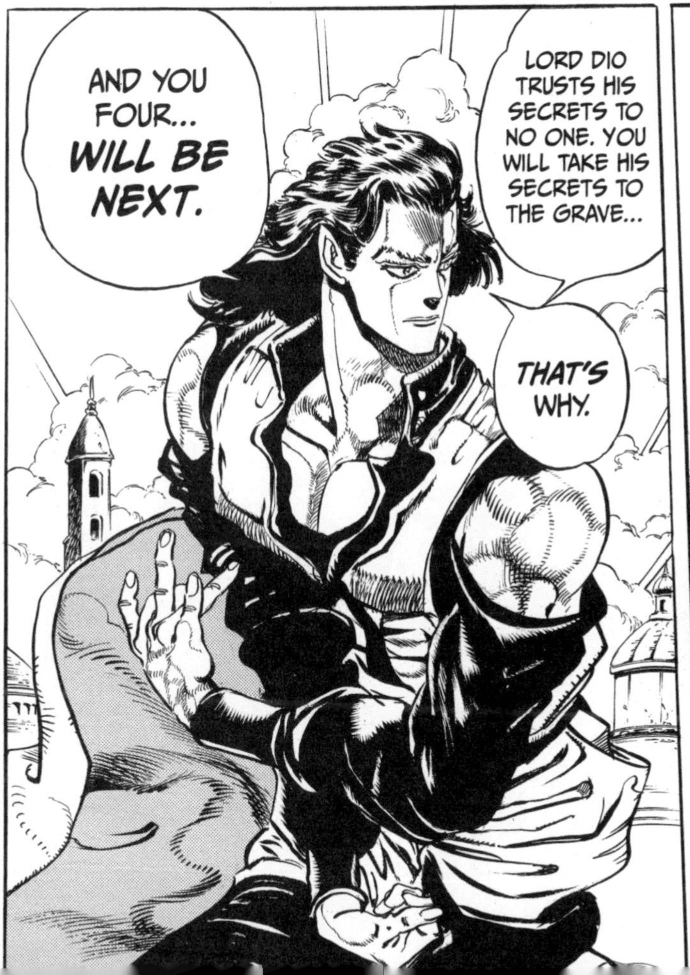
LORD DIO TRUSTS HIS SECRETS TO NO ONE. YOU WILL TAKE HIS SECRETS TO THE GRAVE...
THAT'S WHY.
AND YOU FOUR... WILL BE NEXT.

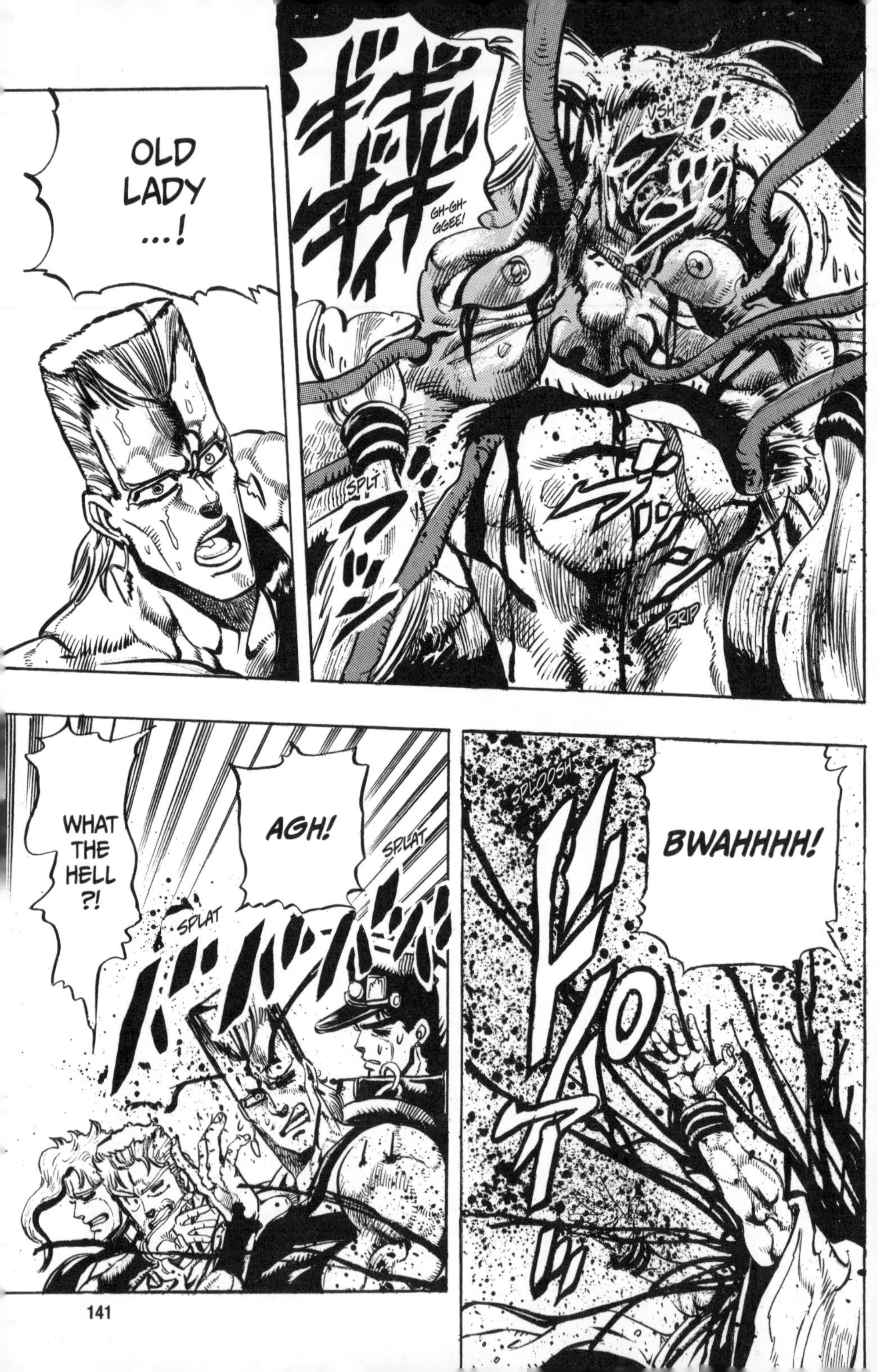
VSH
GH-GH-GGEE!
SPLT
RRIP
OLD LADY ...!
BWAHHHH!
SPLOOSH
AGH!
SPLAT
WHAT THE HELL ?!
SPLAT

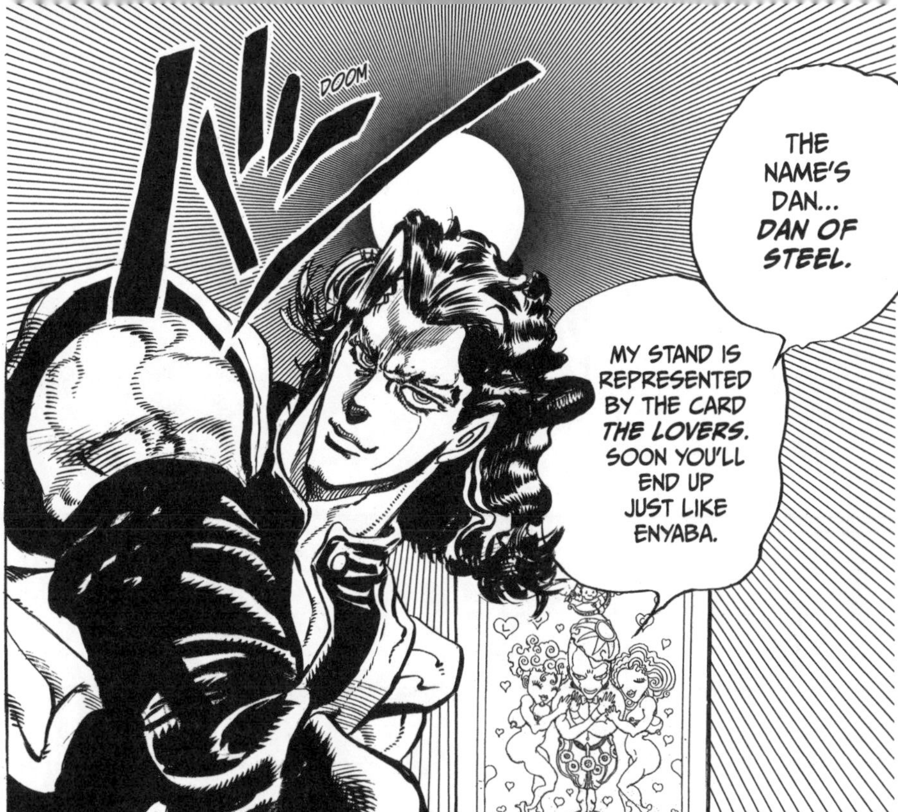
DOOM
THE NAME'S DAN... *DAN OF STEEL.*
MY STAND IS REPRESENTED BY THE CARD *THE LOVERS.* SOON YOU'LL END UP JUST LIKE ENYABA.
THE LOVER

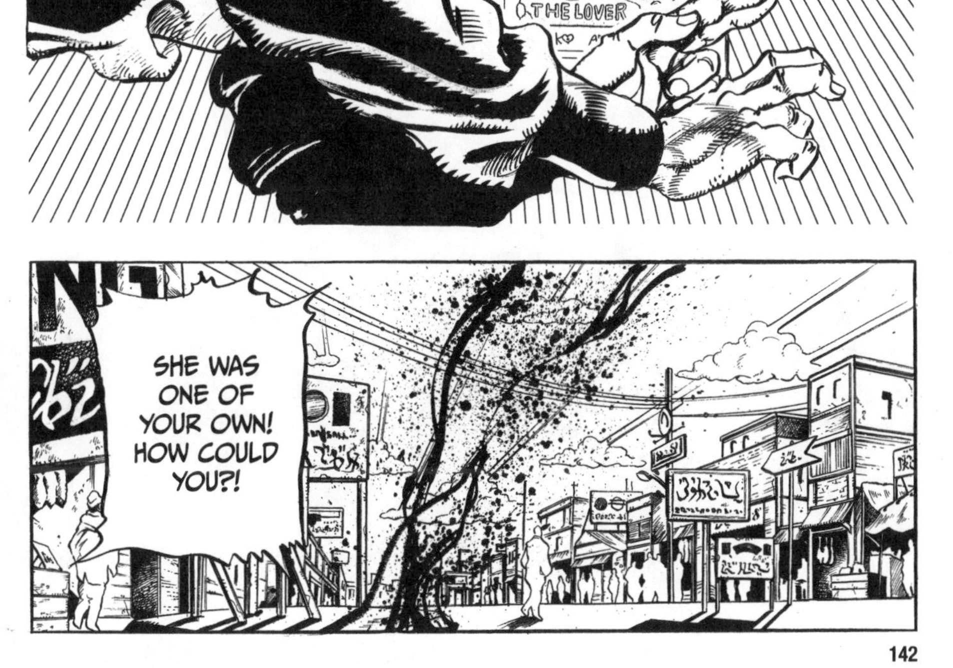
SHE WAS ONE OF YOUR OWN! HOW COULD YOU?!

CHAPTER 48: The Lovers PART 2

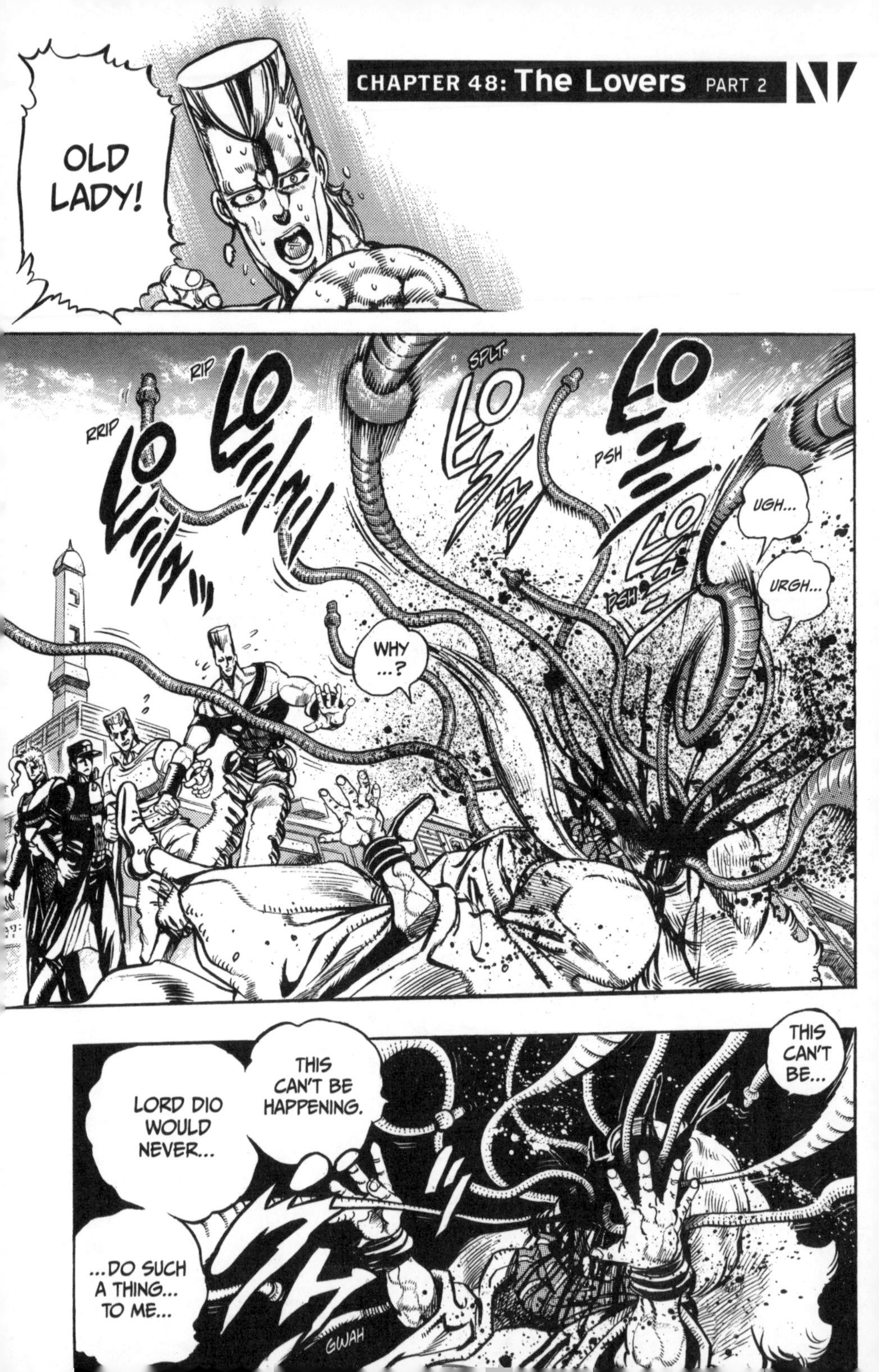
OLD LADY!
PSH
PSH
URGH...
UGH...
SPLT
RIP
RRIP
WHY ...?
THIS CAN'T BE...
THIS CAN'T BE HAPPENING.
LORD DIO WOULD NEVER...
...DO SUCH A THING... TO ME...
GWAH

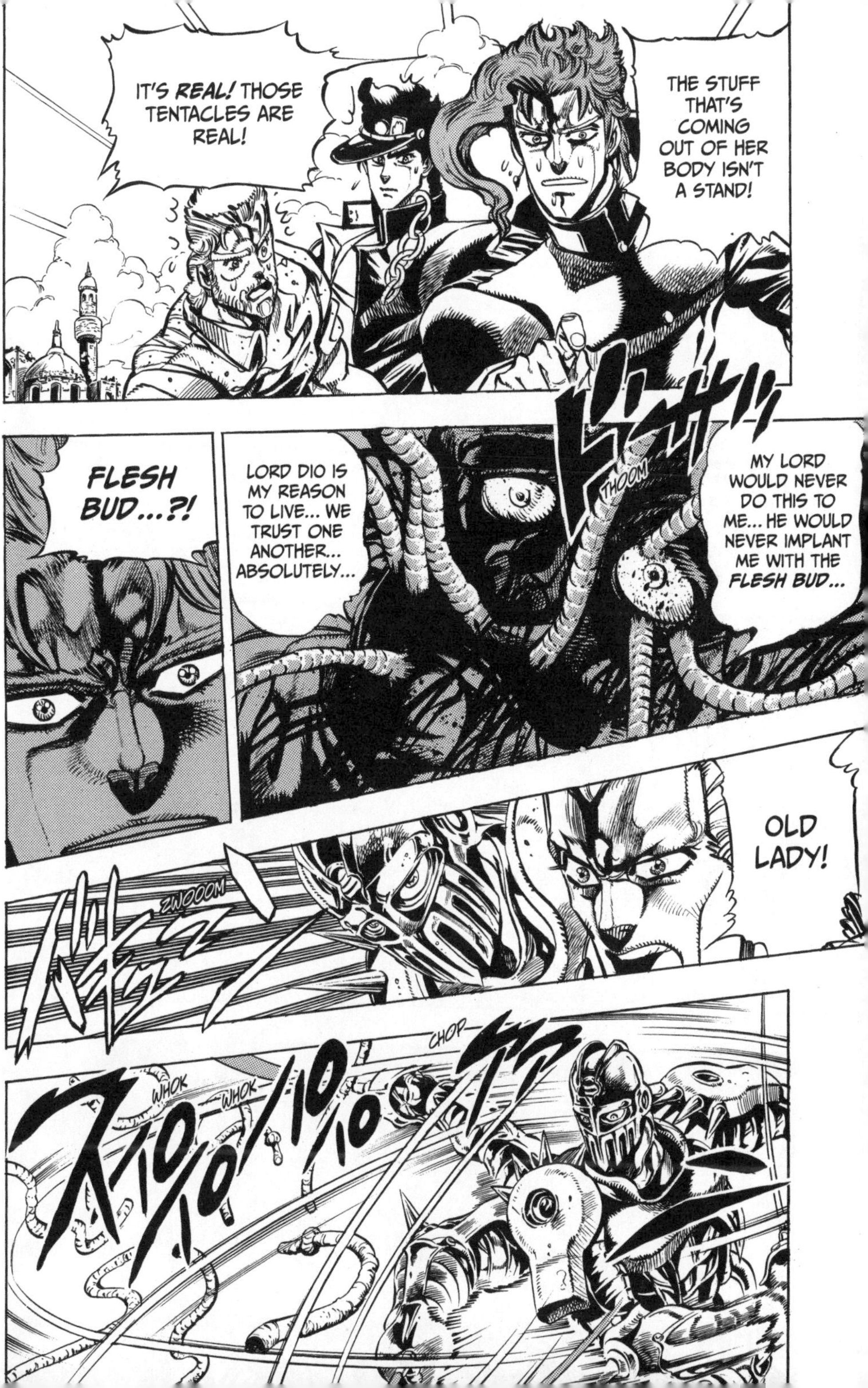

THE STUFF THAT'S COMING OUT OF HER BODY ISN'T A STAND!
IT'S *REAL!* THOSE TENTACLES ARE REAL!
MY LORD WOULD NEVER DO THIS TO ME... HE WOULD NEVER IMPLANT ME WITH THE *FLESH BUD*...
THOOM
LORD DIO IS MY REASON TO LIVE... WE TRUST ONE ANOTHER... ABSOLUTELY...
FLESH BUD...?!
OLD LADY!
ZWOOOM
CHOP
WHOK
WHOK

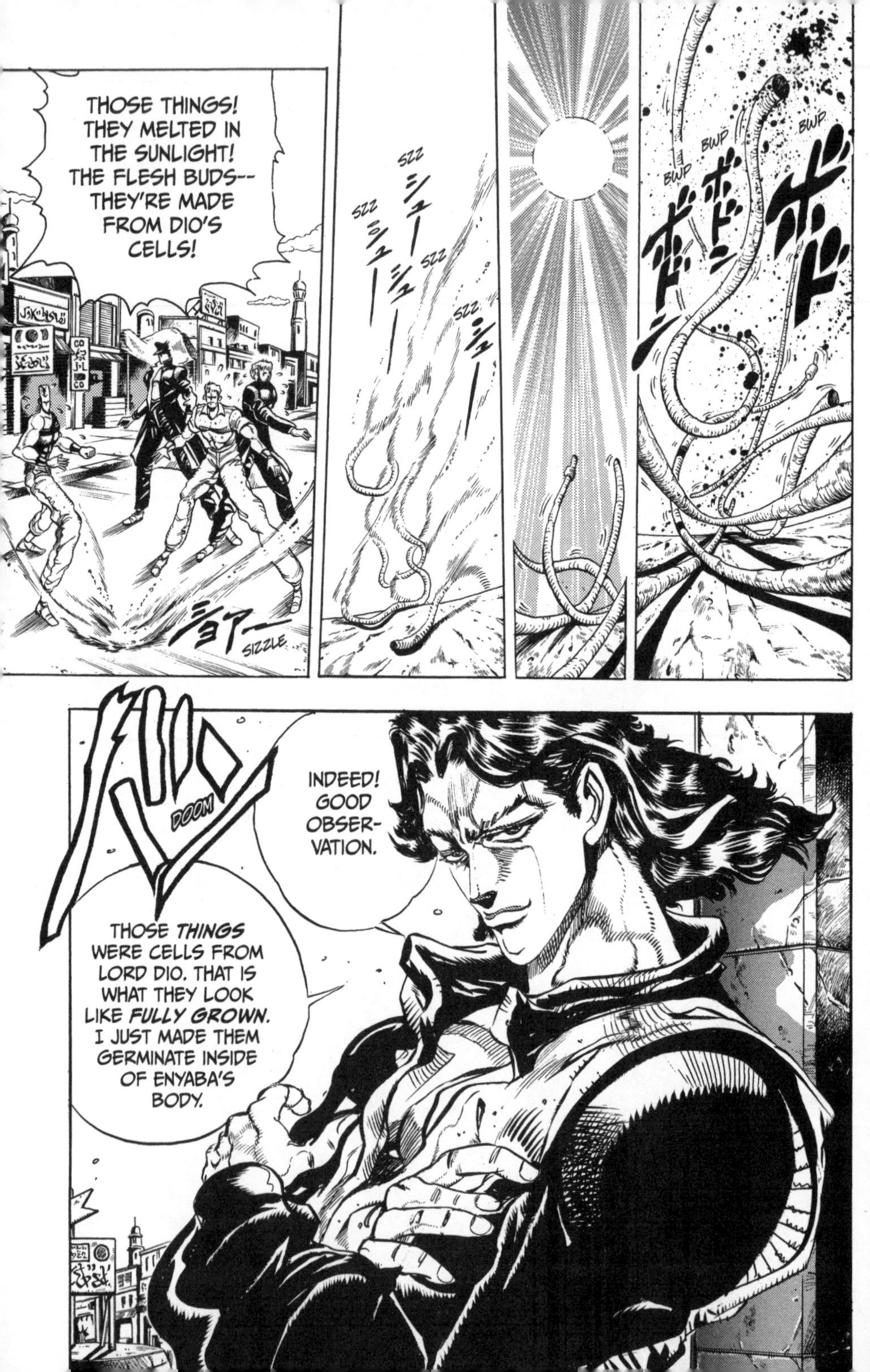
BWP
BWP
BWP
SZZ
SZZ
SZZ
SZZ
THOSE THINGS! THEY MELTED IN THE SUNLIGHT! THE FLESH BUDS-- THEY'RE MADE FROM DIO'S CELLS!
SIZZLE
DOOM
INDEED! GOOD OBSERVATION.
THOSE THINGS WERE CELLS FROM LORD DIO. THAT IS WHAT THEY LOOK LIKE FULLY GROWN. I JUST MADE THEM GERMINATE INSIDE OF ENYABA'S BODY.

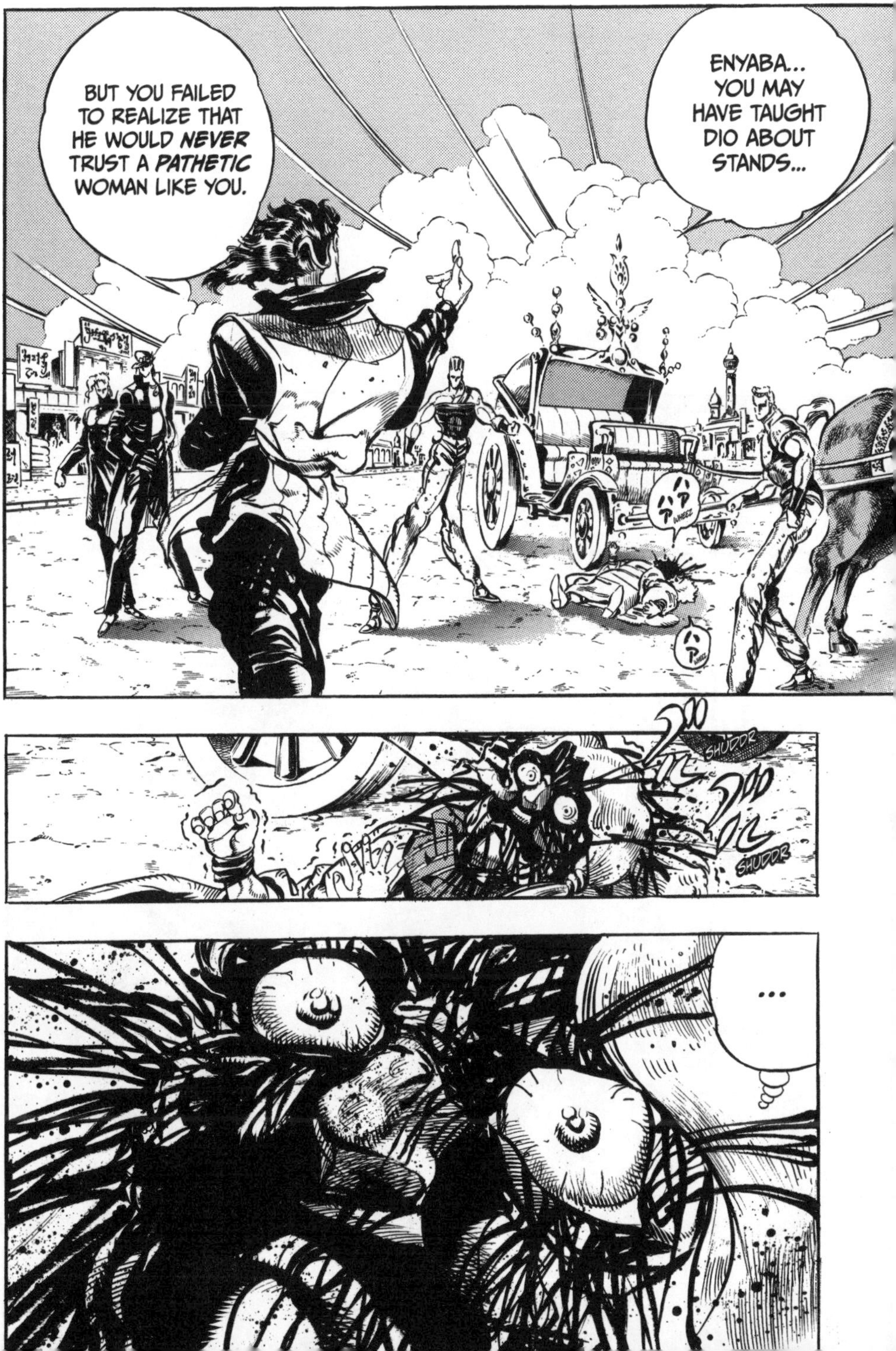
ENYABA... YOU MAY HAVE TAUGHT DIO ABOUT STANDS...
BUT YOU FAILED TO REALIZE THAT HE WOULD *NEVER* TRUST A *PATHETIC* WOMAN LIKE YOU.
WHEEZ
WHEEZ
SHUDDR
SHUDDR
...

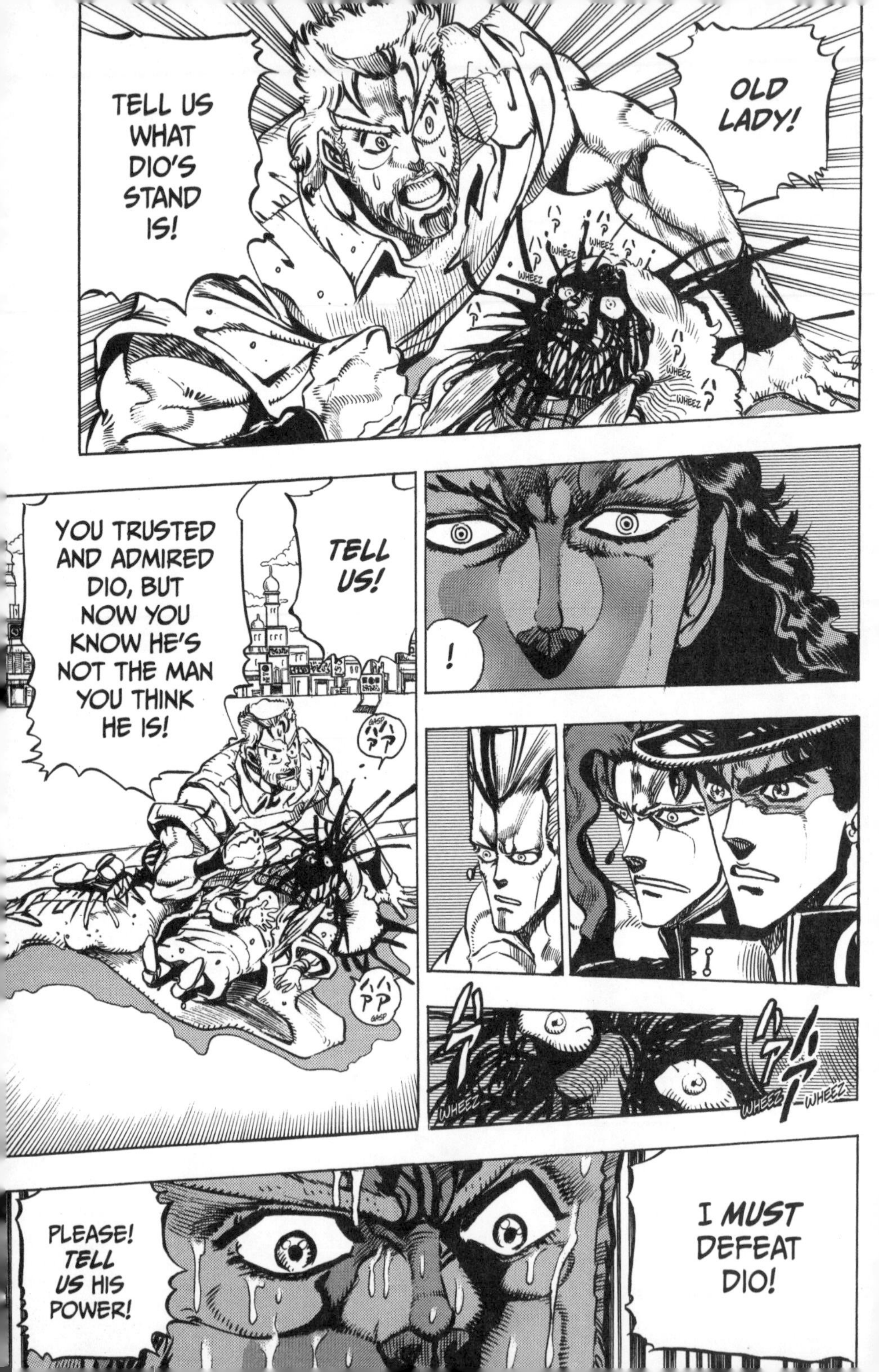
OLD LADY!
TELL US WHAT DIO'S STAND IS!
WHEEZ
WHEEZ
WHEEZ
WHEEZ
WHEEZ
!
WHEEZ
WHEEZ
WHEEZ
TELL US!
YOU TRUSTED AND ADMIRED DIO, BUT NOW YOU KNOW HE'S NOT THE MAN YOU THINK HE IS!
GASP
GASP
I MUST DEFEAT DIO!
PLEASE! TELL US HIS POWER!

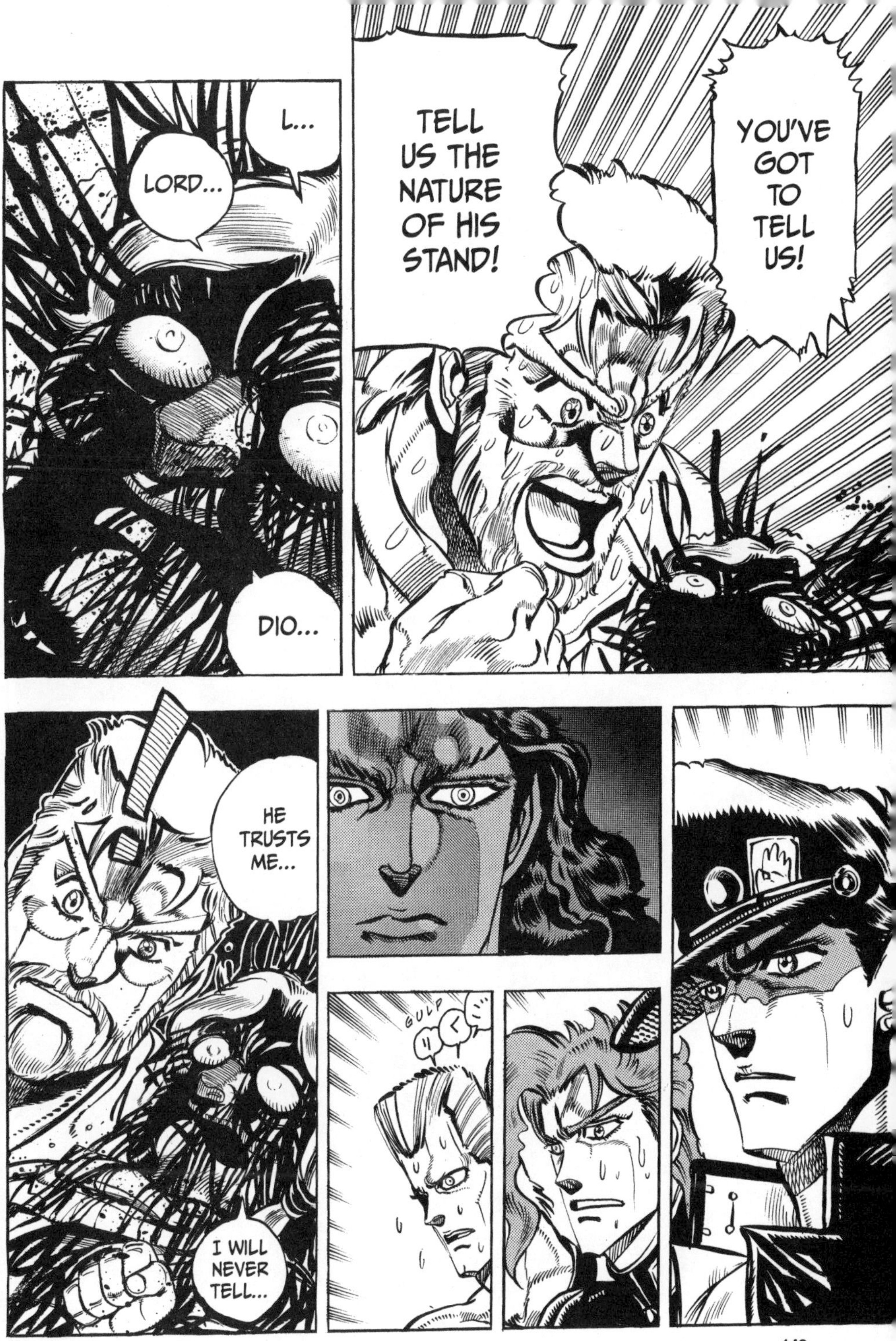
YOU'VE GOT TO TELL US!
TELL US THE NATURE OF HIS STAND!
L...
LORD...
DIO...
GULP
HE TRUSTS ME...
I WILL NEVER TELL...

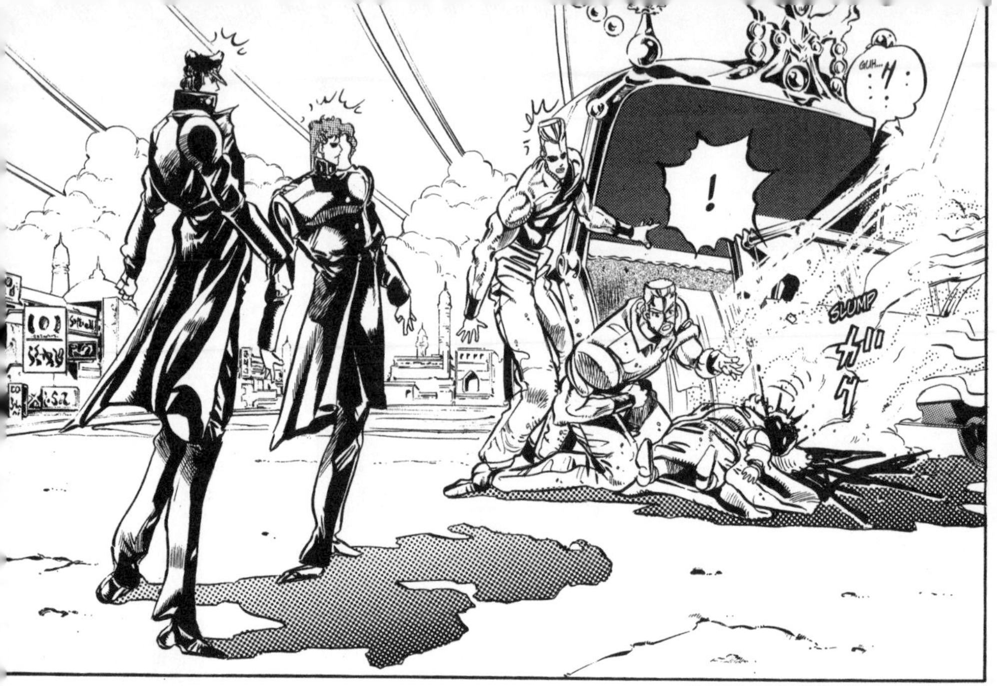
GUH...
!
SLUMP

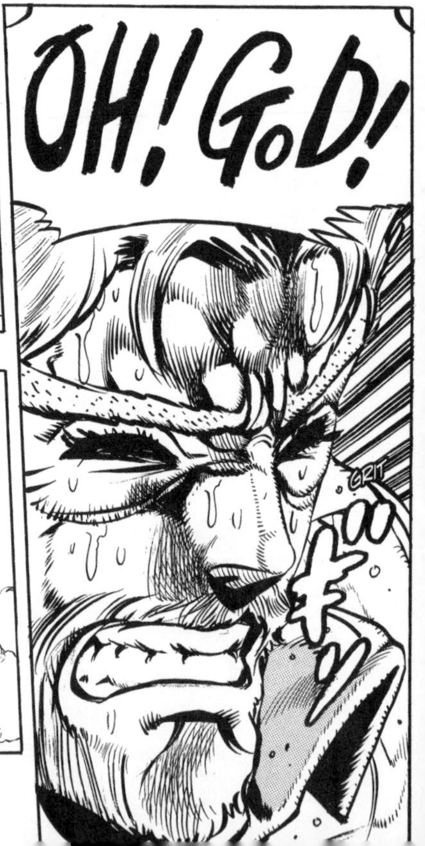
OH! GOD!
GRIT

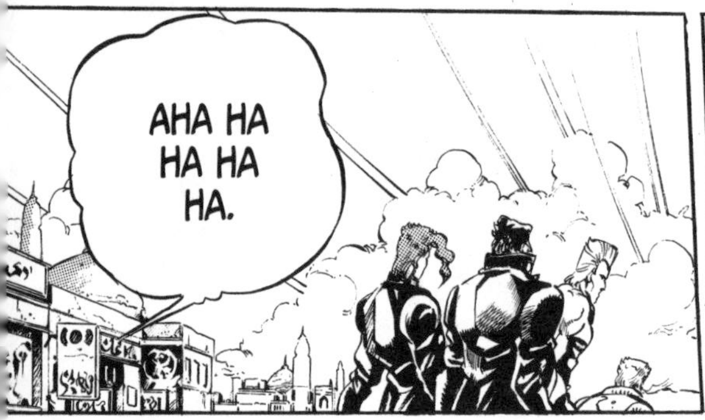
AHA HA HA HA HA.

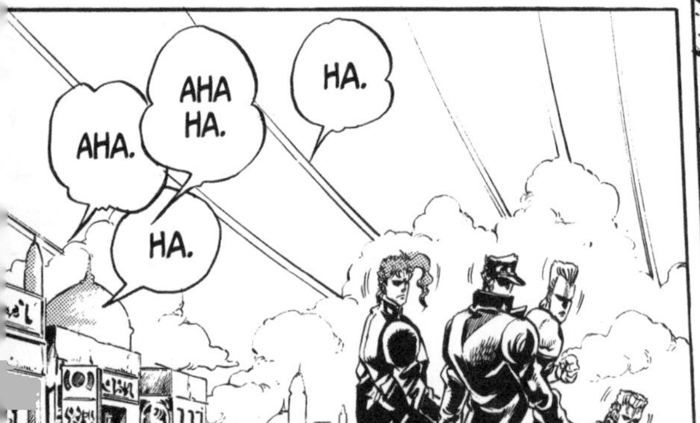
HA.
AHA HA.
AHA.
HA.

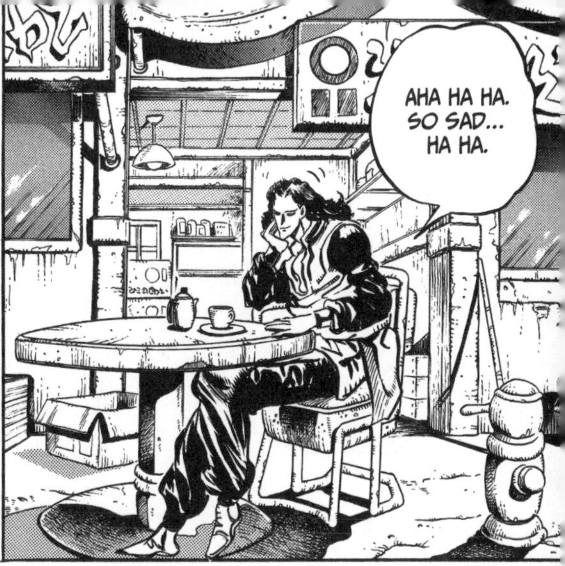
AHA HA HA. SO SAD... HA HA.

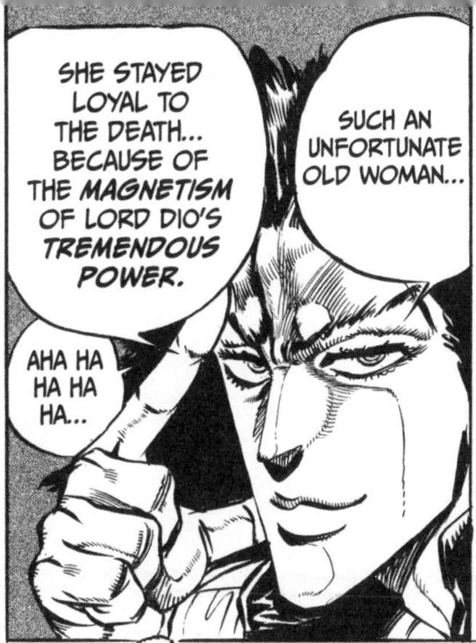
SUCH AN UNFORTUNATE OLD WOMAN...
SHE STAYED LOYAL TO THE DEATH... BECAUSE OF THE *MAGNETISM* OF LORD DIO'S *TREMENDOUS POWER.*
AHA HA HA HA HA...

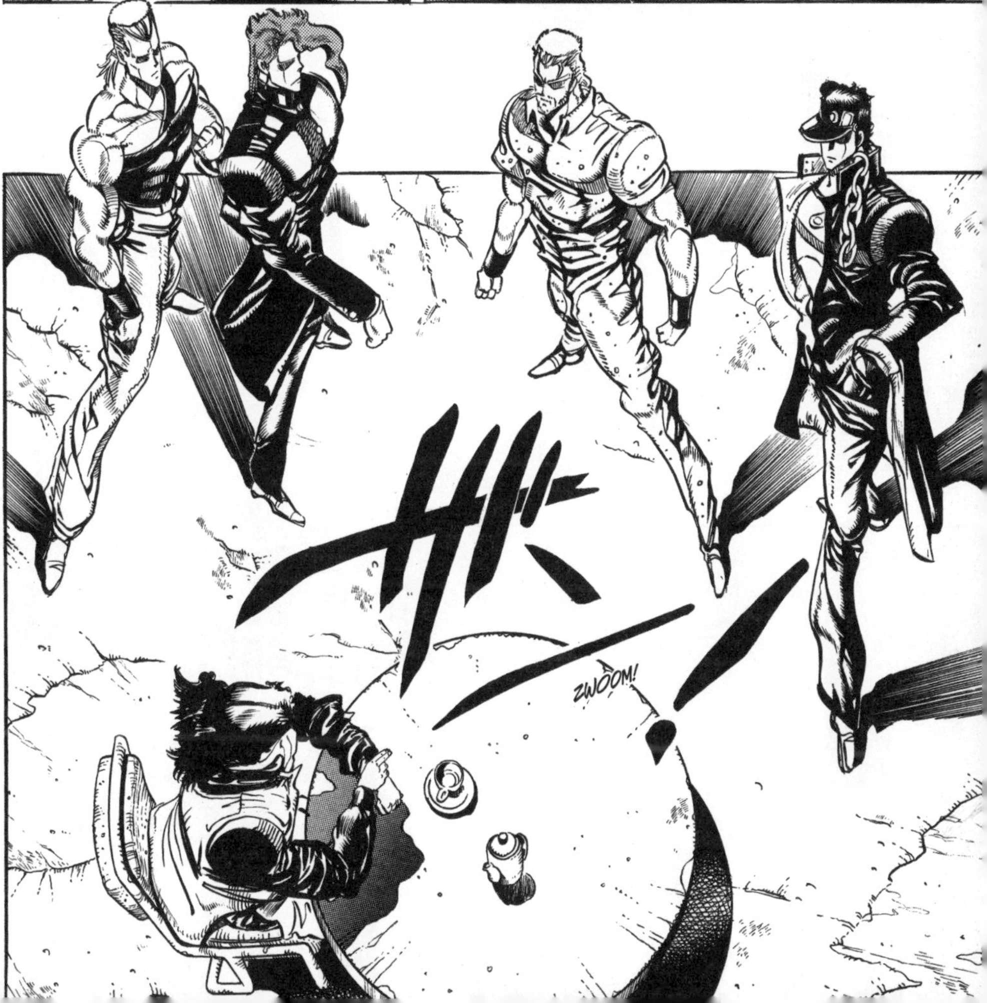
ZWOOM!

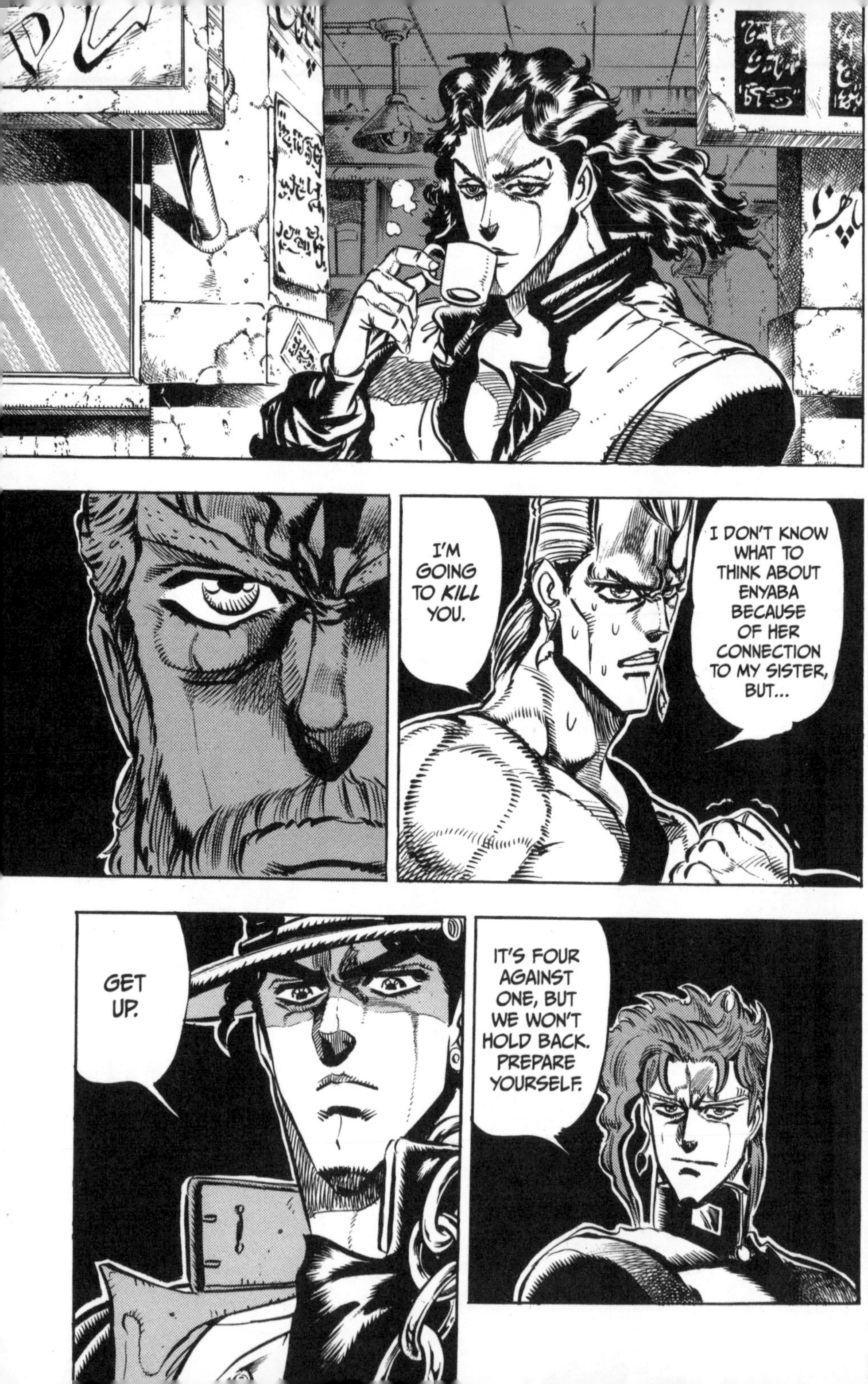
I DON'T KNOW WHAT TO THINK ABOUT ENYABA BECAUSE OF HER CONNECTION TO MY SISTER, BUT...
I'M GOING TO *KILL* YOU.
IT'S FOUR AGAINST ONE, BUT WE WON'T HOLD BACK. PREPARE YOURSELF.
GET UP.

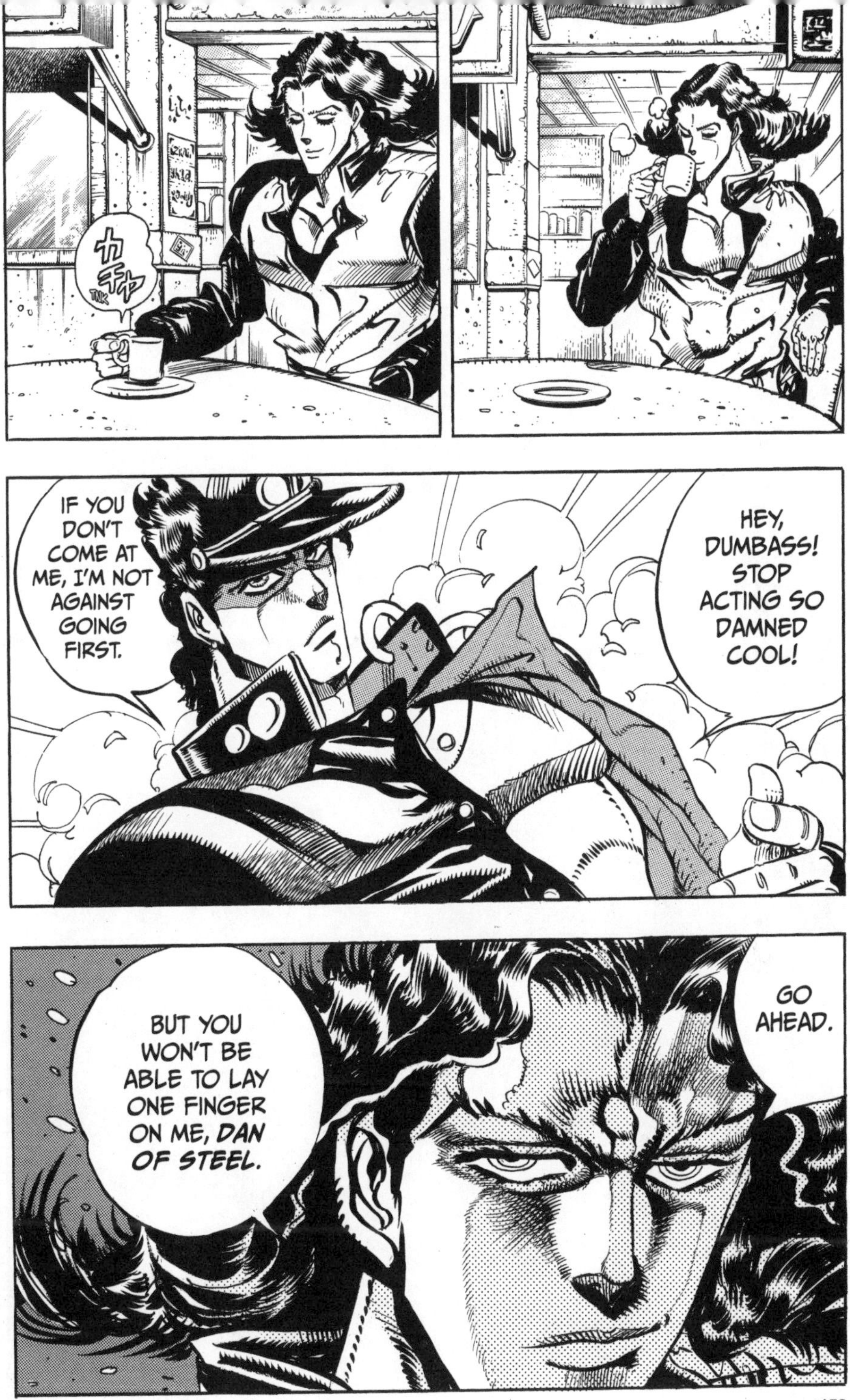
カチャ
TINK
HEY, DUMBASS! STOP ACTING SO DAMNED COOL!
IF YOU DON'T COME AT ME, I'M NOT AGAINST GOING FIRST.
GO AHEAD.
BUT YOU WON'T BE ABLE TO LAY ONE FINGER ON ME, *DAN OF STEEL.*

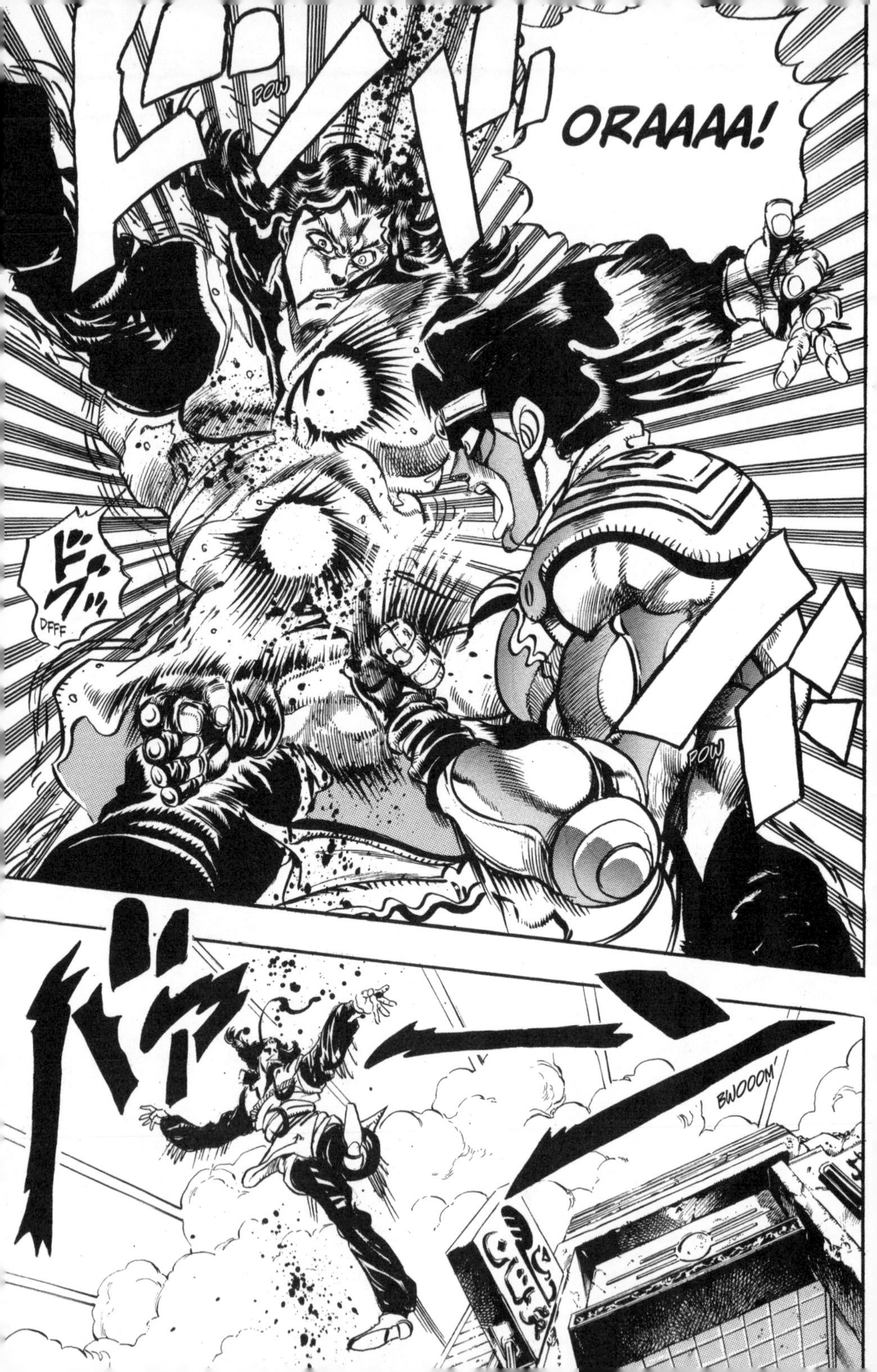
ORAAAA!
POW
POW
ドブッ
DFFF
BWOOOM
バァーン

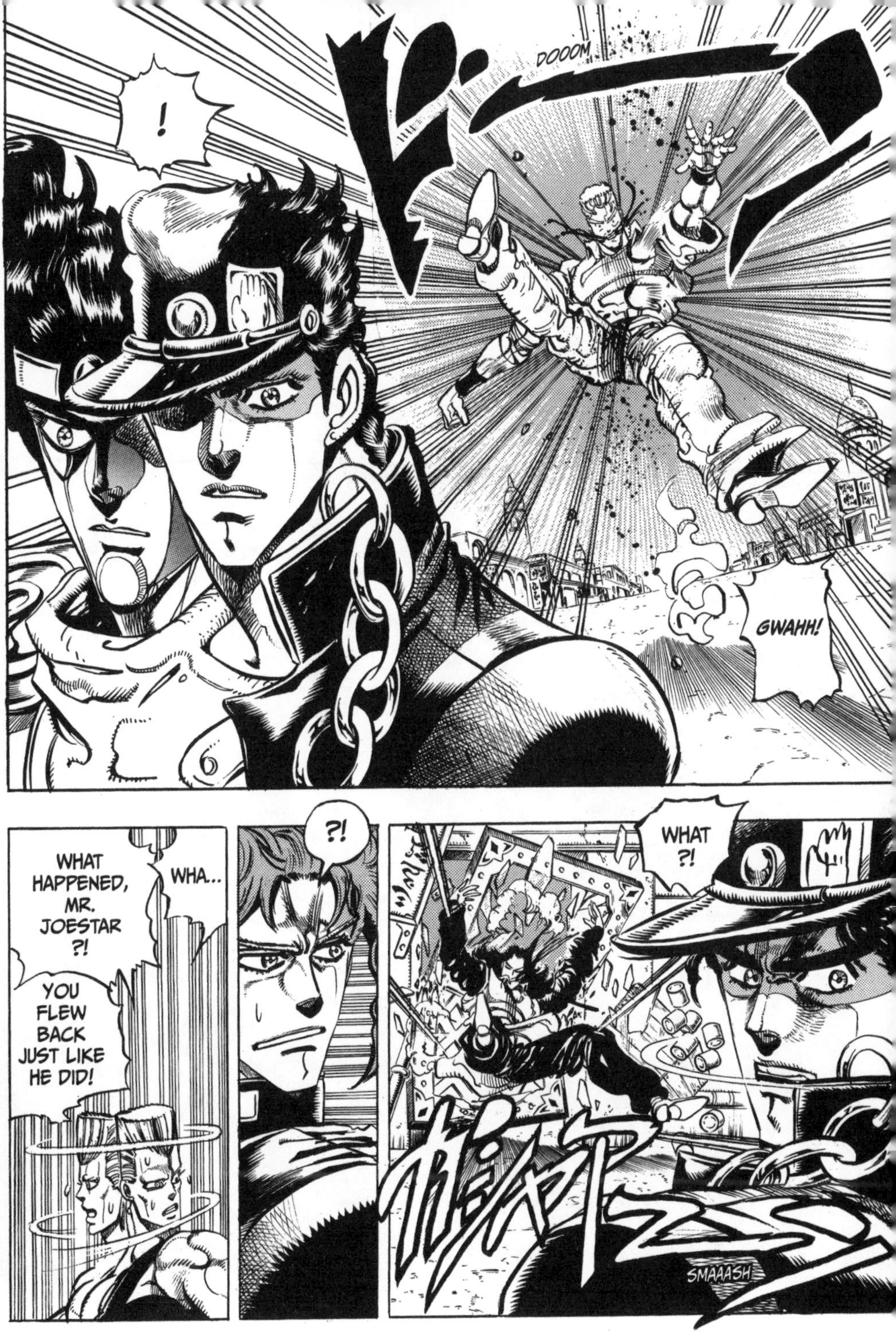
DOOOM
GWAHH!
!
WHAT ?!
SMAAASH
?!
WHA...
WHAT HAPPENED, MR. JOESTAR ?!
YOU FLEW BACK JUST LIKE HE DID!

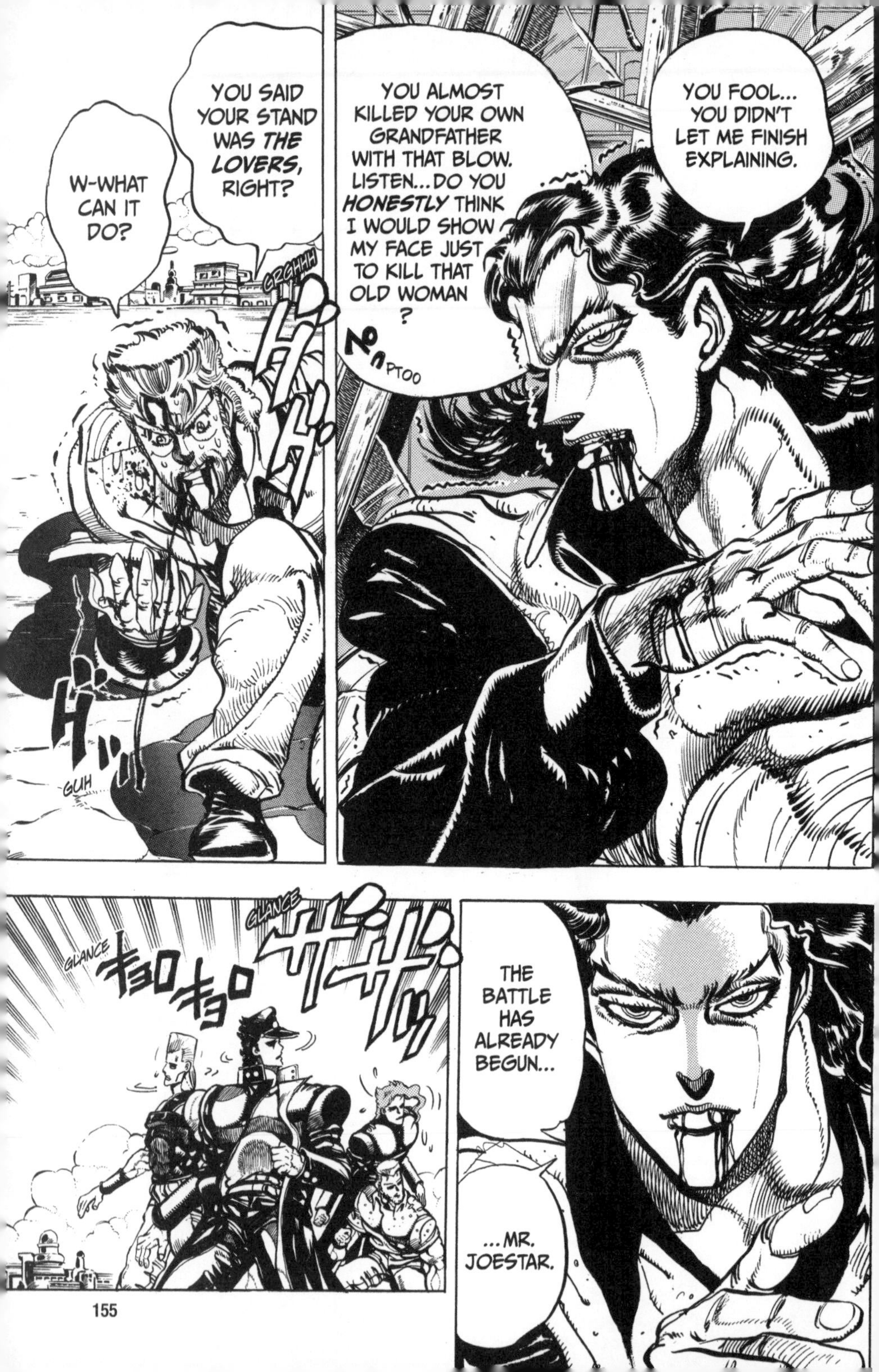
YOU FOOL... YOU DIDN'T LET ME FINISH EXPLAINING.
YOU ALMOST KILLED YOUR OWN GRANDFATHER WITH THAT BLOW. LISTEN...DO YOU *HONESTLY* THINK I WOULD SHOW MY FACE JUST TO KILL THAT OLD WOMAN?
PTOO
YOU SAID YOUR STAND WAS *THE LOVERS,* RIGHT?
GRGHHH
W-WHAT CAN IT DO?
GUH
THE BATTLE HAS ALREADY BEGUN...
...MR. JOESTAR.
GLANCE
GLANCE

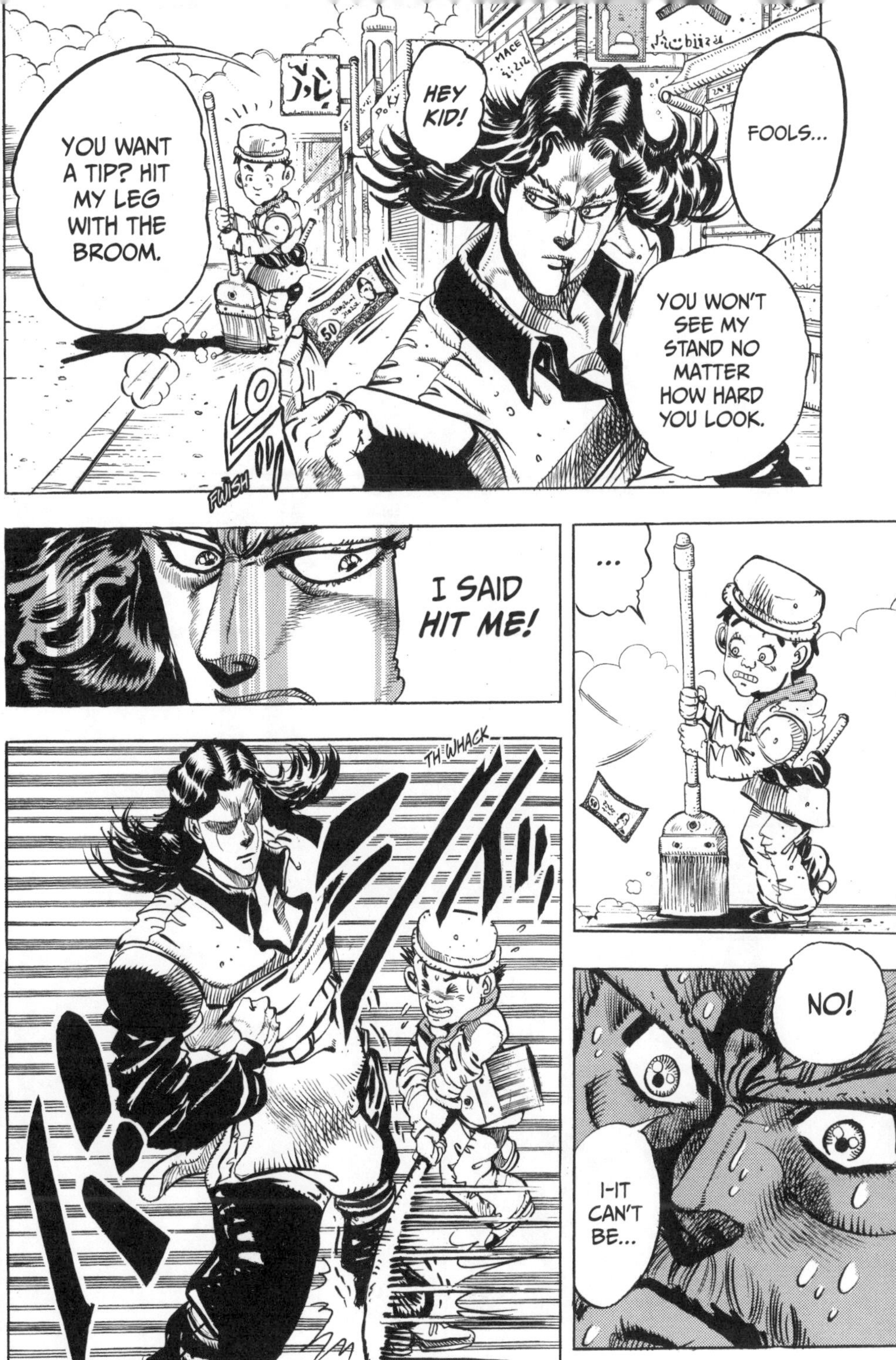

FOOLS...
YOU WON'T SEE MY STAND NO MATTER HOW HARD YOU LOOK.
HEY KID!
YOU WANT A TIP? HIT MY LEG WITH THE BROOM.
FWISH
...
I SAID HIT ME!
NO!
I-IT CAN'T BE...
THWHACK

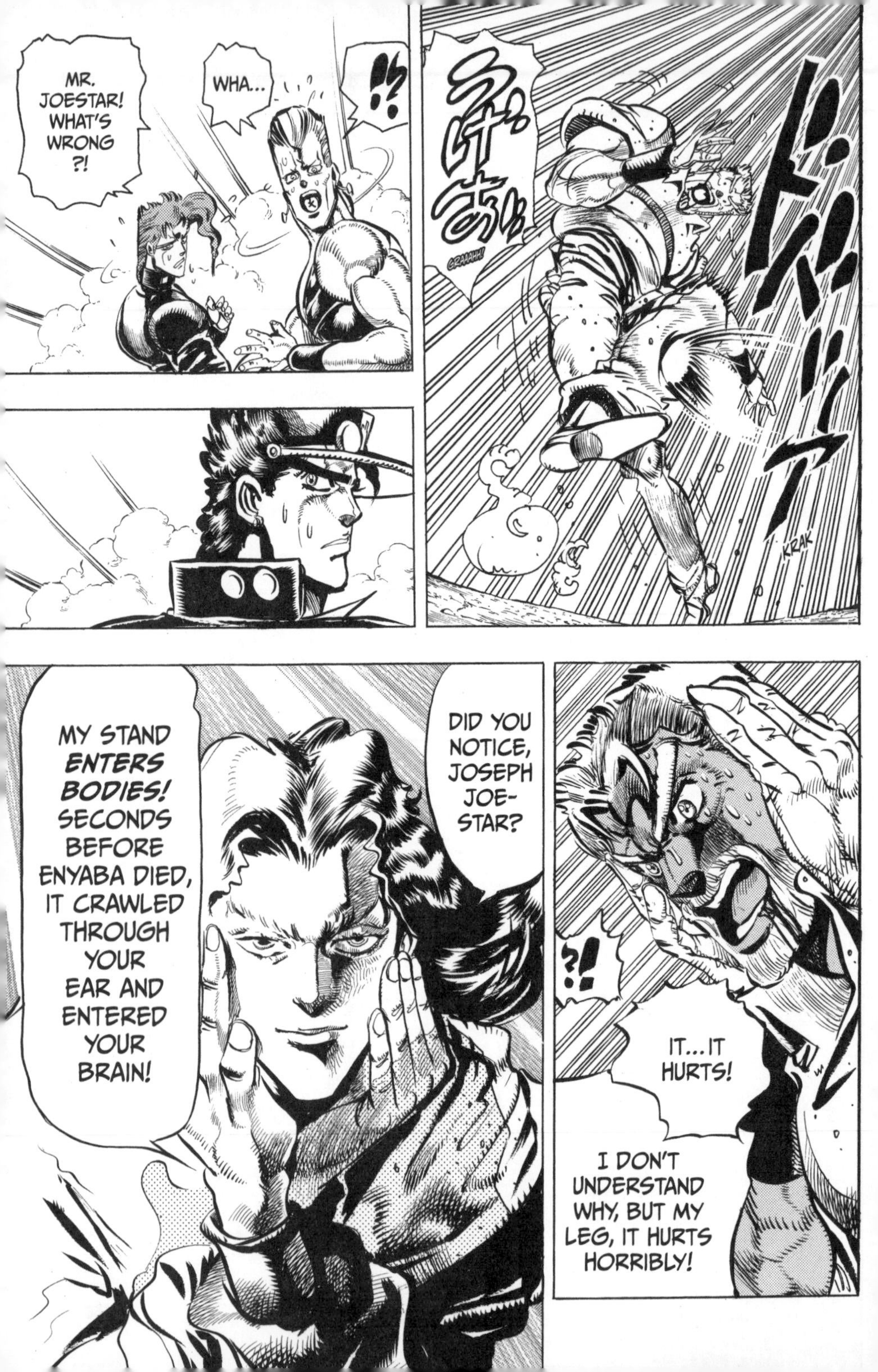
GRAAAHH!
KRAK
!?
WHA...
MR. JOESTAR! WHAT'S WRONG ?!
?!
IT... IT HURTS!
I DON'T UNDERSTAND WHY, BUT MY LEG, IT HURTS HORRIBLY!
DID YOU NOTICE, JOSEPH JOE-STAR?
MY STAND *ENTERS BODIES!* SECONDS BEFORE ENYABA DIED, IT CRAWLED THROUGH YOUR EAR AND ENTERED YOUR BRAIN!

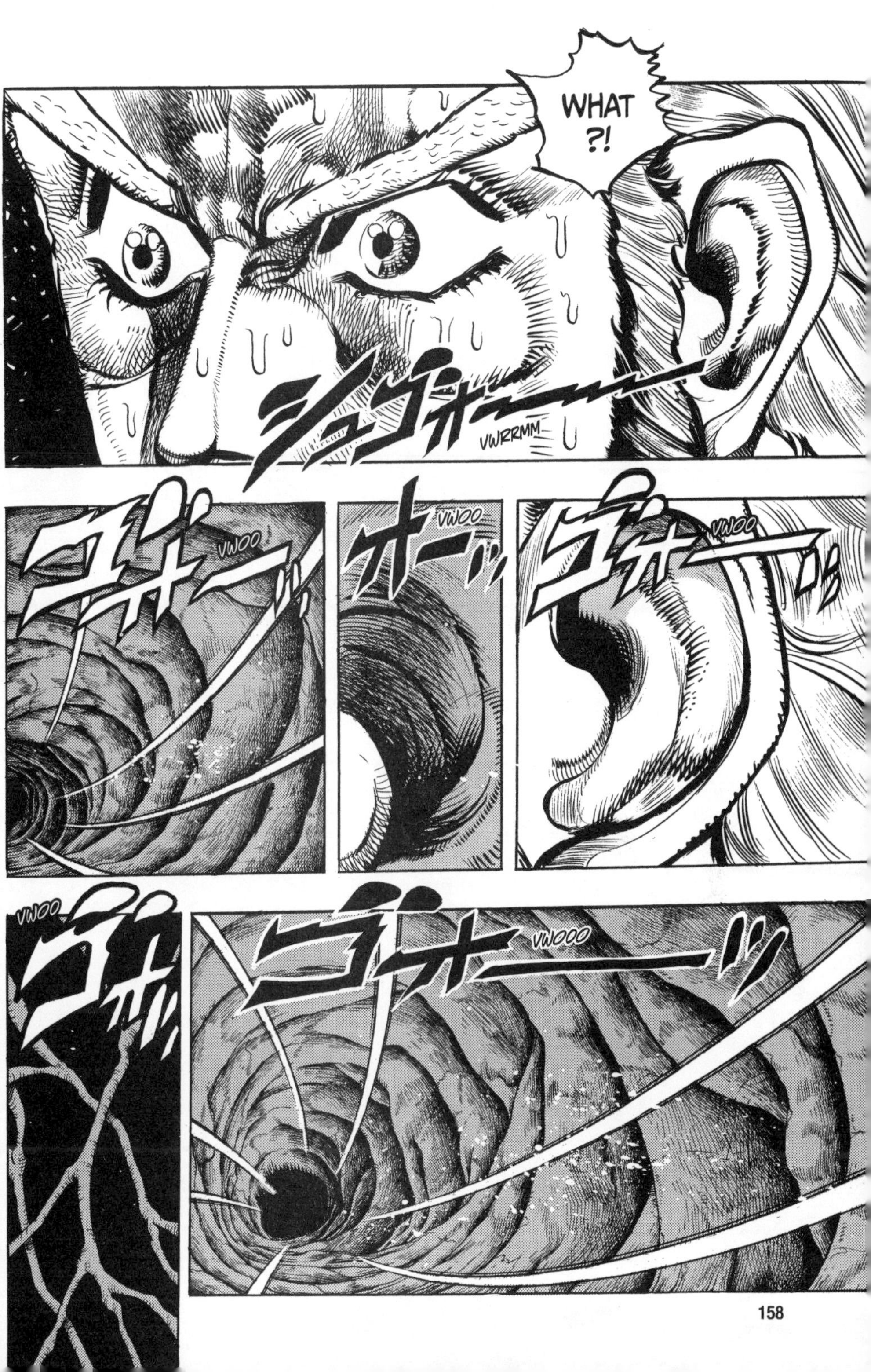
WHAT ?!
VWRRMM
VWOO
VWOO
VWOO
VWOOO
VWOO

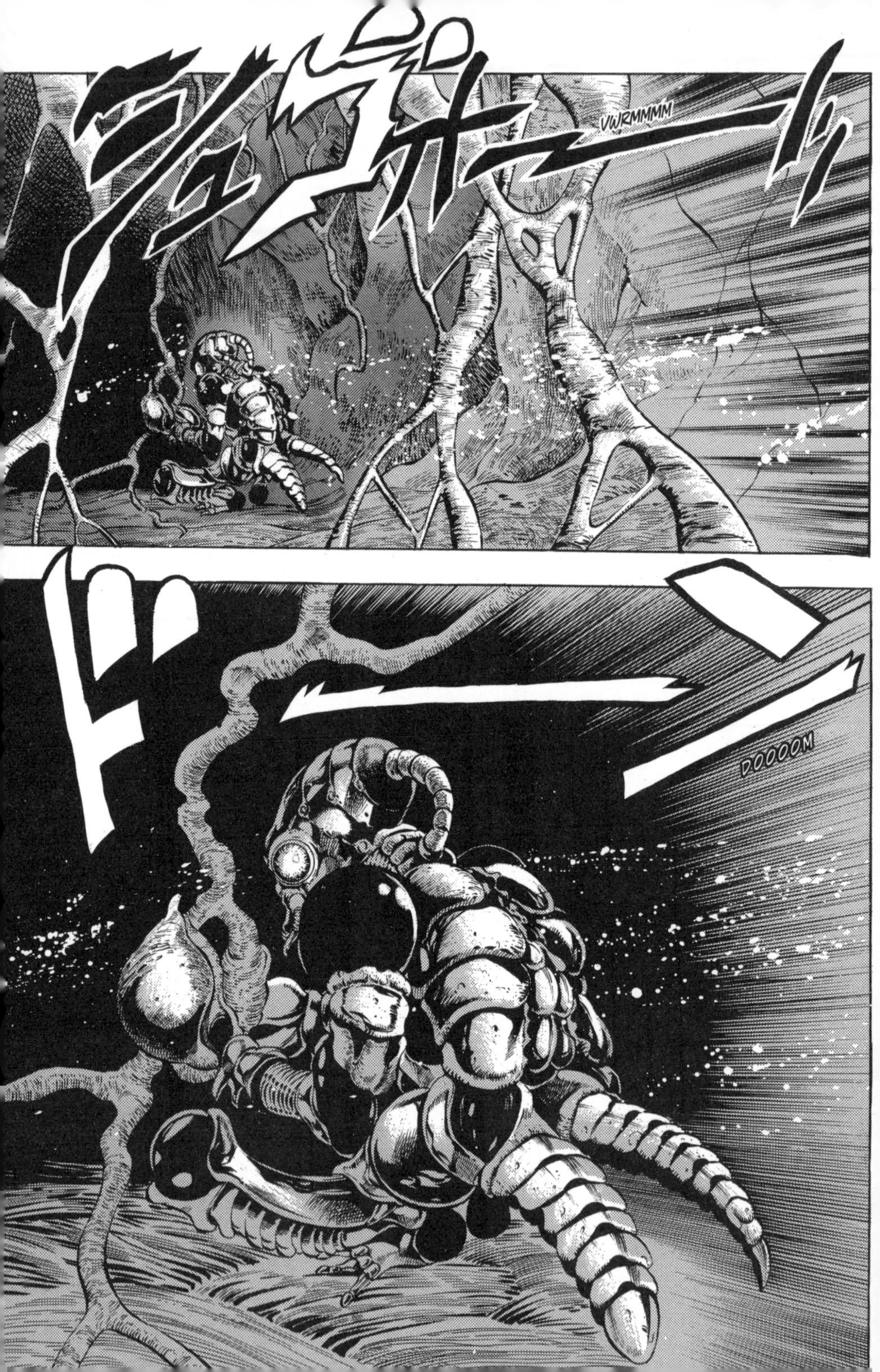
VWRMMMM
ドーン
DOOOOM

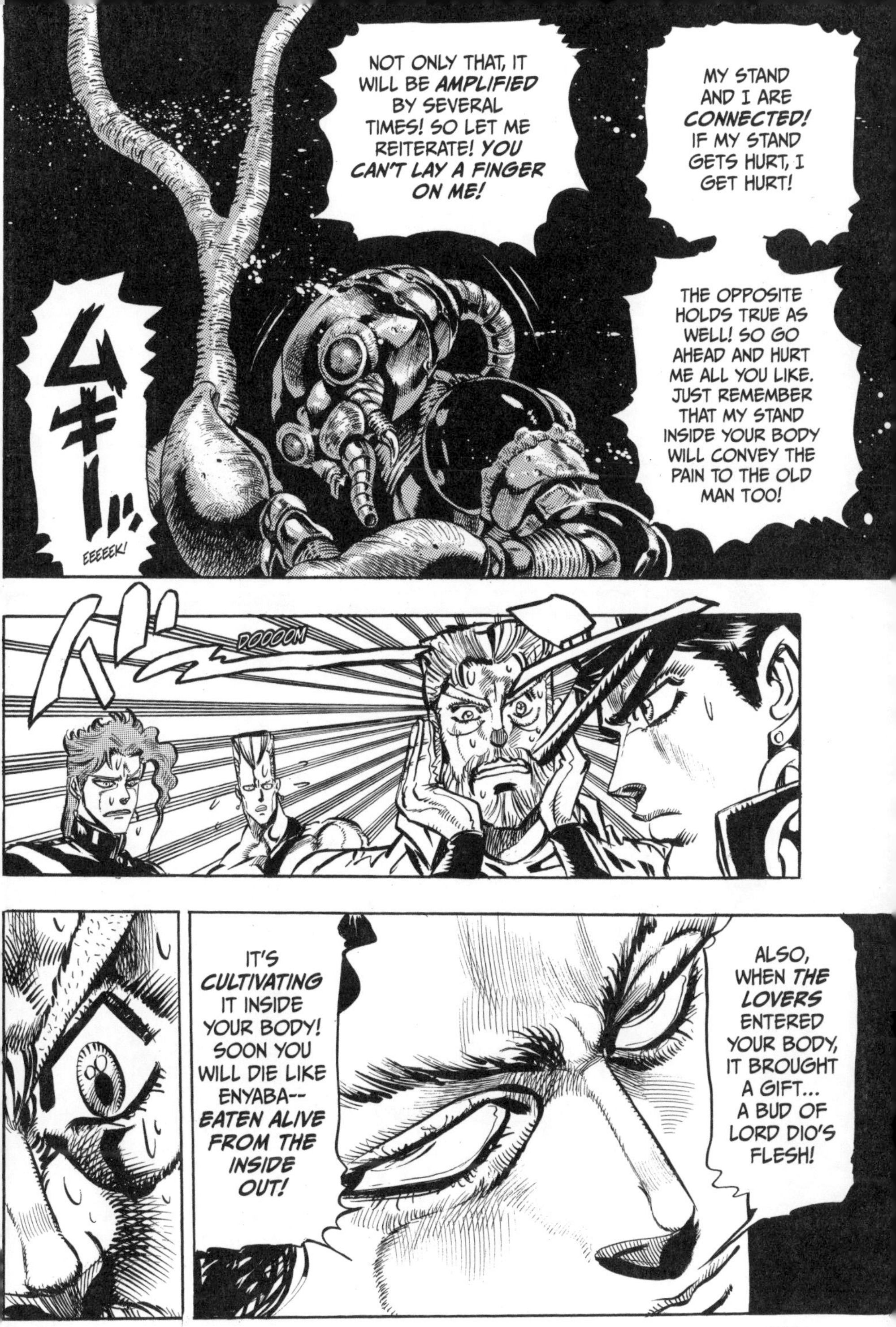
MY STAND AND I ARE CONNECTED! IF MY STAND GETS HURT, I GET HURT!
THE OPPOSITE HOLDS TRUE AS WELL! SO GO AHEAD AND HURT ME ALL YOU LIKE. JUST REMEMBER THAT MY STAND INSIDE YOUR BODY WILL CONVEY THE PAIN TO THE OLD MAN TOO!
NOT ONLY THAT, IT WILL BE AMPLIFIED BY SEVERAL TIMES! SO LET ME REITERATE! YOU CAN'T LAY A FINGER ON ME!
EEEEEK!
DOOOOM
ALSO, WHEN THE LOVERS ENTERED YOUR BODY, IT BROUGHT A GIFT... A BUD OF LORD DIO'S FLESH!
IT'S CULTIVATING IT INSIDE YOUR BODY! SOON YOU WILL DIE LIKE ENYABA-- EATEN ALIVE FROM THE INSIDE OUT!

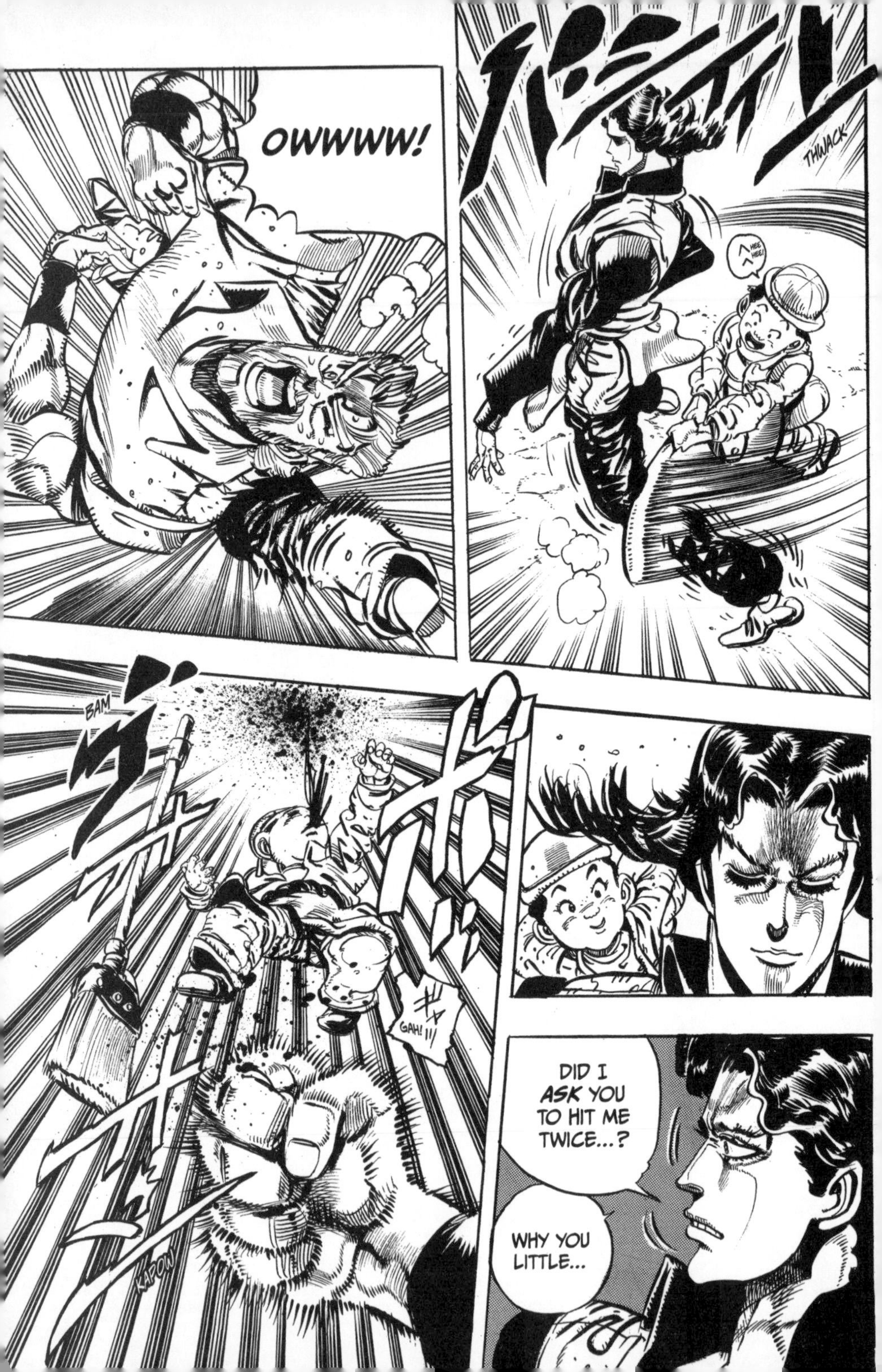
THWACK
HEE HEE!
OWWWW!
DID I ASK YOU TO HIT ME TWICE...?
WHY YOU LITTLE...
BAM
GAH!
KAPOW

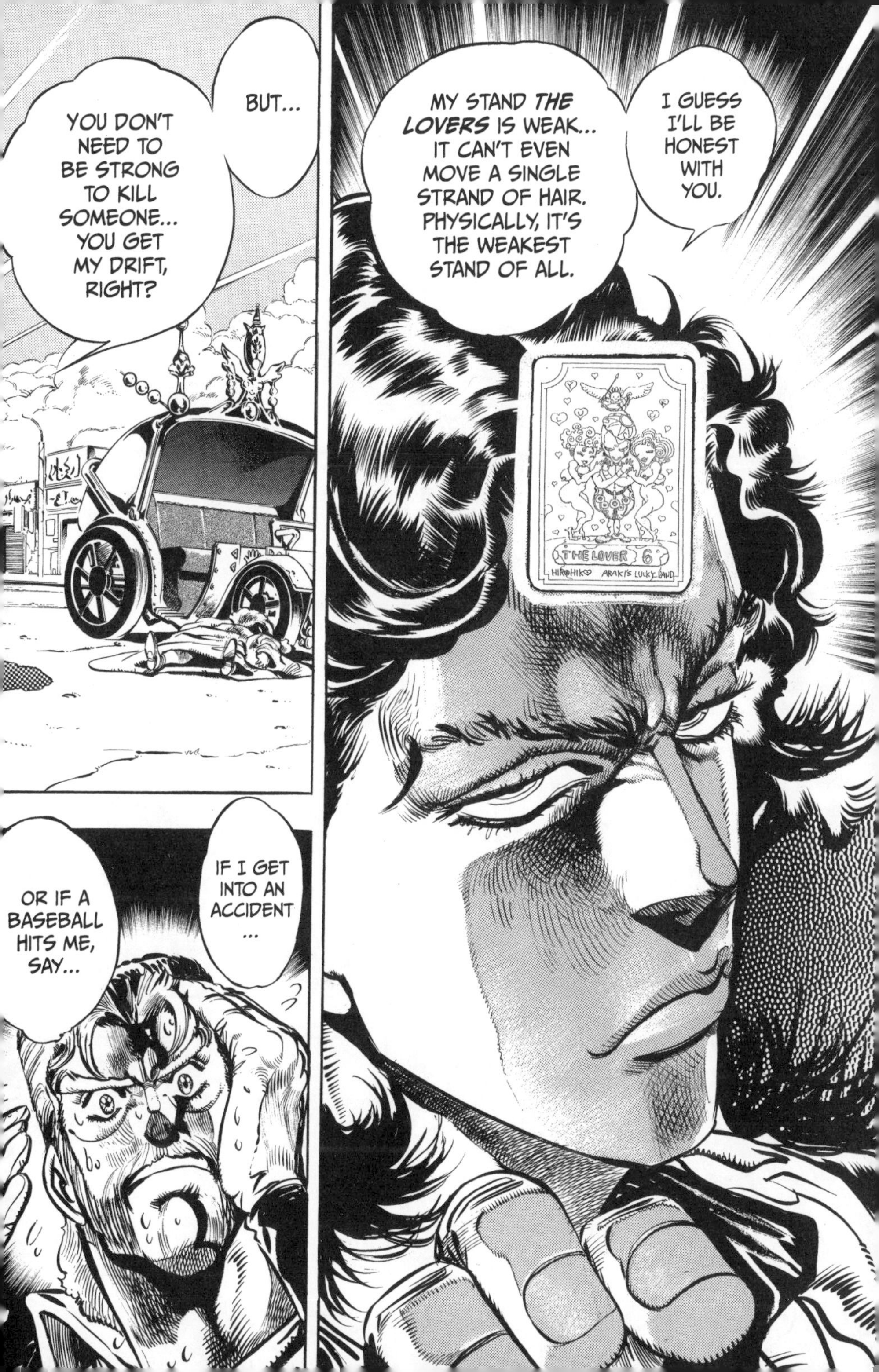
I GUESS I'LL BE HONEST WITH YOU.
MY STAND *THE LOVERS* IS WEAK... IT CAN'T EVEN MOVE A SINGLE STRAND OF HAIR. PHYSICALLY, IT'S THE WEAKEST STAND OF ALL.
THE LOVER 6
HIROHIKO ARAKI'S LUCKY LAND
BUT...
YOU DON'T NEED TO BE STRONG TO KILL SOMEONE... YOU GET MY DRIFT, RIGHT?
IF I GET INTO AN ACCIDENT ...
OR IF A BASEBALL HITS ME, SAY...

CHAPTER 49: The Lovers PART 3

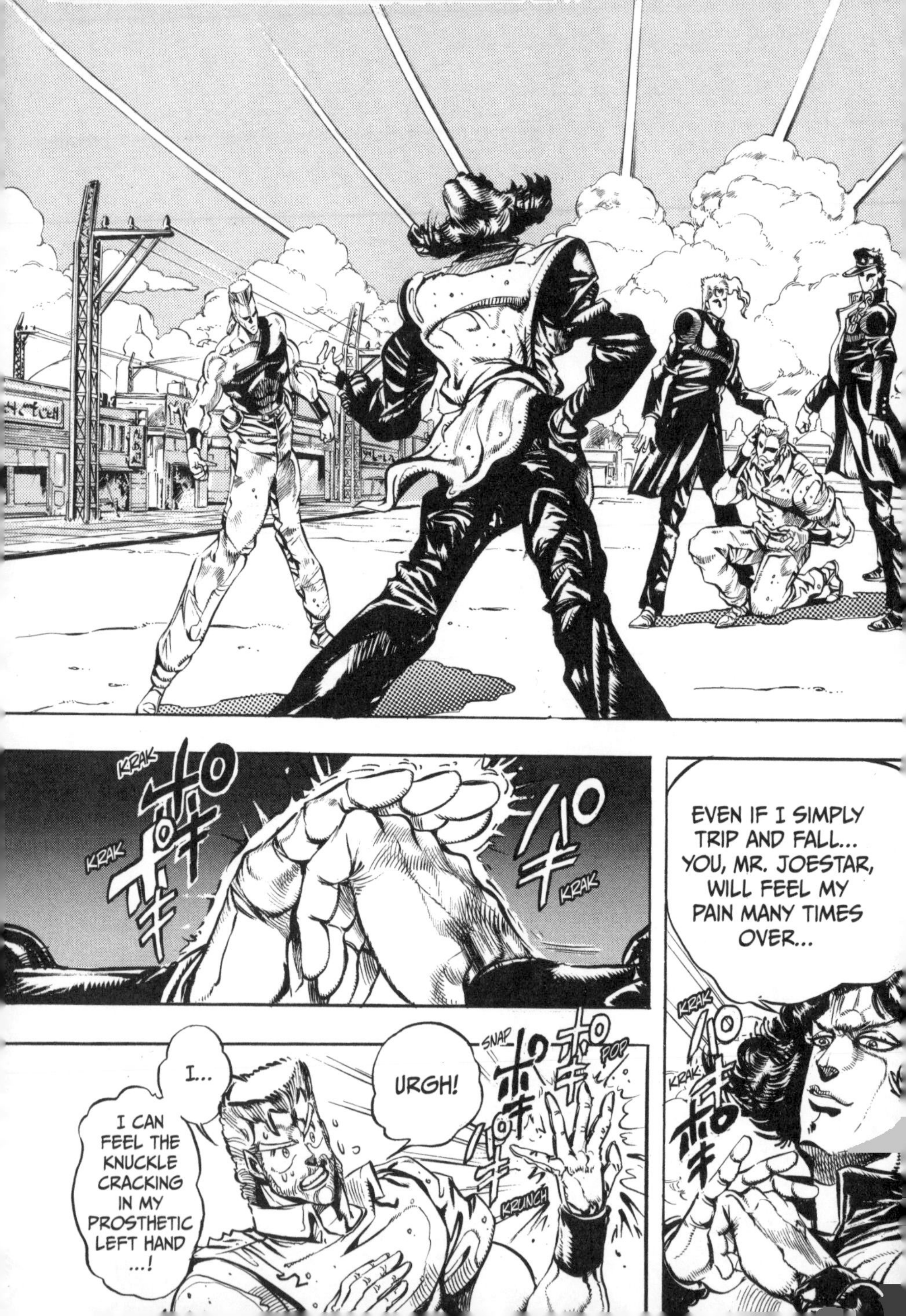
EVEN IF I SIMPLY TRIP AND FALL... YOU, MR. JOESTAR, WILL FEEL MY PAIN MANY TIMES OVER...
KRAK
KRAK
KRAK
KRAK
KRAK
SNAP
POP
KRUNCH
URGH!
I...
I CAN FEEL THE KNUCKLE CRACKING IN MY PROSTHETIC LEFT HAND ...!

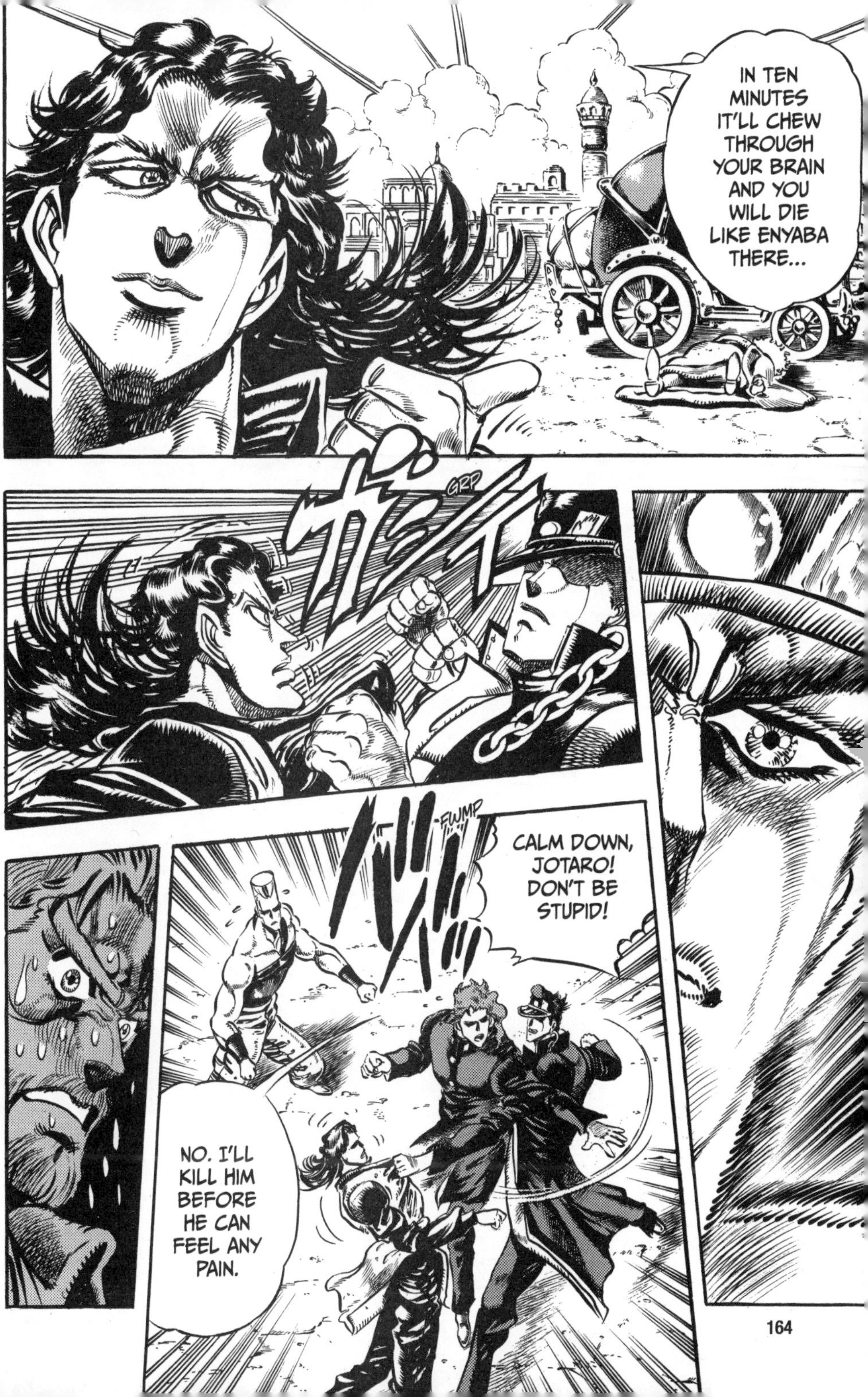
IN TEN MINUTES IT'LL CHEW THROUGH YOUR BRAIN AND YOU WILL DIE LIKE ENYABA THERE...
GRP
FWUMP
CALM DOWN, JOTARO! DON'T BE STUPID!
NO. I'LL KILL HIM BEFORE HE CAN FEEL ANY PAIN.

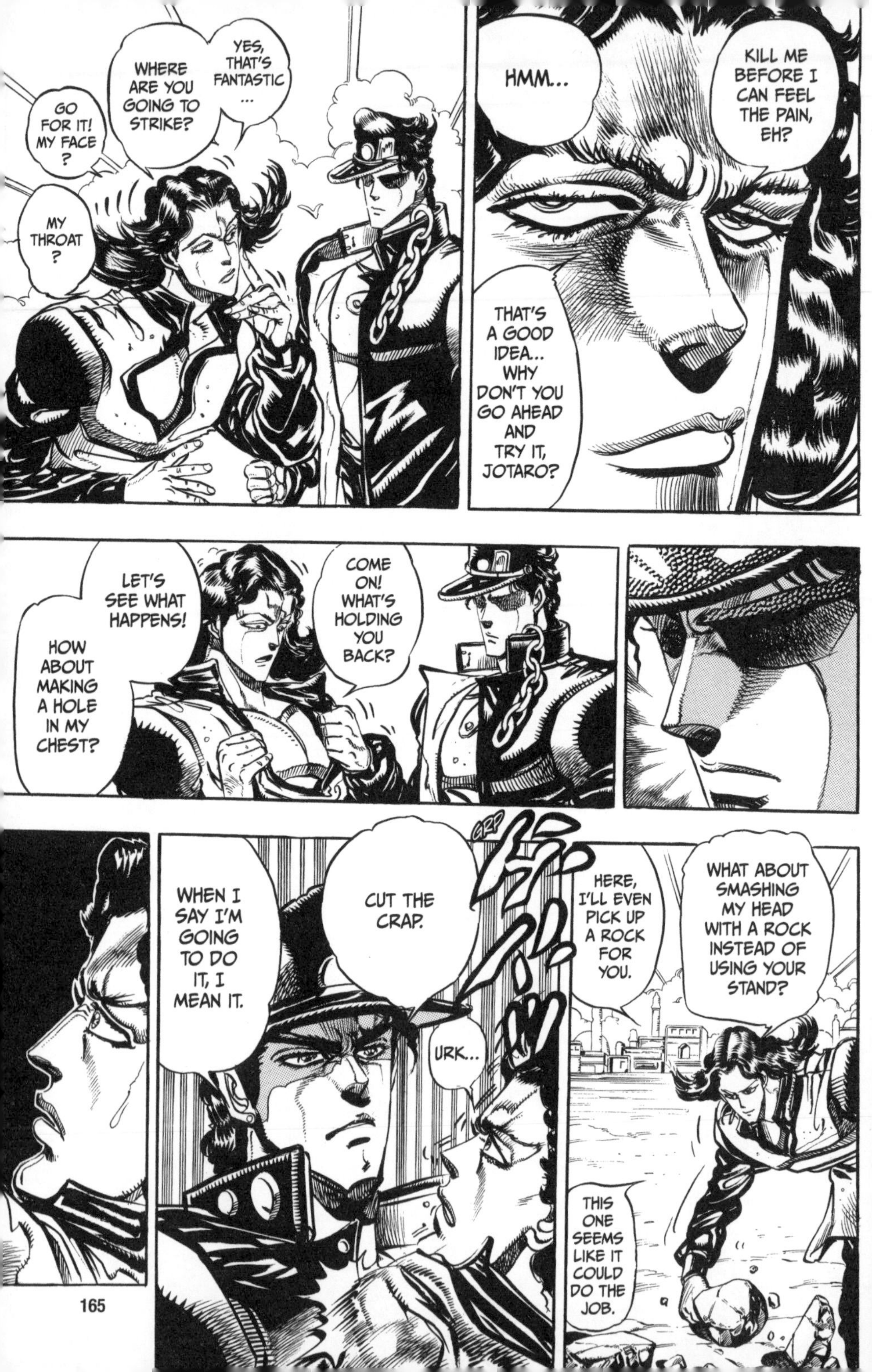
KILL ME BEFORE I CAN FEEL THE PAIN, EH?
HMM...
THAT'S A GOOD IDEA... WHY DON'T YOU GO AHEAD AND TRY IT, JOTARO?
YES, THAT'S FANTASTIC...
WHERE ARE YOU GOING TO STRIKE?
GO FOR IT! MY FACE?
MY THROAT?
COME ON! WHAT'S HOLDING YOU BACK?
LET'S SEE WHAT HAPPENS!
HOW ABOUT MAKING A HOLE IN MY CHEST?
WHAT ABOUT SMASHING MY HEAD WITH A ROCK INSTEAD OF USING YOUR STAND?
HERE, I'LL EVEN PICK UP A ROCK FOR YOU.
THIS ONE SEEMS LIKE IT COULD DO THE JOB.
GRP
CUT THE CRAP.
WHEN I SAY I'M GOING TO DO IT, I MEAN IT.
URK...

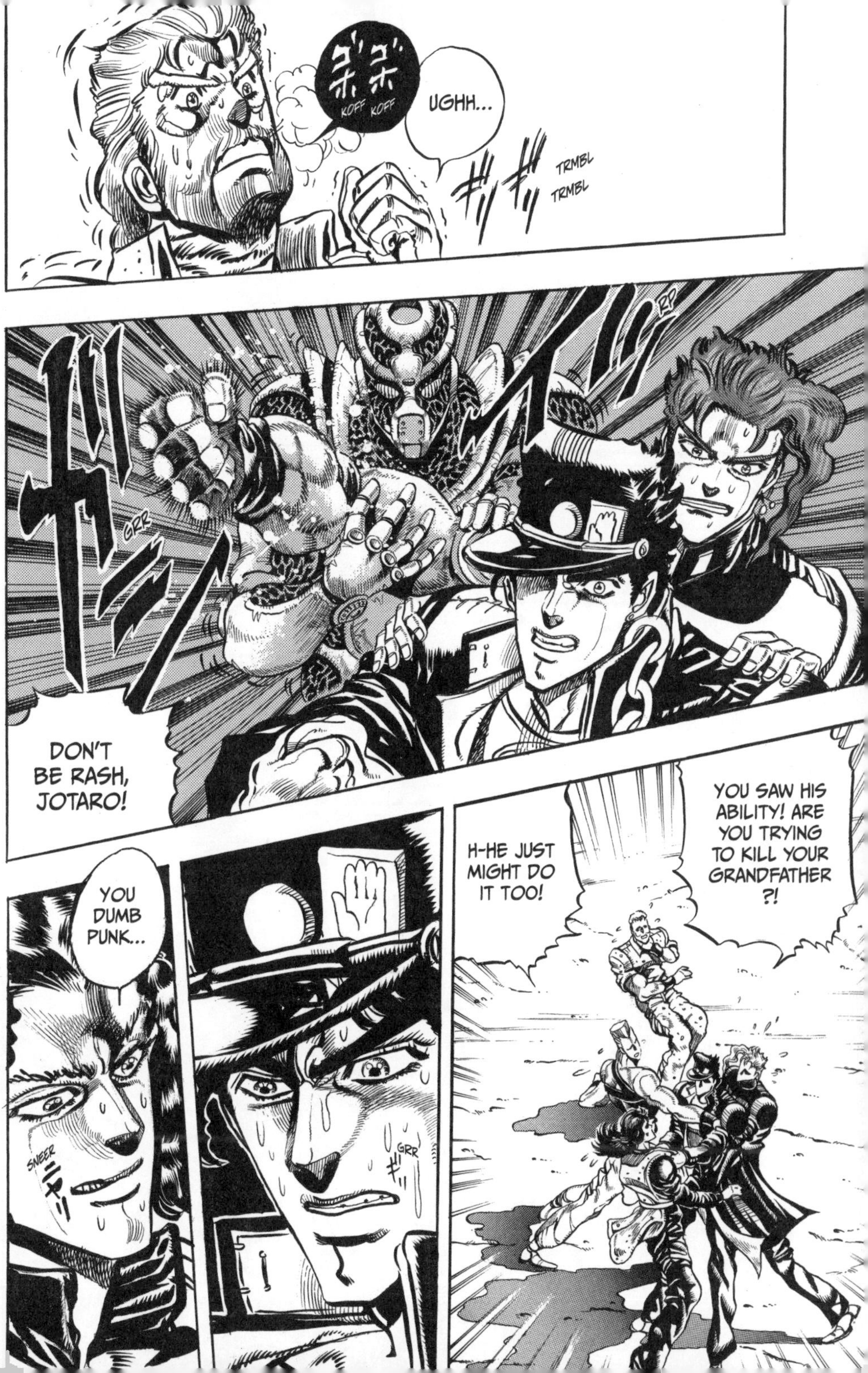

UGHH...
KOFF KOFF
TRMBL
TRMBL
GRR
DON'T BE RASH, JOTARO!
YOU SAW HIS ABILITY! ARE YOU TRYING TO KILL YOUR GRANDFATHER ?!
H-HE JUST MIGHT DO IT TOO!
GRR
YOU DUMB PUNK...
SNEER

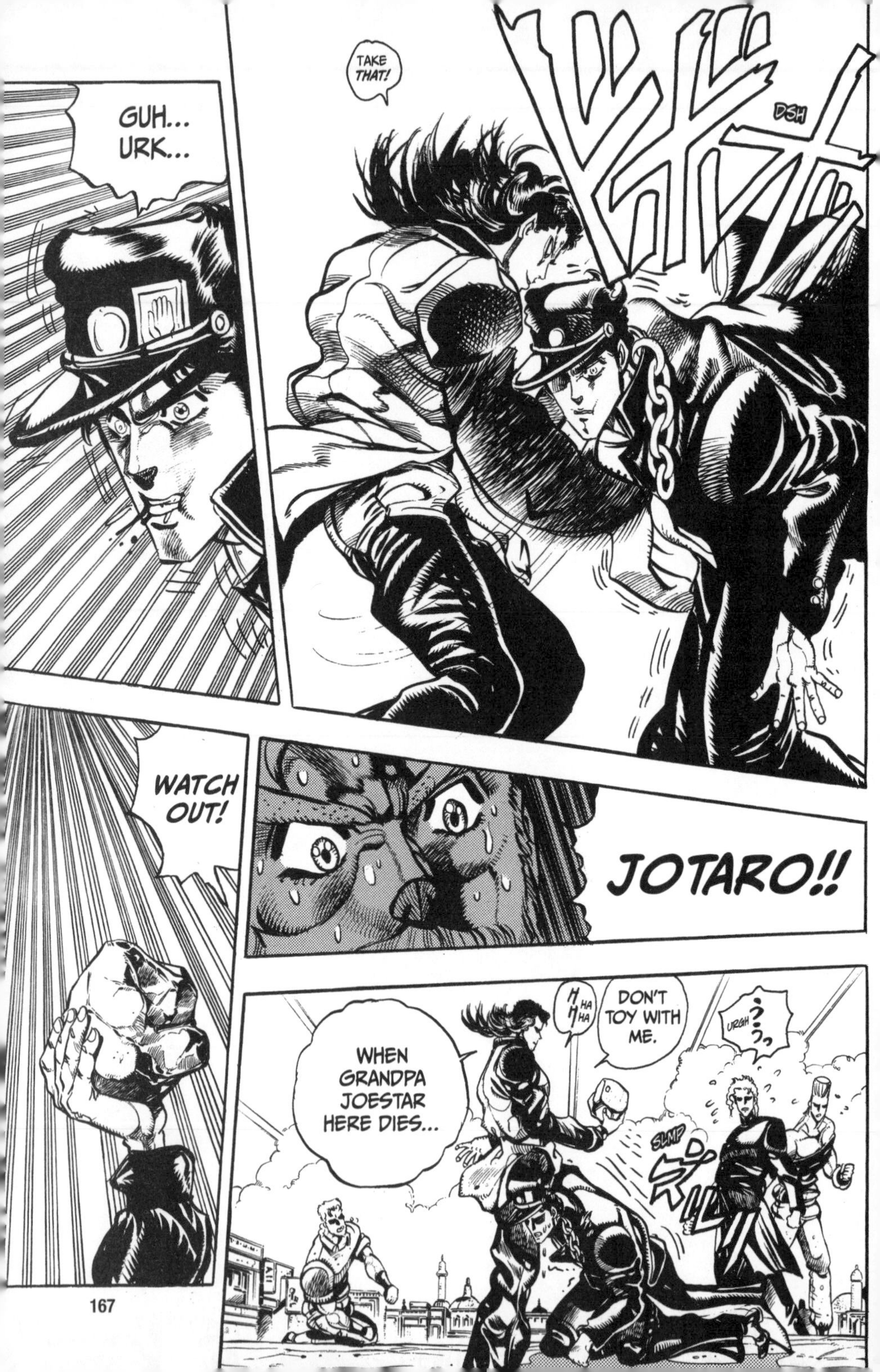
TAKE THAT!
DSH
GUH... URK...
JOTARO!!
URGH
DON'T TOY WITH ME.
HA HA
WHEN GRANDPA JOESTAR HERE DIES...
SLMP
WATCH OUT!

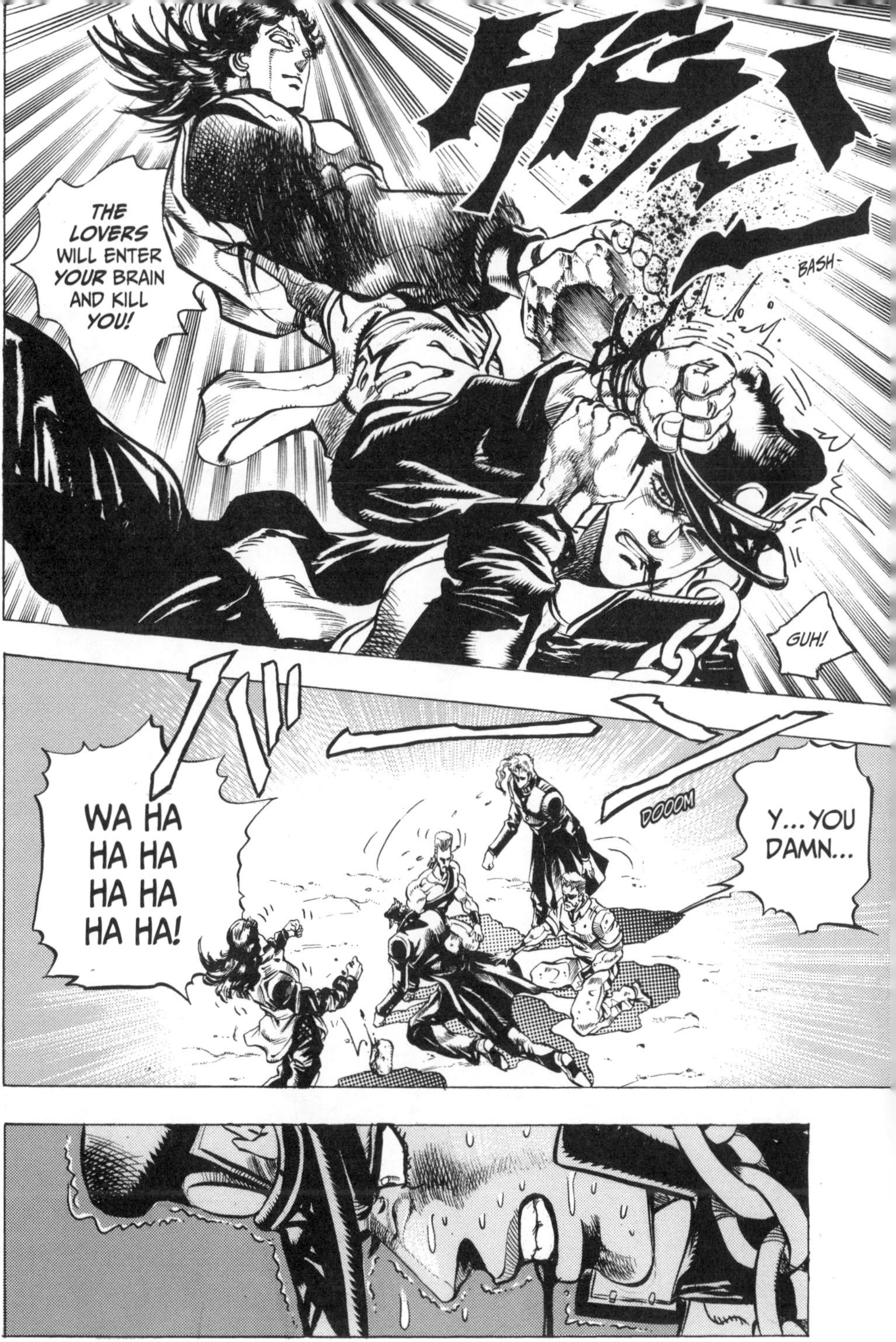
BASH
THE LOVERS WILL ENTER YOUR BRAIN AND KILL YOU!
GUH!
Y...YOU DAMN...
DOOOM
WA HA HA HA HA HA HA HA!

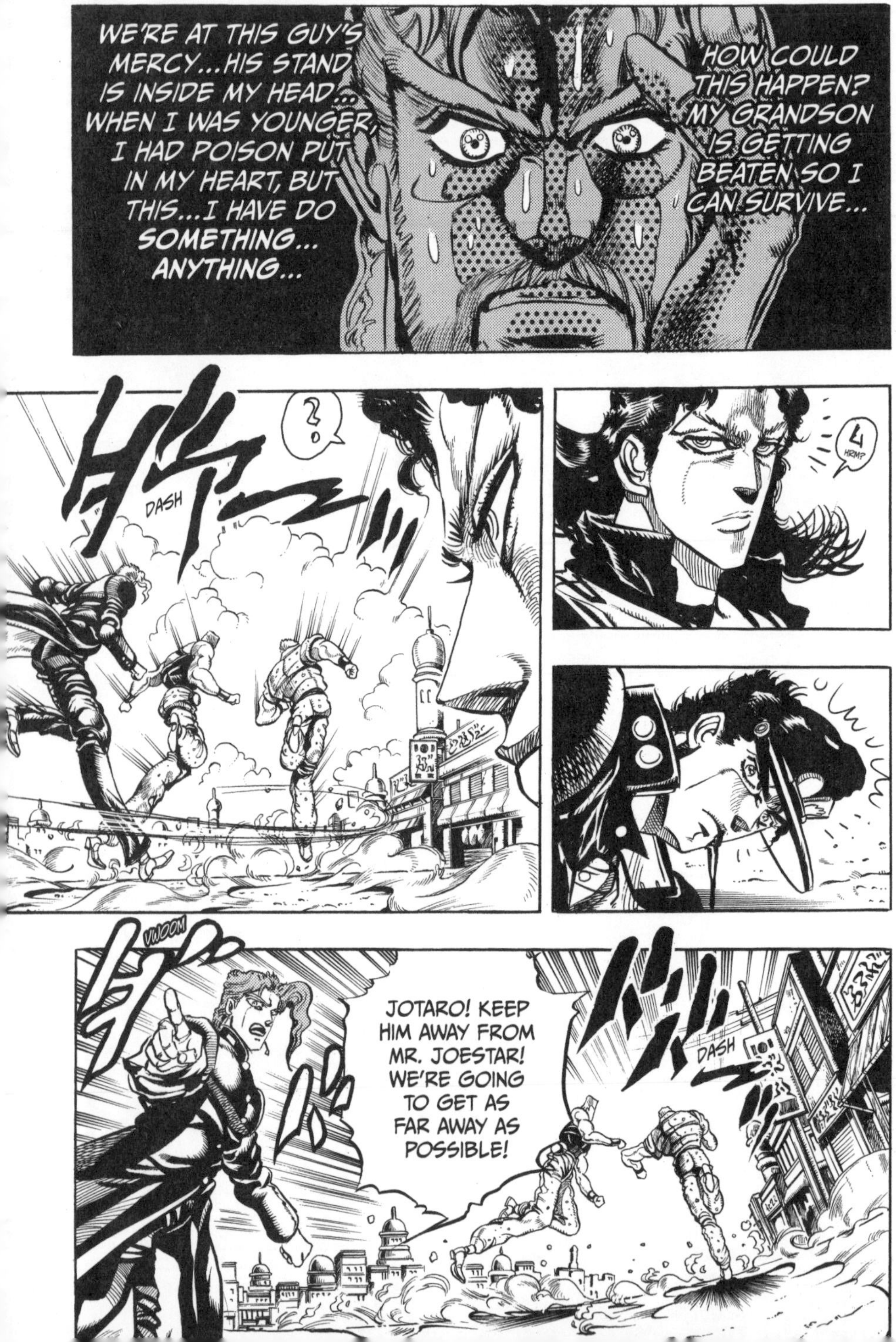
HOW COULD THIS HAPPEN? MY GRANDSON IS GETTING BEATEN SO I CAN SURVIVE...
WE'RE AT THIS GUY'S MERCY...HIS STAND IS INSIDE MY HEAD... WHEN I WAS YOUNGER, I HAD POISON PUT IN MY HEART, BUT THIS...I HAVE DO SOMETHING... ANYTHING...
HRM?
?
DASH
VWOOM
JOTARO! KEEP HIM AWAY FROM MR. JOESTAR! WE'RE GOING TO GET AS FAR AWAY AS POSSIBLE!
DASH

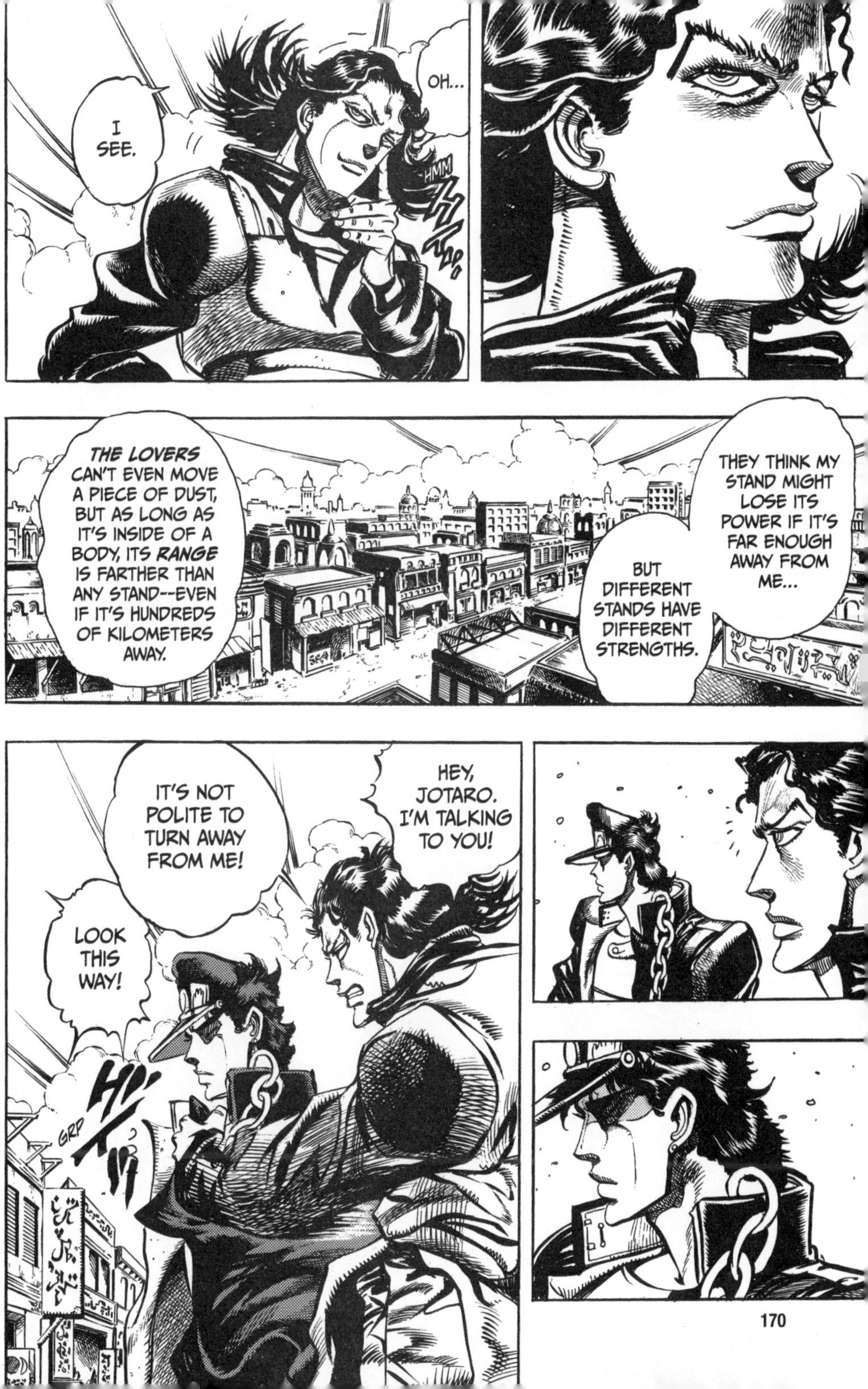
OH...
HMM
I SEE.
THEY THINK MY STAND MIGHT LOSE ITS POWER IF IT'S FAR ENOUGH AWAY FROM ME...
BUT DIFFERENT STANDS HAVE DIFFERENT STRENGTHS.
THE LOVERS CAN'T EVEN MOVE A PIECE OF DUST, BUT AS LONG AS IT'S INSIDE OF A BODY, ITS *RANGE* IS FARTHER THAN ANY STAND--EVEN IF IT'S HUNDREDS OF KILOMETERS AWAY.
HEY, JOTARO. I'M TALKING TO YOU!
IT'S NOT POLITE TO TURN AWAY FROM ME!
LOOK THIS WAY!
GRP

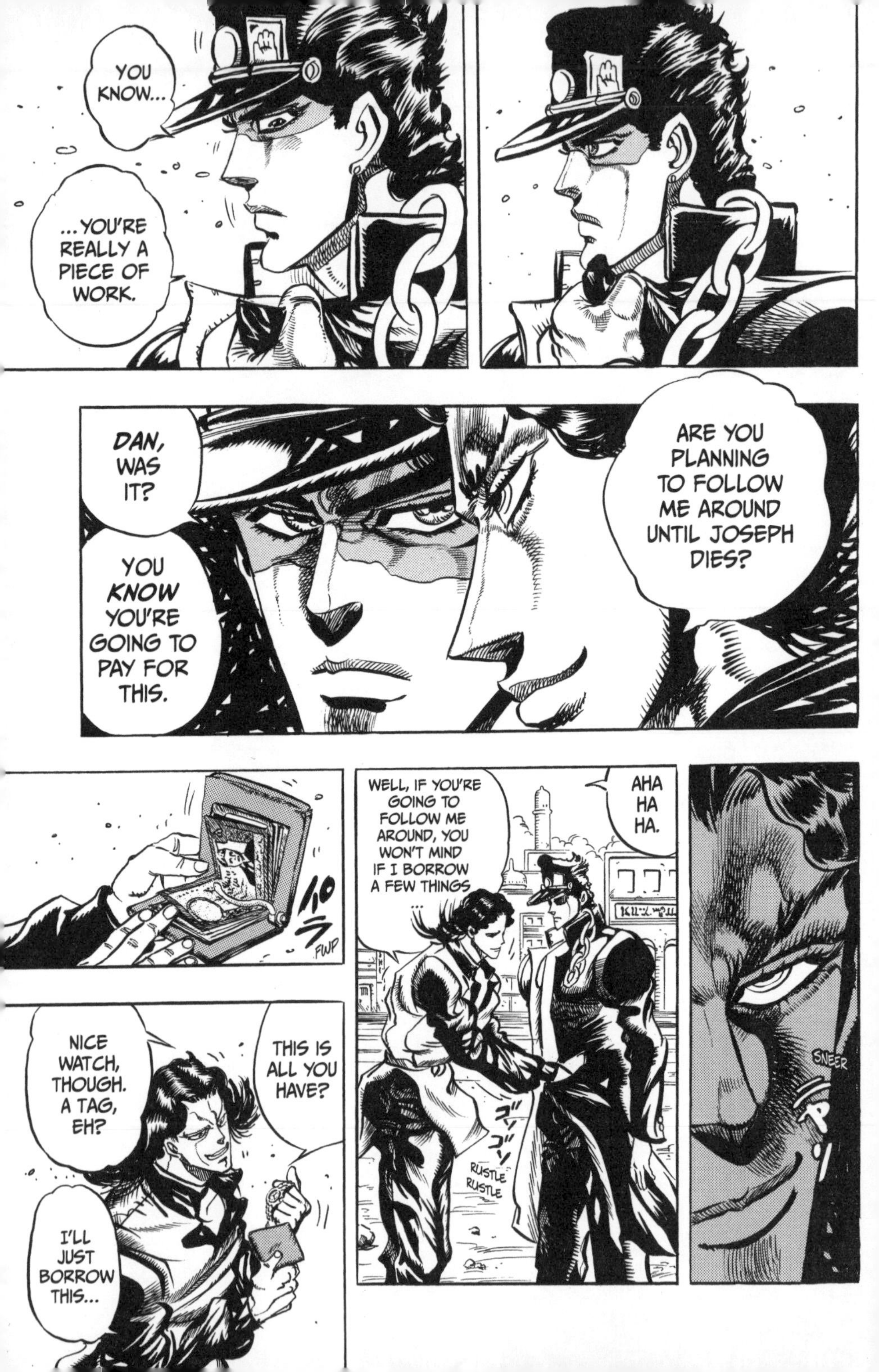
YOU KNOW...
...YOU'RE REALLY A PIECE OF WORK.
ARE YOU PLANNING TO FOLLOW ME AROUND UNTIL JOSEPH DIES?
DAN, WAS IT?
YOU KNOW YOU'RE GOING TO PAY FOR THIS.
SNEER
AHA HA HA.
WELL, IF YOU'RE GOING TO FOLLOW ME AROUND, YOU WON'T MIND IF I BORROW A FEW THINGS...
RUSTLE RUSTLE
FWP
THIS IS ALL YOU HAVE?
NICE WATCH, THOUGH. A TAG, EH?
I'LL JUST BORROW THIS...

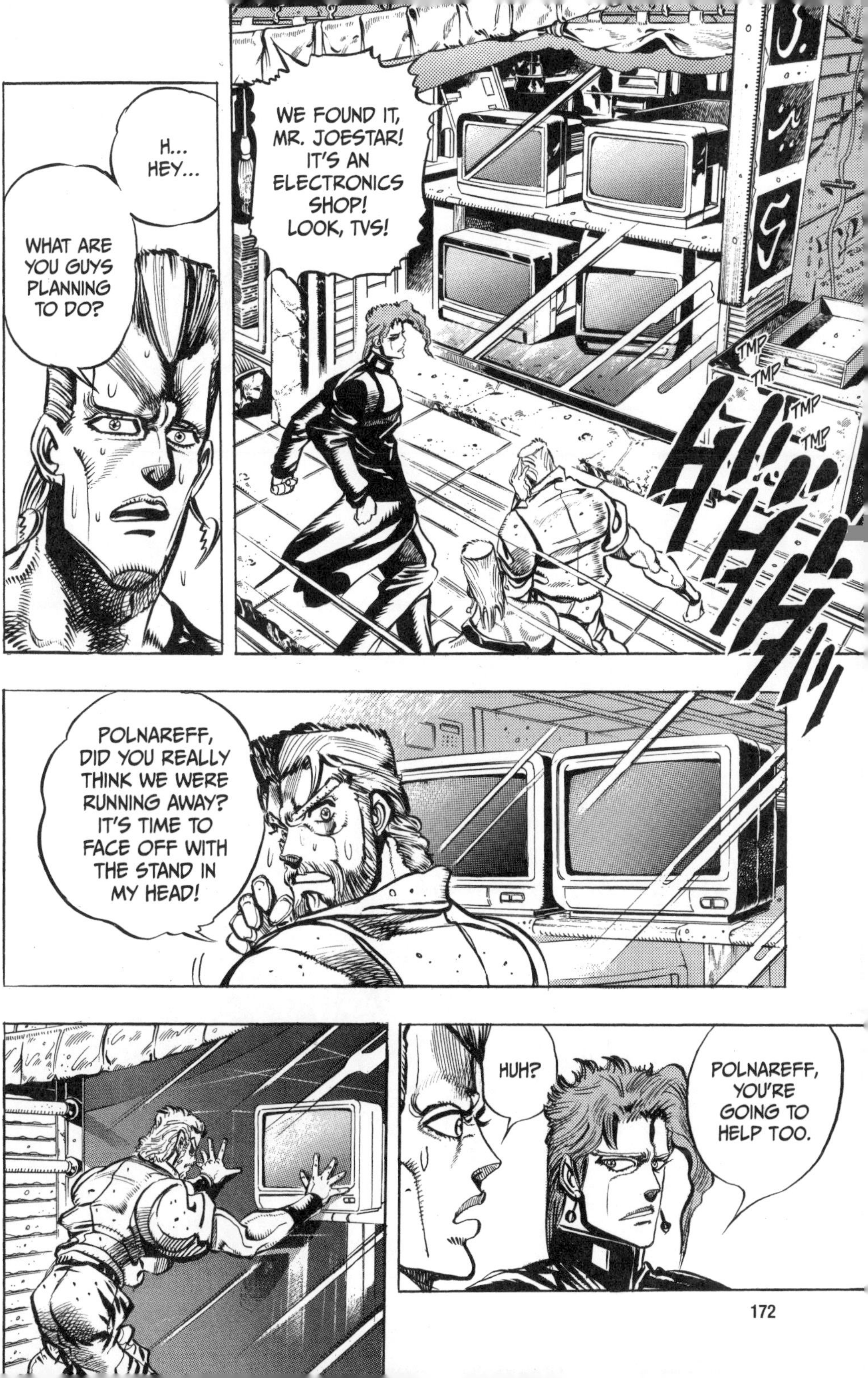
WE FOUND IT, MR. JOESTAR! IT'S AN ELECTRONICS SHOP! LOOK, TVS!
TMP
TMP
TMP
TMP
H... HEY...
WHAT ARE YOU GUYS PLANNING TO DO?
POLNAREFF, DID YOU REALLY THINK WE WERE RUNNING AWAY? IT'S TIME TO FACE OFF WITH THE STAND IN MY HEAD!
POLNAREFF, YOU'RE GOING TO HELP TOO.
HUH?

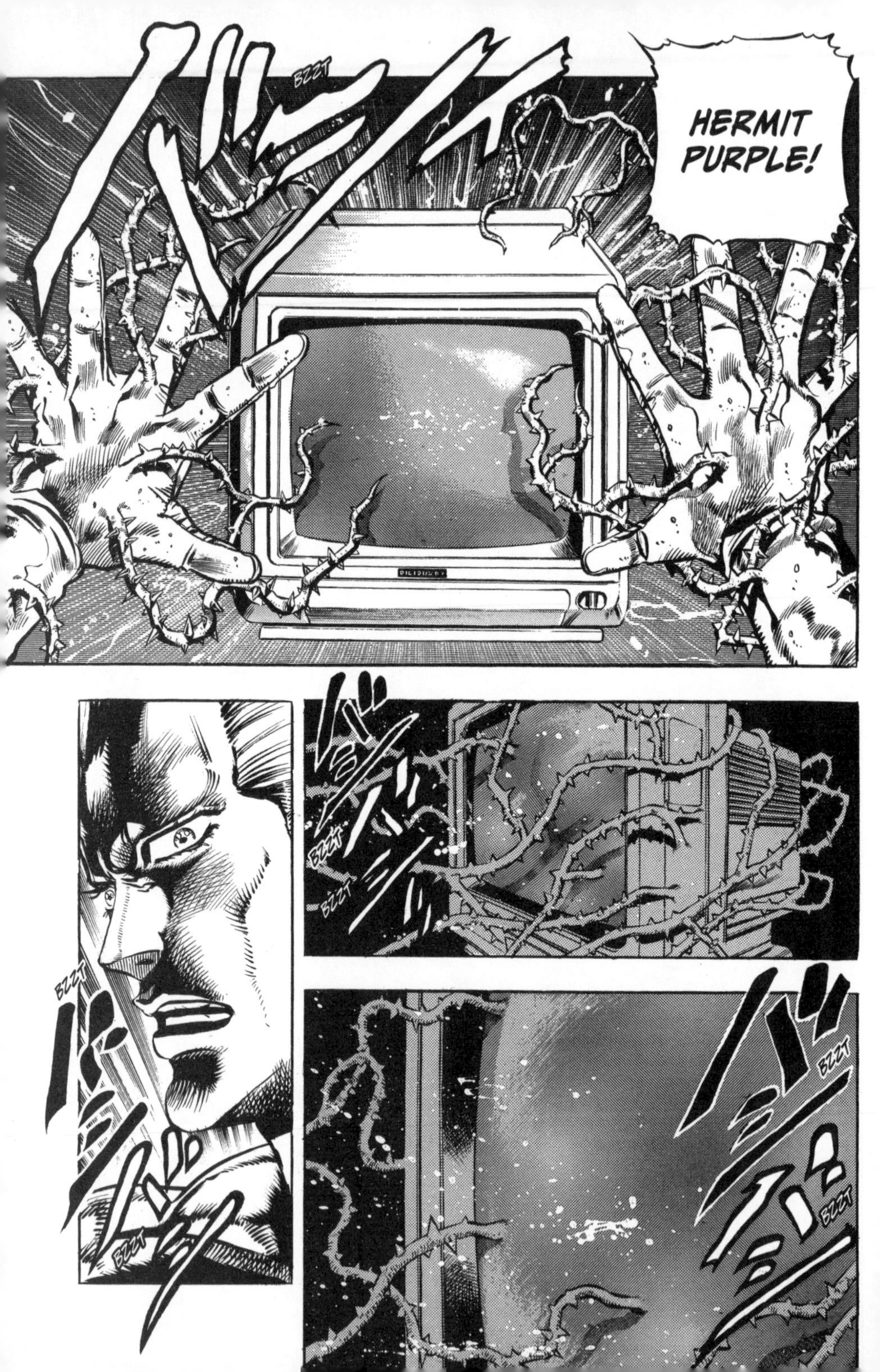
HERMIT PURPLE!
BZZT
BZZT
BZZT
BZZT
BZZT
BZZT
BZZT

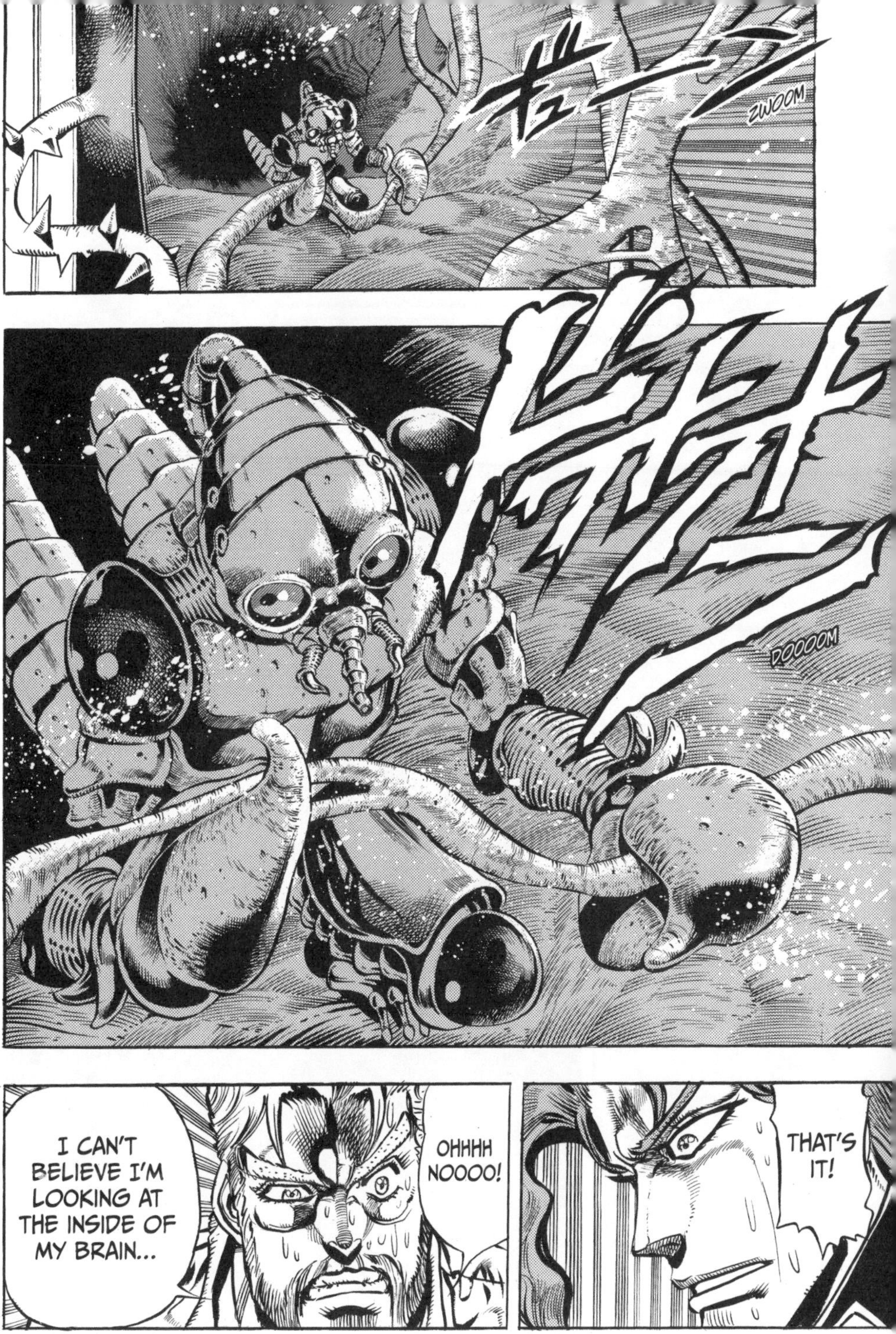
ZWOOM
DOOOOM
THAT'S IT!
OHHHH NOOOO!
I CAN'T BELIEVE I'M LOOKING AT THE INSIDE OF MY BRAIN...

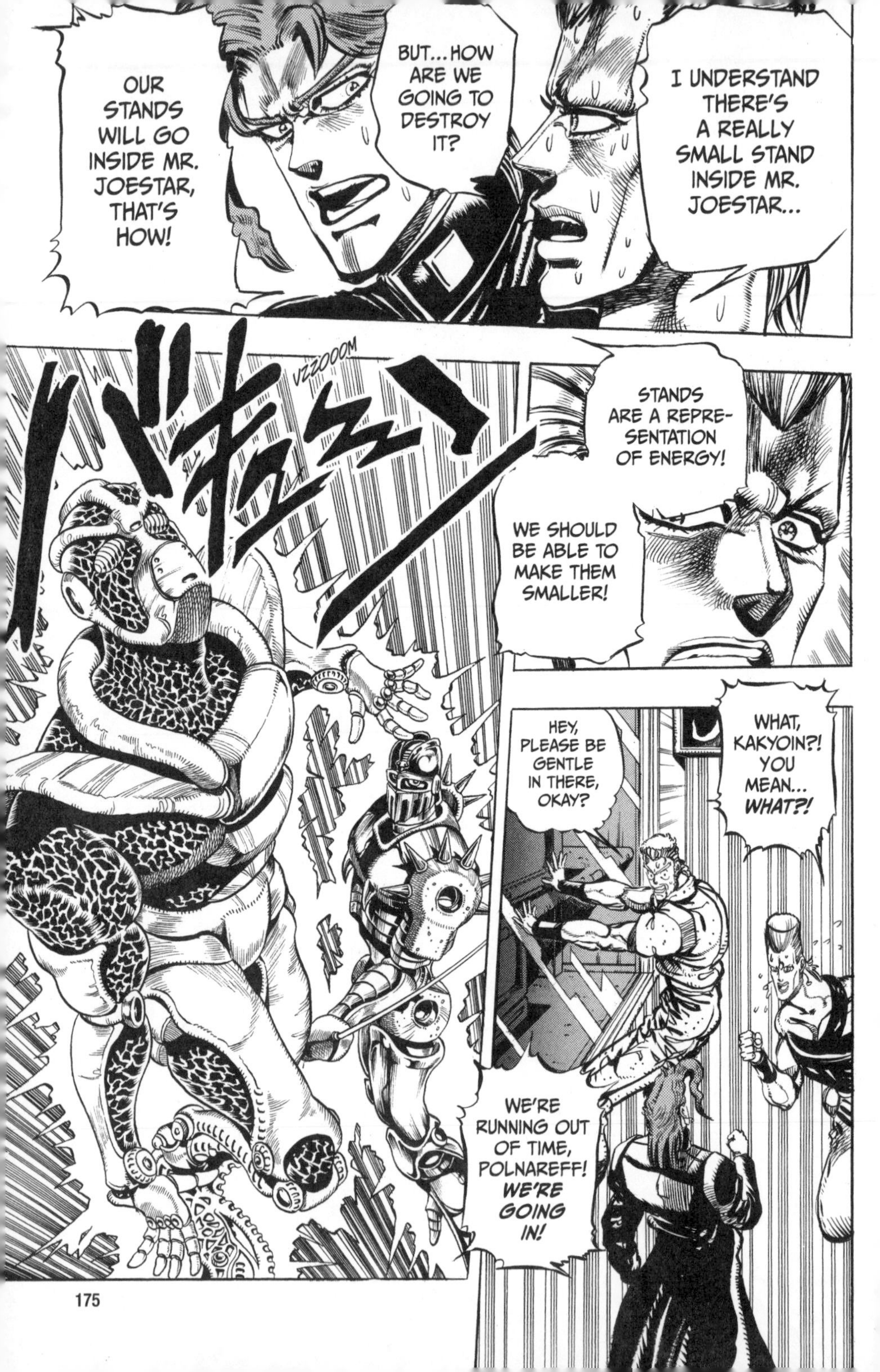
I UNDERSTAND THERE'S A REALLY SMALL STAND INSIDE MR. JOESTAR...
BUT... HOW ARE WE GOING TO DESTROY IT?
OUR STANDS WILL GO INSIDE MR. JOESTAR, THAT'S HOW!
STANDS ARE A REPRESENTATION OF ENERGY!
WE SHOULD BE ABLE TO MAKE THEM SMALLER!
WHAT, KAKYOIN?! YOU MEAN... *WHAT?!*
HEY, PLEASE BE GENTLE IN THERE, OKAY?
WE'RE RUNNING OUT OF TIME, POLNAREFF! *WE'RE GOING IN!*
VZZOOOM

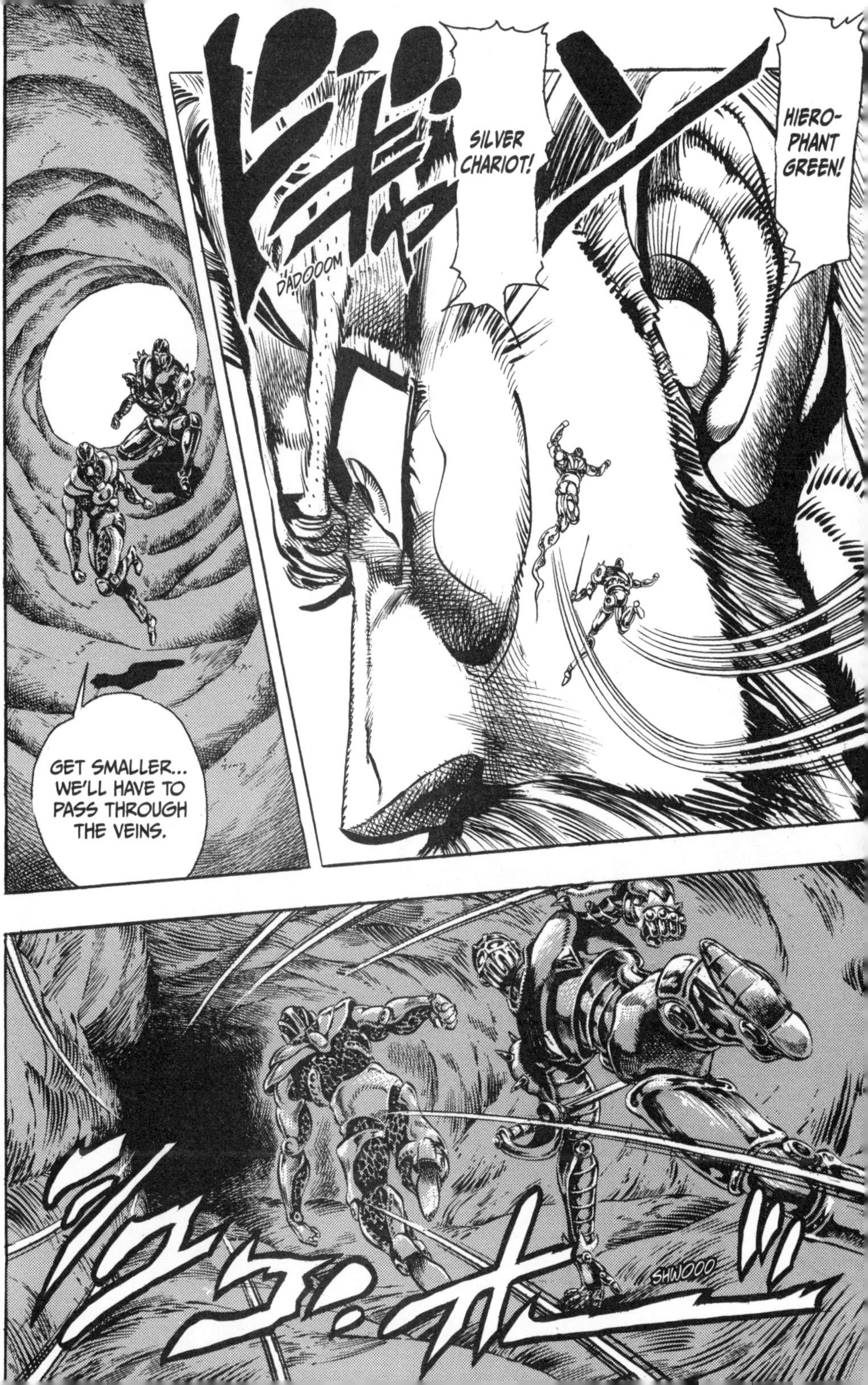
HIERO-PHANT GREEN!
SILVER CHARIOT!
DADOOOM
GET SMALLER... WE'LL HAVE TO PASS THROUGH THE VEINS.
SHWOOO

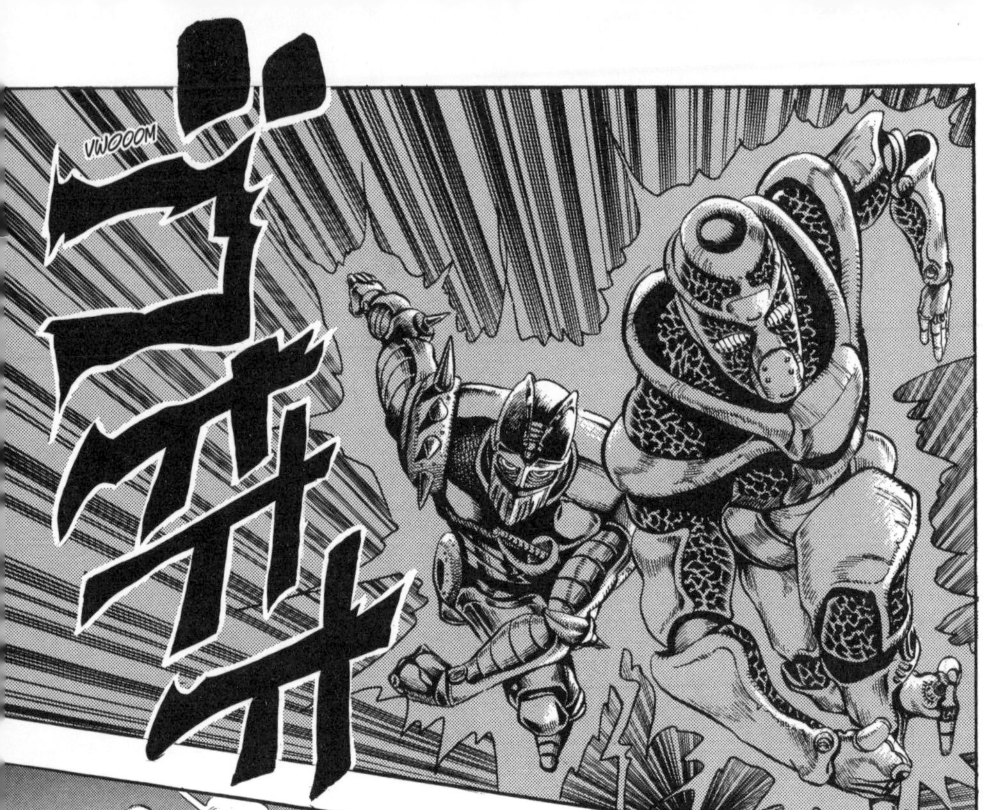
VWOOOM
ゴオオオ

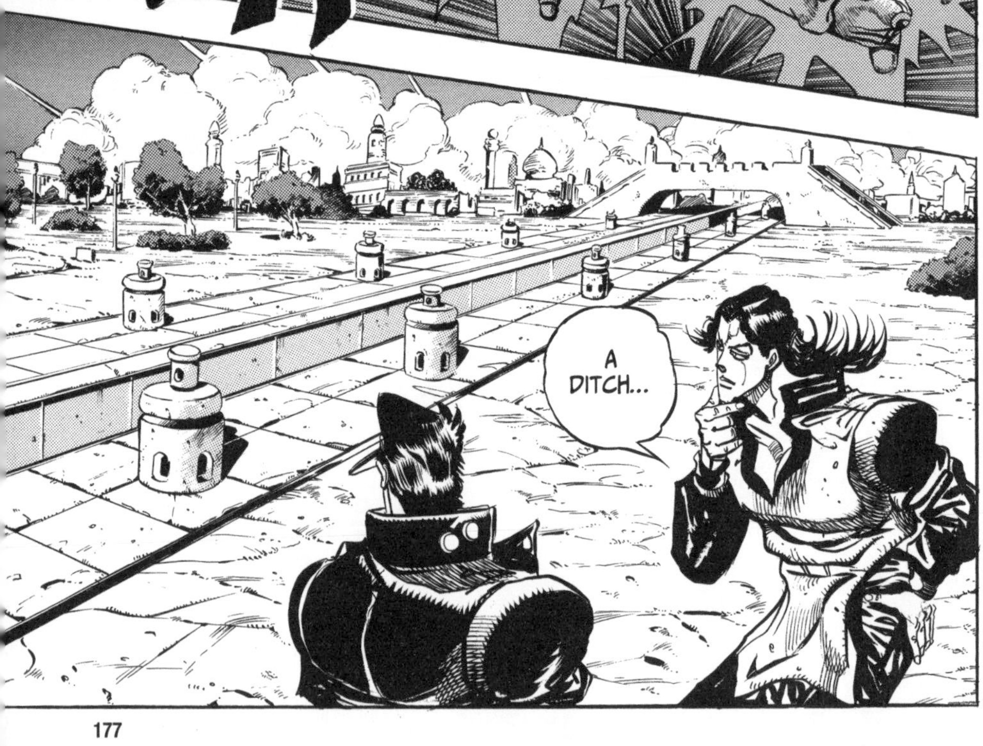
A DITCH...

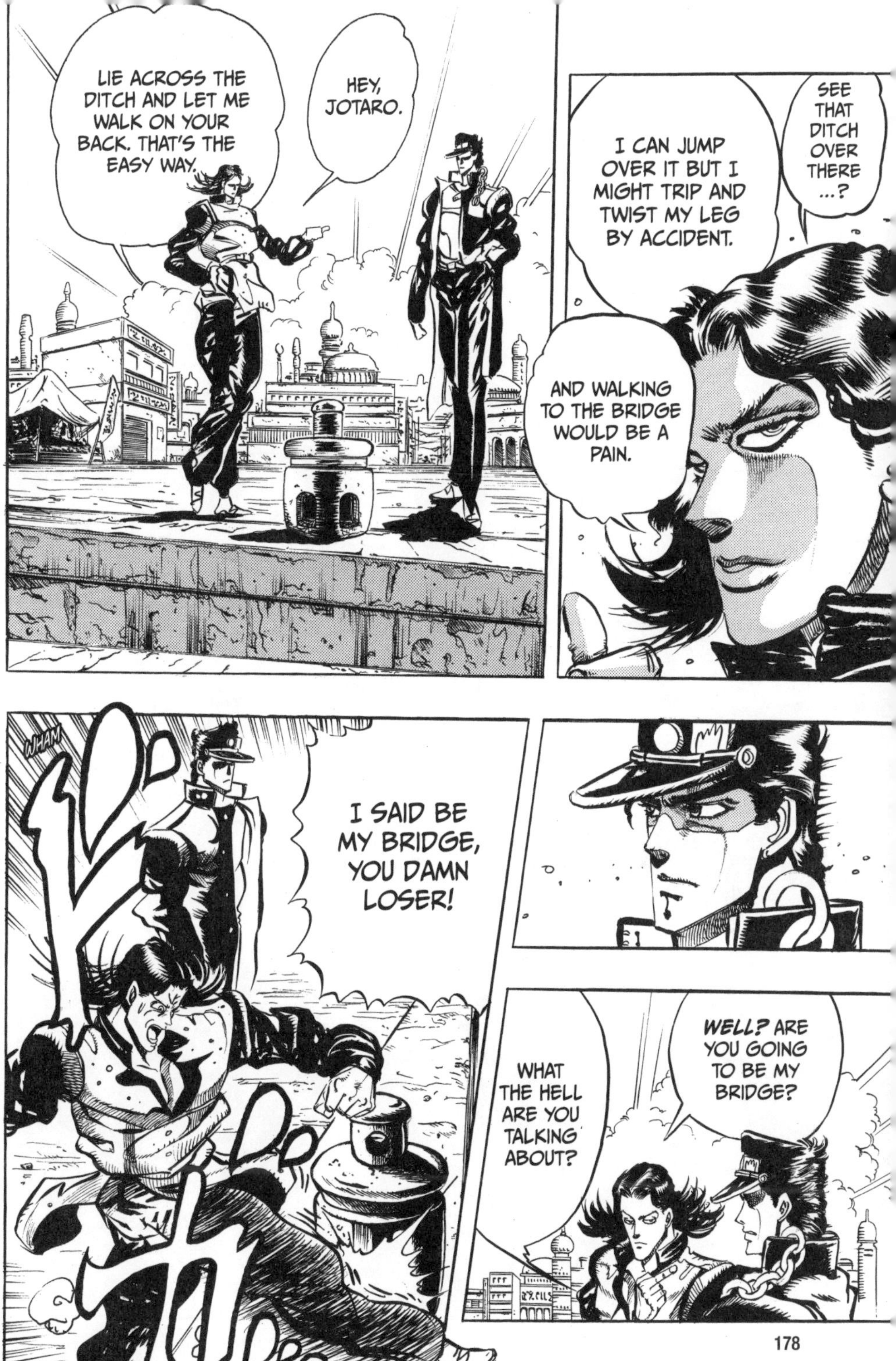
SEE THAT DITCH OVER THERE ...?
I CAN JUMP OVER IT BUT I MIGHT TRIP AND TWIST MY LEG BY ACCIDENT.
AND WALKING TO THE BRIDGE WOULD BE A PAIN.
HEY, JOTARO.
LIE ACROSS THE DITCH AND LET ME WALK ON YOUR BACK. THAT'S THE EASY WAY.
WELL? ARE YOU GOING TO BE MY BRIDGE?
WHAT THE HELL ARE YOU TALKING ABOUT?
I SAID BE MY BRIDGE, YOU DAMN LOSER!
WHAM

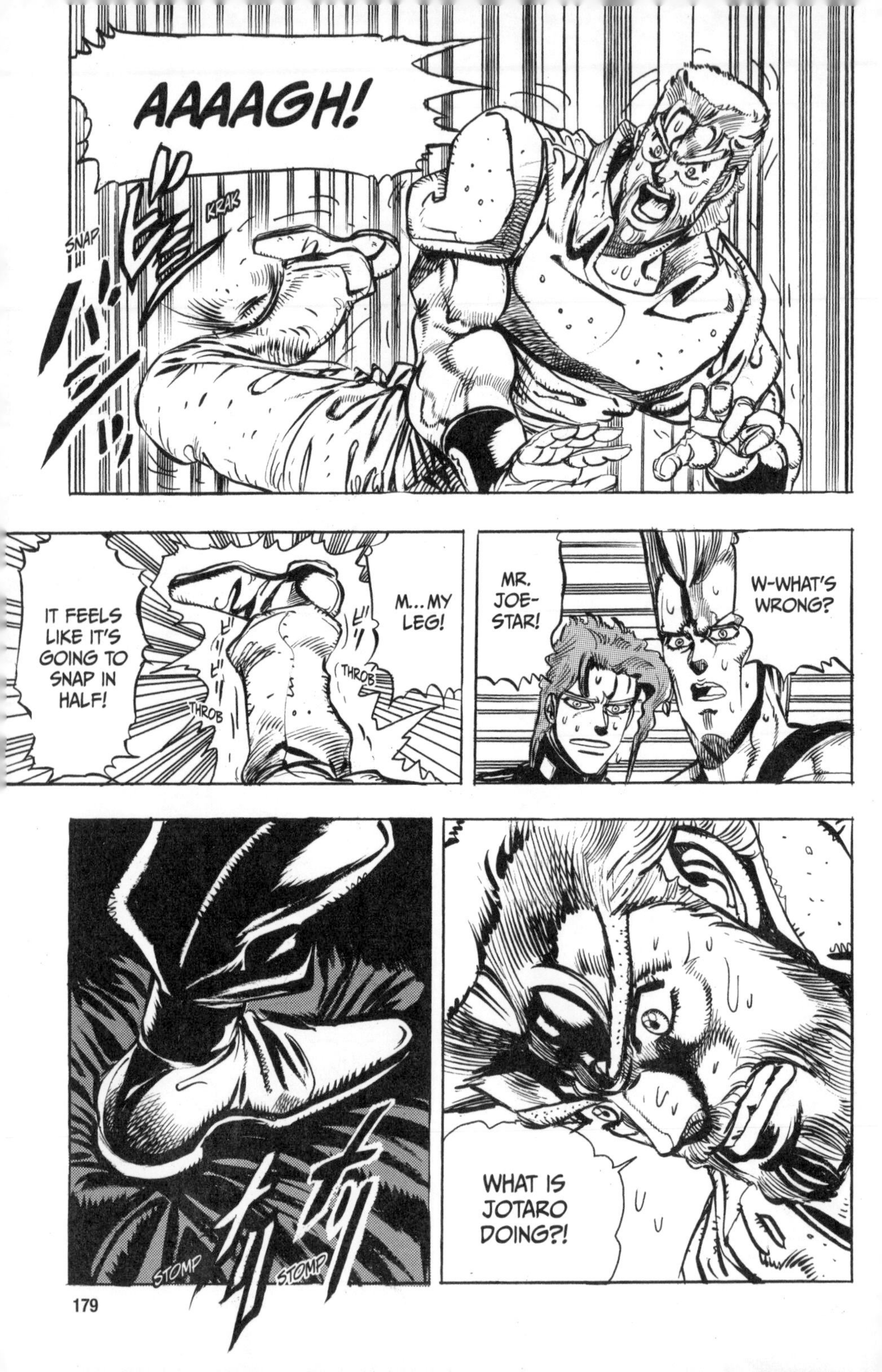
AAAAGH!
SNAP
KRAK
W-WHAT'S WRONG?
MR. JOE-STAR!
M... MY LEG!
IT FEELS LIKE IT'S GOING TO SNAP IN HALF!
THROB
THROB
WHAT IS JOTARO DOING?!
STOMP
STOMP

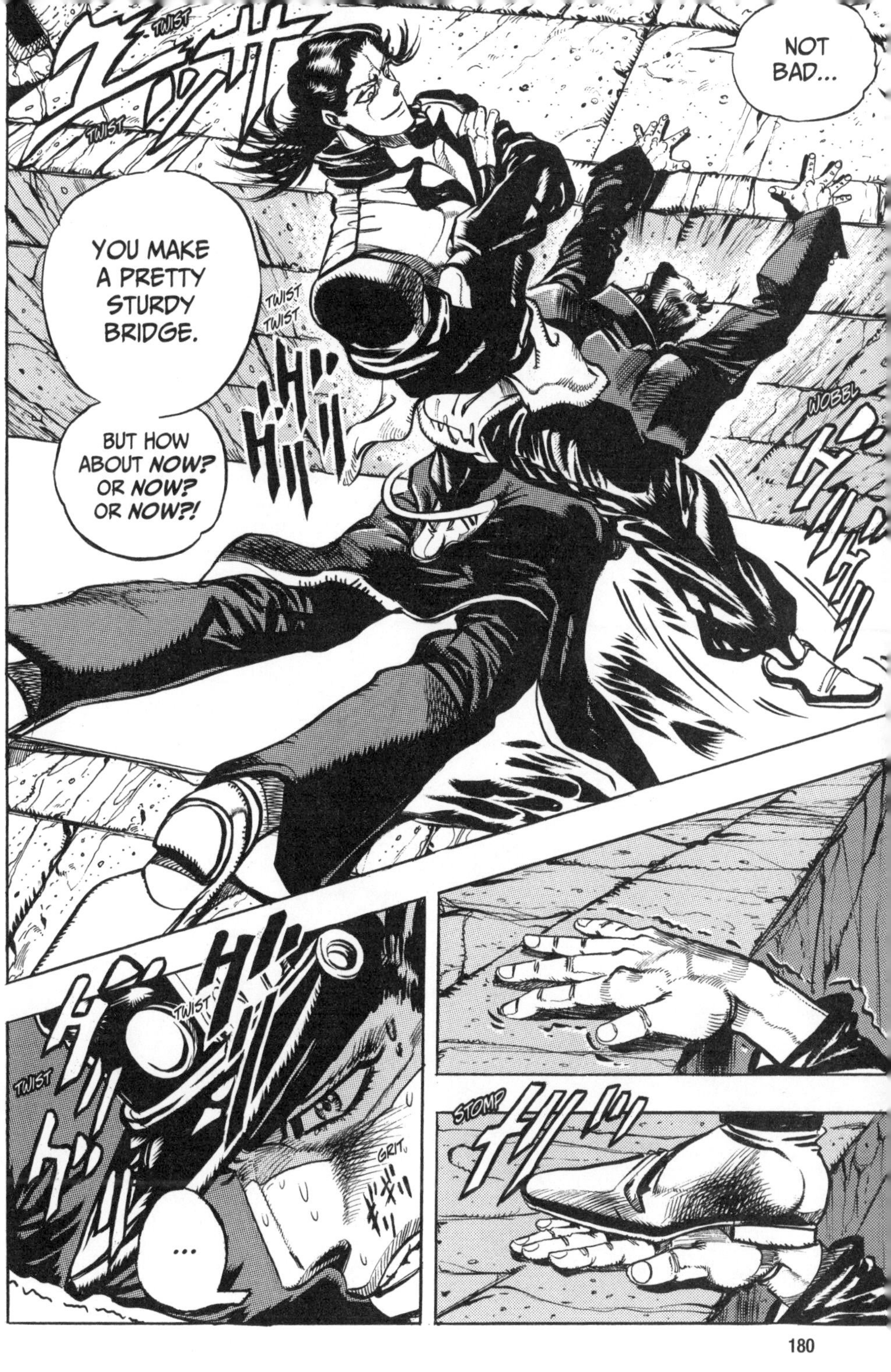
NOT BAD...
TWIST
TWIST
WOBBL
YOU MAKE A PRETTY STURDY BRIDGE.
TWIST
TWIST
BUT HOW ABOUT NOW? OR NOW? OR NOW?!
STOMP
TWIST
TWIST
GRIT
...

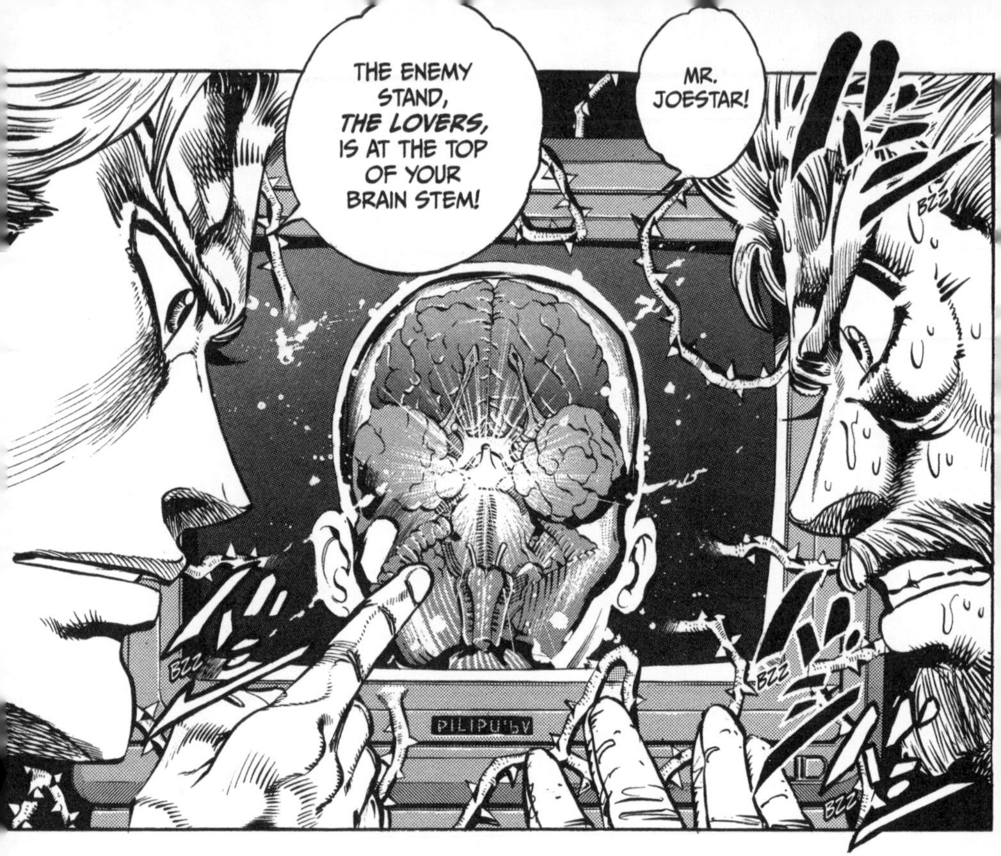
MR. JOESTAR!
THE ENEMY STAND, *THE LOVERS,* IS AT THE TOP OF YOUR BRAIN STEM!
BZZ
BZZ
BZZ
BZZ

CHAPTER 50: The Lovers PART 4

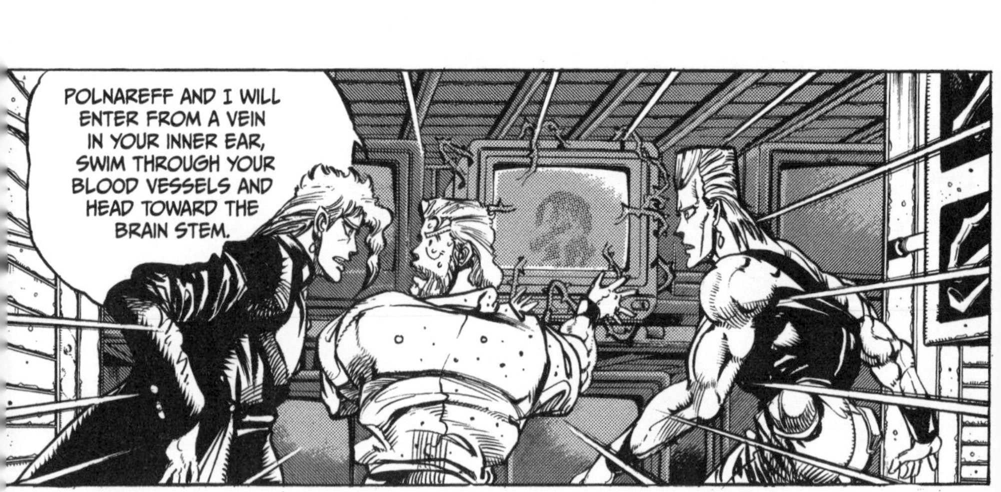
POLNAREFF AND I WILL ENTER FROM A VEIN IN YOUR INNER EAR, SWIM THROUGH YOUR BLOOD VESSELS AND HEAD TOWARD THE BRAIN STEM.

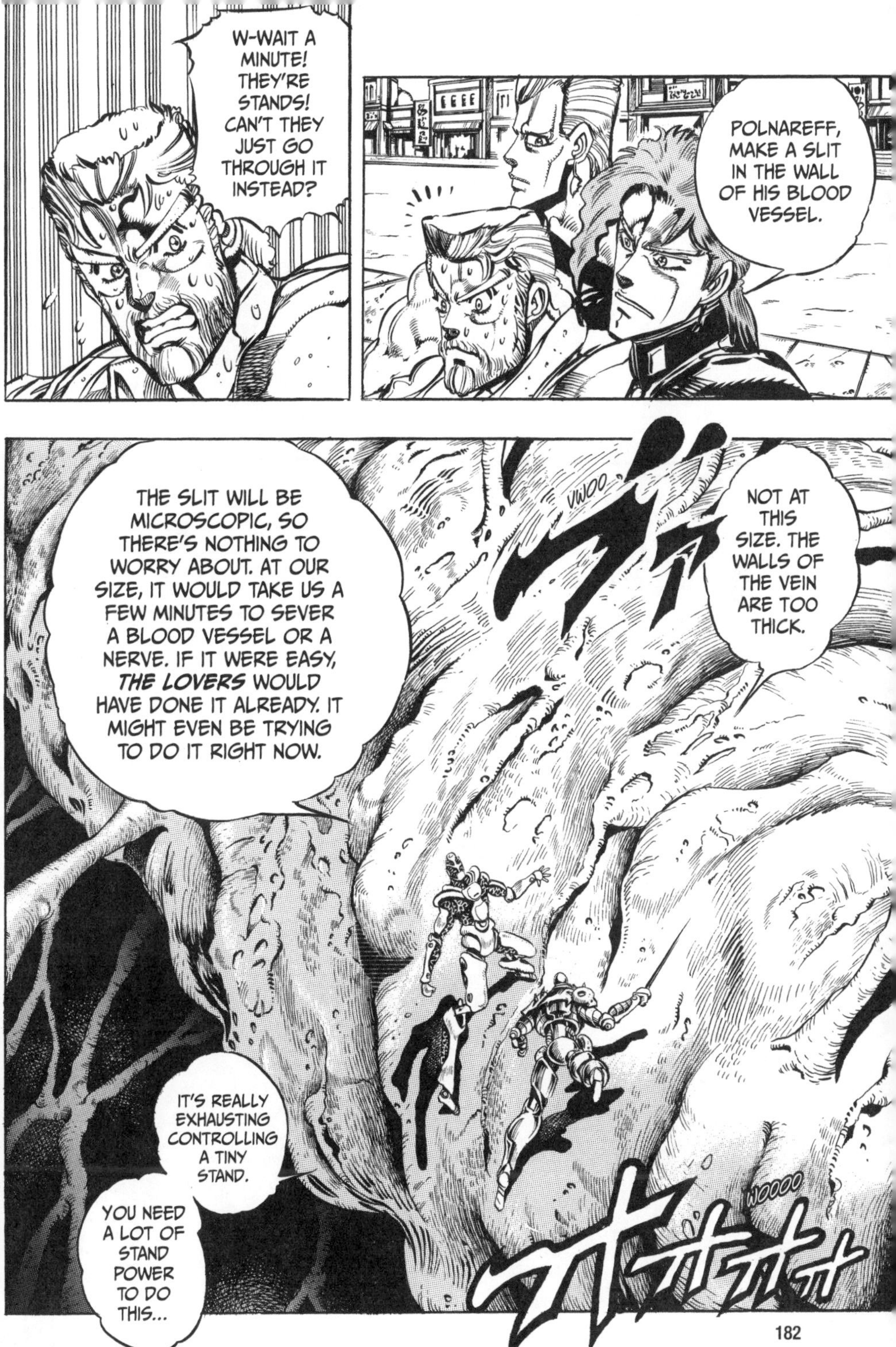
POLNAREFF, MAKE A SLIT IN THE WALL OF HIS BLOOD VESSEL.
W-WAIT A MINUTE! THEY'RE STANDS! CAN'T THEY JUST GO THROUGH IT INSTEAD?
VWOO
NOT AT THIS SIZE. THE WALLS OF THE VEIN ARE TOO THICK.
THE SLIT WILL BE MICROSCOPIC, SO THERE'S NOTHING TO WORRY ABOUT. AT OUR SIZE, IT WOULD TAKE US A FEW MINUTES TO SEVER A BLOOD VESSEL OR A NERVE. IF IT WERE EASY, *THE LOVERS* WOULD HAVE DONE IT ALREADY. IT MIGHT EVEN BE TRYING TO DO IT RIGHT NOW.
WOOOO
IT'S REALLY EXHAUSTING CONTROLLING A TINY STAND.
YOU NEED A LOT OF STAND POWER TO DO THIS...

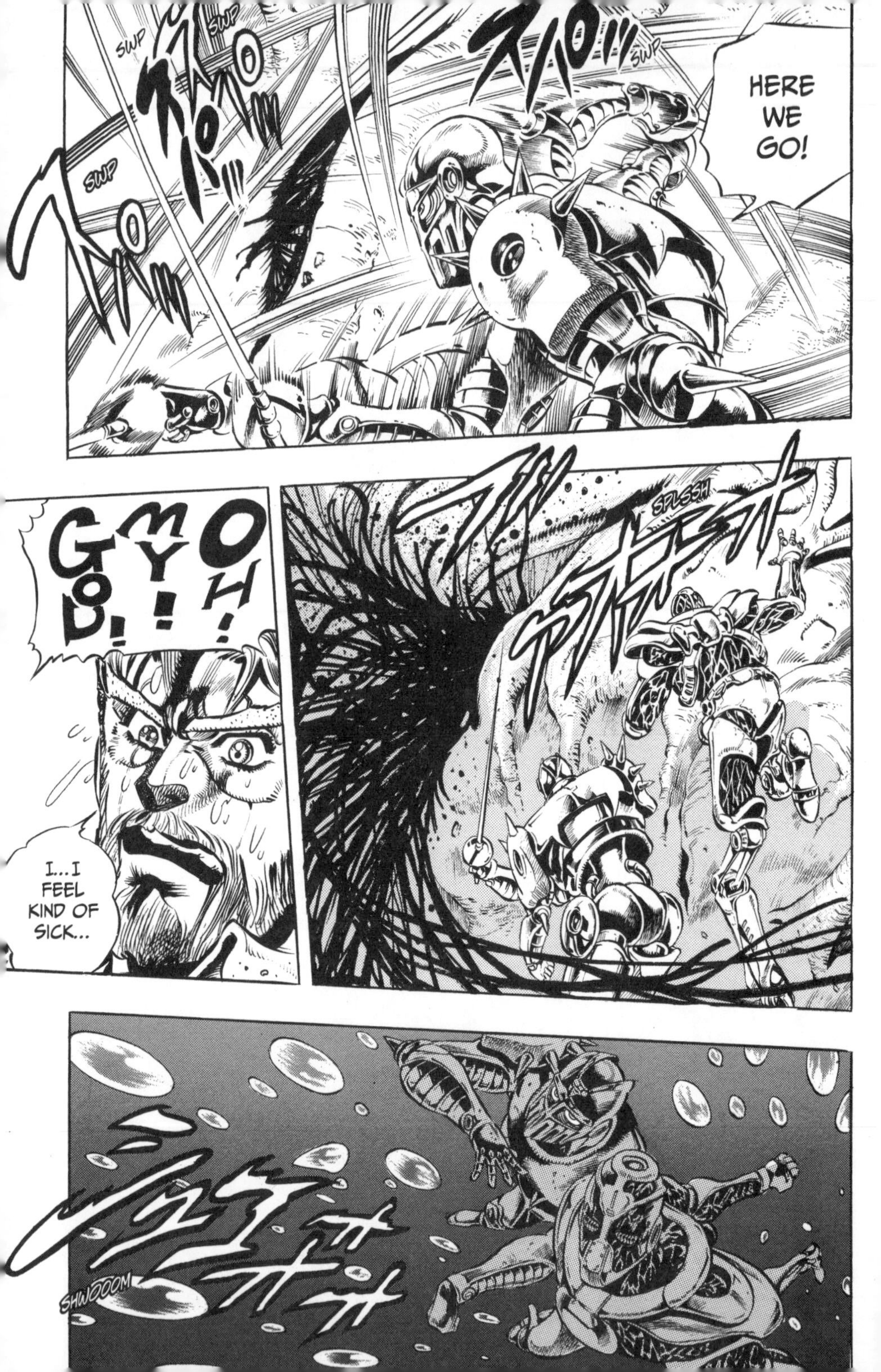
SWP
HERE WE GO!
SWP
SWP
SWP
SPLSSH
OH MY GOD!!
I...I FEEL KIND OF SICK...
SHWOOOM

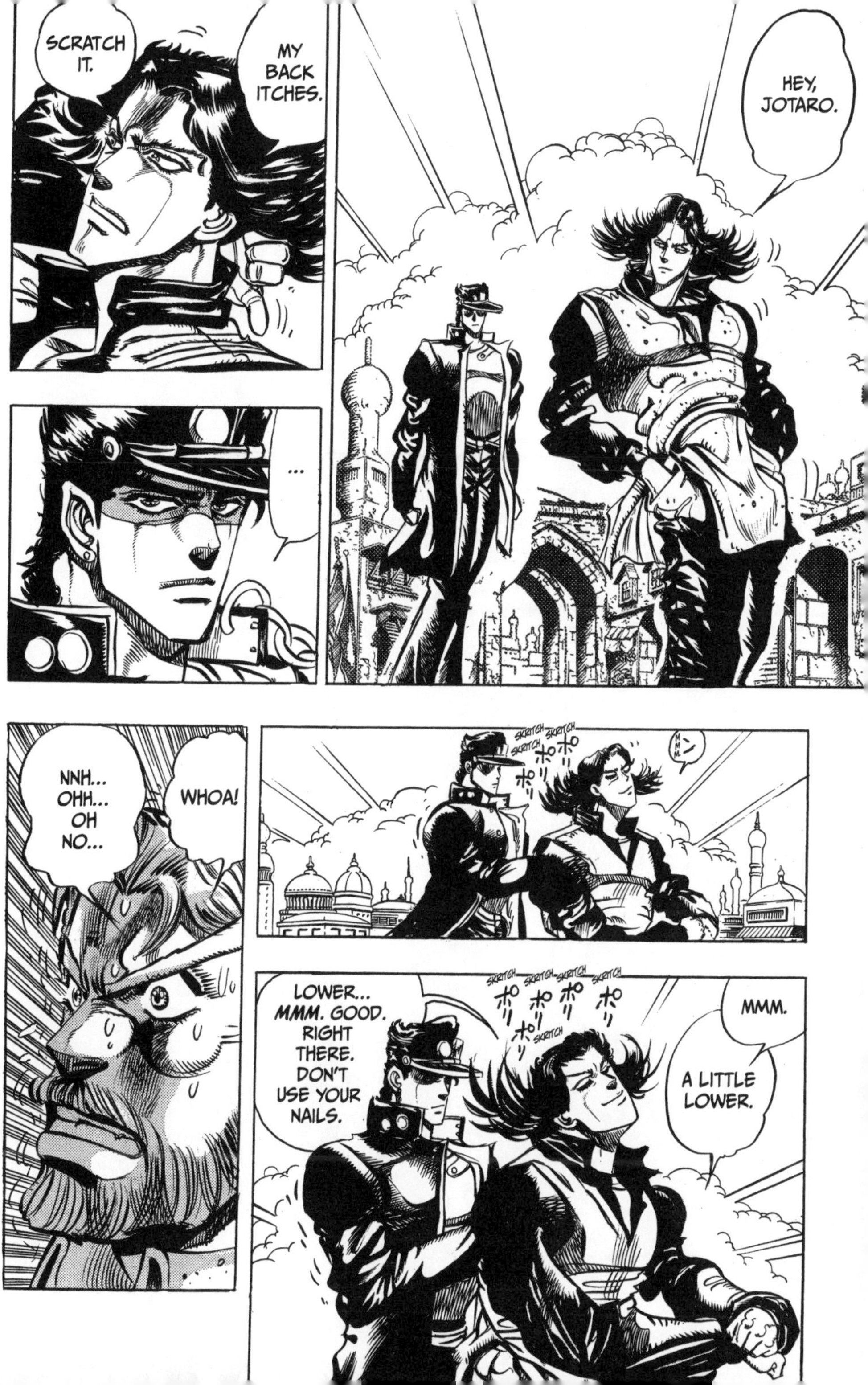
HEY, JOTARO.
MY BACK ITCHES.
SCRATCH IT.
...
SKRITCH SKRITCH SKRITCH
MMM
MMM.
A LITTLE LOWER.
SKRITCH SKRITCH SKRITCH SKRITCH SKRITCH
LOWER... MMM. GOOD. RIGHT THERE. DON'T USE YOUR NAILS.
WHOA!
NNH... OHH... OH NO...

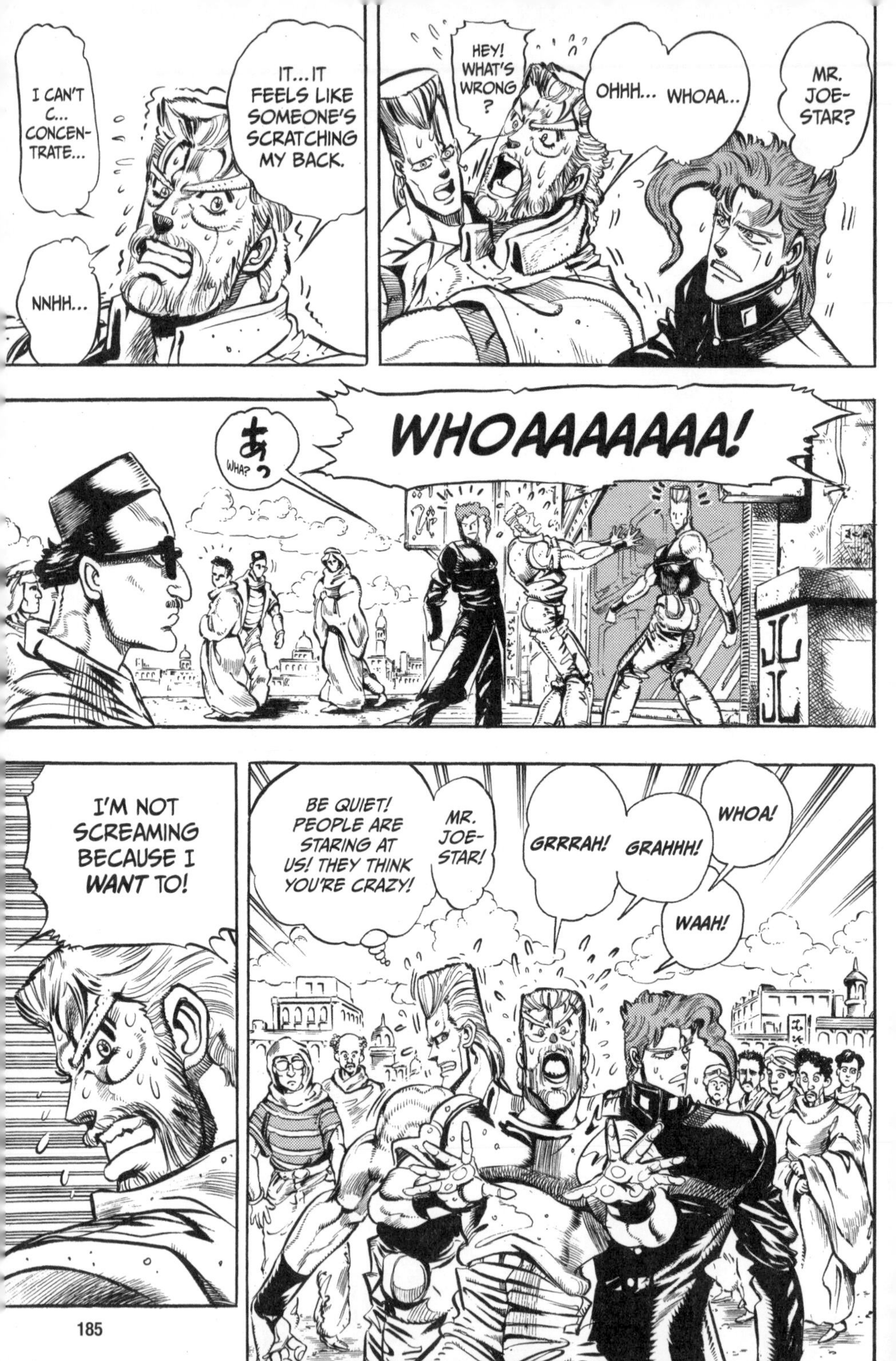
MR. JOE-STAR?
OHHH... WHOAA...
HEY! WHAT'S WRONG?
IT...IT FEELS LIKE SOMEONE'S SCRATCHING MY BACK.
I CAN'T C... CONCENTRATE...
NNHH...
WHOAAAAAAA!
あっ
WHA?
WHOA!
GRAHHH!
GRRRAH!
WAAH!
MR. JOE-STAR!
BE QUIET! PEOPLE ARE STARING AT US! THEY THINK YOU'RE CRAZY!
I'M NOT SCREAMING BECAUSE I WANT TO!

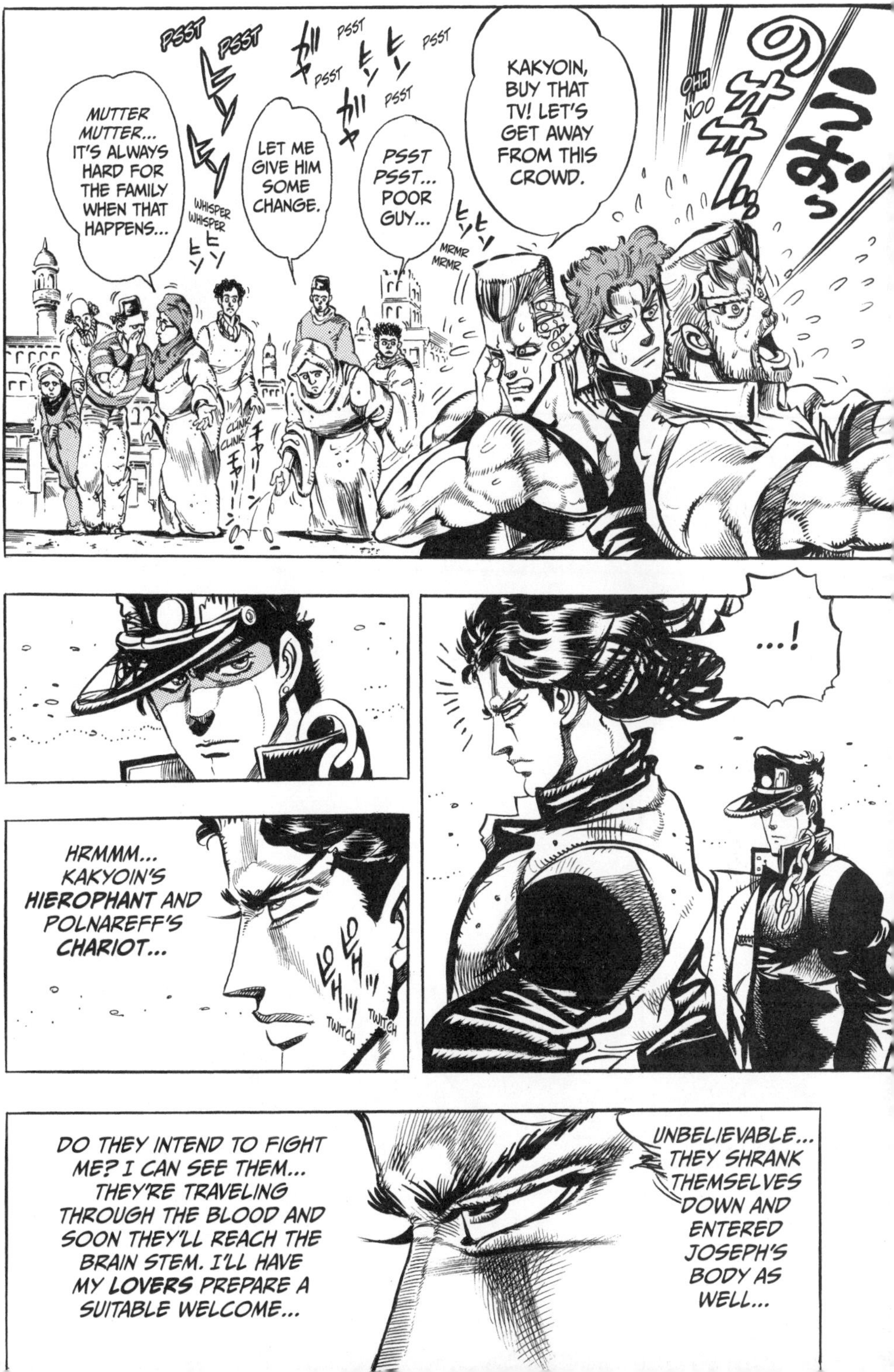
OHH NOO
KAKYOIN, BUY THAT TV! LET'S GET AWAY FROM THIS CROWD.
PSST
PSST
PSST PSST... POOR GUY...
MRMR MRMR
LET ME GIVE HIM SOME CHANGE.
PSST
PSST
WHISPER WHISPER
MUTTER MUTTER... IT'S ALWAYS HARD FOR THE FAMILY WHEN THAT HAPPENS...
CLINK CLINK
...!
HRMMM... KAKYOIN'S HIEROPHANT AND POLNAREFF'S CHARIOT...
TWITCH TWITCH
UNBELIEVABLE... THEY SHRANK THEMSELVES DOWN AND ENTERED JOSEPH'S BODY AS WELL...
DO THEY INTEND TO FIGHT ME? I CAN SEE THEM... THEY'RE TRAVELING THROUGH THE BLOOD AND SOON THEY'LL REACH THE BRAIN STEM. I'LL HAVE MY LOVERS PREPARE A SUITABLE WELCOME...

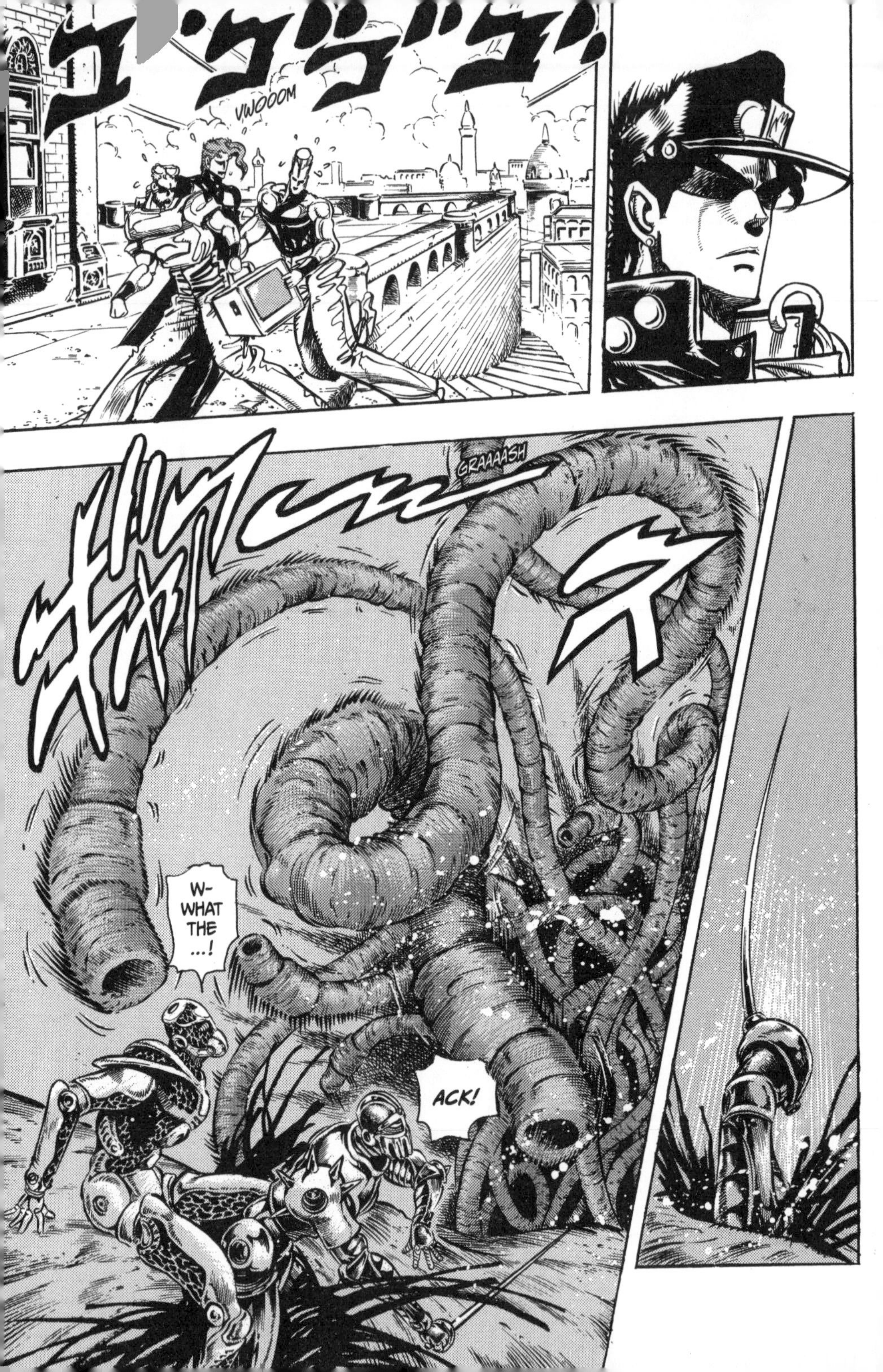
VWOOOM
GRAAAASH
W-WHAT THE ...!
ACK!

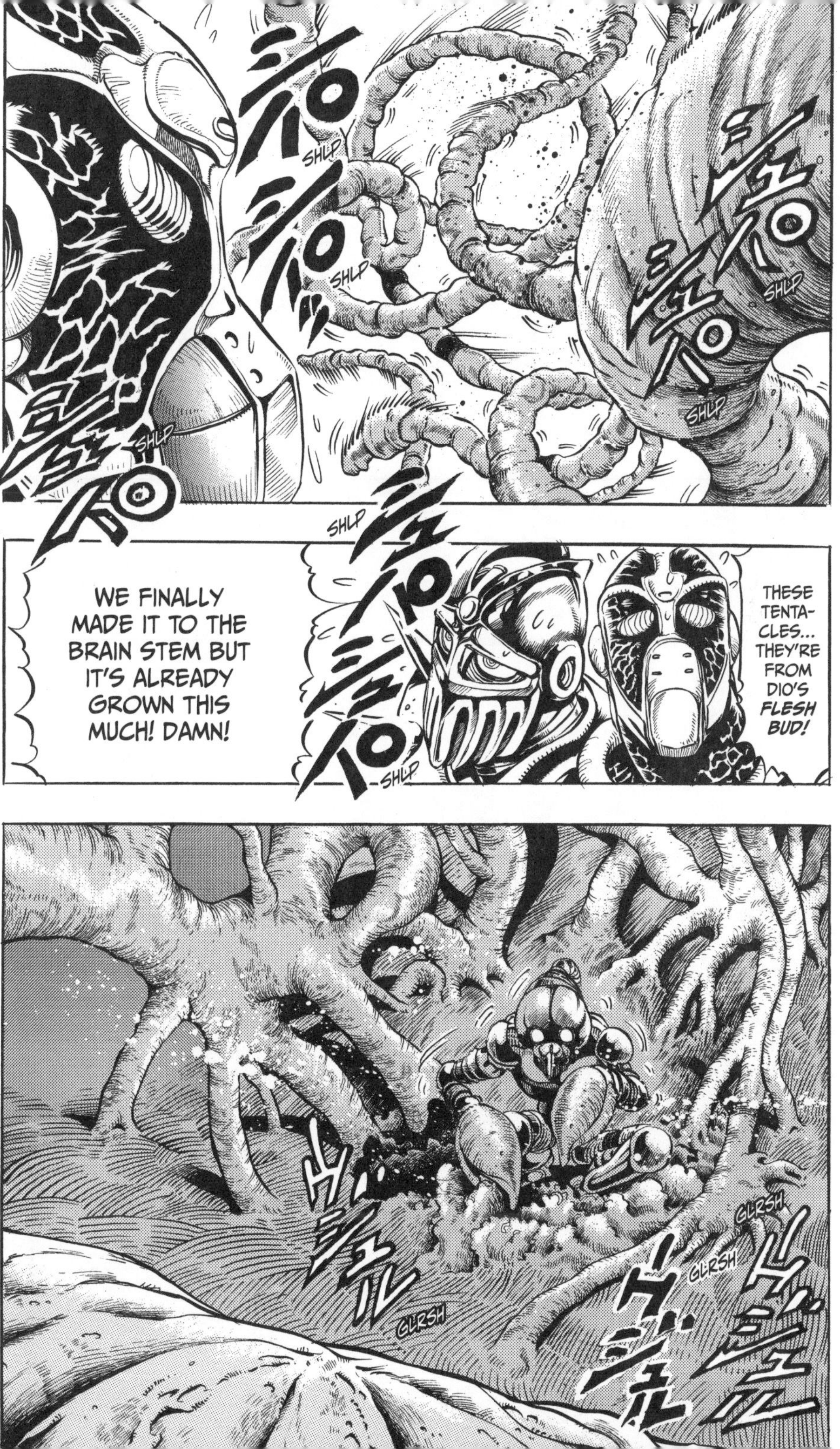
SHLP
SHLP
SHLP
SHLP
SHLP
SHLP
THESE TENTACLES... THEY'RE FROM DIO'S *FLESH BUD!*
WE FINALLY MADE IT TO THE BRAIN STEM BUT IT'S ALREADY GROWN THIS MUCH! DAMN!
SHLP
GLRSH
GLRSH
GLRSH

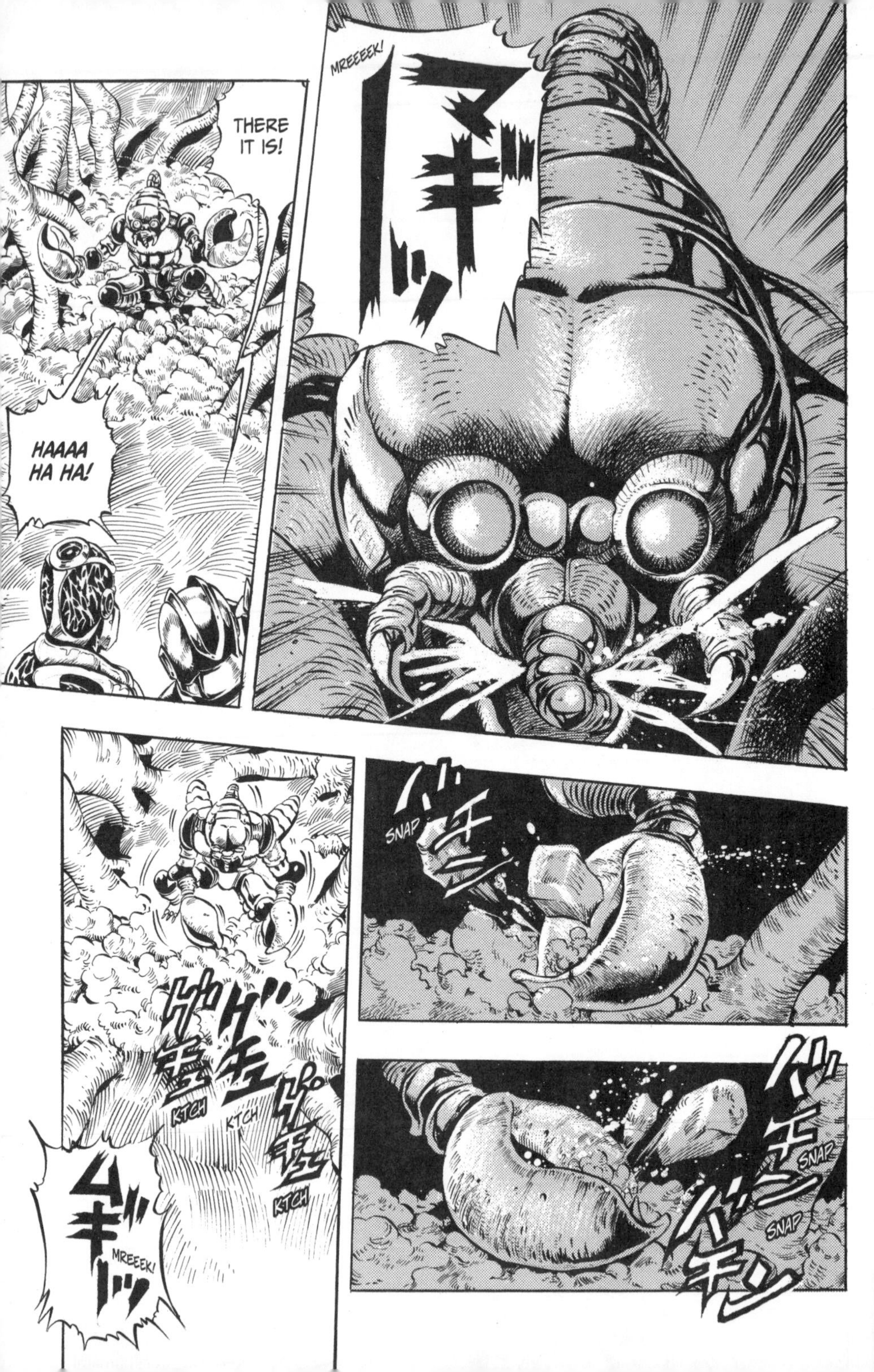
MREEEEK!
THERE IT IS!
HAAAA HA HA!
SNAP
SNAP
SNAP
KTCH
KTCH
KTCH
MREEEK!

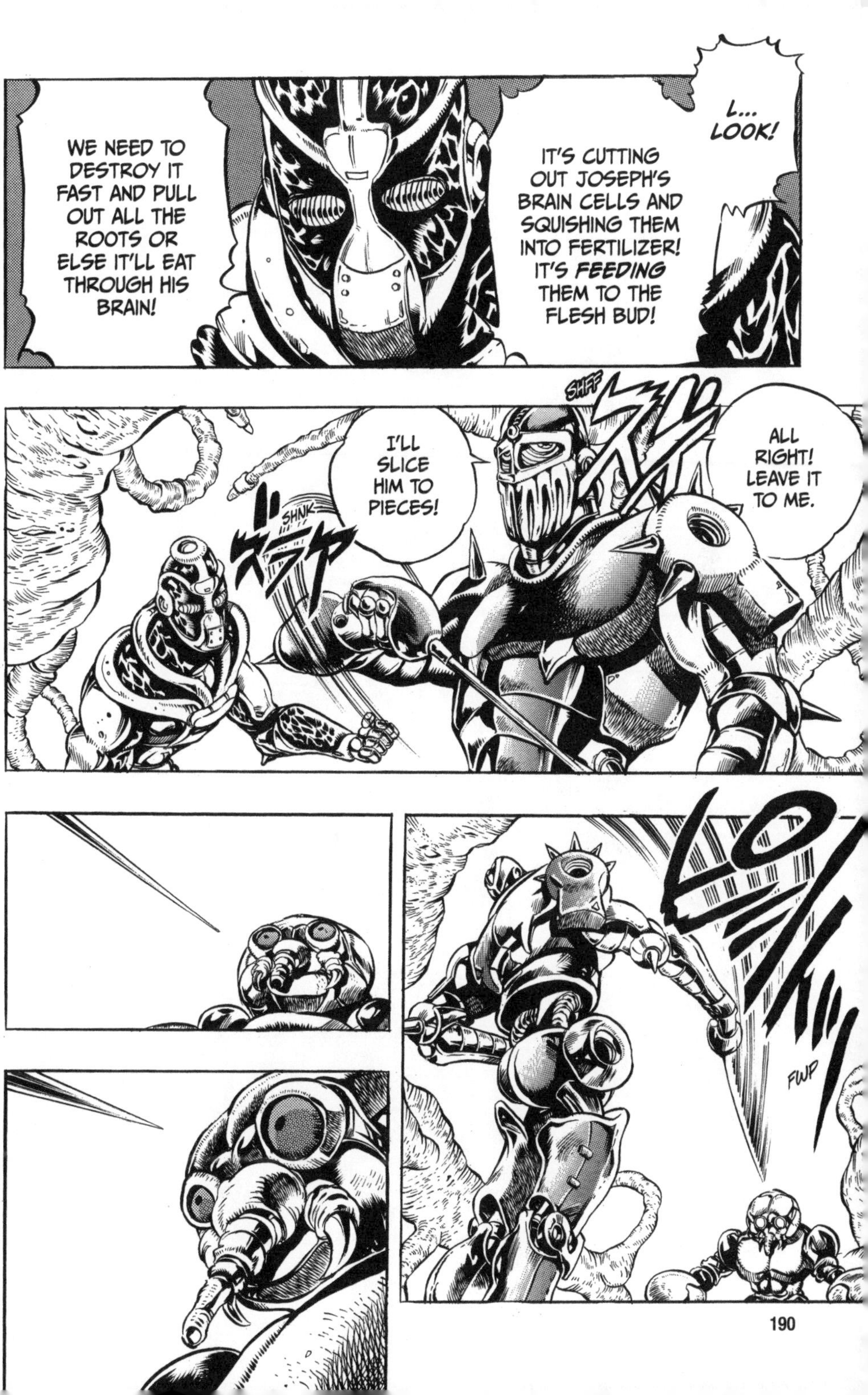
L... LOOK!
IT'S CUTTING OUT JOSEPH'S BRAIN CELLS AND SQUISHING THEM INTO FERTILIZER! IT'S *FEEDING* THEM TO THE FLESH BUD!
WE NEED TO DESTROY IT FAST AND PULL OUT ALL THE ROOTS OR ELSE IT'LL EAT THROUGH HIS BRAIN!
SHFF
ALL RIGHT! LEAVE IT TO ME.
I'LL SLICE HIM TO PIECES!
SHNK
FWP

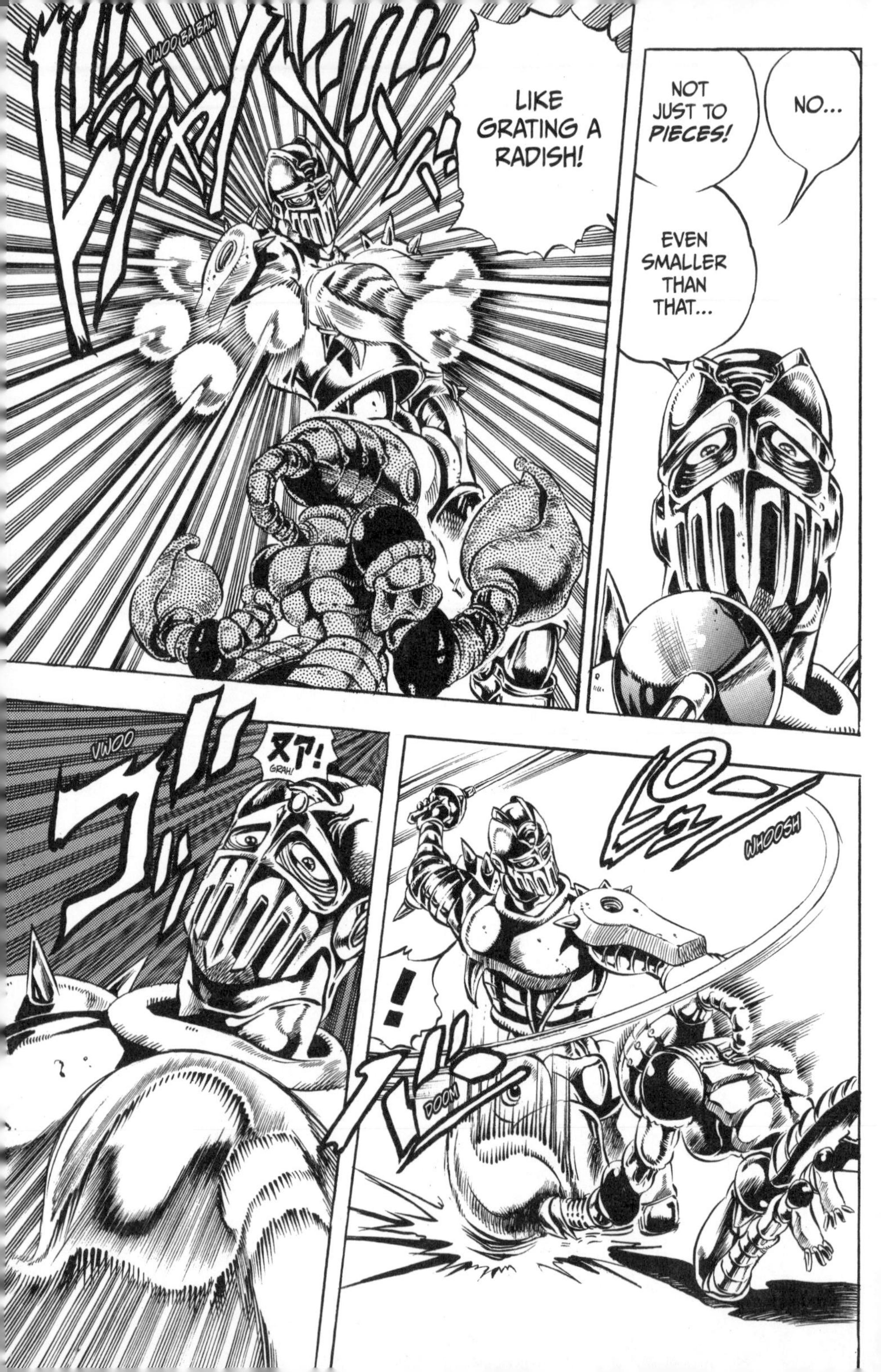
NO...
NOT JUST TO PIECES!
EVEN SMALLER THAN THAT...
LIKE GRATING A RADISH!
VWOO BA BAM
WHOOSH
!
DOOM
ヌア!
GRAH!
VWOO

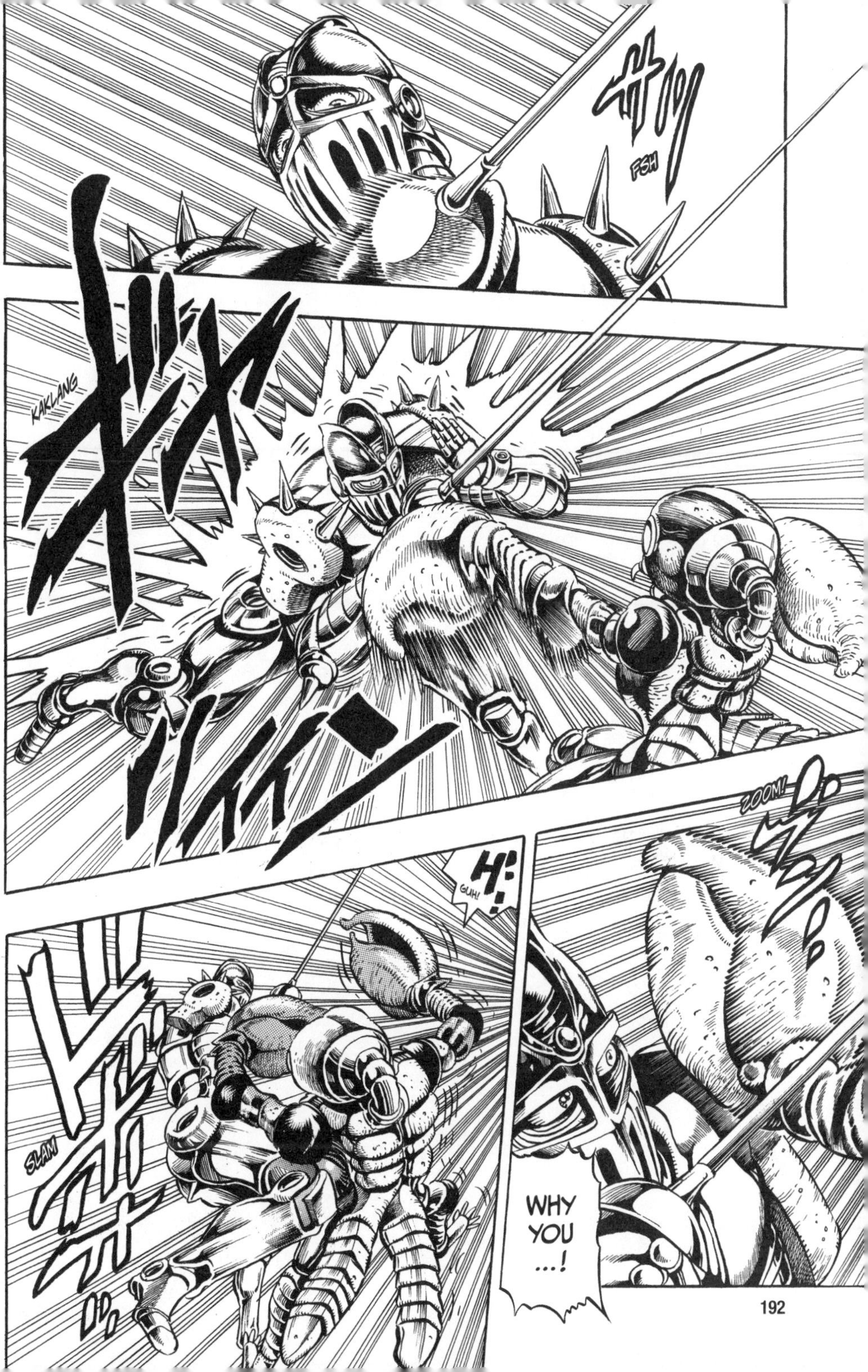
FSH
KAKLANG
ZOOM!
WHY YOU ...!
GUH!
SLAM

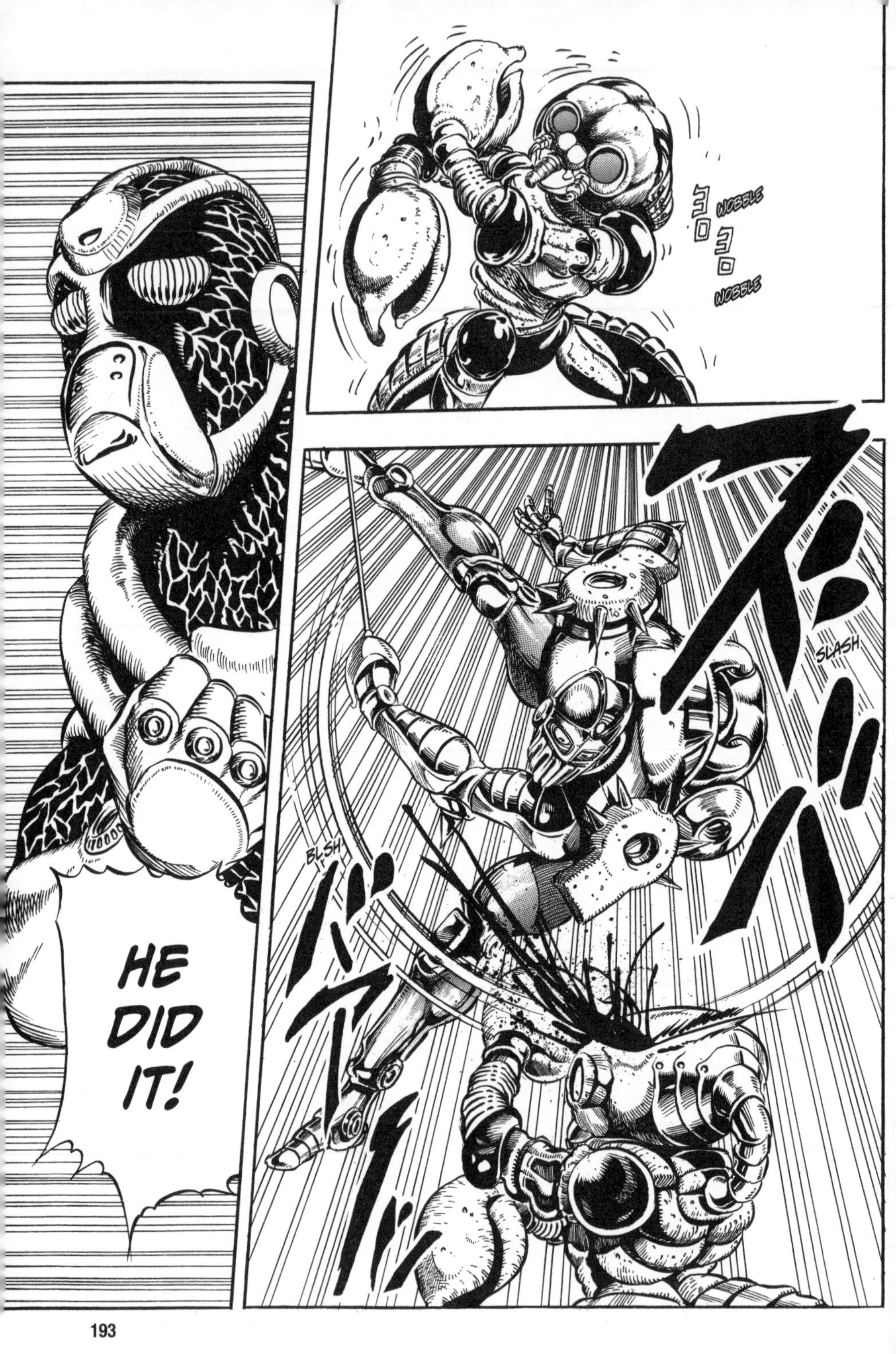
ヨロ
WOBBLE
ヨロ
WOBBLE
SLASH
BLSH
HE DID IT!

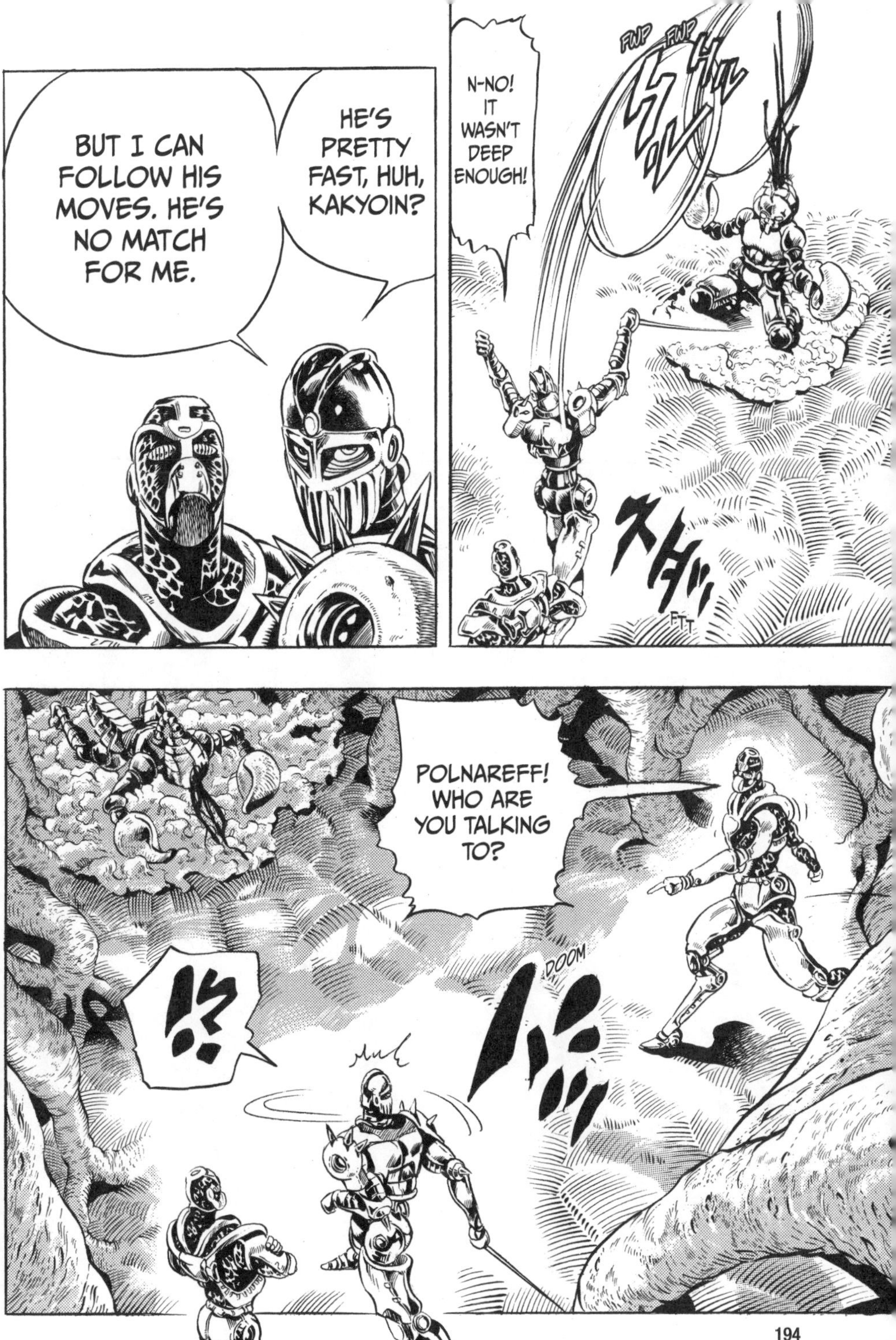
FWP FWP
N-NO! IT WASN'T DEEP ENOUGH!
FTT
HE'S PRETTY FAST, HUH, KAKYOIN?
BUT I CAN FOLLOW HIS MOVES. HE'S NO MATCH FOR ME.
POLNAREFF! WHO ARE YOU TALKING TO?
DOOM
!?

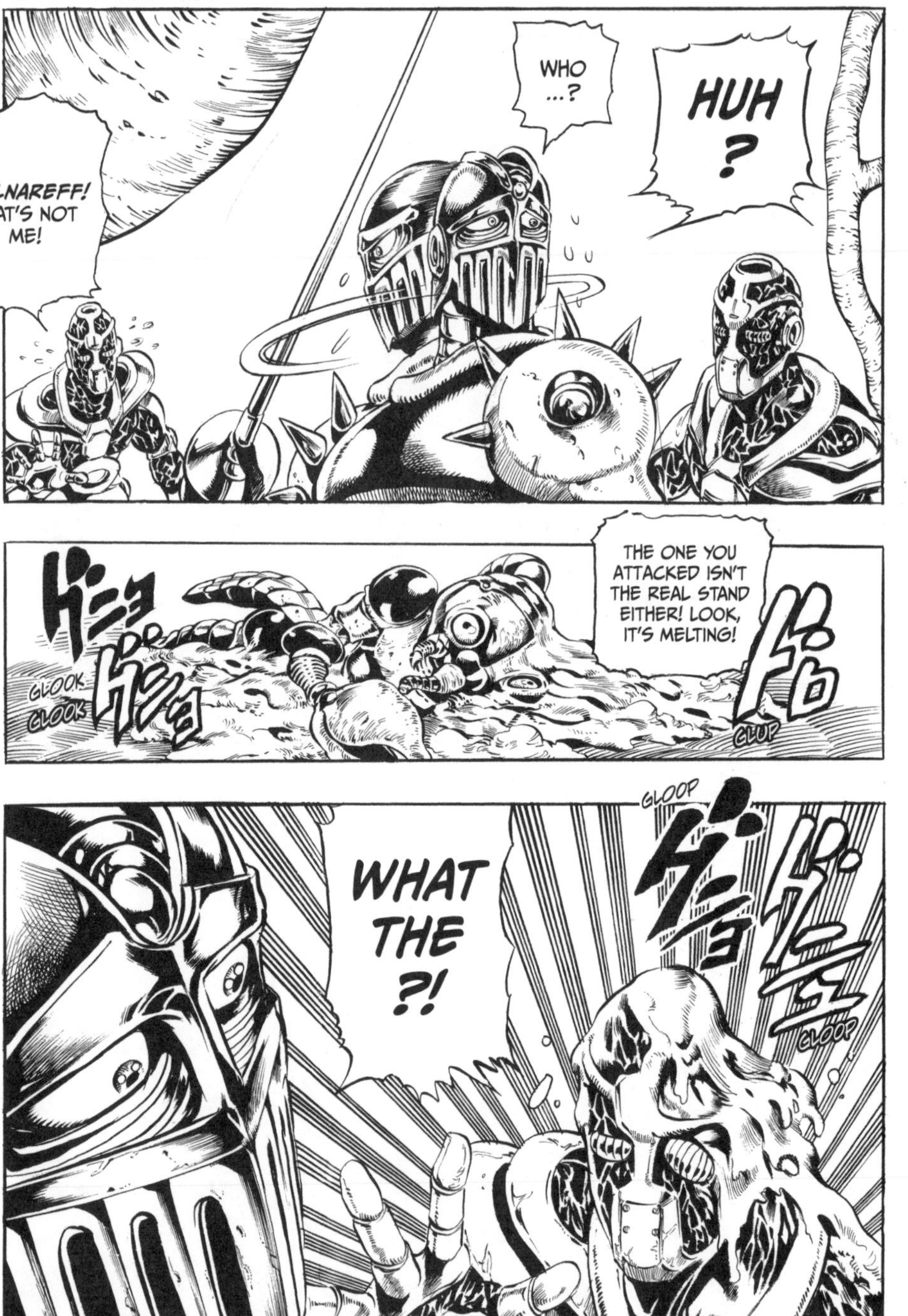
HUH ?
WHO ...?
POLNAREFF! THAT'S NOT ME!
THE ONE YOU ATTACKED ISN'T THE REAL STAND EITHER! LOOK, IT'S MELTING!
GLUP
GLOOK GLOOK
GLOOP
GLOOP
WHAT THE ?!

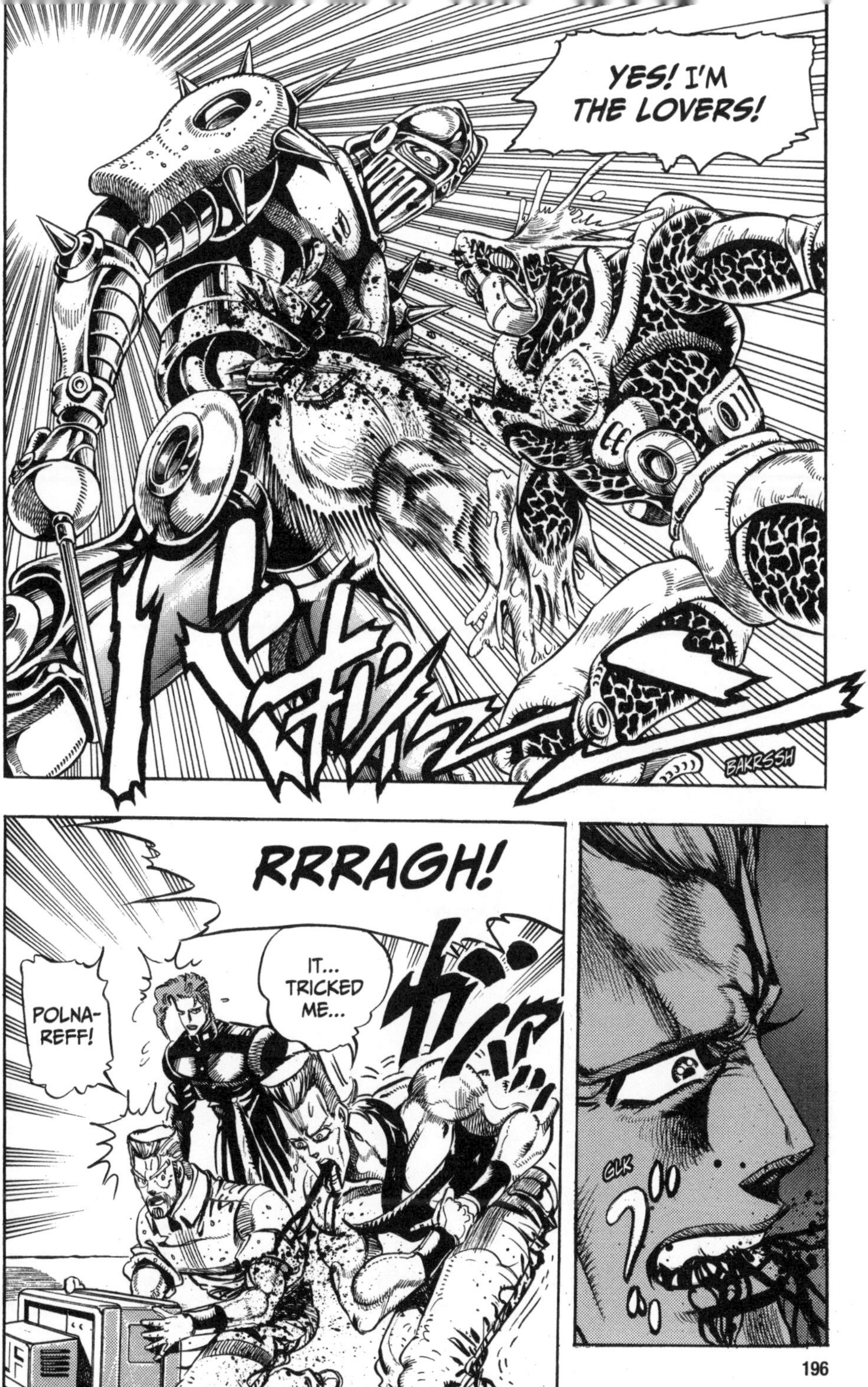
YES! I'M THE LOVERS!
BAKRSSH
CLK
RRRAGH!
IT... TRICKED ME...
POLNA-REFF!

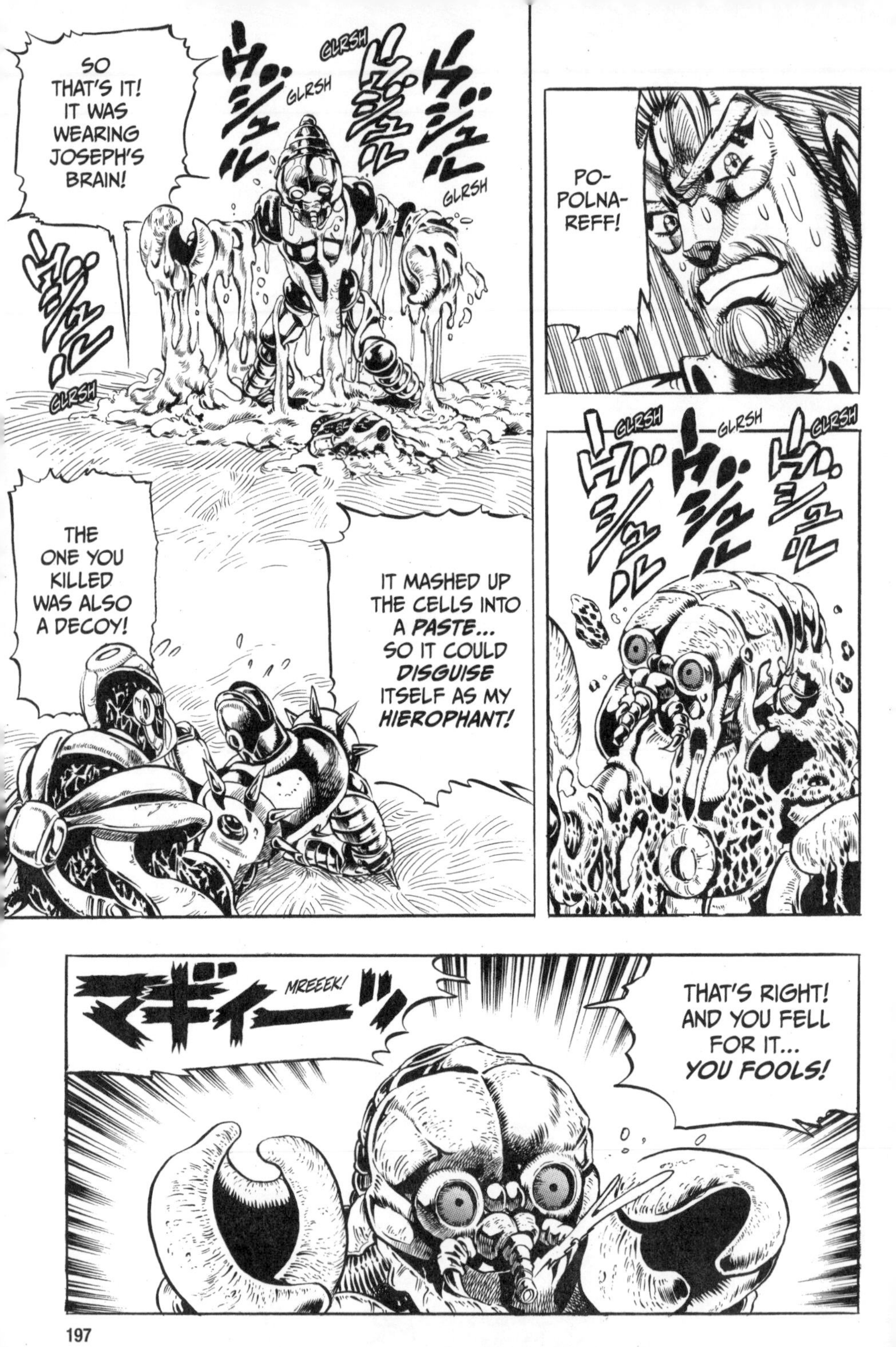
PO-POLNAREFF!
GLRSH
GLRSH
GLRSH
GLRSH
GLRSH
GLRSH
GLRSH
SO THAT'S IT! IT WAS WEARING JOSEPH'S BRAIN!
THE ONE YOU KILLED WAS ALSO A DECOY!
IT MASHED UP THE CELLS INTO A *PASTE*... SO IT COULD *DISGUISE* ITSELF AS MY *HIEROPHANT!*
マギィーッ
MREEEK!
THAT'S RIGHT! AND YOU FELL FOR IT... *YOU FOOLS!*

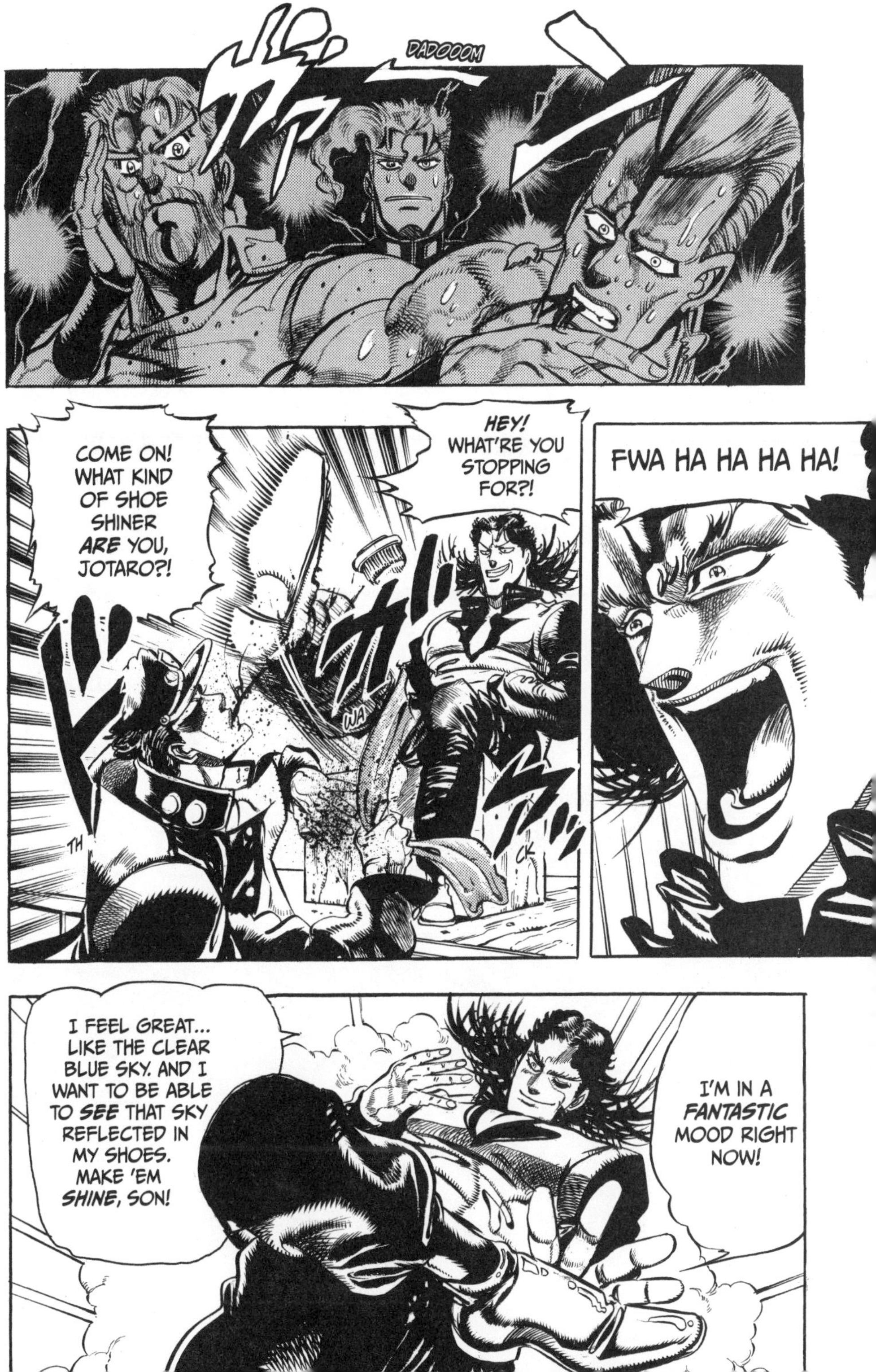
DADOOOM
FWA HA HA HA HA!
HEY! WHAT'RE YOU STOPPING FOR?!
COME ON! WHAT KIND OF SHOE SHINER ARE YOU, JOTARO?!
WA
CK
TH
I'M IN A FANTASTIC MOOD RIGHT NOW!
I FEEL GREAT... LIKE THE CLEAR BLUE SKY. AND I WANT TO BE ABLE TO SEE THAT SKY REFLECTED IN MY SHOES. MAKE 'EM SHINE, SON!

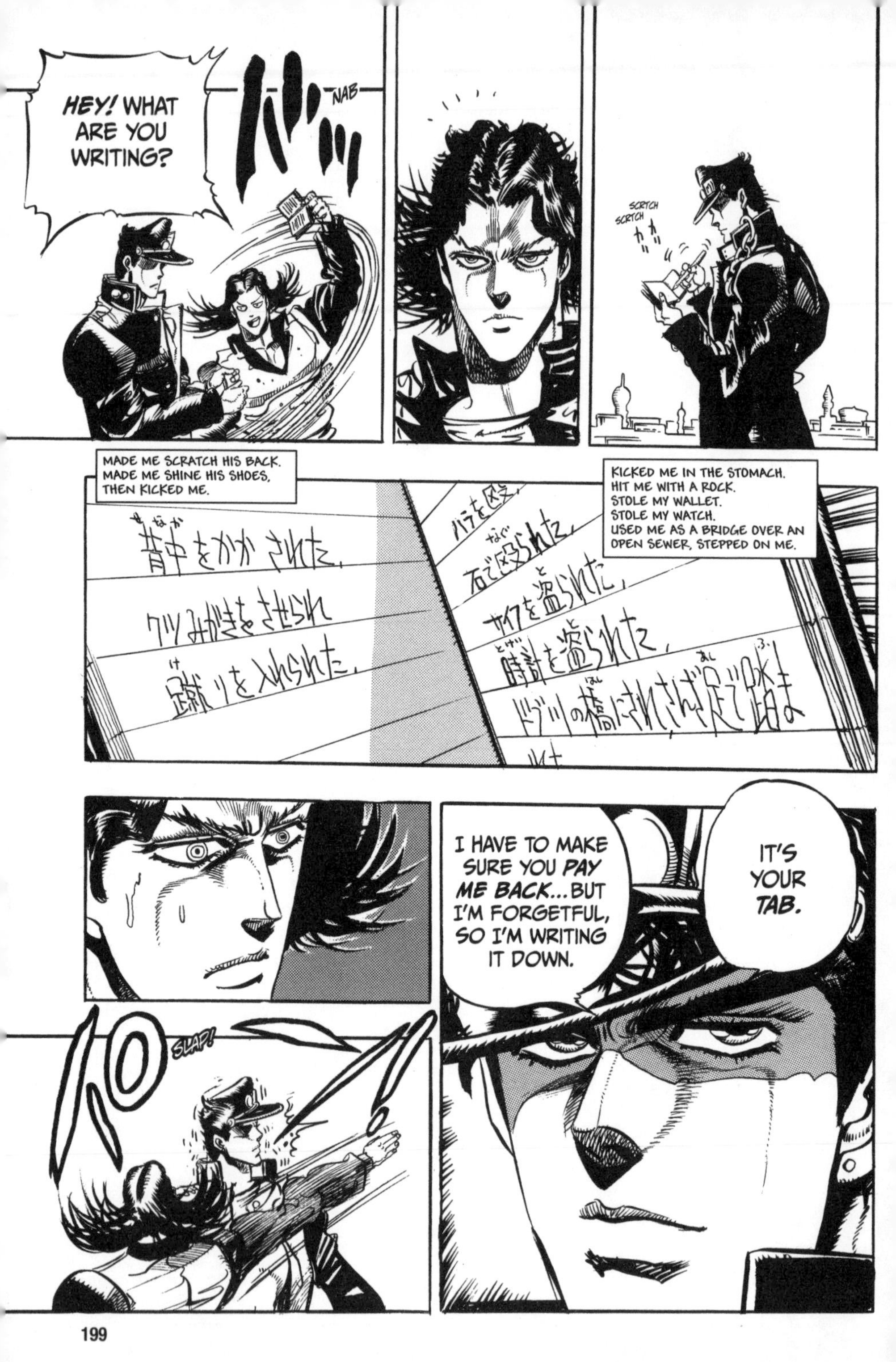
SCRTCH
SCRTCH
NAB
HEY! WHAT ARE YOU WRITING?
MADE ME SCRATCH HIS BACK.
MADE ME SHINE HIS SHOES,
THEN KICKED ME.
KICKED ME IN THE STOMACH.
HIT ME WITH A ROCK.
STOLE MY WALLET.
STOLE MY WATCH.
USED ME AS A BRIDGE OVER AN OPEN SEWER, STEPPED ON ME.
IT'S YOUR TAB.
I HAVE TO MAKE SURE YOU PAY ME BACK...BUT I'M FORGETFUL, SO I'M WRITING IT DOWN.
SLAP!

THE LOVER 6
HIROHIKO ARAKI'S LUCKY LAND

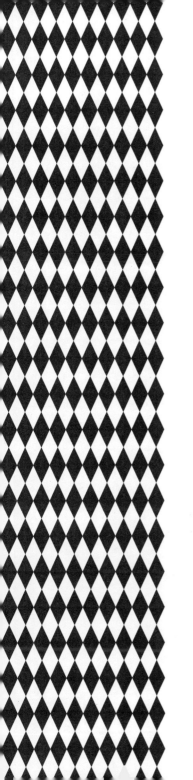

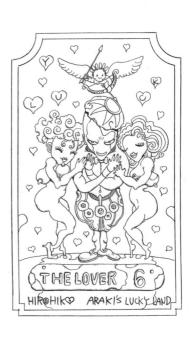

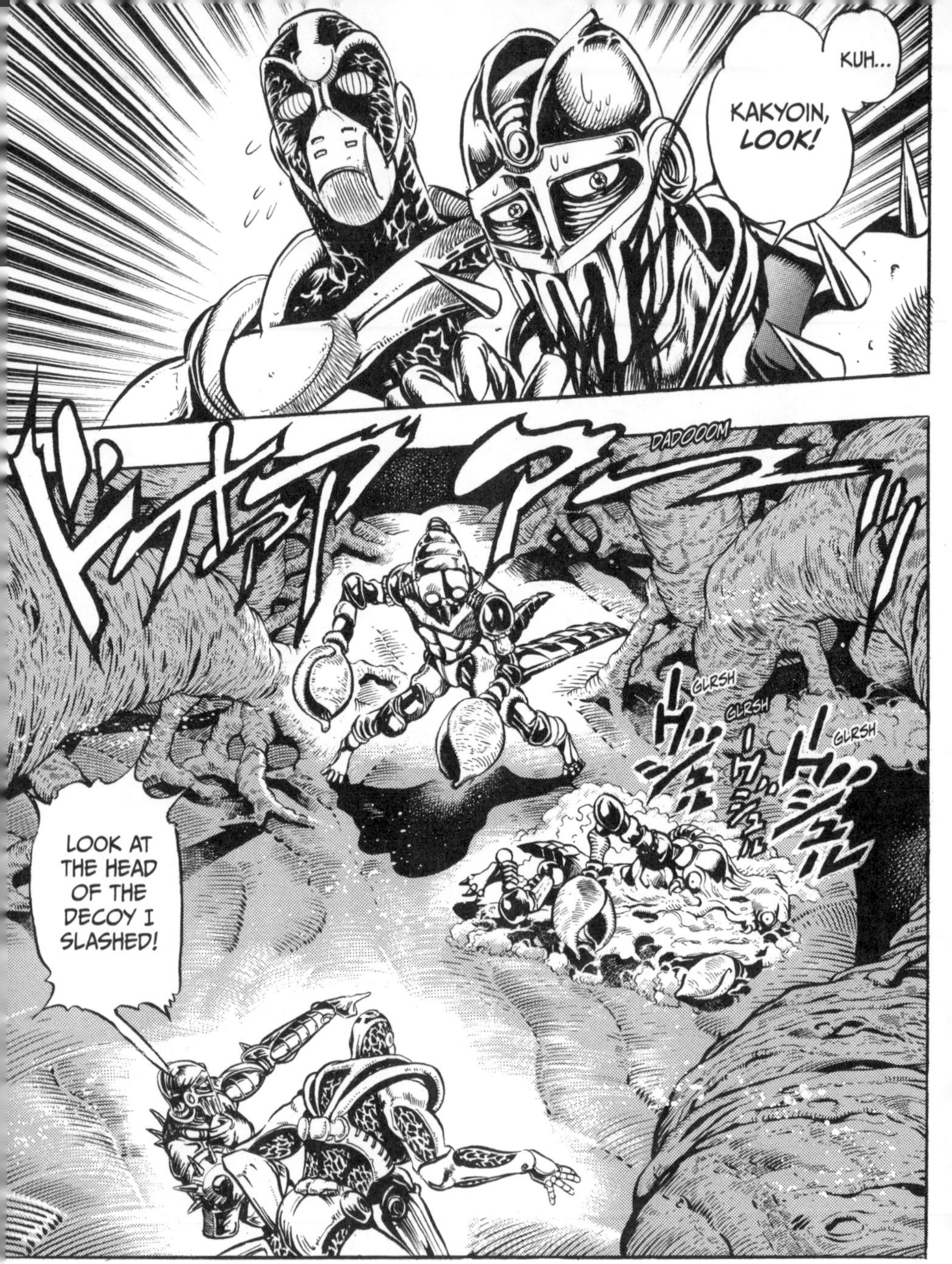
KUH...
KAKYOIN, LOOK!
DADOOOM
GLRSH
GLRSH
GLRSH
LOOK AT THE HEAD OF THE DECOY I SLASHED!

CHAPTER 51: The Lovers PART 5

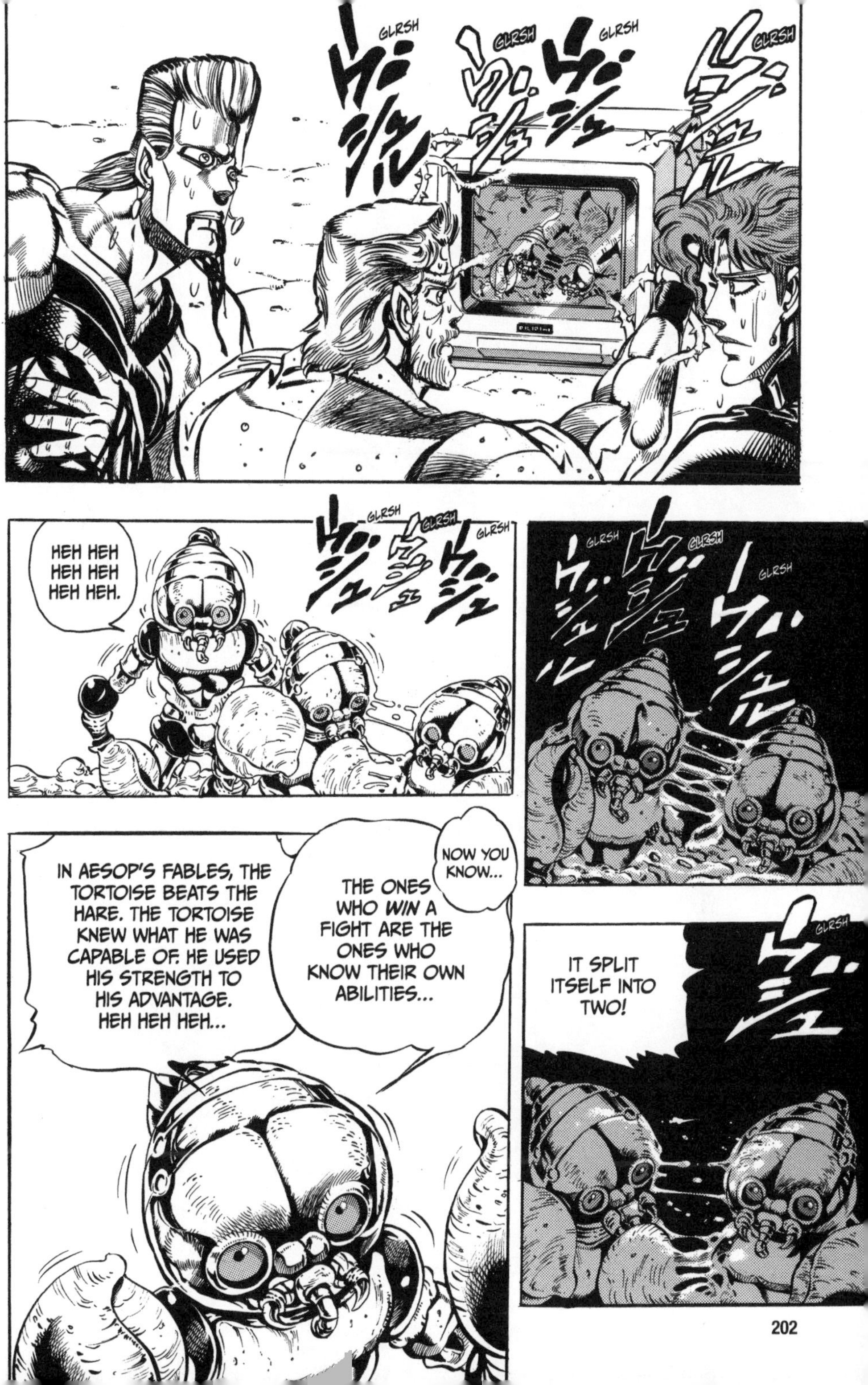
GLRSH
GLRSH
GLRSH
GLRSH
GLRSH
GLRSH
GLRSH
GLRSH
GLRSH
GLRSH
HEH HEH HEH HEH HEH HEH.
GLRSH
IT SPLIT ITSELF INTO TWO!
NOW YOU KNOW...
THE ONES WHO *WIN* A FIGHT ARE THE ONES WHO KNOW THEIR OWN ABILITIES...
IN AESOP'S FABLES, THE TORTOISE BEATS THE HARE. THE TORTOISE KNEW WHAT HE WAS CAPABLE OF. HE USED HIS STRENGTH TO HIS ADVANTAGE. HEH HEH HEH...

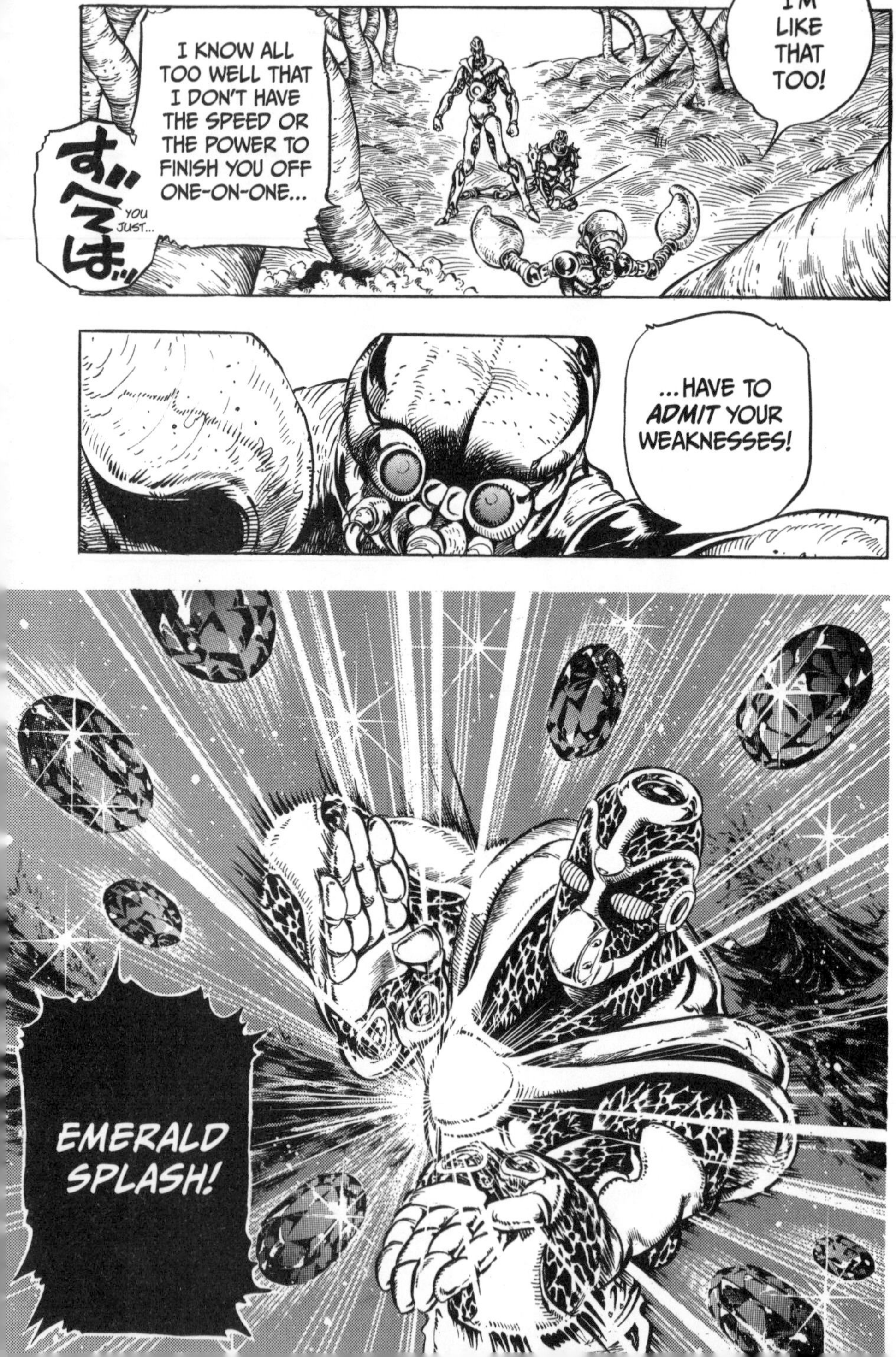
I'M LIKE THAT TOO!
I KNOW ALL TOO WELL THAT I DON'T HAVE THE SPEED OR THE POWER TO FINISH YOU OFF ONE-ON-ONE...
YOU JUST...
...HAVE TO *ADMIT* YOUR WEAKNESSES!
EMERALD SPLASH!

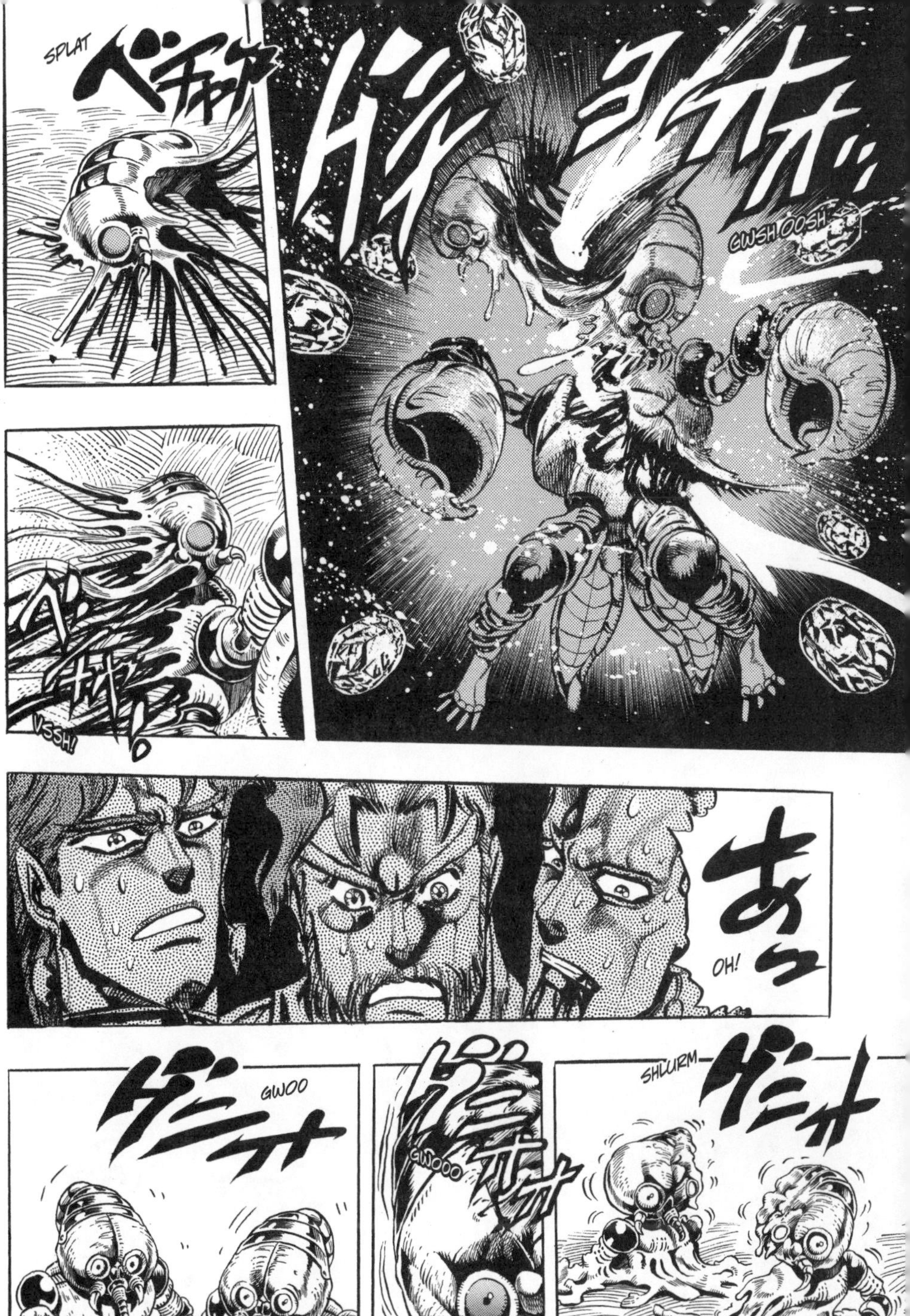
GWSH OOSH
SPLAT
VSSH!
あっ
OH!
SHLURM
GWOOO
GWOO

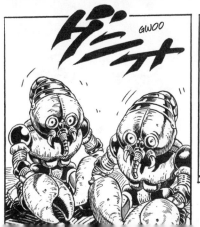

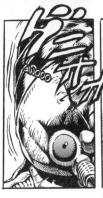

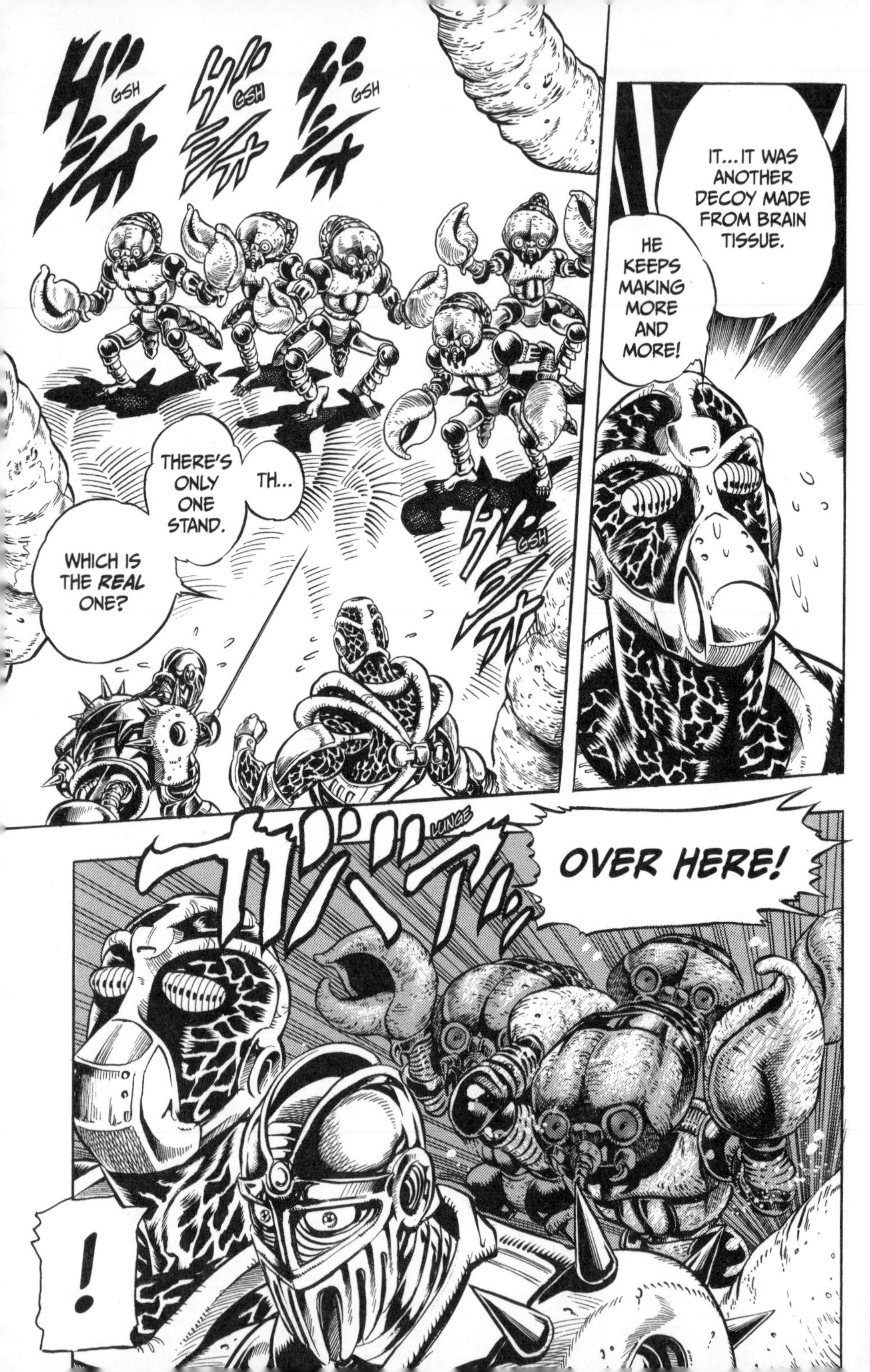
IT...IT WAS ANOTHER DECOY MADE FROM BRAIN TISSUE.
HE KEEPS MAKING MORE AND MORE!
GSH
GSH
GSH
GSH
TH...
THERE'S ONLY ONE STAND.
WHICH IS THE *REAL* ONE?
OVER HERE!
LUNGE
!

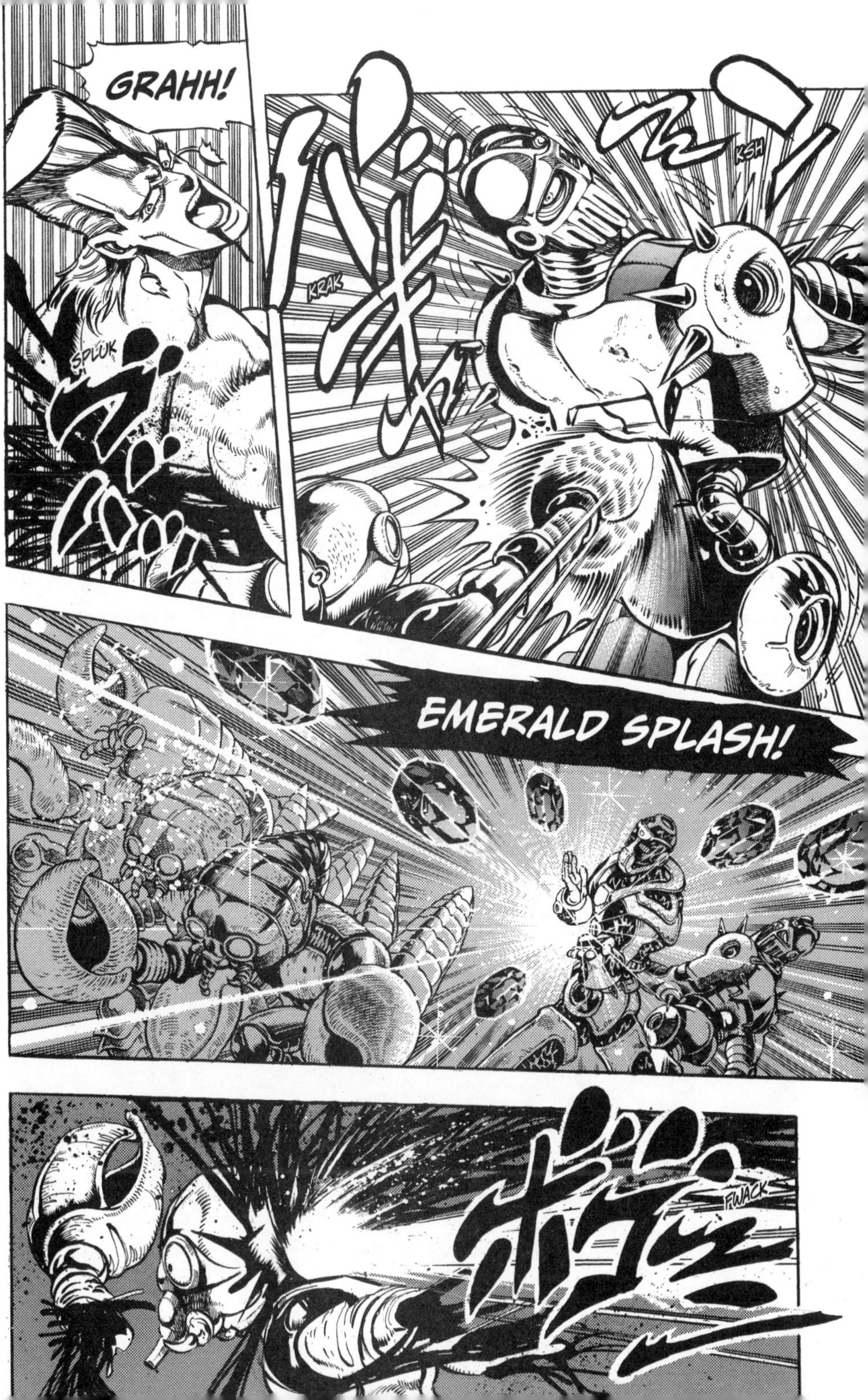
KSH
KRAK
GRAHH!
SPLUK
EMERALD SPLASH!
FWACK

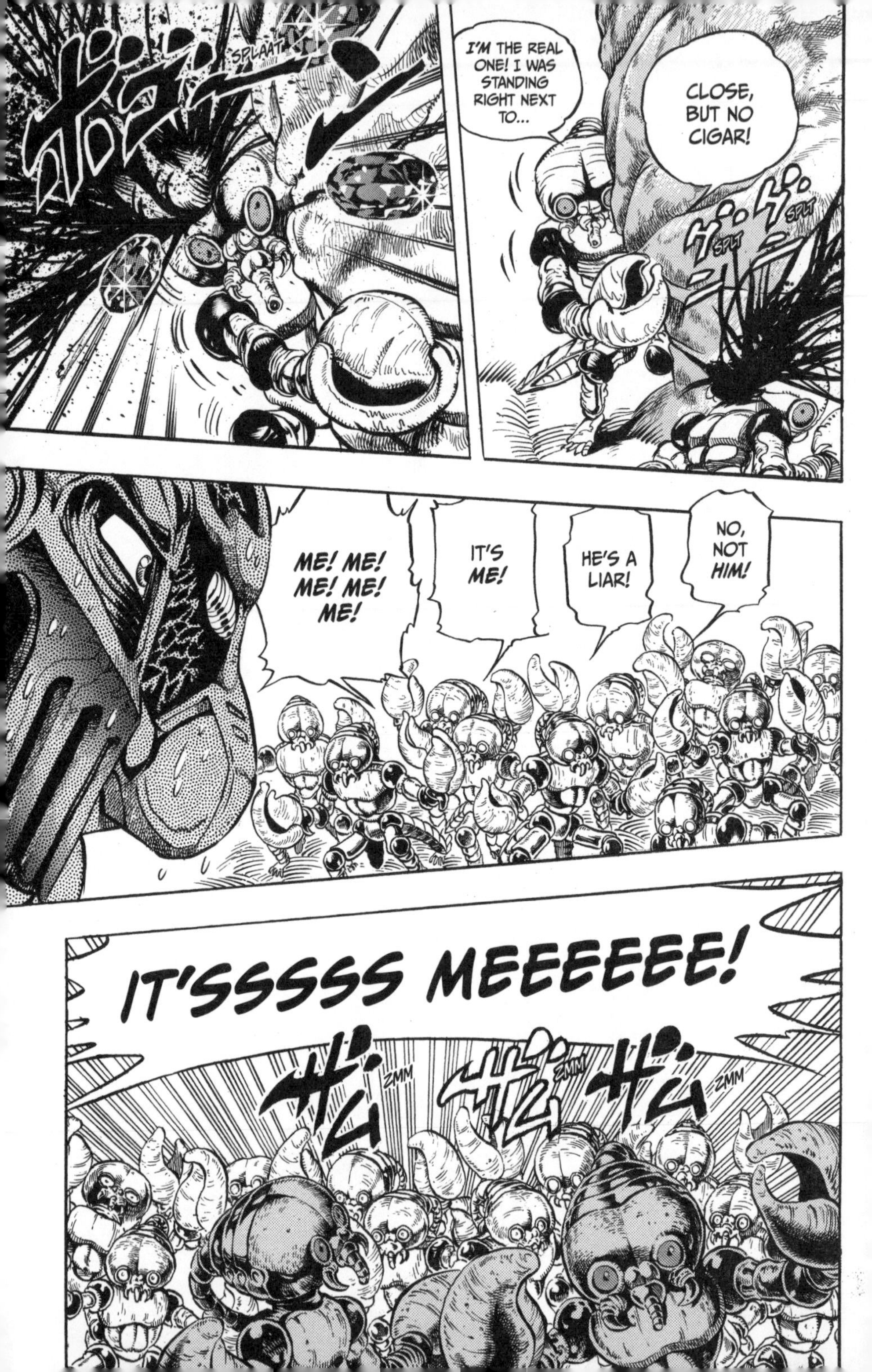
I'M THE REAL ONE! I WAS STANDING RIGHT NEXT TO...
CLOSE, BUT NO CIGAR!
SPLT
SPLT
SPLAAT
NO, NOT HIM!
HE'S A LIAR!
IT'S ME!
ME! ME! ME! ME! ME!
IT'SSSSS MEEEEEEE!
ZMM
ZMM
ZMM

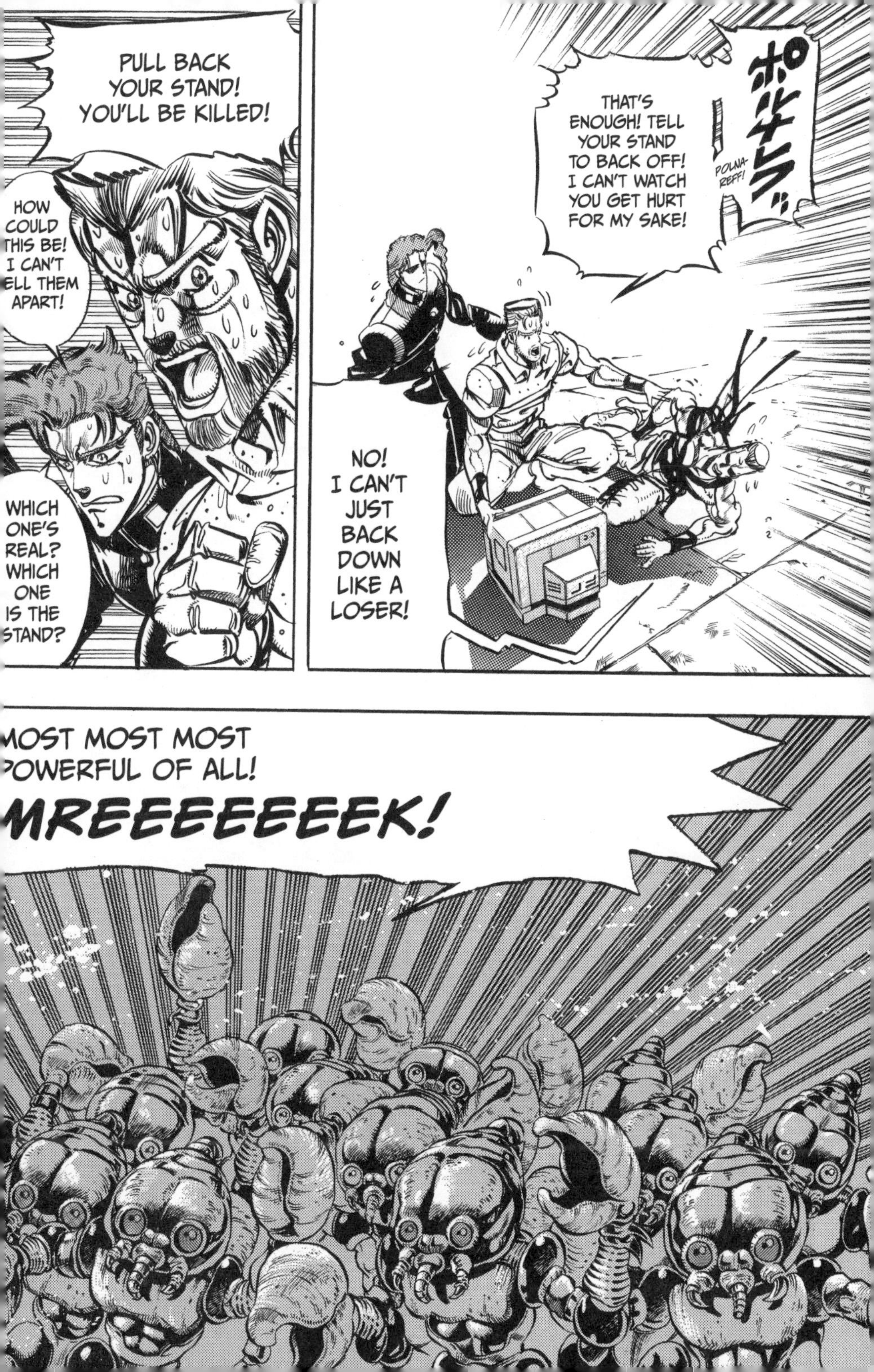
ポルナレフ
POLNAREFF!
THAT'S ENOUGH! TELL YOUR STAND TO BACK OFF! I CAN'T WATCH YOU GET HURT FOR MY SAKE!
NO! I CAN'T JUST BACK DOWN LIKE A LOSER!
PULL BACK YOUR STAND! YOU'LL BE KILLED!
HOW COULD THIS BE! I CAN'T ELL THEM APART!
WHICH ONE'S REAL? WHICH ONE IS THE STAND?
MOST MOST MOST POWERFUL OF ALL!
MREEEEEEEK!

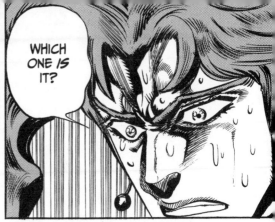

WHICH ONE IS IT?
HEH HEH HEH. NOW YOU SEE...
THE WORLD'S "WEAK-EST" STAND ...
...IS THE MOST MOS
MOST MOST MOST
MOST MOST MOST
MOST MOST MOST

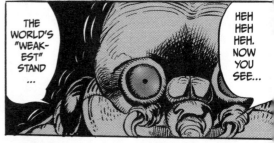

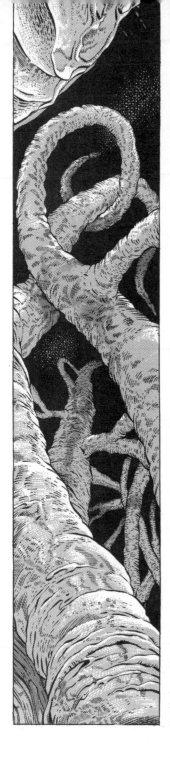

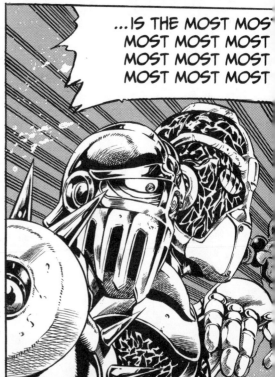

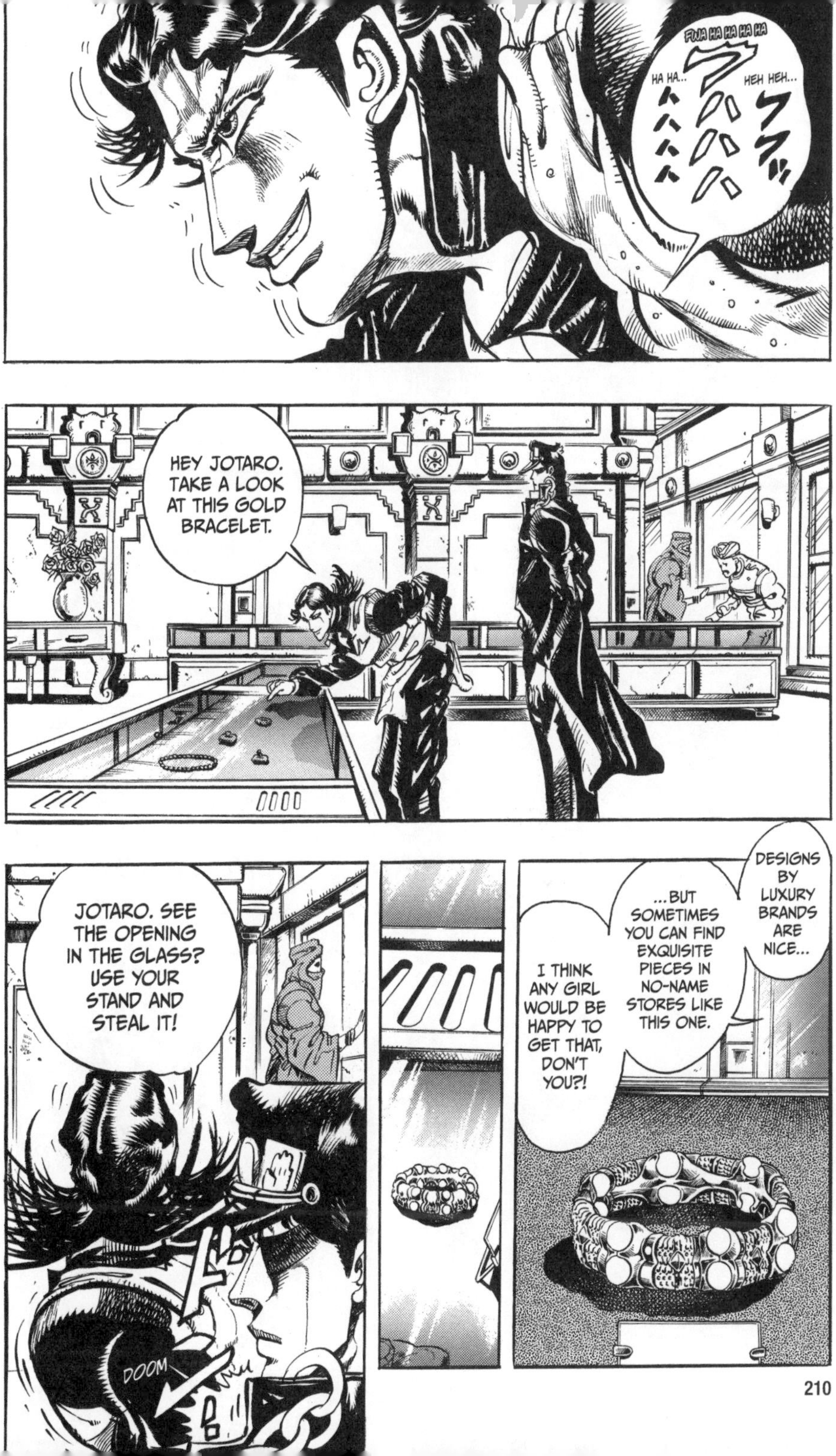
HEH HEH...
FWA HA HA HA HA
HA HA...
HEY JOTARO. TAKE A LOOK AT THIS GOLD BRACELET.
DESIGNS BY LUXURY BRANDS ARE NICE...
...BUT SOMETIMES YOU CAN FIND EXQUISITE PIECES IN NO-NAME STORES LIKE THIS ONE.
I THINK ANY GIRL WOULD BE HAPPY TO GET THAT, DON'T YOU?!
JOTARO. SEE THE OPENING IN THE GLASS? USE YOUR STAND AND STEAL IT!
DOOM

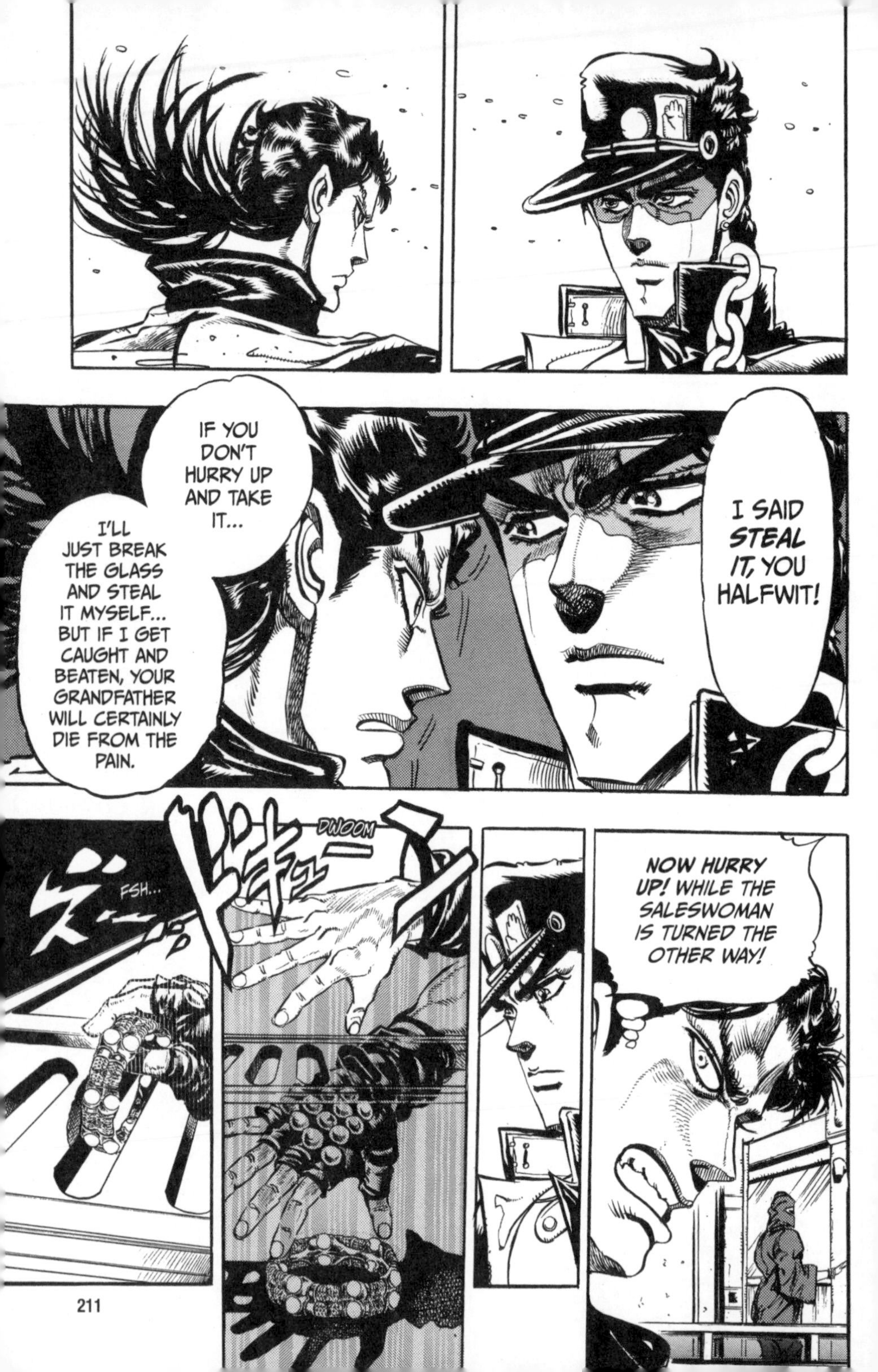

I SAID STEAL IT, YOU HALFWIT!
IF YOU DON'T HURRY UP AND TAKE IT...
I'LL JUST BREAK THE GLASS AND STEAL IT MYSELF... BUT IF I GET CAUGHT AND BEATEN, YOUR GRANDFATHER WILL CERTAINLY DIE FROM THE PAIN.
NOW HURRY UP! WHILE THE SALESWOMAN IS TURNED THE OTHER WAY!
DWOOM
FSH...

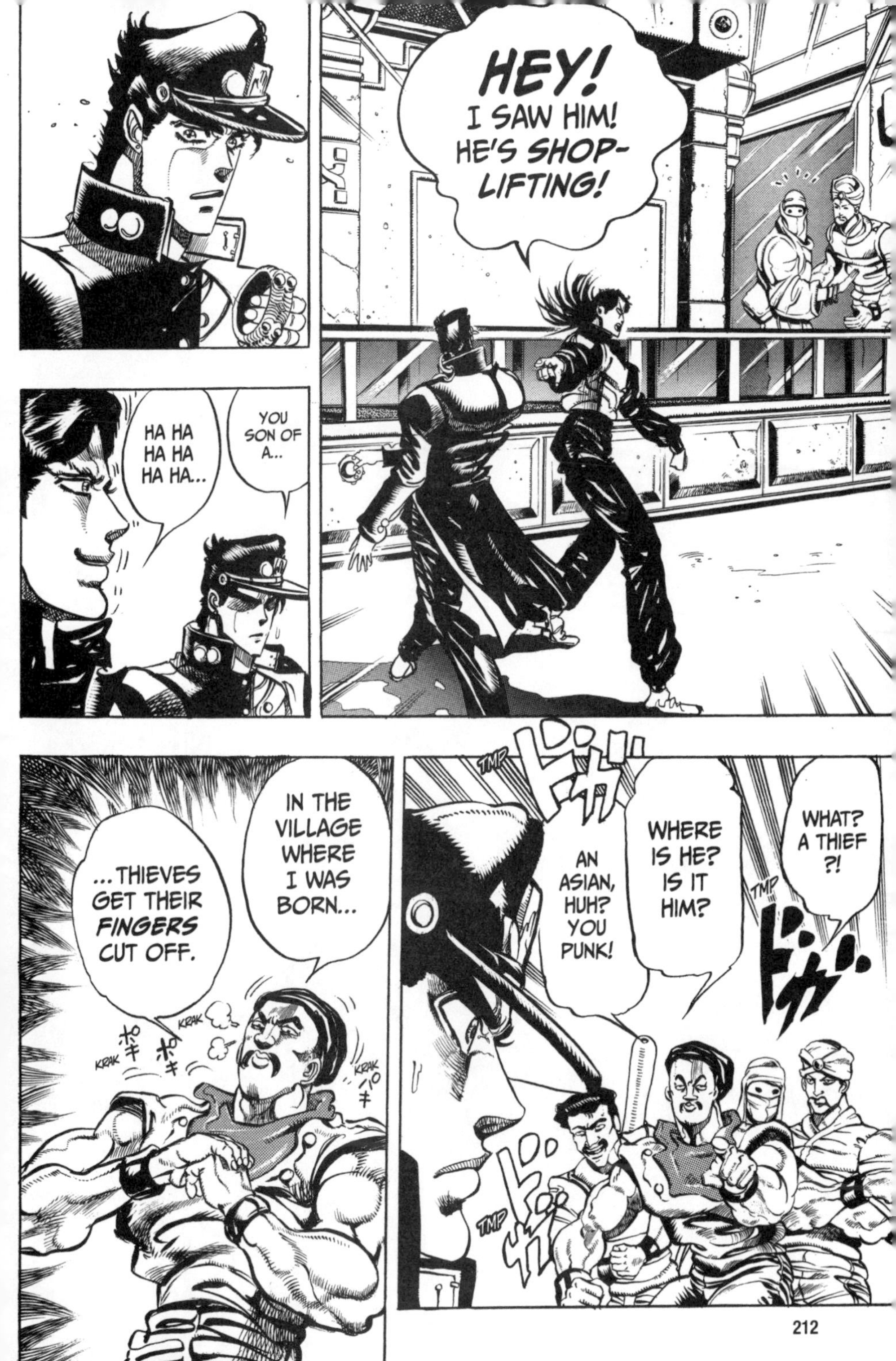
HEY! I SAW HIM! HE'S SHOP-LIFTING!
YOU SON OF A...
HA HA HA HA HA HA...
TMP
WHAT? A THIEF?!
TMP
WHERE IS HE? IS IT HIM?
AN ASIAN, HUH? YOU PUNK!
TMP
IN THE VILLAGE WHERE I WAS BORN...
...THIEVES GET THEIR FINGERS CUT OFF.
KRAK
KRAK
KRAK

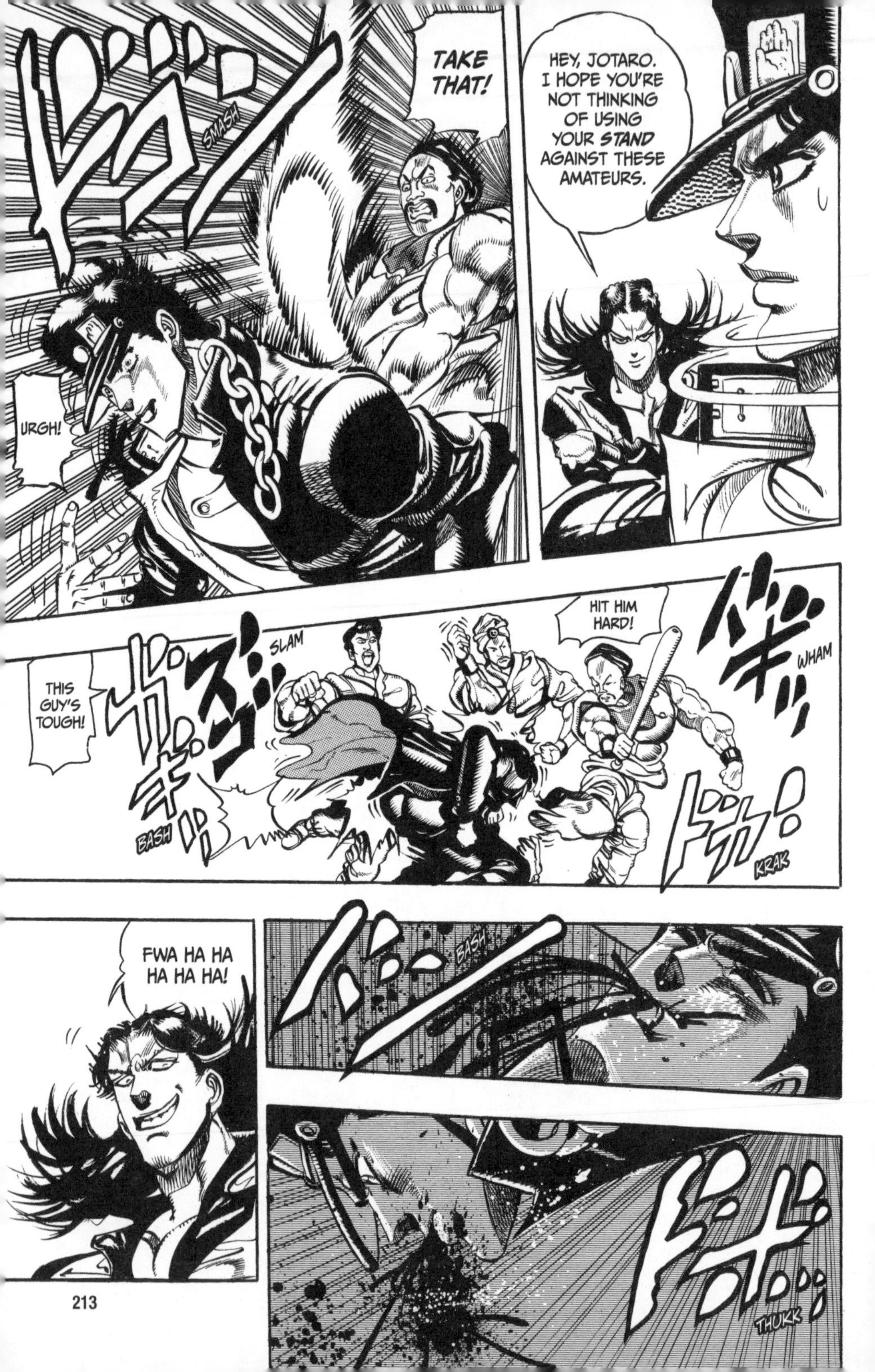
HEY, JOTARO. I HOPE YOU'RE NOT THINKING OF USING YOUR ***STAND*** AGAINST THESE AMATEURS.
TAKE THAT!
SMASH
URGH!
WHAM
HIT HIM HARD!
SLAM
KRAK
THIS GUY'S TOUGH!
BASH
BASH
THUKK
FWA HA HA HA HA HA!

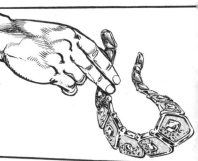

AHA HA HA.

AHA.

AHA HA HA.

HA HA.

THAT SHOULD DO IT. NOW GET THE HELL OUT OF OUR COUNTRY!

WE'LL LET YOU OFF EASY. YOU CAN KEEP YOUR FINGERS FOR NOW.

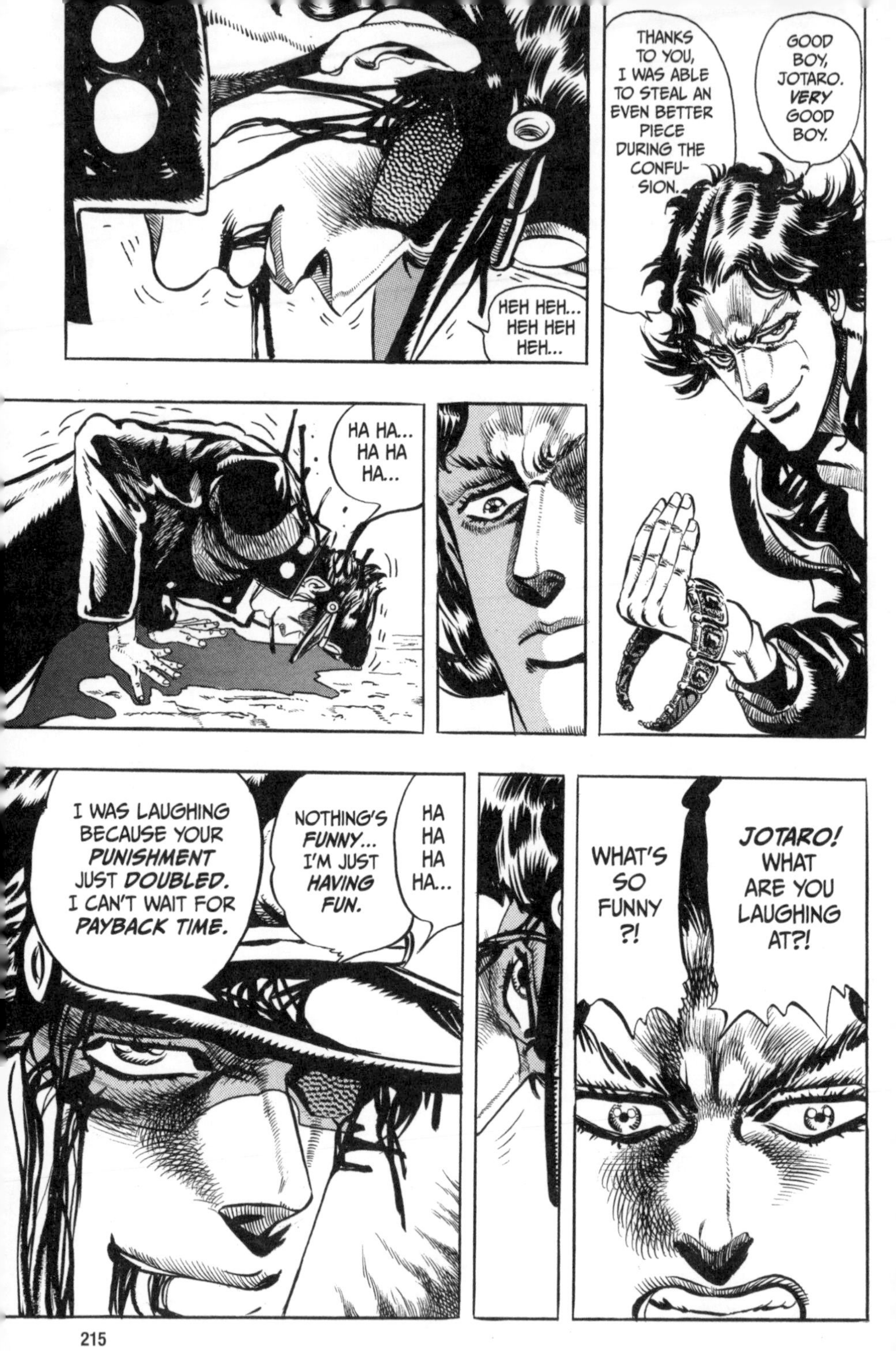
GOOD BOY, JOTARO. VERY GOOD BOY.
THANKS TO YOU, I WAS ABLE TO STEAL AN EVEN BETTER PIECE DURING THE CONFUSION.
HEH HEH... HEH HEH HEH...
HA HA... HA HA HA...
JOTARO! WHAT ARE YOU LAUGHING AT?!
WHAT'S SO FUNNY?!
HA HA HA HA...
NOTHING'S FUNNY... I'M JUST HAVING FUN.
I WAS LAUGHING BECAUSE YOUR PUNISHMENT JUST DOUBLED. I CAN'T WAIT FOR PAYBACK TIME.

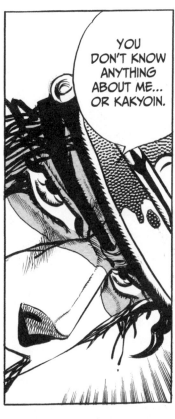

SLAM
WHY YOU!!
I DON'T THINK YOU UNDER-STAND YOUR SITUATION!
OLD MAN JOESTAR IS GOING TO DIE IN A MATTER OF SECONDS, AND THE NEXT ONE TO GO WILL BE...
HA HA HA. NO...
YOU'RE THE ONE WHO DOESN'T UNDERSTAND.
YOU DON'T KNOW ANYTHING ABOUT ME... OR KAKYOIN.
WHAAAAAAT?!
"KNOW THYSELF" IS A GOOD MESSAGE. BUT BEFORE YOU PREACH IT, THINK ABOUT THIS.
YOU DON'T KNOW ENOUGH ABOUT YOUR ENEMIES! YOU SHOULD HAVE DONE YOUR HOMEWORK!

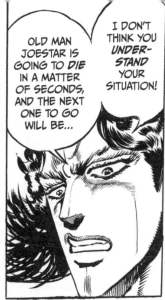

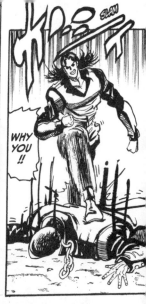

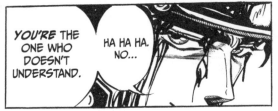

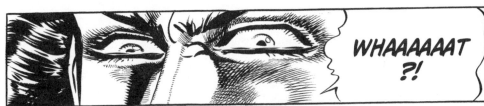

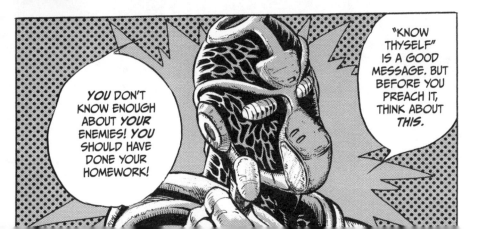

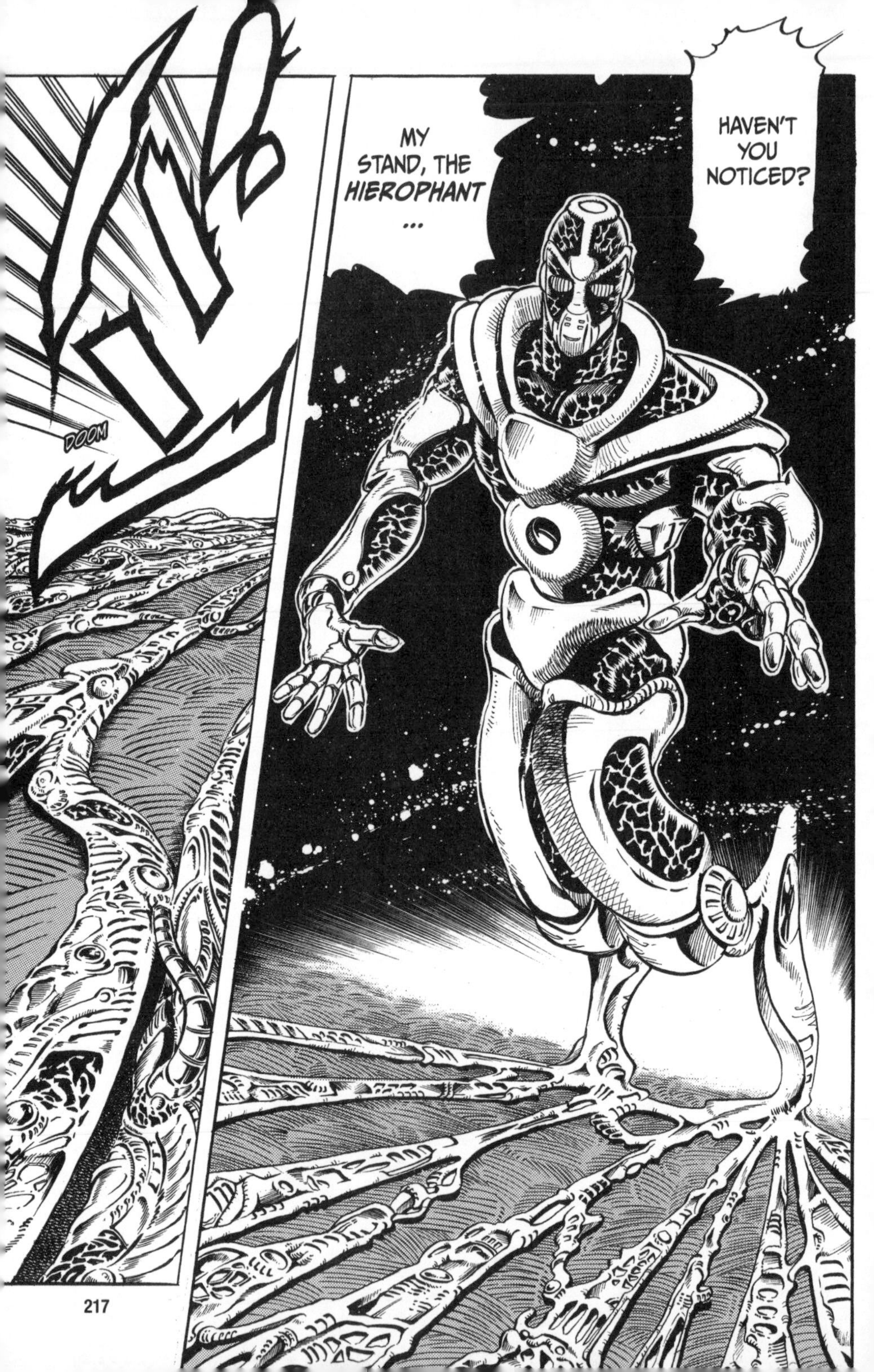
HAVEN'T YOU NOTICED?
MY STAND, THE HIEROPHANT ...
DOOM

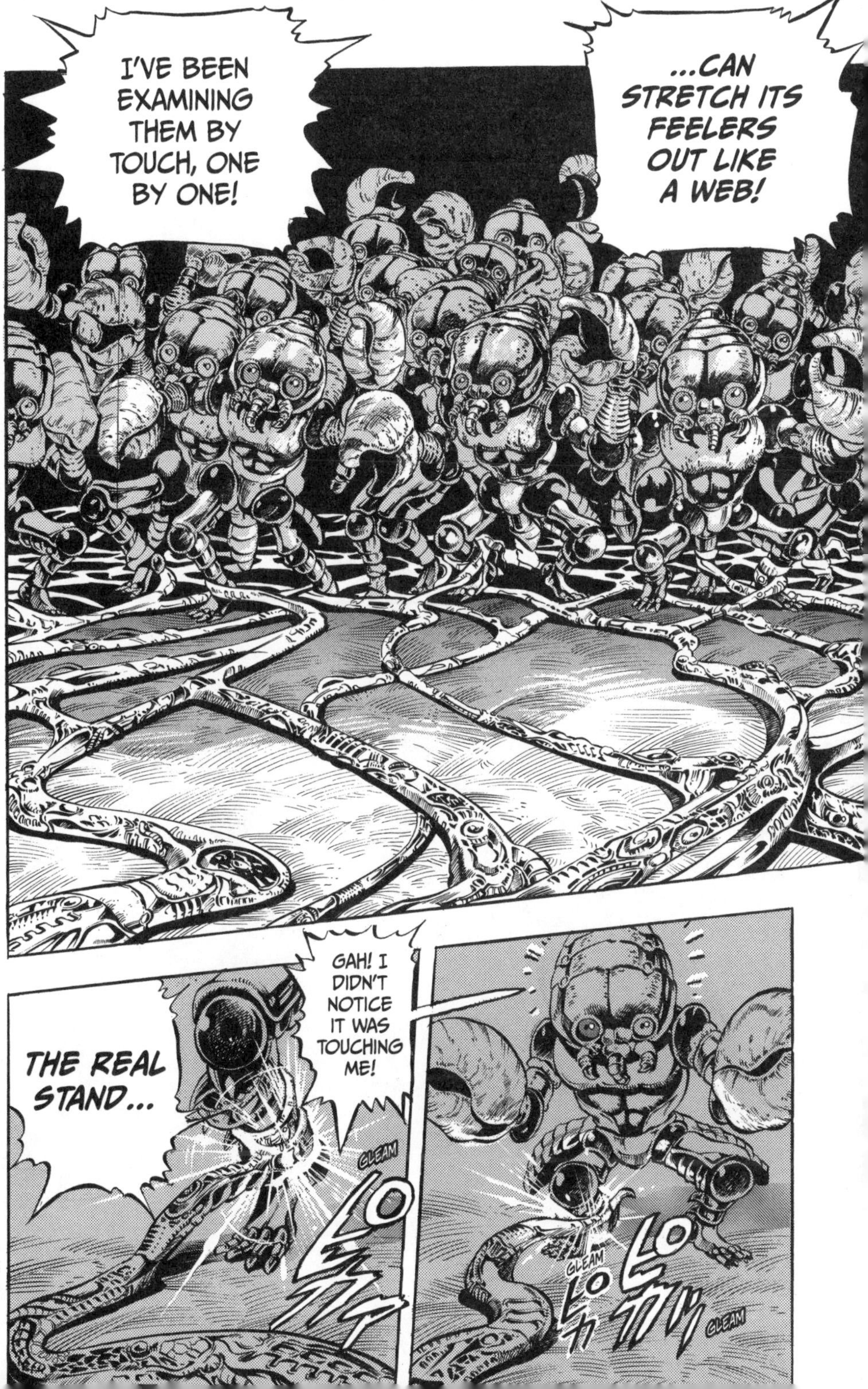
...CAN STRETCH ITS FEELERS OUT LIKE A WEB!
I'VE BEEN EXAMINING THEM BY TOUCH, ONE BY ONE!
GLEAM
GLEAM
GAH! I DIDN'T NOTICE IT WAS TOUCHING ME!
THE REAL STAND...
GLEAM

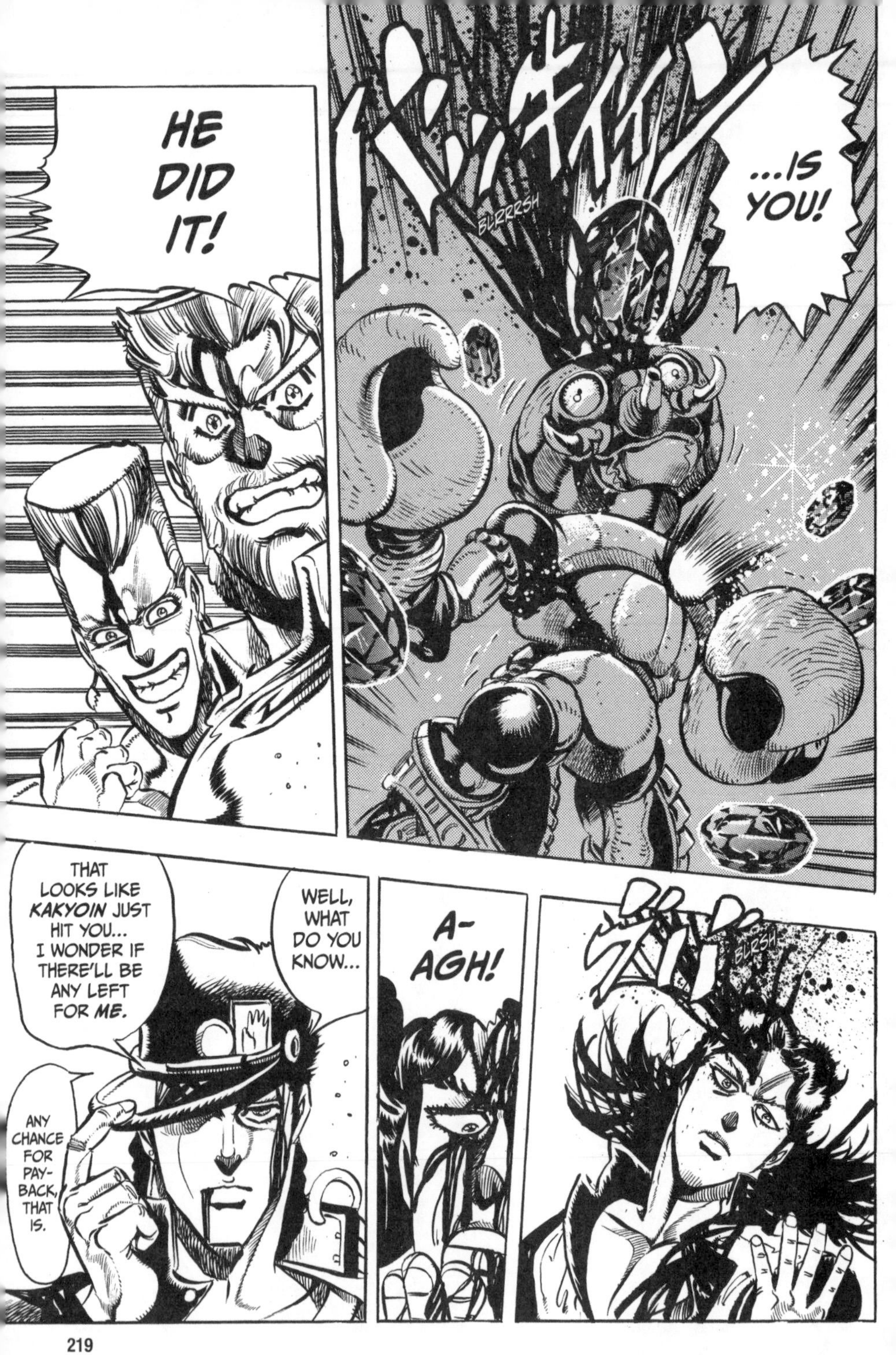
BLRRRSH
...IS YOU!
HE DID IT!
BLRSH
A-AGH!
WELL, WHAT DO YOU KNOW...
THAT LOOKS LIKE KAKYOIN JUST HIT YOU... I WONDER IF THERE'LL BE ANY LEFT FOR ME.
ANY CHANCE FOR PAY-BACK, THAT IS.

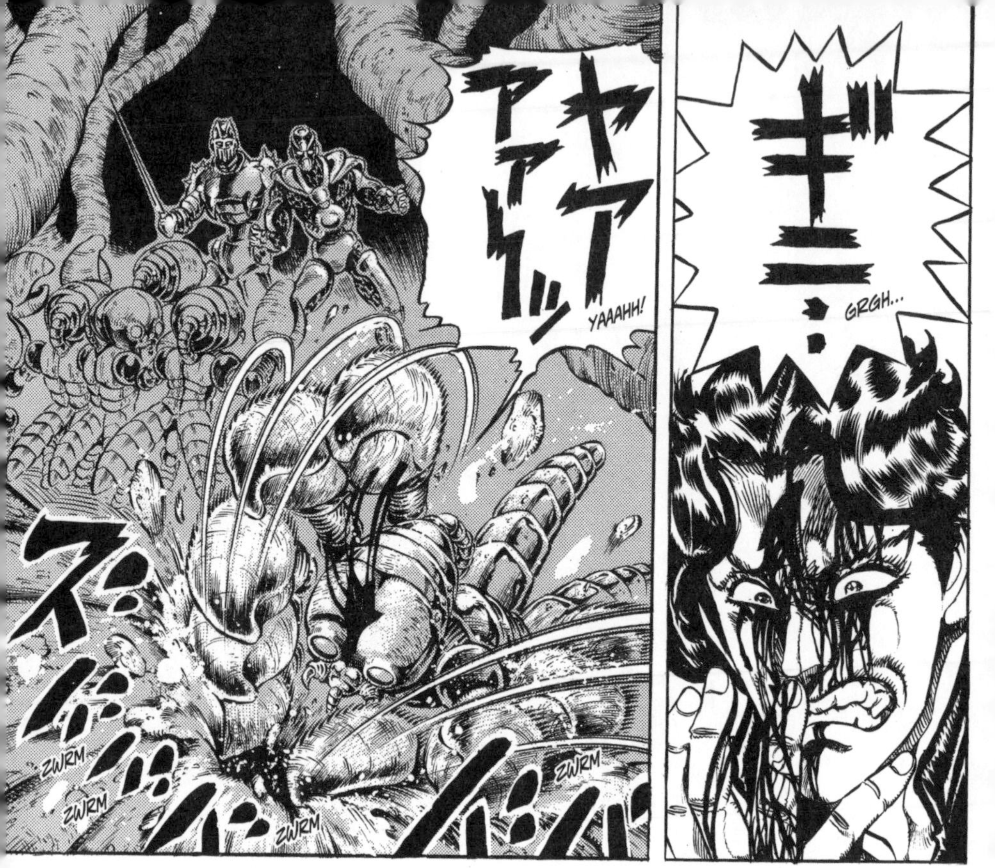
ギー…
GRGH…
ヤアアァッ
YAAAHH!
ズバババ
ZWRM
ZWRM
ZWRM
ZWRM

CHAPTER 52: The Lovers PART 6

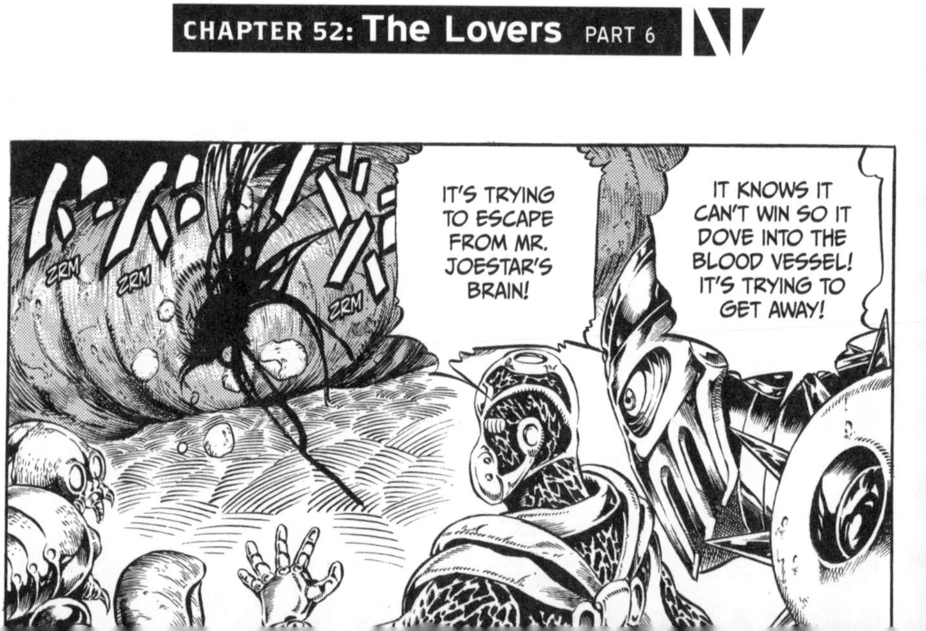
IT KNOWS IT CAN'T WIN SO IT DOVE INTO THE BLOOD VESSEL! IT'S TRYING TO GET AWAY!
IT'S TRYING TO ESCAPE FROM MR. JOESTAR'S BRAIN!
バババ
ZRM
ZRM
ZRM

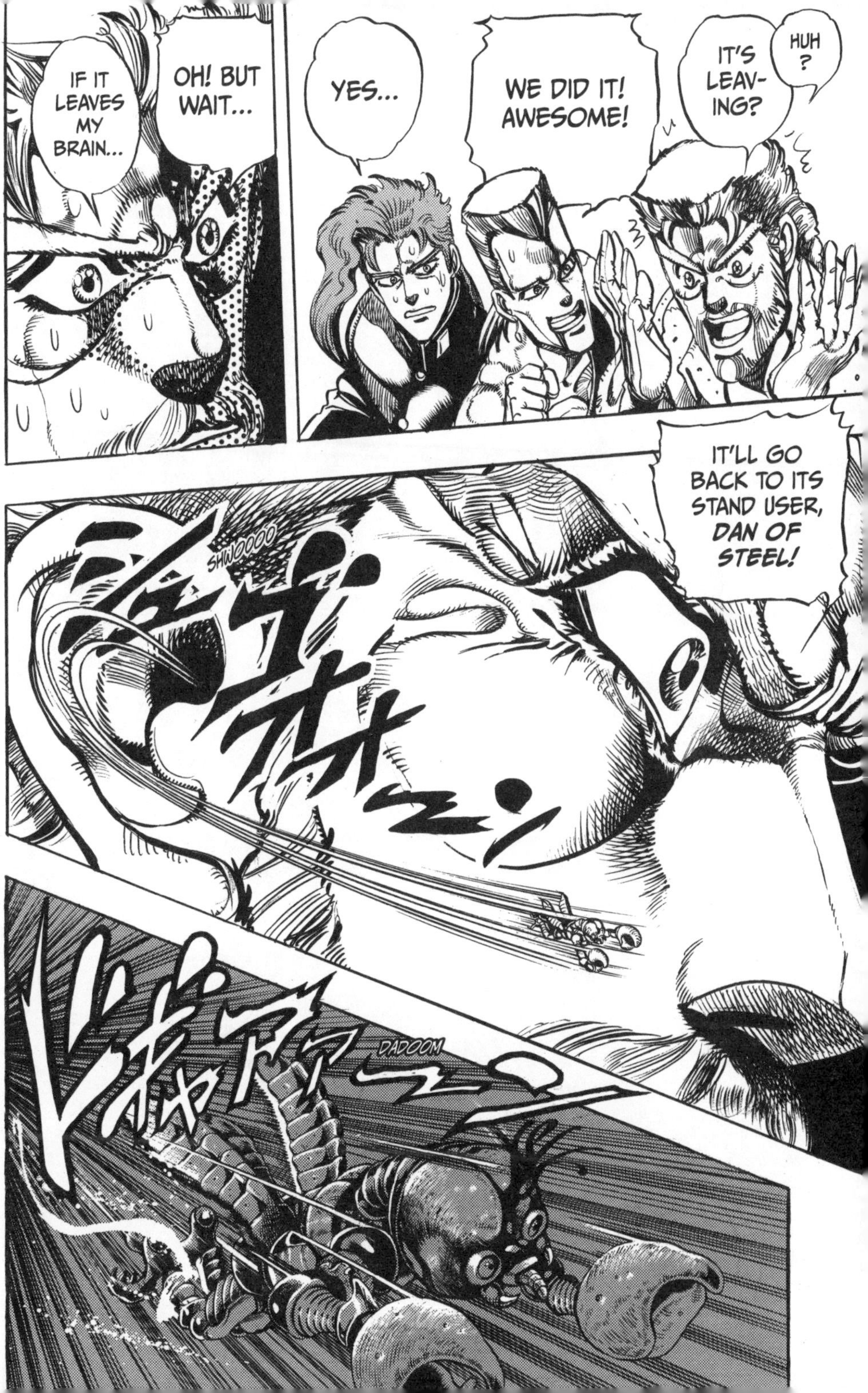
HUH?
IT'S LEAVING?
WE DID IT! AWESOME!
YES...
OH! BUT WAIT...
IF IT LEAVES MY BRAIN...
IT'LL GO BACK TO ITS STAND USER, DAN OF STEEL!
SHWOOOO
DADOOM

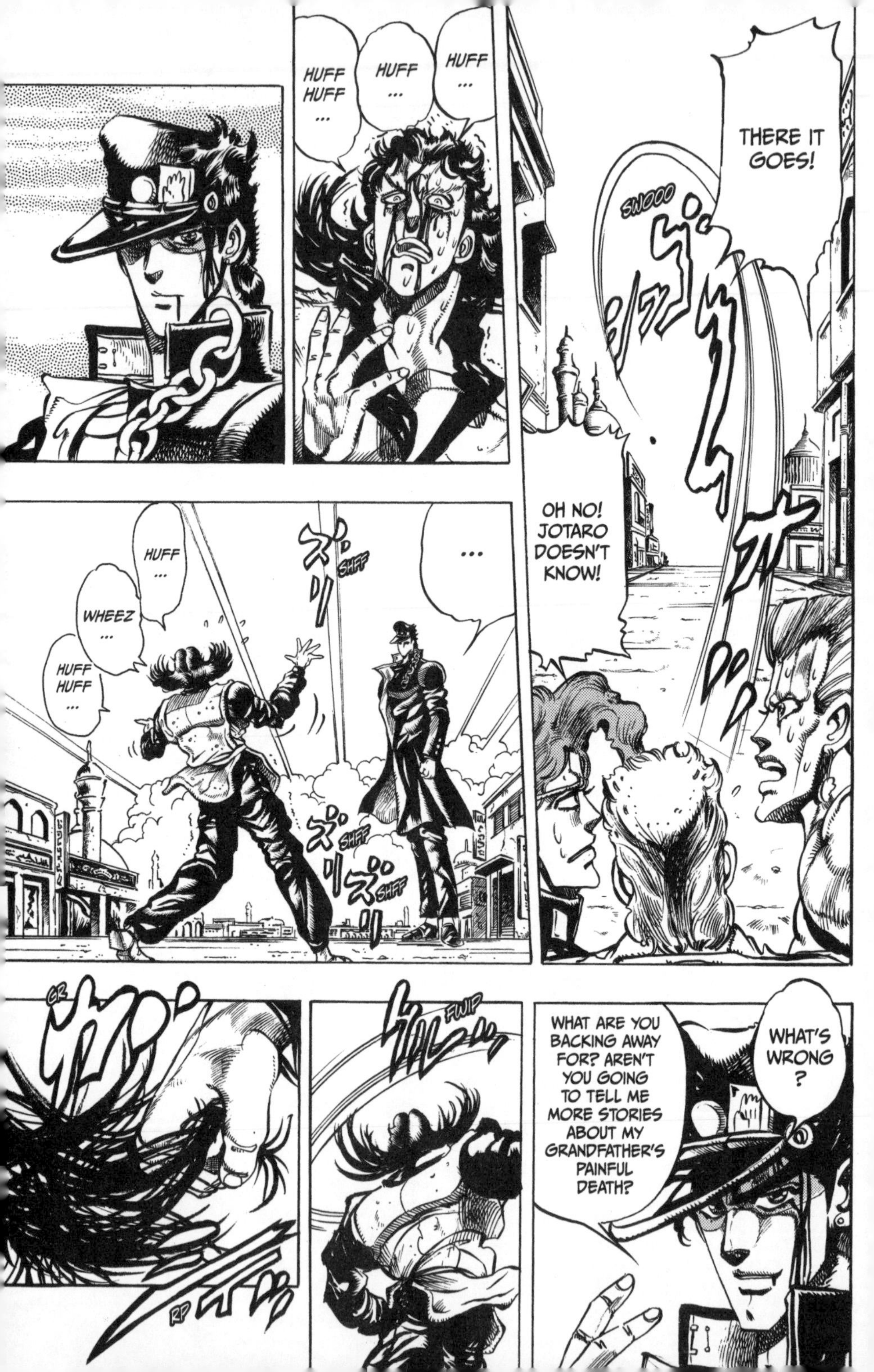
THERE IT GOES!
SWOOO
OH NO! JOTARO DOESN'T KNOW!
HUFF ...
HUFF ...
HUFF HUFF ...
...
SHFF
HUFF ...
WHEEZ ...
HUFF HUFF ...
SHFF
SHFF
WHAT'S WRONG?
WHAT ARE YOU BACKING AWAY FOR? AREN'T YOU GOING TO TELL ME MORE STORIES ABOUT MY GRANDFATHER'S PAINFUL DEATH?
FWIP
GR
RP

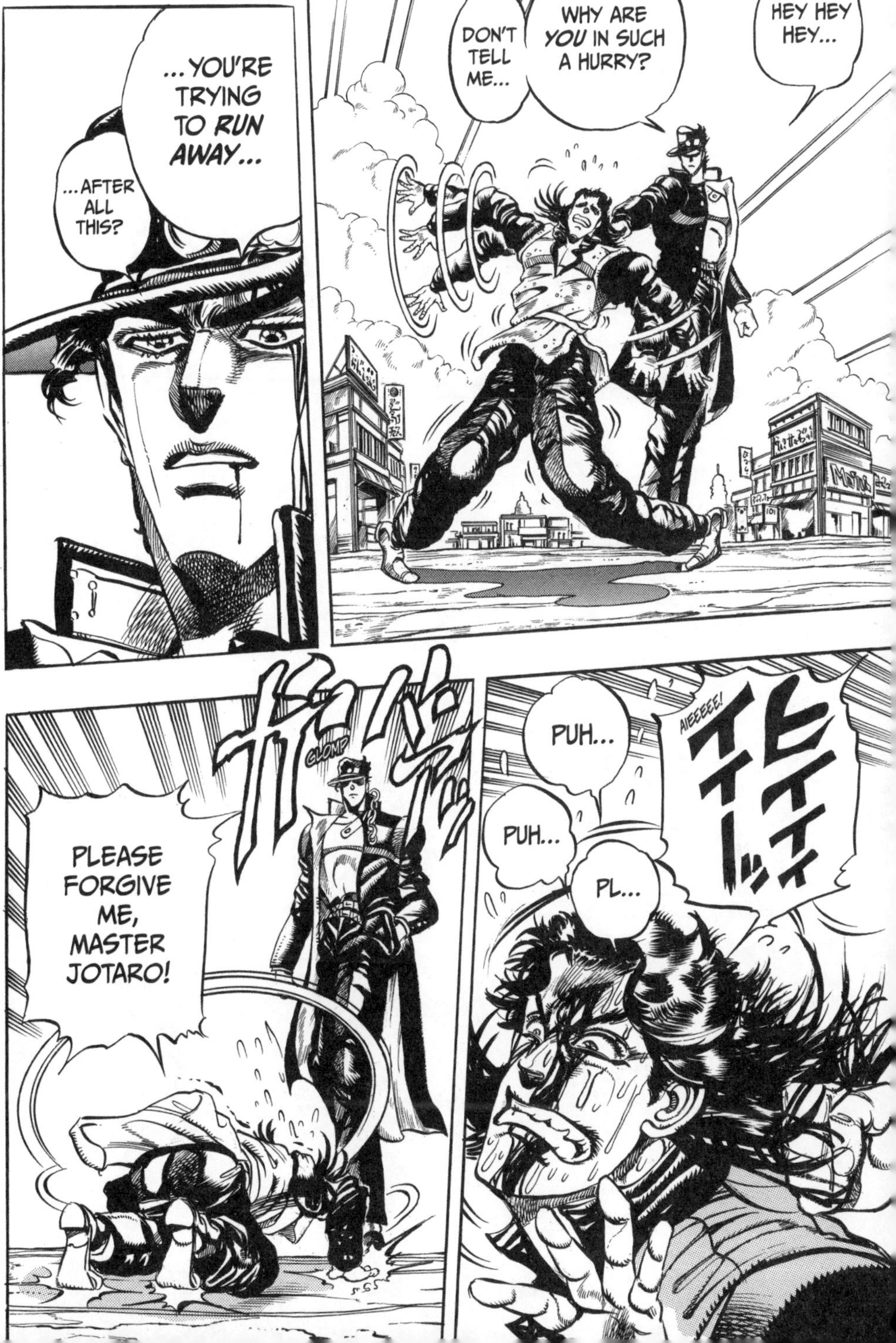
HEY HEY HEY...
WHY ARE YOU IN SUCH A HURRY?
DON'T TELL ME...
...YOU'RE TRYING TO RUN AWAY...
...AFTER ALL THIS?
AIEEEEE!
PUH...
PUH...
PL...
GLOMP
PLEASE FORGIVE ME, MASTER JOTARO!

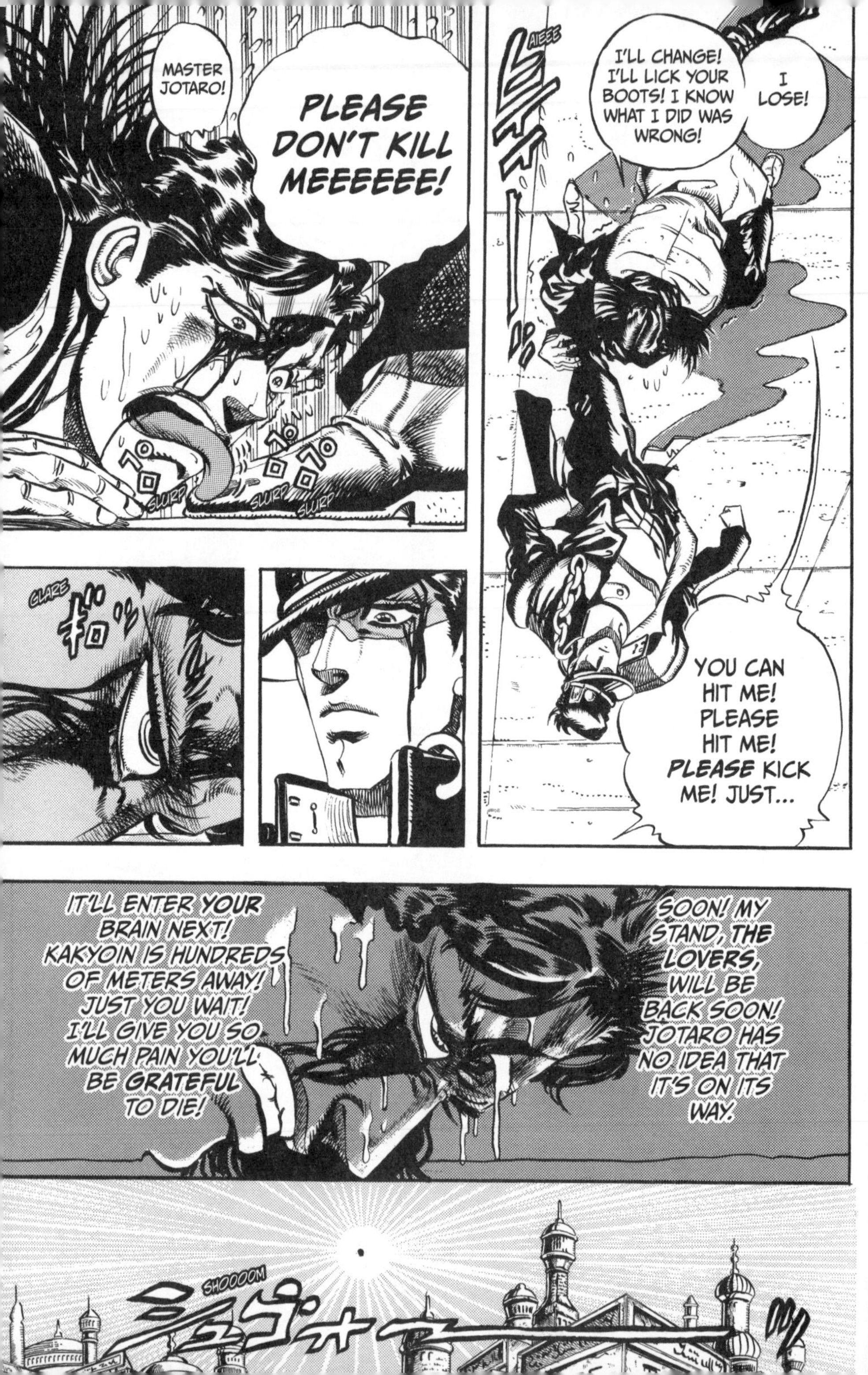
I LOSE!
I'LL CHANGE! I'LL LICK YOUR BOOTS! I KNOW WHAT I DID WAS WRONG!
AIEEE
YOU CAN HIT ME! PLEASE HIT ME! PLEASE KICK ME! JUST...
MASTER JOTARO!
PLEASE DON'T KILL MEEEEEEE!
SLURP
SLURP
SLURP
GLARE
SOON! MY STAND, THE LOVERS, WILL BE BACK SOON! JOTARO HAS NO IDEA THAT IT'S ON ITS WAY.
IT'LL ENTER YOUR BRAIN NEXT! KAKYOIN IS HUNDREDS OF METERS AWAY! JUST YOU WAIT! I'LL GIVE YOU SO MUCH PAIN YOU'LL BE GRATEFUL TO DIE!
SHOOOOM

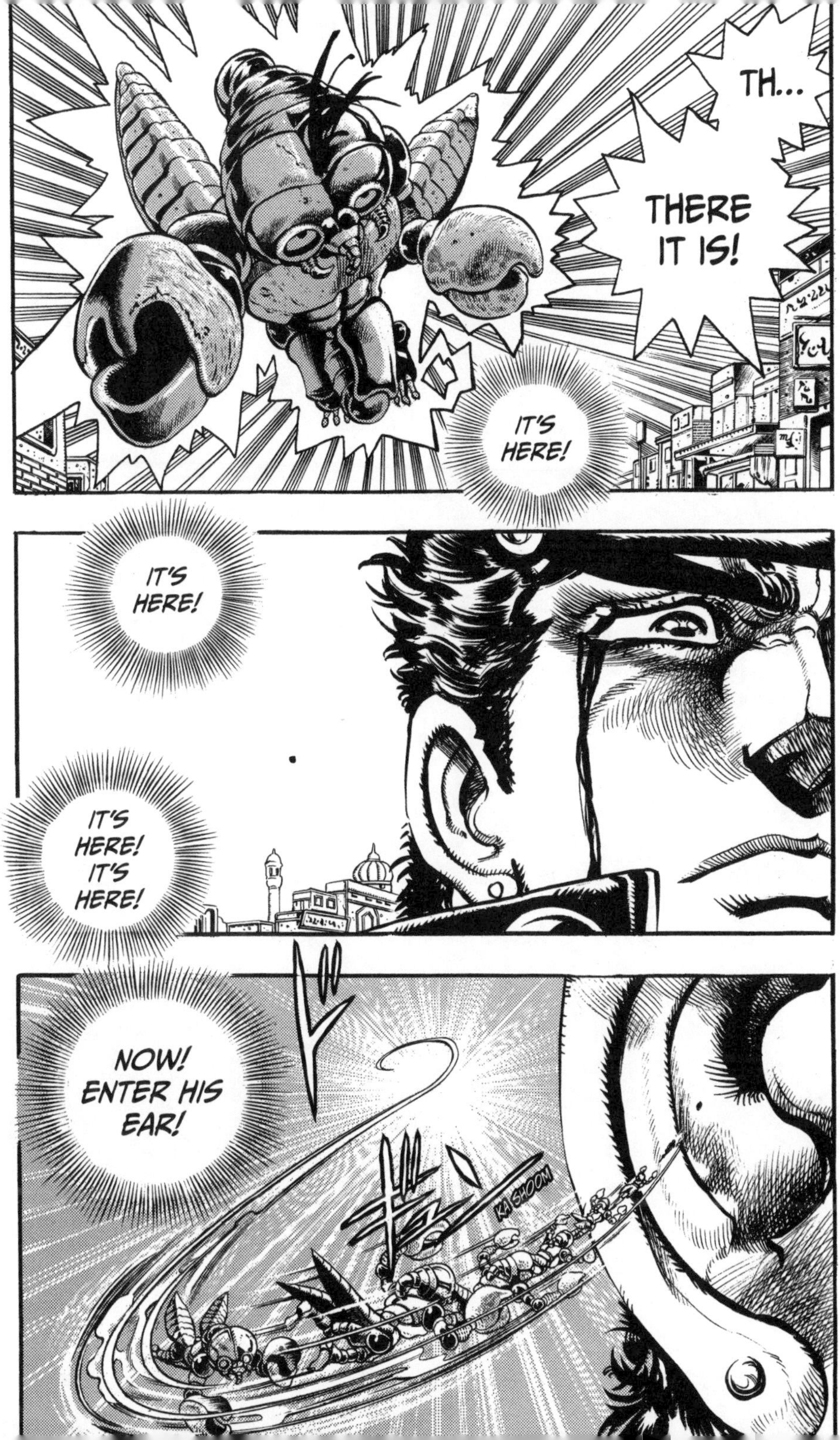
TH...
THERE IT IS!
IT'S HERE!
IT'S HERE!
IT'S HERE! IT'S HERE!
NOW! ENTER HIS EAR!
KA SHOOM

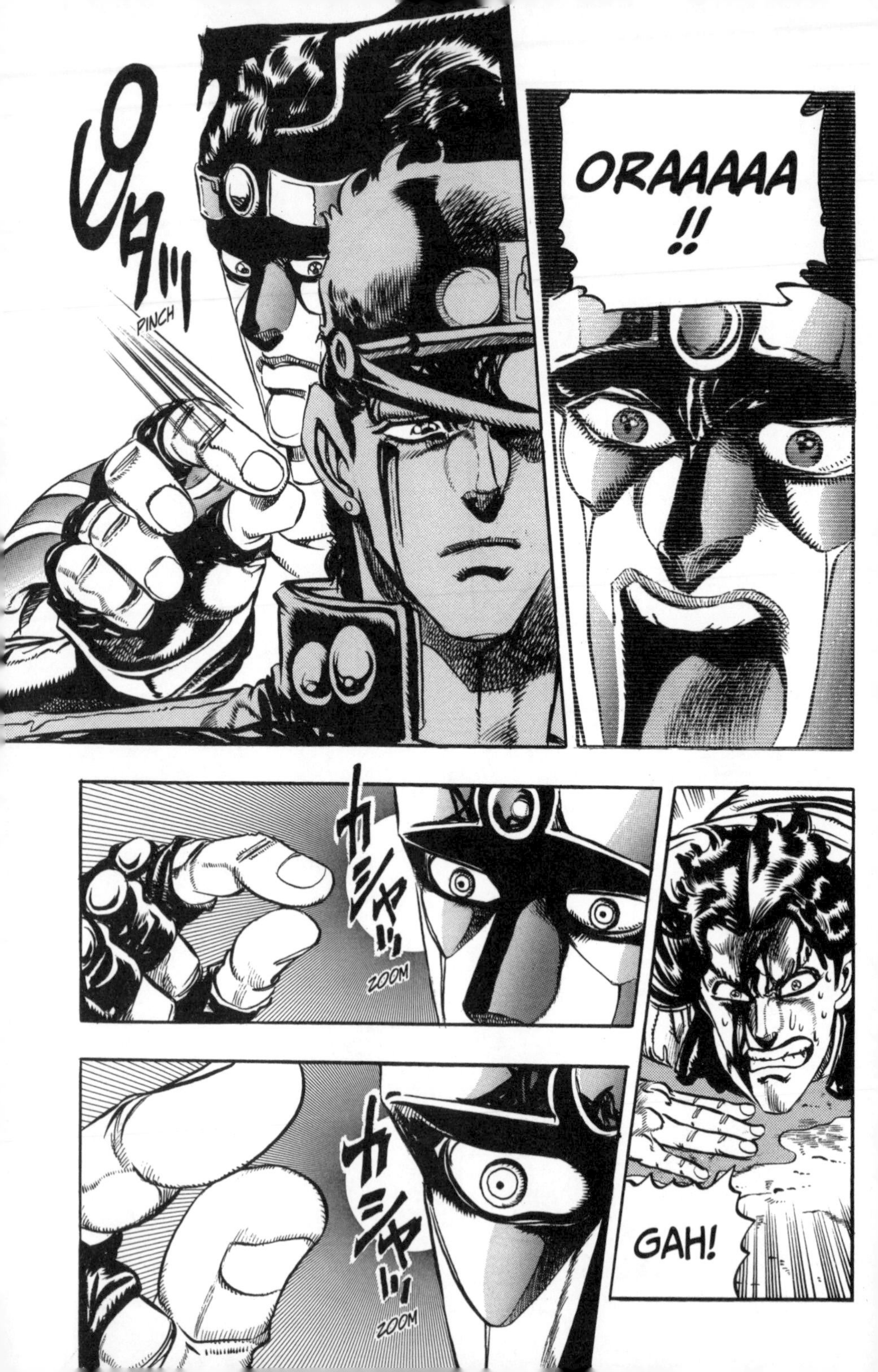
ORAAAAA !!
PINCH
GAH!
カシャッ
ZOOM
カシャッ
ZOOM

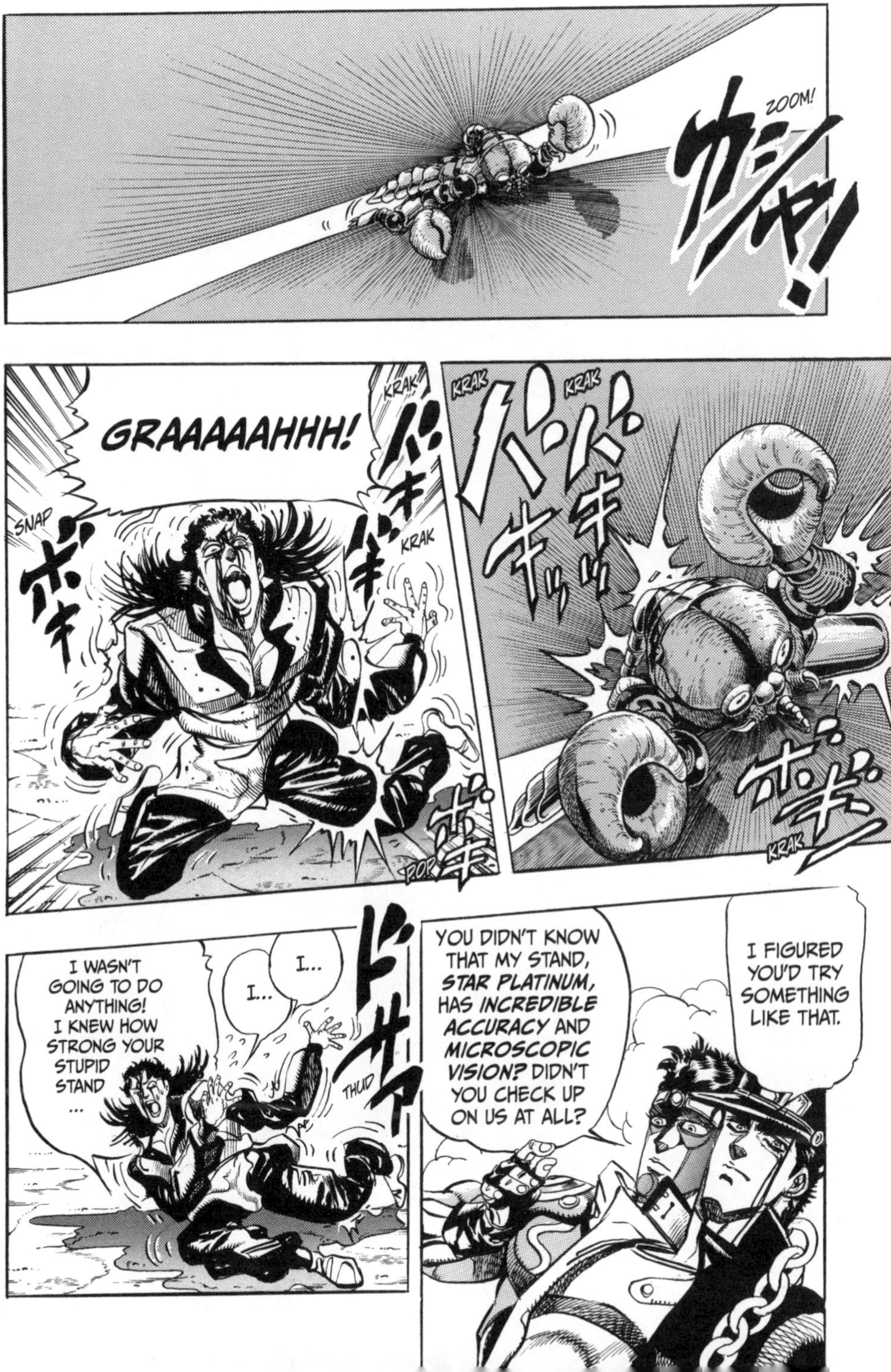
ZOOM!
KRAK
KRAK
KRAK
GRAAAAAHHH!
KRAK
SNAP
KRAK
POP
I FIGURED YOU'D TRY SOMETHING LIKE THAT.
YOU DIDN'T KNOW THAT MY STAND, STAR PLATINUM, HAS INCREDIBLE ACCURACY AND MICROSCOPIC VISION? DIDN'T YOU CHECK UP ON US AT ALL?
I...
I...
I WASN'T GOING TO DO ANYTHING! I KNEW HOW STRONG YOUR STUPID STAND ...
THUD

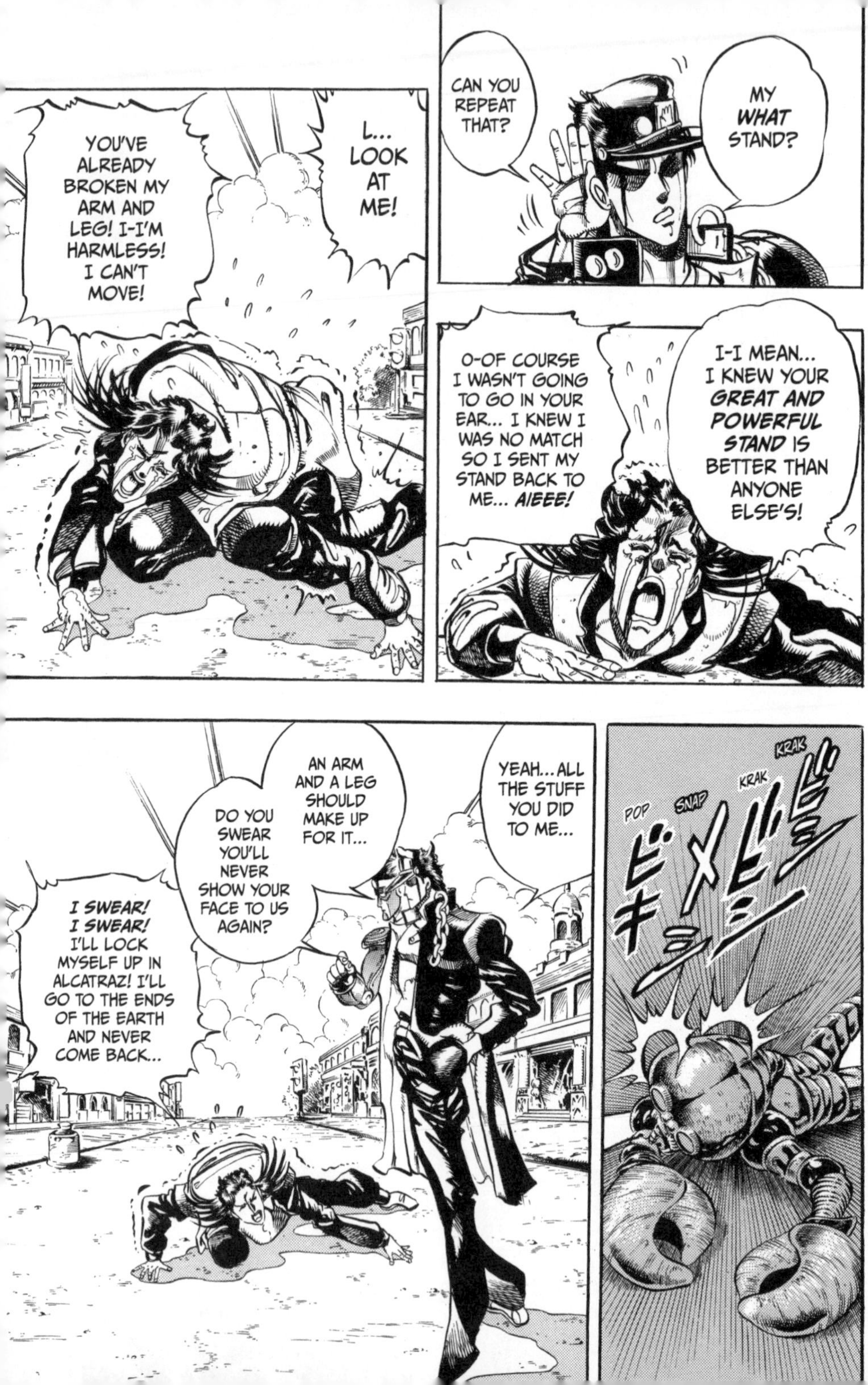
MY *WHAT* STAND?
CAN YOU REPEAT THAT?
I-I MEAN... I KNEW YOUR ***GREAT AND POWERFUL STAND*** IS BETTER THAN ANYONE ELSE'S!
O-OF COURSE I WASN'T GOING TO GO IN YOUR EAR... I KNEW I WAS NO MATCH SO I SENT MY STAND BACK TO ME... ***AIEEE!***
L... LOOK AT ME!
YOU'VE ALREADY BROKEN MY ARM AND LEG! I-I'M HARMLESS! I CAN'T MOVE!
KRAK
KRAK
SNAP
POP
YEAH...ALL THE STUFF YOU DID TO ME...
AN ARM AND A LEG SHOULD MAKE UP FOR IT...
DO YOU SWEAR YOU'LL NEVER SHOW YOUR FACE TO US AGAIN?
I SWEAR! I SWEAR! I'LL LOCK MYSELF UP IN ALCATRAZ! I'LL GO TO THE ENDS OF THE EARTH AND NEVER COME BACK...

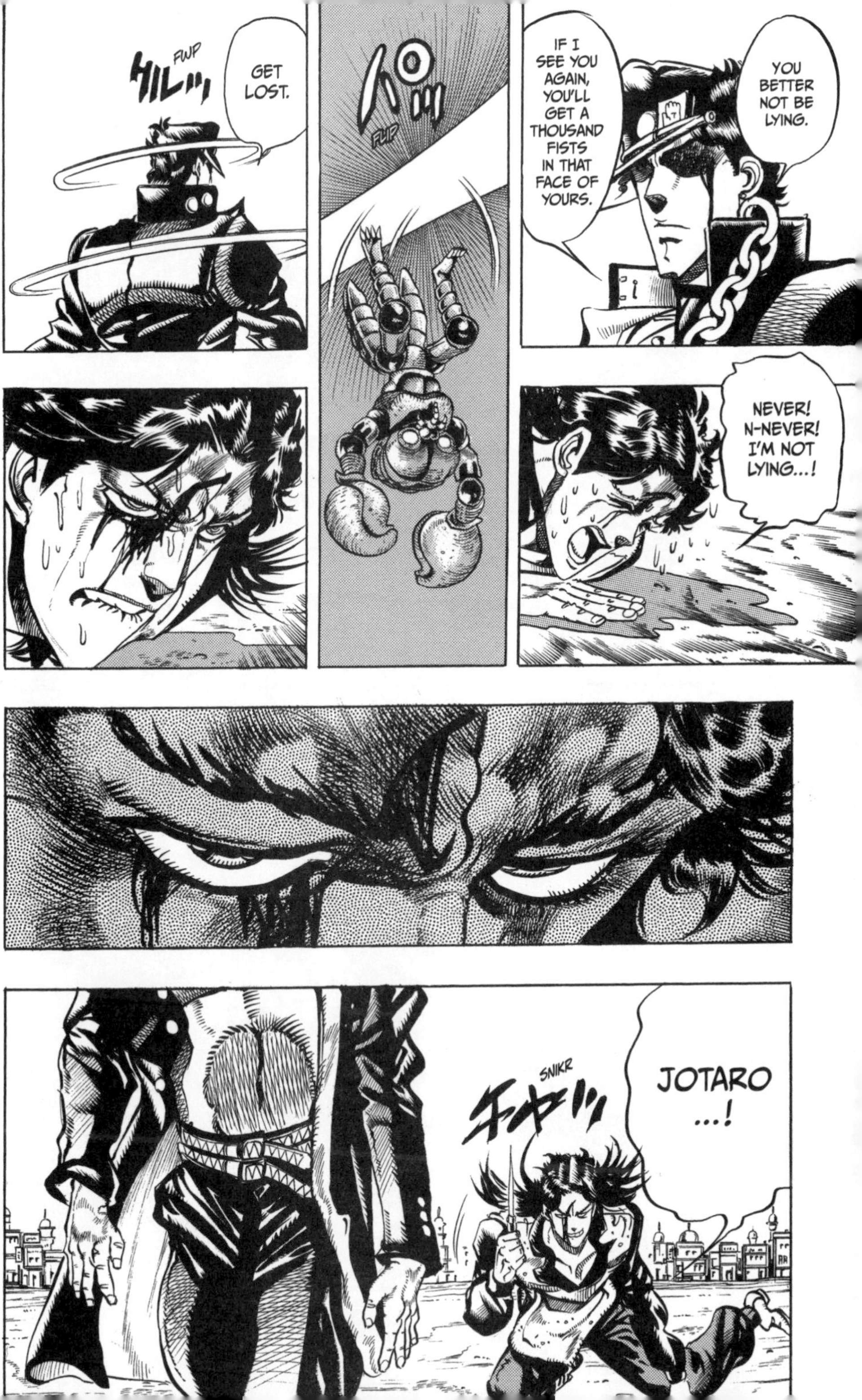
YOU BETTER NOT BE LYING.
IF I SEE YOU AGAIN, YOU'LL GET A THOUSAND FISTS IN THAT FACE OF YOURS.
NEVER! N-NEVER! I'M NOT LYING...!
FWP
FWP
GET LOST.
SNIKR
JOTARO ...!

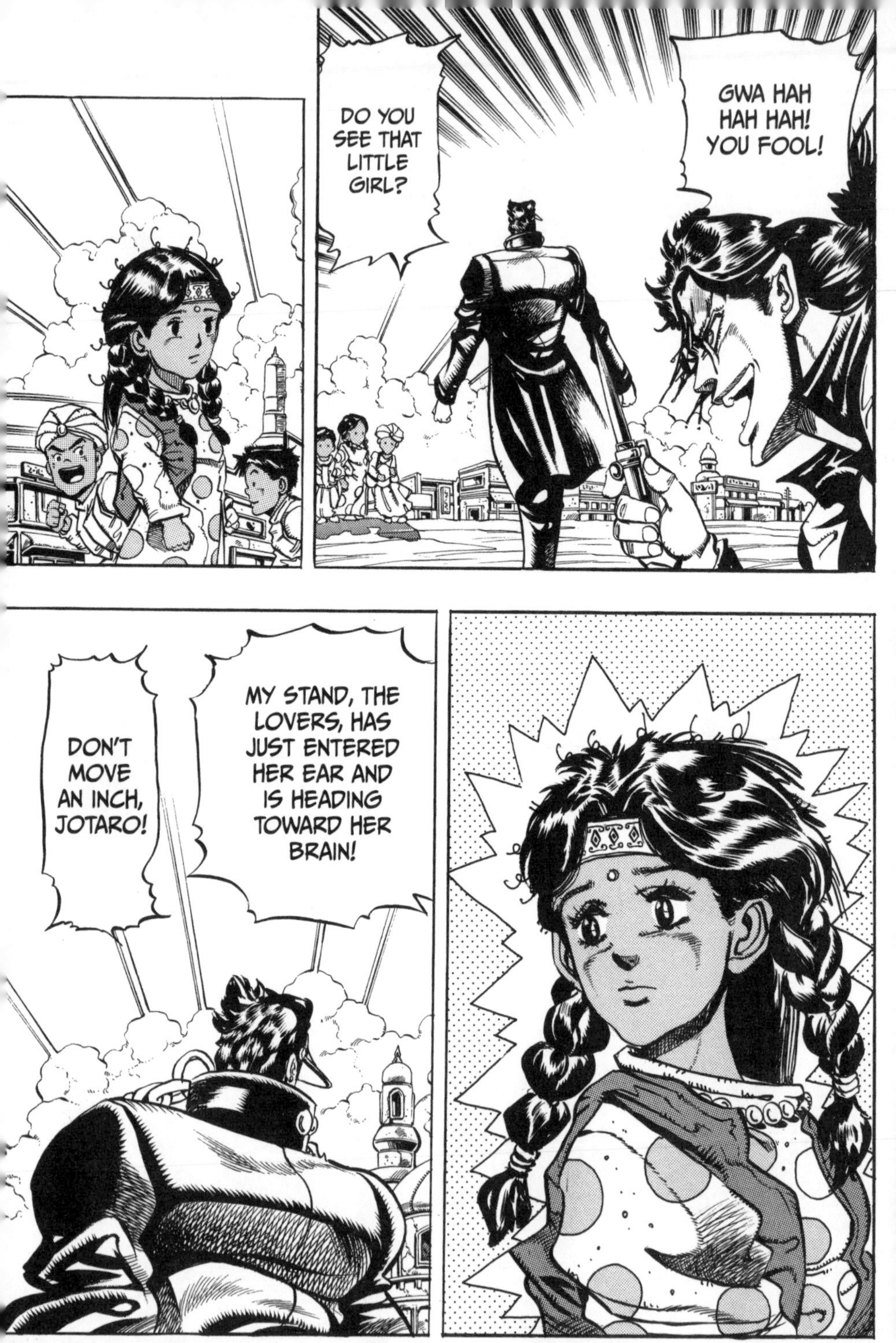
GWA HAH HAH HAH! YOU FOOL!
DO YOU SEE THAT LITTLE GIRL?
MY STAND, THE LOVERS, HAS JUST ENTERED HER EAR AND IS HEADING TOWARD HER BRAIN!
DON'T MOVE AN INCH, JOTARO!

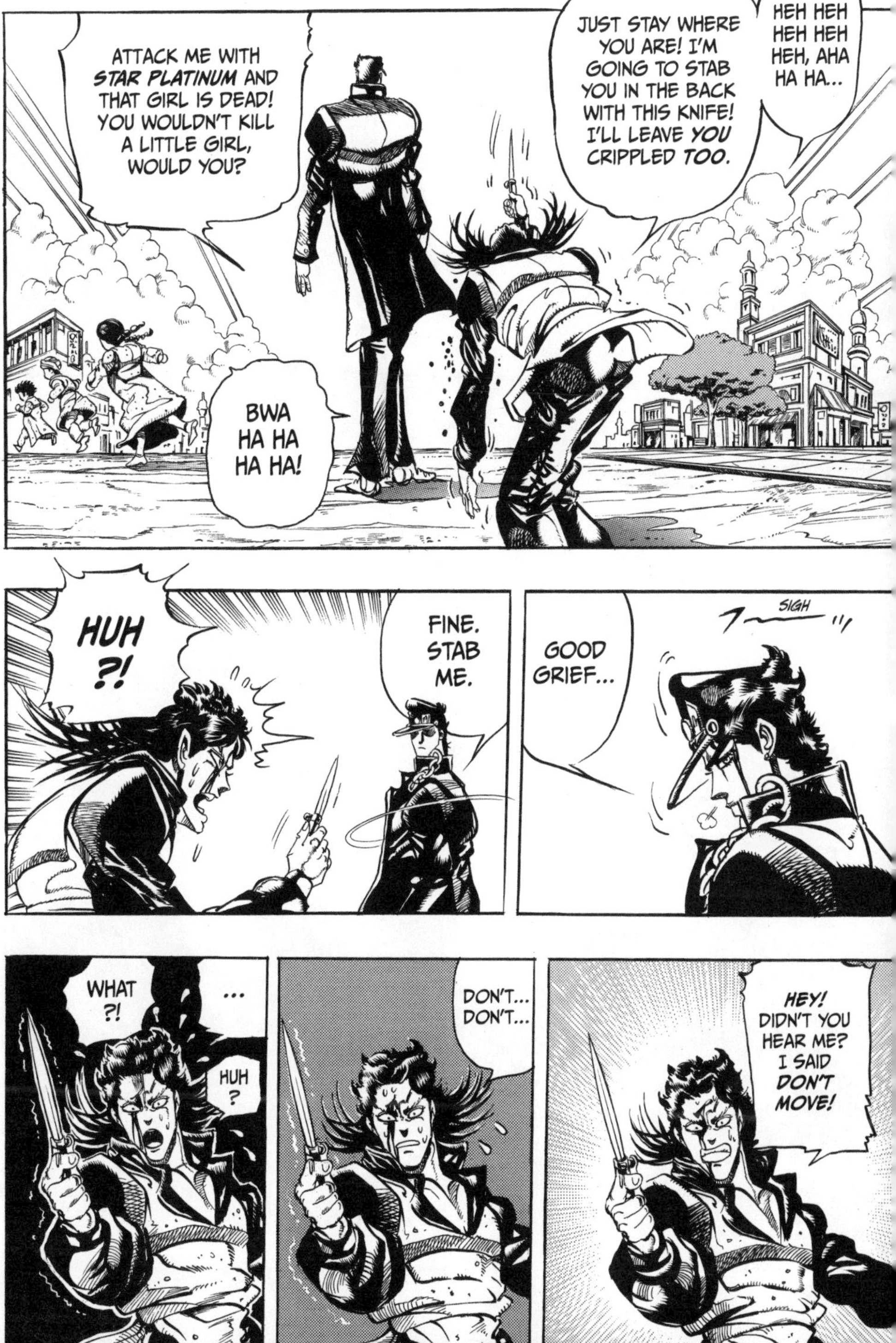
HEH HEH HEH HEH HEH, AHA HA HA...
JUST STAY WHERE YOU ARE! I'M GOING TO STAB YOU IN THE BACK WITH THIS KNIFE! I'LL LEAVE *YOU* CRIPPLED *TOO*.
ATTACK ME WITH *STAR PLATINUM* AND THAT GIRL IS DEAD! YOU WOULDN'T KILL A LITTLE GIRL, WOULD YOU?
BWA HA HA HA HA!
SIGH
GOOD GRIEF...
FINE. STAB ME.
HUH ?!
HEY! DIDN'T YOU HEAR ME? I SAID *DON'T MOVE!*
DON'T... DON'T...
...
WHAT ?!
HUH ?

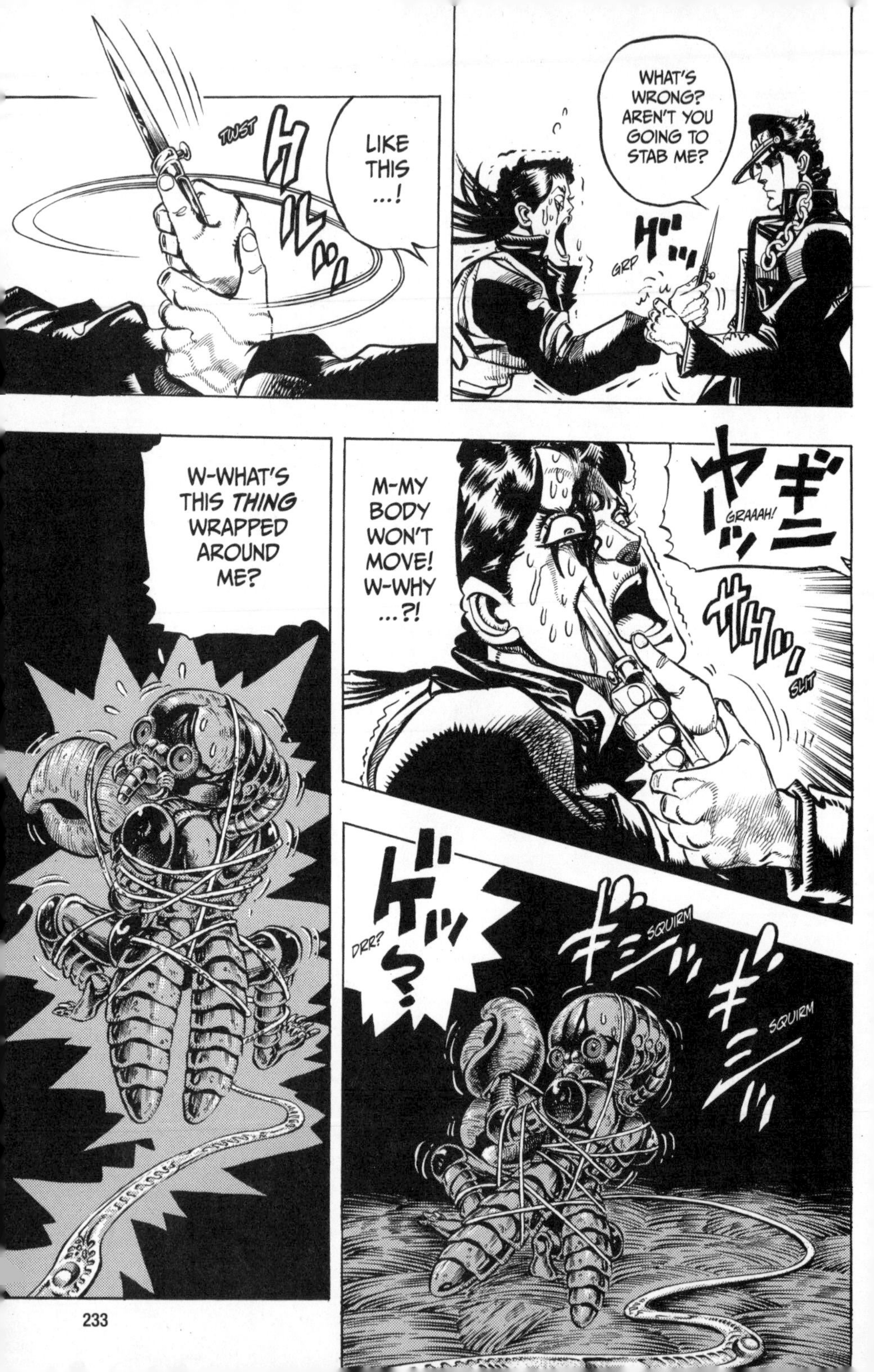
WHAT'S WRONG? AREN'T YOU GOING TO STAB ME?
GRP
LIKE THIS ...!
TWIST
M-MY BODY WON'T MOVE! W-WHY ...?!
GRAAAH!
SLIT
DRR?
SQUIRM
SQUIRM
W-WHAT'S THIS *THING* WRAPPED AROUND ME?

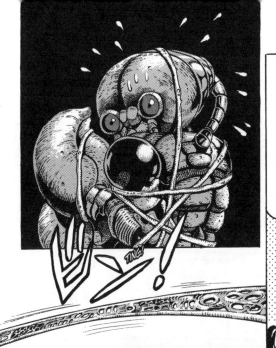

I GUESS YOU DIDN'T EVEN NOTICE ...
KAKYOIN TIED *HIEROPHANT'S* TENTACLES AROUND YOUR STAND'S LEG, REMEMBER? ***WELL, HE NEVER LET GO.***
IT STRETCHES ALL THE WAY BACK TO HIM LIKE A KITE STRING. YOU MUST HAVE BEEN SO ABSORBED YOU DIDN'T REALIZE IT.
TING!
TUG
AH!

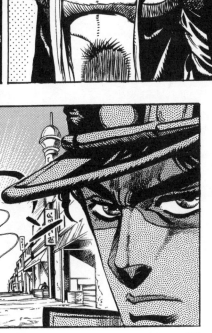

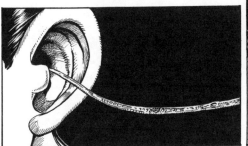

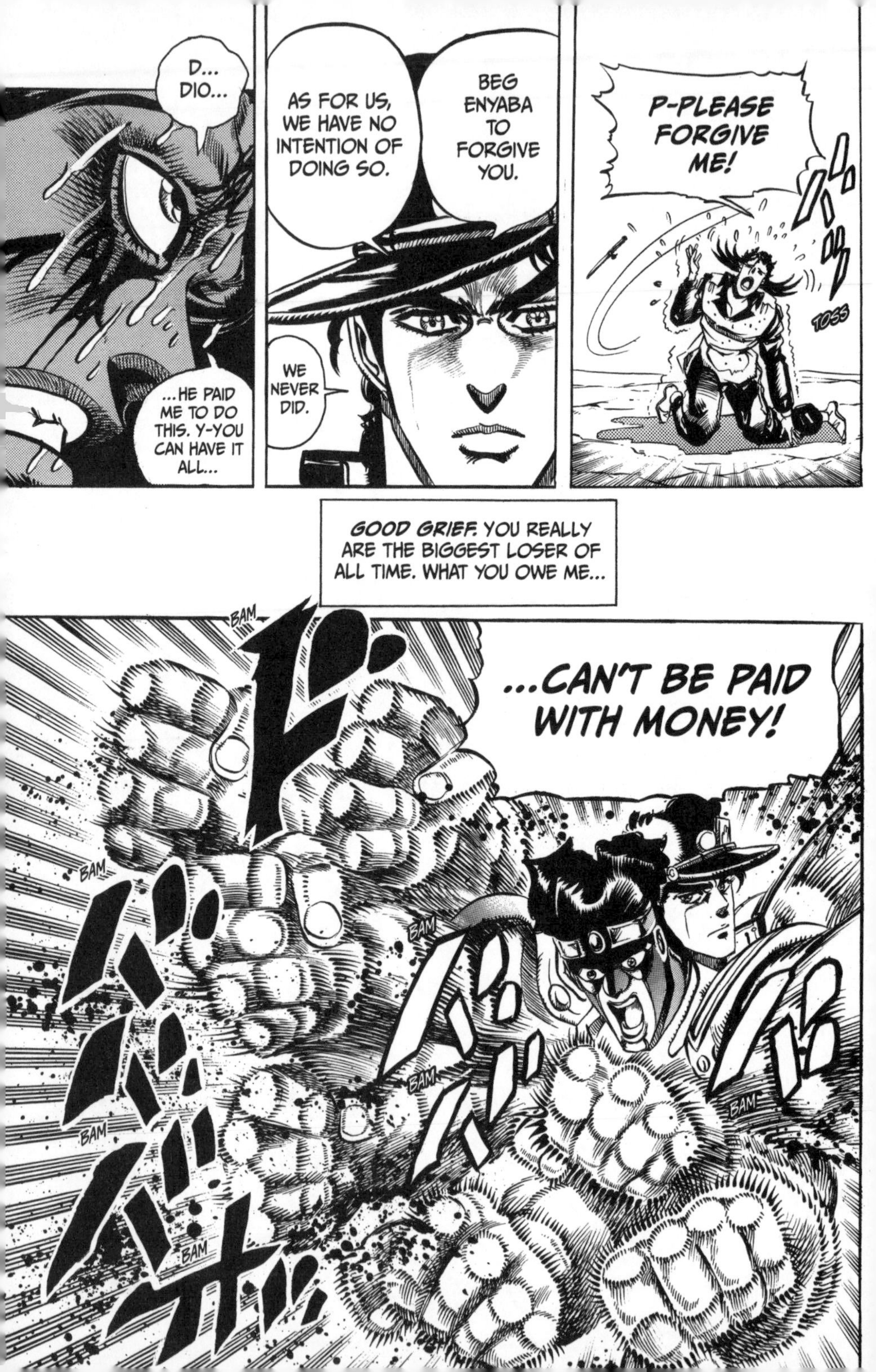
P-PLEASE FORGIVE ME!
TOSS
BEG ENYABA TO FORGIVE YOU.
AS FOR US, WE HAVE NO INTENTION OF DOING SO.
WE NEVER DID.
D... DIO...
...HE PAID ME TO DO THIS. Y-YOU CAN HAVE IT ALL...
GOOD GRIEF. YOU REALLY ARE THE BIGGEST LOSER OF ALL TIME. WHAT YOU OWE ME...
...CAN'T BE PAID WITH MONEY!
BAM
BAM
BAM
BAM
BAM
BAM
BAM

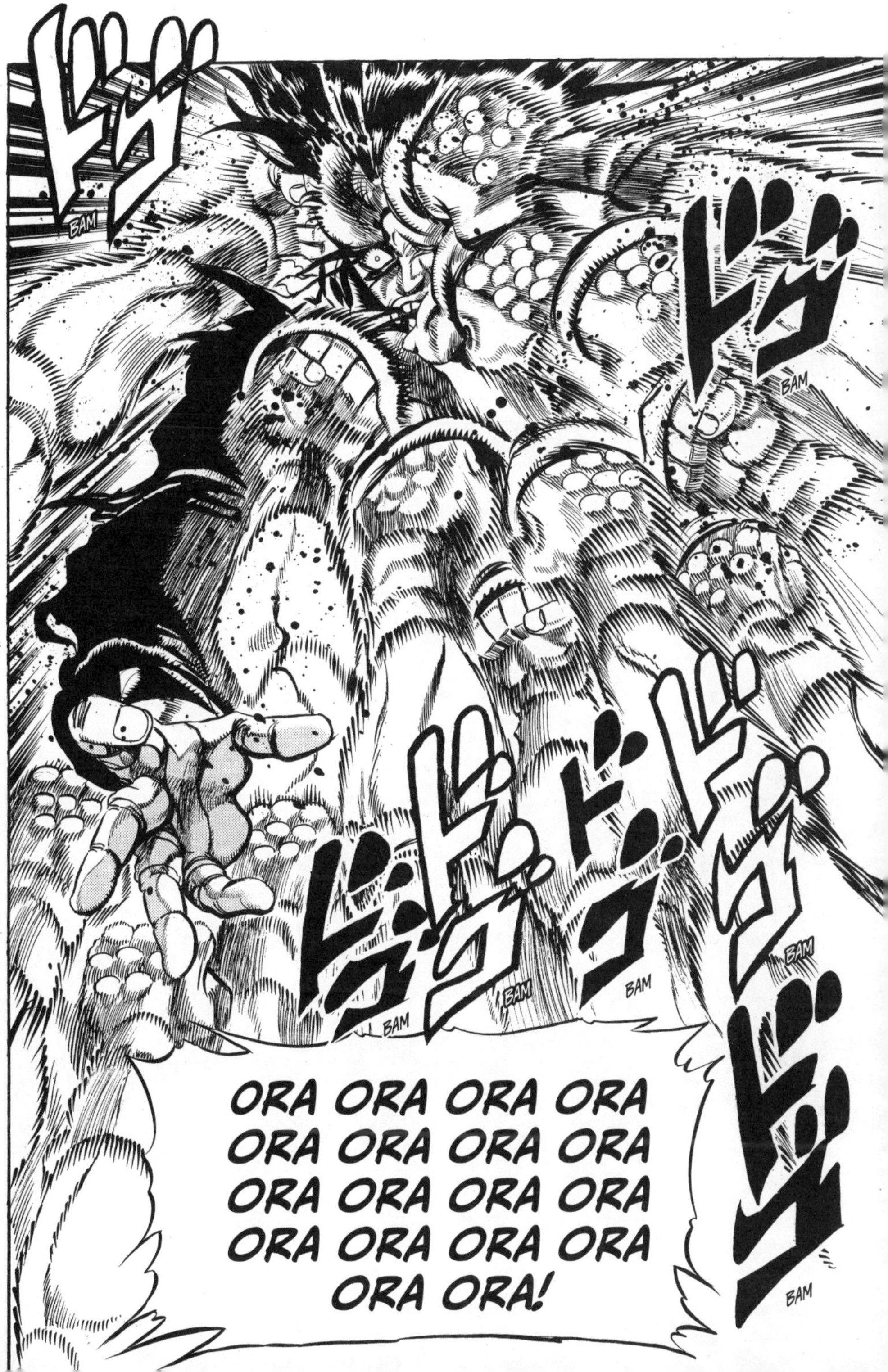
BAM
BAM
BAM
BAM
BAM
BAM
BAM
ORA ORA ORA ORA ORA ORA ORA ORA ORA ORA ORA ORA ORA ORA ORA ORA ORA ORA!

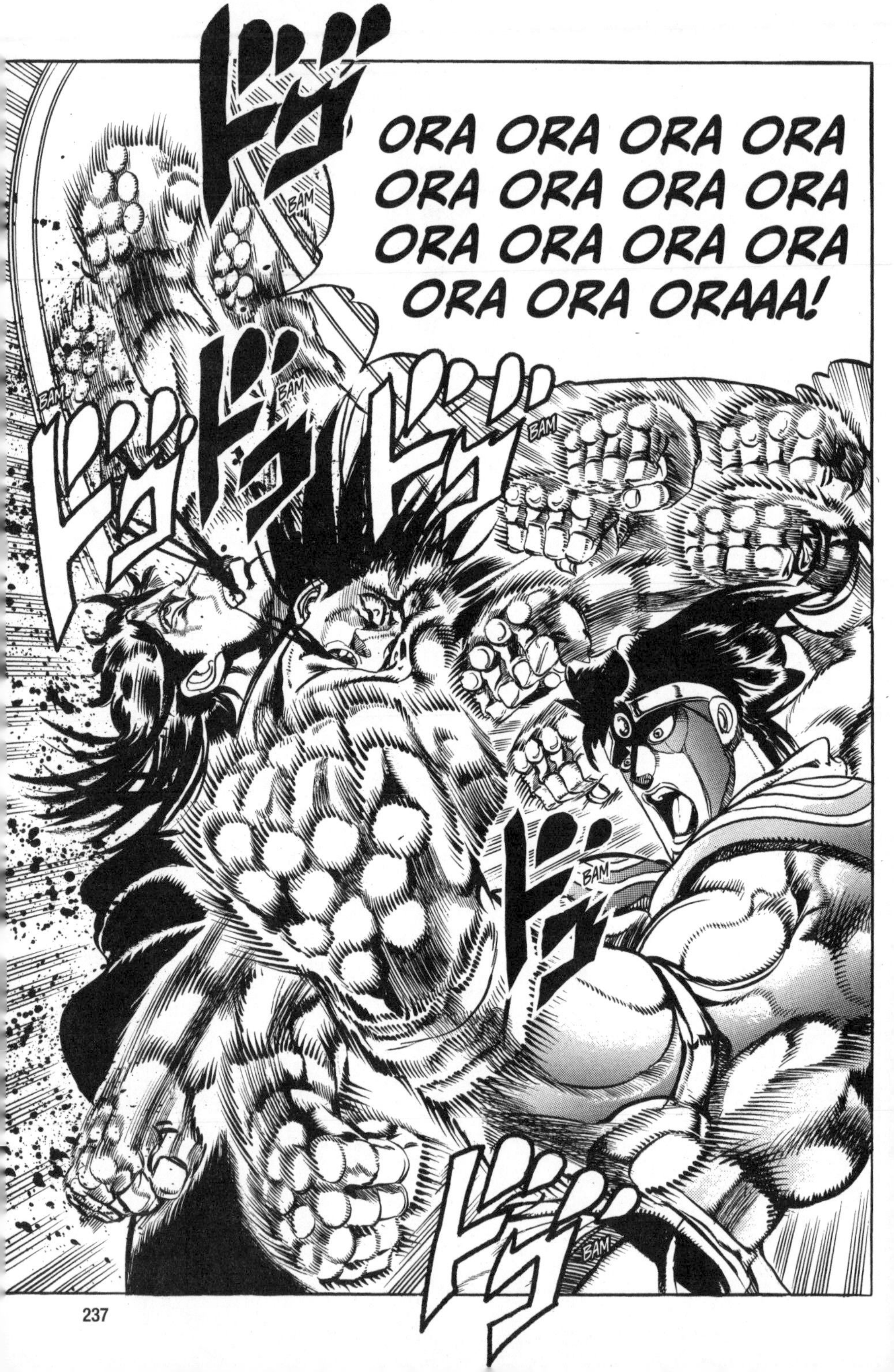
ORA ORA ORA ORA
ORA ORA ORA ORA
ORA ORA ORA ORA
ORA ORA ORAAA!
BAM
BAM
BAM
BAM
BAM
BAM
BAM

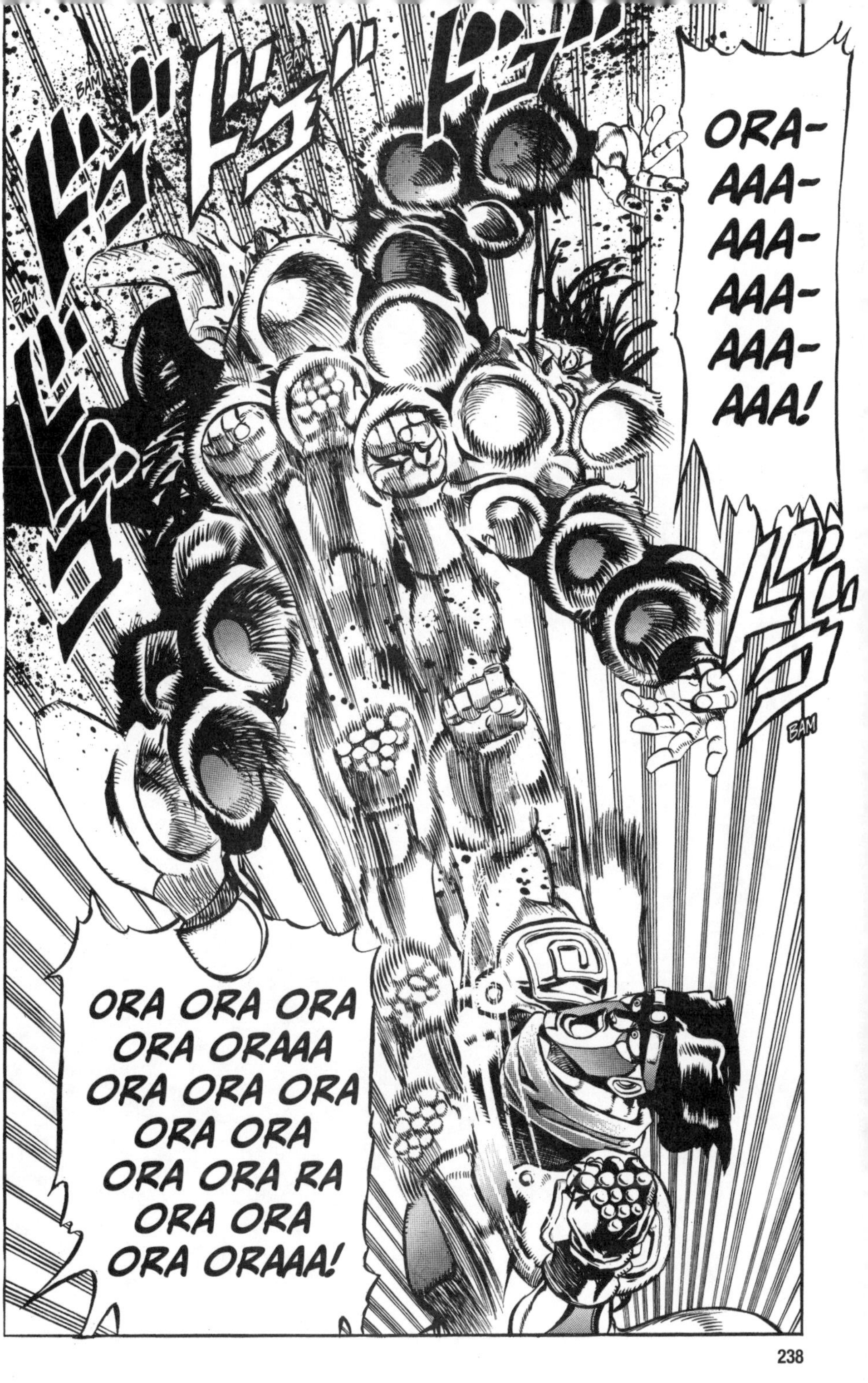
ORA-
AAA-
AAA-
AAA-
AAA-
AAA!
BAM
BAM
BAM
BAM
ORA ORA ORA
ORA ORAAA
ORA ORA ORA
ORA ORA
ORA ORA RA
ORA ORA
ORA ORAAA!

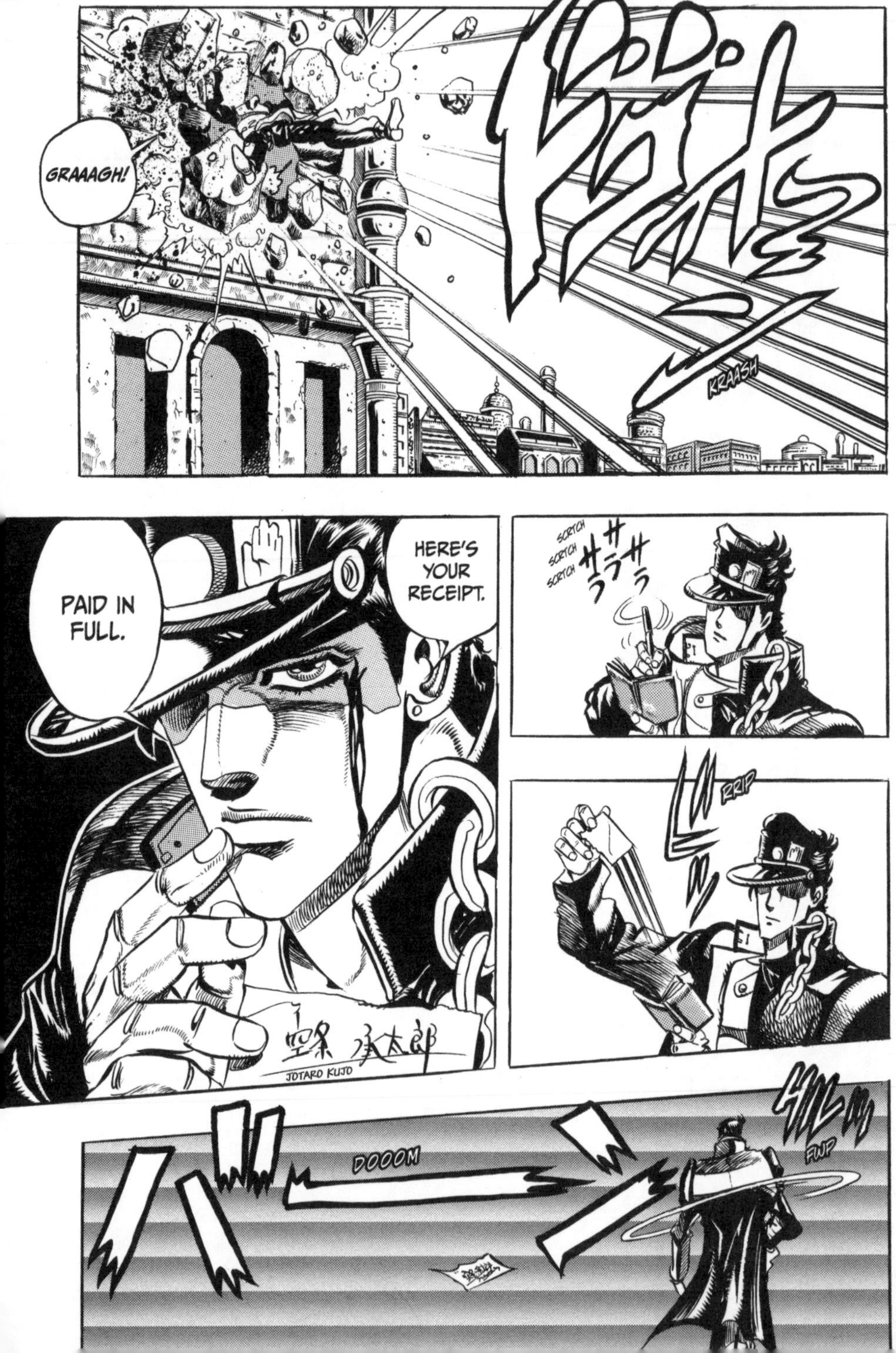
KRAASH
GRAAAGH!
SCORTCH SCORTCH SCORTCH
RRIP
HERE'S YOUR RECEIPT.
PAID IN FULL.
JOTARO KUJO
FWUP
DOOOM

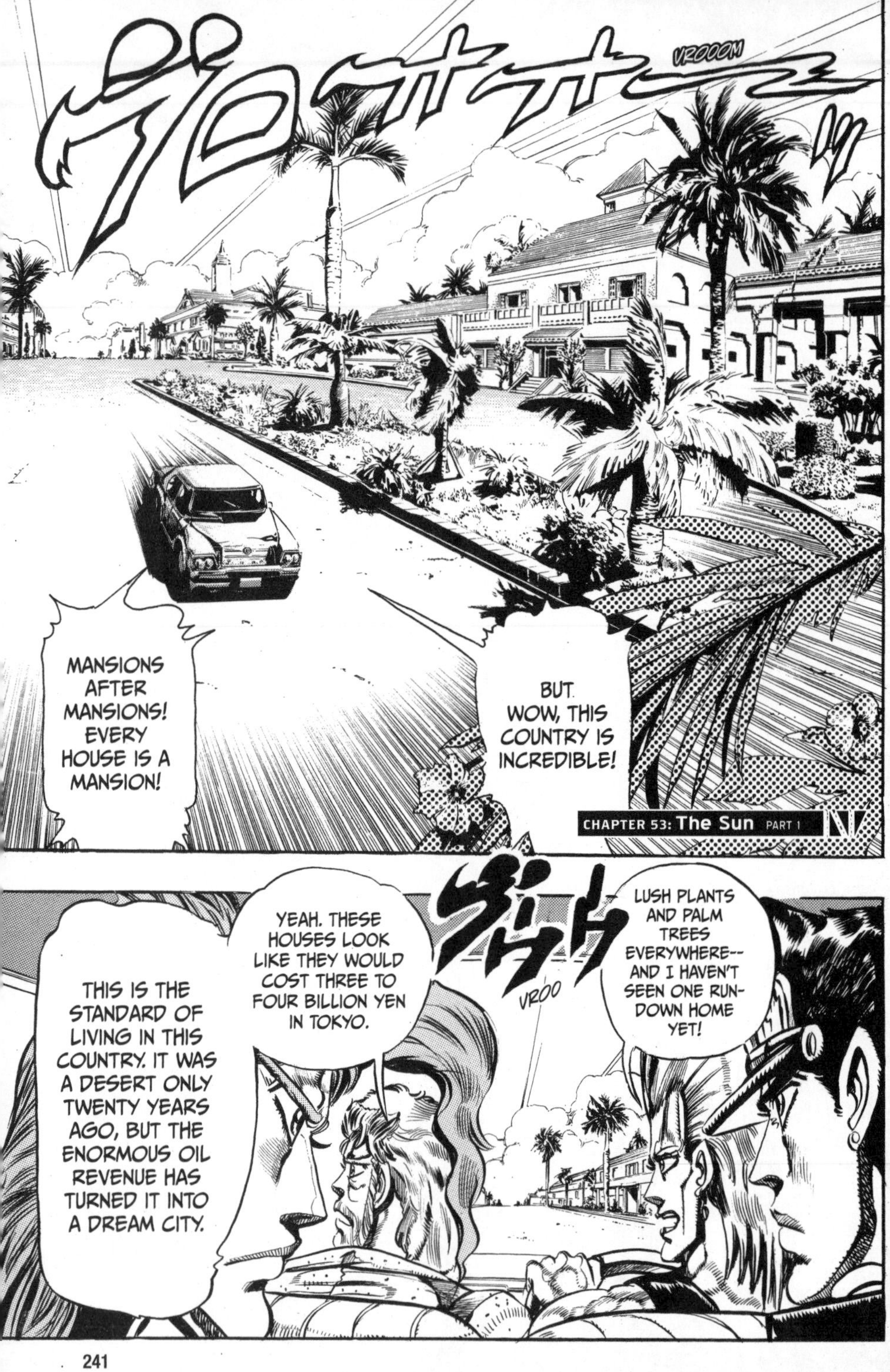
VROOOM
BUT. WOW, THIS COUNTRY IS INCREDIBLE!
MANSIONS AFTER MANSIONS! EVERY HOUSE IS A MANSION!
CHAPTER 53: The Sun PART 1
LUSH PLANTS AND PALM TREES EVERYWHERE-- AND I HAVEN'T SEEN ONE RUN-DOWN HOME YET!
VROO
YEAH. THESE HOUSES LOOK LIKE THEY WOULD COST THREE TO FOUR BILLION YEN IN TOKYO.
THIS IS THE STANDARD OF LIVING IN THIS COUNTRY. IT WAS A DESERT ONLY TWENTY YEARS AGO, BUT THE ENORMOUS OIL REVENUE HAS TURNED IT INTO A DREAM CITY.

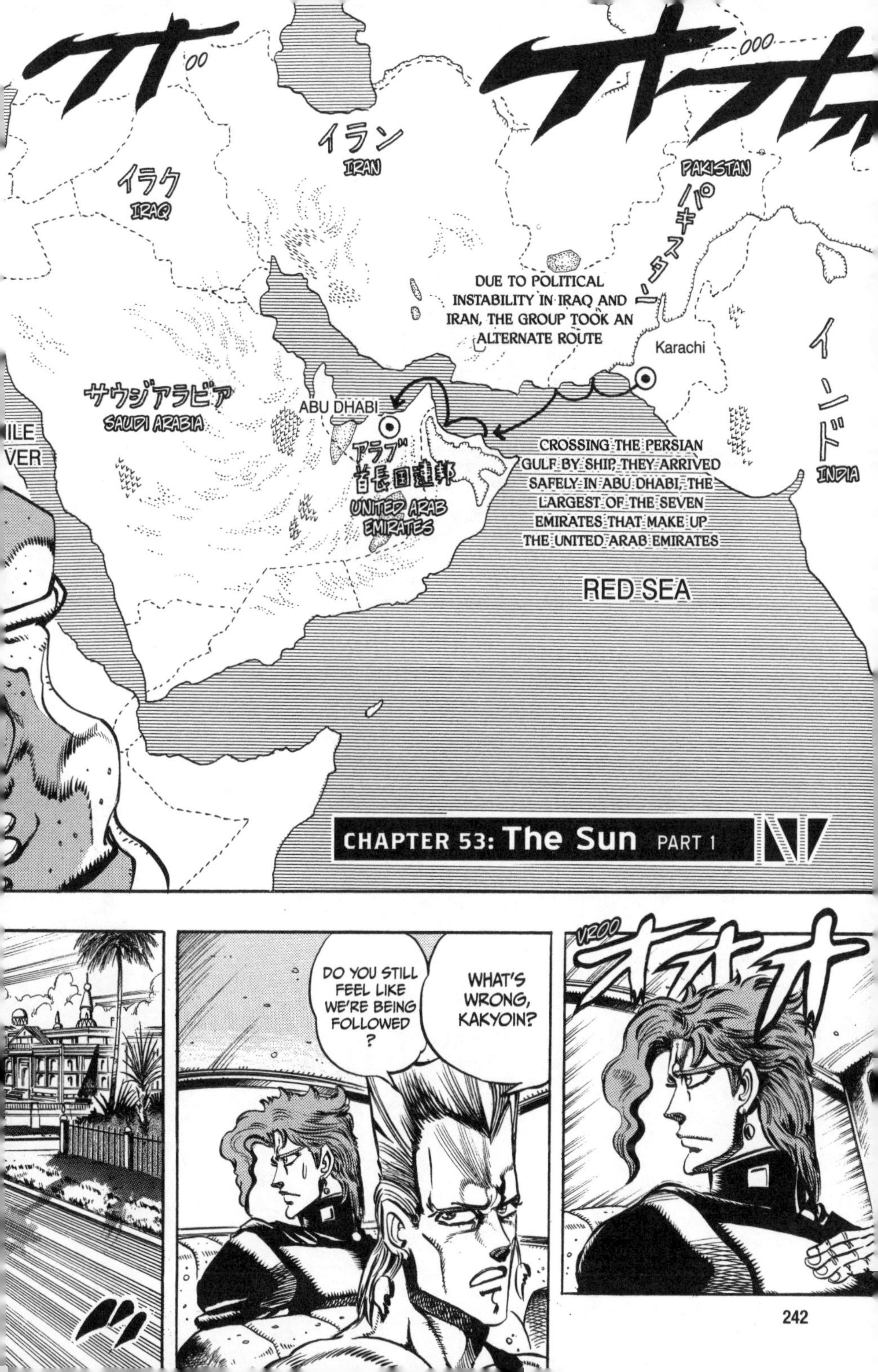
OO
OOO
イラン
IRAN
イラク
IRAQ
PAKISTAN
パキスタン
DUE TO POLITICAL INSTABILITY IN IRAQ AND IRAN, THE GROUP TOOK AN ALTERNATE ROUTE
Karachi
インド
INDIA
サウジアラビア
SAUDI ARABIA
ABU DHABI
アラブ首長国連邦
UNITED ARAB EMIRATES
CROSSING THE PERSIAN GULF BY SHIP, THEY ARRIVED SAFELY IN ABU DHABI, THE LARGEST OF THE SEVEN EMIRATES THAT MAKE UP THE UNITED ARAB EMIRATES
RED SEA
CHAPTER 53: The Sun PART 1
VROO
WHAT'S WRONG, KAKYOIN?
DO YOU STILL FEEL LIKE WE'RE BEING FOLLOWED?

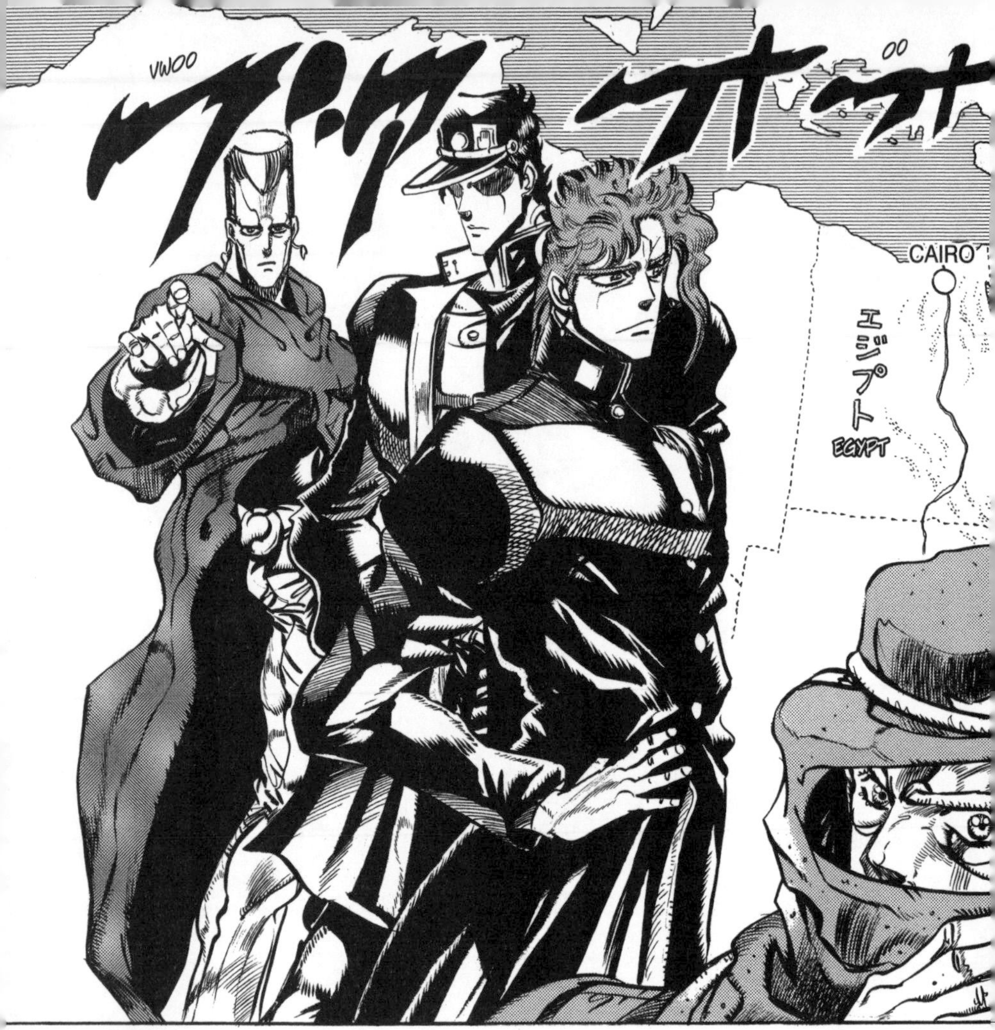
VWOO
OO
CAIRO
エジプト
EGYPT

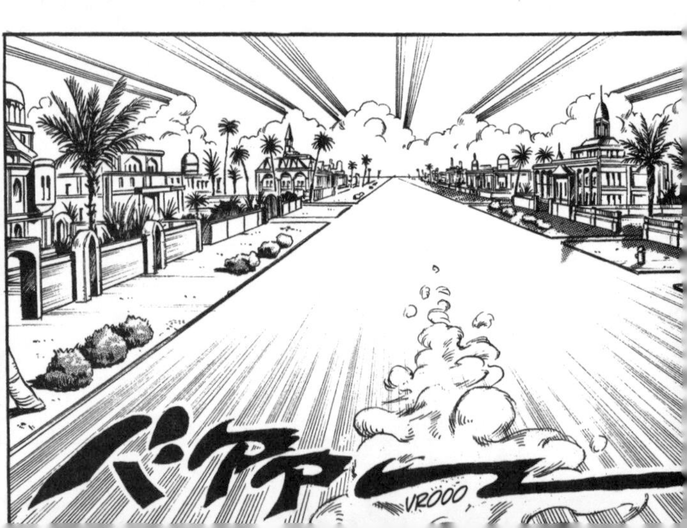
VROOO

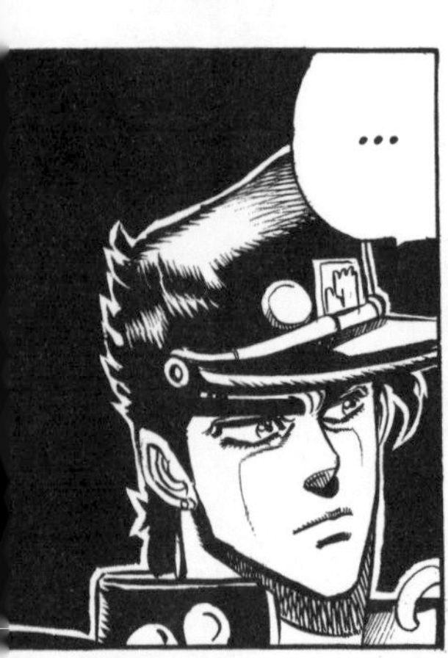
...

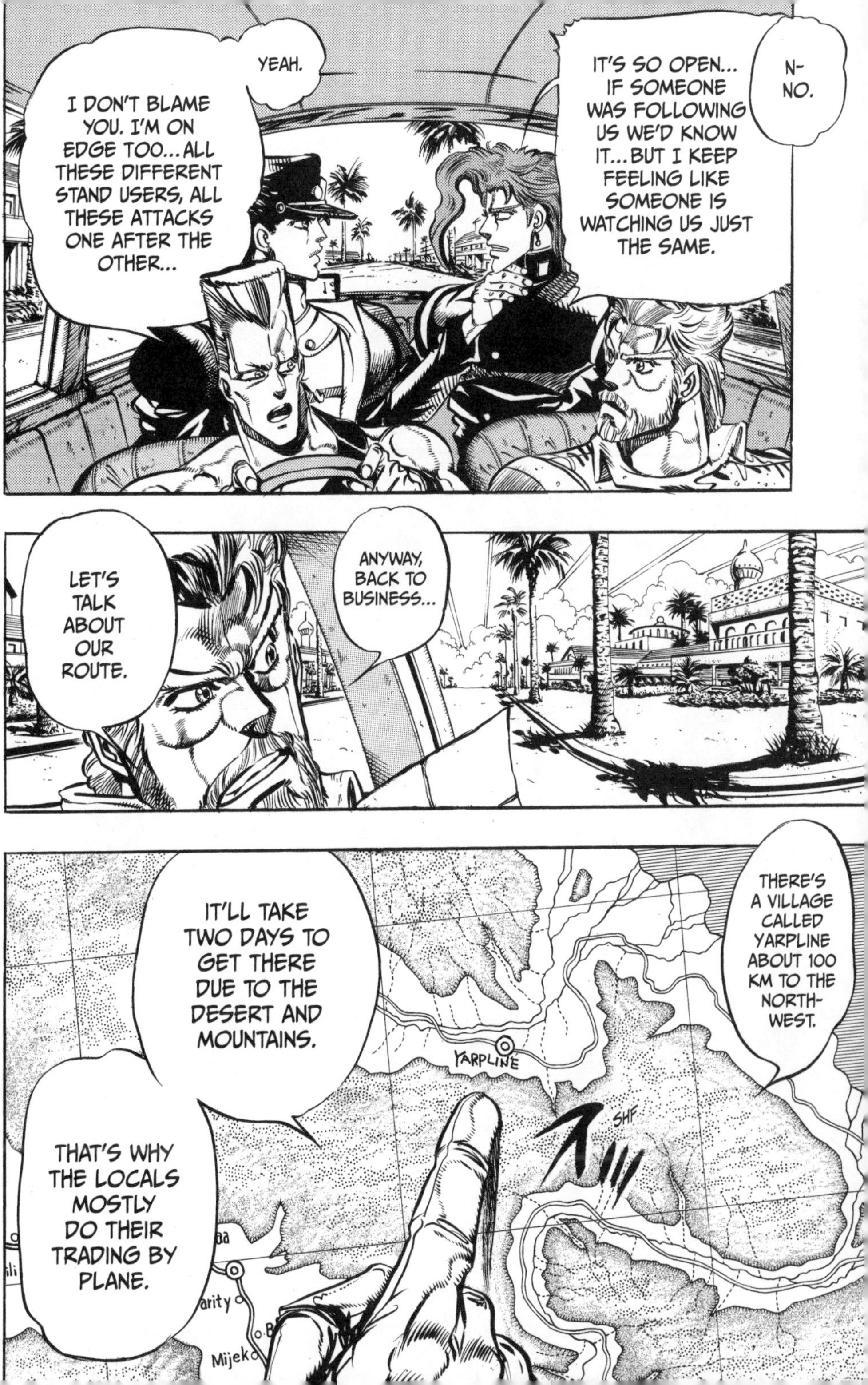
N-NO.
IT'S SO OPEN... IF SOMEONE WAS FOLLOWING US WE'D KNOW IT...BUT I KEEP FEELING LIKE SOMEONE IS WATCHING US JUST THE SAME.
YEAH.
I DON'T BLAME YOU. I'M ON EDGE TOO...ALL THESE DIFFERENT STAND USERS, ALL THESE ATTACKS ONE AFTER THE OTHER...
ANYWAY, BACK TO BUSINESS...
LET'S TALK ABOUT OUR ROUTE.
THERE'S A VILLAGE CALLED YARPLINE ABOUT 100 KM TO THE NORTH-WEST.
YARPLINE
SHF
IT'LL TAKE TWO DAYS TO GET THERE DUE TO THE DESERT AND MOUNTAINS.
THAT'S WHY THE LOCALS MOSTLY DO THEIR TRADING BY PLANE.

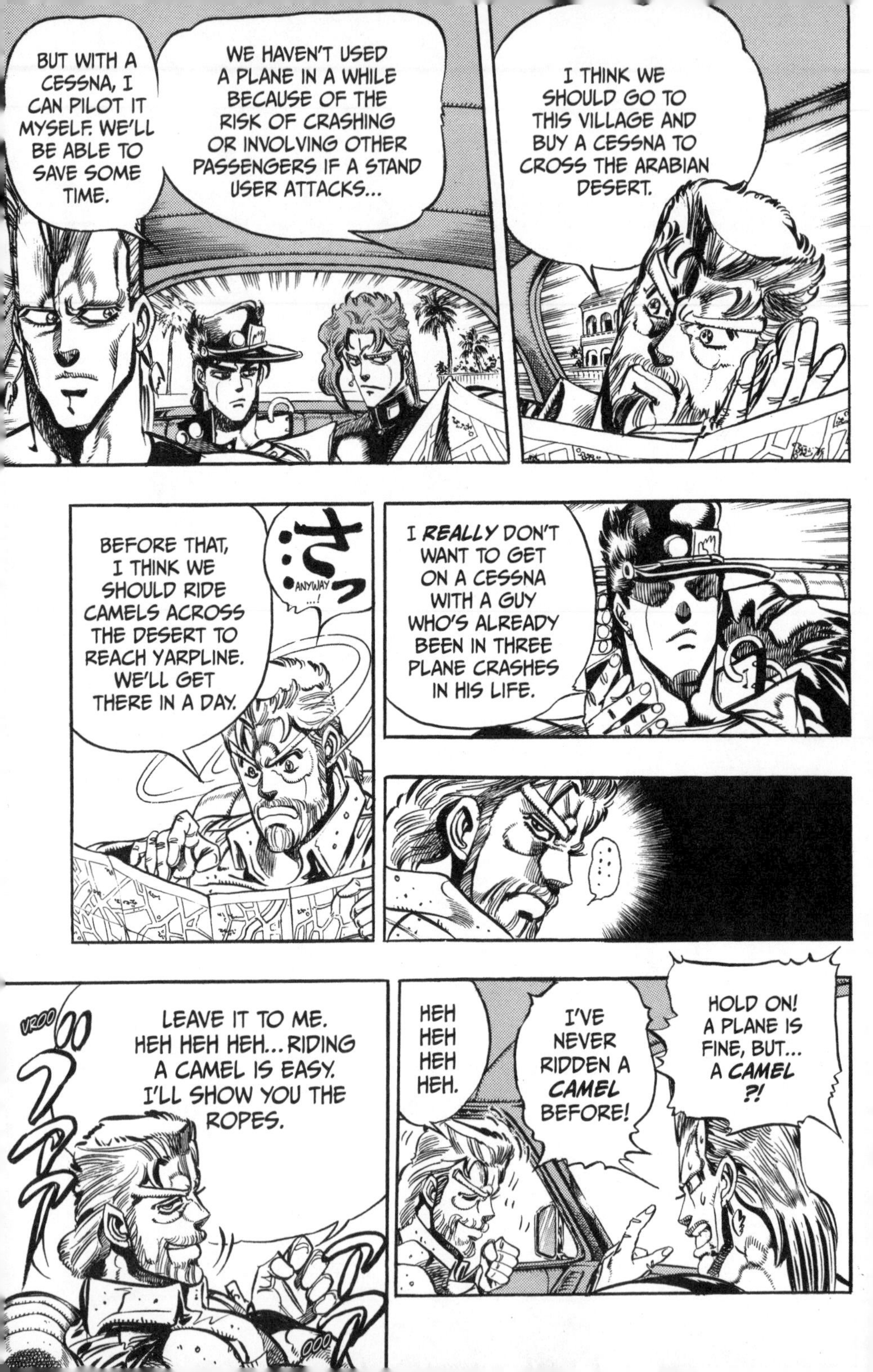
I THINK WE SHOULD GO TO THIS VILLAGE AND BUY A CESSNA TO CROSS THE ARABIAN DESERT.
WE HAVEN'T USED A PLANE IN A WHILE BECAUSE OF THE RISK OF CRASHING OR INVOLVING OTHER PASSENGERS IF A STAND USER ATTACKS...
BUT WITH A CESSNA, I CAN PILOT IT MYSELF. WE'LL BE ABLE TO SAVE SOME TIME.
I ***REALLY*** DON'T WANT TO GET ON A CESSNA WITH A GUY WHO'S ALREADY BEEN IN THREE PLANE CRASHES IN HIS LIFE.
...
さっ
ANYWAY ...!
BEFORE THAT, I THINK WE SHOULD RIDE CAMELS ACROSS THE DESERT TO REACH YARPLINE. WE'LL GET THERE IN A DAY.
HOLD ON! A PLANE IS FINE, BUT... A ***CAMEL*** ?!
I'VE NEVER RIDDEN A ***CAMEL*** BEFORE!
HEH HEH HEH HEH.
VROO
LEAVE IT TO ME. HEH HEH HEH... RIDING A CAMEL IS EASY. I'LL SHOW YOU THE ROPES.

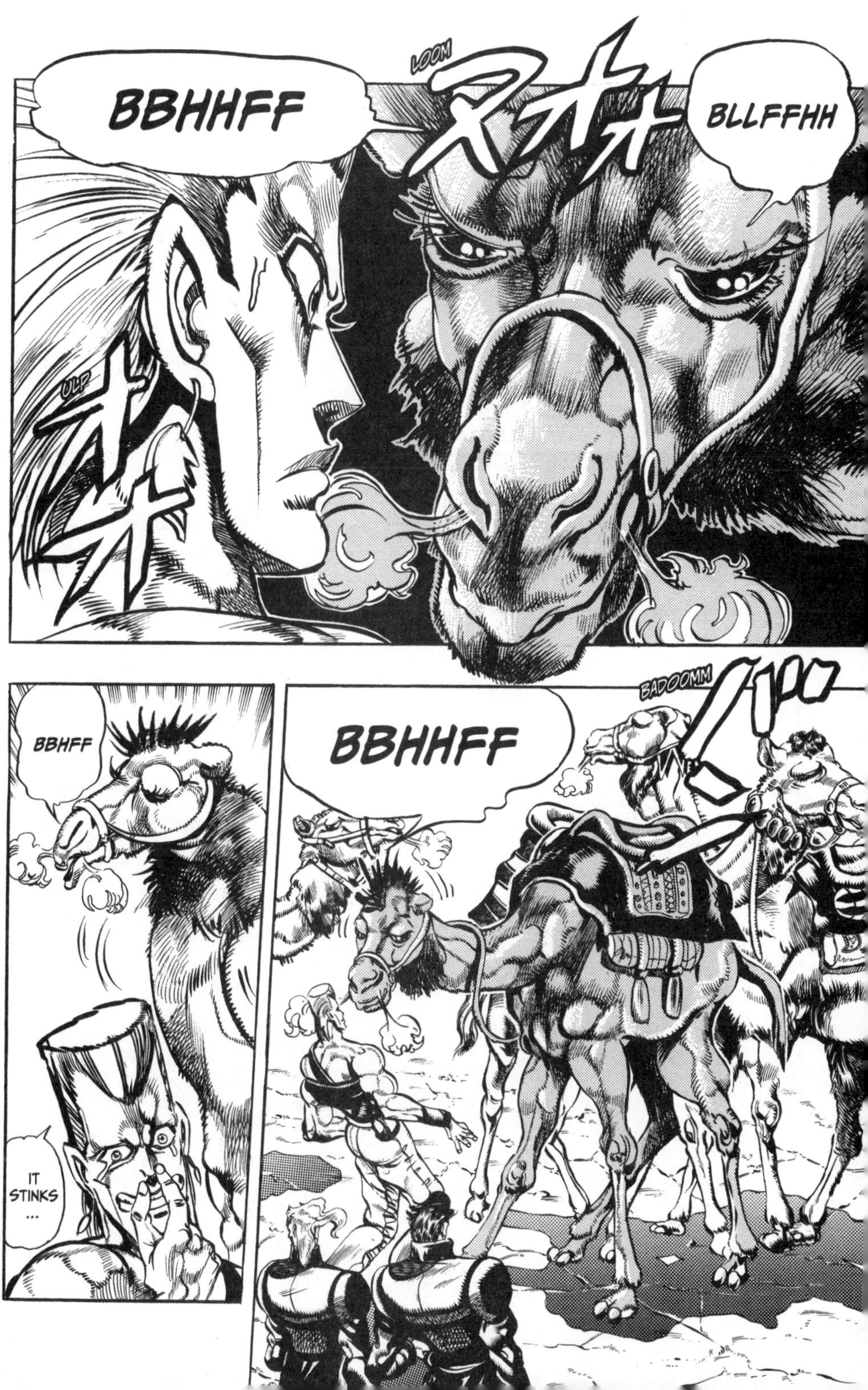
BLLFFHH
LOOM
BBHHFF
ULP
BADOOMM
BBHHFF
BBHFF
IT STINKS ...

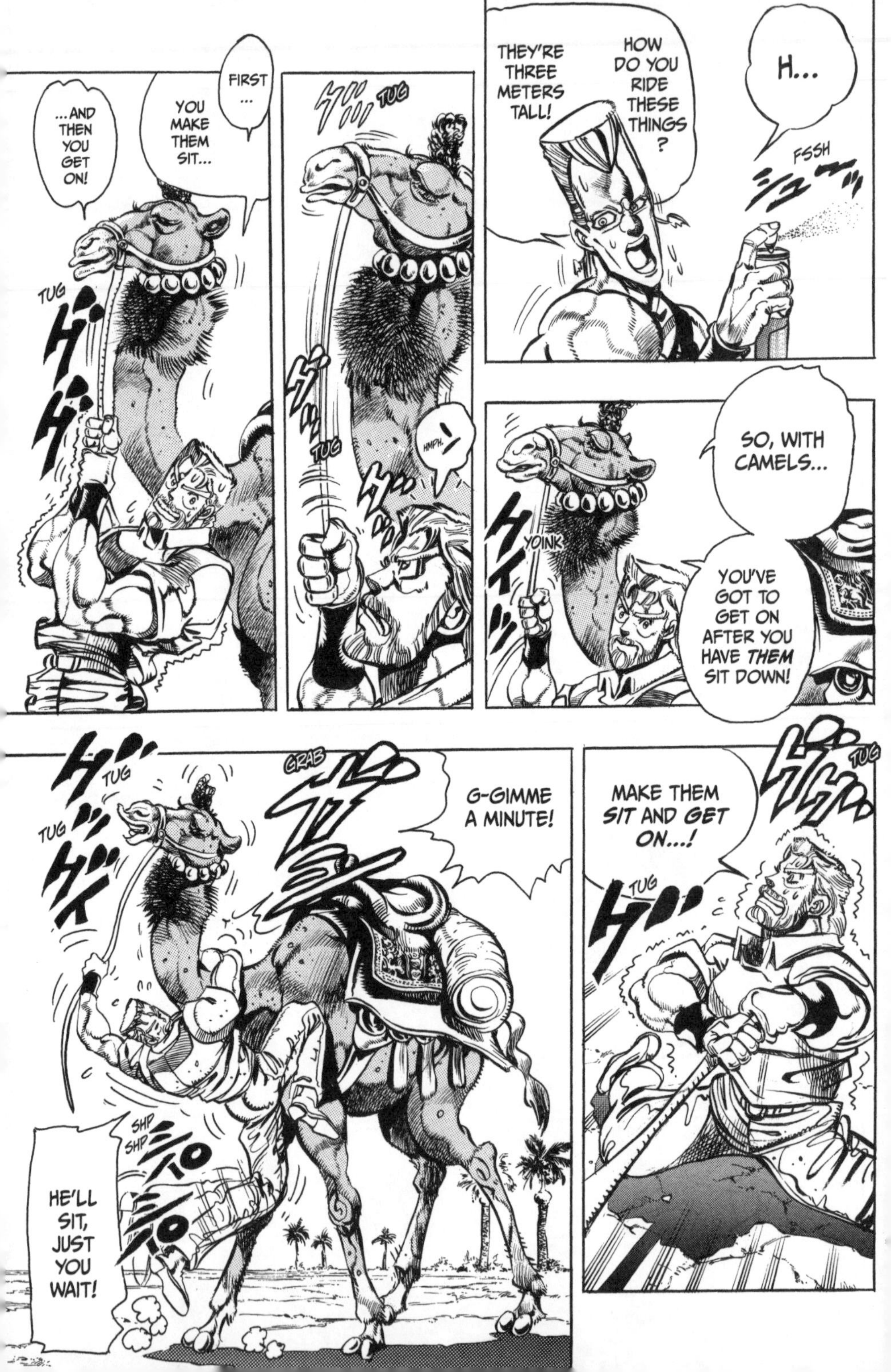
H...
FSSH
HOW DO YOU RIDE THESE THINGS?
THEY'RE THREE METERS TALL!
SO, WITH CAMELS...
YOU'VE GOT TO GET ON AFTER YOU HAVE *THEM* SIT DOWN!
YOINK
TUG
HMPH.
TUG
FIRST...
YOU MAKE THEM SIT...
...AND THEN YOU GET ON!
TUG
TUG
MAKE THEM *SIT* AND *GET ON...!*
TUG
GRAB
G-GIMME A MINUTE!
TUG
TUG
SHP SHP
HE'LL SIT, JUST YOU WAIT!

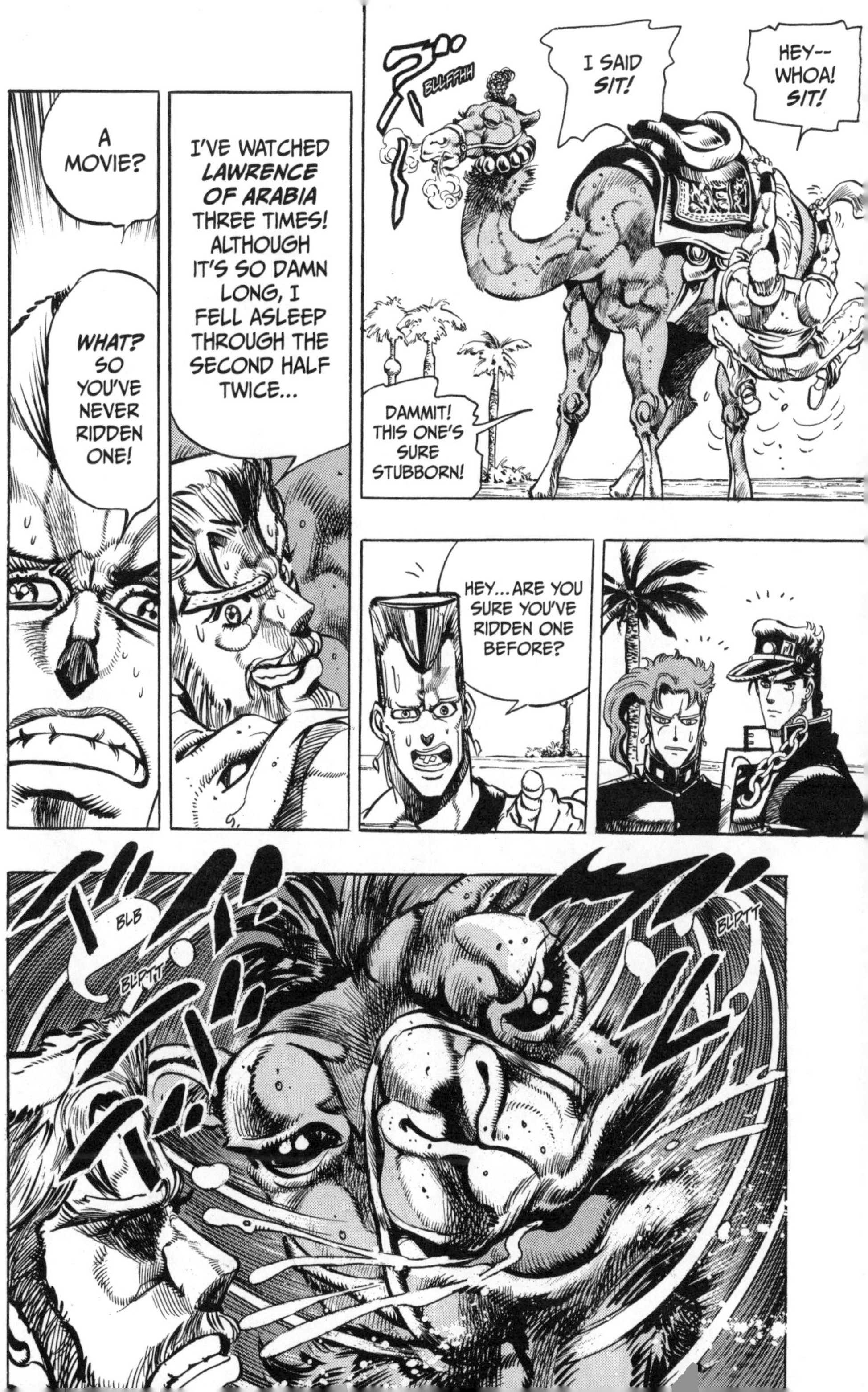
HEY-- WHOA! SIT!
I SAID SIT!
BLLFFHH
DAMMIT! THIS ONE'S SURE STUBBORN!
HEY... ARE YOU SURE YOU'VE RIDDEN ONE BEFORE?
I'VE WATCHED *LAWRENCE OF ARABIA* THREE TIMES! ALTHOUGH IT'S SO DAMN LONG, I FELL ASLEEP THROUGH THE SECOND HALF TWICE...
A MOVIE?
WHAT? SO YOU'VE NEVER RIDDEN ONE!
BLPTT
BLB
BLPTT

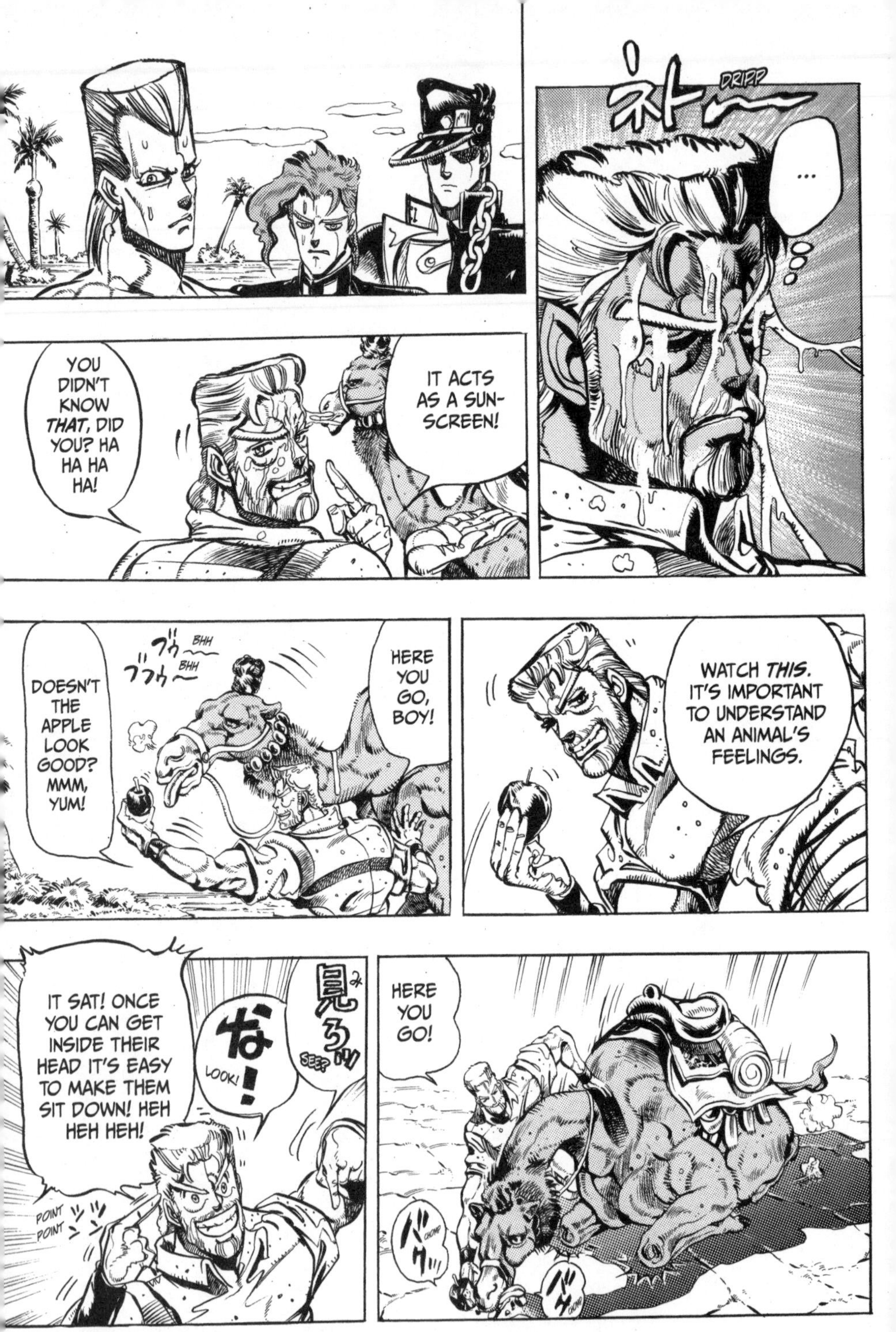

ネト〜 DRIPP
...
IT ACTS AS A SUN-SCREEN!
YOU DIDN'T KNOW *THAT*, DID YOU? HA HA HA HA!
WATCH *THIS*. IT'S IMPORTANT TO UNDERSTAND AN ANIMAL'S FEELINGS.
HERE YOU GO, BOY!
ブゥ〜 BHH
ブフゥ〜 BHH
DOESN'T THE APPLE LOOK GOOD? MMM, YUM!
HERE YOU GO!
バク CHOMP
バク CHOMP
見ろ!!/ SEE?
な! LOOK!
IT SAT! ONCE YOU CAN GET INSIDE THEIR HEAD IT'S EASY TO MAKE THEM SIT DOWN! HEH HEH HEH!
ツツ POINT POINT

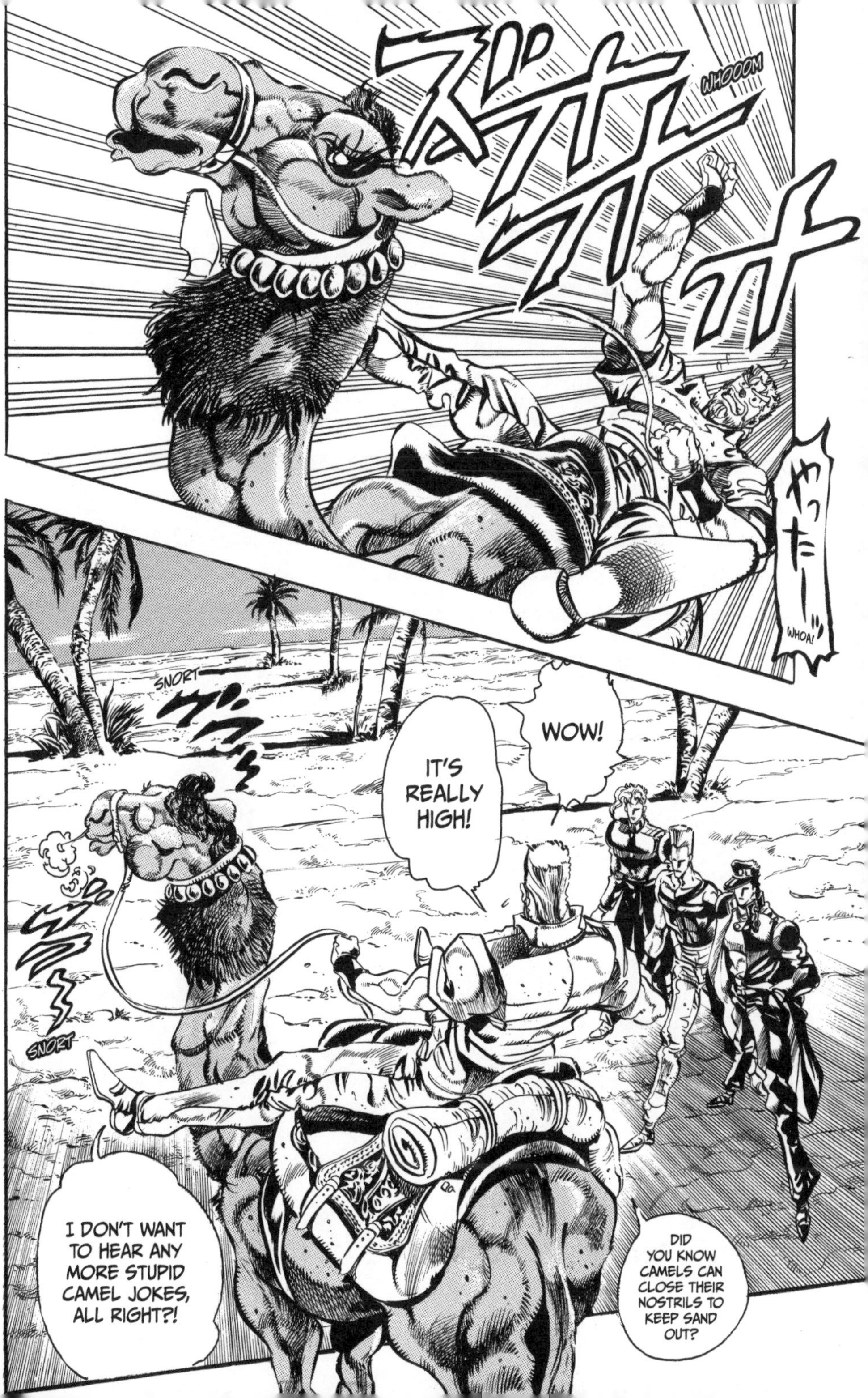
WHOOOM
やったー
WHOA!
WOW!
IT'S REALLY HIGH!
SNORT
SNORT
DID YOU KNOW CAMELS CAN CLOSE THEIR NOSTRILS TO KEEP SAND OUT?
I DON'T WANT TO HEAR ANY MORE STUPID CAMEL JOKES, ALL RIGHT?!

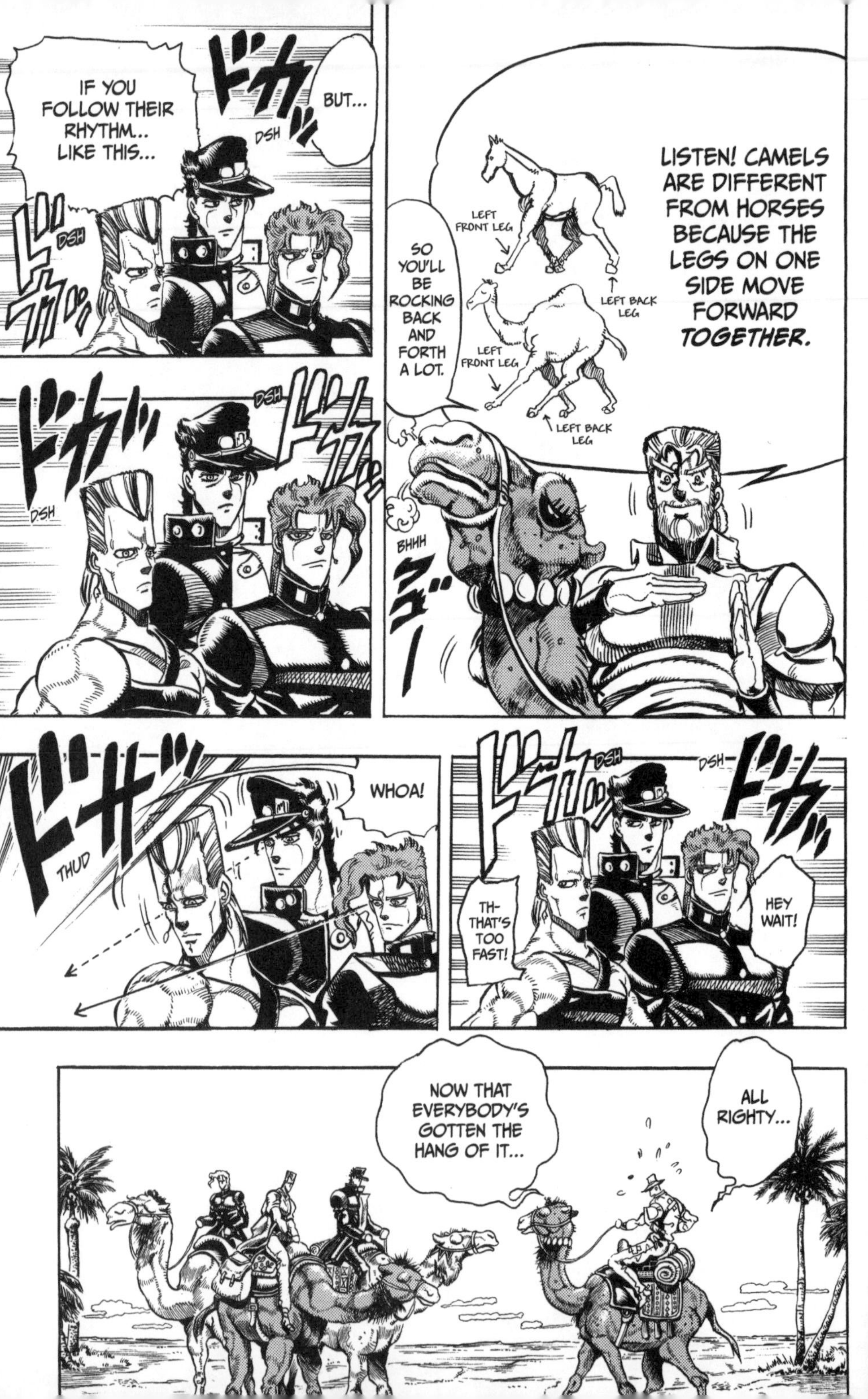
LISTEN! CAMELS ARE DIFFERENT FROM HORSES BECAUSE THE LEGS ON ONE SIDE MOVE FORWARD TOGETHER.
LEFT FRONT LEG
LEFT BACK LEG
LEFT FRONT LEG
LEFT BACK LEG
SO YOU'LL BE ROCKING BACK AND FORTH A LOT.
BHHH
BUT...
DSH
IF YOU FOLLOW THEIR RHYTHM... LIKE THIS...
DSH
DSH
DSH
DSH
DSH
HEY WAIT!
TH-THAT'S TOO FAST!
WHOA!
THUD
ALL RIGHTY...
NOW THAT EVERYBODY'S GOTTEN THE HANG OF IT...

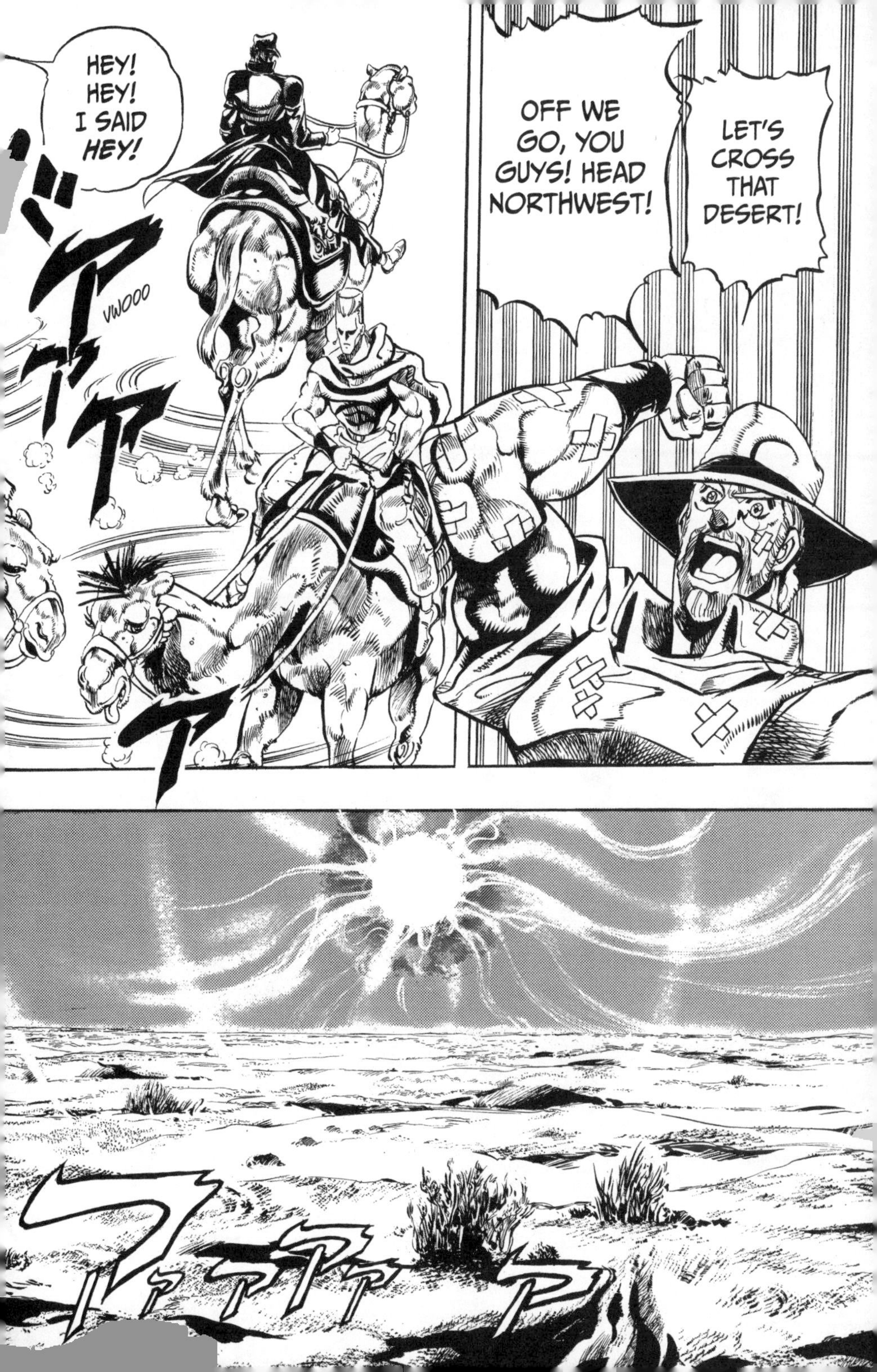
LET'S CROSS THAT DESERT!
OFF WE GO, YOU GUYS! HEAD NORTHWEST!
HEY! HEY! I SAID HEY!
VWOOO

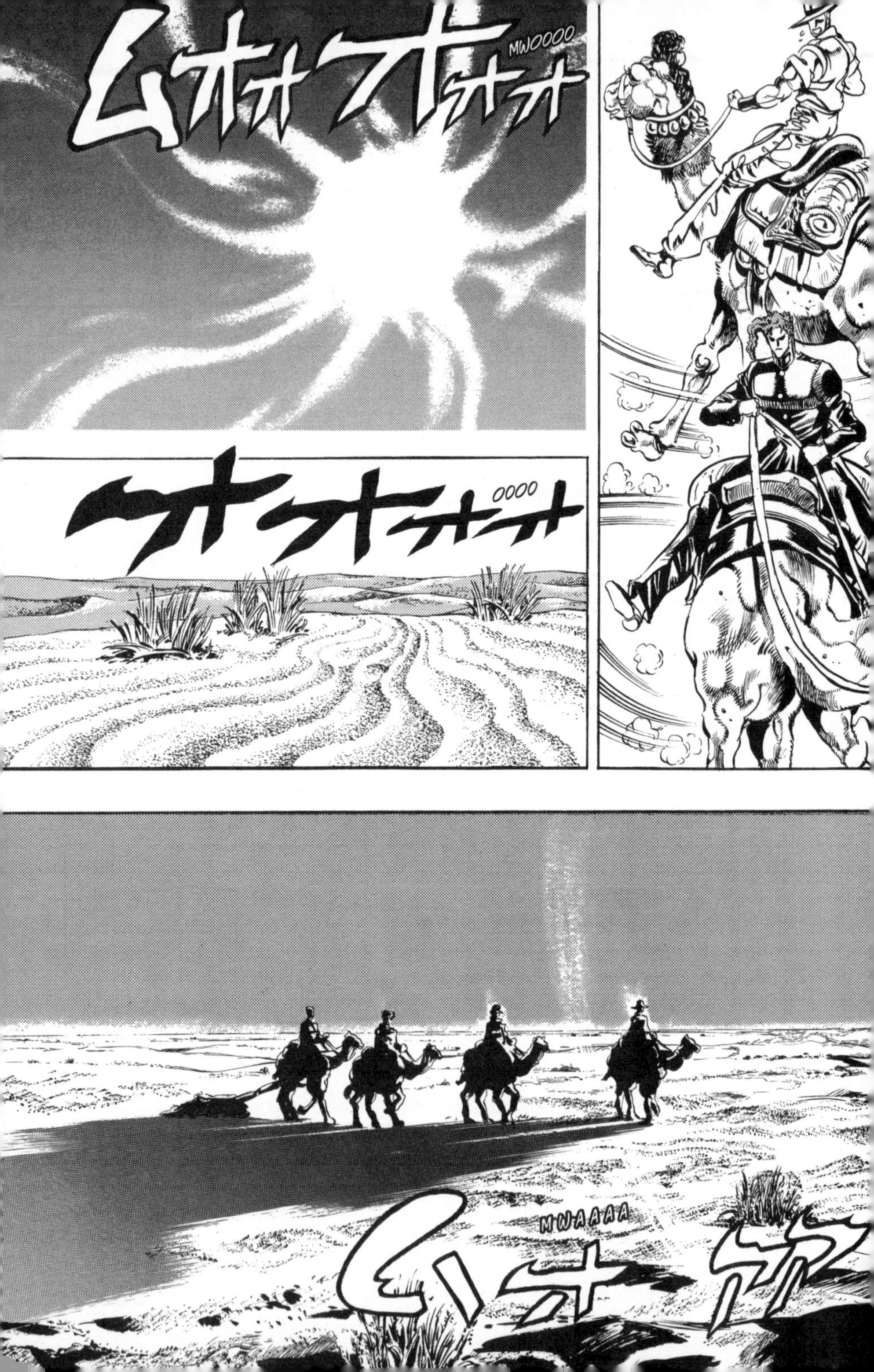
MWOOOO
OOOO
MWAAAA

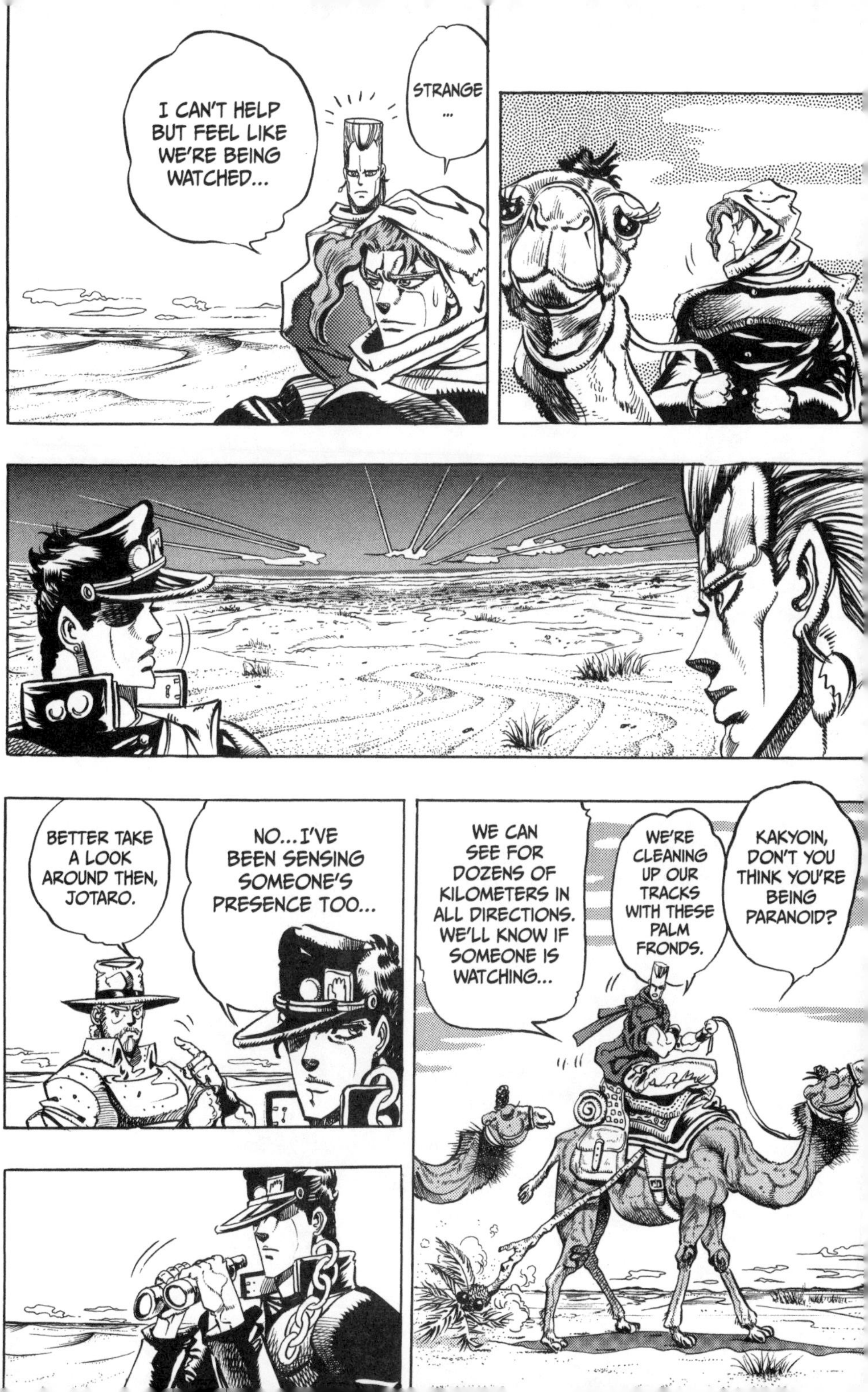
STRANGE ...
I CAN'T HELP BUT FEEL LIKE WE'RE BEING WATCHED...
KAKYOIN, DON'T YOU THINK YOU'RE BEING PARANOID?
WE'RE CLEANING UP OUR TRACKS WITH THESE PALM FRONDS.
WE CAN SEE FOR DOZENS OF KILOMETERS IN ALL DIRECTIONS. WE'LL KNOW IF SOMEONE IS WATCHING...
NO...I'VE BEEN SENSING SOMEONE'S PRESENCE TOO...
BETTER TAKE A LOOK AROUND THEN, JOTARO.

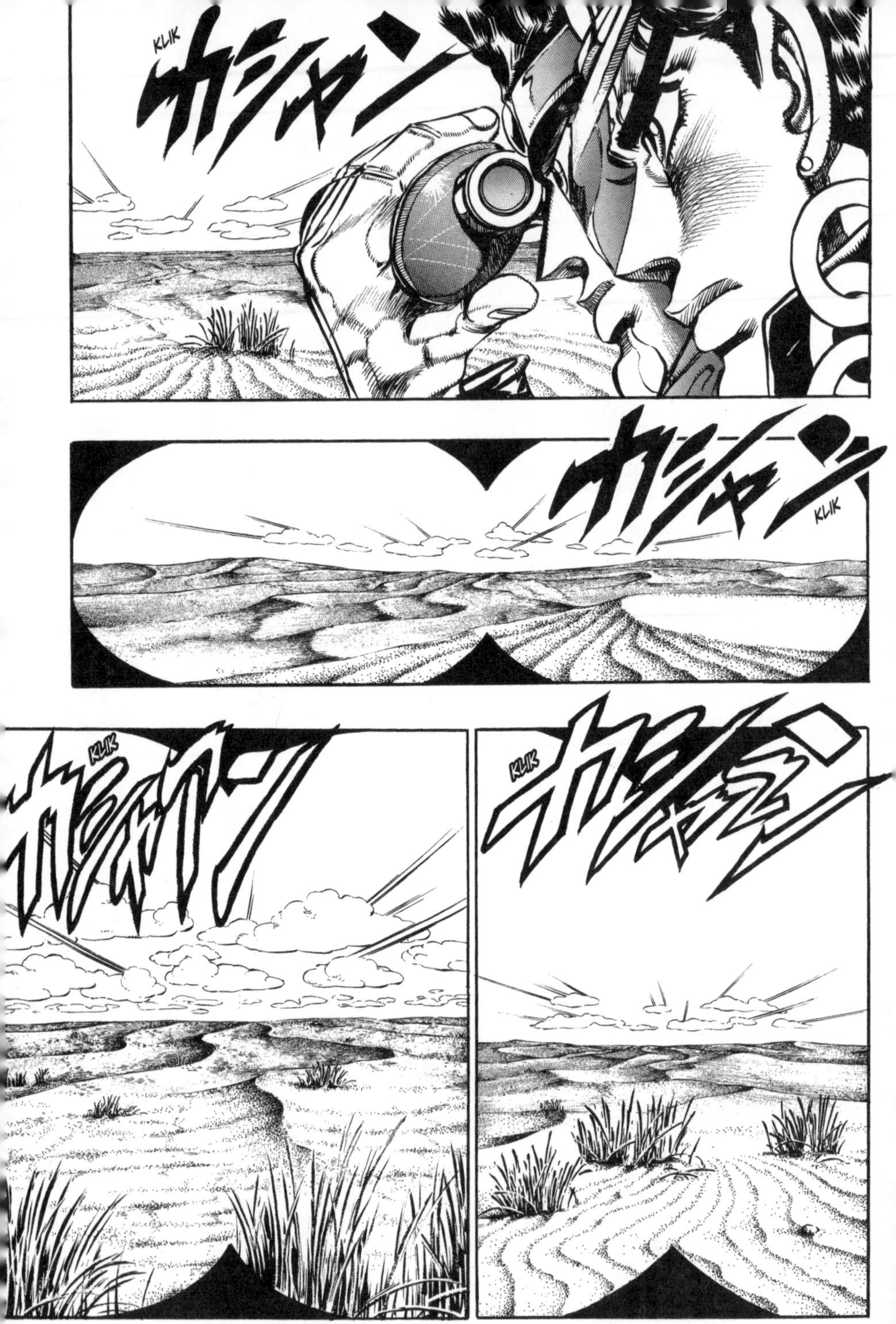

KLIK
カシャン
カシャン
KLIK
KLIK
KLIK

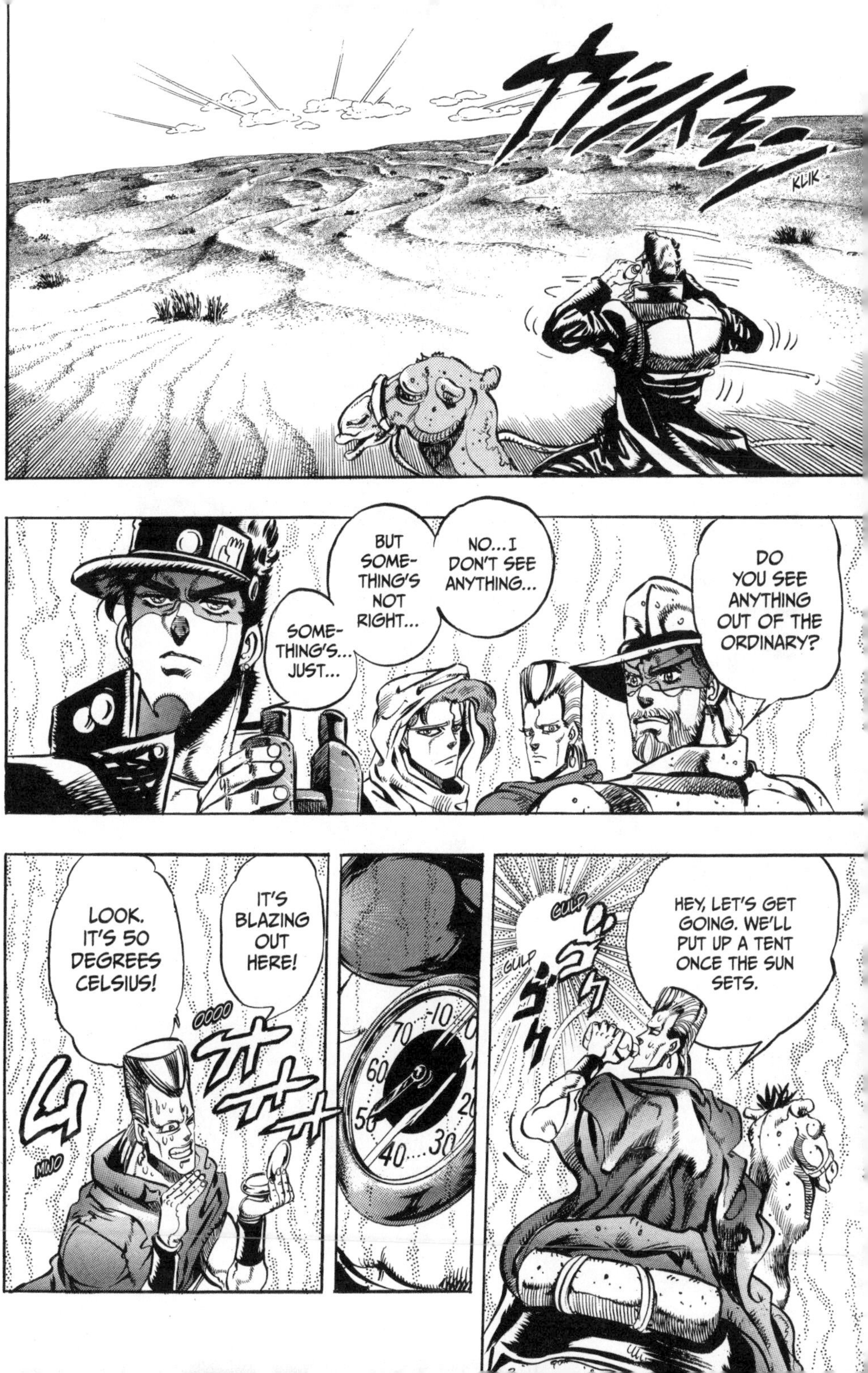
KLIK
DO YOU SEE ANYTHING OUT OF THE ORDINARY?
NO...I DON'T SEE ANYTHING...
BUT SOMETHING'S NOT RIGHT...
SOMETHING'S... JUST...
HEY, LET'S GET GOING. WE'LL PUT UP A TENT ONCE THE SUN SETS.
GULP
GULP
IT'S BLAZING OUT HERE!
LOOK. IT'S 50 DEGREES CELSIUS!
OOOO

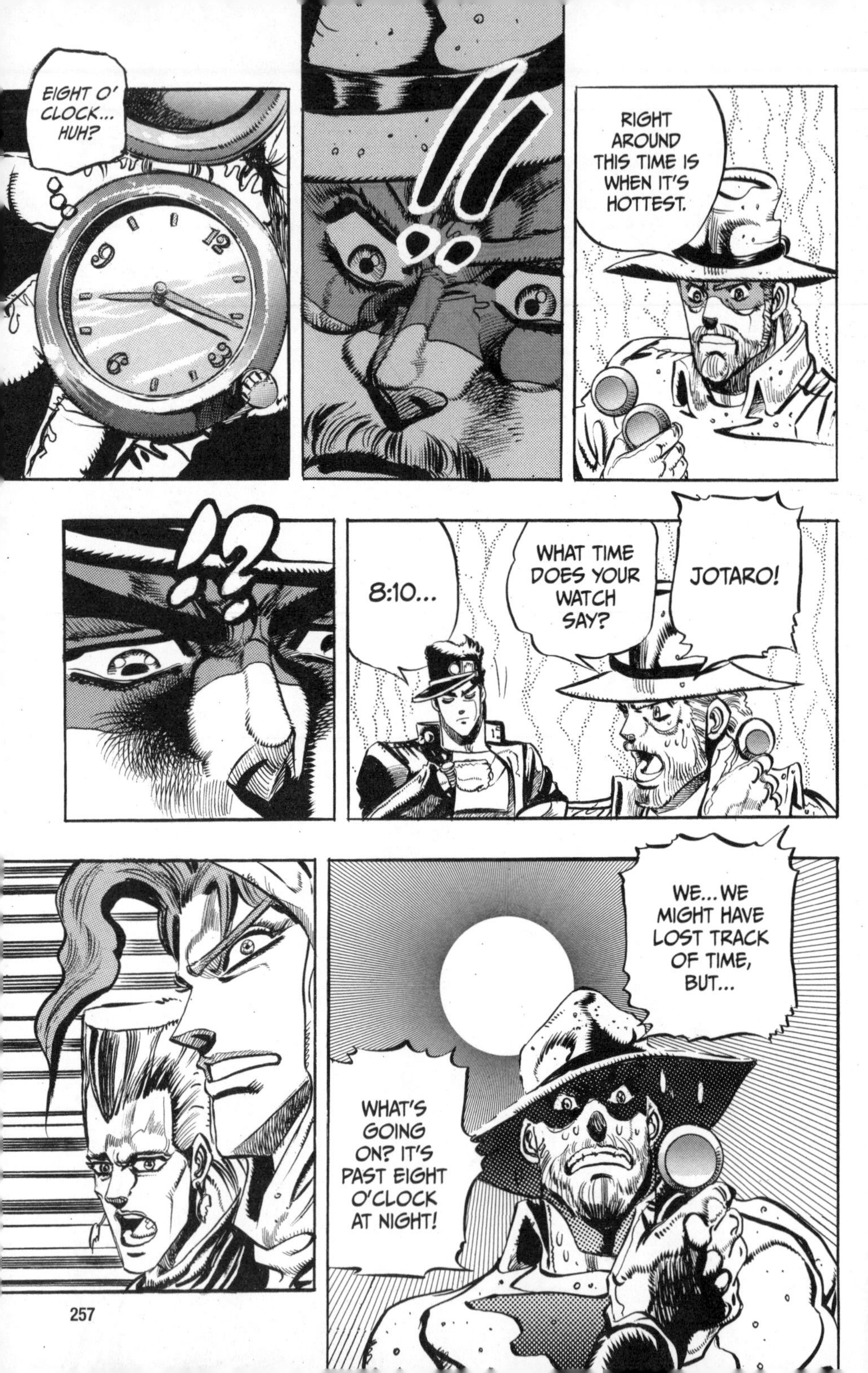
RIGHT AROUND THIS TIME IS WHEN IT'S HOTTEST.
EIGHT O' CLOCK... HUH?
JOTARO!
WHAT TIME DOES YOUR WATCH SAY?
8:10...
WE...WE MIGHT HAVE LOST TRACK OF TIME, BUT...
WHAT'S GOING ON? IT'S PAST EIGHT O'CLOCK AT NIGHT!

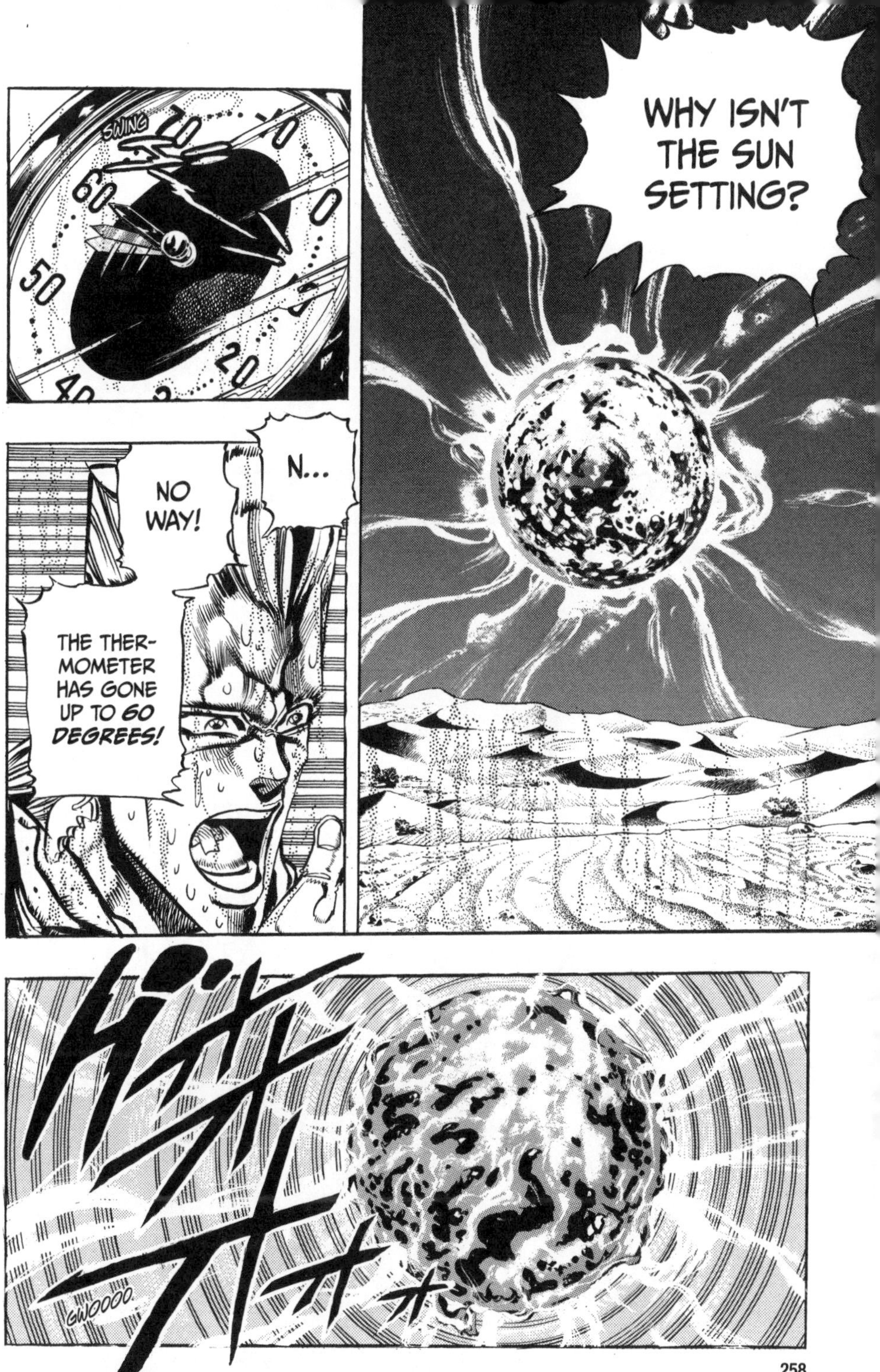
WHY ISN'T THE SUN SETTING?
SWING
N...
NO WAY!
THE THERMOMETER HAS GONE UP TO 60 DEGREES!
GWOOOO

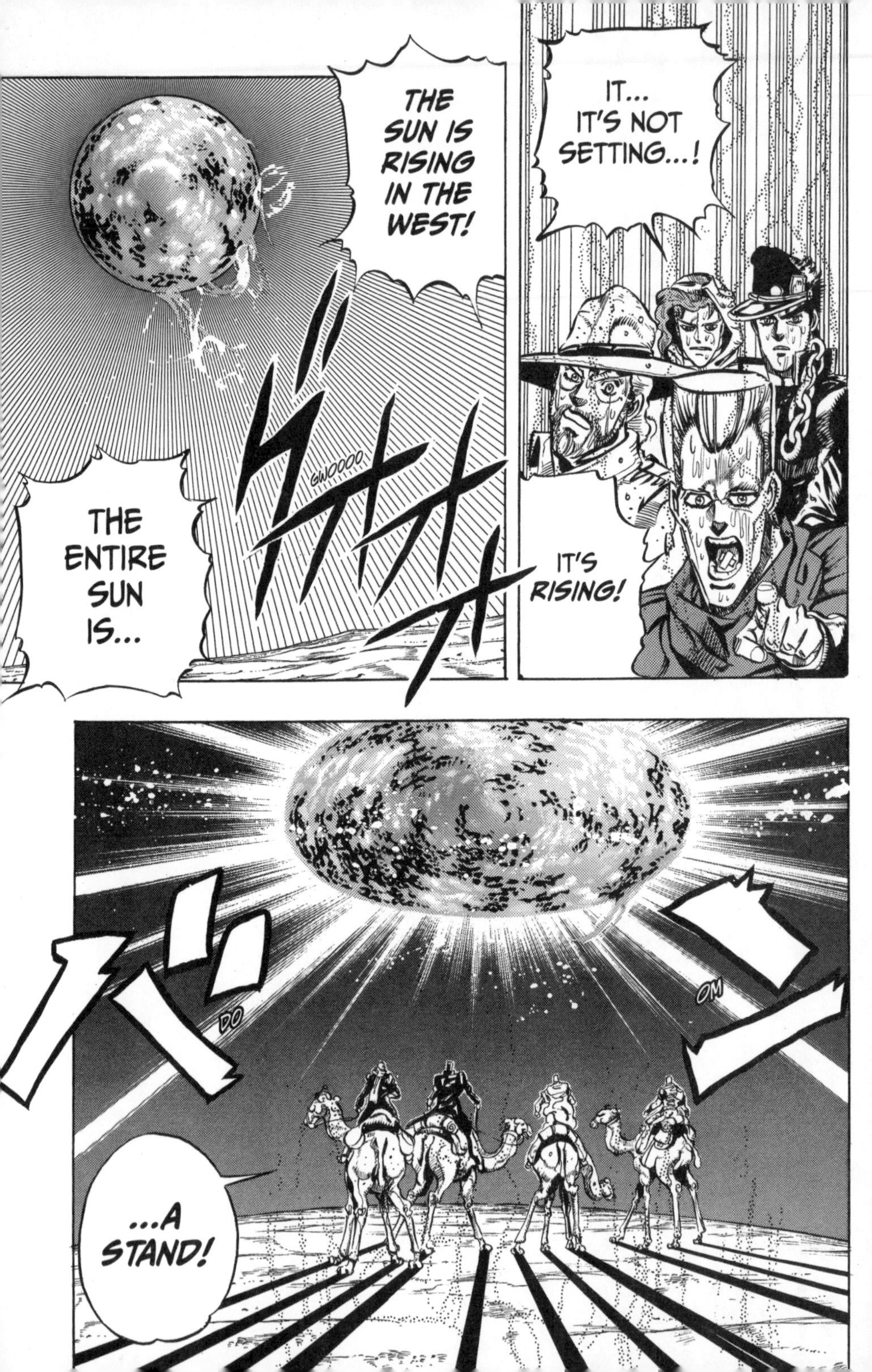
IT... IT'S NOT SETTING...!
IT'S RISING!
THE SUN IS RISING IN THE WEST!
GWOOOO
THE ENTIRE SUN IS...
DO
OM
...A STAND!

LUCKY LAND
THE SUN 19

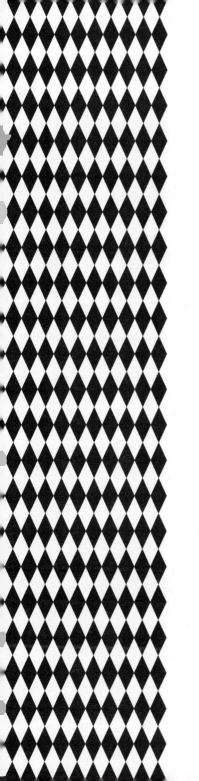

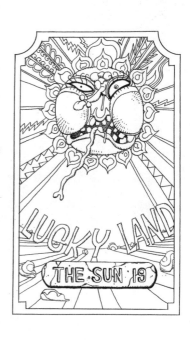

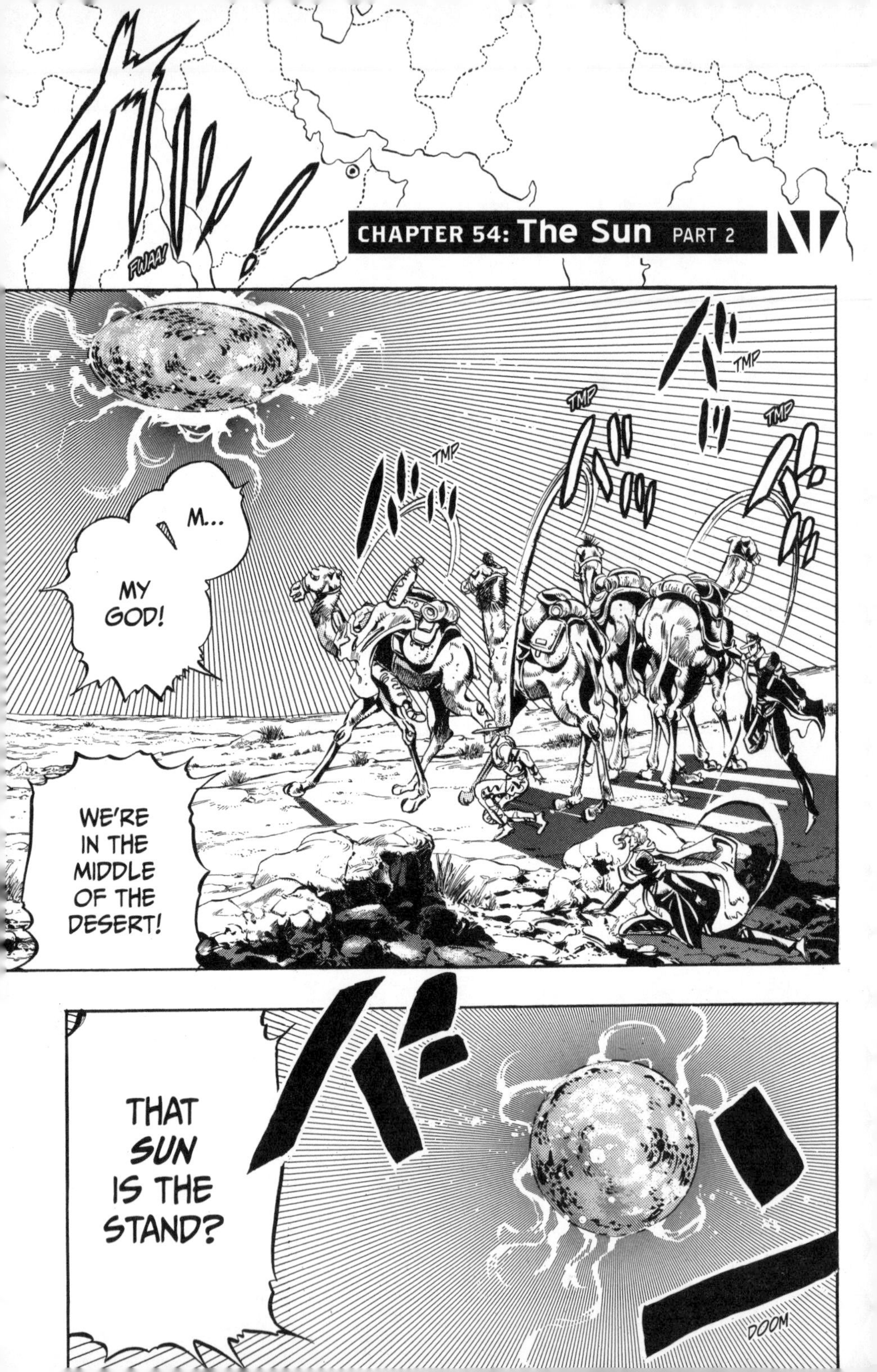
CHAPTER 54: The Sun PART 2
FWAA!
TMP
TMP
TMP
TMP
M...
MY GOD!
WE'RE IN THE MIDDLE OF THE DESERT!
THAT *SUN* IS THE STAND?
DOOM

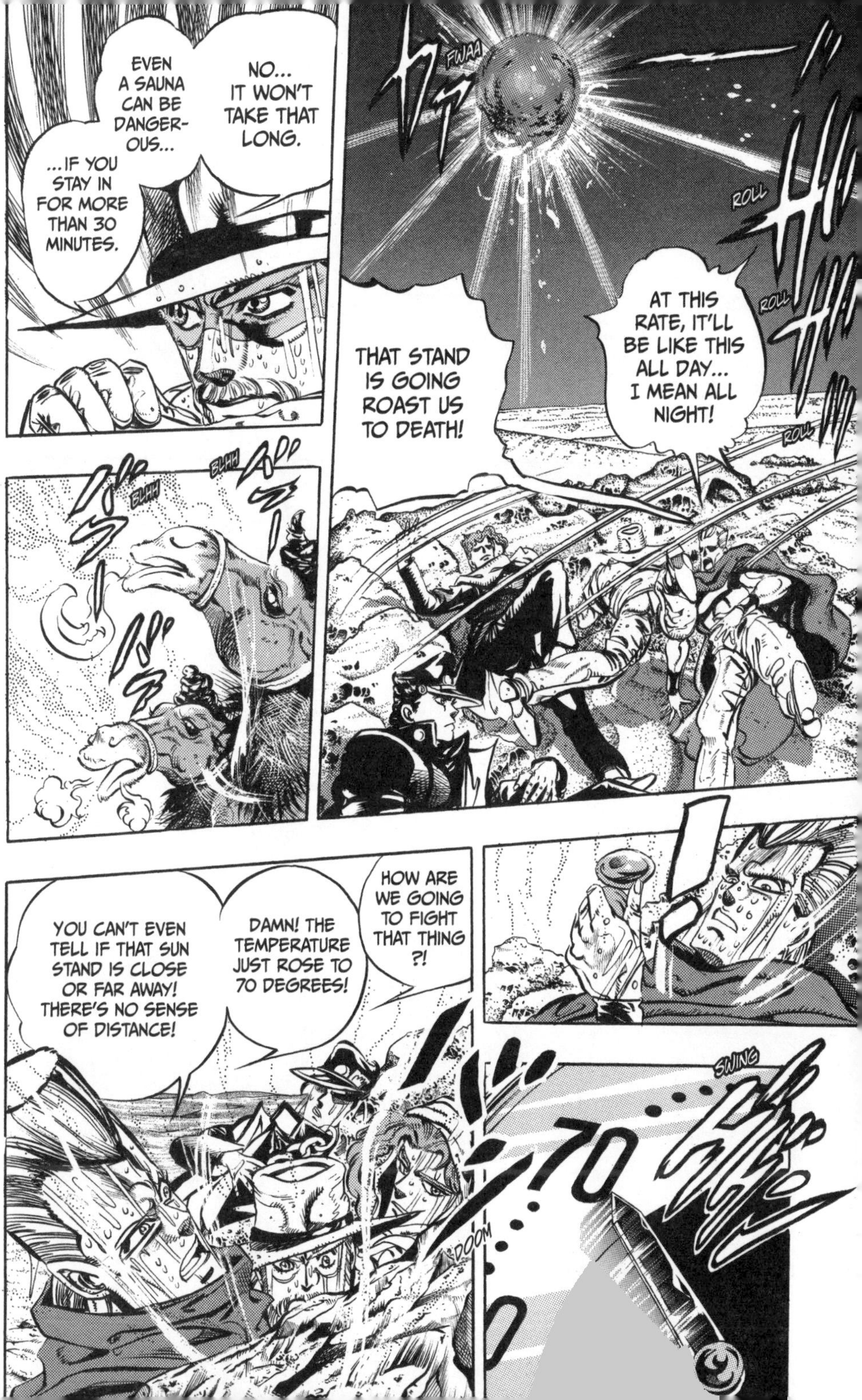
FWAA
ROLL
ROLL
AT THIS RATE, IT'LL BE LIKE THIS ALL DAY... I MEAN ALL NIGHT!
ROLL
THAT STAND IS GOING ROAST US TO DEATH!
NO... IT WON'T TAKE THAT LONG.
EVEN A SAUNA CAN BE DANGER-OUS...
...IF YOU STAY IN FOR MORE THAN 30 MINUTES.
BLHH
BLHH
HOW ARE WE GOING TO FIGHT THAT THING ?!
DAMN! THE TEMPERATURE JUST ROSE TO 70 DEGREES!
YOU CAN'T EVEN TELL IF THAT SUN STAND IS CLOSE OR FAR AWAY! THERE'S NO SENSE OF DISTANCE!
SWING
70
DOOM

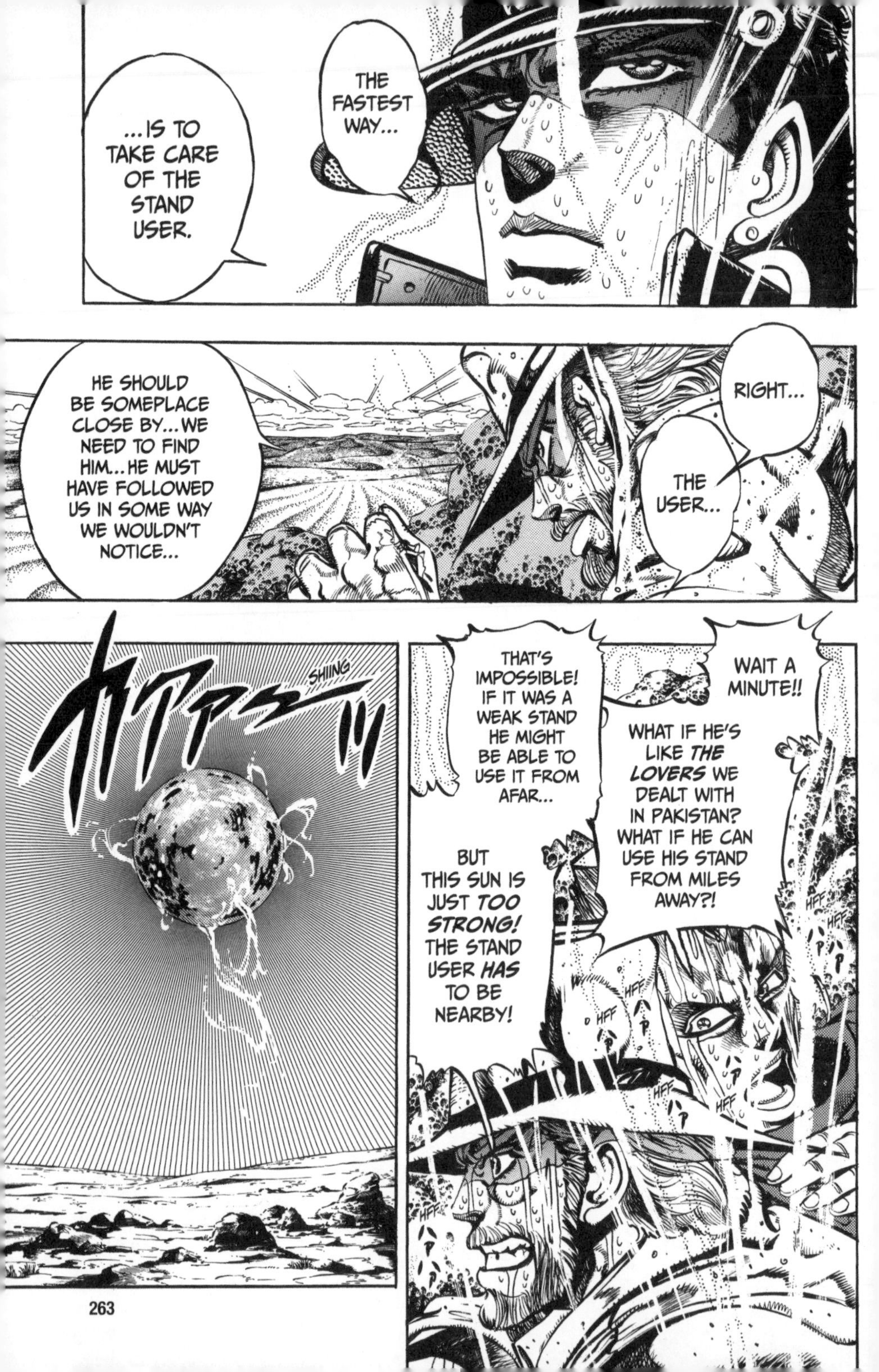
THE FASTEST WAY...
...IS TO TAKE CARE OF THE STAND USER.
RIGHT...
THE USER...
HE SHOULD BE SOMEPLACE CLOSE BY...WE NEED TO FIND HIM...HE MUST HAVE FOLLOWED US IN SOME WAY WE WOULDN'T NOTICE...
WAIT A MINUTE!!
WHAT IF HE'S LIKE *THE LOVERS* WE DEALT WITH IN PAKISTAN? WHAT IF HE CAN USE HIS STAND FROM MILES AWAY?!
THAT'S IMPOSSIBLE! IF IT WAS A WEAK STAND HE MIGHT BE ABLE TO USE IT FROM AFAR...
BUT THIS SUN IS JUST *TOO STRONG!* THE STAND USER *HAS* TO BE NEARBY!
HFF
HFF
HFF
HFF
HFF
HFF
SHIING

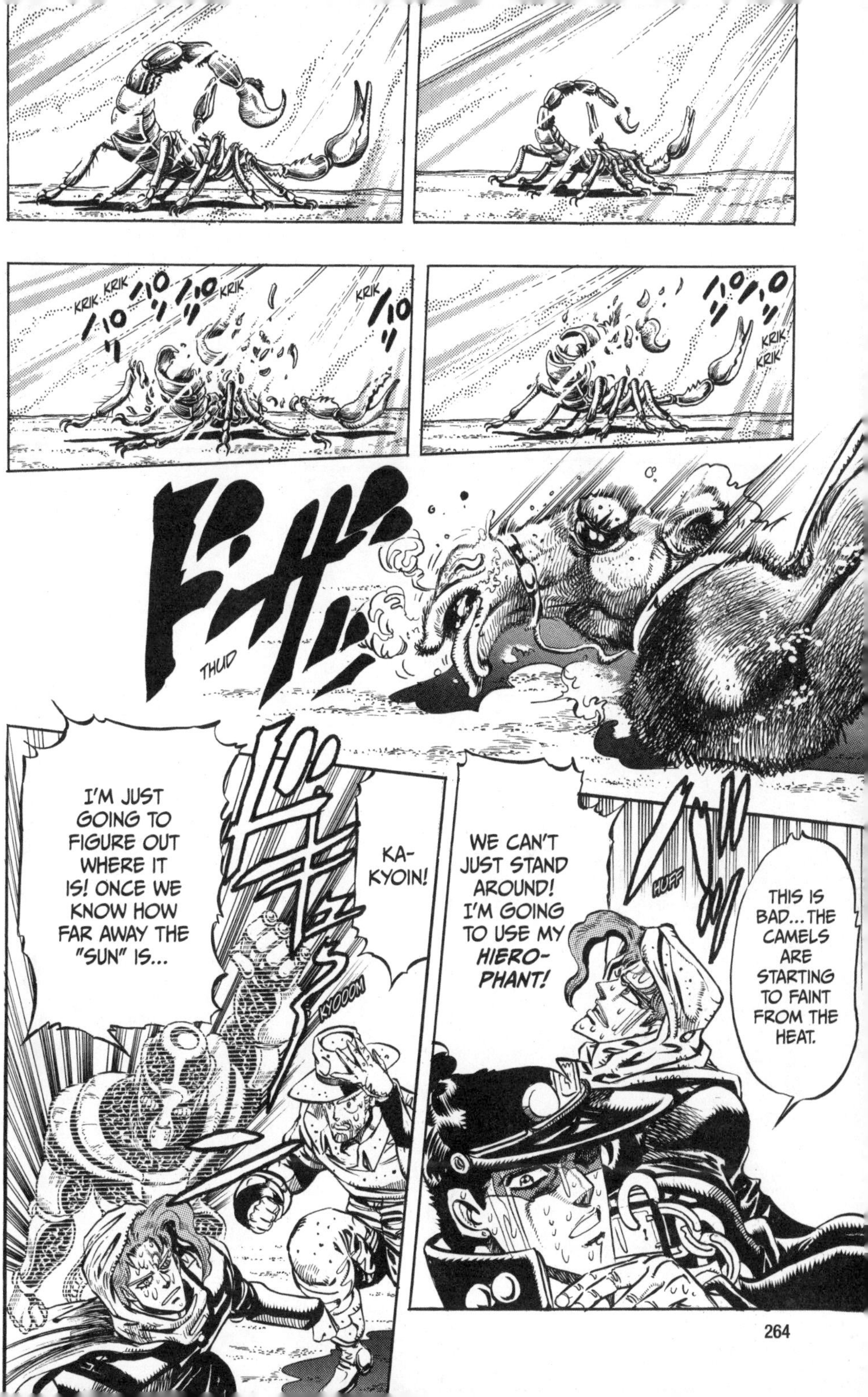
KRIK
KRIK
KRIK
KRIK
KRIK
THUD
THIS IS BAD... THE CAMELS ARE STARTING TO FAINT FROM THE HEAT.
HUFF
WE CAN'T JUST STAND AROUND! I'M GOING TO USE MY *HIEROPHANT!*
KA-KYOIN!
I'M JUST GOING TO FIGURE OUT WHERE IT IS! ONCE WE KNOW HOW FAR AWAY THE "SUN" IS...
KYOOOM

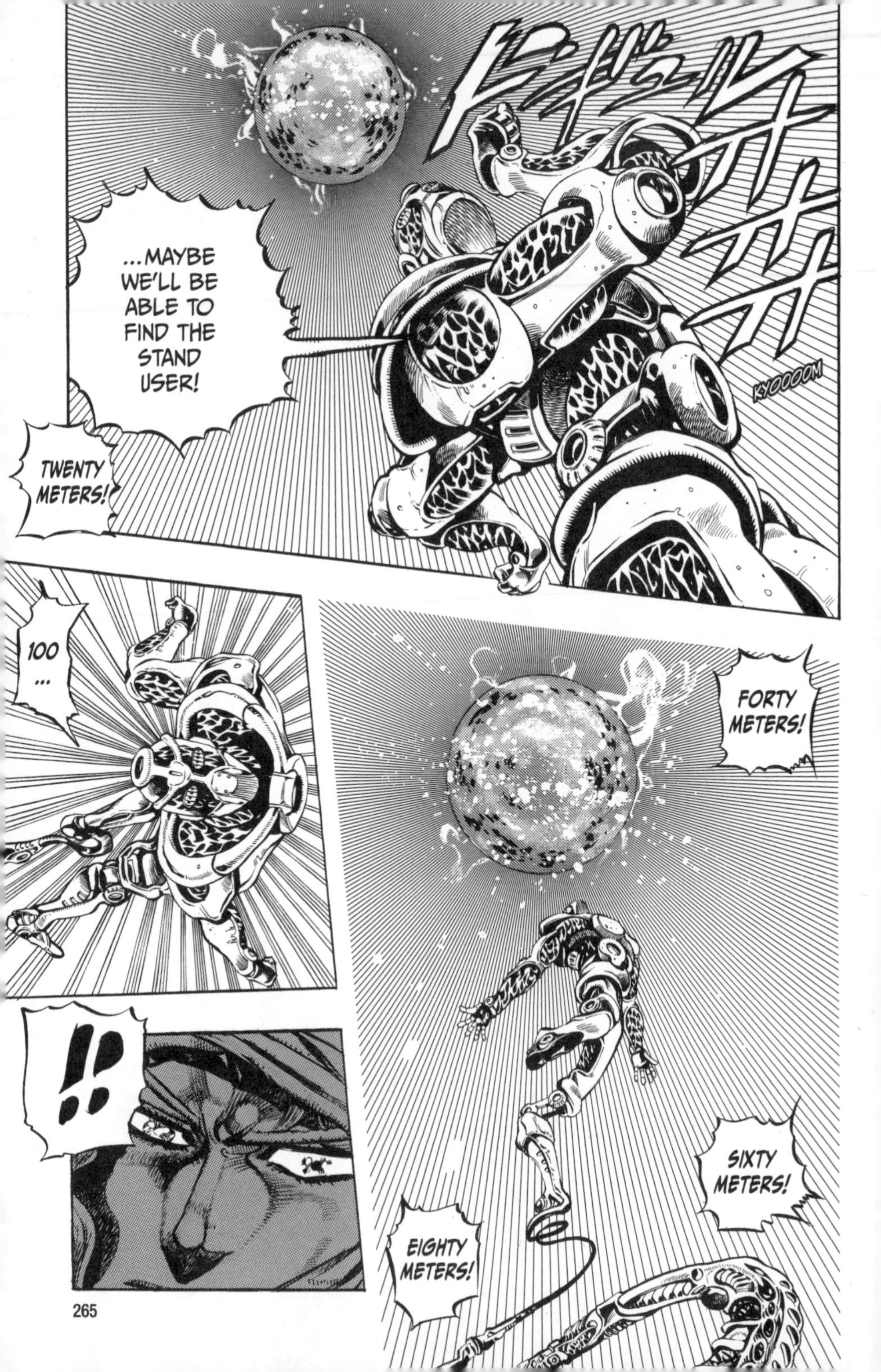
KYOOOOM
...MAYBE WE'LL BE ABLE TO FIND THE STAND USER!
TWENTY METERS!
FORTY METERS!
SIXTY METERS!
EIGHTY METERS!
100 ...
!!

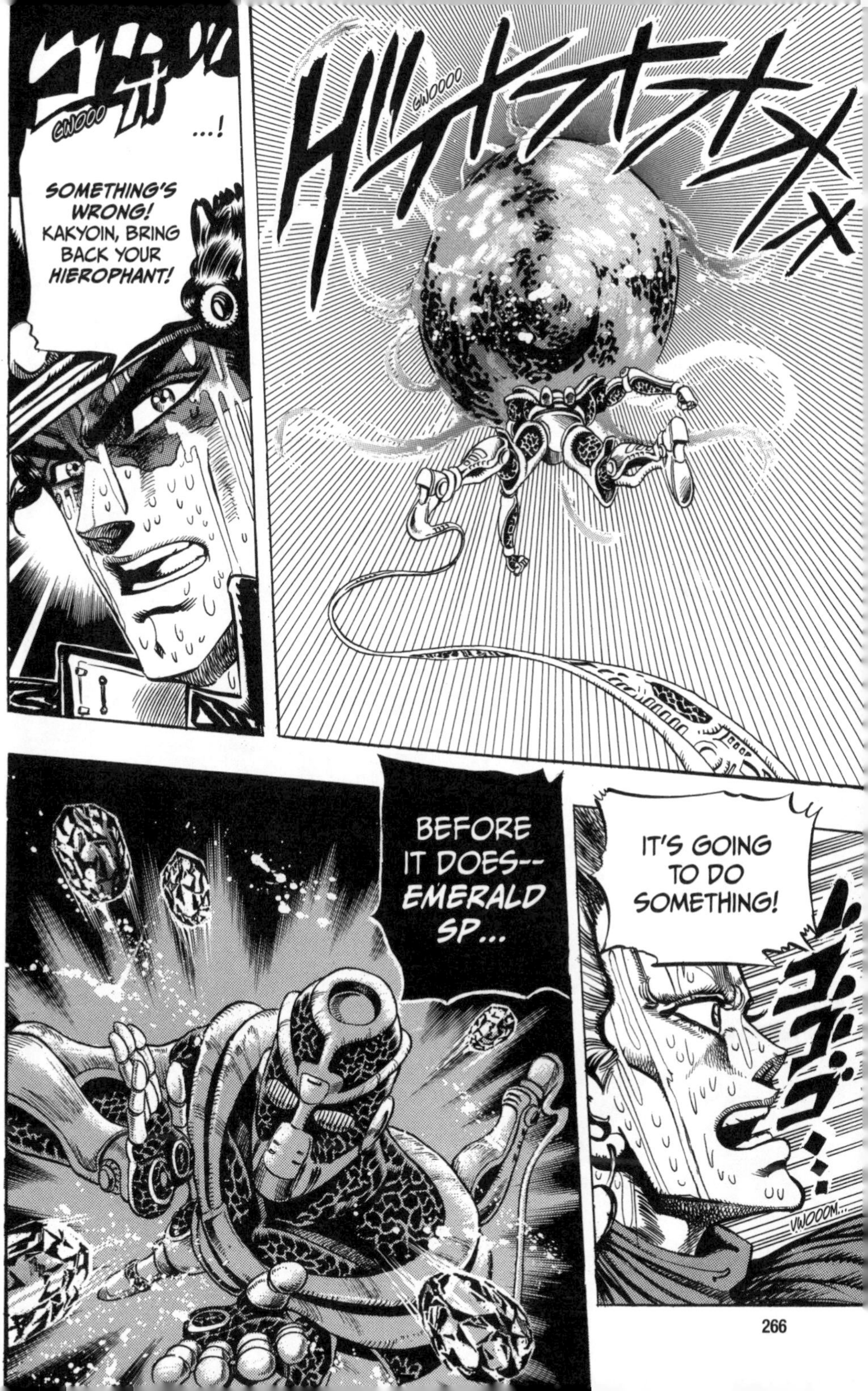
GWOOOO
GWOOO
...!
SOMETHING'S WRONG! KAKYOIN, BRING BACK YOUR HIEROPHANT!
IT'S GOING TO DO SOMETHING!
VWOOOM...
BEFORE IT DOES-- EMERALD SP...

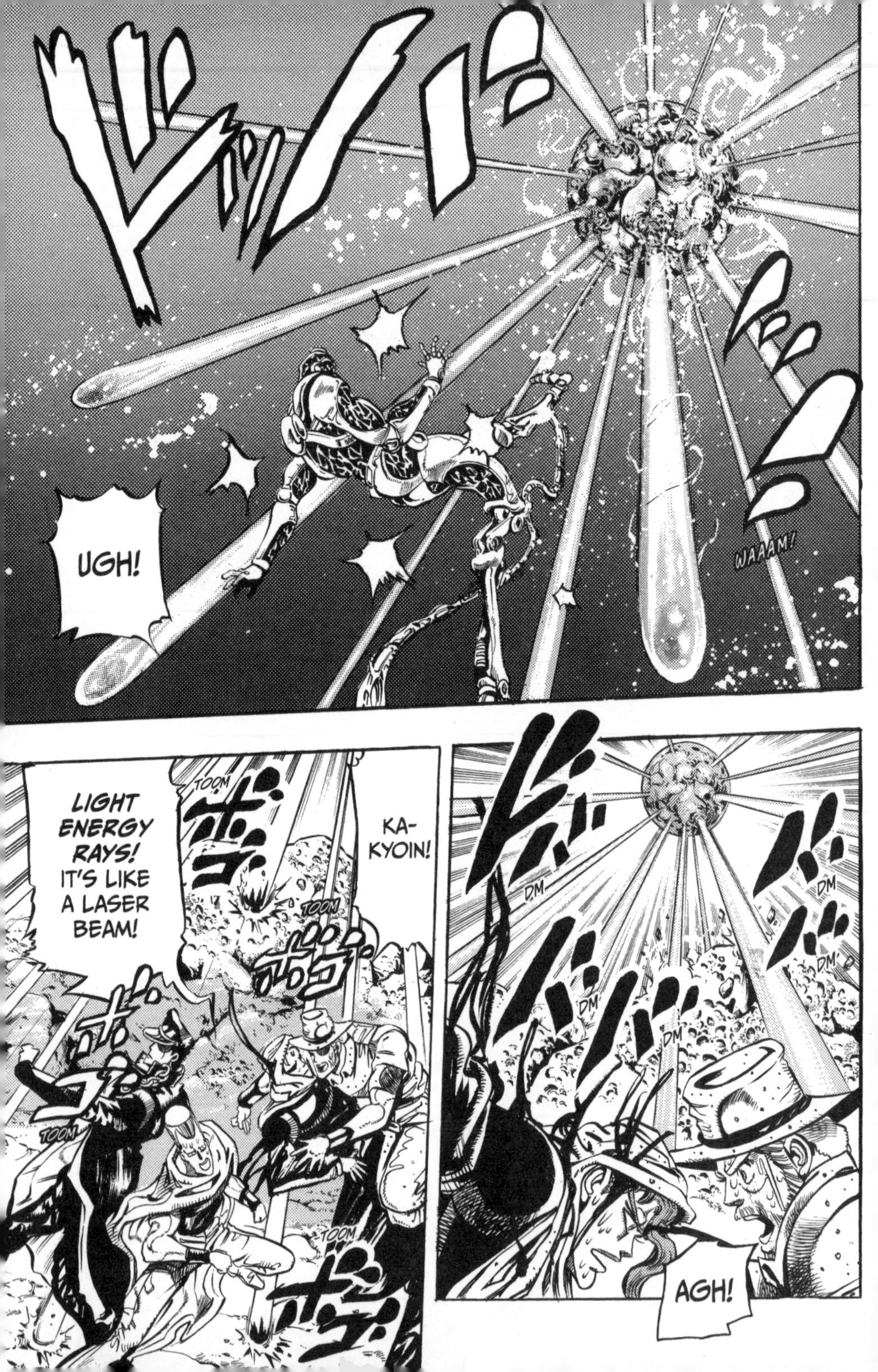
WAAAM!
UGH!
DM
DM
DM
DM
DM
AGH!
TOOM
KA-KYOIN!
LIGHT ENERGY RAYS! IT'S LIKE A LASER BEAM!
TOOM
TOOM
TOOM

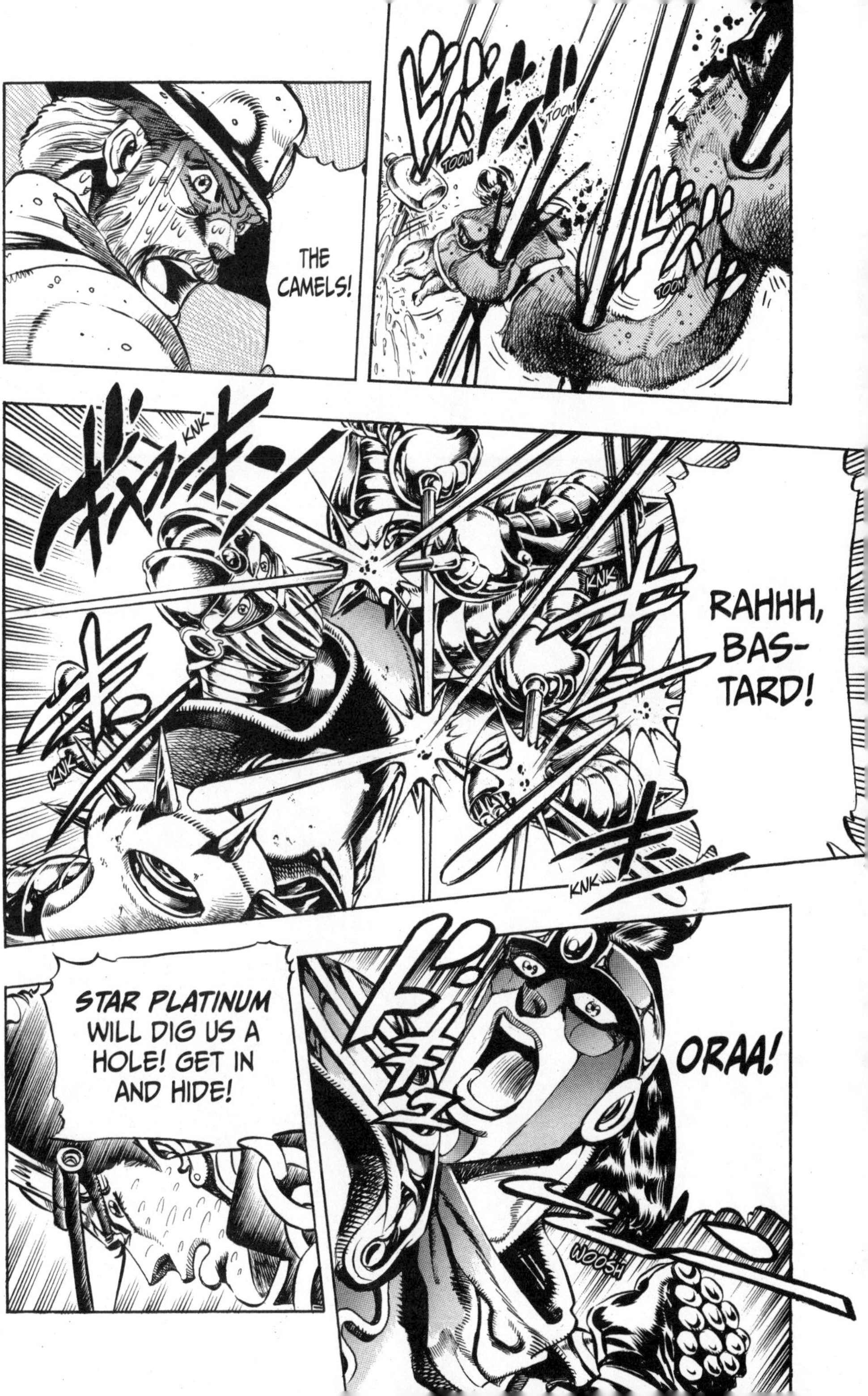
TOOM
TOOM
TOOM
TOOM
THE CAMELS!
KNK
KNK
KNK
KNK
RAHHH, BASTARD!
ORAA!
WOOSH
STAR PLATINUM WILL DIG US A HOLE! GET IN AND HIDE!

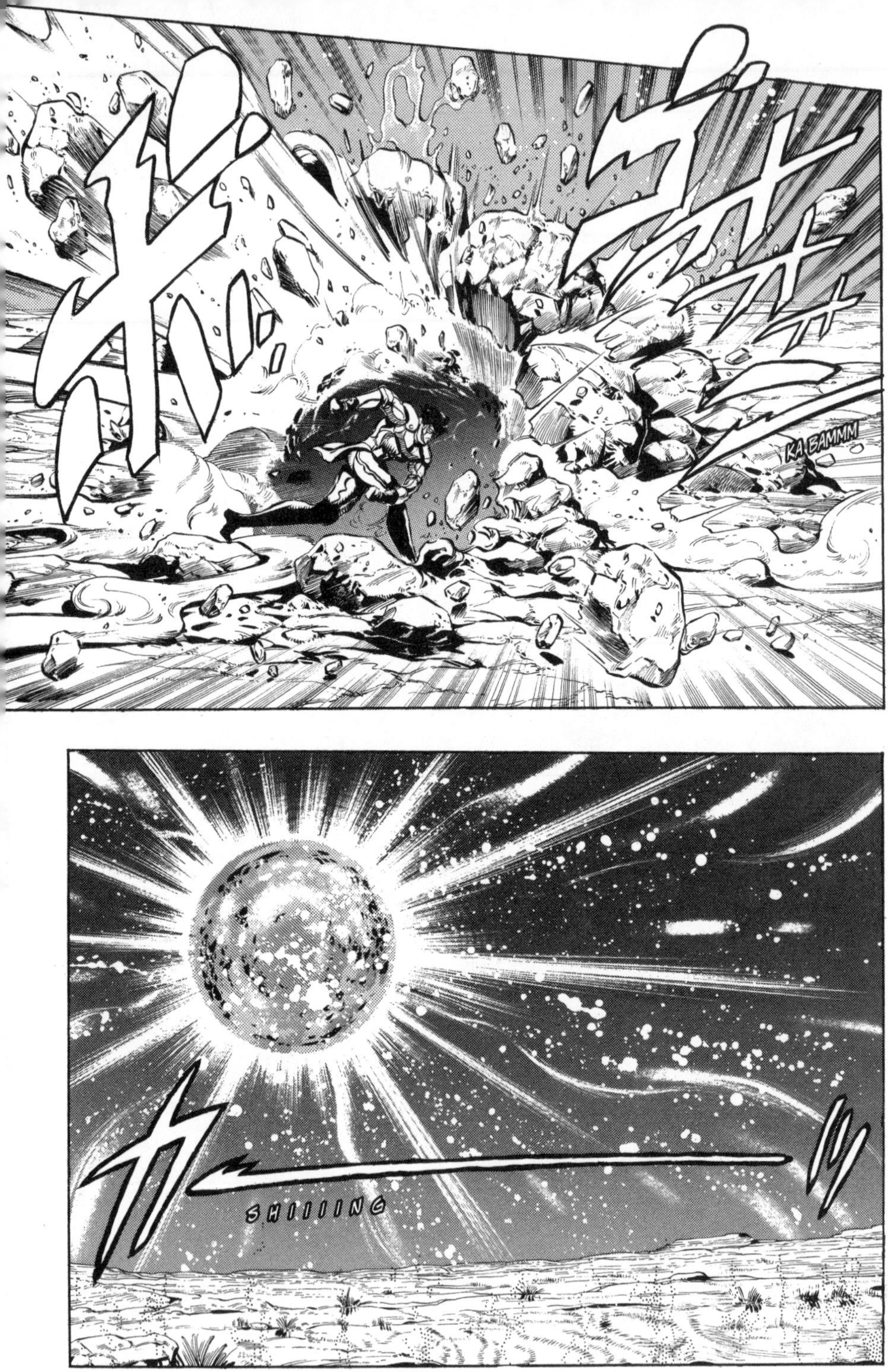
KA BAMMM
SHIIIING

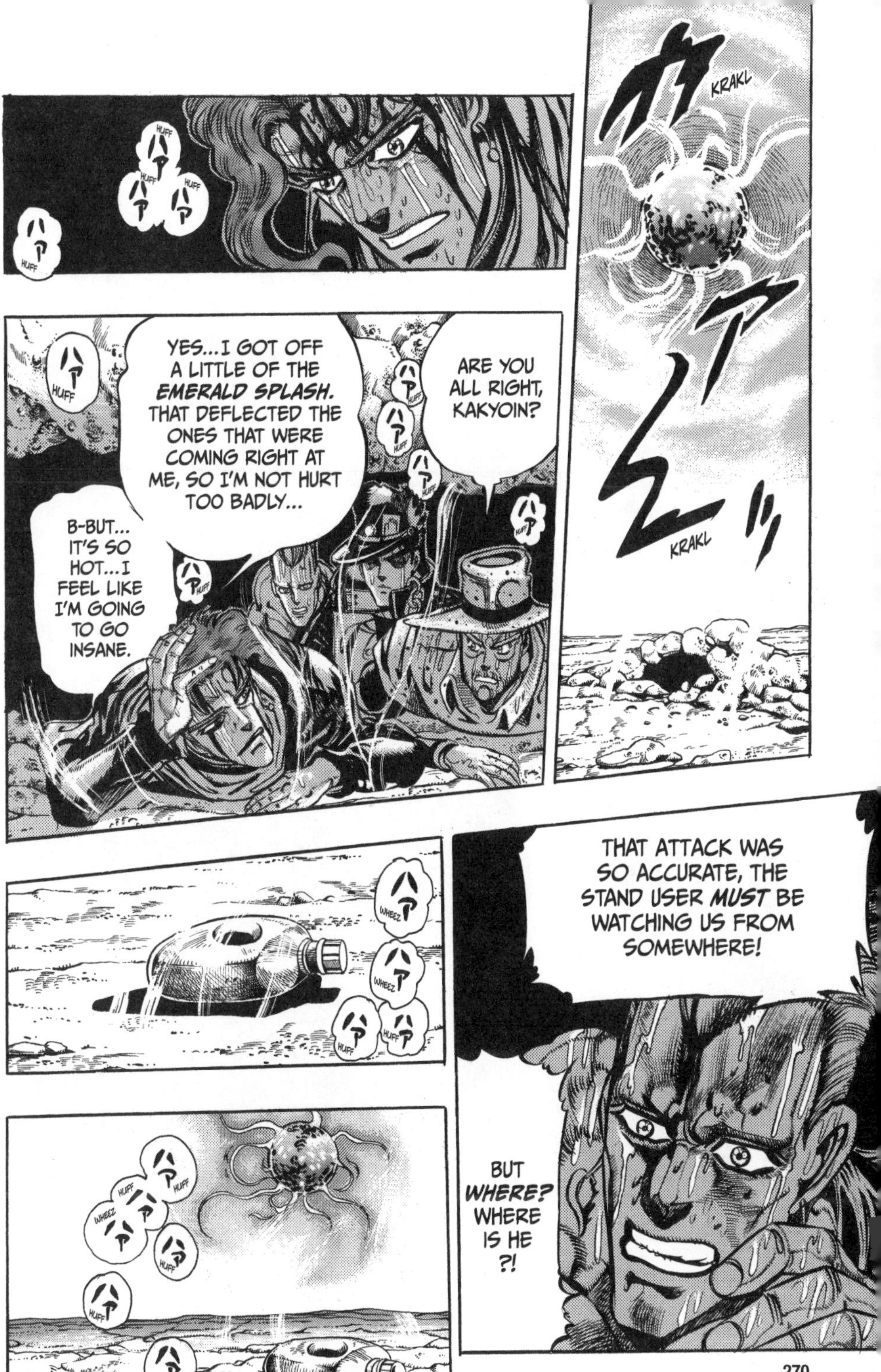
KRAKL
KRAKL
HUFF
HUFF
HUFF
HUFF
ARE YOU ALL RIGHT, KAKYOIN?
YES...I GOT OFF A LITTLE OF THE *EMERALD SPLASH.* THAT DEFLECTED THE ONES THAT WERE COMING RIGHT AT ME, SO I'M NOT HURT TOO BADLY...
B-BUT... IT'S SO HOT...I FEEL LIKE I'M GOING TO GO INSANE.
THAT ATTACK WAS SO ACCURATE, THE STAND USER *MUST* BE WATCHING US FROM SOMEWHERE!
BUT *WHERE?* WHERE IS HE ?!
WHEEZ
WHEEZ
HUFF
HUFF
HUFF
HUFF
WHEEZ
HUFF
HUFF
WHEEZ

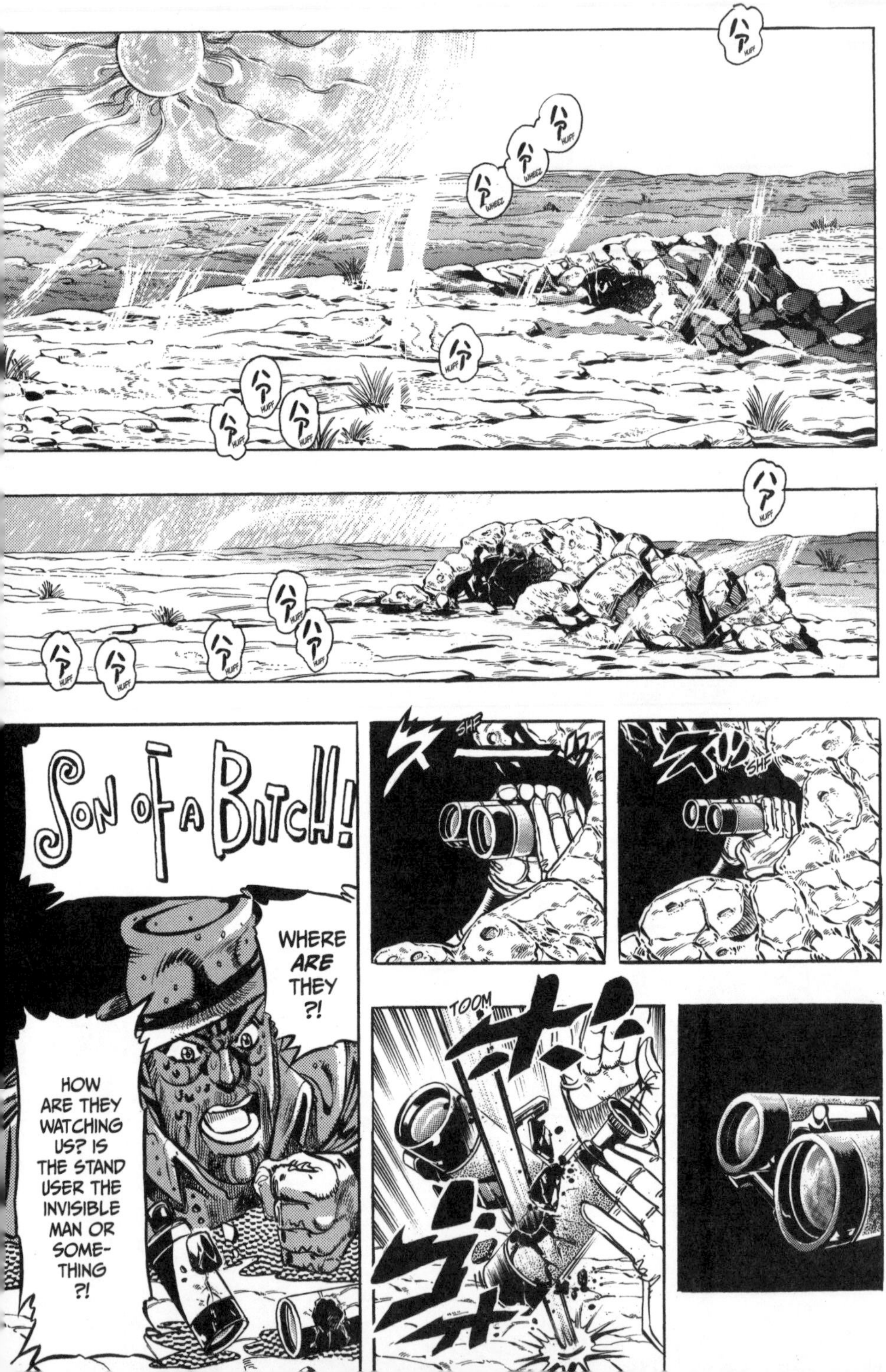
HUFF
HUFF
WHEEZ
WHEEZ
HUFF
HUFF
HUFF
HUFF
HUFF
HUFF
HUFF
HUFF
HUFF
HUFF
SHF
SHF
TOOM
SON OF A BITCH!
WHERE ARE THEY ?!
HOW ARE THEY WATCHING US? IS THE STAND USER THE INVISIBLE MAN OR SOME-THING ?!

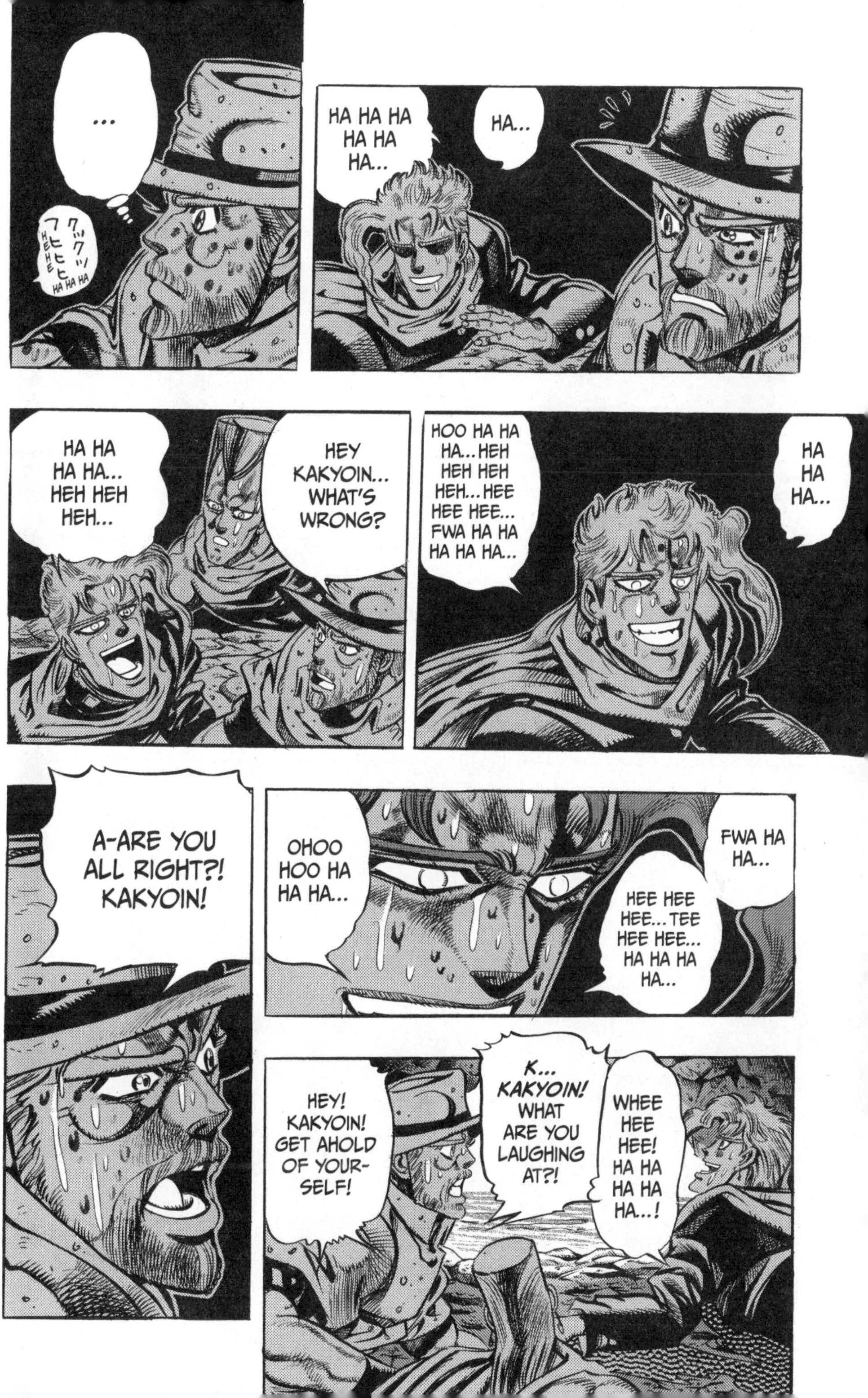
HA...
HA HA HA HA HA HA...
...
クックッ
フヒヒヒ
HEHE HA HA HA
HA HA HA...
HOO HA HA HA...HEH HEH HEH HEH...HEE HEE HEE... FWA HA HA HA HA HA...
HEY KAKYOIN... WHAT'S WRONG?
HA HA HA HA... HEH HEH HEH...
FWA HA HA...
HEE HEE HEE...TEE HEE HEE... HA HA HA HA...
OHOO HOO HA HA HA...
WHEE HEE HEE! HA HA HA HA HA...!
K... KAKYOIN! WHAT ARE YOU LAUGHING AT?!
HEY! KAKYOIN! GET AHOLD OF YOURSELF!
A-ARE YOU ALL RIGHT?! KAKYOIN!

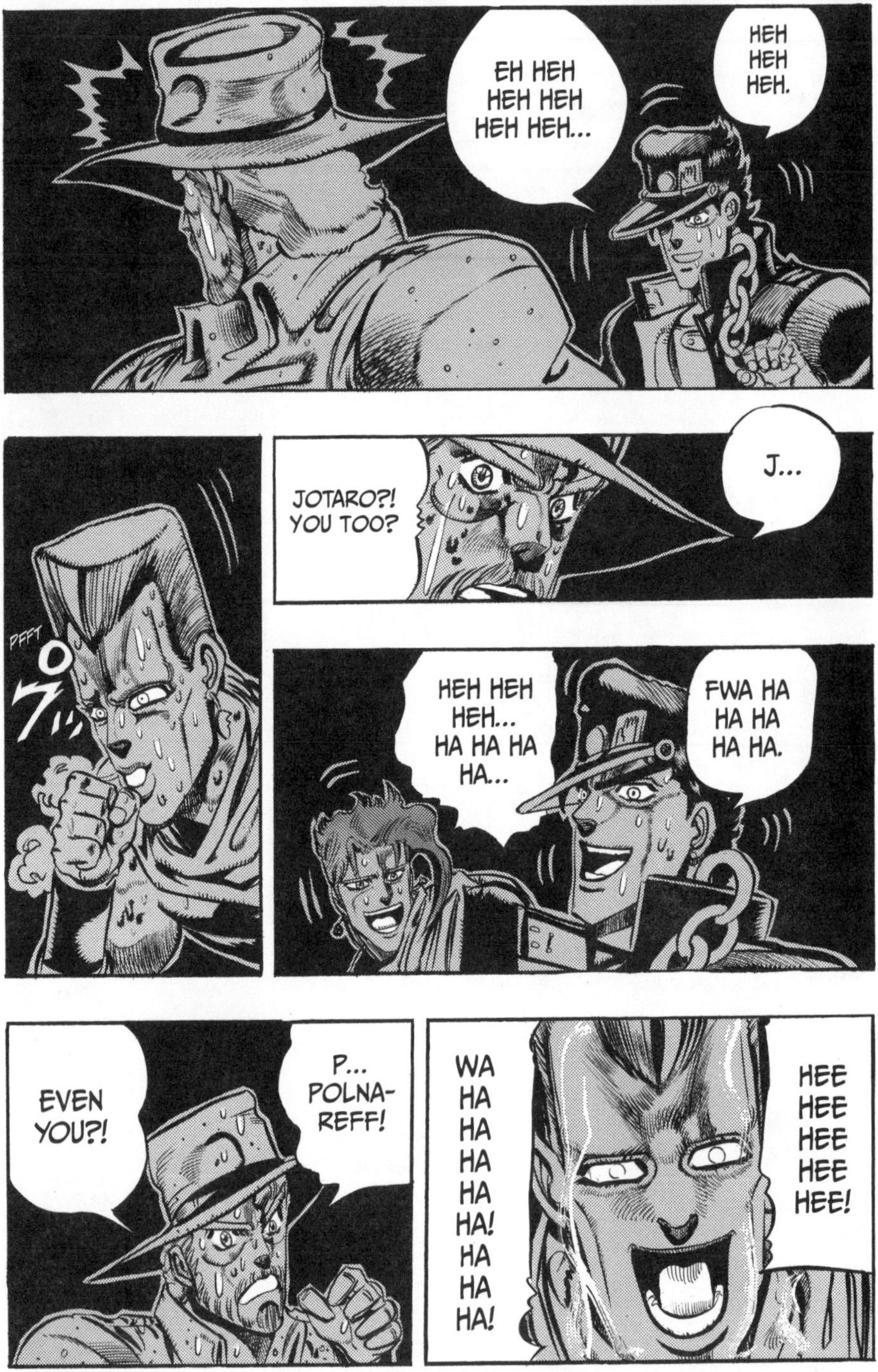
HEH HEH HEH.
EH HEH HEH HEH HEH HEH...
J...
JOTARO?! YOU TOO?
FWA HA HA HA HA HA.
HEH HEH HEH... HA HA HA HA...
PFFT
HEE HEE HEE HEE HEE!
WA HA HA HA HA HA HA! HA HA HA!
P... POLNA-REFF!
EVEN YOU?!

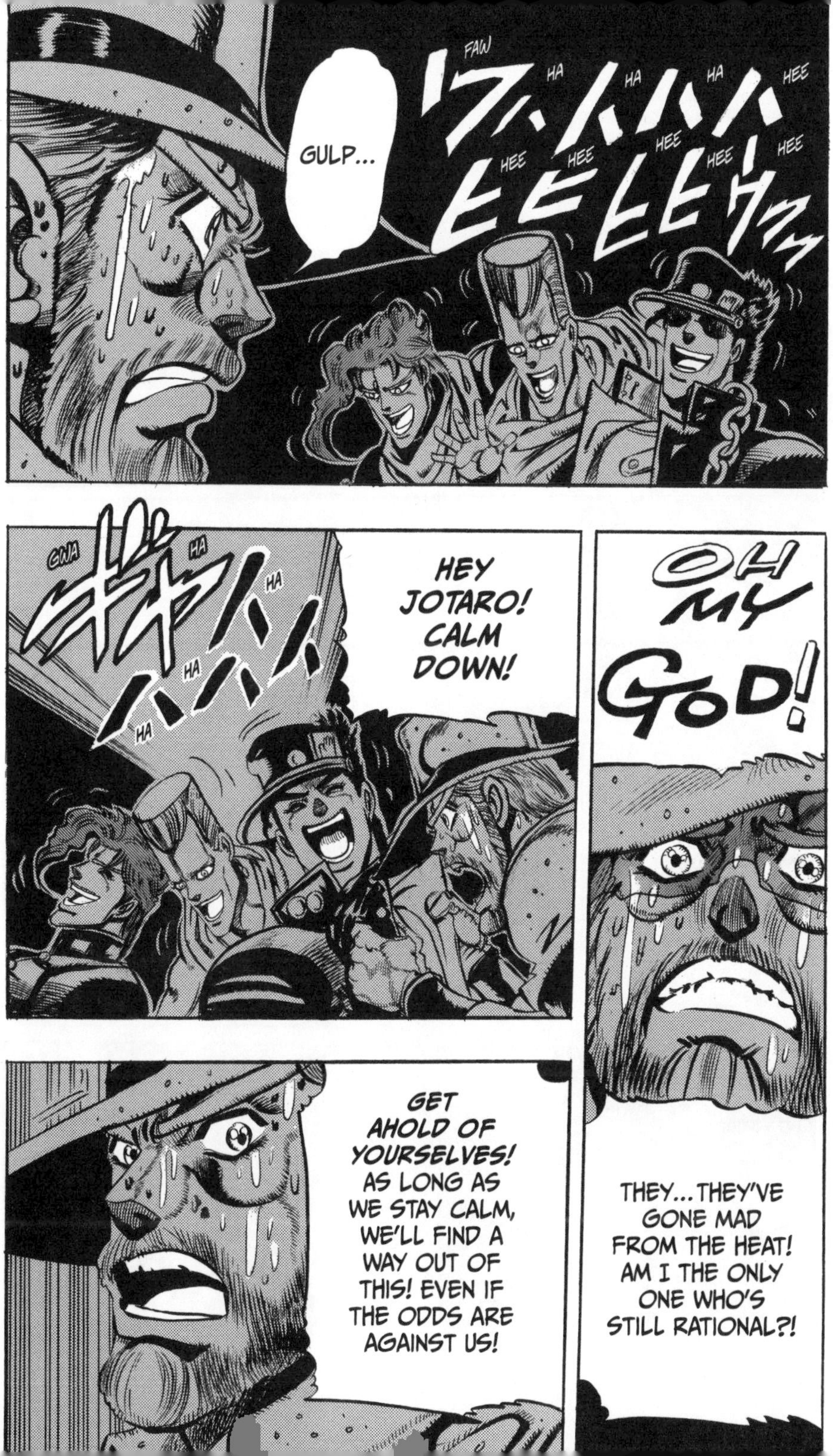
FAW HA HA HA HEE
HEE HEE HEE HEE HEE
GULP...
OH MY GOD!
GWA HA HA HA HA
HEY JOTARO! CALM DOWN!
THEY... THEY'VE GONE MAD FROM THE HEAT! AM I THE ONLY ONE WHO'S STILL RATIONAL?!
GET AHOLD OF YOURSELVES! AS LONG AS WE STAY CALM, WE'LL FIND A WAY OUT OF THIS! EVEN IF THE ODDS ARE AGAINST US!

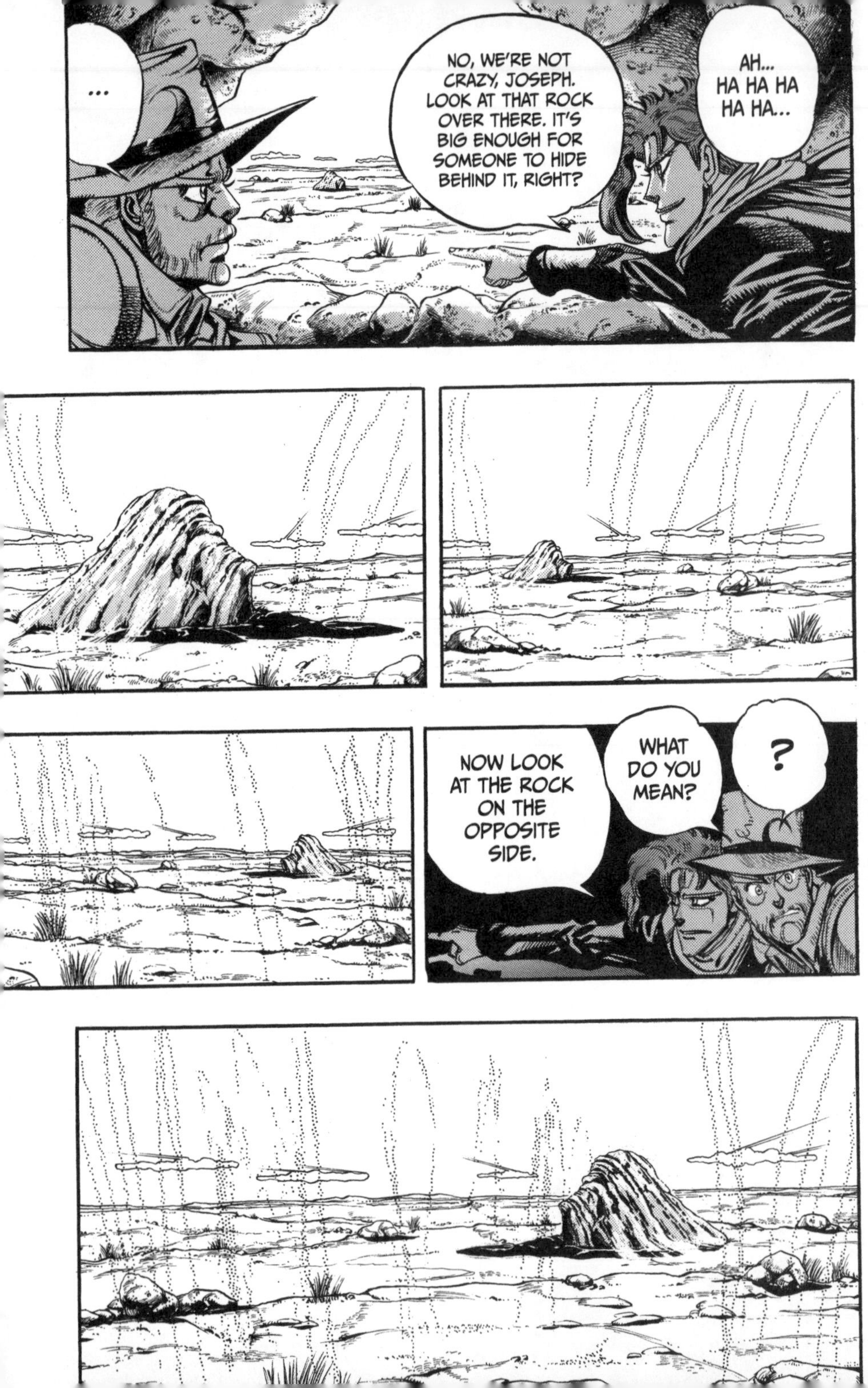
AH... HA HA HA HA HA...
NO, WE'RE NOT CRAZY, JOSEPH. LOOK AT THAT ROCK OVER THERE. IT'S BIG ENOUGH FOR SOMEONE TO HIDE BEHIND IT, RIGHT?
...
?
WHAT DO YOU MEAN?
NOW LOOK AT THE ROCK ON THE OPPOSITE SIDE.

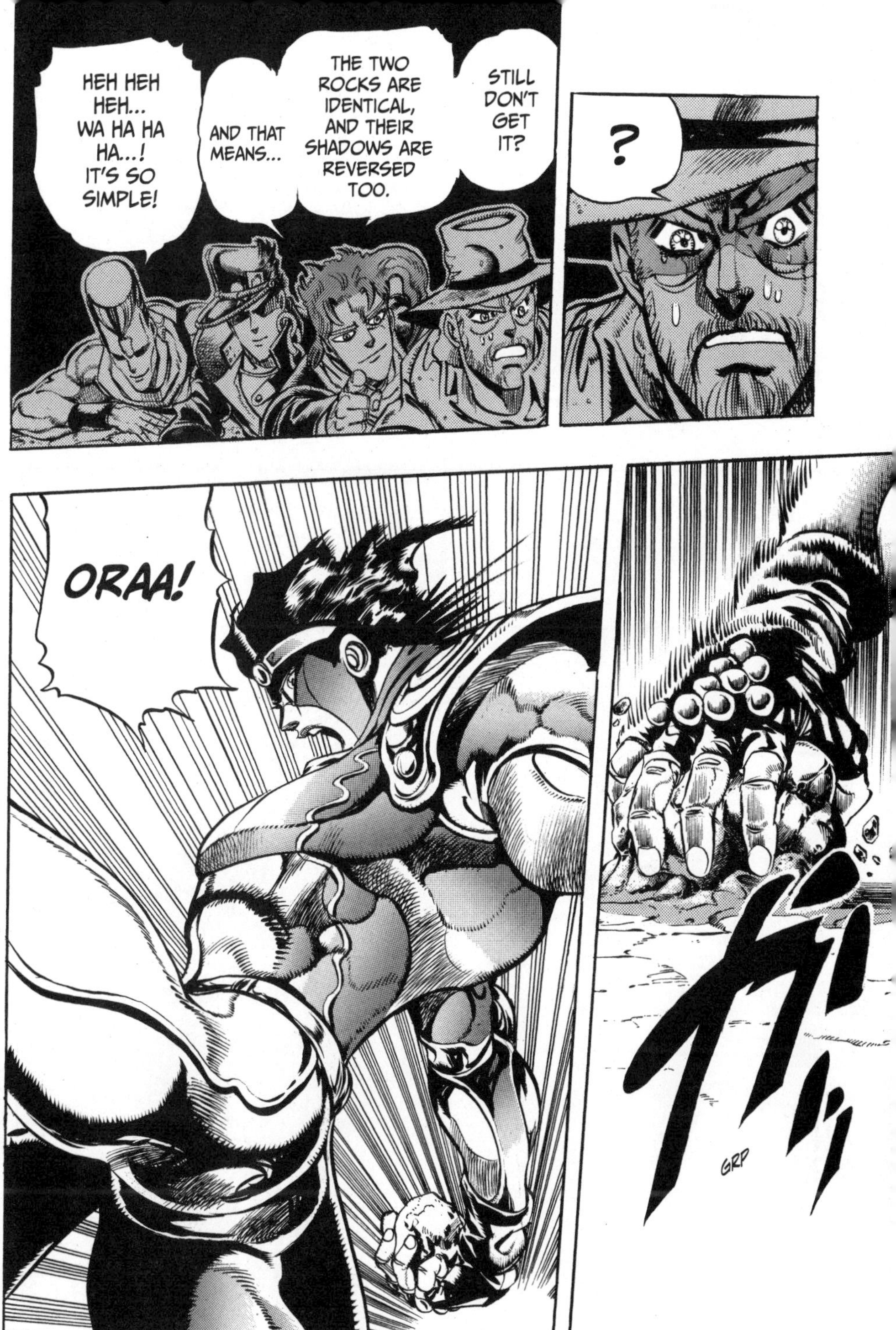
?
STILL DON'T GET IT?
THE TWO ROCKS ARE IDENTICAL, AND THEIR SHADOWS ARE REVERSED TOO.
AND THAT MEANS...
HEH HEH HEH... WA HA HA HA...! IT'S SO SIMPLE!
GRP
ORAA!

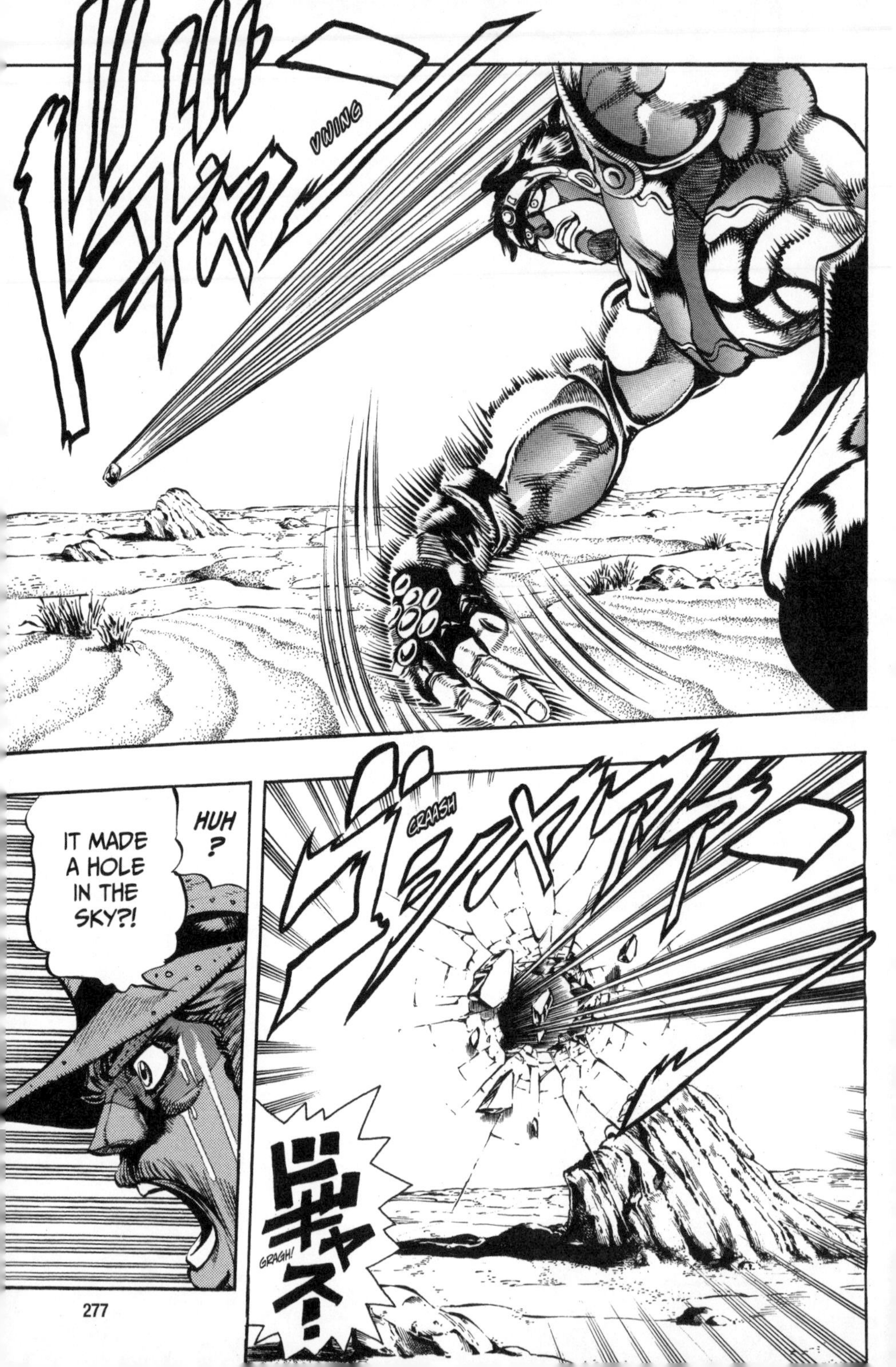
VWING
CRAASH
GRAGH!
HUH?
IT MADE A HOLE IN THE SKY?!

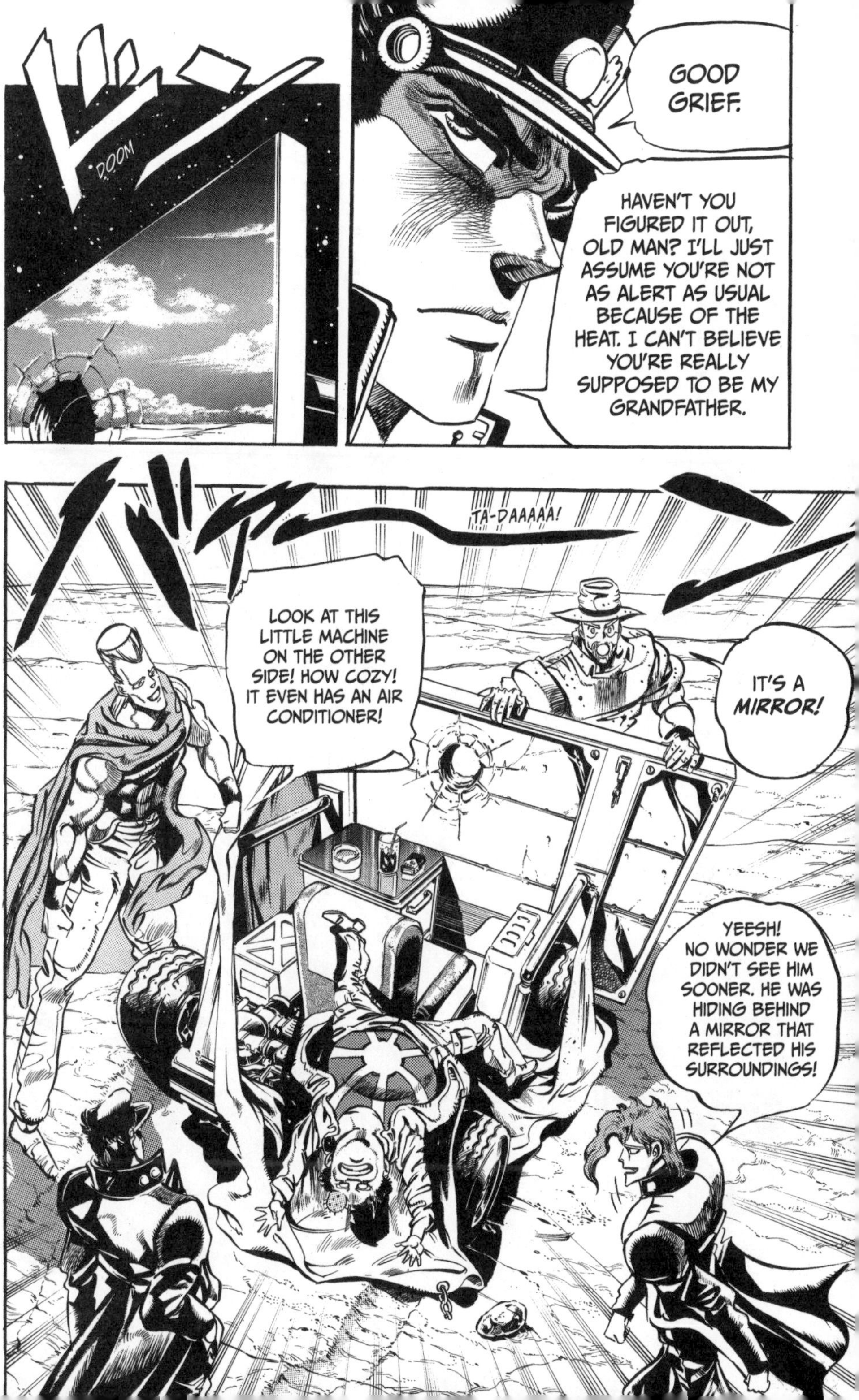
GOOD GRIEF.
HAVEN'T YOU FIGURED IT OUT, OLD MAN? I'LL JUST ASSUME YOU'RE NOT AS ALERT AS USUAL BECAUSE OF THE HEAT. I CAN'T BELIEVE YOU'RE REALLY SUPPOSED TO BE MY GRANDFATHER.
DOOM
TA-DAAAAA!
IT'S A *MIRROR!*
LOOK AT THIS LITTLE MACHINE ON THE OTHER SIDE! HOW COZY! IT EVEN HAS AN AIR CONDITIONER!
YEESH! NO WONDER WE DIDN'T SEE HIM SOONER. HE WAS HIDING BEHIND A MIRROR THAT REFLECTED HIS SURROUNDINGS!

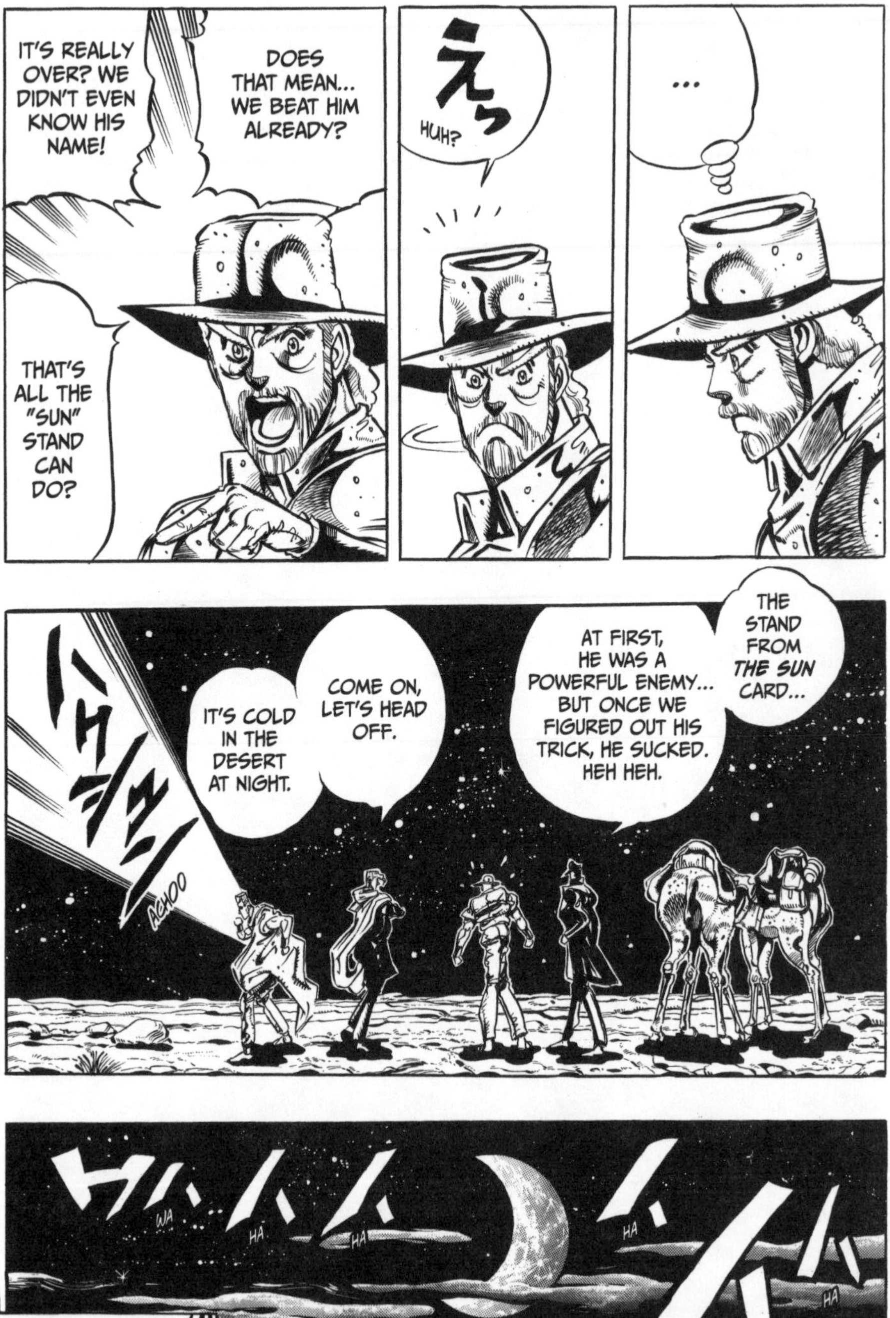
...
えっ
HUH?
DOES THAT MEAN... WE BEAT HIM ALREADY?
IT'S REALLY OVER? WE DIDN'T EVEN KNOW HIS NAME!
THAT'S ALL THE "SUN" STAND CAN DO?
THE STAND FROM *THE SUN* CARD...
AT FIRST, HE WAS A POWERFUL ENEMY... BUT ONCE WE FIGURED OUT HIS TRICK, HE SUCKED. HEH HEH.
COME ON, LET'S HEAD OFF.
IT'S COLD IN THE DESERT AT NIGHT.
ACHOO
WA
HA
HA
HA
HA
HA
To Be Continued
TA-DA! チャンチャン

JoJo's
BIZARRE ADVENTURE

04
END

To Be Continued

JoJo's BIZARRE ADVENTURE

04

En

荒木飛呂彦が
語る
キャラクター
誕生秘話

Hirohiko Araki talks about character creation!

JOJO'S BIZARRE ADVENTURE
PART 3
STARDUST CRUSADERS

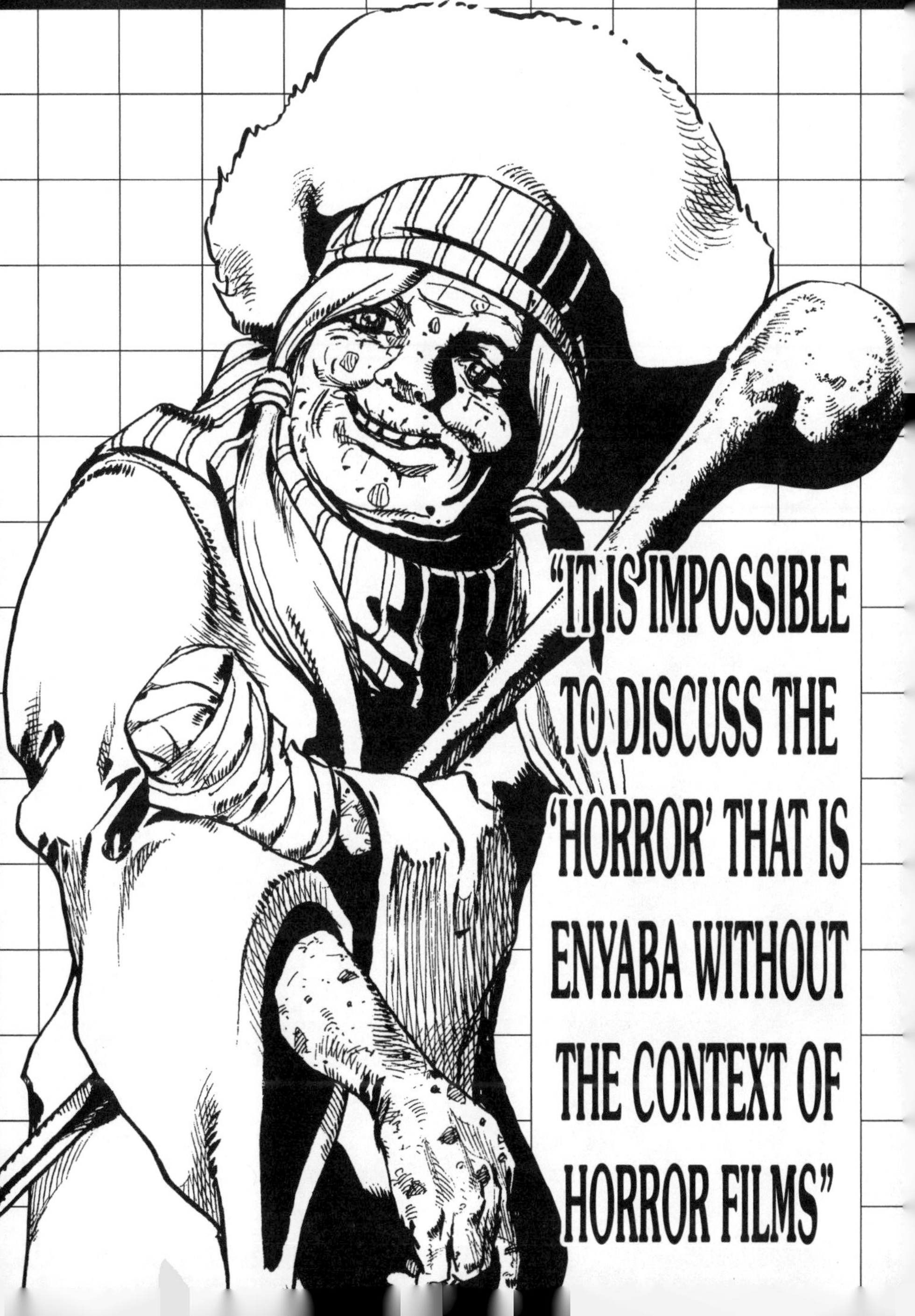

"IT IS IMPOSSIBLE TO DISCUSS THE 'HORROR' THAT IS ENYABA WITHOUT THE CONTEXT OF HORROR FILMS"

En

Eny

Enyaba as a character was born as an answer to the question of who taught DIO about the existence of Stands. I had some of the Stands named after tarot cards, and I also had a vague idea to make a witch-like fortuneteller. I also wanted a scary old woman to be an enemy. After all, I consider horror films to be my teachers and textbooks, and you can't have a horror film without a scary old lady! *JoJo* has had a strong connection to horror films ever since vampires appeared in Part 1, especially when you look at the enemies. As far as Enyaba is concerned, I think I managed to include all the usual tropes you see with scary old ladies in horror films. She hides in waiting for the main characters to show up, she's got a hidden knife, she's ancient, but when it comes down to it, she can be insanely fast (laughs). It's pretty horrifying to run away as fast as you can, but as soon as you turn around, a scary old woman is right there waiting for you!

The same goes for her Stand, Justice. There are several horror films that deal with some sort of unknown virus coming down from space and putting humanity in danger. That was the inspiration for why I had her Stand "infect" the town, and why I had it in the form of "fog." This is a bit off-topic, but I consider Frankenstein's monster, werewolves, and mummies to be the three greatest designs in the world of horror. I think it's absolutely fantastic to imagine how you can start to unwrap one part of a mummy's bandages and it'll just keep going and going. I drew her son Centerfold's Stand, "The Hanged Man," based on a mummy, but I worked the essence of a merman into him as well. Both mother and child are truly denizens of the world of horror, through and through.

Looking back on it now, Enyaba is chock-full of all of my favorite aspects of horror, so I had a fantastic time drawing her, even during the original serialization. I'm still not sure whether she was an appropriate enemy for a *shonen* manga, though. It's pretty "adventurous" to have an old woman as an antagonist for the main character to face off with, after all. The ratings didn't necessarily go up during that time, either (laughs). No matter how much I may like her personally, there's no mistaking that the ability to convey her strength and horror as a character despite the fact that she's an old woman is something unique to *JoJo* due to the existence of Stand battles. I talked about this in Volume 2 of *JoJo* Part 2 when I was discussing Lisa Lisa, but when Part 2 was being serialized, I realized that if you worked in supernatural elements, the outward physical strength of women and children would no longer matter. Stands use the concept of the Hamon and take it to the next level of visual representation. Despite being "just an old woman," she can use her Stand to disguise an entire town. Both Enyaba's looks and the concept of her Stand had a strong impact on readers. One last thing--I think having the mental strength to be able to control an entire town's worth of corpses would match up pretty closely with that which would be needed to stop time.

The story behind the new illustration for JoJo Part 3 04!

Q. Why is an enemy Stand called "Justice"?

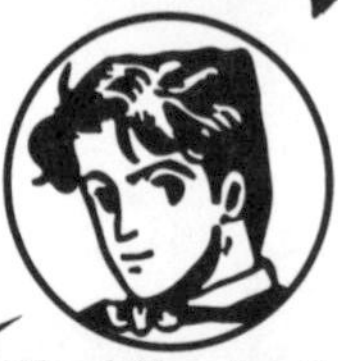

Hirohiko Araki

A. I like that it makes you ponder what "justice" really is.

"Justice" is a subjective thing, after all. Enyaba is on the cover for this volume, so I put a lot of detail into this drawing, including the wrinkles on her face. Her eyes look a bit more friendly than usual, but well...she is this volume's "cover girl" (laughs).

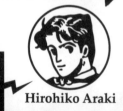

04

JoJo's Bizarre Adventure

Part 3 Stardust Crusaders

BY

HIROHIKO ARAKI

SHONEN JUMP ADVANCED EDITION
Translation ☆ Alexis Kirsch, Mayumi Kobayashi
Editor ☆ Jason Thompson

DELUXE HARDCOVER EDITION
Translation ☆ Evan Galloway
Touch-Up Art & Lettering ☆ Mark McMurray
Design ☆ Izumi Evers
Editor ☆ Urian Brown

Original Japanese cover design by
MITSURU KOBAYASHI (GENI A LÒIDE)

Printed in the U.S.A.

Published by VIZ Media, LLC
P.O. Box 77010
San Francisco, CA 94107

10 9 8 7 6 5
First printing, August 2017
Fifth printing, October 2021

RATED T+ FOR OLDER TEEN ratings.viz.com

PARENTAL ADVISORY
JOJO'S BIZARRE ADVENTURE PART THREE STARDUST CRUSADERS is rated T+ for Older Teen and is recommended for ages 16 and up. This volume contains graphic violence and some mature themes.

VIZ media
www.viz.com

SHONEN JUMP ADVANCED
www.shonenjump.com

JoJo's Bizarre Adventure
PART 3 STARDUST CRUSADERS

OH! GOD!

JO

OH! GOD!

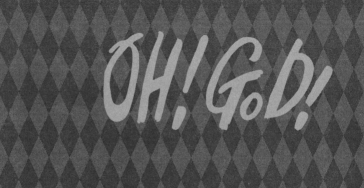

Jo

THIS IS THE LAST PAGE

ドドド

JoJo's Bizarre Adventure
has been printed in the original Japanese format in order to preserve the orientation of the original artwork.

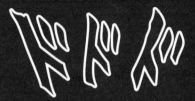

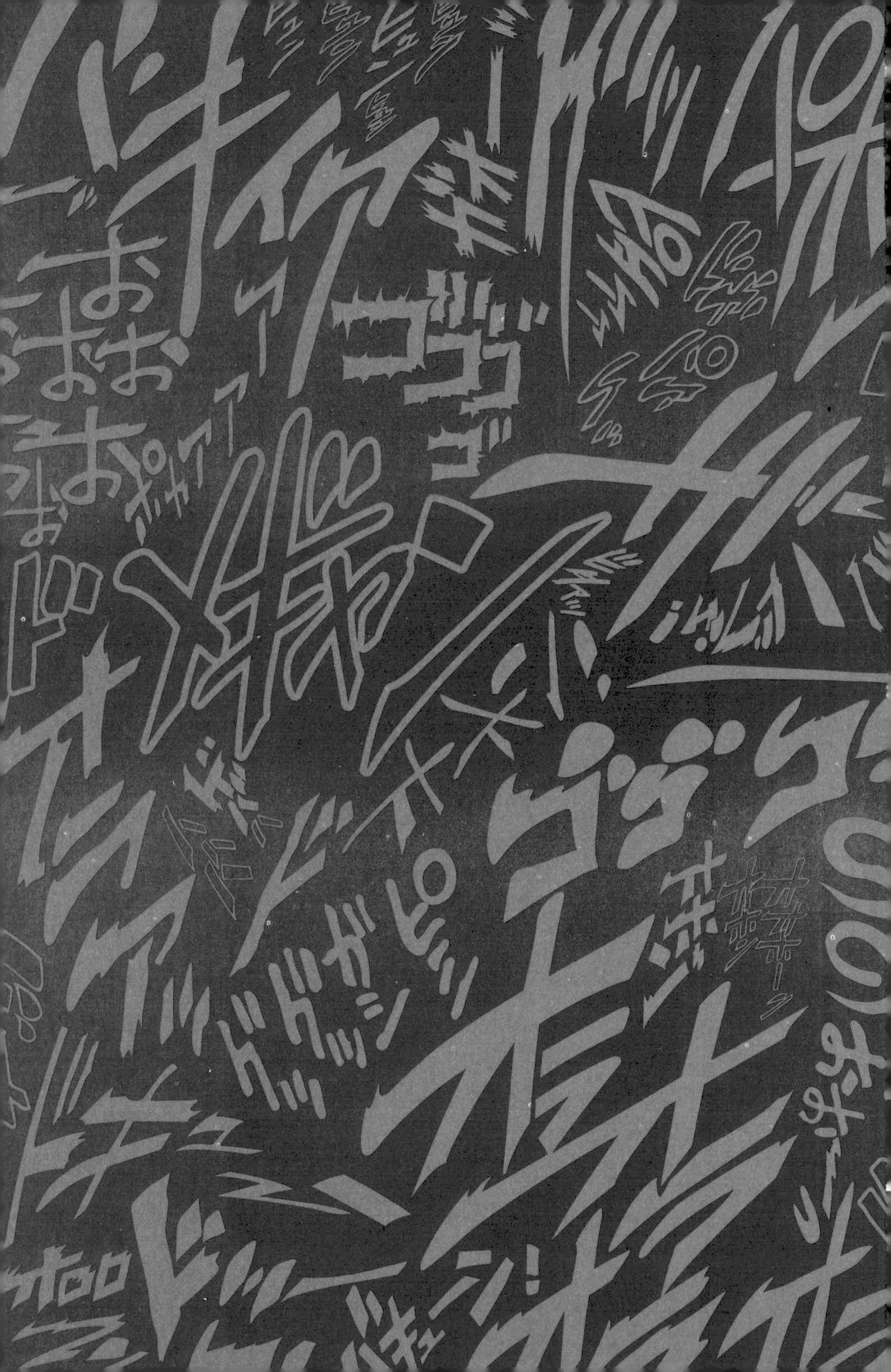